PASSPORT

An Introduction to the Travel and Tourism Industry

CANADIAN EDITION

DAVID W. HOWELL, NIAGARA UNIVERSITY, NEW YORK
ROBERT A. ELLISON, DALHOUSIE UNIVERSITY

CONTRIBUTORS:
DON MACLAURIN, UNIVERSITY OF GUELPH
MARY LEE WHITE, NEW BRUNSWICK COMMUNITY COLLEGE
MARIE RENNIE, NIAGARA COLLEGE OF APPLIED ARTS &TECHNOLOGY

Nelson Canada

I(T)P An International Thomson Publishing Company

Toronto • Albany • Bonn • Boston • Cincinnati • Detroit • London • Madrid • Melbourne
Mexico City • New York • Pacific Grove • Paris • San Francisco • Singapore • Tokyo • Washington

I(T)P™
International Thomson Publishing
The ITP logo is a trademark under licence

© Nelson Canada
A division of Thomson Canada Limited, 1995

Published in 1995 by
Nelson Canada
A division of Thomson Canada Limited
1120 Birchmount Road
Scarborough, Ontario M1K 5G4

Original U.S. edition published by South-Western Publishing Co. Copyright 1993.

All rights reserved. No part of this work covered by the copyrights hereon may be reproduced or used in any form or by any means—graphic, electronic or mechanical, including photocopying, recording, taping or information storage and retrieval systems—without prior written permission of the publisher.

To show your appreciation for the time and effort that the authors and publisher have invested in this book, please choose **not** to photocopy it. Choose instead to add it to your own personal library. The investment will be well worth it.

Every effort has been made to trace ownership of all copyrighted material and to secure permission from copyright holders. In the event of any question arising as to the use of any material, we will be pleased to make the necessary corrections in future printings.

Canadian Cataloguing in Publication Data

Howell, David W., CTC
    Passport: an introduction to the travel and
tourism industry

Canadian ed.
Includes index.
ISBN 0-17-604227-X

1. Travel agents — Vocational guidance — Canada.
2. Tourist trade — Vocational guidance — Canada.
I. Ellison, Robert Anthony, date . II. Title.

G155.5.H6 1995   338.4'791'023   C94-932867-7

Acquisitions Editor	John Horne
Supervising Editor	Rosalyn Steiner
Senior Developmental Editor	Maryrose O'Neill
Senior Production Coordinator	Sheryl Emery
Art Director	Liz Harasymczuk
Cover Design/Interior	Teri McMahon
Cover Photographs	First Light/Koji Yamoshita, Ron Watts, Allen Prier
Composition Analyst	Anita Macklin
Input Operators	Elaine Andrews, Michelle Volk

2 3 4 WC 98 97 96

OTABIND The pages in this book open easily and lie flat, a result of the Otabind bookbinding process. Otabind combines advanced adhesive technology and a free-floating cover to achieve books that last longer and are bound to stay open.
Bound to stay open

CONTENTS

Preface ix
Acknowledgements xi

PART 1   **WELCOME ABOARD**

CHAPTER 1   **The Travel and Tourism Industry** 2
                 The Growth of Travel 2
                 Travel as an Industry 6
                 Profile: Canadian Initiatives in Tourism: Part I 11
                 The Travel Industry in the Marketplace 12
                 Government and the Travel Industry 13
                 Geography and the Travel Industry 15
                 Profile: Thomas Cook 16
                 A Day in the Life of a Receptive Operator 20
                 Worksheets 21

CHAPTER 2   **The Travellers** 25
                 A Brief History of Travel 25
                 Who Travels Today? 26
                 Vacation and Leisure Travellers 29
                 Profile: Isadore Sharp and Four Seasons Hotels 30
                 Domestic Vacation Travel 33
                 Foreign Vacation Travel 34
                 A Day in the Life of Three Travellers 35
                 Inbound Tourism 40
                 Profile: Travel CUTS 43
                 Worksheets 47

CHAPTER 3   **The Channels of Distribution** 51
                 Channels of Distribution 51
                 Nonautomated Systems of Information 54
                 Profile: Dennis Frost 55
                 Automated Systems of Information 58
                 Profile: WORLDSPAN 60
                 Other Uses of Automation 63
                 Career Opportunities 64
                 A Day in the Life of an Airline Reservations Agent 66
                 Worksheets 67

PART 2 TRANSPORTATION AND ACCOMMODATIONS

CHAPTER 4 The Airline Industry 72

A Brief History of Global Aviation 72
Profile: The Boeing Company 76
Types of Air Service 78
Airports: Transportation Terminals for the Skies 80
Profile: Canadian Airlines International 81
Regulation 85
The Product 92
Career Opportunities in the Airline Industry 94
A Day in the Life of a Flight Attendant 95
Worksheets 99

CHAPTER 5 The Surface Travel Industries 103

The Railway Industry 103
Profile: The Chunnel 109
The Motorcoach Industry 112
Profile: Henry Ford 114
The Car Rental Industry 117
Mass Transit Systems 121
Career Opportunities 123
A Day in the Life of a Car Rental Agent 124
Worksheets 127

CHAPTER 6 The Cruise and Steamship Industry 131

The Origins of the Cruise Industry 131
Cruises of Today 135
Profile: *S.S. Norway* 137
Cruise Marketing 142
Profile: Robert Dickinson 144
The Cruise as Product 145
The Channels of Distribution 148
The Regulation and Promotion of Cruises 149
Career Opportunities 150
A Day in the Life of a Purser 152
Worksheets 155

CHAPTER 7 The Hospitality Industry 159

A Brief History of Hospitality 159
Modern Hotels and Motels 161
Hotel Ownership 165
Profile: J. Willard Marriott, Sr. 166
The Hotel/Motel/Resort as a Product 168
Profile: Bed-and-Breakfast 174

CONTENTS

Career Opportunities 177
A Day in the Life of a Front Desk Manager 179
Worksheets 183

PART 3 — TOURISM SYSTEMS AND SERVICES

CHAPTER 8 — Destination Development 188

Destinations Defined 188
Destination Development 190
The Economic Impact of Destination Development 195
Profile: Club Med 196
The Social Impact of Tourism 199
Banff National Park 201
A Day in the Life of a Provincial Tourism Bureau Worker 203
Career Opportunities 204
Worksheets 207

CHAPTER 9 — The Recreation and Leisure System 211

Types of Recreation Systems 211
The Public Recreation and Leisure System 212
Commercial Recreation 218
Profile: Canadian Initiatives in Tourism: Part 2 219
Profile: Cavendish Resort Community 222
Recreation as Product 227
Career Opportunities 227
A Day in the Life of a National Park Interpreter 231
Worksheets 233

CHAPTER 10 — Tours and Charters 237

A Brief History of the Package Tour 237
The Modern Tour 238
Tours, Tours, Tours 240
Profile: Brewster Transportation and Tours 243
The Ingredients of a Tour 246
Profile: Tours for the Physically Challenged 247
Self-Regulation and Ethics 249
The Tour as Product 250
Charters 252
The Channels of Distribution 254
Career Opportunities 255
A Day in the Life of a Tour Manager 256
Worksheets 259

PART 4 — BUSINESS AND PROFESSIONAL TRAVEL

CHAPTER 11 — The Business of Professional Travel ... 264

- Travel for Business ... 264
- The Frequent Business Traveller ... 267
- Transportation Systems and Business Travellers ... 268
- Profile: Frequent Traveller Program ... 271
- Profile: P. Lawson Travel and Carlson Wagonlit Travel ... 273
- Hospitality Services and Business Travellers ... 275
- The Channels of Distribution ... 277
- Career Opportunities ... 279
- A Day in the Life of a Hotel Concierge ... 281
- Worksheets ... 283

CHAPTER 12 — Meetings, Conventions, and Incentive Travel ... 287

- The Where, What, and Why of Meetings ... 287
- The Marketplace ... 291
- Profile: Darlene Stewart ... 292
- The Role of the Meeting Planner ... 295
- A Day in the Life of a Meeting Planner ... 296
- Incentive Travel Programs ... 297
- Trade Shows and Exhibitions ... 299
- The Channels of Distribution ... 300
- Profile: National Trade Shows, Inc. ... 301
- Career Opportunities ... 303
- Worksheets ... 307

PART 5 — THE TRAVEL AND TOURISM MARKETPLACE

CHAPTER 13 — Travel and Tourism Distributors ... 312

- The Travel Agency as Intermediary ... 312
- Types of Travel Agencies ... 315
- Profile: ACTA ... 316
- The Growth of the Travel Agency ... 318
- Opening a Travel Agency ... 321
- Profile: American Express Company ... 322
- How a Travel Agency Functions ... 324
- Other Travel and Tourism Distributors ... 326
- Associations ... 326
- Becoming a Travel Agent ... 327
- Career Opportunities ... 328
- A Day in the Life of a Travel Agent ... 329
- Worksheets ... 331

CONTENTS

CHAPTER 14 — Promotion and Sales 335
- Travel and Tourism Marketing 335
- Profile: Michael Eisner 337
- Advertising 338
- Other Types of Promotion 342
- The Promoters 343
- Profile: I Love New York 346
- Sales 348
- A Day in the Life of an Outside Sales Representative 349
- Career Opportunities 350
- Worksheets 353

CHAPTER 15 — The Future and You 357
- Continued Growth of Travel and Tourism 357
- Increased Recognition 359
- Profile: Dr. Margaret Bateman Ellison 360
- Advanced Technology 362
- A Day in the Life of a Family Hotel Operator 363
- World Problems 365
- Changing Demographics 368
- Increased Education and Professionalism 369
- Profile: Global Trends in Tourism 370
- Conclusion 372
- Worksheets 375

Appendix A — Commonly Used Abbreviations 379
Appendix B — Travel Industry Associations and Organizations 380
Appendix C — Travel and Tourism Publications 386
Appendix D — Occupational Titles in Travel and Tourism 392

GLOSSARY 393
INDEX 401

PREFACE

The first Canadian edition of *Passport: An Introduction to the Travel and Tourism Industry* gives students planning a career in travel and tourism an overview of the industry today. The book is designed to illustrate the roles played by the various components of the travel and tourism industry and to help you decide which of many different career choices best suits you.

This edition builds on the success of the previous two editions published in the United States. The entire text has been updated to reflect the current Canadian travel and tourism industry. The introduction of new systems of automation, current environmental issues of concern to travel professionals, and worldwide political changes will have a great impact on the industry. Every chapter includes new features on personalities and companies that have contributed to the phenomenal success of the travel industry. Many new charts, graphs, and tables have also been added to emphasize key points in the text.

The travel and tourism industry is one of the largest and most dynamic industries in Canada today. For many years it was the "poor relation" among industries, receiving little attention from government and recognized at but a few educational institutions. But now federal, provincial, and local governments are waking up to the fact that this is a major resource that can generate millions of dollars in revenue. At the same time, educational institutions are expanding their programs to include courses in travel and tourism in response both to the increased demand for travel industry professionals and to the need for specialized training for travel professionals.

If you are planning a career as a travel professional, you need to know much more than the travel agent of 25 years ago. While the world has not become any larger, the number of people who travel throughout it certainly has. And the choices available to today's travellers are more varied than ever. Modern transportation makes it possible for people to go virtually anywhere in the world. And the ever-expanding hospitality industry offers them places to stay when they arrive.

With so many places for travellers to go and so many ways of getting there, travel professionals must be acquainted with countless schedules and directories. Fortunately, most of the tasks once done by hand now have been automated. Whether you plan to work in a travel agency, in an airline office, in a hotel, or in one of the many other businesses that make up the travel and tourism industry, you will almost certainly have a computer. Without one, the speed and efficiency that people expect from today's travel professionals would be impossible.

CONTENT AND ORGANIZATION

Passport is divided into five parts and fifteen chapters. Part 1 introduces you to the travel industry as a whole. You will learn about the history of travel and discover the reasons for the growth of travel in the past few decades. The role of government both as regulator and promoter of travel and tourism is discussed. You will also become acquainted with today's travellers. There are three main types of travellers—vacation and leisure, business and professional, and travellers visiting friends and relatives—and each type has different motivations, needs, and expectations. Finally, Part 1 introduces you to the various channels of distribution in the travel industry and to the role of automation in selling and distributing travel products.

Part 2 focuses on transportation and accommodations. Three chapters explore three different kinds of transportation—airlines, ground transportation, and maritime transportation. The history of each is explained briefly, but the emphasis is on exploring the role and significance of each transportation mode today. The effects of airline regulatory reform of the Canadian airline industry are described in depth, and the importance of the car rental industry is discussed. A component of the travel industry that has been experiencing major growth is the cruise industry. You will learn of the efforts being made to expand upon that growth. In the final chapter of Part 2, you will learn about the hospitality industry—hotels, motels, and resorts. This industry, too, has experienced dramatic growth. You'll discover what hotels are doing to attract more business and how the typical hotel is organized.

Tourism systems and services are the subject of Part 3. You will explore what goes into developing a destination for tourism, from providing fresh water and food to building new ports, airports, and hotels. The many different kinds of destinations for tourists are described in detail. These include national parks, theme parks, museums, sports facilities, and shopping malls. Finally, Part 3 discusses tours and charters—packages arranged by travel professionals that include a number of different components such as transportation, accommodations, and sightseeing. You'll learn how these packages are created and how they are sold.

Part 4 is concerned with business travel—an important source of revenue for the travel industry. You'll find out what the airlines and hotel industry have been doing to attract and keep business travellers. You'll also read about the role of the business travel department. Business travel often involves going to meetings and conventions. The many different kinds of meetings are described and the variety of locations for them are discussed. The final section of Part 4 looks at incentive travel—travel offered to corporate employees as a reward for a job well done.

The many different distributors of travel and tourism products are the focus of Part 5. The operations of travel agencies are described in detail and the trend toward specialization within the travel agency industry is discussed. You'll learn how a travel agent sets up a new business and what skills will be sought in new employees. You'll also discover what goes into promoting and selling a travel product—from advertising in newspapers and on television to producing travel videos to conducting public relations campaigns. The final chapter of the book looks into the future of travel and tourism, predicts trends that are likely to change the way travel products are sold and promoted, and suggests ways that travel professionals can prepare for the changes ahead.

Most of the chapters in *Passport* conclude with a section that focuses on the career opportunities in the area under discussion. You'll be gratified at the vast range of jobs offered by the travel and tourism industry. Whether you prefer to work on your own or with others, indoors or outdoors, at home or on the road, there's sure to be a career to suit your tastes and abilities.

LEARNING AIDS

To help you understand what you are reading, a number of learning aids are provided:

Objectives. Each chapter begins with a list of the objectives. These will help you focus on the main points of the chapter and see the sequence of topics to be covered.

Glossary Terms. Every industry has its own language, and the travel and tourism industry is no exception. As you work through this book, you will learn many new words and terms. This task has been made easier for you by highlighting in bold type within the text words and terms that may be unfamiliar to you and by defining them in context. The travel industry also uses many abbreviations and acronyms. These are spelled out for you the first time they are used in any chapter; thereafter the abbreviated forms are used.

Check Your Product Knowledge. To help you check that you have understood what you have just read, review questions are included at the end of each major chapter section. Make sure you can answer the questions at the end of each section before you move on to the next section.

Summary. To help you review content and locate quickly the main ideas in a chapter, a summary is provided, in list format, at the end of each chapter.

Key Terms. Another learning aid is the list of key terms that appears at the end of each chapter. These are the terms that appear in bold type in that chapter. The lists provide an at-a-glance reminder of the chapter content. You may want to look through the list when you complete the chapter and look up any words that you cannot define, either in the chapter itself or in the glossary of terms that appears at the end of the book.

What Do You Think? This end-of-chapter list of discussion questions and critical thinking questions helps you look beyond what you have read in the chapter. The questions challenge you to think about what is happening in the travel and tourism industry and to formulate your own opinions about industry trends.

Dealing with Product and Dealing with People. The end-of-chapter materials conclude with two case studies or activities that challenge you to deal with a hypothetical situation involving a travel product or customer. The purpose of these activities is to help you become familiar with the kind of day-to-day situations that travel professionals encounter.

Special Features. In addition to the text learning aids, each chapter includes three special features designed to entertain as well as instruct. Some "Profile" features focus on the life and achievements of an individual selected for his or her contribution to travel and tourism. Among the individuals you will read about are Isadore Sharp and Thomas Cook. Another "Profile" feature focuses on important and successful companies in the travel world. You'll find out how Banff National Park was developed and how Club Med has grown and evolved over the years. The third kind of feature, called "A Day in the Life of ...," explores the daily routines of people who work in the travel and tourism industry. Among those who describe their jobs are a flight attendant, a ship's purser, and a travel agent.

Worksheets. At the end of each chapter, four worksheets are provided. The worksheets are designed to reinforce what you have learned in the chapter. Some worksheets require you to conduct independent research into travel and tourism facilities in the region where you live. Others challenge you to think beyond what you have been reading by asking you to solve hypothetical problems. And others ask you to locate and use the sources of information that travel professionals use daily. Your instructor will assign the worksheets. Some of them may be used as a basis for classroom discussion. Others may be used as mini-tests and graded by your instructor.

ACKNOWLEDGEMENTS

The author wishes to thank Don MacLaurin of the University of Guelph, Marie Rennie of Niagara College, Mary Lee White of New Brunswick Community College, Vicki Bashita of Trend College, Karen Cathcart of Lambton College, Catherine Volpé of Georgian College, Don Craig of Mount Saint Vincent University, and Carl Kenneth Link of Link Hospitality Consultants Ltd. for reviewing the manuscript and offering valuable suggestions for improvement. I would like to especially thank my "Profile" contributing authors: Don MacLaurin, Marie Rennie, and Mary Lee White.

I wish to thank the Alpina School of Hotel Management in Parpan, Switzerland, for usage of computer facilities while visiting during my sabbatical leave in 1993. Special thanks are due to Maryrose O'Neill (Senior Developmental Editor in the College Division) for her guidance, patience, and understanding—particularly during many long hours of telephone consultation; and also to Rosalyn Steiner (Supervising Editor) for her kind assistance at the production stage. And, as always, my thanks to my wife, Margaret, and to my sons, Scott and Richard, for their encouragement, understanding, and support.

ROBERT A. ELLISON
HALIFAX
DECEMBER 1994

PART 1

Welcome Aboard

CHAPTER 1
The Travel and Tourism Industry

CHAPTER 2
The Travellers

CHAPTER 3
The Channels of Distribution

CHAPTER 1

The Travel and Tourism Industry

"For my part, I travel not to go anywhere, but I go. I travel for travel's sake. The great affair is to go."

Robert Louis Stevenson

OBJECTIVES

When you have completed this chapter, you should be able to do the following:

- State the importance of the travel and tourism industry to Canada.
- List five factors in the growth of the travel industry.
- Explain the travel industry's impact on economics and culture.
- Describe the travel industry in terms of direct and indirect employment.
- Name areas of knowledge important to the travel professional.
- Explain travel as an industry, with seven components that provide products and services enabling people to travel.
- Tell how the travel industry functions in the marketplace.
- List ways in which the government promotes and regulates the travel industry.
- Discuss how geography influences the travel industry.
- List questions about destinations that travel professionals should be able to answer.

Welcome aboard! Bon voyage! With these traditional greetings, passengers on airplanes and cruise ships begin journeys to new destinations. This phrase also welcomes you — a future travel professional — to the travel industry. You have chosen an exciting career. The travel industry is big business. It spans the globe and provides employment and revenue in almost every nation. Furthermore, the travel industry is a dynamic business. According to some sources, it is the largest and fastest growing industry in the world. Figure 1-1 shows how world tourism has grown in the past three decades. The global tourism industry is now the world's largest employer, with one in 15 workers across the planet involved in this industry. The travel and tourism industry is of vital importance to Canada. Its estimated $28.48 billion value in 1992 amounted to more than 4 percent of Canada's gross domestic product of $688.64 billion, according to Statistics Canada. Approximately one Canadian in every ten works in a tourism-related industry, as shown in Table 1-1. That is 1.2 million people. Direct employment accounts for about one-third of that total, or 431,000.

THE GROWTH OF TRAVEL

If you're like most Canadians, you've probably already travelled to many places. Perhaps you spent a summer touring Europe or backpacking in the Rockies. You may have scrapbooks filled with photos and souvenirs of trips to Ottawa, Cavendish Beach, or DisneyWorld. Maybe you're saving money for a cruise to the Bahamas or to Alaska along the coast of British Columbia. Canada is a nation of travellers. Every year, millions of Canadians take business trips. (A trip

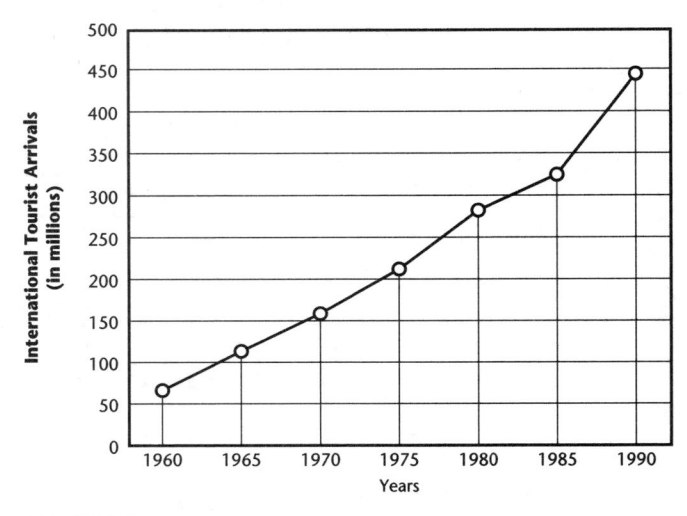

FIGURE 1-1
World Tourism Growth, 1960-90
SOURCE: World Tourism Organization, *Travel Industry World Yearbook*

	Tourism-related employment	Tourism-related employment (%)	Tourism employment	Tourism employment (%)
Food and beverage	596 600	49.7	101 422	23.6
Transportation	275 100	22.9	93 748	21.7
Accommodation	159 700	13.3	137 916	32.0
Attractions	90 700	7.6	42 629	9.9
Adventure tourism and outdoor recreation	50 100	4.2	27 999	6.5
Travel trade	27 200	2.3	27 200	6.3
Total	1 199 400	100.0	430 914	100.0

TABLE 1-1
People in Tourism-Related and Tourism Employment in Canada, 1991
SOURCE: Statistics Canada, *Labour Force Survey*, 1991. Annual Averages (unpublished data)

is defined as travel to a place 25 miles or more from home, excluding commutes to and from work.)

The world is travelling to Canada, too. According to Statistics Canada, more than 36 million international travellers came to Canada in 1991: 33.5 million from the United States (12 million of whom stayed one or more nights), and an additional 2.9 million from other parts of the globe. However, statistics also reveal that on a proportional basis, very few people in our major markets actually travel to Canada. In 1990 only 13.9 percent of Americans visited Canada. Compare this with the 60 percent of Canadians who made an overnight visit to the United States that same year.

Reasons for the Growth of Travel

The modern travel industry began in the late 1950s and early 1960s. Many companies that are now giants in the industry trace their origins to those days. In 1982, Canadians made about 34.8 million trips outside Canada; in 1991 this figure was 82.1 million.

There are several reasons for the growth of the travel industry during the 1950s and 1960s. A relatively peaceful political climate encouraged travel. Stronger economies in the industrialized nations meant that people had more money to spend on travel. The introduction of passenger jet service made travelling faster, less expensive, and more comfortable. Television documentaries on subjects such as the wildlife of Africa, the mountains of Nepal, and the dancers of Bali inspired viewers to visit faraway peoples and lands.

Since 1970 the number of people travelling has grown even more. In both Canada and the United States, the increased ownership of automobiles and improvements in the highway system have enabled more people, especially families, to travel. With more women in the workforce, and lower interest rates (and hence lower mortgage rates), more families can afford to travel. Also, longer paid vacations from work have given people more time to travel. The increase in the number of senior citizens has also been a boon to the travel industry. Retired from jobs and freed from mortgage payments, many older Canadians have the time and money to travel in any season. Finally, the operations of domestic and multinational businesses throughout North America and the world have done much to promote travel.

The Impact of the Growth of Travel

The growth of the travel industry has had a tremendous influence on the economies of Canada and other nations. Worldwide spending for travel in 1993 was an estimated $3.4 trillion. Nations have recognized the potential of travel for improving relations among cultures. Because of the economic and cultural importance of the travel industry, governments around the world are attaching more and more importance to tourism development and promotional planning. Canada, Australia, New Zealand, France, and Greece are just a few of the countries that have created government departments specifically to oversee their tourism industries.

Economic Impact The travel and tourism industry has become a major contributor to the economy of Canada. First, the industry provides employment for about 1.2 million people; many hold jobs that are indirectly related. These numbers translate into billions of dollars in salaries and wages. In turn, workers in the travel and tourism industry pour money back into the economy as they pay taxes or make purchases and investments.

Second, the travel and tourism industry provides profits for hundreds of businesses and corporations. These include airlines and cruise lines; railway, motorcoach, and car rental companies; hotels, motels, and restaurants; amusement and theme parks; shops, museums, and theatres; and the intermediaries, such as travel agents, wholesalers, and tour operators. Table 1-2 shows tourism spending in Canada by overnight travellers by place of origin. The importance of attracting foreign visitors to Canada is demonstrated by the one-third growth in share of spending by visitors from the United States and the doubling in the share of spending by visitors from other countries. The decline in the tourism-related sectors between 1990 and 1991, which was greater than the decline in the total economy, reflects the vulnerability of the tourism industry to economic recession.

The travel and tourism industry has sometimes helped revive economically depressed areas. For example, waterfront restorations featuring shops, restaurants, and entertainment complexes are attracting tourists to the downtown areas of some major North American cities. Marketplace Square in Saint John, New Brunswick, and the Harborplace development in Baltimore, Maryland, which includes the National Aquarium, are fine examples of successful restoration.

Cultural Impact "Understanding through travel is a passport to peace" was the slogan of the European Travel Commission in the 1950s. Through travel, people of different cultures get to know each other, and this knowledge increases the possibility of peaceful co-existence among nations. The Helsinki Accord, signed by 35 nations in 1975, acknowledged the contribution of international travel to the development of mutual understanding. In 1985 the United States and what was then the Soviet Union agreed to expand programs fostering greater travel and people-to-people contact between the two nations. This was the only formal agreement signed at the Geneva summit. In 1989 the Americans and the Soviets met again, in Vancouver at the Conference on Peace and Global Understanding through Tourism, and agreed to greatly expand air service between their two nations. Most of these flights use Canadian airspace. In a large country such as Canada, with its many cultural groups, travel can also ease internal tensions and promote understanding.

Travel Growth and Employment

As the travel industry grows, it generates new jobs. Between 1984 and 1990, employment in tourism industries grew faster than the total workforce, at 26 percent against 15 percent. Conversely, when the recession began in 1990, employment in tourism dropped at a sharper rate (3.4 percent against 1.8 percent).

We will return to the projected growth of tourism employment in Chapter 15.

Direct Employment The travel industry offers an unusually broad range of employment opportunities. Clerks interact with travellers on a daily basis. Others workers, such as hotel managers, accountants, and housekeepers, are employed behind the scenes to ensure the comfort and safety of travellers. Some jobs require a high level of skill and intensive training, others need little skill and virtually no training. The following list indicates some of the employment areas in the travel industry:

- *Managerial* (hotel manager, historic sites supervisor, museum director).
- *Technical* (air traffic controller, safety inspector, motor-coach dispatcher).
- *Marketing and sales* (shop clerk, travel agent, airline reservations agent).
- *Clerical* (motel desk clerk, clerk-typist in a provincial tourism department).
- *Food and beverage preparation and service* (chef, bartender, server).
- *Cleaning service* (housekeeper, room cleaner, aircraft cleaner).
- *Personal service* (flight attendant, bellstaff, social director of a resort).

Overnight travel in Canada by origin	1980	1990	Change (%) 1980–90	Share (%) 1980	Share (%) 1990
	Millions of dollars				
Total	10 415	17 817	71.1	100	100
Canada	8 081	11 870	46.9	78	67
intraprovincial	5 577	8 321	49.2	54	47
interprovincial	2 504	3 549	41.7	24	20
United States[1]	1 594	3 528	121.3	15	20
Other countries[1]	740	2 419	226.9	7	14

[1] Excludes international passenger fares.

TABLE 1-2
Tourism Spending in Canada, 1980–90
SOURCE: Statistics Canada, *Travel-Log* (Winter 1993), Table 1

CHAPTER 1: The Travel and Tourism Industry

- *Mechanical* (airplane mechanic, automobile mechanic, general maintenance worker).
- *Transportation* (airplane pilot, ship captain, bus driver).

The travel and tourism industry provides hundreds of thousands of job opportunities from coast to coast in Canada (Figure 1-2). In fact, the travel and tourism industry is ranked among the top three employers in most provinces. And unlike many other industries, the travel industry offers a high degree of flexibility; there is no need to go where the jobs are, because they are everywhere. So if you want a job in the travel industry, you can probably find one. The travel industry has long provided employment for women and minorities. In addition, it provides many jobs for those between the ages of 16 and 24. Many of these jobs are part-time or seasonal, and enable young people to earn money for education and to explore possible future careers. Another benefit of working in the travel industry is the possibility of free or reduced-rate travel. Many sectors in the travel industry, including airlines, car rental companies, cruise lines, travel agencies, and tour companies, offer privileges to their employees.

Indirect Employment Many people work indirectly in the travel industry. They provide support services for workers who deal directly with the travelling public. Writers and editors for travel publications, researchers for marketing firms, and managers of contract laundry services for hotels are just a few of the many employees in this sector. In addition, certain organizations assist the travel industry in several vital areas. Some plan and finance new attractions. Others train new personnel. Instructors in vocational training programs, real estate developers, and bankers are considered to be employed by travel-related organizations.

ILLUSTRATION 1-1
The growth of the travel industry has had a tremendous influence on the economies of many nations.
SOURCE: Karen O'Neill

Travel Growth and the Travel Professional

As the travel industry grows, it will continue to recruit well-educated and highly motivated men and women for careers as travel professionals. These professionals include travel agents, hotel and restaurant managers, airline pilots, recreation directors, tour operators, and owners of motorcoach companies. Employment growth is shown in Figure 1-3.

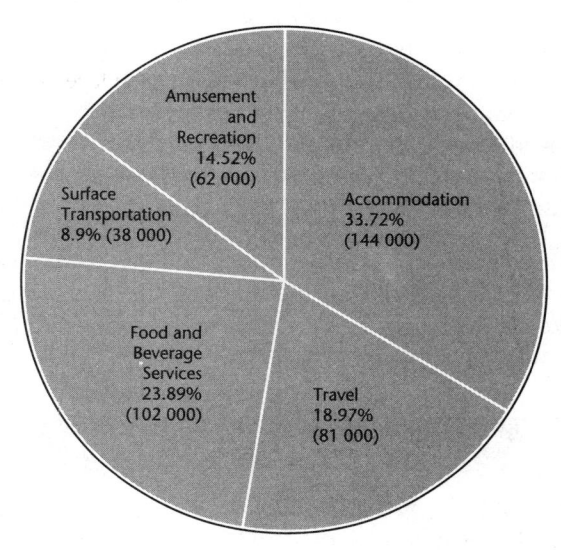

FIGURE 1-2
Estimated Tourism Employment in Canada, 1991
SOURCE: Derived from Statistics Canada, *Travel-Log*, Autumn 1992

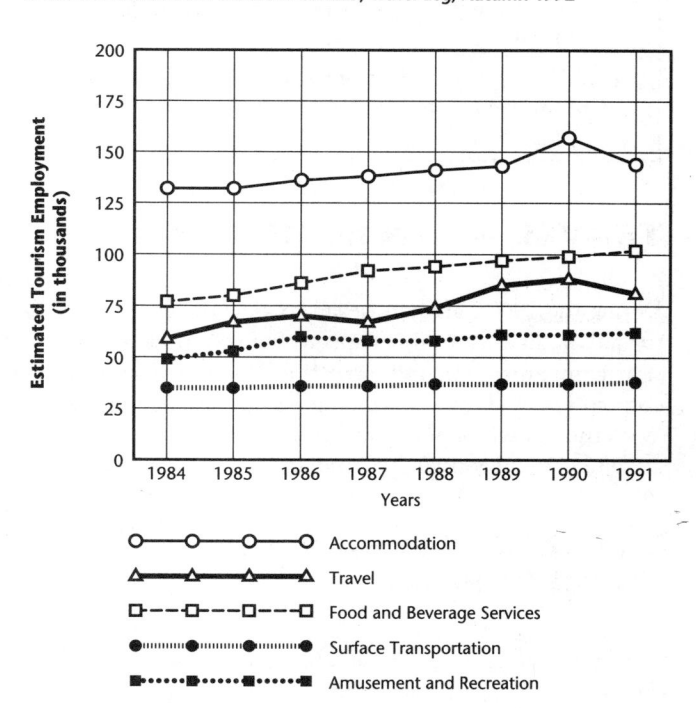

- Amusement and Recreation 14.52% (62 000)
- Surface Transportation 8.9% (38 000)
- Accommodation 33.72% (144 000)
- Food and Beverage Services 23.89% (102 000)
- Travel 18.97% (81 000)

FIGURE 1-3
Growth of Employment in Travel and Tourism in Canada, 1984–91
SOURCE: Statistics Canada, *Travel-Log* (Autumn 1992), Table 2

You might be seeking a career in the travel industry because of its glamorous image — exotic destinations, luxurious cruise ships, high-flying jets, beautiful scenery, ancient castles and cathedrals. The travel industry does, of course, have this attractive side. But it is also a business, and if you are going to be a successful travel professional, you must understand and practise the basics of business. These basics include accounting, financial management, personnel administration, communications, and marketing and sales. An understanding of the relationship between government and the travel business is also necessary. As a travel professional, you must have a sincere desire to help other people. Throughout this book you will find references to the motivations, needs, and expectations (MNEs) of travellers. These three forces shape people's travel plans. Successful travel professionals make a point of understanding the MNEs of the people they serve.

Finally, as a travel professional, you will need to be creative and flexible in keeping up with an industry that is constantly growing and changing. For those who are prepared to make the effort, the travel industry offers many exciting and rewarding opportunities.

CHECK YOUR PRODUCT KNOWLEDGE

1. What are five reasons for the growth of the travel industry in the last 35 years?
2. How has the growth of travel influenced the Canadian economy?
3. How is direct employment in the travel industry different from indirect employment?
4. What are some areas of knowledge with which the travel professional should be acquainted?

TRAVEL AS AN INDUSTRY

During the 1960s, analysts began to view travel as an industry rather than as a miscellaneous collection of transportation companies. An **industry** is a group of businesses or corporations that produce products and services for a profit. With the billions of dollars in income it generates, travel can certainly be categorized as an industry.

The Seven Components of the Travel Industry

The travel industry comprises thousands of companies producing products and services for travellers. These companies range in size from small businesses to multinational corporations. The roadside hamburger stand is just as much a part of the industry as a major airline. (And to a hungry traveller, the hamburger stand may be even more important.) The combined efforts of all these travel and tourism companies enable people to travel from one location to another. This text organizes these companies into seven groups, or components, according to their function (see Figure 1-4). Three components provide the most basic service — transportation (Sector IV in the Canadian employment study classification). These are the components that move people to where they're going and get them from place to place once they arrive:

- *Air transportation and services.*
- *Maritime transportation and services.*
- *Ground transportation and services.*

Two components care for and entertain travellers:

- *The hospitality industry*—Sectors I (accommodation) and II (food and beverage).
- *The tourism industry*—Sectors III (adventure tourism and outdoor recreation) and VI (attractions).

- Air transportation and services
- Maritime transportation and services
- Ground transportation and services
- Hospitality industry
- The tourism industry
- Wholesale and distribution companies
- The travel mart

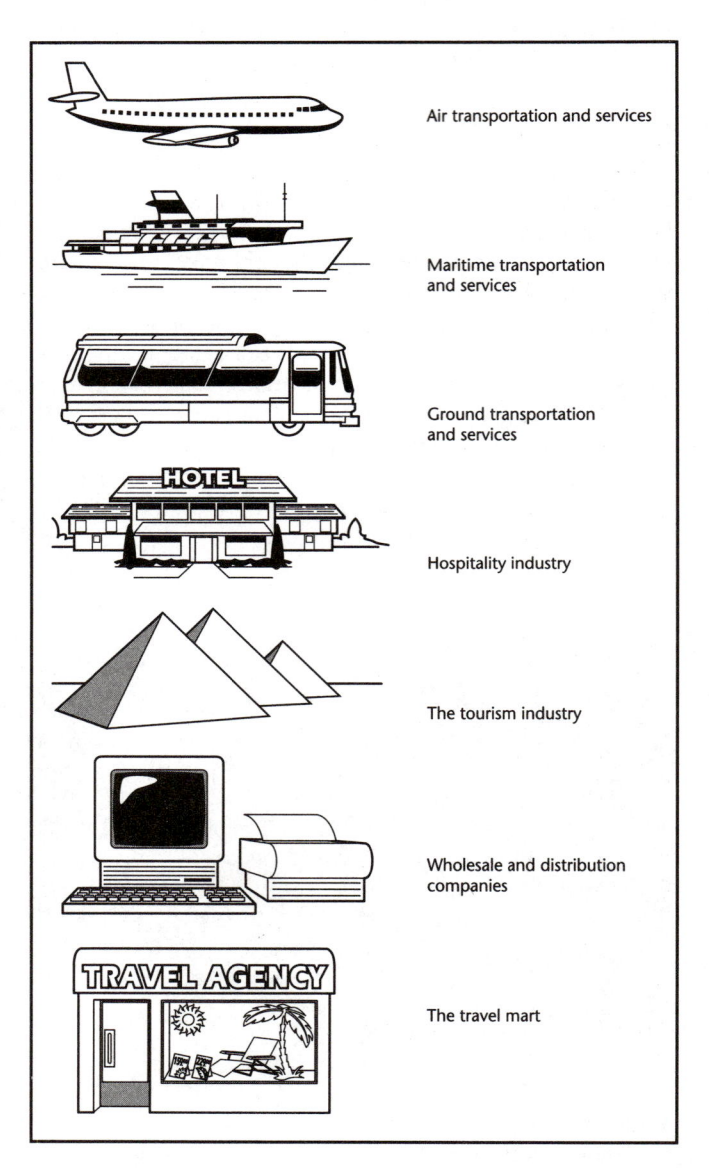

FIGURE 1-4
The Seven Components of the Travel Industry

CHAPTER 1: The Travel and Tourism Industry

Two components provide the means for distributing to travellers the products and services of the other components:

- *Wholesale companies*—Sector V (travel trade).
- *The travel mart*—Sector V (travel trade).

Since the companies are grouped by function, rather than by size, both an international airline with a fleet of 200 airplanes and a one-airplane taxi company would be in the first component. Each provides air transportation for travellers. Likewise, since the highrise hotel and the roadside motel both provide accommodation, they are in the hospitality component, despite the differences in size and scope of operations.

Air Transportation and Services Airplanes are very important to the travel industry. The air transportation component includes scheduled carriers, supplemental carriers, air taxi operators, and aerial sightseeing and excursion companies.

The scheduled carriers are those airline companies, such as Air Canada and Canadian Airlines International, that provide service on a regular basis. The business traveller who needs to get from Calgary to Winnipeg is likely to book a flight on an airline that makes regularly scheduled flights. The two major carriers in Canada fly long-distance international and domestic routes. Other airlines, many of them affiliated with the two major carriers, confine their services to a particular region of Canada, perhaps with some transborder routes to the United States. Air passenger travel in Canada grew from 7 million passengers in 1965 to 36 million in 1988. This includes domestic, transborder, and international trips by Canadian carriers.

Supplemental carriers, or charter companies, provide air travel for groups at net rates that can be lower than regular fares on scheduled airlines. (The rates depend on the number of passengers, length of trip, and destination.) An organization like the Sons of Norway might charter, or hire, an airplane to take its members on a vacation trip to Oslo. The planes used by supplemental carriers are often the same size as those used by scheduled carriers.

Air taxi companies also provide transportation on a charter or contract basis. As the name implies, they function in much the same way as taxis do. Using smaller airplanes, air taxi companies fly passengers or supplies to destinations that may not be accessible to scheduled carriers. For example, business travellers may use an air taxi company to fly to two or three different corporate locations in one day.

Maritime Transportation and Services Sailing is one of the oldest forms of transportation. **Maritime** or ocean-going transportation includes passenger lines, cruise lines, and passenger freighters. This component also includes companies that ferry passengers and cars across lakes, rivers, or channels, as well as companies that provide harbour cruises and riverboat excursions.

Passenger lines, which carry passengers between major ports, flourished in the decade after World War II. However, with the introduction of transatlantic jet service in the late 1950s, passenger liners such as the Empress ships of Canadian Pacific began to disappear. Today, several ships, including the Queen Elizabeth II and Vistafjord (Cunard Lines) and the Royal Princess (Princess Cruise Lines), still offer passenger service between Western Europe and North America.

Many passenger lines survived by changing into cruise lines. Rather than focusing on transportation, cruise lines provide a total travel experience. These floating hotels may offer swimming, sunbathing, dancing, gambling, sumptuous dining, nightclub entertainment, and first-run movies. They dock at ports like Halifax for shopping and sightseeing. Cruises have become very popular for vacations. About 200 cruise ships worldwide offer vacations to the east and west coasts of Canada, the Mexican Riviera, the islands of the Caribbean, and the Greek Islands.

Passenger freighters are cargo ships with some first-class cabins aboard. Passengers can travel anywhere in the world the freighter goes. Because their ports of call can change as business dictates, freighters have more flexible itineraries than cruise ships. For many travellers, that element of surprise adds excitement to the trip.

Ground Transportation and Services Ground transportation (or surface transportation) is so basic that it is almost taken for granted. The various forms of ground transportation are, however, the underpinnings of the entire travel industry. Bus companies, car rental companies, passenger railways, and taxi and limousine companies are included in this component. While the buses and trains used in mass transit systems exist primarily to transport workers to their jobs, they also transport visitors to museums, zoos, theatres, and sporting events in metropolitan areas.

The **motorcoach** or bus industry provides transportation between cities. The intercity bus industry provides the most extensive coverage of any form of public transportation in Canada. Buses serve about 3000 communities, while air and rail each serve about 500, according to the Royal Commission on National Passenger Transportation. Buses have also become popular for escorted one-day trips and for longer vacation trips. Many people, especially senior citizens, enjoy seeing the countryside as they travel but would rather leave the driving to someone else.

Car rental companies such as Avis, Hertz, Thrifty, and Tilden provide important, on-demand transportation for travellers who fly or take the train to their destinations and who then want to drive to their hotel or meeting place. In certain destinations, such as the Maritimes and Florida, rental companies provide transportation for vacation and leisure travellers who are visiting several different cities.

The passenger railway is a vital part of the transportation network in Europe, but far less important in Canada and the United States, where it has been dealt a severe blow by the rise in passenger jet service and by the increasing number of automobiles and buses. Rail passenger traffic declined substantially during the 1960s and 1970s and still further in the 1980s. Passenger totals declined from 6.5 million in 1988 to 3.5 million in 1992. VIA Rail was established as a Crown corporation in 1977 to run trains under contract to Transport Canada. It took over the passenger operations of Canadian National and Canadian Pacific in 1978. Cutbacks in 1990 have left VIA Rail serving mainly the Windsor–Quebec City corridor. There is limited service to Western Canada and the Maritimes.

Another type of ground transportation is the limousine. Some limousines are large luxury automobiles; others are vans. Hotels use limousines to transport guests to and from airports. Restaurants and tourist attractions have also begun to offer limousine service.

The Hospitality Industry Travellers who don't stay with friends and relatives usually depend on the hospitality industry. This component includes such sectors as accommodations (overnight lodging) and food and beverage services (restaurants, takeouts, caterers, taverns, bars, clubs). Resorts, casinos, convention centres, and other meeting places are further examples.

The hospitality industry has a long history. In ancient times, when people began to journey from their homes, they needed shelter. The shelter may have been a roadside inn. Today in Canada there are thousands of establishments that provide shelter, ranging in size from small bed-and-breakfast operations to large convention hotels, such as the Delta Chelsea Inn (the largest hotel in Canada with 1600 rooms) and the Sheraton Centre Hotel and Towers (the largest Sheraton in the world). The Royal York Hotel, the tallest building in the British Empire when it opened in 1929, now has 1500 rooms.

Most hotels and motels are individually owned, but usually as part of a chain. Holiday Inn is the largest chain in the world by the number of rooms; Best Western by the number of properties.

Major hotels are no longer just places to stay overnight. With their beautifully designed interiors, wide variety of restaurants and bars, and many recreational facilities (saunas, swimming pools, fitness centres, tennis courts), some are being marketed as places to spend a weekend vacation. Also, some rely heavily on convention business and provide meeting rooms and exhibition areas.

The Tourism Industry Niagara Falls, the Pyramids of Egypt, and the World Series, in spite of their obvious differences, are alike in that they are all major tourist attractions. The tourism component of the travel industry is concerned with such attractions, and with the adventure and recreational possibilities that draw travellers to an area.

Attractions may be natural or man-made. Every year, thousands of tourists enjoy the beauty of the Rocky Mountains, Montmorency Falls, and other natural or scenic attractions. Constructed tourist attractions include historic buildings (the Historic Properties in Halifax), museums (the Royal Ontario Museum in Toronto), theme parks (Canada's Wonderland), shopping malls (West Edmonton Mall), and recreational facilities (golf courses, tennis courts, marinas). Also, commercial and spectator sports, parades, fairs, plays, festivals, and other events attract tourists who like to get caught up in the action. These events range in size and scope from the Olympics, the Quebec Winter Carnival, and the Grey Cup to small-town fairs and rodeos. The main difference between attractions and events is that attractions are usually permanent while events are usually of limited duration. The category of adventure tourism and recreation includes recreation camps (guest ranches) and sports and recreation (golfing, skiing, curling). Eco-tourism (whale watching, jungle travel) is a rapidly growing activity.

Wholesale Companies Wholesale companies are part of the travel trade sector. They buy the products of the first five components of the travel industry. Because they buy in large quantities, they receive discounts. Wholesalers make a profit by marking up the prices of the products they buy and then selling them through retail travel agencies.

There are three main types of wholesale operations in the travel industry. Charter operators buy airplane seats, hotel rooms, car rentals, and other travel products and sell them to tour operators or to the public. Tour operators assemble transportation, lodging, and sightseeing packages for various groups of travellers; they usually provide the group with an escort or guide. Inbound operators are tour operators who provide specialized travel packages for foreign visitors to Canada.

The Travel Mart The travel mart is the other important part of the travel trade sector in Canada. The word **mart**, short for marketplace, refers to the many outlets through which people can obtain travel information, make reservations, and pay for trips. This component includes retail travel agencies, business travel departments, and travel clubs.

In a retail travel agency, travel agents deal with all kinds of clients — the young couple going on a honeymoon cruise, the retired couple planning a round-the-world trip, the college student going to Europe for the first time. Travel agents help excited travellers plan their trips, make reservations, and obtain tickets.

Retail travel agencies, which operate either independently or as part of a chain, are located in department stores, shopping malls, or suburban or downtown business districts. Some agencies specialize in a specific type of travel: business or pleasure, domestic or international, individual or group. As travel has increased, so has the number of travel agencies. Today, there are more than 5200 travel agencies in Canada.

Some corporations have their own business travel departments (BTDs). BTDs handle the travel arrangements of employees travelling for business purposes. Workers in a BTD do much the same work as travel agents. The main difference is that the customers must be company employees,

CHAPTER 1: The Travel and Tourism Industry

and most of the travel arrangements they make are for business purposes. Travellers can also purchase travel products through a travel club. Travel clubs specialize in selling unsold travel products, such as cabins on a cruise ship or airline tickets to Europe, at discounted prices. To take advantage of these travel bargains, travel club members must pay an annual fee and have flexible schedules so that they can make a trip on short notice.

Interrelationship of Components

Although the seven components of the travel industry operate independently and often compete with each other, they are really part of an overall system. Travellers use more than one component when they travel. For this reason, what affects one component can affect the others. The permanent closing of a tourist attraction such as a ski resort reduces business for the transportation components that brought skiers to the area and for the hospitality businesses that housed and fed them. Likewise, the expansion of a particular component increases business for other components. When the airlines expanded international travel in the early 1960s, North American–based hotel chains also expanded overseas. Holiday Inn now has hotels in more than 50 countries. The IMP Group of Nova Scotia, which operates a Holiday Inn in Halifax, built and now manages Russia's first five-star, Western-style hotel, the 440-suite Aerostar Hotel in Moscow. This is a joint venture with Aeroflot, the Russian airline.

The travel industry has recognized this interrelationship by putting various components together and selling them as a **package**. A package can be an **intermodal package — one that includes more than one form of transportation**. For example, the price of a Caribbean cruise usually includes air fare to and from the point of departure. Or a package might include a day of sightseeing by chartered bus, with lunch at a popular restaurant. Such packages have made travel more convenient and less expensive for many people.

The following case study illustrates the interrelationship between the components of the travel industry:

After seeing a newspaper ad in *The Globe and Mail* for a package tour, Karen Carlson, an accountant from Mississauga, decided to go to Cancun, Mexico. For $1299, she received round-trip airfare, ground transportation to and from the airport, hotel accommodations at the Caribbean Village Playacar, all meals and snacks, and all drinks. The Canadian Automobile Association (CAA) Travel Centre made the arrangements.

On Friday morning, a complimentary van arrived at Ms. Carlson's door and transported her to Terminal 1 of Pearson International Airport in Toronto. She departed on a charter airline. On the plane, she was served a complimentary breakfast and beverage. To get the passengers in the mood for Mexico, the flight attendants taught them some simple phrases in Spanish.

After arriving in Cancun, Ms. Carlson settled into her hotel room and then made a reservation for the 9 P.M. show at the resort. A co-worker had told her not to miss the show, with its authentic Mexican music and dancing. Ms. Carlson was very pleased with her accommodations that week. Her package fare was based upon double occupancy, and she and her room-mate from Thunder Bay, who paid a low connector air fare to Toronto, developed an instant friendship. Both of them spent the first few days around the pool and the beach partaking in a number of activities: snorkelling, sailing, scuba lessons, and tennis. There was nightly entertainment and a manager's cocktail party.

On Tuesday they decided to go sightseeing. They opted for a tour of the ancient Maya ruins at Chichen Itza. A motorcoach picked up Carlson, her room-mate, and others from the tour group at the hotel. As she boarded the bus, Carlson paid the tour guide $35 for the tour. (The full tour price was $50, but a discount coupon for $15 was included as part of her package price.) At noon, the tour bus stopped at a restaurant. The people on the tour ate lunch and browsed in a souvenir shop next to the restaurant. In the afternoon the tour guide led the group through the ruins, describing the sights and providing interesting information about the Mayan people. Carlson found the trip fascinating.

On Thursday, Carlson and her room-mate took a boat ride to Isla Mujeres, a small island. There, they and the others on the boat trip went snorkelling and ate a picnic lunch. The next morning, thoroughly satisfied with her trip, Carlson boarded the charter aircraft for the flight back to Toronto. Many travel professionals working for air, ground, and maritime transportation services, the hospitality and tourism industries, and the travel mart had helped her have a wonderful time.

Travel as a Product and as a Service

Industries generate either products or services. The garment industry makes products, such as suits, dresses, shirts, blouses, and other items of clothing. The health care "industry," for its part, provides services, such as the diagnosis of illness, the relief of pain and discomfort, and the setting of bones.

Some authorities say the travel industry provides products, while others say it provides services. Actually, the travel industry provides both products and services.

Travel as a Product Almost all products are **tangible, that is, they can be seen and touched**. They have weight and occupy space. **Televisions, furniture, clothes, and appliances are all tangible**. The travel industry produces a few tangible products such as food and beverages. However, most of its products are **intangible, that is, they cannot be seen or touched**. Intangible travel products include a flight on an airplane, a stay in a hotel room, a ride on a bus, relaxation on a warm beach, a reunion with family members, fun at a nightclub, a view of the ocean, and much more. None of these things can be weighed or measured or stored in a room. Unlike an old car or a washing machine, travel products cannot be junked. They exist as experiences, which yield to memories.

Travel as a Service A service industry has three special characteristics. First, its employees perform actions that benefit or serve customers. Second, its employees are professionals. They are expected to perform their duties with a high level of expertise and to be able to give their customers information and counsel. Third, a special attitude or relationship exists between the employee performing the service and the customer receiving it. Clearly, these three characteristics describe much of the travel industry.

At the local full-service gas station, the attendant fills your car's fuel tank, cleans the windshield, and checks the oil. All these actions benefit or serve you, the driver. In much the same way, members of the travel industry provide travellers with benefits. They help to plan trips, transport passengers to their destinations, arrange places to stay, and much more.

Travel professionals are like other professionals. Just as a lawyer gives you legal advice and an accountant offers you financial guidance, the travel professional is able to provide the travel products and services that best meet your needs. Doctor–patient, lawyer–client, and teacher–student are familiar professional relationships. Each relationship assumes a certain attitude and way of behaving on the part of the people involved. In the travel industry, the relationship is host–guest, with the travel professional as the host and the

ILLUSTRATION 1-2
Tourist attractions, both natural and constructed, draw travellers to an area.
SOURCE: Karen O'Neill

PROFILE

Canadian Initiatives in Tourism: Part 1

Rodd Hotels and Resorts

Fifty years ago, David Rodd's parents operated a few summer cottages in Winsloe, Prince Edward Island. Today, David Rodd is president of a hospitality chain that offers 750 rooms and employs 800 people in eight properties in P.E.I., Nova Scotia, and New Brunswick.

Keeping up with developing trends has been an important factor in fostering growth, says Rodd, who is currently responding to a changing business market. Some hotel rooms are being converted to suites for business travellers and his recently renovated Rodd Mill River Resort has become P.E.I.'s first full-service facility, offering Maritime businesses an attractive "corporate getaway."

La Station Touristique du Mont Orford

A commitment to planning and expansion has enabled architect Fernand Magnan to create and develop this exceptional tourist complex, which integrates ski facilities, chalets, boutiques, and a year-round resort at Lake Memphremagog in the Estrie region of Quebec. Developed as a four-season destination, La Station Touristique du Mont Orford is one of the largest resorts in Quebec, employing more than 400 in the winter and 150 in the summer season.

With skiing facilities that rate among the world's finest, it is not surprising that in both 1988 and 1989, it was awarded the "Grand Prix du Tourisme" by the Quebec government.

Cullen Country Barns

In the early 1980s, Len Cullen, owner of Weall and Cullen Nurseries Ltd., had space to spare at his Markham, Ontario, nursery and a unique idea for developing a tourist attraction and retail complex. In the highly competitive Metropolitan Toronto area, positioning is crucial. The "barn concept" Cullen created offered quality merchandise, entertainment, gifts, crafts, and restaurants in three interconnected barns.

Since its opening in 1983, Cullen Country Barns has increased its sales 700 percent. It attracts motor-coach tours to the Markham–Unionville area and provides employment for 500 people. Cullen Country Barns has won many awards, including a place on *The Financial Post*'s list of the Best 100 Companies to Work For in Canada.

SOURCE: Information Canada. Reproduced with permission of the Minister of Supply and Services Canada, 1990

traveller as the guest. This relationship assumes that the host will focus attention on the needs and welfare of the guest and strive to make his or her travel experience happy and fulfilling. Travel professionals *must* maintain this relationship if they want customers to return.

> **CHECK YOUR PRODUCT KNOWLEDGE**
>
> 1. Why is travel called an industry?
> 2. What criterion is used to assign a particular travel company to a component?
> 3. How are wholesale companies and the travel mart different from the other components?
> 4. In what ways does the travel industry provide products?
> 5. In what ways is travel a service industry?

THE TRAVEL INDUSTRY IN THE MARKETPLACE

When the word marketplace is mentioned, some people imagine a town square filled with flower carts, vegetable stands, and crafts. They can almost hear the noisy merchants selling their goods and see the crowds clamouring to get a better look.

A marketplace, however, can be anywhere buyers and sellers meet to exchange goods and services for money — a high-priced boutique, a Salvation Army outlet, a grocery store, a gas station. In the travel industry, the marketplace may be an office in a travel agency. The sellers are wholesale distributors and retail companies; they sell products and services supplied by air, maritime, and ground transportation companies and by the hospitality and tourism industries. The buyers are the travellers.

Free Enterprise or Mixed Enterprise?

The Canadian government owns Wood Buffalo National Park, Fortress Louisbourg, and the National Art Gallery, as well as many other parks, monuments, and historic attractions. In addition, federal, provincial, territorial, and municipal funds are used to build and operate public transit systems, airports, docks, harbours, and highways. The federal government owns the CNR, along whose tracks most VIA Rail trains operate.

However, these examples of government ownership of travel enterprises and infrastructure really illustrate the exception. Most of the travel and tourism businesses in Canada are privately owned and operated. This is in contrast to many countries, where most travel enterprises are owned and operated by government.

Some people would argue that the travel and tourism industry in Canada functions within the **free enterprise system**. In such a system, privately owned businesses are allowed to compete with each other in the marketplace with minimal government interference. Owners are free to make as much money as they can.

To the extent it is part of the free enterprise system, the Canadian travel and tourism industry is a business like any other business. To stay in business, companies must produce good products and services, sell them at a fair price, and earn a profit. The possibility of making a profit is an incentive for owners of travel companies to put forth their best efforts. Many economists believe that the free enterprise system is more efficient than a government-controlled system, better suited to change, and more conducive to growth. Others would argue that the travel and tourism industry in Canada functions within a mixed enterprise system, in that governments own and operate the parks, museums, and historic attractions, as well as the infrastructure. Governments opened a casino in Montreal in 1993 and another in Windsor in 1994. They are increasingly involved in the promotion of travel and tourism. Government ownership and funding coupled with privately owned businesses in the tourism industry yields a combination called the mixed enterprise system.

The Four Ps of Marketing

Marketing refers to those activities which direct the flow of goods and services from the producer to the consumer. To market products and services, travel professionals must coordinate the four Ps of marketing:

- product
- price
- place
- promotion

The focus of marketing is on the consumer. The coordination of the four Ps, known as the marketing mix, must satisfy the needs, wants, and desires of the market target. Therefore, to satisfactorily blend the elements of the marketing mix, the travel professional must understand buyer behaviour.

A travel agent probably wouldn't have much success trying to sell a disco-till-dawn singles' cruise to an elderly couple. The successful travel professional knows how to bring the right product or service to the right place at the right time at the right price.

Product This category includes all products and services provided by the components of the travel industry. Products range from a bus ride across town to an ocean cruise around the world. If you think about the seats available on just one bus, you realize that there are hundreds of millions of travel products and services for sale at any given time and that these can be sold over and over.

CHAPTER 1: The Travel and Tourism Industry   13

Price This category is the cost of the product or service to the consumer. The price is based on the supplier's expenses in producing the product and the distributor's expenses in marketing it. With the growth of travel and increased competition for the travel dollar, the price of travel products today is quite reasonable. Open your newspaper to the travel ads, and you will be amazed at how far you can go for just $300.

Place This category refers to any marketplace within the channel of distribution where the buyer and the provider are brought together by a seller. This may be a retail travel agency, a business travel department, a travel club, a ticket counter, or a telephone line between the buyer and the provider—for example, VIA Rail, in which case the provider is the seller. Sellers set up their marketplaces in locations that are convenient to most buyers. With increased competition in the marketplace, sellers are looking for new places to distribute products and services. Already, at some supermarkets, you can purchase bus tickets along with your bread and milk.

Promotion This category refers to the ways in which sellers create consumer interest. To inform consumers that various products and services are available, sellers advertise on television and radio and in newspapers and magazines. To create even more excitement, they may also offer special deals, such as two airline tickets for the price of one. (Air Canada did this on Canada Day in 1991.) Giving away trips for two as door prizes at charitable fundraisers has become a popular form of promotion.

This category includes the very important area of marketing research. Researchers interview travellers at airports and resorts, conduct surveys aboard buses and airplanes, and leave questionnaires in hotel and motel rooms. The point of this research is to learn more about the consumer's preferences and buying and trip-planning behaviour. This information is used to increase the consumer's satisfaction by improving existing travel products and services and planning new ones.

CHECK YOUR PRODUCT KNOWLEDGE

1. In the travel industry, where is the marketplace? Who are the buyers? Who are the sellers? What do they exchange?
2. How is the travel marketplace in Canada different from the travel marketplace in many other countries?
3. What are the four Ps of marketing? Why are they important?

GOVERNMENT AND THE TRAVEL INDUSTRY

Although the majority of travel enterprises in Canada are privately owned, they are not allowed to do absolutely anything they want. Local, provincial/territorial, and federal governments promote and regulate many travel enterprises, whatever their size and location. Knowing how the government affects the travel and tourism industry is an important part of your product knowledge.

Government and Promotion

Recognizing the economic benefits, the government promotes travel and tourism by providing facilities, publicity, and concessions and incentives.

Facilities The government raises and budgets tax dollars for building, maintaining, and operating facilities that enable people to travel. The funding for intercity roads, airports, and river and harbour facilities is provided by various levels of government. The federal government, through Transport Canada, finances all air traffic control operations. Governments also finance facilities, such as convention centres and stadiums, that will bring visitors to a given area. Parks, monuments, historic sites, recreational areas, and scenic trails and waterways are also provided by government.

The federal government has set aside about 130 000 square kilometres of land for public recreation and enjoyment, under the administration of Parks Canada. That is an area about the size of England. Canada has the largest system of national parks in the world.

Publicity People living in Michigan probably saw a television ad inviting them to visit Ontario. Those living in New England probably saw an ad extolling the wonders of Atlantic Canada. By calling a special toll-free number, potential visitors could order a travel packet containing more tourist information.

These are examples of how government tourism offices advertise attractions and events to stimulate tourism. As they look for ways to replace jobs lost in agriculture, fishing, forestry, and manufacturing, provincial governments in particular are encouraging visitors.

Concessions and Incentives Federal, provincial, and local governments help the travel and tourism industry to grow by offering concessions and incentives. To attract a travel company to an area, the local government may reduce or waive taxes for a certain time, thus enabling the company to use more of its financial resources in getting started.

In late 1993 the Ontario government announced a $50 million contribution toward the expansion of the Metro Toronto Convention Centre. This will encourage businesses, professional organizations, and trade shows to hold their conventions and conferences in downtown Toronto. This will in turn benefit the hotels, restaurants, retail outlets, taxi companies, and public transportation systems in the city centre.

Finally, the federal government aids the travel and tourism industry by giving travellers incentives to spend more money. Tax-free shopping at duty-free shops in international airports is an example of this form of government support.

Government Regulation

To ensure public safety and to maintain an orderly system, the government requires licences and certificates, imposes rules and regulations, levies taxes and fees, and controls international travel.

Licences and Certificates To drive a car legally in Canada, you must pass a written examination and a road test. This process is overseen by the provincial governments, which also administer tests and issue licences to all bus drivers and chauffeurs, and many other vehicle operators. A licence indicates that the person has completed the necessary training and possesses the skills required to operate the vehicle safely. Airline pilots and railway engineers must also be tested and licensed. Their licences are issued by the federal government.

Just as you must obtain a licence to drive your car, all vehicles used in the travel industry must be registered with the government. Also, vehicles used for public transportation are subject to periodic safety inspections, and transportation companies must be certified before they can do business.

Another type of licensing applies to the hospitality industry. Local governments issue food and liquor licences to restaurants and bars. These licences enable the government to control the number, location, and hours of such establishments. In addition, bars and restaurants must conform to government safety and health standards. For instance, food must be stored at proper temperatures, and employees must wash their hands before handling food. To ensure the customers' safety in case of a fire, bars and restaurants must have the proper number of exits specified by government guidelines.

Rules and Regulations To prevent monopolistic practices and unfair pricing, the government requires transportation companies to keep their tariffs (schedules of rates) on public file. It also approves or refuses to approve fares, routes, and hours of operation; and allows or disallows corporate mergers. Since 1988, however, the federal government has eased its regulation of the transportation industry. The National Transportation Agency regulates the airlines and railways. The provincial governments oversee the motorcoach industry, which is still highly regulated in several provinces. They also monitor working conditions in the travel industry and enforce minimum wage laws.

Taxes and Fees If you've ever driven down a toll highway or crossed a toll bridge, you know that having an ample supply of quarters, dimes, and nickels will speed your journey along. The new Highway 407, an east-west bypass road north of Toronto, will be a toll road. Tolls are one way a government can raise money. It can also levy taxes and charge fees for the use of other facilities; for example, there are airport landing fees and port and harbour charges. The revenue from sales taxes on travel products — such as restaurant meals and hotel room stays — also goes to government. Taxes and fees, if too high, can discourage companies and travellers.

ILLUSTRATION 1-3
Canadian provincial governments promote travel and tourism by advertising, allocating funds for tourism offices, and offering concessions and incentives to the travel industry.
SOURCE: Nova Scotia Department of Tourism and Culture

CHAPTER 1: The Travel and Tourism Industry

International Travel The federal government encourages foreign travellers to visit Canada. Some visitors, however, are definitely *not* welcome. These include cocaine smugglers, illegal immigrants, and people with certain infectious diseases. By issuing visas and other documents, the government controls who enters the country.

Through customs inspections and border checks, the federal government attempts to control what products travellers bring into the country. For example, illegal drugs, explosives, and insect-infested fruit are dangerous to the health and welfare of Canadians and are not allowed.

Of course, before any travel can occur between Canada and another country, the two nations must have extended diplomatic recognition to each other. They must also have negotiated agreements on commerce, navigation, visa issuance, and consular and air transport rights.

CHECK YOUR PRODUCT KNOWLEDGE

1. Why does the government get involved in the travel industry?
2. In what way does the government promote travel?
3. In what four ways does the government regulate travel?

GEOGRAPHY AND THE TRAVEL INDUSTRY

As a travel professional, you should know geography. This does not mean that you must be able to plot the latitude and longitude of individual cities or memorize every country's chief exports and imports. Rather, you must know enough geography to give a traveller an idea of what to expect at his or her destination, and to make recommendations for travel there. Furthermore, you need to understand how geography influences the travel industry as a whole.

Destination Geography

Many travel professionals deal in destinations, or places. Most travellers are not familiar with the destinations they have chosen. As a result, travel professionals must be able to answer questions regarding three aspects of the destination: location, culture, and physical conditions.

Location Location refers to a traveller's most basic question about his or her destination: Where is it? A travel agent must be able to locate the place on a map and show the client its position in relation to other cities, regions, or countries.

The next question is this: How do I get there? The travel agent must be able to plan an **itinerary**, or route, for the journey. Along with this, the travel agent must know how accessible a particular destination is. Some travellers will choose only direct flights to well-travelled places, while others will seek out adventure in remote areas.

Having arrived at a destination, a traveller will expect to find other travel professionals who can answer more specific questions. For example, a business traveller will want to know where the factories, office buildings, and convention centres are, and how to get to them.

Culture Culture refers to the political, historical, social, artistic, and religious characteristics of travel destinations. Travellers will ask questions such as these: What should I see and do? Will I be able to communicate with the people? What kind of food can I expect? How much money will I need? Is it safe to drink the water? Travel professionals use their knowledge to inform travellers about local customs and prepare them for various differences. If travel agents suspect that a destination will cause severe cultural shock, they may suggest an alternative one. For example, they may discourage people who would be upset by crowds or by poverty from visiting certain cities in Asia.

Physical Conditions Physical conditions involve climate and terrain. Travellers will ask what the weather is like, and what clothes to bring. Travel professionals should be able to inform travellers about the average temperature and rainfall

ILLUSTRATION 1-4
The travel professional must possess in-depth knowledge of geographic areas, including their location, culture, and physical geography.

PROFILE

Thomas Cook

Thomas Cook, founder of the world's first travel agency and entrepreneur extraordinaire, was born in England in 1808. Cook quit school at the age of ten and worked at a series of jobs, including gardening, fruit selling, and bookselling. In 1828, at the age of 20, he became a Baptist missionary and an ardent supporter of the temperance movement. It was his interest in the cause of temperance that began his career in travel.

One day, in the early summer of 1841, Cook was on his way to a temperance meeting in Leicester. At the time he was working for a Baptist publisher in Loughborough, about ten miles away. An idea occurred to him: Why not arrange for a special train between Loughborough and Leicester for those who planned to attend the upcoming quarterly temperance meeting in Leicester? Cook approached the Midland Counties Railway company with his idea. The company agreed, and Cook advertised the arrangement. On July 5, the historic excursion took place—historic because it was the first publicly advertised excursion train to run in England.

Conditions were a bit rough. The 570 travellers were crammed into nine "tubs"—seatless third-class carriages open to the elements. Already, however, Cook's planning skills were evident. He had negotiated a specially reduced fare of one shilling per person for the trip. He also arranged for a picnic lunch to be served before the afternoon procession, and at the end of the line he set out tea for 1,000 people. Despite the primitive conditions of the ride, the trip was a reasonable success. By 1844, the railway had agreed to run the excursion regularly if Cook would guarantee the passengers. And he did, having by now left the ministry to start his own travel agency.

In the next several years, Cook organized other temperance-related tours. They were especially popular with people of limited income, who had never before had the opportunity to travel. As his agency grew, it began to serve all kinds of travellers, no longer limiting itself to the cause of temperance.

Cook's excursions did not venture outside the British Isles until he conducted excursions from Leicester to the French port of Calais for the Paris Exposition of 1855, a kind of world's fair. Foreseeing the business possibilities in European travel, the next year he organized "A Great Circular Tour of the Continent." Cook led the tour himself but, because he knew no foreign languages, also employed an interpreter. The tour left from Harwich, England, and moved through Belgium, Germany, and France, finally ending back at the English port of Southampton. So many travellers signed up for the tour that a repeat tour had to be scheduled six weeks later to take care of the overflow.

It took a few years for Cook's agency to institute regular service to Europe. Cook personally conducted another tour to Switzerland in July 1864, the same year his son, John Mason Cook, joined him in his firm (which became Thomas Cook & Son). John Mason Cook specialized in promoting the company's American tours. He did much to make Thomas Cook & Son a worldwide travel agency.

Extremely energetic and a top organizer, Thomas Cook used his group purchasing power to gain concessions from railroad companies and hotels. His agency was soon so dominant that he was able to impose on many hotels his system of accommodation cards. These were somewhat like coupons. They entitled Cook's clients to reduced rates on rooms in hotels throughout the world. Cook was not, however, without his critics. One writer compared his group tours to cattle drives. Yet business thrived. Thomas Cook died in 1892, and his business passed to his son. Today there are Thomas Cook & Son branches all over the world.

Cook's enterprising spirit changed the face of travel. He was responsible for the coining of a new phrase, the "Cook's tour," which means a whirlwind tour that lightly touches down in many places. In a larger sense, Cook was important because of the pioneering role he played in the area of organized mass travel. Thanks to Thomas Cook, the age of the grand tour gave way to the age of tourism.

of the destination. They should also advise travellers about any conditions that will seem unusual. For example, people who go to the Scandinavian countries (the "Land of the Midnight Sun") in the summertime should be aware that there will be almost 24 hours of daylight every day. Windows in hotel rooms there are equipped with blackout curtains to prevent sunlight from disturbing sleep at night. Canada has seven major physiographic regions: Arctic Tundra; Cordillera; Interior Plains; Canadian Shield; Hudson Bay Lowlands; St. Lawrence Lowlands; and Appalachian.

System Geography

In addition to knowing about specific destinations, travel professionals need a broad overview of the influence of geography on travel. All travel components operate within a geographic system, or area. Each system has its own climate, terrain, and political and cultural divisions that determine the level of tourist activity and the kinds of travel enterprises needed. As travellers move from geographic system to geographic system, the kinds and types of components needed may change.

Physical Conditions Climate is a major influence on travel. Warmer climates tend to draw more travellers than do colder ones. In Europe, vacationers flock to the sunny Mediterranean. About 10 percent of Canadians take a winter vacation to a southern location. In the United States the warm states of Florida, California, and Texas account for more than one-quarter of tourism receipts. Despite the distance from Canada, Florida attracted 2.4 million Canadians in 1991. This state accounted for more than one-third of the person-nights and one-quarter of the dollars ($2.1 billion) that Canadians spent staying one or more nights in the United States that year. Seasonal variations affect transportation and accommodation rates. Rates are generally lower in the off-season. Travel professionals should know what an area is like during the off-season. Some travellers may prefer to take advantage of the less crowded conditions and lower rates.

Terrain, too, is a major influence on travel. Some fortunate areas have a marvellous natural attraction that stimulates tourism; Percé Rock, 500 metres long, 100 metres wide, and 70 metres high, off the Gaspé Peninsula, is a major tourist destination in Quebec, both as a natural attraction and as a bird sanctuary. Travel enterprises in a mountainous area will take advantage of the terrain by building ski resorts. An area with many lakes will build a resort industry offering swimming, water-skiing, and fishing.

The climate and terrain of the Laurentian "playground," just north of Montreal, encouraged the development of both a winter and a summer resort industry. Also, the spectacular fall foliage there attracts tourists from eastern Canada and the United States. The terrain determines how accessible an area is: few people vacation in the Amazon Basin because the dense jungle makes travel difficult. Terrain dictates transportation. If a large body of water lies between the starting point and the destination, the travel professional may need to arrange ferry transportation. A prime example in Canada is the ferry crossing from Sydney, Nova Scotia, to Port aux Basques, Newfoundland. Automobile travellers need to budget two extra travel days for the 18-hour return trip on the ferry.

Culture Geographic areas have political boundaries: city; province, state, or canton; country. Governments influence how open or how closed an area is and place restrictions on travellers. Travel industries in Western Europe, for instance, are more highly developed than in Eastern Europe because, until very recently, the governments of the East European nations restricted travel. Travel to the Persian Gulf was severely restricted in the early 1990s when war broke out. The governments of many nations advised their citizens to stay away from the area.

Travel professionals need to inform clients about the requirements for passing from one political jurisdiction to another. For international travel, this means helping clients obtain passports, visas, and other travel permits; informing them about necessary vaccinations; and explaining customs regulations. Travel professionals should be able to explain how to exchange currency. People who are travelling between provinces in this country may also require certain information, such as differences in health coverage and costs.

Location Location influences travel and the type of travel components. Remote, underdeveloped locations may have a standard of living different from what a traveller is used to. Items commonplace to the traveller, such as toothpaste, toilet paper, and ketchup, may be unavailable or very expensive. Travel professionals need to prepare travellers for these differences.

Smaller countries with high standards of living and high population densities generate the most international travel. The countries of Western Europe are the best example; travellers can cross several international boundaries in a short amount of time. Canada and the United States do not generate as much international travel because of their large size and greater isolation. Australia and New Zealand are two good examples of geographic isolation hampering international tourism—although this is now changing.

Learning About Destinations and Systems

Learning about geography is an ongoing process. The travel professional must keep up-to-date because destinations and systems are constantly changing. For example, if hotel workers in Montreal are on strike, creating chaos in that city's hospitality industry, a travel professional will probably suggest that clients postpone a vacation trip to the Montreal area. Similarly, a political disturbance, a natural disaster, or an unfavourable shift in the currency exchange rate might temporarily discourage travellers from going to a particular destination.

A travel professional should also know when a destination is likely to be saturated — that is, when there are too many people for the area to handle comfortably. In the summertime, London is extremely crowded with tourists. The number of tour buses visiting the Changing of the Guard at Buckingham Palace each day must now be rationed. British tourism officials are promoting visits to the quaint hamlets outside London instead.

If a destination has become polluted, travel professionals should know so that they can advise clients. Some travellers will be very upset to see how acid rain is destroying many beautiful buildings and works of art in many European cities. They may be dismayed by the litter in many national parks in the United States. This presents an opportunity for federal and provincial tourism officials to position Canada in the minds of international travellers as a country with relatively unspoiled natural beauty and clean and well-kept cities.

A travel professional can keep up with destinations and systems in several ways. One way is through visits. Travel professionals can take familiarization trips (**FAM trips**) to inspect hotels and restaurants, sample attractions, and experience the local culture. FAM trips are sponsored by airlines, resorts, and other travel and tourism suppliers to showcase established vacation spots and to help develop new destinations. They enable travel professionals to determine whether these areas meet their clients' vacation needs. Travel professionals can also learn about destinations on personal vacation trips. Or they can learn from the travel experiences of other professionals or clients who have recently returned from trips.

It is impossible, however, for travel professionals to obtain firsthand accounts of every destination. Another way to find out about destinations is through written sources:

- atlases
- brochures (from government tourist offices, tour operators, or suppliers)
- guidebooks
- trade publications
- travel magazines
- travel sections of newspapers

A third way to learn about destinations is through membership in professional organizations.

> **CHECK YOUR PRODUCT KNOWLEDGE**
>
> 1. Why is a knowledge of geography important for the travel professional?
> 2. What are three ways the travel professional can learn more about destinations and systems?
> 3. What topics relevant to the travel industry does geography include?

Summary

- The travel industry has grown tremendously in the past 35 years.
- A calm political climate throughout most of the world, improvements in transportation, a rise in personal incomes, and an increase in leisure time have all stimulated the growth of travel.
- The travel industry offers a variety of job opportunities requiring a range of skills, training, and experience.
- Travel professionals must possess a knowledge of business, psychology, and geography. They must be able to adapt to a dynamic industry and understand the consumer's motivations, needs, and expectations (MNEs).
- Travel is an industry because it comprises companies that work as a profit-making system to provide travellers with products and services.
- Travel companies can be grouped by function into seven components. Three components furnish transportation, two provide accommodation and entertainment, and two distribute travel products and services.
- Travel products are mainly intangible. They include a ride on a train, a visit to a national park, a stay in a hotel.
- Travel services provide benefits to travellers. They are performed by professionals within a host–guest relationship.
- The travel industry in Canada and the United States functions within a free enterprise system in which privately owned businesses compete with a minimum of government interference.
- To be successful in the marketplace, the travel professional must bring the right product or service to the right marketplace at the right time and right price. The travel professional must also promote the product and determine whether it satisfies the consumer.
- Recognizing the travel industry's potential to generate jobs, the government promotes travel by providing facilities, publicity, and concessions and incentives.

- The government regulates travel by requiring licences and certificates, imposing rules and regulations, levying taxes and fees, and controlling international travel. Government regulation seeks to protect the health, safety, and welfare of citizens.
- The climate, terrain, location, and politics of a geographic area affect the level and type of travel activity.
- The travel professional must be able to give travellers a clear picture of any destination. Knowledge of the location, culture, and physical conditions enables travel professionals to do this.

Key Terms

trip
industry
charter
maritime
ground transportation
motorcoach
mart
package
intermodal package
tangible
intangible
free enterprise system
tariff
itinerary
FAM trip

What Do You Think?

1. Do you think the travel industry will continue to grow? Why or why not?
2. Which of the seven components of the travel industry do you think will experience the most growth? Why?
3. Should the federal government spend more money or less money on travel and tourism? Give reasons for your answer.
4. Why, do you think, are accurate travel statistics hard to find?
5. What are some of the main attractions of a career in travel and tourism?

Dealing with Product

Welcome to "Yourtown." At the end of each chapter, you will be asked to do some problem-solving involving both the travel product and the people who buy and use this product. Quite often, you will be asked to refer to "Yourtown," meaning either your hometown or the city or town where you are studying.

Let's begin by examining travel and intangible products. Why do we consider travel to be an intangible product? What types of intangible products (besides the travel industry) are available in Yourtown? Are these intangible products similar to or different from travel products?

Next, think of the various components of the travel industry that you were introduced to in this chapter. Once again, using Yourtown as a reference point, list as many examples as you can of each of these components and the products that each one offers to the travellers of Yourtown.

Dealing with People

Every traveller has his or her own motivations, needs, and expectations. However, these MNEs are situational — they will vary with the type of traveller and the type of travel. Put yourself to the test in the following brief self-study. The motivations for each trip are given. What do you think your expectations would be if you were travelling from Yourtown to these places?

1. Paris and Rome for a two-week vacation.
2. Edmonton for a wedding.
3. Toronto for a sales meeting.
4. Baltimore for the Grey Cup.
5. Halifax for a job interview.
6. Vancouver to begin a cruise.

Use your imagination. Are you the same person in each of these scenarios? What does this exercise tell you about the statement that "the travel professional must possess a knowledge of business, psychology, and geography"?

A DAY IN THE LIFE OF

A Receptive Operator

I own a tour business, but my business differs from other tour operators in two important ways. First, I don't sell tours to the general public; I sell to other tour operators, bus companies, and travel agents. Second, I specialize in one particular geographic area, the New England area. The terms *receptive operator, reception services,* and *destination manager* all refer to people like me who specialize in serving travellers in one small geographic vicinity.

I am one of about 160 receptive operators in the United States. We are a very recent but growing addition to the travel industry. We are a sort of wholesaler or sub-contractor of tours. Let's assume that you own a tour business called All-Star Tours. You have a group of retired people who want to tour New England during the fall when the leaves change colour. However, your regular tour packages do not include any tours of New England.

You could either turn down the group or hire a tour company like mine to conduct the tour. If you hire my company, my tour director will meet your busload of tourists at the start of the tour and conduct it for you. The tour director will welcome your guests "on behalf of All-Star Tours." Your clients will never know that they are actually being served by my company.

There are several advantages to using receptive operators. The major advantage is that because I specialize in one particular geographic area, I am able to provide the highest quality tours of that area. I know all of the hotels, restaurants, and tourist attractions there. My tour guides are the most knowledgeable about the history and development of the region. I give local hotels and restaurants a lot of business; they, in turn, give me superb service and special discount rates that I can pass on to my customers and they can pass on to theirs.

Another advantage is that I can be much more flexible than regular tour operators. I can custom tailor my tours to meet the needs and interests of the group. Because of this ability, I am often called upon to provide tours for foreign visitors to the United States. I recently tailored a tour for a group of German bankers and another for a group of Japanese industrialists. I employ only about eight full-time workers, but my payroll includes several part-time tour directors who speak German, French, Japanese, Spanish, and other languages.

My full-time employees spend their day arranging tours, negotiating with hotels and restaurants, writing brochures, seeking out new attractions and routes, and so on. I spend the bulk of my day in sales activities. I may be on the phone all day calling bus companies, travel agents, and tour operators. I want as many of these companies as possible to be aware of my agency's services so that when they need me, they know where to find me.

I also spend a lot of time at travel industry conferences and trade shows. For example, I attend the World Travel Market trade show in London each year. I run a booth at the show where I can meet British travel agents and tour operators and familiarize them with my services.

I wasn't always a receptive operator. I started out as a tour escort. Then I had my own tour company for a while. You really need experience as a tour operator before trying to specialize in receptive services. In addition, you need as much experience as you can get in running a small business. You have to know how to estimate profits and expenses and how to manage people and perform the necessary paperwork to run a business. And, of course, you must know how to organize and conduct tours.

Running a receptive services business is a very risky venture. It is usually seasonal, which means that it makes money only a few months of each year, but it must employ workers and spend money year-round. Despite these drawbacks, I enjoy being a receptive operator very much because I like being able to serve people and I like being my own boss. I am very proud of my geographic region and gain a great deal of satisfaction showing it to visitors. I also love to travel myself so I know what other travellers want and expect from a well-run tour.

CHAPTER 1: The Travel and Tourism Industry   Name: _____

WORKSHEET 1-1 Travel and the Economy

The travel industry has a huge impact on the economy or the United States. The table below shows the amount of money taken in by selected components of the travel industry in recent years. Study the table and then answer the questions that follow.

Business Receipts of Travel Industry Components, 1975–88

	RECEIPTS (IN MILLIONS OF DOLLARS)				
Year	Air Transportation	Ground Transportation	Hospitality	Tourism	TOTAL
1975	10,301	1,409	64,069	18,760	94,539
1980	23,405	2,081	116,890	29,409	171,785
1982	25,488	2,283	137,342	34,661	199,774
1984	31,437	2,551	158,489	39,484	231,961
1986	33,846	2,466	181,189	45,532	263,033
1988	41,654	2,467	211,812	53,922	309,855

SOURCE: U.S. Travel Data Center, Washington, D.C. *The 1988–89 Economic Review of Travel in America*

1. What were the total United States industry receipts in 1988?
2. What was the overall pattern of travel receipts from 1975 to 1988?
3. Which component nearly tripled its receipts between 1975 and 1988?
4. What happened to air transportation receipts between 1975 and 1988?
5. Which component showed the lowest total receipts between 1975 and 1988?

Construct a table or graph to show the growth of tourism in Yourtown. The information could be in terms of number of visitors, amount of revenue generated by local travel components, or number of people employed locally by the travel industry. Contact Yourtown's chamber of commerce for appropriate data.

21

CHAPTER 1: The Travel and Tourism Industry   Name: _____

WORKSHEET 1-2 Destination Geography

First, choose a travel destination—the more exotic and unfamiliar to you the better. Then do research on this destination so that you can draw up a geographic profile that would be useful to a tourist.

LOCAL GEOGRAPHY

1. Name of destination
2. Location of destination
3. How to get there

CULTURAL GEOGRAPHY

4. Language(s) spoken
5. General health conditions
6. Type of food
7. Type of clothing worn
8. Currency used and exchange rate in dollars
9. Cost of living
10. Availability of basic items
11. Unusual conditions or customs

PHYSICAL GEOGRAPHY

12. Climate, in winter and summer
13. On-season and off-season
14. Clothing needed
15. Terrain
16. Local transportation

CHAPTER 2

The Travellers

"The world is a great book, of which they who never stir from home read only a page."

St. Augustine of Hippo

OBJECTIVES

When you have completed this chapter, you should be able to do the following:

- Explain how the concept of travel has changed through the ages.
- Describe the three main groups of travellers and their motivations, needs, and expectations (MNEs).
- Explain why people travel for pleasure in terms of both Stanley Plog's theory of personality types and Abraham Maslow's theory of need satisfaction.
- Explain why the travel industry classifies travellers into groups, or segments, and how it obtains information about each segment.
- List some of the reasons why Canadians might be interested in travelling within Canada.
- Discuss the special issues of international travel, such as documentation, customs regulations, common health problems, and foreign currencies.
- Define inbound tourism and describe the MNEs of travellers who come to Canada.

Passengers on Flight 723 from Vancouver are deplaning at Gate 11 on the concourse of Terminal 3 in Toronto. Glancing at her watch, a business executive hurries down the ramp. She is followed by a group of tourists who are loaded down with cameras and flight bags. Next comes a young family—the mother is carrying an infant, while the father is trying to hang on to a rambunctious two-year-old. Also among the passengers are a newly married couple returning from a cruise to Alaska and an elderly woman whose granddaughter attends the University of Victoria. When most of the passengers have deplaned, a flight attendant comes down the ramp guiding a young man in a wheelchair.

These are modern-day travellers. As a travel professional, you must get to know these people in order to serve them. You must know who they are, why they travel, and where they go.

A BRIEF HISTORY OF TRAVEL

Throughout history, there have been travellers. The Old Testament describes the journey of the Israelites from Egypt to the Promised Land. The walls of a temple in Luxor, Egypt, chronicle the pleasure cruise of Queen Hatshepsut to the ancient land of Punt (now Somalia). History books give accounts of famous travellers, such as the Vikings, Marco Polo, and Christopher Columbus. Fossil remains of *Homo erectus* have been found in western Europe, Africa, and China—revealing that even prehistoric people were travellers.

Requirements for Travel

In the time of the Roman Empire, a wealthy citizen could travel quite easily. The Roman government had built a magnificent network of roads. Fresh relays of horses were available every five or six miles. A single system of currency throughout the empire facilitated payments for food and lodging. Most important, the *Pax Romana*, or Roman peace, guaranteed travellers a high degree of safety.

In order for travel to flourish, there must be an efficient transportation system and an atmosphere of peace and political stability. Travel—especially travel for pleasure—also requires economic prosperity and sufficient leisure time. When the Roman Empire declined, so did travel. The wealthy class disappeared, roads deteriorated, and the countryside was overrun by brigands and robbers.

In the Dark Ages that followed (approximately A.D. 500 to 1450), travel became what it has generally been throughout history—dangerous and difficult. In fact, the word travel, which was coined during this time, comes from a root word meaning "heavy labour." Peasants rarely left their villages. When merchants and clergy had to travel, they did so on foot or in crude ox-drawn carts over rough terrain.

It was not until the Industrial Revolution, which began in the mid-1700s in Europe, that travel started to be more common. Around that time, a series of developments in transportation—the stagecoach, then the steamboat, and finally the railway—made travel easier in North America as well as in Europe. In addition to technological changes, social changes contributed to the growth of travel. A middle class, with money and leisure time, was developing. Wishing to escape occasionally from bleak city life, these people retreated to seaside resorts for recreation.

In the 20th century the development of automobiles and motorcoaches created a demand for better roads, and people were soon driving all over Canada and the United States. With the first transatlantic passenger-jet flight in the late 1950s, fast, comfortable, and economical international travel became possible.

In the last 35 years, the volume of travel has increased tremendously. Partly the result of improvements in transportation, this increase is also attributable to economic prosperity and social change. Earlier, only wealthy people travelled for pleasure; in today's industrial societies, people from most economic classes have money to spend on travel. Many households have more than one person working, and thus providing disposable income for travel. Paid annual vacations and holidays give people more leisure time for travel. People are better educated today. In general, the more education a person receives, the more likely he or she is to travel. People are also living longer. Many senior citizens, having retired from the workforce and paid off their mortgages, can take trips any time of the year. For most Canadians, travel has become a normal expectation associated with the good life.

Reasons for Travel

Throughout history, most travel was done out of necessity rather than for pleasure. People travelled to satisfy basic needs for survival. They were searching for food and shelter or fleeing from enemies. Many people travelled in search of a better life. Perhaps they were looking for gold, silver, and other treasures that would make them rich. Or they were scouting for fertile farmland to which they could move their families.

This is not to say that no one ever travelled just for the fun of it. Even in ancient times, some pleasure travel occurred. During a typical season, 700,000 tourists crowded into Ephesus, a city in Asia Minor, where they were entertained by acrobats, animal acts, jugglers, and magicians. Wealthy Romans made excursions to Greece to take in the Olympic Games, theatrical productions, and festivals.

Of course, some people travelled just out of curiosity. They wanted to know what lay beyond the horizon or around the bend in the road. Perhaps some sailors joined the crews of the *Niña*, *Pinta*, and *Santa Maria* in 1492 because they wanted to find out what would happen when the ships reached the edge of the world.

There have been other motivations for travel as well. During the Middle Ages, people went on pilgrimages to holy cities and shrines. They did so to pay homage to a saint or to fulfil a vow. Some pilgrims dressed in sackcloth and walked barefoot as a sign of penance. The passport originated in 1388, when Richard II required English pilgrims to obtain and carry permits before they could travel to France. The Crusades (1095–1291), during which Christians attempted to wrest control of the Holy Land from the Muslims, were the most ambitious religious journeys of all.

Travel for the purpose of conducting trade—in other words, business travel—has been going on for centuries. Traders from Phoenicia, a civilization that existed from 1100 to 332 B.C., sailed from port to port in the Mediterranean world. Early travel in China and India was based on trade.

Notions about cures for ailments of the body have also influenced travel. To relieve his rheumatism, the Roman emperor Caracalla (A.D. 188–217) journeyed to mineral springs located north of Rome. Juan Ponce de Leon, a Spanish conquistador, discovered Florida in 1513 while searching for the Fountain of Youth. In the 1800s it was fashionable for members of the European aristocracy to visit various German spas (different spas claimed to treat different maladies). These people sipped mineral water all day and then entertained themselves with banquets, dancing, and gambling all night.

Destinations of historic and cultural significance have attracted travellers through the ages. This reason for travel originated with the Grand Tour during the Renaissance and Elizabethan eras. As part of their education, the sons of the British aristocracy travelled extensively in Europe. Accompanied by tutors and servants, these young gentlemen visited cathedrals, castles, and galleries, especially those of France and Italy. They learned to speak several languages and were introduced to Europe's aristocracy. The Grand Tour usually took three years.

> **CHECK YOUR PRODUCT KNOWLEDGE**
>
> 1. How is the modern concept of travel different from that of the Middle Ages?
> 2. In order for travel to occur on a wide scale, what conditions are necessary?
> 3. What have been some reasons for travel throughout history?

WHO TRAVELS TODAY?

In the past, wealthy travellers had similar expectations of travel. For example, in the 1920s, anyone who was anybody took the grand tour of Europe. It was fairly easy for hotel managers, captains of cruise ships, and other travel professionals to anticipate the needs of these travellers and to serve them satisfactorily.

CHAPTER 2: The Travellers

Today's travellers are not so similar in nature; they form a larger and more diverse group of people. However, as a travel professional, you can begin to know today's travellers and their MNEs by dividing travellers into three general categories: the vacation and leisure traveller; the business and professional traveller; and the traveller visiting friends and relatives. Figure 2-1 shows the percentage of trips taken in each of these categories. You will soon learn more about the individual differences within these three categories.

The Vacation and Leisure Traveller

The following people represent the vacation and leisure travel segment: the family spending a week in Florida at DisneyWorld; the college student spending the summer exploring Europe; the retired couple taking a one-week cruise to Bermuda. Rather than lying in a hammock in the backyard, they use their leisure time to travel.

Discretionary Travel Vacation and leisure travel is often called discretionary travel. The word discretion refers to the ability to make a choice, judgment, or decision. (You may have heard someone say, "Use your own discretion," when you've had a decision to make.) Vacation and leisure travellers take trips because they want to—travel is voluntary for them. They choose whether to stay at home, drive to the Laurentians, or fly to the Caribbean.

Likewise, the money that vacation and leisure travellers spend is called discretionary income. Discretionary income is the money that's left over after the necessities of life—shelter, food, clothing—have been purchased. People choose how they want to spend their discretionary income. Some choose to spend it on travel; others may choose to spend it on a boat, or a second home. Since there is much competition from many industries for consumer's discretionary income, the components of the travel industry work together to persuade consumers to spend their money on travel.

The Pleasure Seekers In general, vacation and leisure travellers seek pleasure and relaxation. However, since the concept of pleasure varies from individual to individual, one person's idea of the perfect vacation is another person's idea of a total waste of time and money. Some travellers enjoy exploring ancient ruins, while others prefer sunbathing by the ocean. More will be said about specific motivations for pleasure travel later in this chapter.

Another feature of vacation and leisure travel is that the pleasure comes not only during the trip but also before and after. Planning the itinerary, shopping for clothes to take along, and researching the destination can be as enjoyable as

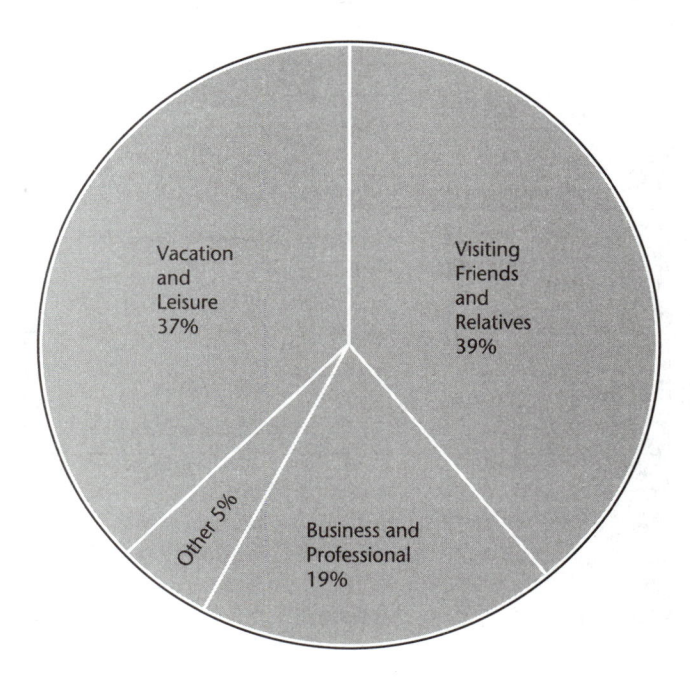

FIGURE 2-1
Why People Travel
SOURCE: U.S. Travel Data Center

- Vacation and Leisure 37%
- Visiting Friends and Relatives 39%
- Business and Professional 19%
- Other 5%

ILLUSTRATION 2-1
Vacation travellers travel because they want to.
SOURCE: Karen O'Neill

the trip itself. Once back home, putting together a scrapbook about the trip or talking about it with friends and relatives sustains the pleasure.

Purchasing Travel Products and Services When they purchase travel products and services, vacation and leisure travellers are essentially buying an experience they hope will be pleasurable. To satisfy their needs, vacation and leisure travellers will select products and services from several of the travel components. They will certainly select products from the tourism component, such as tickets to a theme park or a concert. They will probably purchase hospitality products and services, although some vacationers travel by recreational vehicle and camp along the way. Depending on the size of the group, the type of trip, the distance of the destination, and the time involved, vacation travellers may or may not choose air transportation. For example, even though air transportation is sometimes less expensive, families who want to visit many sites en route to their destination will find it more convenient to travel by automobile.

Vacation and leisure travellers have time to shop around for the product that best suits their needs. Often they wait for discounted prices or a last-minute sale before they choose a trip. Their schedules are more flexible than those of business and professional travellers, so they can take advantage of the travel restrictions that accompany discounted airfares. Vacation and leisure travellers are likely to purchase a package of travel products, including transportation, accommodations, and sightseeing.

The Business and Professional Traveller

The sales representative who sells pharmaceutical products to physicians and pharmacists throughout New Brunswick, Nova Scotia, and Prince Edward Island; the efficiency expert who inspects operations at a company's branch locations; and the manager of a Manitoba farmers' co-op who must attend parliamentary hearings in Ottawa are all business travellers.

Business travel is **nondiscretionary travel**. Business travellers usually do not have a choice about whether or not they want to travel, nor do they usually decide *where* they want to travel. Travel is part of their job description. They must travel to get their job done.

A variation of business travel is professional travel. Professional travellers attend conventions and seminars related to their work. These meetings usually provide participants with information and skills to help them perform their jobs better. For example, a physician may attend a medical convention to obtain the latest information on the treatment of allergies. A sales representative may attend a seminar on how to improve selling skills.

Professional travel is also nondiscretionary in the sense that travellers do not decide the date or location of the convention or seminar. At the same time, it is discretionary in that attendance at conventions and seminars is often optional. Some professional travellers are also business travellers, and vice versa. For example, a salesperson who often travels for business may also attend an annual sales convention.

Time is very important for business and professional travellers. They must arrive at meetings on time. They must get their work done on time. Since every minute away from their home office costs money, they can't afford to waste time on delays and errors.

When they purchase travel products and services, business and professional travellers are essentially buying time. Products that furnish speed, efficiency, and convenience of location provide them with time. Business and professional travellers generally purchase air transportation to and from their destination, a rental car for on-demand local transportation, and accommodations in a major hotel near their meeting site.

ILLUSTRATION 2-2
For business travellers, travel is part of a day's work.
SOURCE: IBM Canada Limited

The schedules of business and professional travellers are less flexible than those of vacation and leisure travellers. Often, because they can't plan their trips far in advance, they can't take advantage of discount airfares and other bargains. To obtain speed, efficiency, and convenience, business and professional travellers must often pay higher prices for travel products and services. Chapters 11 and 12 describe the MNEs of this group of travellers in more detail.

The Traveller Visiting Friends and Relatives

The father who takes his children to Saskatchewan every summer to visit their grandparents; alumni who attend their college's reunion; and the son and daughter who return home because their father is ill are all travellers visiting friends and relatives.

Travellers visiting friends and relatives (often referred to as VFRs) form the largest group of travellers. VFR travel may be discretionary or nondiscretionary, depending on the reasons for the trip. If a traveller must go out of town because of an emergency, such as an illness or a death in the family, then the travel is nondiscretionary. If a traveller wants to visit high school friends or spend some time with family members simply to enjoy their company, the travel is discretionary.

Travellers who visit friends and relatives for pleasure are like leisure travellers in their purchase of travel products. Travellers who visit friends and relatives because of an emergency are more like business travellers, with an added element of stress. In either case, they are likely to purchase only transportation, and perhaps some tourism products. The friends and relatives usually supply the accommodations (a spare bedroom or the living-room sofa) and meals.

CHECK YOUR PRODUCT KNOWLEDGE

1. Name the three main groups of modern-day travellers.
2. What is the purpose of dividing travellers into these groups?
3. List the characteristics of each group.

VACATION AND LEISURE TRAVELLERS

Imagine that you're a travel agent in a retail travel agency. A woman who appears to be in her late thirties comes into your office. She introduces herself as Mrs. O'Neill and says she wants help planning a trip to Mexico. You begin to reach for the brochures describing family vacations in Mexico, but Mrs. O'Neill says she'll be travelling without her family. You then ask if she's seeking a sun vacation on the Mexican Riviera, but that's not it either. Mrs. O'Neill tells you she's bored with the routine of everyday life. What she really wants is a vacation experience that will challenge her mind and imagination. After thinking for a moment, you suggest that she go to Mexico to study the architectural legacy of the Aztecs. Mrs. O'Neill thinks that is a wonderful idea.

Discovering a vacation traveller's motives for travelling is very important. A travel agent needs this information in order to sell the client the right travel product for his or her needs. In case of Mrs. O'Neill, a family vacation tour or a resort vacation would clearly have been the wrong product.

To define the product further, the travel agent needs to ask questions relating to the client's background and lifestyle. You would ask Mrs. O'Neill questions such as these: Do you want to travel alone or with a group? What kind of accommodations do you want? About how much money do you want to spend? How long do you want to stay? After discussing these questions, you and Mrs. O'Neill may well agree that she should join a study tour to Mexico that is being organized by the Museum of Civilization in Hull, Quebec.

Why Do They Travel?

In the dining room of a resort hotel in Balestrand, Norway, the guests are enjoying a Sunday evening smorgasbord. If you were to ask each traveller why he or she came to Norway, you would get different responses. For example, Vern Olson, a dairy farmer from Ontario, wants to visit the village from which his ancestors emigrated. He's also interested in learning more about Norwegian folklore and music. Recently widowed, Dora Larson is seeking companionship from other members of her tour group. Travel posters showing magnificent mountains and fjords convinced Brian and Melissa West to make a trip to Norway. Peter Holm, a college student from Manitoba, wants to hike up to the glaciers. And, after teaching junior high students for nine months, Bill Horvath is hoping this trip will restore his frazzled nerves.

Underlying these stated objectives may be deeper motives. For example, Andrea Stevenson enjoys the feeling of importance she gets when people wait on her. Ray and Maryann Kerncamp decided to go to Norway because last year their neighbours made a similar trip. And Mark Williams, a middle-aged bachelor, is secretly hoping to find romance.

There are many reasons for vacation and leisure travel, and travel experts have many ways of listing or organizing them. In recent years, however, two theories for explaining why people travel have gained widespread acceptance. One theory is offered by psychologist Stanley Plog, the other by sociologist Abraham Maslow.

Stanley Plog According to Plog, an individual's personality determines his or her motivation for travel and choice of destination. Plog uses a continuum to describe vacation and

PROFILE

Isadore Sharp and Four Seasons Hotels

In 1992, Isadore Sharp was named CEO of the Year by *The Financial Post*. In September 1993, 30 of Isadore Sharp's Four Seasons hotels were listed among the top hotels in the Americas, Europe, and the Asia–Pacific region by *International Investor*. In October of the same year, *Condé Nast Traveler* reported that 7 of the top 25 hotels and resorts in the world were part of the Four Seasons group, and named the Four Seasons Wailea in Maui the best resort in the world. The quality of Sharp's hotels and of his leadership are now hallmarks of the chain he founded and runs.

Isadore Sharp grew up in Toronto and earned a degree in architecture from Ryerson Polytechnical Institute in 1952. After graduating, he joined his father's small construction firm. Sharp built his first motel in the early 1960s, on Jarvis Street in downtown Toronto. It had 165 rooms. The venture was considered by some to be risky; it was, after all, in one of the least affluent neighbourhoods in the city and far from the business district. But from the start, Sharp was an innovator, and his instincts have seldom failed him. As soon as his first motel was well established, he built the Inn on the Park in Toronto's northern suburbs. This hotel is built on a high point of land and has beautifully landscaped grounds. Despite initial scepticism about its location, the hotel flourished. In 1970, he decided to expand outside of Toronto and built the five-star Inn on the Park (now called the Four Seasons London) in London, England. Once again, there were those who thought he couldn't succeed. Why build a five-star hotel in a city that already offered several luxury hotels? But Sharp had recognized a need for a quality modern hotel in keeping with the style of the day. Once again, he was right — the Four Seasons London was a success.

Sharp's company has changed over the years. In the 1970s, Four Seasons decided to "only operate medium-sized hotels of exceptional quality." Then, during the 1980s, the company changed focus so that it managed hotels instead of owning them. The company prospered by applying its sense of quality and style to other companies' properties. However, in the summer of 1992, Four Seasons expanded into Asia by acquiring Regent Hotels International of Hong Kong. Some of this chain's hotels are luxury hotels on a grand scale. (A budget room at the Hong Kong Regent costs $350 a night; a suite costs $1,600.)

One of the most important ingredients in the success of Four Seasons has been its commitment to a very high quality of service. It is the kind of service that has inspired loyalty among guests and made the company's name one of the most respected in the international hotel business. Hotel staff and management pride themselves on their fast, friendly, and tactful service. Four Seasons Hotels offer 24-hour room service, good to outstanding restaurants, and small services such as terry-cloth bathrobes in all rooms and complimentary overnight shoeshines. Also, Four Seasons concierges are among the most highly skilled and dedicated in the world. They must be knowledgeable and helpful, must have a ready command of the geography and amenities of their city, must speak at least one foreign language, and, above all, must be able to maintain their professionalism and grace under fire. As Gander Lurer of the Four Seasons in Washington, D.C., says, "Our clientele expects the best. We never say no, never say can't."

Not surprisingly, the company has also been successful as an employer, and has one of the lowest turnover rates in the hotel industry. Four Seasons locker rooms and staff cafeterias are nearly as well appointed as the guest facilities. Employees are valued highly and are treated accordingly. According to Sharp's executive assistant, "You read all these buzz words today like empowerment; [he] was doing it before they coined the phrases."

Today, Isadore Sharp's Four Seasons/Regent Hotels and Resorts is a multimillion-dollar hotel empire that spans the globe, managing 43 hotels in 17 countries. Sharp's innovation, daring, and commitment to quality offer an inspiring example of a Canadian succeeding in the global market.

leisure travellers (Figure 2-2 shows the continuum, along with possible destinations for each personality type).

At one end of the continuum is the **allocentric personality** (*allo-* means "varied in form"). Allocentric personalities seek adventure, variety, and excitement. They want to experience totally different cultures and environments. They may choose to visit an isolated hill tribe in India and stay in native lodgings, eat native food, and participate in native dances and ceremonies. Allocentric personalities shun traditional destinations and modes of transportation. They may be seen driving a jeep across the Sahara or paddling a dugout canoe on the inland rivers of Brazil. Allocentric personalities are trend setters—they help to establish new destinations. When those destinations become popular with other travellers, allocentrics move on to explore new territory.

At the opposite end of the continuum is the **psychocentric personality** (*psyche* means "self"). Psychocentric personalities, who tend to focus their thoughts on themselves and their families, don't travel much. When they do go away, they don't venture too far from home. For example, if they live in the Maritimes, they might travel to Saint John, Halifax, or Charlottetown. Psychocentric personalities need consistency and reliability in their travel products. Often, they return to the same place year after year. They don't want to experiment with accommodations, food, or entertainment. Nor do they want to experience personal stress or encounter unusual situations.

Falling between these two extremes is the **midcentric personality**. Most vacation and leisure travellers fit into this category. Midcentric personalities travel in order to obtain a break from their everyday routines. They want to strike a healthy balance between work and recreation. Midcentric personalities aren't afraid to try new travel experiences as long as these experiences are not too bizarre or challenging. The environment can't seem too foreign—a fast-food restaurant in the midst of 17th-century buildings is reassuring to them. Midcentric personalities often go where their friends have gone. They tend to travel to familiar destinations such as the Caribbean, Hawaii, and Great Britain. They might go to Hong Kong, Tokyo, and Manila, but most places in the Far East are too extreme for them.

Abraham Maslow Maslow's theory centres on the belief that needs satisfaction motivates human behaviour. Maslow developed five areas of human needs and arranged them in a hierarchy. (Figure 2-3 shows this hierarchy.) As if climbing a ladder, individuals start at the bottom of the hierarchy and work their way up. The needs at a lower level must be met before the individual can proceed to a higher level. In other words, individuals must satisfy their needs for food, shelter, and clothing before seeking safety and security. Once their needs for safety and security have been met, they are free to seek love and the company of other people, and so on.

Maslow's theory suggests that vacation and leisure travellers are motivated by the desire to satisfy needs. People who lack money for food, shelter, and clothing can't travel for pleasure. But after basic physical and emotional needs have been met, travel meets people's needs for esteem, respect, and self-actualization. (Self-actualization is Maslow's term for the highest level of personal fulfilment.)

Travellers who feel a need to be with other people may purchase an escorted group tour or a cruise with many planned activities. Travellers who feel a need for respect may purchase a travel product that will impress their friends and associates. This might be a trip to an exotic destination or a stay at a ritzy resort or hotel. Travellers who feel a need for self-actualization are beyond trying to impress their friends. Instead, they want a travel product that will help them develop physically, mentally, or spiritually. They might choose a bicycle tour through Ireland, a study tour of France's châteaux, or a trip to Mecca.

Maslow's hierarchy of needs operates on different levels for different activities at different times. The hierarchy also operates within a single travel experience. For example, sudden terrorist activities at a destination will bring a vacationer's needs back down to the level of safety and security—at such times, the needs for esteem, respect, and self-actualization must be set aside. While on vacation in Europe, a traveller may receive news that a family member has become seriously ill. The traveller's needs then descend to the basic emotional ones, as he or she attempts to deal with the crisis.

In addition to planning travel products and services to meet human needs, travel professionals must recognize when needs change and adapt their products and services accordingly. In the case of a traveller with a critically ill relative, a hotel manager might arrange for long-distance telephone calls, and the tour escort might arrange for quick transportation back home to Canada.

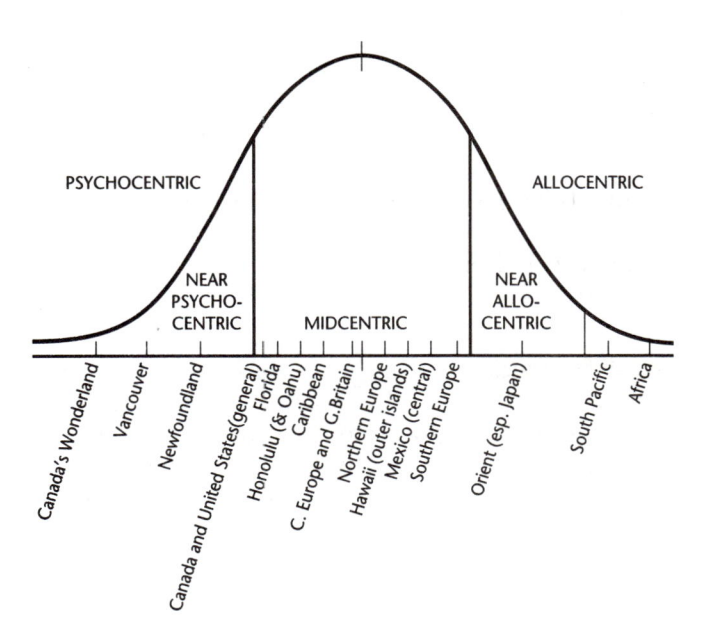

FIGURE 2-2
Plog's Continuum of Vacation and Leisure Travellers
SOURCE: © *The Cornell Quarterly.* Used by permission. All rights reserved.

```
              /\
             /  \
            /Self-\
           /Actual-\
          / ization \
         /-----------\
        / Respect of  \
       /    Others     \
      /-----------------\
     / Self-Esteem/Self- \
    /       Respect       \
   /-----------------------\
  /   Love (Affection,      \
 /        Belonging)         \
/-----------------------------\
/      Safety (Home, Job)      \
/-------------------------------\
/ Physiological Needs (Food, Water) \
-------------------------------------
```

FIGURE 2-3
Maslow's Hierarchy of Needs
SOURCE: "Hierarchy of Needs," from *Motivation and Personality* by Abraham H. Maslow. Copyright 1954 by Harper & Row Publishers. Copyright © 1970 by Abraham H. Maslow. Reprinted by permission of HarperCollins Publishers.

Who Are the Travellers?

Modern-day travellers are a diverse group of people with varying MNEs. Consequently, the travel industry doesn't create one product and try to sell it to everybody. The industry recognizes, for example, that young, unmarried people form a market different from the ones for senior citizens and young families. The realization that the travel market is really many submarkets has fostered a concept known as **market segmentation**.

Thousands of market segments exist, and there is no standard classification system. As you've seen, a general classification system is that of vacation and leisure traveller, business and professional traveller, and traveller visiting friends and relatives. But each of these can be further divided into segments according to travel habits and preferences, mode of transportation used, how travel arrangements are made, class of service purchased, and so on. Furthermore, each component of the travel industry may have one or more ways of segmenting its own market. For example, airlines classify their customers into first-class, business-class, and economy-class. But they also categorize them according to destinations and routes.

The travel industry depends on two kinds of marketing research in identifying and describing each market segment. **Primary research** is carried out by the travel industry itself. For instance, airlines, buses, and cruise ships—or marketing firms hired by them—conduct on-board surveys of passengers. Hotels leave questionnaires in guests' rooms and periodically review their guest ledgers. Airlines and hotels interview travellers at airports and resorts. Another kind of research, called **secondary research**, is based on information from other sources, such as the regular census conducted by the federal government or studies conducted by the Canadian Tourism Research Institute of the Conference Board of Canada.

The travellers in a particular market segment are assumed to have similar purchasing habits. With the information gathered during market research, the travel industry can tailor specific products for that segment and plan specific marketing strategies. The information collected is in the form of demographics and psychographics.

Demographics Demographics are statistics and facts that describe a human population by age, income, sex, marital status, size of family, education, occupation, residence, ethnic origin, religion, and so on. Using demographic information, the travel industry can describe vacation and leisure travellers with statements such as the following:

- More urban dwellers travel than rural dwellers.
- People with college degrees are more likely to travel than people without college degrees.
- Blue-collar workers tend to prefer group travel; executives and professionals tend to prefer more individualized travel.
- There is a strong relationship between travel and age—approximately 71 percent of the 18–24 age group travels, 70 percent of the 25–49 age group, 64 percent of the 50–64 age group, and 38 percent of the 65-and-over age group.
- Well-educated people with high incomes tend to travel by air and stay in hotels; people with lower incomes and less education tend to travel by car or bus and stay with family and friends.
- Most overseas travellers have travelled abroad in the past.

Demographic information can also uncover potentially lucrative markets for the travel industry. For instance, recent Statistics Canada data reveal that there are about 3.3 million challenged people in Canada. Many of these people would be willing to travel if the travel industry provided products and services to meet their needs. Travel enterprises are now reaching out to this market segment by modifying structures to allow for wheelchair access, allowing a helper to travel at a reduced price, and offering tours geared to the challenged. Winter Park, in Colorado, offers special ski programs for blind people and other challenged vacationers.

Psychographics Demographics, which provide objective information, can't fully describe market segments. **Psychographics** furnish more subjective information. Psychographic research asks travellers to reveal their activities, interests, and opinions. Such information may suggest, for instance, that young people travel to experience excitement, independence, and new environments.

Psychographic information also relates an individual's life stage, or position in the life cycle, to travel. Because they have more time and money, young single people and young, newly married, childless couples tend to travel more for pleasure. Married couples with dependent children, and single parents, tend to travel less. When they do travel, they go by car or camper and stay with friends and relatives. Recently retired people and older married couples with no dependent children return to pleasure travel, buying air transportation and cruises.

Psychographic information is also useful in uncovering the attitudes of nontravellers. A great many people do not travel, even though they have the time and money. Barriers to travel may include fear of the unknown, fear of flying, lack of interest, or even uneasiness about how to tip in a restaurant. Once such barriers are revealed, products and services can be designed to overcome them. Airlines, for example, introduced in-flight movies partly to keep nervous passengers from thinking about their fear of flying. Nontravellers represent a vast, untapped resource for the travel industry.

Psychographics show what travellers expect from their vacation experiences. The travel industry seeks to market its products and services based on these expectations. If a traveller is seeking glamour and romance, then the product might be a trip to Paris, with accommodations in an elegant hotel. If a traveller is seeking outdoor adventure, then the product might be a white-water rafting trip in Quebec.

CHECK YOUR PRODUCT KNOWLEDGE

1. Why is it important for the travel professional to understand why people travel?
2. According to Stanley Plog, what determines an individual's choice of travel experience and destination?
3. Why does the travel industry divide the travel market into segments?
4. What two methods of research are used to obtain information about travellers?
5. What is the difference between demographic information and psychographic information?

DOMESTIC VACATION TRAVEL

Where do vacation and leisure travellers go? Canadians travel within their own country, to the United States, and to other countries. Travellers from the United States and other countries visit Canada.

See Canada

Domestic travel has always been popular among vacation and leisure travellers.

Because of its vast size, Canada offers a diversity of travel experiences. Travellers can enjoy the seashore of Prince Edward Island, the plains of Saskatchewan, the mountains of British Columbia, and the badlands of Alberta. Lake Louise, Niagara Falls, and the tides on the Bay of Fundy are just a few of this nation's natural wonders. The climate also varies widely in Canada. The moderate climate of the lower mainland in British Columbia, the hot, dry summer weather on the Prairies, and the cold, snowy winters of Quebec have created different and interesting lifestyles and activities. Descendants of the early settlers of Canada have maintained their ethnic traditions in many regions. The following examples, in somewhat chronological order, are illustrative: the Acadians and French Canadians in New Brunswick and Quebec; the English, Scots, and Irish in Atlantic Canada; the Chinese and Japanese in British Columbia; the Ukrainians in Alberta; and the Germans and Italians in southern Ontario. This diversity has been reinforced and modified by immigration since World War II. Thus, travellers in Canada can sample cultures from all over the world.

Many Canadians, especially families with young children, find it less expensive to travel within Canada.

SOURCE: Calgary Exhibition and Stampede

ILLUSTRATION 2-3

Because Canada is so large, it offers a variety of sights, climates, and cultures to domestic and foreign travellers.
SOURCE: Courtesy Tourism Nova Scotia

Vacationers can usually save money travelling by passenger car or recreational vehicle. A good system of roads, with restaurants and motels along the way, makes highway travel pleasant. In fact, highway travellers represent the largest segment of this country's tourists.

Many Canadians also find domestic travel more convenient. Travellers who stay in Canada rather than go overseas don't have to apply for passports, get inoculated against diseases, or exchange their currency. They don't have to worry about understanding another language.

Recognizing the economic benefits of tourism, many provinces are developing even more of their resources to entertain domestic travellers and to encourage visitors from the United States. Provincial tourism offices are vigorously promoting their provinces' attractions, especially through television advertising in neighbouring provinces and states.

In addition, world events influence the travel plans of vacationers. In the early 1990s, the war in the Persian Gulf and threats of terrorism caused some Canadians to cancel overseas travel plans. Also, when the value of the dollar declines abroad, as it did in the early 1990s, Canadians tend to stay home.

Where Do Travellers Go?

The following are just a handful of Canada's many tourist attractions: Vancouver Island's Douglas firs; the Calgary Stampede; the Museum of Civilization; Parliament Hill; Upper Canada Village; the Skydome; Peggys Cove; Signal Hill; the Laurentians. Chapter 9 will give you an overview of the wide variety of public and commercial tourist attractions in Canada.

> **CHECK YOUR PRODUCT KNOWLEDGE**
> 1. What is meant by domestic tourism?
> 2. What factors favour domestic tourism in Canada?
> 3. Which provinces tend to draw the most vacation and leisure travellers? Why?

FOREIGN VACATION TRAVEL

Canada has much to offer vacation and leisure travellers. But there are certain sights and experiences that are available only through travel to foreign countries. There is just one Eiffel Tower, and people must go to Paris to see it. Only India has the Taj Mahal. For many people, books and television documentaries about foreign countries can't replace the excitement of experiencing a different culture firsthand. Many Canadians dream about going to faraway places and consider their lives incomplete until they've travelled abroad.

In 1991, Canadians made more than 82 million person-trips to foreign countries. The vast majority of these trips (79 million) were to the United States; of these trips, 60 million were same-day. The number of Canadians making same-day trips to the United States in 1991 was 60 percent higher than in 1988 (when the figure was 37 million). In the same period, shoppers' spending on these cross-border trips increased by more than 260 percent, to $1.7 billion. Reasons for the dramatic increase included an increase in the value of the Canadian dollar, higher taxes in Canada (with the introduction of the goods and services tax), lower prices in the United States (particularly for gasoline, tobacco, alcohol, poultry, and dairy products), and higher after-tax incomes.

Travel to the United States for one or more nights almost doubled between 1982 and 1991, to 19 million trips. Canadians travel to the United States to visit friends and relatives, for extended shopping trips, to see the countryside and attractions, and to find fun in the sun during the long Canadian winters.

Canadians make extended shopping trips to outlet malls in the United States. Others travel to see plays on Broadway, to experience Disneyland in California and DisneyWorld in Florida, or to try their luck at gambling in Las Vegas. Some from the Lakehead and the Prairies travel to Minneapolis, Milwaukee, and Chicago to see the Toronto Blue Jays play. Popular winter destinations for Canadians—including "snowbirds" who winter for several months in the United States—are Florida, California, Arizona, and Hawaii. Canadians travel to the United States for camping and hiking in the summer, to admire the changing foliage in the autumn, to ski in winter, and to enjoy an earlier spring.

Travel to the United States requires little documentation. Canadians should be prepared to show proof of citizenship at border crossings. Airlines flying transborder routes will insist that each traveller have a birth certificate or passport. A new concern of Canadians in the 1990s is how much medical coverage they enjoy while outside their home province.

Travel to countries other than the United States is a small portion of Canadians' total foreign travel—about 2.8 million trips in 1991. However, spending per trip is considerably more, at $1,166 (compared with $29.20 for a same-day trip and $410.50 for a longer trip to the United States). Major travel destinations include the United Kingdom, Europe, and the Far East. This reflects both traditional and more recent sources of immigration and business travel. Popular winter sun destinations are Mexico and the Caribbean.

Canada's travel deficit expanded fourfold in less than a decade, from about $2 billion per year in the mid-1980s to more than $8 billion in 1992. While foreign tourists spent $8 billion in Canada in 1992, Canadians spent more than $16 billion outside the country.

Compared with domestic tourism, travel to other countries usually requires far more preparation. Travellers must prepare various documents, obtain traveller's cheques or exchange currency, take precautions to safeguard their

A DAY IN THE LIFE OF

Three Travellers

Woman Business Traveller: I spend about 15 days out of each month travelling for business. Usually I know my travel plans well in advance, so my travel agent can get good flights and prices for me. Last week, for instance, I spent three days in Halifax. I arranged that trip six weeks ago, and my agent got discount rates for me. Nowadays, there can be a penalty for cancellations, so I have to make sure that I know exactly what I'll be doing. Sometimes, of course, I need to make last-minute plans or make changes during a trip. The agency's toll-free number helps when I have to make changes from far away.

My travel agent keeps a file on me. She knows that I prefer to fly business class, and that I prefer certain airlines because I have some frequent flier bonuses to build on. She even knows that I prefer an aisle seat. When she books a flight for me, she gets a seat assignment and boarding pass in advance so that I don't have to stand in line when I arrive at the airport.

My agent also knows my hotel needs and makes the necessary reservations. She knows that my first requirement is that the hotel be near my meeting location. But I insist on certain standards. I don't like eating alone in hotel restaurants, so room service is important, especially since I often have to spend the evening before a meeting reading papers and preparing. Sometimes I have to meet with clients in my hotel room. When I know that will happen, I ask my agent to book a suite for me. I also like to exercise while I'm away, so I want a hotel with a swimming pool and an exercise room.

The primary thing I look to my travel agent for, though, is a trouble-free trip: direct flights or good connections, a comfortable hotel, and no surprises.

Emergency Traveller: Recently, my husband and I had to make an unexpected trip to Winnipeg to attend my uncle's funeral. Since I was appointed executor of his will, we also had to spend some time there sorting matters out. We had only two days' notice before the trip, but our travel agent was able to make good arrangements.

In our case, we had little flexibility—we had to get from Saint John to Winnipeg as quickly as possible. We also needed a rental car. I was pleased that the travel agent saved us money by finding a discounted airfare for our flight and by getting us a subcompact rental car. We had only two suitcases, and all we needed the car for was to get us around town. It certainly wasn't a pleasure trip, and we didn't expect to do any sightseeing.

Our agent was also helpful in suggesting that we should not book a round-trip flight. Sure enough, the settlements didn't go quite as smoothly as we had hoped, and we had to stay a day or two longer than we'd anticipated. Waiting to book the flight until we knew our departure date was a good idea.

An experienced travel agent made an unpleasant trip a lot easier. The agent's understanding of the purpose of our trip and our travelling needs really helped us out. The next time we take a vacation, I know where we'll go to make our travel arrangements.

Family Vacation Traveller: Finally, our family was able to take the vacation we'd been planning for some time—a trip to Disneyland. It was a package tour with the flight to Los Angeles, the bus trip to Anaheim, and the accommodations all included in one price. Our travel agent suggested this particular package when we told her we wanted to go to Disneyland. It was a good choice. It gave us enough structure to have something to do when we wanted it, and enough freedom to explore other avenues if we wished.

The flight was our kids' first, and the airline we were booked on seemed to take a special interest in children. The hotel we stayed in was fantastic—two well-guarded swimming pools, several game rooms, shuttle service to Disneyland, and state-certified child care for a nominal fee—a great help for our one "parents' night out." We would never have found such a perfect place on our own.

I really have to hand it to our travel agent, in fact, for sizing up our family and its needs after only a short conversation. We've never had a better time on a vacation. Of course, there's always next year.

Country	Receipts	Rank
United States	40 579	1
France	20 187	2
Italy	19 738	3
Spain	18 593	4
United Kingdom	15 000	5
Austria	13 017	6
Germany	10 683	7
Switzerland	6 839	8
Canada	6 374	9
Mexico	5 324	10
Netherlands	3 615	15
Japan	3 578	16
Sweden	2 895	22

TABLE 2-1
World's Top International Tourism Dollars in 1990
SOURCE: Derived from Statistics Canada, *Travel-Log*, Winter 1993.

health, and inform themselves about customs regulations. There are several publications that feature the concerns of the foreign traveller. These include *"I Declare,"* available free from Revenue Canada, Customs and Excise. As a travel professional, you must be able to assist travellers with special aspects of foreign travel so that they have a safe and pleasant trip. Canada ranked ninth in international tourism receipts in 1990 (Table 2-1).

Documentation

Documentation refers to government-issued papers used to identify travellers. These documents include passports, visas, tourist cards, and vaccination certificates. When travellers enter or leave a country, immigration officials ask to see these papers. Documentation enables governments to regulate travel.

Passport A passport enables travellers to pass through ports, that is, to enter a foreign country and to return to their native country. By means of passports, governments approve the travel of their citizens and request protection for them while they are travelling abroad.

Countries that do not have diplomatic relations with each other do not honour each other's passports. When a country is experiencing political upheaval or terrorism, or when there is some other condition that makes travel difficult, a government may issue a travel advisory. For example, in the early 1990s, the U.S. State Department advised Americans against travelling to the war-torn countries of the Middle East. In some cases a government will ban travel altogether, so that any of its citizens travelling to the restricted area do so at their own risk. These travel advisories are made available to travel agents through the trade press and by computer.

Every individual must have his or her own passport—family passports are no longer issued. To obtain a Canadian passport, a citizen picks up an application form in person at a passport office, federal court building, or post office. Along with the completed application, the person must submit the following:

- *Proof of citizenship* (original birth certificate; or, if born in Quebec, a record of birth issued by a religious, municipal, or judicial authority of the province of Quebec; or, a certificate of Canadian citizenship).
- *Two recent photos* (between 43 mm x 54 mm and 50 mm x 70 mm).
- *Declaration of Guarantor* (who must have known the applicant personally for at least two years, be a Canadian citizen residing in Canada; be included in one of a specified group, and sign the declaration and the back of one photograph).
- *fee* (for adults 18 years and older, currently $35).

Since it can take two weeks to process an application mailed to the Passport Office (address: Department of Foreign Affairs and International Trade Canada, Ottawa K1A 0G3), travellers should apply for a passport well ahead of their scheduled departure. A passport can be obtained through a regional office in a shorter time period. Passports are valid for five years.

A passport comes in the form of a wallet-sized booklet, which travellers should carry on their person at all times. If they lose any of their documentation while travelling overseas, they should go immediately to the nearest Canadian embassy or consulate and report the loss. There is a Canadian embassy in almost every major world capital. Each **embassy** is the official residence of the Canadian ambassador for that country. It also houses diplomats and other officials. **Consulates**, which are like branch offices of embassies, are found in major cities other than the capital. Just as Canada has embassies in foreign capitals, so do foreign countries have embassies in Ottawa. Both embassies and consulates can assist tourists travelling in foreign countries.

Visa A passport is issued by the traveller's own government; a **visa** is issued by a foreign government. A visa is a stamp or endorsement placed in the traveller's passport that specifies the conditions for entering a country.

Vacation and leisure travellers apply either for a transit visa, which allows them just enough time to pass through a country, or for a tourist visa, which allows them to stay in the country for a specific period of time. Travellers to Russia, for instance, can obtain a one-month tourist visa for between $15 and $25. Tourist visas generally permit multiple entries, that is, travellers can leave the country on side trips and then return. Other types of visas may be required for those who intend to conduct business, attend school, or establish long-term residence in a foreign country.

About 60 percent of the world's countries still require tourist visas. This is beginning to change, however. Canadian citizens no longer need tourist visas to travel to most countries in Western Europe. Travellers can obtain visas directly from a foreign country's embassy or through a travel agency or visa service. Since visas are stamped into travellers' passports, the passport must be sent along with the visa application. This means that the process for obtaining a passport should be started even earlier when one or more visas are needed.

Proof of Citizenship When relations are friendly between certain countries, such as between Canada and the United States, a passport is not necessary. Instead, travellers on vacation who stay less than six months may simply carry some **proof of citizenship**. An expired passport, a birth certificate, or a certificate of Canadian citizenship may be used. Note that a driver's licence is *not* proof of citizenship.

Tourist Card Another type of document is a **tourist card**. Along with proof of citizenship, it can be used instead of a passport in some countries, such as Mexico. Travellers can obtain a tourist card from the foreign government's embassy or through a travel agency or airline.

Vaccination Certificate For travel to certain countries, travellers need immunizations, or shots, to protect themselves from various diseases and to prevent the spread of disease. An **International Certificate of Vaccination** verifies that a traveller has received the proper immunizations. The certificate is a passport-sized yellow pamphlet with space to list the date of each vaccination and its date of expiration. Many travellers use this "yellow card" to record other health information, such as any medications that must be taken frequently.

Immunizations are no longer required for direct travel between Canada and other developed nations, such as Japan and the countries of Western Europe. Even so, health officials recommend that travellers be sure they have received routine childhood vaccinations and have kept up with booster shots. For instance, adults should have a diphtheria–tetanus booster every ten years.

Some countries in Africa and Asia may require cholera vaccinations. Countries in Africa and South America may require yellow fever vaccinations. To help prevent hepatitis, an injection of gamma globulin is recommended for travellers who will be visiting the rural areas of underdeveloped countries, where sanitary conditions are often poor.

Since vaccination requirements change with the current health situation, travellers should get up-to-date information from public health departments. Canadians can get this information from provincial or federal health officers or contact Health and Welfare Canada, Ottawa K1A 0K9.

Customs

Just as governments regulate who may leave and who may enter a country, they also regulate what goods may be brought in and what goods may be taken out. Such regulations are referred to as **customs**. Immigration and customs are usually handled as a single process, although they may involve two or more government bureaus or agencies working together. In Canada, immigration procedures are handled by the Canada Immigration Centres within the Ministry of Employment and Immigration; customs matters are handled by Customs Canada; and passports are issued to Canadian citizens by a special office in Foreign Affairs and International Trade Canada.

Outgoing customs checks seek to prevent travellers from taking certain items out of a country. For example, some countries prohibit travellers from removing archaeological treasures, even if the traveller has paid for them. Incoming customs checks seek to discourage travellers from purchasing too many foreign-made items to the detriment of domestic manufacturers. These checks also seek to prevent the importation of items harmful to humans, animals, or plants.

Duty-Free Purchases Travellers pay a **duty**, or tax, on items purchased abroad. However, under present Customs Canada regulations, travellers returning to Canada are allowed **duty-free** purchases, the actual amount depending on the length of absence.

After 24 hours' absence or more, any number of times per year, a Canadian may bring in goods to the value of $20

ILLUSTRATION 2-4
A visa is one of several means for a government to regulate travel in and out of its country.

ILLUSTRATION 2-5
Customs officers regulate what goods may be taken out of or brought into a country.
SOURCE: Ernie Sparks/Revenue Canada

(except tobacco products and alcoholic beverages). A written declaration may be required. After 48 hours or longer, any number of times per year, a Canadian may bring in goods to the value of $100. A written declaration may be required. After seven days or longer, once every calendar year, a Canadian may bring in goods to the value of $300. A written declaration will be required. To calculate the number of days, exclude the date of departure but include the date of return. It is dates that matter, not times. For example, leave Friday the 7th, return Friday the 14th.

Returning travellers do not have to pay any taxes on these duty-free purchases. Goods that are brought in under the $20 or $100 exemption must accompany the traveller in hand or checked luggage in all cases. The goods that are claimed under the $300 exemption may follow by mail or other means. Duty and taxes will have to be paid on the value of goods exceeding the exemption for duty-free purchases. Value for duty is sometimes referred to as customs value and is the amount on which the percentage duty rates are calculated. Generally, value for duty is based on the price the traveller pays (in Canadian dollars) for imported goods. In most cases, the foreign sales tax added to or included in the price paid for the imported goods is part of the value on which Canadian duty and GST are paid. Some provinces also collect the provincial sales tax on imported goods.

Duty-Free Shops The duty-free shops in international airports, sell merchandise at reduced prices to departing travellers. Many travellers believe that they won't have to pay duty on items purchased in these shops. This is not true—items purchased in foreign duty-free shops are subject to customs regulations upon the traveller's return home. "Duty-free" means that the seller hasn't been required to pay a duty on the merchandise and thus can sell it at reduced prices. In addition, the traveller does not have to pay sales tax on the merchandise.

Departure Taxes Most countries charge some kind of **departure tax**. Visitors to a country are expected to pay this tax when they leave. Usually it is not a large sum—the equivalent of between $2 and $25. Governments use the revenues from departure taxes to help fund their work in promoting and regulating tourism. After Vancouver's airport was privatized, the Vancouver International Airport Authority levied a departure tax to pay for the renovation and expansion of the terminal facilities and runways.

Forbidden and Restricted Purchases Some items, such as clothing, handbags, and textiles, are subject to import controls under the Export and Import Permits Act. Depending on the value and quantity of the goods the traveller intends to import, an import permit may be required, even if the traveller qualifies for a personal exemption. For more information, contact the local Customs office or the Special Trade Relations Bureau, Foreign Affairs and International Trade Canada, Ottawa K1A 0G2.

Certain objects, such as antiquities and cultural objects, may not be imported to Canada. If a traveller plans to purchase such goods, which could be considered historically significant in their country of origin, the traveller should first obtain more information by contacting Movable Cultural Property, c/o Department of Communications, Cultural Affairs, 500–300 Slater Street, Ottawa K1A 0C8.

There are restrictions on the international movement of certain agricultural products and animals. These include livestock (including pets), meat and meat products, and plants (and the earth, sand, or other substances in which they are packed). For specific information, the traveller should contact the Food Protection and Inspection Branch, Agriculture Canada, Ottawa K1A 0C5.

Canada is a member of the Committee on International Trade in Endangered Species (CITES). It is also a signatory to an international agreement restricting the sale and movement of an increasing number of endangered animals, birds, reptiles, fish, insects, and plants. These restrictions extend to any products made from the fur, skin, feathers, bone, or other parts of these creatures. Thus, if a traveller purchases a leopard-skin coat while abroad, Customs Canada officials will confiscate it without reimbursement, even if the purchase was legal where made. To avoid losing hundreds of dollars in purchases, travellers should know what is on the list of endangered species. Canadians seeking information may contact the Convention Administrator, Canadian Wildlife Service, Environment Canada, Ottawa K1A 0H3.

Common Health Problems

All travellers before leaving their own country should consider medical care. This is especially true for those who have a pre-existing medical condition that might flare up while they are away. Travellers can prepare for such an emergency by getting a directory of overseas doctors. A list can be obtained from the International Association for Medical

CHAPTER 2: The Travellers

Assistance to Travellers (IAMAT), which has its Canadian headquarters in Guelph, Ontario), or from the World Medical Association, or the International Health Care Service.

Diarrhea Whether it's called Montezuma's Revenge or Delhi Belly, diarrhea is one of the most common illnesses of people travelling abroad. The cause is usually an unfamiliar intestinal bacteria picked up from untreated water or unclean food. Symptoms may also include fever and vomiting.

Travellers can often help prevent diarrhea by watching their eating and drinking habits. They should avoid dairy products unless they're sure the milk or cream was pasteurized. They should also avoid cold foods such as sliced meats and hard-boiled eggs, unless they're certain of the refrigeration. Raw or undercooked meats and raw fruits and vegetables may also cause problems. Most travellers have heard "Don't drink the water," but not all travellers realize that they must also be careful about the ice added to beverages. In addition, travellers should be careful not to swallow any water when brushing their teeth.

If diarrhea does occur, it's vital to prevent dehydration. Diarrhea victims should drink plenty of liquids—tea, bottled water, soda pop, or broth. Over-the-counter diarrhea medicines are available. If symptoms persist longer than three days, a physician should be consulted. The nearest Canadian embassy or consulate will have a list of local doctors.

Dysynchronosis The symptoms of this traveller's malady are irregular sleeping habits and physical exhaustion. Dysynchronosis (meaning "time out of sync") sounds frightful until you hear its common name—"jet lag."

Jet lag happens when a traveller passes through several time zones in a short period of time. This confuses the body's biological clock. For instance, a traveller who takes off from Toronto at 6:30 P.M. and flies nonstop to London arrives at 2 A.M. Toronto time, but 7 A.M. London time. The traveller is ready for bed, while Londoners are ready for a full day's activities. It will take two or three days for the traveller's biological clock to reset itself to the new time schedule.

To minimize the effects of jet lag, some authorities suggest that, before departing, travellers gradually adjust their eating and sleeping hours to those of their destination. However, this is often difficult to do, especially in the busy and exciting week before departure. Travellers should try not to become overtired on the day of departure. During the flight, they should drink plenty of nonalcoholic liquids and try to doze for a while. Sleeping pills, motion sickness medicine, tobacco, and caffeine tend to aggravate jet lag.

On arrival, travellers should not attempt a full day of sightseeing. Nor should they sleep themselves out, or they will be wide-awake at the wrong times. Instead, they should rest for two or three hours and then force themselves to get up and pursue some activity, such as a short sightseeing trip.

Sleepy travellers should not try to drive a car the first day or two—especially in the British Isles, where Canadians must adjust to driving on the left!

Motion Sickness In the movies, motion sickness is often treated with humour. The audience laughs when it sees passengers on a cruise ship moaning and groaning in their berths or turning green and hanging their heads over the railing. But in real life, motion sickness is miserable.

Motion sickness is caused by the effect of motion on the fluid in the inner ear. Its symptoms are dizziness, nausea, vomiting, and fatigue. Travellers can become sick while riding in an airplane, car, train, or boat.

Prescription and over-the-counter drugs are available to minimize the effects of motion sickness. One popular prescription medication comes in the form of a small adhesive patch, which the traveller places behind the ear. The medication is slowly released into the bloodstream for 72 hours. The patch must be applied from 4 to 16 hours before exposure to motion. Acupressure wristbands have also gained popularity in recent years.

Altitude Sickness Travellers to Mexico City (2261 metres), La Paz, Bolivia (3636 metres), and other high-altitude destinations may experience breathlessness, headache, heart pains, nausea, and severe fatigue. Altitude sickness develops when the body doesn't receive enough oxygen. Although sea-level air and high-mountain air contain the same percentage of oxygen, the reduced air pressure at higher altitudes makes oxygen less available to the lungs.

After two to six days, the traveller's lungs and heart will become accustomed to the higher altitude. To prevent acute altitude sickness, vacationers should rest during the first day, eat and drink with moderation, and have their main meal at midday. Stopping to rest during the ascent or descent—even staying overnight at a lower altitude—helps the body adjust to the change in altitude. Skiers and mountain climbers should limit strenuous activity to half a day during the first 24 to 48 hours. For people who must travel directly to high altitudes, a prescription drug called acetazolamide is available.

Foreign Currency

Travellers should be familiar with the currency used in countries they plan to visit and its value in Canadian dollars. A money-conversion chart or a small programmable exchange calculator would be handy for travellers to take with them.

When exchanging dollars, travellers are actually buying a foreign currency. How much foreign currency Canadian dollars will buy depends on the current rate of exchange.

Today, one Canadian dollar might buy 5 French francs. In two months, it might buy 8, but in four months, it might buy only 4. Political, social, and economic factors contribute to fluctuating exchange rates.

The rate of exchange often determines where travellers go. Canadian travellers tend to go to places where the dollar buys more and to stay away from places where it buys less. Since the mid-1970s, Mexico has been a travel bargain for Canadians because of the steady devaluation of the peso. (By early 1991 the Mexican peso had fallen to about 2960 to the dollar.) Sometimes the exchange rate changes drastically while travellers are on vacation, so that they either run out of money or find themselves with more money to spend.

There are four ways to exchange money, and travellers will probably want to use a combination of these methods:

- Obtain foreign currency before departure. It's a good idea to purchase a small amount of foreign currency before leaving home. On arrival, travellers will be able to pay for a taxi or a telephone call immediately. This is an especially good idea if they will be arriving at night or on the weekend, when banks and exchange offices are closed.
- Use a credit card and be billed later in Canadian dollars. By paying for major purchases, such as hotels and airfare, with a credit card, travellers can spread the cost of a trip over time. The exchange rate is the rate in effect on the day the bill is posted; this may or may not be the rate that was in effect the day of the purchase.
- Buy traveller's cheques in foreign currency before departure. When cashing these abroad, travellers won't be charged a conversion fee. Foreign traveller's cheques and currencies are available from the international banking departments of major banks and from foreign exchange companies.
- Buy traveller's cheques in U.S. dollars and exchange them for cash as needed. These cheques are good anywhere, and any left over can be used when travellers return home.

In addition to knowing *how* to exchange their money, travellers should know *where* to exchange money overseas. For example, banks offer the best exchange rates, but they also have limited hours, and travellers often have to stand in line and go through a formal procedure. As an alternative, they can cash traveller's cheques at their hotel. This is convenient, but hotels charge a service fee.

Finally, travellers must know whether a country limits the amount of its own currency that may be brought in and out. Canadian travellers to the United States should also be aware of this: U.S. Customs requires travellers, on departure or arrival, to report if they are holding more than $10 000 in any kind of monetary form (American or foreign currency or coin, traveller's cheques, money orders, investment securities, and so on). Some countries require travellers to purchase in advance set amounts of nonexportable currency.

Foreign Languages

Some travellers worry about being able to communicate in a foreign country, while others consider this part of the fun of travelling abroad. In the developed nations, where English is widely spoken, communication is generally not a major problem, especially if travellers are part of a tour group and hotels and attractions have been selected to cater to American and Canadian tourists. Often, signs using pictographs guide travellers to restrooms, exits, subways, and other important destinations. Many Canadians are bilingual in French and English, which also helps in foreign travel.

However, tourists will find that they are well received if they can speak at least a few words of the native tongue, such as "Good morning," "How are you?" and "Thank you." Being able to identify foreign words on menus and street signs will make travelling safer and more pleasant. Foreign-language dictionaries are available to help travellers learn the meaning of important words and phrases. Also, in many parts of Canada, foreign-language classes geared to the needs of travellers are available.

Travellers who intend to rent a car should learn the international road signs before leaving home — not while they're driving on the Autobahn (German expressway) for the first time! Canadians driving to the United States will have to adjust, or adjust back to, the use of miles for measuring distance.

CHECK YOUR PRODUCT KNOWLEDGE

1. Name five types of documentation. What is the purpose of each?
2. What are the two purposes of customs regulations for travellers entering Canada?
3. Name four health problems common among international travellers.
4. What are four ways to exchange money?
5. List categories of foreign words and phrases a traveller should know.

INBOUND TOURISM

What do you know about the lifestyle of a British working-class person? Can you speak French? What type of food does a German prefer? How do Japanese customs differ from Canadian customs?

As a travel professional, you will help Canadian citizens to travel domestically and internationally. But you may also have an opportunity to assist people from other countries who visit Canada. **Inbound tourism,** or vacation and leisure travel to Canada, is a rapidly growing segment of the travel market. Figure 2-4 shows the growth of tourism between Canada and the United States in recent years; Figure 2-5 shows the growth of tourism between Canada and all other countries. To design appropriate products and services for inbound tourists, travel professionals must get to know the needs of these travellers as well.

Who Are the Travellers?

Between 1986 and 1991 the number of foreign visitors to Canada actually declined by nearly 10 percent. In 1991 approximately 37 million foreign travellers visited Canada, spending $6.7 billion. The majority of the travellers were from the United States—33.5 million, including 21.5 million on same-day trips. There were 3.2 million visitors from other countries. About 10 percent of these visits — 331,000 — were same-day. This indicates they piggybacked a trip to Canada while visiting the United States. Most of the 3.2 million visitors to Canada from countries other than the United States were from Europe, mainly the United Kingdom, France, and Germany. There is an increasing number of visitors from Asia, with those from Japan and Hong Kong predominating.

Inbound Travel to the United States Between 1985 and 1990 the number of foreign visitors to the United States increased by more than 50 percent. In 1990 approximately 40 million foreign travellers visited the United States, spending more than $44 billion. There were 17 million visitors from Canada (staying one or more nights), 8 million from Mexico, and 15 million from overseas. Most of the European visitors were from the United Kingdom, most of the Asian visitors from Japan.

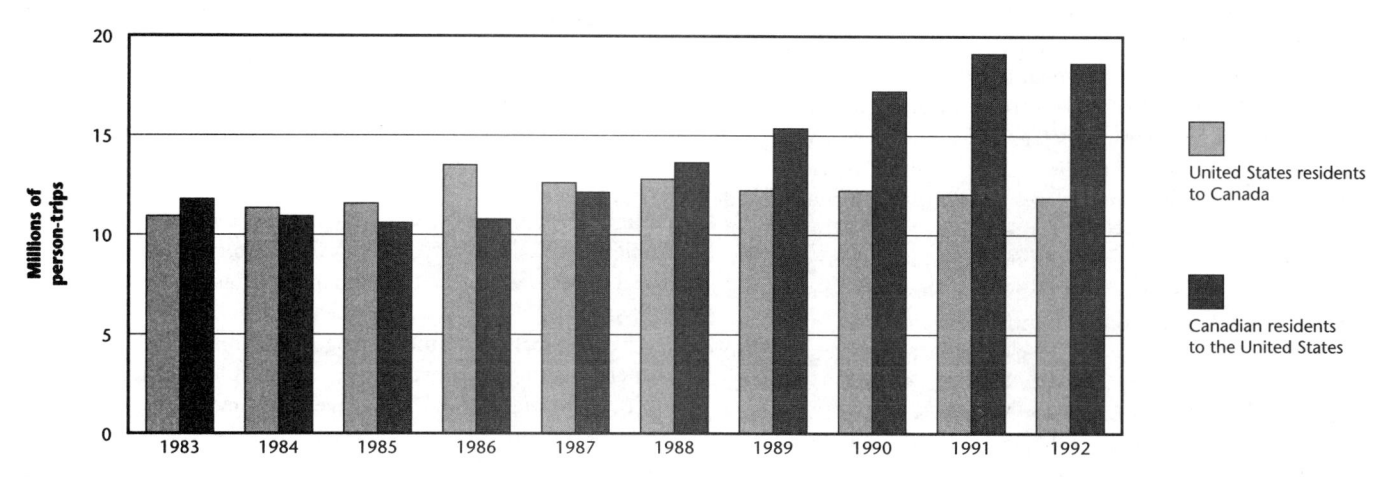

FIGURE 2-4
Trips of One or More Nights Between Canada and the United States, 1983-92
SOURCE: Statistics Canada, Touriscope International Travel, Catalogue 66–201, November 1993

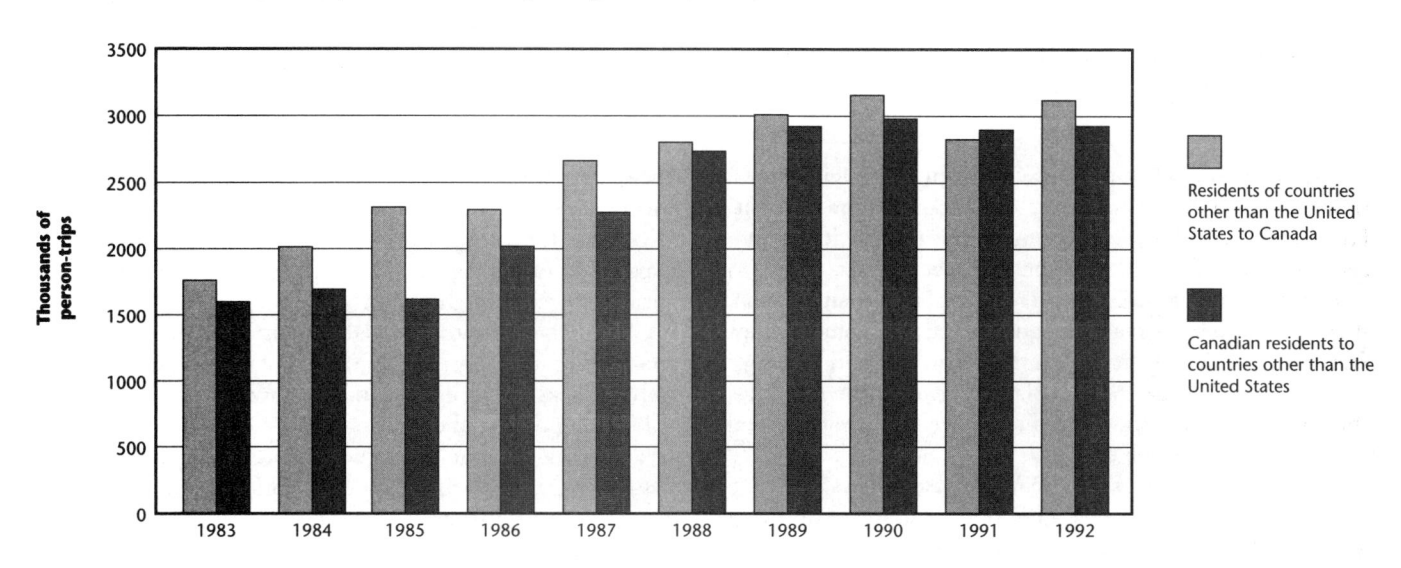

FIGURE 2-5
Trips of One or More Nights Between Canada and Countries Other than the United States, 1983–92
SOURCE: Statistics Canada, Touriscope International Travel, Catalogue 66–201, November 1993

	1980	1989	% change
United States	10 963	12 196	11.2
All Overseas	1 822	2 972	63.1
United Kingdom	489	570	16.6
West Germany	189	269	42.3
France	114	245	114.9
Japan	123	390	217.0
Total	12 785	15 168	18.6

TABLE 2-2

International Travel to Canada, 1980–89 (thousands of person-visits of more than one night)
SOURCE: *Tourism on the Threshold,* Industry Canada

For the most part, visitors to the United States are from highly developed, industrialized countries where there is a high standard of living and people have time and money to travel. For example, 95 percent of England's blue-collar workers receive four weeks of paid vacation annually. The rise in personal affluence, the decline of the American dollar, and low transoceanic airfares make travel to the United States feasible for thousands of tourists. A visit to the United States now costs Europeans only a little more than a trip in their own hemisphere. Canadians and Mexicans can visit at even less cost because their countries are closer.

There is an opportunity for Canada to market itself to these overseas visitors to the United States. Statistics Canada counts the spending by foreign visitors in Canada as exports and the spending by Canadians abroad as imports. Canada could reduce its $8 billion travel deficit by persuading these overseas visitors to make a side trip to Canada even if the United States is still their primary destination. Innovative advertising and travel packages will be necessary.

Why Do They Travel?

According to Statistics Canada, 15 percent of foreign visitors come to Canada for business, 22 percent come to visit friends and relatives, 56 percent come for vacation and leisure travel, and 7 percent come for other reasons.

Vacation and leisure travellers from abroad visit Canada for some of the same reasons Canadians travel domestically. They enjoy the diversity of climate, culture, and scenery. The image of Canada as a land of plenty excites the imagination of international travellers and makes them want to see the country for themselves.

A kind of reverse motivation also exists. Just as Canadians often journey abroad to find their ancestral roots, foreign tourists often want to see the land to which their relatives emigrated. Reunions with family members are a common reason for visiting Canada. Canadians travel abroad to see old castles, cathedrals, and fortresses; foreign tourists are attracted by this country's youthfulness. They want to see Canada's architecture, technology, and pace of life. Even though Canada is relatively young, its history of western expansion fascinates foreign tourists. So does the culture of its native peoples.

Where Do They Travel?

In 1991 Ontario was the entry point for 67 percent of tourists from the United States and 54 percent of overseas tourists. This reflects the close proximity of Ontario to the largest target market in the United States, and the fact that most immigrants to Canada have settled in Ontario. British Columbia is the point of entry for most visitors from Asia and for about 20 percent of visitors from the United States. The primary destinations for these travellers include the lower mainland, Vancouver Island, and the Okanagan Valley (in British Columbia), and Banff and Jasper national parks, Edmonton and Calgary (in Alberta). The Calgary Stampede is especially popular. American visitors still predominate in Quebec even though that province has succeeded recently in doubling the number of travellers from Europe over a five-year period. Montreal, with the Jazz Festival and the Just-for-Laughs Comedy Festival, is the major destination. The ancient walled city of Quebec, the Eastern Townships, and the Laurentians are the other prime destinations in that province.

Billboards in Maine during the summer of 1993 urged Americans to go to sleep in the good ol' U.S. of A. and wake up in a "foreign land." The advertising campaign by Prince of Fundy Cruise Lines for its service between Portland, Maine, and Yarmouth, Nova Scotia, was an example of aggressive marketing to attract tourists to Atlantic Canada. Most travel within Atlantic Canada is by regional residents, followed by Ontarians, then Americans. A surprising number of Japanese visitors travel to Prince Edward Island because so many young Japanese girls identify with Anne of Green Gables.

Receptive Operators Just as a trip abroad represents a dream come true for Canadian travellers, so, too, does a trip to Canada for foreign travellers. The **receptive operator** is responsible for seeing that the dreams of international visitors don't become nightmares.

Receptive operators specialize in arranging tours for visitors from other countries. They usually work in cooperation with overseas operators to plan and market tours. In addition to handling the usual details of a tour—checking the itinerary; making arrangements with hotels, bus companies, restaurants, and tourist attractions; pricing out the tour—they arrange for the special needs of the tour group, such as multilingual guides and interpreters. Foreign companies can set up their own receptive services in this country (Japan, for example, has operators on the West Coast), or Canadian travel agencies can specialize in another country's visitors.

PROFILE

Travel CUTS

Canadian students have long recognized that education extends beyond the classroom and that travel is an intrinsic part of the educational process. Travel is a learning opportunity that broadens cultural contact, enhances understanding, and contributes to making the world a better place. Over 40 years ago, Canadian students established a national student travel bureau. This was the beginning of Travel CUTS (Voyages Campus in Québec).

Today, Travel CUTS is wholly owned and operated by the Canadian Federation of Students (CFS), Canada's national student organization. As Canada's only national student travel bureau, Travel CUTS provides unique student-oriented products and services to over 200 000 students each year. It develops and promotes student fares on airlines and trains, student discount cards, and student tour packages.

Travel CUTS is affiliated with over 600 international student travel bureaux through the International Student Travel Confederation (ISTC). This means that Travel CUTS can negotiate and provide a worldwide network of student fares on air and surface transportation, as well as the International Student Identity Card (ISIC) and student travel insurance.

The Student Traveller, published by the CFS, is Canada's only magazine for student and budget travellers. It is published twice a year and distributed free of charge at Travel CUTS offices and university and college campuses across Canada. A version in French, *L'Étudiant Voyageur*, is produced and distributed at Voyages Campus offices.

The International Student Identity Card (ISIC) is the only recognized proof of full-time student status in over 70 countries around the world, including Canada (through the Student Saver Card program). The ISIC is distributed in Canada at all Travel CUTS offices and at many student associations. Students purchasing an ISIC receive a copy of the *ISIC World Travel Handbook*, which includes an ISIC directory that lists addresses and telephone numbers of ISIC offices in major cities around the world. Soon they will also receive the *Canada Student Travel Handbook*. This guidebook will list discounts across Canada that are available to student travellers.

Bon Voyage Travel Insurance is designed especially for student travellers. It covers trip cancellation or interruption, personal accidents, loss of baggage and personal effects, and medical expenses.

The Student Work Abroad Program (SWAP) provides students with the opportunity to work abroad in one of 11 destinations: Britain, Ireland, Finland, Germany, France, the Netherlands, Jamaica, Japan, Australia, New Zealand, and the United States.

The Volunteer Abroad Program allows students to travel to the United States and Europe and volunteer time to worthwhile environmental or community service projects.

Youth Standby fares are available exclusively through Travel CUTS. Flights are available one-way or return, are valid up to one year, and are at prices below youth standby tickets.

With the number of visitors increasing, the receptive operator is growing in importance.

Until recently, foreign vacation and leisure travel in Canada consisted of a "grand tour." Travellers typically visited Montreal, Ottawa, Toronto, Niagara Falls, Vancouver, and a national park such as Banff or Jasper. Receptive operators were located mainly in Vancouver, Toronto, and Montreal, Canada's three main cities.

This situation is beginning to change. Today, international visitors are looking for new destinations in Canada. They want to go to the East Coast, the North, and farther inland and see how people in this country live. This interest in other destinations creates more opportunities for regional receptive operators, who know their own areas better and can plan more efficient and interesting tours.

Increasing Marketability Inbound tourism represents an important source of jobs and revenue. To capture and maintain this lucrative market, the travel industry and the Canadian public must overcome this country's shortcomings as a tourist destination.

Language is perhaps the biggest barrier to overcome. When travelling to well-developed destinations overseas, most people from Canada expect to encounter English-speaking personnel in hotels and restaurants and at tourist attractions. Bilingual Canadians have a second language to use. The reverse is not true for the international traveller to Canada. This person does not expect to speak his or her own language here. To minimize language difficulties for foreign visitors, the travel industry should consider taking the following steps:

- Use internationally recognized pictographs in restaurants, hotels, and bars.
- Print menus in other languages, or provide photos.
- Provide multilingual travel personnel, and encourage more Canadians to become multilingual, especially at popular tourist destinations.
- Provide a public translating service at travel destinations. Foreign visitors could bring printed materials to the service centre for translation. Hotels, restaurants, and receptive operators could send menus, itineraries, and general instructions to the centre for translation into the foreign language.

Other improvements that might be made include the following:

- Make the exchange of money easier at airports and in banks and hotels.
- Explain tipping customs and sales taxes.
- Improve the intercity railroad system, since foreign visitors are accustomed to rail travel.
- Have conversion tables for the metric system available.
- Train waiters, waitresses, bellstaff, bartenders, salespeople, and others to be friendly and patient in assisting international travellers.

The Canadian public must learn to realize the extent and importance of inbound tourism. All citizens, not just travel professionals, need to assume the role of gracious host in welcoming foreign guests.

> **CHECK YOUR PRODUCT KNOWLEDGE**
>
> 1. From what countries do most of our international visitors come?
> 2. What factors are contributing to the fluctuation in the number of foreign travellers to Canada?
> 3. List four reasons why people from other countries want to visit Canada.
> 4. Why are regional receptive operators becoming more important?
> 5. What improvements could be made in Canada to minimize difficulties for foreign visitors?

Summary

- People have travelled throughout history for a variety of reasons. For most of history, travel was difficult and dangerous.
- For travel to flourish, there must be an efficient system of transportation and protection for travellers. Pleasure travel also requires that people have leisure time and money to spend.
- Largely because of economic prosperity, more people in industrialized societies are travelling than ever before. For them, travel has become a symbol of the good life.
- Modern-day travellers form a diverse group. Travel professionals must match appropriate products and services to each traveller's motivations, needs, and expectations (MNEs).
- There are three main groups of travellers. For vacation and leisure travellers, travel is discretionary, or voluntary. For business and professional travellers, it is nondiscretionary. For travellers visiting friends and relatives, travel may be discretionary or nondiscretionary.
- Many types of experiences, such as learning about other cultures, participating in sports, and being with other people, give vacation and leisure travellers pleasure. According to Stanley Plog, an individual's personality (allocentric, psychocentric, or midcentric) determines travel motivation and choice of destination. According to Abraham Maslow's theory of needs satisfaction, people travel for pleasure in order to satisfy needs for social interaction, self-esteem, respect, and self-actualization.
- The travel industry designs products and services to meet the needs of particular market segments. Demographics (statistical information) and psychographics (information on interests and attitudes) help the industry understand the marketplace.

CHAPTER 2: The Travellers

- Most Canadian vacation and leisure travellers take trips within Canada or to the United States. Destinations offering beautiful scenery, sunshine, and culture attract the most visitors.
- Vacation and leisure travel abroad offers unique experiences. International travel, however, requires more preparation, such as obtaining documentation, learning customs regulations, taking measures to safeguard health, exchanging currency, and learning some basic phrases in a foreign language. Travel professionals must be able to assist travellers with these preparations.
- Inbound tourism has been increasing. To maintain this market segment, travel professionals must also become familiar with the MNEs of international visitors.

Key Terms

discretionary travel
nondiscretionary travel
allocentric personality
psychocentric personality
midcentric personality
market segmentation
primary research
secondary research
demographics
psychographics
passport
embassy
consulate
visa
proof of citizenship
tourist card
International Certificate of Vaccination
customs
duty
duty-free
departure tax
inbound tourism
receptive operator

What Do You Think?

1. What are some current examples of people travelling to meet the basic need for survival?
2. According to Plog's theory, what type of personality is Mrs. O'Neill (see page 29)? What needs is she satisfying according to Maslow's theory? Explain your point of view.
3. How might a tour to Toronto for senior citizens be different from a tour for young singles to the same destination?
4. In arranging an international journey for a client, what are the responsibilities of the travel agent?
5. How do customs regulations reflect the views of a government?
6. What is the purpose of confiscating products made from endangered animals?
7. In promoting inbound tourism, how does the Canadian government compare with the governments of other developed nations?
8. What can be done to encourage more people who live in Canada to become multilingual? Which languages should be stressed?

Dealing with Product

Travel and tourism products do not exist in a vacuum. They are often affected by events that take place half a world away. Consider the following:

In 1990, Iraq invaded Kuwait. After several months of negotiations, the United States and its allies launched a war against Iraq, with the intent of driving Iraq out of Kuwait. Many countries were involved in the war, including Canada, Great Britain, France, Italy, and Saudi Arabia.

What impact did this fighting have on international travel? Did each of the three primary types of travellers react in the same way? What impact did this fighting have on domestic travel? In what ways might a war on the other side of the world cause changes in the price of travel products in Yourtown?

Dealing with People

It is often said that the three most important ingredients in pleasure travel are time, money, and education. The more of each the better. Unfortunately, most of us either never seem to have enough, or have plenty of one and not enough of the others. First, let's look at time and money.

How would you describe the following prospective travellers in terms of time and money? What vacation and leisure travel products would you recommend for these travellers?

- a college student
- a dairy farmer
- a high school teacher
- an orthopedic surgeon
- a factory worker
- the owner of a laundry and dry-cleaning company

Now—how do you think that education affects a person's travel plans? Can you find any relationship between education and the profiles provided by Plog and Maslow?

CHAPTER 2: The Travellers   Name: _____

WORKSHEET 2-1 Foreign Travel: FAM Trip

The decline of communism in Eastern Europe has opened up new and exciting opportunities for travel. Imagine that your travel agency has sent you on a FAM trip to Prague in the Czech Republic. Use the space below to record your findings.

1. How to get there from Yourtown
   _____
   _____

2. How to obtain a visa
   _____
   _____

3. Currency used and exchange rate in dollars
   _____
   _____

4. Customs rules
   _____
   _____

5. What clothes to pack
   _____
   _____

6. Where to stay
   _____
   _____

7. Recommended restaurants
   _____
   _____

8. Things to see and do in the city
   _____
   _____

9. How to get around the city
   _____
   _____

10. What to do in case of a medical emergency
    _____
    _____

11. Additional tourist information
    _____
    _____

CHAPTER 2: The Travellers

Name: _____

WORKSHEET 2-2 Travel Canada: Tourist Attractions

Canada has a variety of tourist attractions. Some attractions provide breathtaking scenery, others provide fun **and relaxation, and still** others provide a glimpse of our nation's history. The chart below lists a few of this country's outstanding tourist attractions. **Use** travel guides and encyclopedias to help you locate and describe each attraction.

Fathers Of Confederation National Historic Site

Location _____
Description _____
_____
_____
_____
_____
_____

Big Muddy Badlands

Location _____
Description _____
_____
_____
_____
_____
_____

Ontario Science Centre

Location _____
Description _____
_____
_____
_____
_____
_____

Museum Of Civilization

Location _____
Description _____
_____
_____
_____
_____
_____

Whitehorse

Location _____
Description _____
_____
_____
_____
_____
_____

Stanley Park

Location _____
Description _____
_____
_____
_____
_____
_____

Mount Robson

Location _____
Description _____
_____
_____
_____
_____
_____

Percé Rock

Location _____
Description _____
_____
_____
_____
_____
_____

CHAPTER 3

The Channels Of Distribution

"Free market competition, freely advertised, is consumerism at its best."

J. Kesner Kahn

OBJECTIVES

When you have completed this chapter, you should be able to do the following:

- Explain how travel retailers differ from retailers in other industries.
- Distinguish between the three different systems of distribution.
- List the primary printed references available to travel professionals.
- Distinguish between the informational functions of a computer reservations system and its transactual functions.
- Outline the development of automated reservations systems.
- List the major CRS vendors.
- Describe the relationship between host vendors and co-hosts.
- Discuss the issue of bias.
- Distinguish between teleticketing machines and satellite ticket printers.
- Show how automated back-office systems can facilitate a travel agency's internal operations.
- Explain how hotel and car rental reservations systems differ from airline CRSs.

Every industry has products that it attempts to sell to consumers at a profit. Most industries sell tangible products. The automobile industry sells cars and trucks, the garment industry sells clothes, the food-processing industry sells food products. The products of the travel and tourism industry are usually intangible—such as a flight on an airplane, a stay at a hotel, the use of a rental car, a complete tour package, and so on.

Travel products are perishable. They must be sold within a certain period of time or they become worthless. An empty seat on an airplane can never be sold once the flight has taken off. Some travel products are also seasonal: in great demand during certain times of the year and unattractive at others. A trip to the Prince Edward Island seashore is a seasonal product.

Like other industries, the travel industry uses a system of distribution to move its products and services from producer to consumer. Manufacturing industries typically use wholesalers and retailers as **intermediaries**, or links, between the producer and the consumer. The wholesaler purchases products from the manufacturer and sells them to the retailer. The retailer in turn sells the products to the consumer. The sales distribution system of the travel industry also involves intermediaries, such as tour operators (wholesalers) and travel agents (retailers).

An important difference between the travel industry and other industries is the status of the retailer. A traditional retailer buys goods and services and sells them to the consumer with markup. Travel retailers, however, do *not* buy goods and services, nor do they mark up the price. Instead, they are paid a **commission**, or a percentage of the selling price, by the supplier or wholesaler. Travel retailers are most commonly called travel "agents" because they act as agents for the supplier or wholesaler. Another difference between the travel industry and most other industries is that the consumer can bypass the intermediaries and purchase the product directly from the supplier.

In this chapter, you'll learn how the different channels of distribution used in the travel industry are structured. You'll also learn about the increasing use of automation in getting the travel product from the supplier to the consumer.

CHANNELS OF DISTRIBUTION

There are three main channels of distribution in the travel industry. These can be defined by level of complexity:

- *Unilateral*, involving no intermediaries between supplier and consumer.

- *Bilevel*, involving one intermediary.
- *Multilevel*, involving two or more intermediaries.

Consumers are free to choose the channel they prefer. Whether they buy a travel product directly from the supplier or through an intermediary, identical products usually cost the same. This feature is unique to the travel industry.

Unilateral Distribution System

The unilateral system is the simplest of the three distribution systems (see Figure 3-1). It involves the direct sale of travel products and services by the supplier to the consumer. Suppliers include airlines, railways, bus companies, cruise lines, car rental firms, hotels, resorts, sightseeing companies, and so on.

Customers can either telephone the supplier to make a reservation or go in person to the ticket or sales outlet. Most major suppliers in the travel industry maintain national and regional sales offices. Some own or lease counter space in airports, hotels, convention centres, and other high-visibility locations.

In recent years, suppliers have begun to experiment with automated methods of direct distribution. Automated ticketing machines (similar to automated teller machines) have been installed at airports, railway stations, and ticket offices in major cities. It is expected that they will become widely available in the near future. Teleshopping—the use of personal computers for obtaining flight information and for making reservations—is already possible through several software packages, including Prodigy and CompuServe. Though still in its early stages, teleshopping is likely to have far-reaching effects on the way travel products and information are distributed in the future.

The unilateral system of distribution is ideal for simple travel arrangements, such as domestic airline reservations and hotel bookings. More complex arrangements, such as cruises and tour packages, generally require the assistance of a travel agent or other sales intermediary.

The greatest advantage of the unilateral system is its simplicity. Suppliers deal directly with consumers, thereby minimizing the misunderstandings that are possible when a third party is involved. Many clients prefer to talk directly to the supplier because they feel that this allows them greater personal control over the transaction.

Suppliers make a greater net profit per unit sale if they sell directly to the traveller. Suppose, for example, that Annette Bondi wants to fly from Edmonton to Toronto on Air Canada. The quoted fare is $600. If she buys the ticket directly from Air Canada, she will pay the airline $600. If she decides to book the flight through a travel agency, it will still cost her the same amount, but Air Canada will not receive the full $600. The reason is that airlines (and other suppliers) have to pay a commission to travel agents to compensate them for making the booking. If Air Canada pays 10 percent commission, the travel agency will receive $60. In other words, Air Canada earns only $540 on the sale instead of $600. You can understand why airlines like to sell directly to the traveller.

In the unilateral system the supplier has the opportunity to make additional sales. When dealing directly with Bondi, Air Canada may well convince her to book her return trip to Edmonton on Air Canada or to upgrade her seat.

Bilevel Distribution System

Two main forces work against the unilateral system of distribution. First, many suppliers cannot afford to maintain regional sales offices and must therefore rely on intermediaries to get their products to the consumer. In addition, many travellers would rather make their travel arrangements through a retail agency than deal directly with the supplier.

The bilevel distribution system usually involves a travel agent as intermediary (see Figure 3-2). The agent represents the suppliers and sells their travel services to the consumer. Suppliers also use business travel departments (BTDs) as distribution channels. In-house BTDs sell travel products and services to employees of large corporations. Tour operators may also serve as intermediaries, buying travel products from various suppliers and packaging them for sale directly to the consumer.

A recent development has been the use of supermarkets, department stores, and other retail outlets to distribute travel products (especially airline tickets). Some American supermarket chains sell certificates that are redeemable for discounted airline tickets. A supermarket in the Netherlands has even experimented with selling package tours in cans. The cans contain tickets and travel itineraries and are placed on the shelves alongside more traditional grocery products. It is conceivable that suppliers will look to similar retail outlets to distribute an ever-widening variety of travel products. This will make life more convenient for travel consumers but may eventually take business away from travel agencies.

The recent success of **video marketing**—whereby television cable channels show a catalogue of items on the screen—has not gone unnoticed by the travel industry. In fact, The Travel Channel in New York City is an all-travel

FIGURE 3-1
Unilateral Distribution System

Supplier → Consumer

FIGURE 3-2
Bilevel Distribution System

Supplier → Retailer → Consumer

video marketing channel. It shows travel films and promotes tours and other travel products.

For the consumer, the bilevel system's greatest advantage is that most travel intermediaries can provide professional assistance and personalized advice. In the present deregulated marketplace, the traveller faces a baffling maze of airfares. One airline may offer a bargain fare to Toronto, but only if you book a month in advance, travel on a Wednesday, and return on a Monday. Another airline offers an unbeatable fare to Miami, but the fine print reveals that you can fly only from Montreal and must stay in Miami for a minimum of seven days. Professional travel agents have the expertise to make sense of the airfare maze and to recommend arrangements to suit the needs and budgets of individual travellers.

Travel intermediaries can also provide the traveller with information on a greater variety of travel options than can any single supplier. An example will illustrate this point. John Roth wants to take his family to DisneyWorld for a week's vacation, but he is not sure where to stay. If he has the time, patience, and money for long-distance telephone calls, Roth can call several hotels and motels in the area to find suitable accommodations. His other option is to call or visit a local travel agency and explain his specific needs. The agent will be able to eliminate those hotels that are beyond his budget or unsuitable for other reasons. If Roth plans to fly to DisneyWorld, the agent will also be able to make the necessary flight arrangements and possibly reserve a rental car for the family's use. In other words, Roth can make all his travel plans in one simple step, instead of calling a host of different suppliers.

Since travel retailers do not charge clients for their services, Roth is not paying any extra for his family's trip. Only if the agent has to make overseas phone calls, or if a particularly complicated itinerary is involved, will the customer be charged.

Travel intermediaries usually have more influence with suppliers than do individual travellers. Suppliers value retail intermediaries as an important source of volume bookings and generally give preferential treatment to these customers. If space is limited—as is often the case during peak seasons—the traveller who books through an intermediary is more likely to get a seat on a plane or a room in a hotel than is a traveller who books independently. Suppliers cannot afford to disappoint the intermediaries. You perhaps have heard of travellers who have been "bumped" from flights or who turn up at a hotel to find that the front desk has no record of their reservation. Often, these are clients who have booked independently.

It is clear that the bilevel distribution system holds a number of distinct advantages for the consumer. What about the supplier? Travel intermediaries are an extension of the supplier's own sales force; in some cases, they are the sole sales force. In the latter case, the supplier has no sales overhead except for the commissions that it pays to retailers. Many suppliers would rather pay commissions to travel agents than maintain a network of sales offices that require full-time reservations staff. This is particularly true of smaller suppliers.

Airline commissions are the major source of travel agency revenues, accounting for almost two-thirds of total receipts. Since deregulation, suppliers have been free to choose how much commission they pay, although 10 percent remains the standard rate. Some suppliers also offer **overrides** to travel agents in addition to regular commissions. An override is a volume incentive and is usually paid on a graduated scale (for example, 1 percent for sales between $10,000 and $20,000, 2 percent for sales between $20,000 and $30,000, and so on).

Multilevel Distribution System

The multilevel system is the most complex type of distribution system. It involves the intervention of two or more intermediaries between the supplier and the consumer (see Figure 3-3). The system is most commonly used for the distribution of tour packages. Suppliers sell their products and services to tour operators (i.e., wholesalers). These in turn package the various components into a tour (transportation, accommodations, meals, sightseeing services, transfers, and so forth). The operator then sells the tour to the consumer through a retail outlet (usually a travel agency).

An additional intermediary is sometimes involved in the planning of a tour package. This intermediary can be an incentive travel company, a meeting/convention planner, a travel club, or some other **specialty channeler**. All intervene between the retailer and the consumer.

For the consumer, the advantages of the multilevel system are similar to those of the bilevel system. An additional advantage arises from the role of the wholesaler in the distribution process. Wholesalers buy travel services and products in bulk from suppliers. Advance sales, and the savings that arise from bulk buying, enable suppliers to offer their services to wholesalers at substantially reduced prices. Unlike the retailer, the wholesaler is not paid a commission by the supplier. Instead, the wholesaler makes its profit by marking up the price of the product. The markup must be high enough to cover overhead and commissions paid to travel agents and other retailers. Even after markup, the final package is still cheaper than if the traveller had bought the various components directly from the suppliers.

As we have seen, the multilevel system involves the greatest number of distribution channels. Occasionally, one company acquires several different channels of distribution. Each channel can then be used to promote the services and products supplied by the other channels within the group. This concept is known as **vertical marketing**. One of the first companies to form a vertical marketing operation was Canadian Pacific. CP owned and operated an airline (CPAir), a railway (CPRail), a shipping line, and a hotel company. CPAir is now part of Canadian Airlines International.

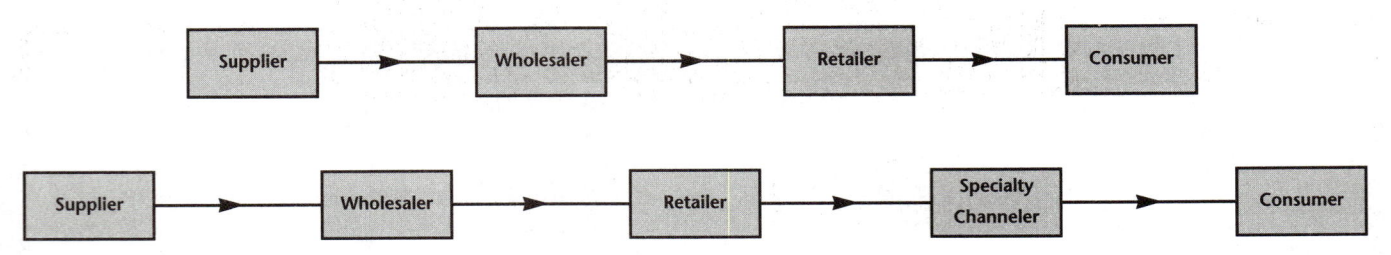

FIGURE 3-3
Multilevel Distribution Systems

In many cases, a single member of the distribution channel will sell products from other suppliers as well as its own products. Most of the large airlines, for example, sell hotel rooms, car rentals, and tour packages in addition to airline tickets. Similarly, American Express sells airline tickets and hotel accommodations as well as escorted tours. Cruise lines sell airline tickets as well as cruises. This means that a traveller can usually buy a package of two or more products from almost any part of the distribution channel.

> **CHECK YOUR PRODUCT KNOWLEDGE**
>
> 1. What advantages does the unilateral distribution system offer to consumers and to suppliers?
> 2. How will the growing use of automated ticketing machines, personal computers, and supermarkets as channels of distribution affect the role of travel agents?
> 3. What is the difference between the bilevel system of distribution and the multilevel system?
> 4. What is meant by vertical marketing?

NONAUTOMATED SYSTEMS OF INFORMATION

To operate successfully, the travel industry depends on a continuous flow of information from supplier to consumer. The information must be accurate and up-to-date, especially since fares and schedules can change overnight. What is this information? And how do travel retailers and consumers get access to it? We'll answer these two questions in this section. Although almost all travel agencies now use automated information systems, it is still important for today's travel professional to know about nonautomated systems. That way, in the event of a computer breakdown or similar problem, the travel professional will still be able to obtain current information. Let's take a look at how travel agencies operated before automated systems came into wide use.

Types of Information

Daralyn Walker wanted to fly from Charlottetown, Prince Edward Island to Calgary, Alberta. In the past, she made travel arrangements through a local agency—let's call it Alpha Travel. She had always been happy with their service and decided to use them again to make her reservation. Having established where Walker wanted to go (Calgary) and where she wanted to fly from (Charlottetown), the agent at Alpha Travel had to determine the following:

- Which airlines had flights from Charlottetown to Calgary.
- The seat availability on these flights.
- The fares of the different flights to Calgary.
- When the flights left Charlottetown and arrived in Calgary.
- How the flights got to Calgary—were they direct, or was a connecting flight necessary?
- Where the relevant flight information could be found.
- Walker also wanted to arrange hotel accommodations and to rent a car in Calgary. Where could the agent find information on hotel and rental car availability and rates?

Alpha Travel was a nonautomated agency—that is, it did not have access to a computer reservations system. As a result, the agent had to rely on printed reference sources and on telephone inquiries to suppliers.

Primary Printed References

A nonautomated travel agency needs a large number of printed reference works. All of these works must be updated regularly.

Airlines There are three main sources of information on flight schedules and fares:

- timetables and fare sheets
- airline guides
- tariffs

PROFILE

Dennis Frost

Written by Don MacLaurin

Dennis Frost developed an interest in the motorcoach business at a very young age. He grew up in Peterborough, Ontario and as a child loved to watch buses from the nearby Trentway Bus Lines garage travel past his house. Frost and his brothers would race across the front yard to wave to the drivers, hoping they would sound the horn as a drive-by greeting. Little did he know that he would be supervising Trentway drivers less than 20 years later.

Frost's first job, in 1981, was as a weekend bus washer with Trentway. His older brother had the job but was ready to quit and asked him if he would like to replace him. That same day, Frost rode his bicycle 10 kilometres to the bus garage and informed the supervisor he was there to take over his brother's night shift at the wash rack. After a quick phone call was made to the owner, he was granted permission to wash buses for the weekend. He has been with the company ever since.

That weekend job led to additional work during summer holidays, preparing school buses for the next school year. His role as bus washer expanded; soon he was picking up and delivering parts, helping the mechanics, and performing general property maintenance.

Talking to the motorcoach drivers as they returned from their trips throughout North America, Dennis realized there was a potential career for himself in the motorcoach and tour business. He wanted an educational program to complement his career choice, and after high school, enrolled in the Tourism and Hospitality Management Program at Sir Sandford Fleming College in Peterborough.

While he attended college, Trentway continued to employ him part-time. The small company with the green, gold, and white buses was growing. It soon acquired Wagar Coach Lines of Napanee, Ontario, and changed its name to the present Trentway-Wagar. This purchase enlarged the company's market to include the Peterborough–Toronto–Kingston triangle. Access to the huge Metro Toronto market was gained later, with the purchase of Charterways Transportation's Toronto Division. In 1993, the company purchased Canada Coach Lines of Hamilton. Trentway-Wagar's present fleet of 90 blue, beige, and purple coaches now dominates the "Golden Horseshoe," where more than one-third of Canada's population resides. Its modern fleet is now one of the five largest motorcoach operations in Canada.

After graduating from Sir Sandford's tourism program in 1988, Dennis decided to accept a position with Trentway-Wagar in the dispatch and operations department. This is the heart of a transportation company—the place on which all other company operations depend. The job involved servicing customer requests for tours, charters, and line run operations. (Line runs are intercity, point-to-point, regularly scheduled bus services.) He also worked with drivers, scheduling and confirming work assignments, dispatching and client or driver requests, and writing incident reports for any unusual occurrences.

Frost was promoted to customer relations representative in 1991. This position placed him squarely in the public eye, where communications and relationship-building are critical to success. He represented Trentway-Wagar at trade shows and visited customers to research their special needs, wants, and suggestions. Often, he would take a motorcoach directly to a client to demonstrate the comfort, safety, and other advantages of a modern, $300,000 luxury motorcoach. After visiting clients, he would help the charter department enter the pertinent booking information on the company's customized computer reservations system.

In 1993, Frost was presented with the biggest challenge of his career—the position of district manager for Trentway-Wagar's new operation in Hamilton, Ontario. His first task was to hire and train new drivers. Line runs and bus parcel express (BPX) comprise a significant portion of this company division. He manages a unionized workforce and all customer relations within the area bordered by Niagara Falls, Buffalo, Hamilton, Kitchener, Guelph, and western Ontario.

Seventy percent of Frost's time is devoted to problem solving. Long work hours are required to ensure the company's high service standards. Its motorcoaches are in motion 24 hours a day, 365 days a year throughout North America. Vehicle breakdowns and passenger complaints sometimes arise despite rigorous standards. The buses must be clean and well maintained at all times.

Frost believes he is fortunate to have an employer that has provided him with substantial career opportunities. He recommends that tourism program graduates set realistic career goals. Hard work, patience, and dedication are essential.

A boyhood dream, a professional education, a progressive employer, and a willingness to learn every facet of a dynamic business from the ground up have propelled Dennis Frost to his present position.

Timetables and fare sheets are published by all major airlines and distributed to travel agencies on a regular basis. The material must be updated every time there is a change of schedule or change of fare. Individual timetables and fare sheets show information for only the issuing carrier. To get a comparative picture of all the available schedules from a single source, the agent must consult the *Official Airline Guide* (OAG), published by Official Airline Guides Inc. This is available in North American and world editions and lists all scheduled flights. The North American edition is updated every two weeks; the world edition is updated once a month.

Tariffs list scheduled airfares and provide a summary of rules and regulations that apply to the flights. There are two main types of tariff. The *ATPCO Tariff*, issued by the Airline Tariff Publishing Company, lists American flights. International tariffs are published by individual international carriers such as Air Canada, Canadian Airlines International, Lufthansa, Swissair, and SAS, or by a consortium of foreign airlines. Of all printed reference sources, tariffs are the most likely to become fully automated. Since the passage of the Airline Deregulation Act in the United States in 1978, carriers in the United States have been allowed to set their own fares. The New Canadian Air Policy of 1984 (NCAP) allowed scheduled carriers complete downward pricing flexibility. It also limited price increases to an objective measure of the rise in price of the factors of production (not including labour). The National Transportation Act of 1987 gave the airlines complete pricing freedom beginning in January 1988.

It is much easier to update a computer every time a fare changes than it is to reprint a tariff. As a result, printed tariffs are rarely used by the travel industry today. (Note: Canadian carriers are no longer required to file tariffs with the government; however, fares and rates must be published, with accessible records kept at the airline's offices for at least three years.)

Ground Transportation

Ground transportation includes railways, intercity buses, rental cars, and mass transit and public transportation systems. Information on schedules and fares can be found in the following sources:

- timetables
- rail and bus guides
- car rental rate sheets

All ground transportation companies (such as VIA Rail) publish timetables that are updated as schedules change. The *Official Railway Guide* is the primary source for VIA (in Canada) and Amtrak (in the United States) schedules and fares. It also contains information on commuter rail services in major North American cities. Rail services worldwide are listed in the *Thomas Cook Overseas Timetable*.

Russell's Official National Motor Coach Guide lists domestic long-distance bus schedules. Car rental companies clearly have no need to publish timetables, but they must distribute information on rates to travel intermediaries. Car rental rate sheets issued by individual companies, such as Avis and Hertz, serve this purpose.

Cruise Lines The major printed reference sources for information on cruises are these:

- brochures
- official cruise guides

Cruise lines rely heavily on retailers to distribute their products. (Travel agents account for 95 percent of total cruise sales.) Individual companies supply agencies with lavish brochures detailing the season's cruise offerings, complete with sailing times, deck plans, rates, and related information. Official publications include the *Official Steamship Guide International* and the *Worldwide Cruise and Shipline Guide*. Both contain listings of cruise schedules throughout the world.

Hotels and Resorts Information on hotel and resort rates and services is available from two types of printed sources:

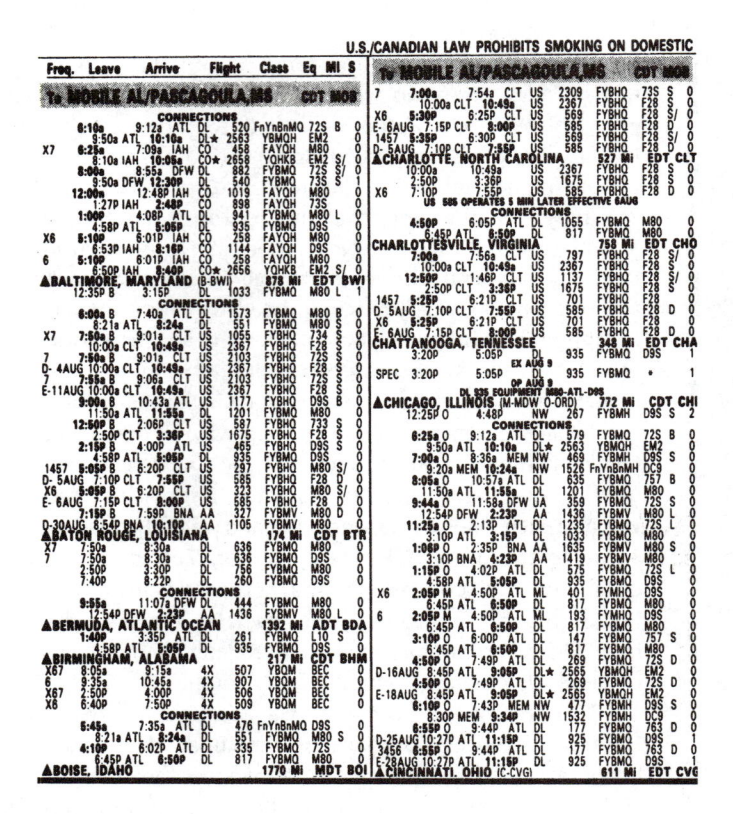

ILLUSTRATION 3-1

Printed references are essential sources of transportation schedules and fare information. Shown here is a portion of the *Official Airline Guide*.

SOURCE: Reprinted by special permission from the August 1, 1991, issue of the *OAG Desktop Flight—North American Edition*. Copyright © 1991, Official Airlines Guides. All rights reserved.

- brochures
- guides and manuals

Hotel brochures serve a function similar to cruise brochures. They not only provide information on individual properties but are also used as a selling tool. Brochures stress the hotel's most attractive features in the hope that travellers will be encouraged to stay at the property.

More objective sources are the various official guides and manuals. These include the *Hotel and Travel Index*, the *Official Hotel Resort Guide*, and the *OAG Travel Planner Hotel and Motel Red Book*.

Tours There are four sources of information on tour packages:

- brochures
- tour manuals
- catalogues
- tariffs

Most of the major tour operators, such as American Express and Thomas Cook, put out glamorous brochures each season with listings of rates and itineraries. A variety of tours are described in the *Consolidated Tour Manual* and the *Official Tour Directory*. A recent innovation in the United States and Canada is the use of mail-order catalogues listing tour packages. Catalogues have been used successfully in Europe for many years.

Travel agents have access to tariffs, which quote net tour prices. The net price is the noncommissionable price that the supplier charges the retailer. The retailer then adds a markup before quoting the price to the client. Confidential tariffs are issued by individual tour operators. These provide listings of tours and excursions, giving net prices.

Telephone Service and the Reservations Centre

With a nonautomated reservations system, after the travel agent obtains the relevant information and discusses options with the client, he or she is ready to make the reservation. Let's return to our earlier example. Daralyn Walker wanted to fly from Charlottetown to Calgary. The agent at Alpha Travel informed her that two airlines had connecting flights to Calgary on the day she wanted to travel. Walker chose the 9:30 a.m. Air Atlantic/Canadian Airlines flight because it was the most convenient time for her.

The agent then telephoned the Canadian Airlines reservations centre to determine if there was a seat available on the preferred flight. There was, so Daralyn Walker's name went on the **manifest**, or passenger list. If the flight had been full, her name could have been placed on the **wait list**. (A wait list is like the numbering system used in a bakery or delicatessen. As each passenger on the list is accommodated, or cancels, the others move up one place.) As an alternative to the wait list, she could have decided to fly at a later time or with a different airline.

When the agent called Canadian Airlines, he or she probably dialled a toll-free number. Most of the major suppliers—particularly airlines, hotel chains, and car rental companies—have a toll-free number. This number allows consumers and retailers to call the reservations centre free of charge from anywhere in the country. It is a valuable marketing tool for suppliers. A supplier without a toll-free number is at a distinct disadvantage. Only a few very small suppliers don't have one.

Toll-free numbers not only help suppliers but also offer considerable savings to the travel agent. During the course of a working day, a travel agent in a nonautomated setting often makes more than 100 calls to suppliers. Bills for long-distance calls can quickly add up, eating into an agency's profits. When all of those calls are to toll-free numbers, they don't cost the agency a cent.

Once a reservation has been made and a fare or rate established in a nonautomated setting, some sort of document must be issued. Such documents include standard airline tickets, rail and motorcoach tickets, and vouchers or coupons to be exchanged for car rentals, package tours, cruises, and hotel accommodations. In a nonautomated agency, the ticketing process is often done manually.

ILLUSTRATION 3-2
Tour brochures are informative marketing tools that contain attractive photographs with listings of rates and itineraries.
Source: Karen O'Neill

> **CHECK YOUR PRODUCT KNOWLEDGE**
>
> 1. What type of information does an agent need before he or she can book a flight?
> 2. In a nonautomated setting, where could an agent find information on (a) ground transportation, (b) hotels, and (c) tours?
> 3. How are toll-free numbers useful for (a) suppliers and (b) travel agents?

AUTOMATED SYSTEMS OF INFORMATION

The past fifteen years have witnessed tremendous growth in the automation of travel industry operations. When we talk about automation in the travel industry, we are referring primarily to the use of airline computer systems. These systems have been developed to facilitate operations in two distinct areas:

- *External functions*, which relate directly to the consumer (such as reservations and ticketing).
- *Internal functions*, which relate to the efficient operation of the company itself (such as accounting and management).

In this section, we will look closely at the external functions of the computer systems.

The Computer Reservations System

A **computer reservations system (CRS)** can be visualized as a huge general store that stocks an almost unlimited variety of travel products and services in one central location. The owner of the store is most commonly an airline. The airline sells not only its own products but also the flights of other airlines, as well as the products of travel suppliers such as hotels, car rental companies, and tour operators.

It is estimated that between 98 and 99 percent of travel agencies now use CRSs. To understand why CRSs are so popular, we must first establish what they are capable of doing. A CRS offers both informational and transactual functions. Informational functions allow the travel agent to obtain up-to-date information on schedules, availability, and fares. In this way the CRS replaces the printed reference sources. Transactual functions allow the travel agent to print tickets, invoices, and itineraries, and to book reservations. A number of travel agents have joined the Travel Agents Computer Society (TACOS), which provides information on system suppliers and vendors.

CRS vendors typically lease computer hardware to travel agencies for a monthly fee. The hardware includes keyboard, video display or CRT (cathode ray tube), modem, and printer. Using this equipment, the agent can communicate directly with the system's central processing unit (CPU) and memory.

Many travel agencies now purchase their own personal computers (PCs) to access their CRS vendor. "Intelligent" PCs are more versatile than "dumb" terminals in that they can perform many other functions, such as accounting and management. Most travel agencies now use PCs.

An agency's in-house computer consolidates the many steps that must be taken in making manual reservations. You will recall that our Alpha Travel agent, working in a nonautomated setting, had to first consult printed reference sources, then call the airline to confirm availability and make the reservation. An agent in today's automated agency can communicate directly with the CRS through the computer keyboard. Information on routes, schedules, fares, and availability for participating airlines is displayed instantly on the screen. The agent can make the reservation with the push of a few keys and create a **passenger name record (PNR)** for the client. The PNR is a complete record of the client's travel plans, which can be retrieved at any time for additions, changes, or cancellations. Its equivalent in the nonautomated system was the reservations card.

If the computer is linked to an in-house printer, it can automatically print airline tickets, boarding passes, and invoices or itineraries as soon as the flight reservation is made. Reservations for hotels, rental cars, and other services

ILLUSTRATION 3-3
Travel agents can use a CRS to obtain information on flight schedules, fares, and availability; make reservations; and even print tickets and travel documents at the touch of a button.
SOURCE: Courtesy P. Lawson Travel

can also be made at the same time through the same CRS. The additional data is stored on the PNR.

The obvious advantage to computer reservations systems is the savings in time they allow. An agent can complete the reservation and ticketing process in a fraction of the time it used to take. This makes for increased productivity and sales.

The Airline as Vendor

The airlines were the first organizations to develop automated reservations systems, and they have remained firmly in the forefront as vendors of CRSs. As **host vendor**, the operating airline receives revenue from three main sources:

- Participating airlines, which pay to have their schedules displayed through the CRS.
- Nonairline suppliers, such as hotels and car rental agencies, which pay to have their services displayed.
- Travel agencies that subscribe to the CRS.

Each CRS allows access only to those suppliers that have agreements with the host vendor. Information on nonparticipating suppliers must be secured by other means.

Before we consider the different systems available, we'll look briefly at the way airlines developed their own CRSs.

History of Automation Airlines recognized the value of computer technology in the reservations process as early as the 1950s. At first, individual carriers used in-house computers to keep track of the number of seats available on certain busy flights. The next stage involved developing reservations systems to which travel agents could have direct access. The problem was that each airline used a different automated system, which made it impossible to coordinate reservations in a single network.

Clearly, no agency could afford to purchase a computer terminal for each of the airlines it needed to contact. What was needed was a common automated reservations system that incorporated the schedules and fares of all the major airlines. The American Society of Travel Agents (ASTA), the largest agency trade group in the United States, launched a joint agent–carrier project to test the feasibility of a multi-access system. The project collapsed in 1976.

That same year, United, American, and TWA began installing their own competing reservations systems in travel agencies throughout the United States. These sophisticated CRSs differed from earlier systems in that they allowed access to several airlines, not just to the host airline, as well as to nonairline suppliers. Most agencies today subscribe to one or more of the major airline CRSs.

Major American CRS Vendors The original airline CRSs introduced in 1976 were APOLLO (United), SABRE (American), and PARS (TWA). They were later joined by DATAS II (Delta) and System One (Eastern). In 1987, Northwest became a co-owner of PARS with TWA.

SABRE (Semi-Automated Business Research Environment) is the world's largest private real-time computer network and travel information database. It is the most popular CRS among travel agencies, with about 14 000 American subscribers. The heart of the SABRE network is the Tulsa Computer Center in Tulsa, Oklahoma, which processes a staggering 107 million transactions a day. Using SABRE, an agent can check schedules for 650 airlines worldwide, make reservations for more than 300 airlines, book rooms at more than 22 000 hotel properties, and reserve vehicles from 60 car rental agencies. The system also allows agents to buy Amtrak and Eurail tickets, tour packages, cruises, and tickets to Broadway shows. You can even charter a private jet through SABRE.

APOLLO is just behind SABRE in popularity, with approximately 11 500 travel agency subscribers in the United States. It has similar capabilities to those of the SABRE system. APOLLO offers direct access to most major air carriers, 19 000 hotel properties worldwide, and 35 car rental agencies. Rail, limousine, entertainment, and tour companies also participate in APOLLO.

In 1990, PARS and DATAS II joined forces to create WORLDSPAN, a new CRS vendor with 10 000 agency subscribers. This new CRS is operated by WORLDSPAN Travel Agency Information Services, an independent company.

System One is the smallest CRS, with 7100 agency users in the United States. With System One, travel agents have direct access to 42 airlines worldwide, 135 hotel chains representing 18 000 properties, 40 car rental companies, and 20 other suppliers, including cruise lines and tour operators.

Most of the major vendors are developing second-generation computer products to further upgrade their capabilities. Focalpoint (Covia) and WORLDSPAN LAN are two examples. These systems are intended to supplement the existing systems rather than to replace them.

Canadian CRS Vendors Gemini, a partnership controlled equally by Air Canada, PWA Corp., and the Covia Group (which is controlled by United Airlines of Elk Grove, Illinois) was the major computer reservations company operating in Canada. AMR, the parent of American Airlines, agreed in 1992 to buy one-third of PWA's Canadian Airlines for $246 million provided that Canadian's internal computer-reservations business were moved from Gemini to AMR's Sabre division. However, Canadian Airlines had a five-year obligation to Gemini.

In early 1994, Air Canada took over Canadian's share of Gemini after a federal ruling in Ottawa released Canadian from its obligation to Gemini. Air Canada also took over Covia's shares in Gemini. Then it split Gemini into two companies. The first one, Galileo Canada, is the CRS for Air Canada and provides travel agencies with travel information and reservations and ticketing services. The second part of Gemini was purchased by IBM Canada for $50 million and

PROFILE

WORLDSPAN

It is now possible for a travel agent to boot up a computer and find the cheapest airfare to Acapulco, Mexico, show a client the floor plan of a cruise ship, and book a tour, hotel room, and rental car—all within a matter of seconds.

Thanks to increased competition, the services provided by computer reservations systems (CRSs) are getting better and better. A major development among American CRSs came in 1990 when three airlines—Northwest, Delta, and TWA—formed an independent company to produce and market a new computer reservations system.

The new company, WORLDSPAN Travel Agency Information Services, is spending millions of dollars to develop a new state-of-the-art CRS. The new company is made up of two existing CRSs, DATAS II (Delta Automated Travel Account System) and PARS (Programmed Airline Reservations System). The company built the new data centre in Atlanta, Georgia.

The creation of WORLDSPAN has had an enormous impact on the CRS industry. The merger of PARS and DATAS II reduced the number of American CRSs from five to four. At the same time, it has created a stronger CRS industry by allowing the four companies to compete on a more even footing. DATAS II had been the smallest CRS company among the five, with only 3500 clients. The combining of DATAS II and PARS has made WORLDSPAN the third-largest CRS in the United States. SABRE, owned by American Airlines, is the largest CRS; APOLLO is the second-largest; and System One is the fourth-largest.

Many travel agents expect to see much more competition among the four CRS companies in the 1990s. The payoff, for travel agents and their clients, will be more and better services in the coming years. The four companies are developing or already have produced several new programs that will enable travel agents and airlines to better serve their clients.

WORLDSPAN will be a completely neutral CRS. Although WORLDSPAN is principally owned by three airlines, the new company promises to offer equal access to all suppliers of travel products and services, including rival airlines. In a move toward increasing globalization, WORLDSPAN recently purchased a 5 percent share in Abacus, a CRS serving Asia and the Pacific. In turn, the Singapore-based Abacus purchased a 5 percent ownership in WORLDSPAN. This agreement will allow both companies to capitalize on the increase in international travel that is expected to continue through the decade.

With the improved services offered by WORLDSPAN and the other CRSs, travel agents have a great deal of information about major airlines, hotel chains, car rental agencies, tour operators, and cruise lines at their fingertips. They can serve their clients quickly and efficiently and be certain that they are assembling the lowest-cost package for each client.

CRSs are improving in other ways as well. They already offer programs that search out the lowest fares before and after a selected travel time. This enables clients to fly more cheaply if they are willing to leave a few hours earlier or later than planned. The CRS companies are also working to speed up the booking and confirmation process for airlines and hotels. All four CRS companies offer a computer service provided by THISCo—The Hotel Industry Switching Company. This service enables travel agencies and airlines to book rooms for customers in 15 major hotel chains. While the ability to book hotel rooms is not new, the THISCo program allows travel agents to confirm reservations at an amazing speed—within three seconds.

Another factor that may soon spur competition among CRSs is a proposed government regulation that will limit contracts between the CRS companies and their clients to three years instead of five. If a travel agent feels its current CRS vendor isn't keeping up with new developments, that agent will be free to switch to a new company after three years. This change, if made, will encourage CRS companies to continue to look for new ways to better serve their clients.

will provide that company with additional telecommunications and data processing for its global information superhighway.

The CRS for Canadian Airlines is SABRE, which has more than 109 000 terminals in more than 25 100 locations in 65 countries. The CRS for Air Canada is Galileo Canada, part of the Galileo International CRS. Galileo International claimed it had a 30 percent market share in 1994, against SABRE's estimated 40 percent.

Major Foreign CRS Vendors A number of foreign airlines sell their own CRSs. These include the following:

- ResAid (Scandinavian Airlines)
- TraviSwiss (Swissair)
- Jalcom-3 (Japan Air Lines)
- Resana (All Nippon Airways)
- Galileo International (12 European, Canadian, and American airlines), formerly Galileo Distribution Systems (originally Alitalia, British Airways, KLM, and Swissair)
- Amadeus Consortium (Air France, Iberia, Lufthansa, and SAS)
- Abacus (Cathay Pacific, Singapore Airlines)
- Fantasia (Qantas)
- Infini (Abacus, All Nippon)

The use of American systems in overseas markets has been a source of concern for foreign airlines, particularly in Europe and Canada. European CRSs can offer more complete local listings, but they cannot match the worldwide information listings and reservations capabilities of SABRE, APOLLO, and WORLDSPAN. Problems were created for Canadian travellers in 1993 when flights to Cuba were blocked out of CRS listings.

In order to avoid losing control of their distribution network and millions of dollars in revenues, in the mid-1980s European airlines started to develop a joint-venture reservations system to compete with the American CRSs. After that plan fell through, some of the foreign CRS vendors formed alliances with American vendors.

Co-hosts and Shared Databases An airline that does not have its own CRS can participate in a computer reservations system at one of four levels:

1. The least expensive level permits a display of the airline's schedules but not of availability.
2. The next level permits a display of schedules and availability, but reservations cannot be confirmed instantly.
3. The third level permits the airline to provide instant confirmation of reservations.
4. The most expensive level permits the airline to provide the same information and services as those offered by the host airline.

An airline that participates at the fourth level is known as a **co-host**. Co-hosts pay part of the cost of developing the

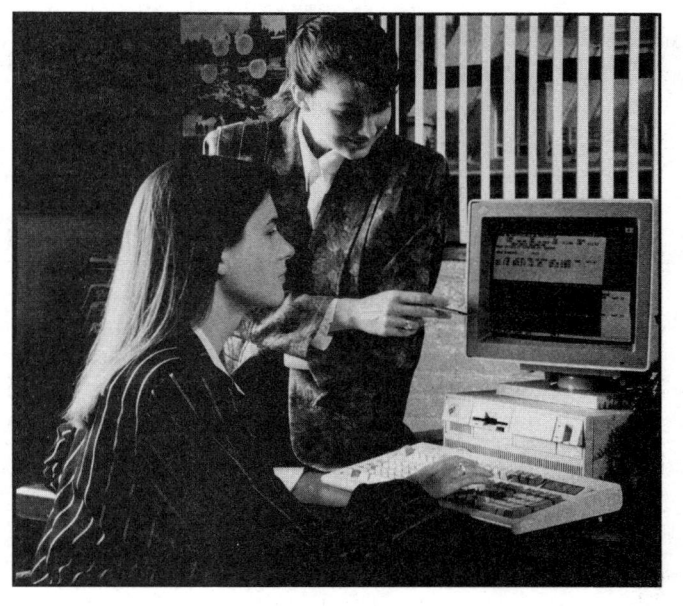

ILLUSTRATION 3-4
This Galileo Canada reservation system computer is connected to a network of over 100 000 terminals in 32 000 travel agencies around the world.
SOURCE Galileo Canada

system. In return, they get to share the database, and their information is given preferential display over other carriers.

The Issue of Bias Bias has been a controversial topic in the automated travel industry ever since the first CRSs were introduced in 1976. Bias refers to the preferential display of host-carrier flight schedules on the video display over the schedules of competing airlines. A hypothetical example will illustrate the point.

A travel agent using SABRE requests flight availability from Los Angeles to Miami on a specific date. There may be 30 flights to Miami on that day, but the video display can display only six to eight flights at a time. Because SABRE is owned by American Airlines, it is clearly in their interest to display their own flights first. Let's assume that American has six flights available to Miami: they would all be shown on the first display. The agent could request to see the second, third, and fourth displays for additional flights, but studies indicate that most bookings are made from the first display. If American did display its own flights first, as in this example, the company would be guilty of bias.

In response to the problem in the United States, the Civil Aeronautics Board (CAB) issued a series of rules in 1984 to eliminate bias from reservations systems. Host carriers are no longer permitted to display their own flights preferentially, nor those of co-host carriers. The CAB rulings have not been entirely effective, however, and bias remains a problem in the computerized travel industry.

The New Canadian Air Policy of 1984 called for the formation of a task force to establish adequate safeguards against bias in Air Canada's computer reservations system.

Teleticketing

Teleticketing, in use since 1960, is the simplest and least expensive form of automation available to travel agents. It permits subscribers to have airline tickets printed on a machine in the agency office. Teleticketing machines, which can be leased or purchased, are linked to the airline CRS by telephone line. When an agent makes a reservation by phone, he or she can ask for the ticketing information to be relayed directly to the in-house teleticketing machine. Unlike automated reservations systems, teleticketing only allows one-way communication—from the airline system to the agency. (CRSs allow two-way communication between the airline and the agency.)

Teleticketing machines are useful for small agencies that do not have the volume of business to warrant the expense of a CRS. Larger agencies that have subscribed to CRSs since 1976 usually hang on to their teleticketing machines, especially if they own them. Even though CRSs linked to printers have made them obsolete, they still come in handy if the in-house computer breaks down.

Satellite Ticket Printer

The **satellite ticket printer (STP)** made its first appearance in 1986. STPs allow travel agents to deliver tickets electronically to a client's premises by a process similar to teleticketing. STPs, however, are run by travel agents, not by airlines. The machines have proved particularly popular for in-plant industrial locations, such as those in industrial parks. With a growth rate of almost 79 percent in 1989, STPs are the fastest-growing category of travel agency location. There were 3840 STPs at the end of 1989 (see Figure 3-4).

Electronic Ticket Delivery Network

A very recent form of automation is the **electronic ticket delivery network (ETDN)**. These ticket printers enable travel agents to make deliveries to travellers, especially business travellers, who need same-day or next-day tickets. ETDNs are similar to STPs but are not owned by travel agencies. In the near future, ETDN ticket printers will be found in such varied locations as hotels, shopping malls, office buildings, and supermarkets.

Automated Ticketing Machine

Automated ticketing machines (ATMs) directly connected to a CRS are another recent development. Unlike STPs, ATMs are owned and operated by individual airlines. By inserting a credit card into the ATM, a customer can gain access to flight information, make a reservation, and receive a ticket and boarding pass. ATMs are found primarily in major airports, but industry analysts predict that self-service machines will eventually be installed in supermarkets, shopping centres, hotel lobbies, banks, and elsewhere. We can also expect to see machines that are shared by a number of different suppliers. These will allow consumers to buy a complete travel package from a single automated location.

CHECK YOUR PRODUCT KNOWLEDGE

1. Why do travel agencies subscribe to computer reservations systems?
2. Name the major computer reservations system available in Canada.
3. Name the four major computer reservations systems available in the United States.
4. What is meant by bias?
5. How do teleticketing machines, STPs, ETDNs, and ATMs differ?

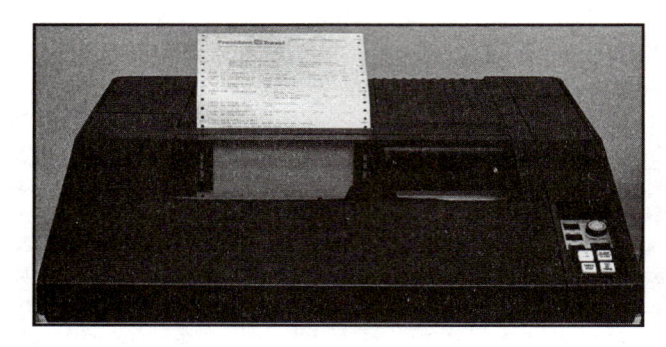

ILLUSTRATION 3-5
The satellite ticket printer is the fastest-growing category of travel agency location.

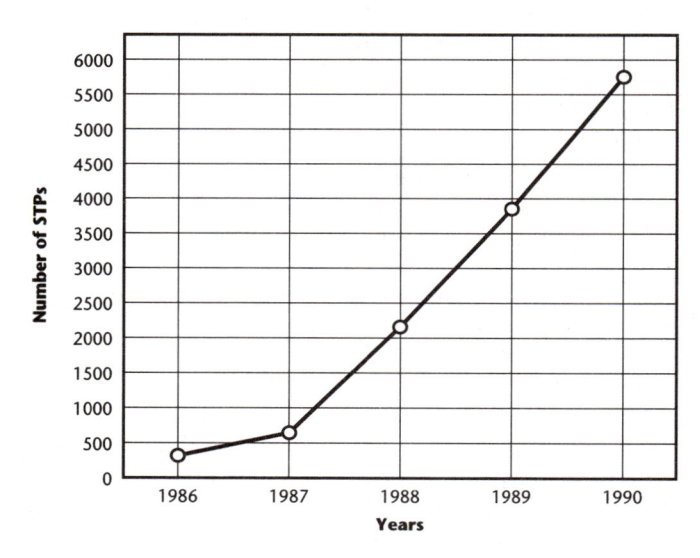

FIGURE 3-4
Growth of Satellite Ticket Printers
SOURCE: Airlines Reporting Corporation

OTHER USES OF AUTOMATION

So far, we have focused on the uses of automation for information, reservations, and ticketing services, with specific reference to airline CRSs. In this section you will learn how computer technology has been applied to back office functions. You will also read about the CRSs of nonairline suppliers, such as hotels and car rental agencies.

Back Office Systems

As the name suggests, **back office systems** involve functions performed behind the scenes. These functions are concerned not with the customer but with the efficient operation of the agency.

Back office systems are sometimes known as computerized accounting systems, or travel agency management systems. This will give you an idea of what the systems are primarily used for, which is performing accounting and management functions.

Accounting functions include listing accounts receivable and accounts payable, writing cheques, keeping general ledgers, and preparing balance sheets and financial statements. Some packages also include software for maintaining agency payrolls.

The management functions of automated back office systems allow reports to be compiled for the use of the agency's management—for example, reports on productivity per employee, on the sources of all commissions earned, on the volume of business with individual suppliers, on future sales projections, and so on. Many back office packages also include software for word processing and mail-list management.

The advantages of automated back office systems are similar to those of computer reservations systems: they involve increased efficiency and productivity. Agencies have been slower to automate back office functions than those directly relevant to the consumer, such as reservations and ticketing. More than half of all domestic travel agencies currently use computerized accounting and management systems (compared with the 98 percent using CRSs). Sales of software packages are, however, rapidly increasing, according to most vendors.

Back office systems are available both from vendors of CRSs and from independent companies. One of the first systems to be developed was ADS (Agency DataSystems), marketed by American Airlines, the same airline that sells the SABRE reservations system.

Most automated back office systems **interface** with one or more CRSs. This means that information can be "exported" from the reservations system to the accounting/management system. Suppose that an agency subscribes both to SABRE and to ADS. When an agent makes a reservation and a ticket is printed through SABRE, the information is automatically relayed to ADS. The back room system records the sale, notes the commission, credits the agent who made the sale, and compiles reports from the data supplied. In this way, the front room reservations system and the back room system are linked.

Uses of Automation by Nonairline Suppliers

Earlier in this chapter, you read that airline CRSs can display the products and services of nonairline suppliers. A travel agent with access to a computer reservations system can, for example, make room reservations for most major domestic hotel chains.

In addition, some suppliers, particularly hotels and car rental agencies, have developed their own automated reservations systems. Holiday Inn's Holidex system, introduced in 1964, was a pioneer in hotel CRSs. Holidex links 1600 Holiday Inn properties worldwide with a central computer in Memphis, Tennessee. About 40 percent of all Holiday Inn reservations are made through Holidex. Reservations systems have also been installed by chains such as Sheraton, Hilton, Westin, and Delta.

Hotel reservations systems are accessed by hotel employees at the client's request, which can be made by phone or in person. All hotel reservations systems operate on a single level, which means that only the services of the host vendor can be booked on individual CRSs. For example, reservations for a room in a Sheraton hotel cannot be made using

ILLUSTRATION 3-6
A hotel reservations agent uses computers to check room availability and book reservations at the request of customers, travel agents, and airlines.

the Holidex reservations system. Nor can a flight reservation be made using a hotel system. This is an important difference between airline CRSs and hotel CRSs. The advantage of making a hotel reservation through a hotel system is that the hotel CRS has the most up-to-date information on room availability. Airline systems are not usually updated automatically every time a reservation is made through a hotel CRS.

Car rental reservations systems function in much the same way as hotel systems. Avis's Wizard Direct Input Reservation System, for example, can be used for booking Avis cars only.

Amtrak also has its own automated reservations system, known as ARROW. Initially, ARROW was purely informational, providing travel agents with information on train schedules, fares, and so on. However, travel agents are now allowed to print Amtrak tickets, using the same standard ticket stock that they use for issuing airline tickets. Like the hotel and car rental CRSs, ARROW is a single-level system. Via Rail is currently implementing a more comprehensive automated reservations system.

CHECK YOUR PRODUCT KNOWLEDGE

1. What are automated back office systems used for?
2. What is meant by interfacing?
3. How do hotel reservations systems differ from airline CRSs?

CAREER OPPORTUNITIES

All the major suppliers employ large staffs of reservations agents. In this section we will look at the nature of the work of those who book reservations in the airline industry, the accommodations industry, the car rental industry, the tour industry, and the cruise industry.

The reservations systems of most suppliers are now computerized. Job applicants are expected to have a working knowledge of computers and computer terminology. Some of the larger suppliers offer training courses for new reservations agents to familiarize them with the CRS. Keyboarding skills are necessary for reservations agents, and office experience is helpful. Some suppliers prefer to hire applicants who have had two years of college or university; for others, a high school diploma is sufficient.

Airline Reservations Agents Airline reservations staff typically work at large central offices and spend much of their time in front of video displays. They take telephone calls from travel agents and consumers who want to book flights. Using a computer keyboard, they check flight schedules, availability, and fares and then reserve seats for passengers.

Hotel Reservations Agents Hotel reservations staff, working in reservations centres, answer telephone calls from travel agents, airlines, and members of the public requesting room reservations. Agents check room availability on a video display and book accommodations accordingly.

Car Rental Reservations Agents Car rental reservations staff also work over the phone with travel agents, airlines, and the public. They check the availability of cars at the location requested. When making a reservation, they enter the length of time the car will be rented as well as the location to which the car will be returned. (Rental cars do not have to be dropped off at the same place they are picked up.) Any relevant flight information is also recorded.

Most car rental reservations systems are centralized. Avis reservations agents, for example, work at the central Avis reservations office in Tulsa, Oklahoma.

Tour Operator Reservations Agents Reservations agents employed by tour operators work in much the same way as other reservations agents. They check the availability of tours and confirm reservations over the telephone.

Cruise Line Reservations Agents Reservations agents working for cruise lines explain to clients what the cruise line offers and when its various cruises take place. They also take reservations and handle routine inquiries. Most cruise line reservations agents work with travel agents, not directly with consumers.

Computer Careers The number of jobs available for reservations agents is expected to decline as a result of automation. Fewer agents will be needed to operate the computers. At the same time, however, automation in the travel industry has opened up a whole new field of computer-related careers. CRS vendors employ people to train potential users of their systems. They also employ programmers, equipment installers, service professionals, and sales and marketing representatives. All of these jobs generally require some experience with travel agency operations or airline reservations systems.

Summary

- The travel industry uses three main systems of distribution to move its products from producer to consumer.
- Regardless of the system used, identical products will usually cost the consumer the same amount.
- The unilateral system involves the direct sale of travel products and services from supplier to consumer.
- The bilevel system most often involves a travel agent as intermediary. The agent is paid a commission by the supplier.
- The multilevel system involves the intervention of two or more intermediaries, most often a tour wholesaler and a retail travel agency.

- A single member of the distribution channel can sell products from other suppliers as well as the member's own products.
- The travel industry depends on a continuous flow of up-to-date information from supplier to consumer.
- In a nonautomated agency, travel agents have access to information through printed reference sources. Reservations are made by telephone.
- In an automated agency, travel agents have access to information through a computer reservations system. Printed reference sources are used for supplementary information.
- A CRS allows travel agents to make reservations and to ticket electronically.
- Airlines are the principal vendors of computer reservations systems.
- The five major international reservations systems are SABRE, Galileo Canada, APOLLO, System One, and WORLDSPAN.
- Air Canada now uses Galileo Canada, and Canadian Airlines uses SABRE (Galileo Canada).
- CRSs allow access to participating airlines and nonairline suppliers.
- Tickets can be delivered electronically to various locations by teleticketing machines, satellite ticket printers (STPs), electronic ticket delivery networks (ETDNs), and automated ticketing machines (ATMs).
- Automated back office systems, marketed by CRS vendors as well as independent companies, have been developed to perform travel agency accounting and management functions.
- Back office systems interface with one or more reservations systems.
- Many hotel chains and car rental agencies have their own automated reservations systems.

Key Terms

intermediary
commission
teleshopping
video marketing
override
specialty channeler
vertical marketing
manifest
wait list
computer reservations system (CRS)
passenger name record (PNR)
host vendor
co-host
bias
teleticketing
satellite ticket printer (STP)
electronic ticket delivery network (ETDN)
automated ticketing machine (ATM)
back office system
interface

What Do You Think?

1. Retail outlets such as supermarkets and department stores are being used as distribution points for travel products. Automated ticketing machines (ATMs) and personal computers are being used for direct ticketing and direct reservations. What effect do you think that these developments will have on the travel industry as a whole and on travel agencies in particular?
2. Why do you think that it has proved so difficult for passenger airlines to come to an agreement on a neutral reservations system?
3. Do you think that CRS vendors should be allowed to display their own flights preferentially?
4. Why might a travel agency choose to subscribe to more than one computer reservations system?
5. Why do you think that airlines have played such a prominent role in the development of automated reservations systems?

Dealing with Product

The word *perishable* seems appropriate for describing dairy products and fresh-cut flowers, but how can this term apply to travel products as well? After all, most hotels are made with iron girders and tons of brick and mortar, ocean liners weigh thousands of tonnes, and airplanes are crafted from the strongest metals. Nevertheless, many marketing specialists will tell you that few products are as perishable as an airplane seat, a hotel bed, or a berth on a cruise ship. What do you suppose they mean by *perishability*? In what ways are travel products seasonal? How does seasonality affect the supply, demand, and cost of a travel product? What impact do you think nonrefundable cancellation penalties would have on perishables?

Dealing with People

You are a regional sales manager with a major airline. You have just received a telephone call from the president of a ski club in Yourtown. It seems the club plans to promote a ski group this winter and they would like to use your airline. You can expect at least 75 passengers, and perhaps as many as 100 will participate—that's a good day's work!

The president of the ski club has assured you that no travel agency is involved; in fact, the club has always dealt directly with air carriers and has never used a travel agency. There are ten travel agencies in Yourtown, each one well qualified to handle this group. Should you recommend that the president use a travel agent, who might be able to get better flights with another airline? Or should you just accept the order and thereby increase your profit margin? What will you tell the travel agency managers when they hear of this group?

A DAY IN THE LIFE OF

An Airline Reservations Agent

If you're planning a trip that involves flying, I may be the first person you contact. I'm a reservations agent with a major airline. The telephone and the computer are the main tools of my trade. In many ways, I am the airline's "voice." I represent the airline every time I answer the phone and deal with a caller. Every caller is a potential customer, whether that person is a travel agent, an individual passenger, or someone from a business travel department.

It's my job to make sure that callers become customers. To many callers, I am the first contact they have with the airline. So it's very important that I deal with every call professionally, efficiently, and courteously.

In addition to knowing when and where we fly, I also have a host of information available about flights offered by other airlines and about rental cars, tours, and hotels and motels. Many people who call for flight information are pleasantly surprised to discover that I can also arrange for rental cars and accommodations. I can even book them onto sightseeing tours. Our prices for these services are very competitive, since the airline negotiates bulk discounts with rental car companies, tour operators, and hotels and motels. Individuals might pay a lot more if they dealt with the suppliers themselves. So in addition to representing the airline and helping callers book seats on flights, I also sell the other services we offer. These telephone sales are an important aspect of my job.

The computer I use at work enables me to access all the information I need to help callers. All the information about our flights, fares, arrival and departure times, and other services is entered into the computer. I can find out anything I need to know at the touch of a few keys. With a typical call, I first find out where the person wants to go and when he or she wants to depart. I also need to know the length of stay at the destination so that I can check to see whether we can offer special fares. Once I have that information, I can give the cost of travelling in first, business, and economy class. I also explain any special fares. The APEX fares, for example, are cheaper than economy fares, but they have several restrictions, including an advance payment requirement and a no-cancellation policy.

To make a reservation, I type the caller's name, address, and phone number into the computer. This file is called the passenger name record, or PNR. I specify the flight the caller is taking, noting the flight number, departure date and time, and arrival time. I also handle seat assignments. Most passengers request an aisle or a window seat. Others also want to know what type of plane they will be flying on. On our 747s, passengers who want more room can elect to sit in the back of the plane, where the side rows contain only two seats. Others may request seats at the front of each section, where there is more leg room. If there will be any small children travelling, I make special arrangements for them. Finally, I make arrangements for other passenger requests, such as special meals or a wheelchair to and from the aircraft. It's my job to process this information properly to ensure that the passenger has the best possible flight.

Since our airline provides reservations information 16 hours a day, 7 days a week, 365 days a year, I work several different shifts. I like the flexibility that gives me, and I enjoy sometimes being off during the week when everyone else is working. While I enjoy my job, I like being part of a large organization that offers me several different career paths. I have the opportunity to build on what I have learned as a reservations agent or I can continue in my present position. Reservations agents can go on to become sales representatives, or senior agents who supervise shifts and help set policy for the entire department.

I like helping people plan their business trips and vacations. I am always pleased when they benefit from all of the extras the airline has to offer, such as our discount accommodations and tours. Each year, a good reservations agent helps thousands of travellers get off to the right start. That's a big responsibility, but it's an interesting and challenging way to earn a living.

CHAPTER 3: The Channels of Distribution   Name: _____

WORKSHEET 3-1 Perishable Product

You have read about the perishable nature of travel products. One kind of intermediary that takes advantage of this perishability is the travel club. Travel clubs offer discounted travel products, such as seats on a charter airplane or cabins on a cruise ship, on very short notice. Look in a local magazine or the travel section of a newspaper and find an ad for such a travel club. Contact the club and get the following information:

Name of travel club

Annual membership fee

Services offered

How members find out what is available

How far in advance members can make plans

Possible savings

What characteristics identify people who can take advantage of clubs like this? What groups of people have these characteristics?

Can you think of any ways to extend the advantage of last-minute buying to other travellers?

    The Yourtown Chamber of Commerce has asked you for your ideas on ways to extend the tourist season. Lower airfares to your area and the absence of crowds are two advantages of off-season travel. What existing but underappreciated aspects of Yourtown's off-season life could you publicize? What special events or activities could Yourtown offer to attract visitors beyond the usual tourist season?

CHAPTER 3: The Channels of Distribution   Name: _____

WORKSHEET 3-2 Specialty Channeler

Imagine that you work as a specialty channeller who creates packages and tours for special-interest groups. Use brochures, tour manuals, catalogues, and other printed references to find a package or tour for each of the following groups. In the space provided, briefly describe the package or tour and the reference you used.

1. White-water rafting enthusiasts

2. Theatregoers

3. Physically challenged campers

4. Avid baseball fans

5. Young singles

6. Families who want to experience a cruise

7. Novice skiers

8. Wine connoisseurs

9. Mystery lovers

10. Canadian history buffs

PART 2

Transportation and Accommodations

CHAPTER 4
The Airline Industry

CHAPTER 5
The Surface Travel Industries

CHAPTER 6
The Cruise and Steamship Industry

CHAPTER 7
The Hospitality Industry

CHAPTER 4

The Airline Industry

"Aviation was the combination of an undeveloped science with an art, resulting in adventure for the mind and body that brought stimulation to the spirit."
Charles Lindbergh

OBJECTIVES

When you have finished this chapter, you should be able to do the following:

- Name aircraft and events significant in the development of the airline industry.
- Distinguish between types of aircraft in service today.
- Define air carrier aviation and general aviation, and describe the types of services each provides.
- Identify the parts of an airport.
- Describe types of air routes.
- Compare multilateral agreements with bilateral agreements, and explain how they make the international air system work.
- Discuss the role of the International Air Transport Association.
- Summarize federal regulation of the Canadian airline industry since 1919, and of the American airline industry since 1925.
- Discuss the effects of the 1978 Airline Deregulation Act in the United States, and of airline regulatory reform in the 1980s in Canada.
- List factors that influence airfares.
- Explain how IATA calculates international airfares.

Canada and Canadians participated in the development of the aviation industry almost from its inception. Alexander Graham Bell recruited two young Canadian engineers, John McCurdy and F. W. Baldwin, to participate in his Aerial Experimental Association in 1907. This group built a number of successful aircraft. Baldwin flew the Red Wing in the United States in 1908. The first manned flight in Canada was made by John McCurdy, who flew a Silver Dart over Baddeck Bay, Nova Scotia, in 1909. The first commercial cargo flight in Canada took place in 1913, when Montreal newspapers were carried from Montreal to Ottawa.

In 1914, in Florida, Tony Jannus flew passengers, one at a time, across Tampa Bay in his seaplane. He charged five dollars for the 35-kilometre trip from St. Petersburg to Tampa. Jannus's one-man company was the first scheduled airline, or air transportation system, in the United States. Canada's first commercial passenger flight took place in 1920, when two bush pilots flew a fur buyer north to The Pas, Manitoba, from Winnipeg. Since then, the domestic airline industry in both Canada and the United States has grown tremendously. The airline industry today employs thousands of people to fly passengers and cargo to destinations throughout Canada and the United States.

International aviation—involving planes that leave the airspace of one country and enter the airspace of another—has grown simultaneously with domestic aviation. As a result, almost every part of the world is now accessible to aircraft. The growth in air travel has been the single most important factor in the development of the modern travel industry. It is the central ingredient on which so much else depends, including the hospitality industry, the tour industry, the cruise industry, and the car rental industry.

A BRIEF HISTORY OF GLOBAL AVIATION

Transporting passengers and cargo by air has been possible, practically speaking, only in the last 60 years. But human beings have dreamed of flying since ancient times. The first successful flight of a manned aircraft occurred in 1783, when two Frenchmen floated 300 feet above Paris in a hot-air balloon. Other important milestones in the history of aviation are shown in Figure 4-1.

Subsequent experiments with hot-air balloons led to the development of the airship, a lighter-than-air craft. For a time in the 1920s and 1930s, airships fitted with engines and propellers seemed a viable means of long-distance air transportation. With the explosion of the German-built

Hindenburg in 1937, however, interest in airships as passenger carriers declined.

Early Airplanes

Early experiments with airplanes were to prove of much greater significance in the development of air transportation. The earliest planes were gliders—aircraft without engines. The first successful manned glider flights were made in the 1890s by pioneers such as Otto Lilienthal of Germany and Octave Chanute of the United States. Their achievements inspired Americans Orville and Wilbur Wright to turn their attention from manufacturing bicycles to building gliders. The Wright brothers developed a glider that could be controlled in flight, then added a 12-horsepower gasoline engine to create the first airplane, the *Flyer*.

The *Flyer*'s historic first flight, lasting just 12 seconds, was made on December 17, 1903, at Kitty Hawk, North Carolina. The entire 36-metre flight could have been made within the cabin of a Boeing 747. By 1905 the Wright brothers had developed a fully manoeuvrable biplane (a plane with two pairs of wings) that could stay in flight for more than half an hour. Experiments in other countries led to the development of monoplanes (with one pair of wings), four-engine planes, and planes of monocoque construction (a tubelike design that eliminated the need for body braces).

World War I greatly advanced the development of the airplane, as warring nations manufactured fighter planes and bombers equipped with more powerful engines and all-metal bodies. During the course of the war, average airplane speeds increased from 105 kilometres an hour to 210 kilometres an hour.

Between the Wars

Organized airline service developed rapidly in Europe after World War I. At first, the airlines used surplus warplanes. Then they began to incorporate newer-model transports such as the trimotor. Government subsidies accelerated the growth of airline, so that by 1921, Europe's major cities were linked by ten airlines.

Commercial airline service did not get under way in the United States until 1926, when the government began offering subsidies to private airline companies to carry mail. The Ford Trimotor, introduced the same year, was the first American aircraft designed primarily to carry passengers (a maximum of ten per flight).

In Canada, the airline industry expanded rapidly between 1920 and 1937. It was composed mainly of a large number of small carriers flying north–south routes, carrying traffic to and from the railways. A government-owned carrier, Trans-Canada Airlines, now Air Canada, was formed in 1937 as a subsidiary of Canadian National Railways. It was given a monopoly on transcontinental and international routes.

The pioneering flights of Charles Lindbergh, Amelia Earhart, and others captured the imagination of the American public and created wider acceptance of the airplane. Between 1926 and 1930 the number of people travelling by air each year increased from 6000 to 400 000. The introduction in 1936 of the Douglas DC-3, which could carry 21 people, further accelerated the growth of air travel. This twin-engine transport, which could fly at 270 kilometres an hour, incorporated all the major technological advances of the time and acquired a reputation for incomparable comfort and safety. For a while, the DC-3 was to the airline industry what the Model T Ford was to the automobile industry: it enabled airlines to make a profit. The DC-3 is still used in many parts of the world today.

By the late 1930s the United States had assumed world leadership in commercial aviation. American Airlines, Eastern Airlines, TWA, and United Airlines were the big names in domestic operations, while Pan Am was the major

1900 — First successful airplane flight at Kitty Hawk.

1910 — First international flight—Louis Blériot.
— First transcontinental flight across the United States.

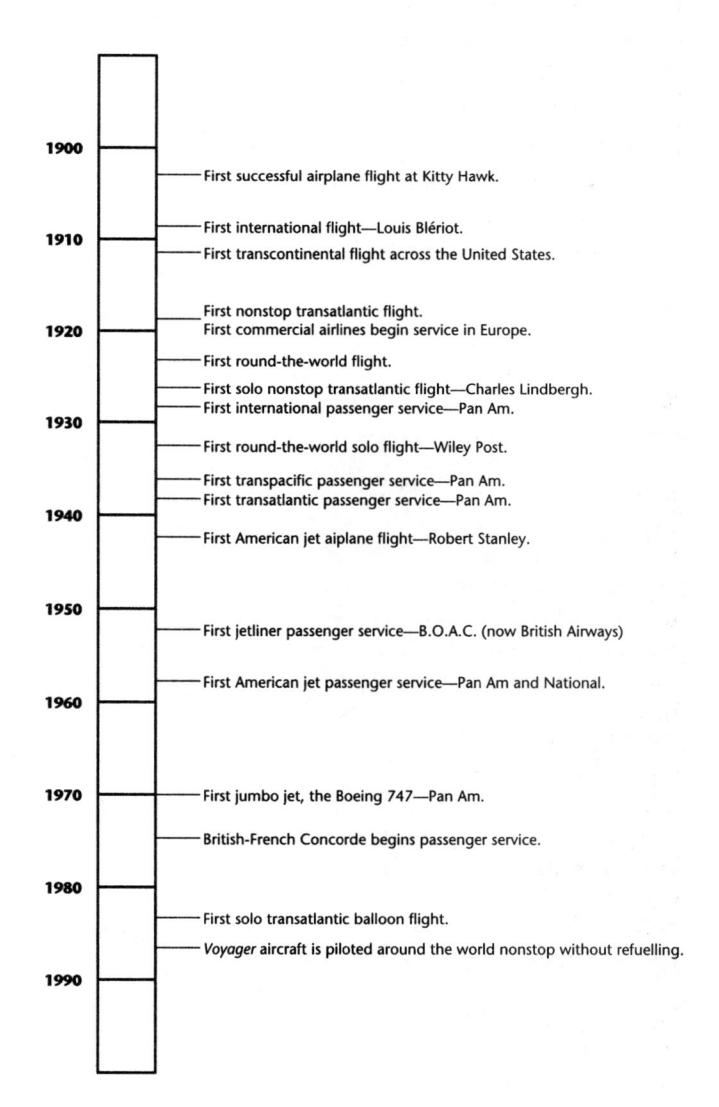

1920 — First nonstop transatlantic flight.
— First commercial airlines begin service in Europe.
— First round-the-world flight.
— First solo nonstop transatlantic flight—Charles Lindbergh.
— First international passenger service—Pan Am.

1930 — First round-the-world solo flight—Wiley Post.
— First transpacific passenger service—Pan Am.
— First transatlantic passenger service—Pan Am.

1940 — First American jet aiplane flight—Robert Stanley.

1950 — First jetliner passenger service—B.O.A.C. (now British Airways).
— First American jet passenger service—Pan Am and National.

1960

1970 — First jumbo jet, the Boeing 747—Pan Am.
— British-French Concorde begins passenger service.

1980 — First solo transatlantic balloon flight.
— *Voyager* aircraft is piloted around the world nonstop without refuelling.

1990

FIGURE 4-1
Milestones in Aviation History

international carrier, flying routes from Alaska to South America. Pan Am introduced transpacific passenger service to Asia in 1937 and transatlantic service to Europe two years later. Concerns in Canada that Canadians were crossing the border to fly on American carriers were a factor in the formation of Trans-Canada Airlines in 1937. TCA was given a monopoly on transcontinental and international routes. The Canadian Pacific Railway purchased 11 small airline firms in 1941 and operated them as United Air Services until 1942, when the name was changed to Canadian Pacific Airlines (CP Air).

World War II to the Present

World War II played a major role in the growth of the commercial airline industry. As happened in World War I, warfare accelerated the development of more advanced airplanes that could fly faster and higher, as well as farther without refuelling. After the war, these improvements were applied to commercial planes. In 1947, United Airlines and American Airlines inaugurated coast-to-coast American service with the Douglas DC-6—a plane with a capacity of 55 passengers and a cruising speed of 480 kilometres an hour at 6000 metres. Nonstop transoceanic transports such as the Douglas DC-7, Boeing 377 Stratocruiser, and Lockheed Super-Constellation were developed, all of which could carry 100 passengers at similar speeds.

In addition to improved airplane design, the war produced trained pilots anxious to transfer their skills to commercial aviation. Surplus warplanes, which could be purchased cheaply, enabled many airline companies to start up, especially smaller regional airlines and charter companies. One further effect of the war was to increase public confidence in the airplane as a means of transportation. Several Canadian airlines started after World War II. Central British Columbia Airways was formed in 1946, and renamed Pacific Western Airlines in 1953. Eastern Provincial Airways began as a Newfoundland-based bush line in 1949.

ILLUSTRATION 4-1

Improved airplane design, trained pilots, and an increase in public confidence in air travel all contributed to the growth of commercial aviation during the years after World War II.
SOURCE: Neg. 24948/National Aviation Museum Archives

ILLUSTRATION 4-2
The late-model 767 is designed to be more economical than earlier planes for fuel consumption and personnel.
SOURCE: Courtesy Canadian Airlines International Ltd.

CHAPTER 4: The Airline Industry

The Jet Age Although privately owned American companies continued to dominate the air, by the 1950s there was an increase in the number of foreign airlines flying international routes. Most of these airlines were government owned and operated. Foreign manufacturers, most notably the British, led the way in the development of jet airliners for commercial use. The Vickers Viscount (the first turboprop) and the de Havilland Comet (the first turbojet) were introduced in 1952.

The Avro Jetliner, designed and built in Canada, first flew on August 10, 1949, just days after the British de Havilland Comet on July 27, 1949. This flight of the Avro Jetliner was the first flight of a jet passenger plane in North America. In 1950 it made the first international jet flight in North America, from Toronto to New York. Unfortunately, the Avro Jetliner did not enter commercial production; instead, Avro turned its attention to the building of military planes for the Korean War. Canadian airlines bought foreign-built aircraft. The United States did not have a jet transport in commercial service until 1958, when Pan Am launched the Boeing 707 on transatlantic routes and National inaugurated DC-8 flights on domestic routes. The 707, with its 180-person capacity, was to have a revolutionary effect on the growth of international tourism. At a speed

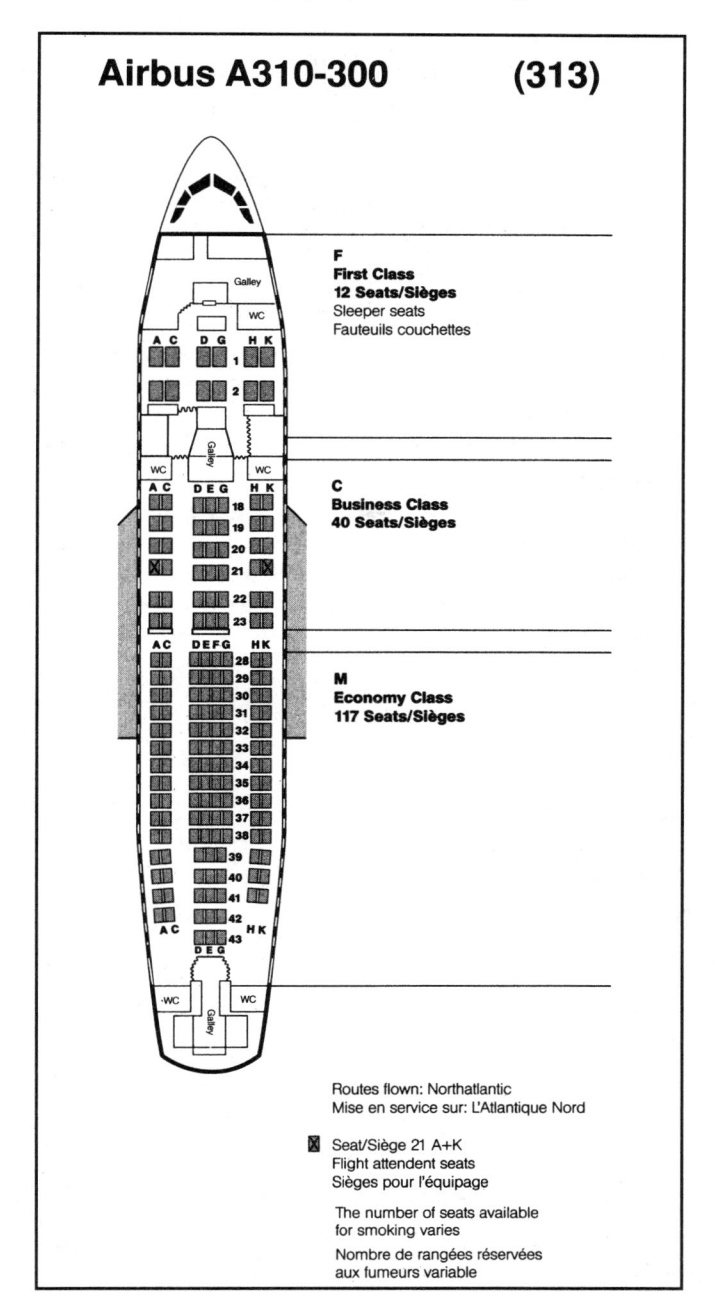

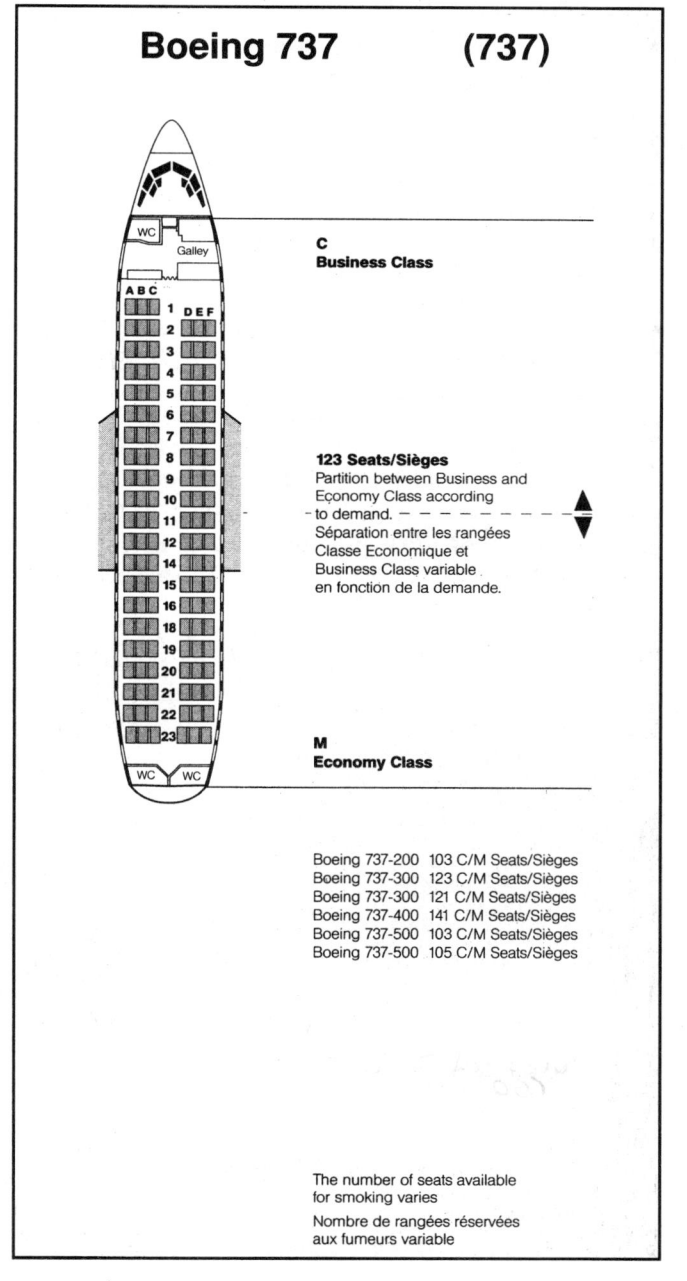

ILLUSTRATION 4-3
Note the comparative sizes and seating configurations of Lufthansa's Boeing 737 City Jet and Airbus A310-300.
SOURCE: Lufthansa German Airlines.

PROFILE

The Boeing Company

Boeing is the world's leading manufacturer of airplanes for commercial travel. It was founded in 1916, only 13 years after the Wright brothers made their first flight. In those days, airplanes were still very crude, handmade machines. William E. Boeing, the son of a wealthy lumber-company owner, took up flying as a hobby when he was 34. He quickly became dissatisfied with the planes he was flying and decided he could build a better one himself.

Boeing set to work with an associate, G. Conrad Westervelt, to construct two airplanes at a Seattle, Washington shipyard. They finished the first plane, which they called the B&W, in 1916. It was a bi-wing float plane with an open cockpit. The B&W was the beginning of the Boeing Company.

The following year, 1917, the United States entered World War I. The U.S. Navy, which had a sudden urgent need for training planes, ordered 52 planes from Boeing. Those planes, an improved version of the B&W, were called Model Cs. The planes were assigned a Navy serial number, 699, so they became known as C-699s. When Boeing built an additional Model C for himself, he named it the C-700. The Boeing Company still uses numbers in the 700s to designate its jetliners. If you have flown on a commercial airline, you have probably flown on a Boeing 707, 727, 737, 747, 757, or 767.

In 1927, Boeing won a contract to fly airmail between San Francisco and Chicago. His company produced 24 new airplanes, Model 40As, in six months to begin the new service. The Model 40As were open-cockpit biplanes with wheels rather than pontoons. They could carry almost 550 kilograms of mail. Tucked away under the wings was a small closed compartment that could carry two very brave passengers. The Model 40As were the first planes to be used for regular long-distance passenger and mail service.

The Model 40As were soon outdated, however. In 1928, Boeing produced a greatly improved passenger plane called the Model 80. This plane was still a bi-wing, but it had three engines and a cabin large enough to carry 12 passengers. The cabin included upholstered seats, a toilet, running water, and reading lamps. By the standards of the time, the Model 80 was the state of the art in luxury and comfort. The new plane also included two other innovations in air transportation: an enclosed cockpit for the two-person crew and registered nurses—the first flight attendants—to wait on the passengers.

Since the 1930s, the Boeing Company has continued to develop new, improved airplanes, both for commercial airlines and for the military. These include the famed Pan American clipper ships in the 1930s, the Stratocruiser airliners in the 1940s, and the Dash 80, the first jet airliner, in the 1950s. During World War II, 12 000 Boeing B-17 bombers—the famed Flying Fortresses—were produced to meet the needs of America's war effort. Boeing now builds Chinook helicopters for the military.

The Everett plant normally produces five jumbo 747s and five wide-body 767s each month. Boeing delivers nearly two airplanes per working day to airlines in countries such as Singapore, Britain, Algeria, Japan, and Brazil. The company has also been awarded contracts to design and build pressurized modules for the proposed NASA space station. These modules will provide living and work space for future astronauts. Perhaps someday Boeing airships will fly passengers to space stations for vacations that are truly "out of this world."

of 980 kilometres an hour, the turbojet could fly from New York City to Europe in just over seven hours. The fastest propeller-driven plane took 18 hours. A comparable trip on an ocean liner took four days. Faster flights meant that airlines could offer more flights. Increased passenger volume in turn reduced airfares and expanded flight schedules.

The expansion of jet service signalled the decline of ocean-going passenger ships as a means of point-to-point international travel. Jets also undercut rail and bus service for domestic travel. By the late 1960s all the major airlines were operating with large jet-powered planes, and many of the smaller airlines were using small- to medium-range jets.

Jumbo Jets, Airbuses, and Supersonic Transports Improvements in jet performance and comfort led to the development of huge, wide-bodied jets in the early 1970s. The first jumbo jet—the four-engine Boeing 747—was put into service by Pan Am in 1970. It could carry as many as 500 passengers. Europe's answer to the jumbo jet was the Airbus, launched in 1974. Built for fuel efficiency as well as passenger capacity, the Airbus A-300 was the first twin-engine, wide-bodied jet. It was produced by Air Industrie, a consortium of Western European companies.

International cooperation between Britain and France produced the Concorde, a supersonic transport (SST). Distinguished by its beaklike nose, the Concorde carries 125 passengers at a speed of 2150 kilimetres an hour, which is much faster than the speed of sound. The British–French SST began passenger service in 1976, shortly after the Russian SST, the Tupolev-144, was introduced. The development of an American SST was halted in 1971 when the U.S. Senate refused to grant further funds. The refusal followed public protests against the loud sonic booms caused by the fast-flying SSTs.

The 1980s and Beyond In the history of the airplane, bigger, faster, and higher have been the key terms. This trend may continue—designers and manufacturers are considering a hypersonic transport, a plane that would travel six times the speed of sound at an altitude of over 36 000 metres. At the same time, economic circumstances may dictate that fuel efficiency be given priority in future designs. Faced with rising costs and falling profits, many airlines are turning to cheaper, more fuel-efficient planes that require smaller air and ground crews and less maintenance. The MD-80; Boeing 737-300, 757, and 767; and Airbus A-310 are examples of jets that have been designed for fuel-efficient operation in recent years. Each of these aircraft is designed to carry 180 or more passengers and is powered by two engines and flown by only two flight officers. The 767 can make international long-haul flights. In 1994, Boeing unveiled the 777, an airplane designed on a computer, as its new long-distance aircraft.

Another trend is toward increasing privatization of overseas airlines. Airlines in the United States have long been privately owned; now a number of foreign governments are transferring airline ownership and operations from the public to the private sector. British Airways and Air Canada are examples of government-run airlines that have passed into private hands.

Types of Aircraft

In this book, aircraft will be described in two ways: by type of engine and by purpose.

Engine Type Modern airplanes either have jet engines or are propeller-driven. Both types are in service worldwide.

Jet aircraft, powered by turbine engines producing tremendous thrust, can cruise at 800 kilometres an hour. Cabins are pressurized so that the aircraft can fly at high altitudes (10 000 metres and above). **Pressurization** means an artificial increase in the cabin air pressure so that it is almost the same as at ground level. Because jets provide speed and comfort, they are used for long-distance and medium-range domestic and international flights. Because they have fewer moving parts, jet engines require less maintenance than the gasoline-powered piston engines that propeller planes use. Also, they can be operated for more hours per day.

The turbojet was the first successful jet engine. Although it is still used on some planes, it has been superseded by the turbofan engine, which operates more efficiently (and more quietly) at low speeds.

More than 6000 jet aircraft are currently in operation worldwide. Most of them were manufactured in the United States by Boeing or McDonnell Douglas. In recent years, European manufacturers such as British Aerospace and Airbus Industrie have begun to offer strong competition to these two American giants of the jet aircraft industry.

Propeller-driven airplanes, or props, fly more slowly and at lower altitude than jets. Props can be divided into two categories: those with piston-powered engines plus one or more propellers (small airplanes); and those with turbine engines plus propellers, known as turboprops (medium-sized planes). Most turboprops and some piston-powered aircraft are pressurized. However, several models are not pressurized and must therefore fly below 4000 metres, often in the weather rather than above it.

For the first 50 years of modern aviation, all airplanes were piston-powered. Airplanes powered by turboprop engines entered commercial service in the 1950s. Jet aircraft replaced turboprops for long-distance flights during the 1960s, but many turboprops are still in use over shorter distances (650 kilometres or less). Some turboprops are pressurized and fly above bad weather. New propeller-driven aircraft are being designed for the growing regional and commuter airlines. Manufacturers outside the United States are earning a large share of this market. For example, Embraer's Bandeirante, a twin-turboprop light transport, made in Brazil, has been sold to 21 countries. Other manufacturers include Casa of Spain, Fokker of the Netherlands, and Short Brothers of Northern Ireland. de Havilland of Canada has built and marketed the DH8-100 Dash 8, which seats 37 and the DH8-300, which seats 50.

Purpose Aircraft can be further classified according to the particular market they are designed to serve.

- *Short-haul flights.* The regional/commuter market is served by a variety of single- and twin-engine planes carrying between 19 and 60 passengers on short-haul flights of 160 kilometres or less. The de Havilland Dash 8-100 and Dash 8-300, manufactured in Toronto, carry 30 and 50 passengers respectively.
- *Short- to medium-range flights.* Twin-jets, such as the McDonnell Douglas DC-9 and the Boeing 737, operate within the short to medium range (1600 kilometres or less) and usually carry between 100 and 160 passengers. There are more 737s flying today than any other type of commercial aircraft. The Boeing 727, a three-engine jet, usually provides service on flights of 3200 kilometres or less and carries up to 180 passengers.
- *Long-haul flights.* The long-haul transcontinental and intercontinental market is served by the largest jets of all—the twin-jets (the Boeing 767 and the new 777, and Airbus A-300), tri-jets (the DC-10, McDonnell Douglas MD-11, and Lockheed L-1011), and four-engine jets (the Boeing 747 and McDonnell Douglas DC-8). These planes vary in capacity from 180 to 500 passengers and fly within the range of 5000 to 11 500 kilometres.
- *Special purpose flights.* This category includes flights by helicopters, seaplanes, and amphibious vehicles. There are several all-helicopter and all-seaplane airlines in several countries.

CHECK YOUR PRODUCT KNOWLEDGE

1. How did World War II influence the development of the commercial airline industry?
2. What effects did the inauguration of passenger jet service in the 1950s have on the travel industry?
3. What is the main difference between North American airlines and those in other countries?
4. Name four types of airplane engines.

TYPES OF AIR SERVICE

Within Canada and the United States, airplanes and other aircraft provide services in two broad areas—civilian and military. Civilian services can be further divided into air carrier aviation and general aviation.

Air Carrier Aviation

Air carrier aviation refers to privately owned companies that offer for-hire public transportation of passengers, cargo, and mail. Canada has 303 public airline carriers, according to the Royal Commission on National Passenger Transportation. An air carrier, also known as a **common carrier,** can be a small company with 100 employees and a dozen aircraft, or it can be a huge conglomerate with 40 000 employees and hundreds of aircraft. Airlines such as Air Canada, Canadian Airlines, United, and USAir belong in the category of air carrier aviation.

Some airplanes are designed to transport passengers only. Others have removable seats, extra-wide doors, and machinery for loading and unloading so that they can transport either passengers or cargo. Still others are designed solely to transport cargo. These airplanes look like passenger airplanes except they have no windows. The largest cargo planes, such as the Boeing 747F, can carry 100 tonnes 6500 kilometres nonstop. Typical airline cargo includes goods that must be delivered quickly (flowers, fruits, vegetables), lightweight but expensive goods (electronic equipment, machine parts), and business documents. In recent years, small-package carriers that guarantee overnight delivery to major cities across Canada and the United States have found a lucrative market. These include Federal Express, UPS, Purolator, and Emery.

Air carriers provide services on either a scheduled or a nonscheduled basis. Most airlines are **scheduled airlines,** which set arrival and departure times for all their flights. Timetables are extremely important to scheduled carriers; most of their flights depart and arrive on time 90 percent of the time. Nonscheduled airlines, also called **supplemental airlines** or **charter airlines,** provide air travel at lower rates than regular fare on scheduled airlines. Planes can be chartered from supplemental airlines or from airlines operating scheduled flights.

Classification Systems in the United States The classification system in the United States was originally set up on a geographical basis. The Civil Aeronautics Board (CAB) awarded "certificates of convenience and necessity" to domestic airlines; these certificates assigned airlines to specific routes. Northwest Orient, for example, was given control of the route from Minneapolis–St. Paul to Seattle. To indicate their size and scope, certified air carriers providing scheduled services came to be classified along geographical lines:

- *Trunk airlines.* These were the heart of the airline industry—the large airlines (such as American, United, and Delta) with long-distance routes between major metropolitan areas and medium-sized cities and some international flights.
- *Intra-Hawaiian and intra-Alaskan airlines.* These operated only within Hawaii or Alaska.

CHAPTER 4: The Airline Industry

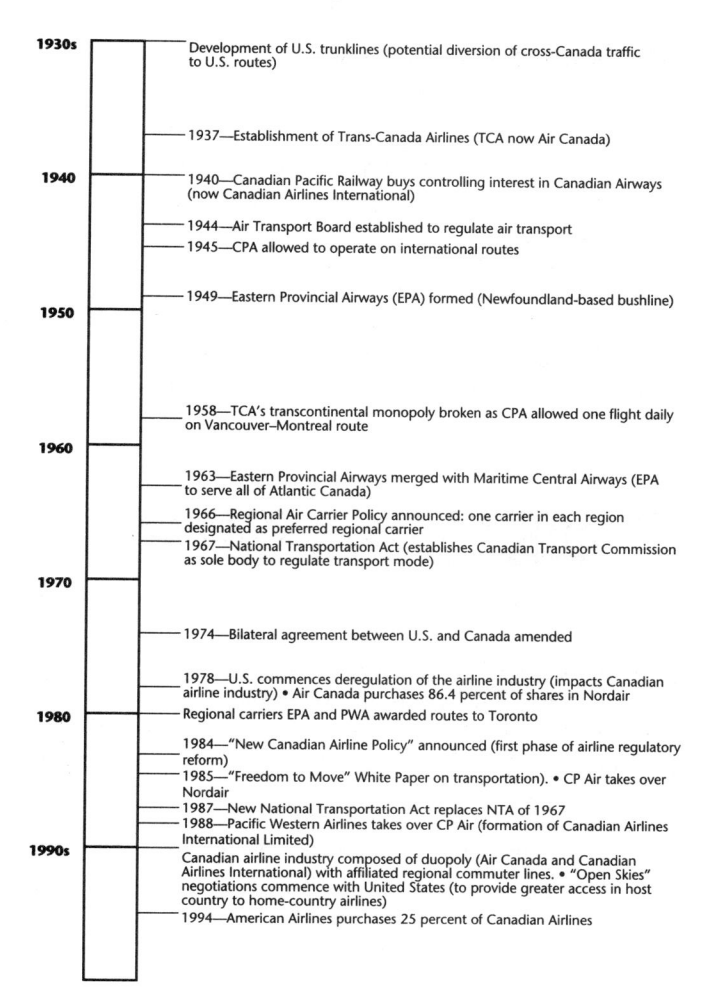

FIGURE 4-2
The Development of the Canadian Airline Industry

- **1930s**—Development of U.S. trunklines (potential diversion of cross-Canada traffic to U.S. routes)
- **1937**—Establishment of Trans-Canada Airlines (TCA now Air Canada)
- **1940**—Canadian Pacific Railway buys controlling interest in Canadian Airways (now Canadian Airlines International)
- **1944**—Air Transport Board established to regulate air transport
- **1945**—CPA allowed to operate on international routes
- **1949**—Eastern Provincial Airways (EPA) formed (Newfoundland-based bushline)
- **1958**—TCA's transcontinental monopoly broken as CPA allowed one flight daily on Vancouver–Montreal route
- **1963**—Eastern Provincial Airways merged with Maritime Central Airways (EPA to serve all of Atlantic Canada)
- **1966**—Regional Air Carrier Policy announced: one carrier in each region designated as preferred regional carrier
- **1967**—National Transportation Act (establishes Canadian Transport Commission as sole body to regulate transport mode)
- **1974**—Bilateral agreement between U.S. and Canada amended
- **1978**—U.S. commences deregulation of the airline industry (impacts Canadian airline industry) • Air Canada purchases 86.4 percent of shares in Nordair
- Regional carriers EPA and PWA awarded routes to Toronto
- **1984**—"New Canadian Airline Policy" announced (first phase of airline regulatory reform)
- **1985**—"Freedom to Move" White Paper on transportation. • CP Air takes over Nordair
- **1987**—New National Transportation Act replaces NTA of 1967
- **1988**—Pacific Western Airlines takes over CP Air (formation of Canadian Airlines International Limited)
- **1990s**—Canadian airline industry composed of duopoly (Air Canada and Canadian Airlines International) with affiliated regional commuter lines. • "Open Skies" negotiations commence with United States (to provide greater access in host country to home-country airlines)
- **1994**—American Airlines purchases 25 percent of Canadian Airlines

- *Regional airlines.* These served a specific area of the country. For example, Allegheny Airlines served the northeastern United States, while Southern served the South. Regionals were feeders for the trunk lines.
- *Local and/or commuter airlines.* These flew to the smaller communities that the regionals could not serve profitably.

Since the Airline Deregulation Act of 1978, these geographical distinctions have become blurred. For instance, airlines formerly allowed to operate only within Hawaii now provide service to the mainland. Former regional airlines have developed services between major cities in competition with the trunk airlines. Consequently, air carriers are now classified on the basis of revenue or annual earnings.

- Major air carriers earn $1 billion or more yearly.
- National air carriers earn $75 million to $1 billion yearly.
- Large regional/commuter carriers earn $10 million to $75 million yearly.
- Medium-sized regional/commuter carriers earn less than $10 million yearly.

A classification system based on revenue is more realistic and flexible, and more accurately describes what is happening in the industry. If business is brisk, a regional carrier could be a national carrier next year. Conversely, a major carrier could drop to a national carrier if sales are low. It should be noted that every major carrier in the United States is also an international carrier, that is, it operates scheduled services to foreign nations. Even some national carriers have international flights.

Classification Systems in Canada Airlines in Canada came to be classified in much the same way as those in the United States. An airline applied to the Canadian Transport Commission for operating authority under the terms of the National Transportation Act of 1967. This application was granted only if the applicant could prove the service was and would be required. This was a test of "public convenience and necessity." All fares had to be filed and could be disallowed if found to be unjust or unreasonable. Carriers were typically classified on a geographic basis. See Figure 4-2.

- *National carriers.* The two major carriers were Air Canada and CP Air (now Canadian Airlines). Both had long-distance routes between major and medium-sized cities, as well as extensive international routes.
- *Regional airlines.* These served particular regions of the country under the Regional Air Carrier Policy of 1966.

Airline	Region
Pacific Western	British Columbia and Alberta
Transair	Prairies and northwestern Ontario
Nordair	Ontario and northwestern Quebec
Quebecair	Quebec east of Montreal
Eastern Provincial	The Atlantic provinces and Montreal

- *Local and/or commuter airlines.* These flew to smaller communities not served by the regionals—for example, Air Maritime served the Maritimes.

Since the National Transportation Act of 1987, there have been different rules for southern and northern Canada. The National Transportation Agency must grant an applicant a licence to operate in southern Canada if it is a Canadian company and can prove it is "fit, willing, and able." That means it must have an operating certificate from Transport Canada and sufficient liability insurance. However, existing carriers in northern Canada can block a new applicant if they can prove that the new licence would lead to a significant reduction in the level of service, or create instability.

In the 1990s, Canada essentially has two national carriers, Air Canada and Canadian Airlines, with affiliated regional airlines. Most of these regional carriers offer transborder services and also operate local and commuter services, and this has blurred the traditional classification system. (See the section "The Canadian Airline Industry in the 1990s" later in this chapter.)

International Air Carriers No nation has as many airlines as the United States, and very few have as many as Canada; indeed, most have only one. Even the leading industrial nations rarely have more than three carriers. Typically, such nations have one long-haul/international, one regional/commuter, and one all-charter operator. Switzerland, for example, is represented by Swissair (long haul), Crossair (regional), and Balair (charter).

General Aviation

General aviation refers to all civilian aircraft except those used by the commercial airlines. In terms of revenue, general aviation is far less important than air carrier aviation. In terms of number of aircraft, however, it is of far greater significance. More than 95 percent of the 224 000 aircraft in the United States and the 25 000 aircraft in Canada are classified as general aviation aircraft. Of these, more than half are single-engine, propeller-driven planes seating from one to six passengers. Few general aviation aircraft fly in the jet routes, which begin at 6000 metres.

Categories of Aircraft General aviation aircraft provide a mix of public (for-hire) and private services. They can be divided into six broad categories, according to use:

- *Air taxis* operate on a charter, contract, or demand basis and provide access to almost 14 000 airports. Note: the air carriers offer scheduled service to only about 600 airports in the United States and 449 in Canada. They range in size from single- or twin-engine propeller-driven aircraft to small jets.
- *Corporate airplanes* fly a company's managers, salespeople, and other employees to out-of-town meetings and assignments. Nearly all of the Fortune 500 companies operate their own private fleets. These aircraft include business jets, such as the Canadair Challenger and the Cessna Citation, as well as light twin-engines and helicopters.
- *Special-services planes* are used for aerial photography, pipeline and power line patrol, fire prevention and firefighting, law enforcement, emergency medical services, traffic reporting, crop dusting and spraying, conservation, and much more.
- *Flight instruction aircraft* range from primary two-place trainers to complex aircraft used for professional training and proficiency programs.
- *Privately owned planes* are used for personal transportation, which can involve business or pleasure.
- *Sports planes*, such as the 250-pound ultralight, provide recreation for their owners.

General aviation is seldom as well developed or diversified in other countries as it is in Canada and the United States.

Relationship to Air Carrier Aviation Although travel professionals are primarily interested in air carrier aviation, a knowledge of general aviation is important for several reasons. First, general aviation aircraft provide access to air travel for people in areas of the country that are not served by scheduled airlines. Second, general aviation is a nationwide training school for pilots, mechanics, and technicians. Third, many domestic airlines, especially scheduled regional and commuter airlines, evolve out of general aviation. Finally, general aviation provides a career path. Many workers gain experience in general aviation and then move on to employment in air carrier aviation.

CHECK YOUR PRODUCT KNOWLEDGE

1. What is the difference between air carrier aviation and general aviation?
2. Why did airline classification change from a system based on geography to one based on revenue?
3. How is general aviation important to air carrier aviation?

AIRPORTS: TRANSPORTATION TERMINALS FOR THE SKIES

The world's major airports are international crossroads, handling thousands of passengers and hundreds of flights each day to every corner of the globe. Figure 4-3 lists the world's ten busiest airports in 1989. At Chicago's O'Hare International Airport, the world's busiest, a plane takes off or lands every 23 seconds. Some international airports resemble cities. Germany's Frankfurt-am-Main Airport, for example, features 12 restaurants, 10 snack bars, a variety of boutiques, medical and dental offices, banks, a supermarket, a disco, and four movie theatres.

In Canada, approximately 40 percent of air travel (5.5 million passengers) takes place along ten routes involving eight large Canadian cities: Vancouver, Calgary, Edmonton, Winnipeg, Toronto, Ottawa, Montreal, and Halifax. The busiest route is Montreal–Toronto (10%), followed by Toronto–Vancouver (6%), Ottawa–Toronto (6%), Calgary–Toronto (4%), Calgary–Vancouver (3%), Toronto–Winnipeg (3%), Edmonton–Toronto (3%), Edmonton–Vancouver (3%), and Halifax–Toronto (2%). At the opposite extreme are the thousands of small private airfields with no scheduled flights, limited facilities, and little daily activity.

PROFILE

Canadian Airlines International

Written by Marie Rennie

According to the World Tourism Organization (WTO), there were an estimated 500 million tourist arrivals worldwide in 1993. In the same year, international tourism receipts hit just over $324 billion. The WTO predicts there will be 661 million arrivals worldwide in the year 2000, and 937 million in 2010. In 1993, Canadian Airlines International Ltd. carried more than 7 million passengers to the 148 destinations it serves in 17 countries on five continents.

In 1987, five airlines were amalgamated to form Canadian, which is a principal subsidiary of Pacific West Airlines (PWA) Corporation. At the beginning of the 1990s, the world airline industry entered a financial slump that saw some of the best-known airlines disappear. In the face of new industry realities, over the next three years, Canadian streamlined its operations, initiated a voluntary financial restructuring of more than $700 million in debt, and negotiated a ground-breaking agreement with AMR Corporation that included a $246 million equity investment by AMR.

Meanwhile, in a display of support that was unprecedented in Canada, Canadian's 15 000 employees elected to invest $200 million to become shareholders in Canadian. This ownership has fostered a sense of responsibility that is demonstrated by every employer–owner in the company—a committed responsibility to cut costs, improve procedures, and provide superior customer service.

In April 1994, Kevin Jenkins was appointed president and chief executive officer of both PWA Corporation and Canadian Airlines International. Jenkins has been involved with the company since 1985, when it was known as Pacific Western Airlines. Jenkins, who has an M.B.A. from Harvard University, is also a member of the executive committee of the International Air Transport Association (IATA), and a past member of the board of directors of the Air Transport Association of Canada (ATAC).

Canadian has 14 790 employees, while Canadian Regional airlines has 1700, and Canadian Holidays has 700. The company has 80 aircraft ranging from DC-10-30s to 767-300s. Canadian flies to five continents, and its OTP (on-time performance) is the best of any major scheduled carrier in Canada.

In order to expand its international network and enhance customer service, Canadian has developed strategic alliances with some of the world's finest airlines, such as Air New Zealand, Mandarin Airlines, Qantas, Lufthansa, and Varig. These alliances increase the frequency of flights to international destinations and ensure a high standard of customer service for Canadian flights abroad.

Canadian is preparing a comprehensive agreement with AMR Corporation. At press time, the deal with AMR—the parent company of American Airlines—has two components. The first is an equity investment that will see AMR invest $246 million in Canadian in exchange for a 25 percent voting interest in the airline. The second component includes a commercial services agreement under which Canadian will receive information technology services as part of a 20-year contract. The transition to AMR systems will be one of the most significant systems changes in airline history. The services agreement will affect almost every aspect of Canadian's operations, ultimately streamlining operations for the benefit of customers and significantly reducing Canadian's operating costs.

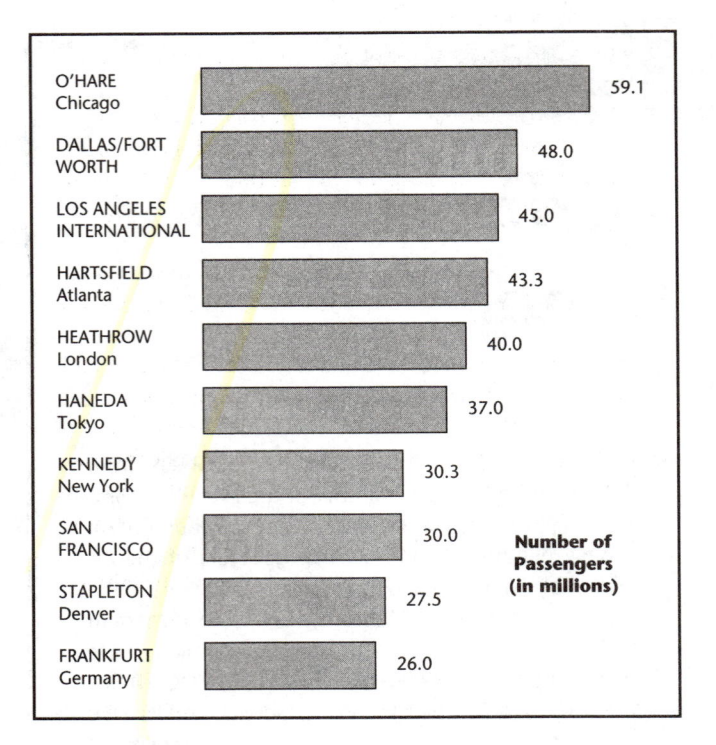

FIGURE 4-3
The World's Ten Busiest Airports, 1989
SOURCE: Airport Operators Council International

Airport	Number of Passengers (in millions)
O'HARE Chicago	59.1
DALLAS/FORT WORTH	48.0
LOS ANGELES INTERNATIONAL	45.0
HARTSFIELD Atlanta	43.3
HEATHROW London	40.0
HANEDA Tokyo	37.0
KENNEDY New York	30.3
SAN FRANCISCO	30.0
STAPLETON Denver	27.5
FRANKFURT Germany	26.0

Types of Airports

Civilian airports can be classified into two types: air carrier airports and general aviation airports. Air carrier airports, of which there are approximately 450 in Canada and 570 in the United States, are used by scheduled airlines—the majors, nationals, and regionals. They can also serve general aviation aircraft, especially corporate airplanes. General aviation airports—often unpaved and unlighted—serve all types of aircraft except scheduled airline planes.

Airport Ownership

In Canada and the United States, a railway company owns not only the trains it operates but also the tracks and stations its trains use. Bus companies generally own the stations out of which their buses operate. The same is not true for airports; very few airlines own and operate the airports they serve. Instead, they rent space.

In Canada, the Aeronautics Act governs ground and air services and facilities. Transport Canada may own and manage airports and is responsible for the air navigation system. In 1987 the federal Minister of Transport announced an initiative whereby Transport Canada airports could be leased to local airport authorities. Vancouver International Airport has since been leased in this way. Terminal 3 at Toronto's Pearson International Airport was developed by the private sector but is still owned by the Canadian government. All provinces except New Brunswick and Prince Edward Island have established, operated, and funded airports to a certain degree.

In the United States most airports are small, privately owned facilities. Their owners primarily serve the recreational flyers who are part of general aviation. There are, however, more than 5000 publicly owned and operated airports in the United States. These include all large airports serving metropolitan areas. Publicly owned airports are administered by state, county, or city governments. Airports often enter into a contract with a **fixed-base operator (FBO)**. The FBO sells fuel, rents hangar space to aircraft owners, provides maintenance and repairs, and gives flying lessons. The FBO pays rent (and usually a percentage of gross revenue) to the airport.

Air carriers pay for use of the airport through landing fees, rents on counter and office space, and fuel and registration taxes. As landlord, the governing authority also charges rent to car rental companies, coffee shops and stores, and other concessions in and around the terminal building.

Airport Location

Because of the space required by runways, even the smallest airport needs four acres of land. Medium-sized airports require 200 to 600 hectares, while large airports require 6000 hectares. Dallas–Fort Worth Airport, the largest airport in the United States, covers 7000 hectares of land—more than 45 square kilometres. Mirabel Airport, near Montreal, would have been larger than Dallas–Fort Worth if it had been fully developed. Originally, it was intended that it should handle all overseas flights, but many of these flights now land and take off elsewhere, so Mirabel has not expanded as originally anticipated.

The large amount of land required by airports makes them difficult to site and construct. The rapid growth of airline traffic and the increase in the size of airplanes have together created a constant demand for more space. Also, train and bus stations can be sited in downtown areas, while airports must usually be built in outlying districts. In the 1940s and 1950s, airports were constructed on what were then the outskirts of metropolitan areas. Airports remained on these sites while suburbs sprang up around them in the 1960s and 1970s. As a result, many communities today must contend with the noise and congestion caused by nearby airports.

The Layout of an Airport

Airports vary in layout depending on their size and the time they were built. Early airports were far simpler in design than those being built today.

The Terminal Building The terminal building is the heart of the airport complex. It is where passengers purchase or present their tickets, check in or retrieve baggage, and board or leave an airplane. In addition to ticket counters and waiting areas, the terminal building will have a weather station, a briefing room for pilots, a dispatch office for communicating with ticket counters and planes, and the office of the airport manager. In the terminal buildings at major airports are also found car rental agencies, shops, restaurants, cocktail lounges, and banks.

The first air terminals were long, straight buildings. People entered in the front and walked out to airplanes parked in back. With the growth of air traffic, pierlike extensions flanked by parking bays were added to the back of the terminal building. This configuration allowed the airport to increase the number of gates for boarding and deplaning. Most major airports follow this type of terminal design.

To avoid long walks along piers, the satellite design was introduced in the 1960s. Passengers check in at ticket desks in a main terminal building. Then they go by way of moving sidewalks or underground trains to satellite buildings to board their flights. Dorval Airport at Montreal and Seattle–Tacoma International Airport follow this arrangement. Another design features a row of terminals shaped like rings or horseshoes. Passengers enter the terminal at the gate marked for their flight and walk only a short distance.

Other Parts of an Airport In addition to the passenger terminals and parking lots, major airports have the following areas:

- The cargo terminal—one or more separate buildings where mail or freight is processed.
- The control tower—the nerve centre of the airport, usually adjacent to the passenger terminal. From the glass-enclosed top level, or cab, air traffic controllers use radar, radio, and signal lights to direct traffic in the air and on the ground.
- Hangars—the buildings where planes are stored and repaired. The hangars must be far enough from the runways to avoid interference.
- Runways—the strips of land on which airplanes land and from which they take off. Runways must be long enough and wide enough to accommodate the airplanes using them. Transport Canada sets size specifications. There must also be a clear zone at either end of the runway. To accommodate a jumbo jet, a runway, including its clear zone, might be 6.5 kilometres in length.
- The loading apron—the parking area at the terminal gate where the airplane is refuelled, loaded, and boarded.
- Taxiways—lanes for the airplane to use when going from the apron to the runway or from the runway to the hangar.

Airports and Route Structures

An airline route is the path an airplane takes in delivering its services. Airports are the delivery points along the path.

ILLUSTRATION 4-4
Manufacturers are designing new propeller-driven aircraft for the growing regional and commuter airlines. Here Pem-Air's Beech-King Air 100 loads passengers in Pembroke, Ontario.
SOURCE: Courtesy: Pem-Air

To make the most efficient use of their airplanes, airline managers plan routes carefully, using three main patterns or structures.

When an airplane flies to a destination in one direction and then turns around and repeats the flight in the opposite direction, it has completed a ==linear route.== A linear route may have intermediate stops, which generate additional revenue at little cost. An example is Calgary–Edmonton–Yellowknife–Norman Wells–Inuvik.

On a ==hub-and-spoke route,== a major airport becomes the centre point for arrivals from and departures to many other airports. This airport is like the hub of a wagon wheel: the smaller airports that surround it form the rim, and the flights that connect it to the rim are the spokes. These route structures in turn overlap to create an ever-widening air-route system. For example, the airport at Calgary, Alberta, is the hub for flights to the smaller cities around it. In turn, Toronto is a hub city with Calgary on its rim, and London, England, is a hub city with Toronto on its rim. In this last case, the airport at Toronto functions as a ==gateway airport== in that it services scheduled international flights.

With the increase in international tourism, many cities have had to expand their airport facilities, and some now have more than one airport. In Montreal, for example, Mirabel Airport handles long-distance international flights, while Dorval handles domestic flights as well as transborder flights to the United States.

A third type of route structure combines the linear and the hub-and-spoke models. As many flights as possible are scheduled to arrive in a particular city (the hub) at the same time. The same planes depart one hour later on linear routes to their originating cities after picking up passengers from connecting flights. For example, Passenger 1 arrives in Toronto on plane A from Calgary. She immediately boards plane B, which is returning to Halifax, while Passenger 2, who just got off plane C from London, Ontario, catches plane A, which is returning to Calgary.

Security at Airports

International airports have become global crossroads; they have also become killing grounds for disputes half a world away. Bombings, shootings, and hijackings have prompted governments and airport officials to tighten security at international airports.

In June 1985, after terrorists hijacked a TWA jet shortly after takeoff from Athens, Greece, even stricter security measures were imposed. These focused on thorough inspection of passenger baggage. Individual airports have instituted further precautions, such as the requirement that all passengers pass through metal detectors before boarding. Some have also hired security coordinators, who monitor the servicing and loading of planes and use dogs to sniff out explosives. At some airports, police in armoured trucks meet and dispatch airplanes arriving from nations associated with terrorists.

Some analysts predict that airports of the future will be located in isolated areas surrounded by electrified barbed-wire fences. Soon, also, terminals may be designed so that passengers funnel through checkpoints, and lockers, rest rooms, restaurants, and other potential hiding places may be placed behind secure checkpoints.

ILLUSTRATION 4-5
The largest airport in the United States is Dallas–Fort Worth, which occupies 1080 hectares.
SOURCE: American Airlines

ILLUSTRATION 4-6
To reduce the danger of skyjacking, all airports have installed rigorous security check systems.
SOURCE: Toronto, Pearson Internationl Airport

> **CHECK YOUR PRODUCT KNOWLEDGE**
>
> 1. What are the classifications for civilian airports?
> 2. Who owns the airports in the United States? in Canada?
> 3. List the main parts of an airport.
> 4. What are three types of airline route structures?

REGULATION

Governments have been involved in the regulation of the airline industry since the early days of aviation. We can identify three different levels of regulation. On the highest level, commercial flights between countries are regulated by international agreements. On the next level, individual governments enforce economic and air safety regulations within each country. And on a third level, governments regulate international travellers by requiring them to carry documentation and observe health and customs regulations. The regulation of international travellers was discussed in detail in Chapter 2.

How the International System Works

In August 1983, Korean Air Lines flight 007 was returning to Seoul when it wandered into Soviet airspace. A missile-firing Soviet interceptor shot the plane down, killing all 269 people aboard. Throughout the world, people were outraged. By launching a military attack on a defenceless civilian airplane, the Soviet Union had violated a basic rule of the air.

Early in the development of international aviation, governments realized that uniform rules would be necessary to ensure the smooth operation of airlines between countries. Over the years, a system for conducting international aviation has evolved through three channels:

- Multilateral agreements reached at worldwide conferences.
- The negotiation of bilateral agreements.
- Membership in international organizations.

At the present time, the international system is a compromise between total government control and totally independent decision-making by the airlines.

Worldwide Conferences Just as each nation claims ownership of the soil within its boundaries and of the sea close to its borders, it also claims ownership of its skies. The fundamental principle of sovereign skies, first affirmed at the Paris Convention on the Regulation of Aerial Navigation in 1919 and reaffirmed at subsequent conventions, requires countries to negotiate the mutual use of airspace. According to this principle, a country must be *invited* to fly through the airspace of another. Thus, when the Soviets shot down KAL 007, they did have the right to regulate the entry of a foreign aircraft into their territory. But they did not, by international custom, have the right to do it in such a drastic manner.

Another important principle established at the Paris Convention was that every aircraft must have a nationality. In other words, an aircraft must be validly registered in a specific nation and accountable to that nation for its operations. This principle is especially important in the event of an infraction of international air law.

The Havana Convention of 1928 resulted in the standardization of operating procedures, such as issuing tickets and checking baggage. This agreement enabled international airlines to work together more easily.

The 1929 Warsaw Convention on International Carriage by Air established limits to liability in the event that a passenger is injured or killed, or baggage or cargo is lost or damaged. This agreement was amended in 1955 by The Hague Protocol and again in 1971 by the Guatemala City Protocol.

The agreements reached at these conventions are multilateral, or many-sided. That is, they involve more than two nations and are equally binding on all nations that sign them. More recent conventions have established procedures for dealing with hijackings and other crimes committed aboard international flights.

The Freedoms of the Air Toward the close of World War II, representatives of all the member countries of the United Nations, except the Soviet Union, gathered in Chicago to renew the principles of international air law. Among other accomplishments, the Chicago Convention of 1944 formulated the Five Freedoms, which have greatly affected international aviation. Also called the Flying Freedoms, these statements categorized the ways in which a carrier of one nation can pass through, land in, and depart from the sovereignty of another nation. They provide a basis for international negotiations. Over the years, three unofficial freedoms have been added to the list.

Figure 4-4 summarizes the eight freedoms and gives an example of each. The first two freedoms are called transit rights and have been widely accepted on a multilateral basis. Freedoms three, four, five, and six are called traffic rights and have not been completely accepted. The seventh and eighth freedoms are allowed only under special circumstances.

Bilateral Agreements Shortly after the Chicago Convention, nations began to understand the need for bilateral, or two-sided, aviation agreements. In 1946, the United States and the United Kingdom negotiated a bilateral agreement that became a model for subsequent agreements. Signed in Bermuda and referred to as the Bermuda System, this agreement incorporates the spirit of the Flying Freedoms.

Negotiating an airline agreement between nations is similar to negotiating a trade pact or a peace treaty. During the negotiations, the governments decide on the routes to be served and the airports to be used. The frequency and capacity of flights, and restrictions for taking off and landing, are also determined. In addition, the agreement specifies the procedure for approving fares and tariffs. Usually, the airlines are asked to consult about fares with the International Air Transport Association (IATA). In the United States, the government decides which airlines get the new routes established through bilateral agreements.

Canada and the United States last negotiated a bilateral agreement in 1966. It was amended in 1974. More routes to the United States were opened; most were granted to Air Canada, which at the time was owned by the federal government. Canada and the United States have been attempting to negotiate a new bilateral agreement, Open Skies, for several years.

International Air Transport Association IATA is an airline service organization with headquarters in Montreal. It was founded in 1919 by a group of European airlines and reorganized in 1945. Today, approximately 200 of the world's

---

First Freedom. The right of an airline to overfly one country to get to another.
Second Freedom. The right of an airline to land in another country for a technical stopover (fuel, maintenance) but not to pick up or drop off traffic.
Third Freedom. The right of an airline, registered in country X, to drop off traffic from country X into country Y.
Fourth Freedom. The right of an airline, registered in country X, to carry traffic back to country X from country Y.
Fifth Freedom. The right of an airline, registered in country X, to collect traffic in country Y and fly on to country Z, as long as the flight either originates or terminates in country X.
Sixth Freedom. The right of an airline, registered in country X, to carry traffic to a gateway—a point in country X—and then abroad. The traffic has neither its origin nor ultimate destination in country X.
Seventh Freedom. The right of an airline, registered in country X, to operate entirely outside of country X in carrying traffic between two other countries.
Eighth Freedom. The right of an airline, registered in country X, to carry traffic between any two points in the same foreign country.

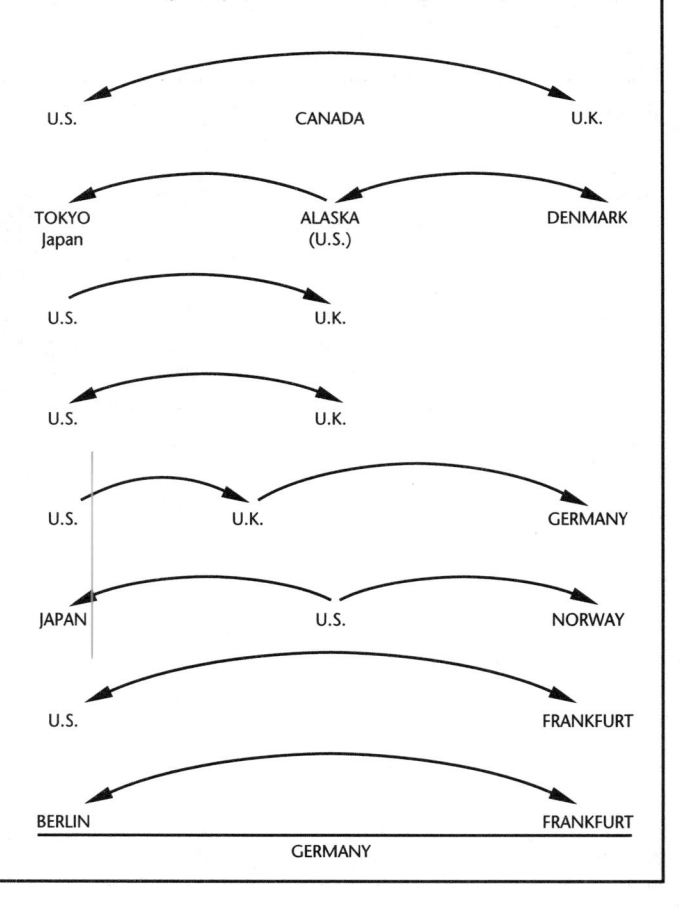

Examples of Freedoms of the Air

First Freedom. Delta Airlines departs from Atlanta and overflies Canada en rouge to London.
Second Freedom. Japan Airlines departs from Copenhagen, Denmark, and lands in Anchorage, Alaska, en route to Tokyo. The stop in Alaska is for fuel and a crew change. Japan Airlines is not allowed to carry passengers or cargo to or from Anchorage.
Third Freedom. Delta Airlines departs from Atlanta and carries American citizens to London.
Fourth Freedom. Delta Airlines departs from London and carries British subjects to the United States.
Fifth Freedom. Delta Airlines departs from Atlanta, stops en route in London, and boards passengers there for its continuation to Frankfurt, Germany.
Sixth Freedom. Northwest Airlines, carrying Norwegian passengers from Oslo bound for Tokyo may stop over in Minneapolis/St. Paul, Minnesota, a gateway city.
Seventh Freedom. British Airways flies nonstop from Frankfurt, Germany, to Washington, D.C., without stopping in Great Britain.
Eigth Freedom. Air France, a French carrier, carries traffic between Frankfurt and Berlin—all within Germany.

FIGURE 4-4
The Eight Freedoms of the Air

airlines belong to IATA, either as full members or as associate members. Although more Third World airlines are joining, IATA is basically controlled by its European members.

IATA performs several important functions for members, including these:

- To provide a forum for airlines to meet and discuss mutual concerns.
- To recommend fares and tariffs for government approval.
- To represent the airlines in travel agency affairs.
- To promote air safety.
- To encourage worldwide air travel.

Another important organization is the International Civil Aviation Organization (ICAO), also based in Montreal. Founded by the Chicago Convention, the ICAO is now an agency of the United Nations. When the former Soviet Union joined in 1970, membership became almost universal. ICAO is primarily concerned with setting standards for aviation equipment and operations. It also organizes world conferences and mediates disputes between members.

Traffic Conferences To make air travel easier to describe and organize, IATA has divided the global airline community into three areas, shown in Figure 4-5.

The United States has frequently disagreed with the airfares established by IATA and has negotiated bilateral pacts to bypass them.

Most of IATA's members are **flag carriers,** or national airlines representing individual nations. For example, El Al is the flag carrier for Israel, and Japan Air Lines (JAL) is the flag carrier for Japan. Scandinavian Airlines (SAS) is a cooperative venture involving Norway, Sweden, and Denmark. (That is why the flags of all three nations are painted on the tail of SAS aircraft.) All carriers registered in other nations are known in the United States as **foreign flags.** A large number of flag carriers are owned or subsidized by the government. Because they receive funding from their governments, flag carriers can offer lower fares, and survive despite financial losses. Also, when flag carriers go to an IATA rate-setting meeting, they know in advance what rates their governments will accept. The privately owned airlines of the United States believe that this situation is unfair and damaging. For these reasons, the United States reserves the right to disallow airfares to and from that country, which are unrealistically low.

Pressures on IATA During the 1970s, several American airlines dropped out of IATA because of the organization's inability to control several forces in the marketplace. One of these forces was the growth in nonscheduled, or charter, flights. A second force was the increase in the sale of dis-

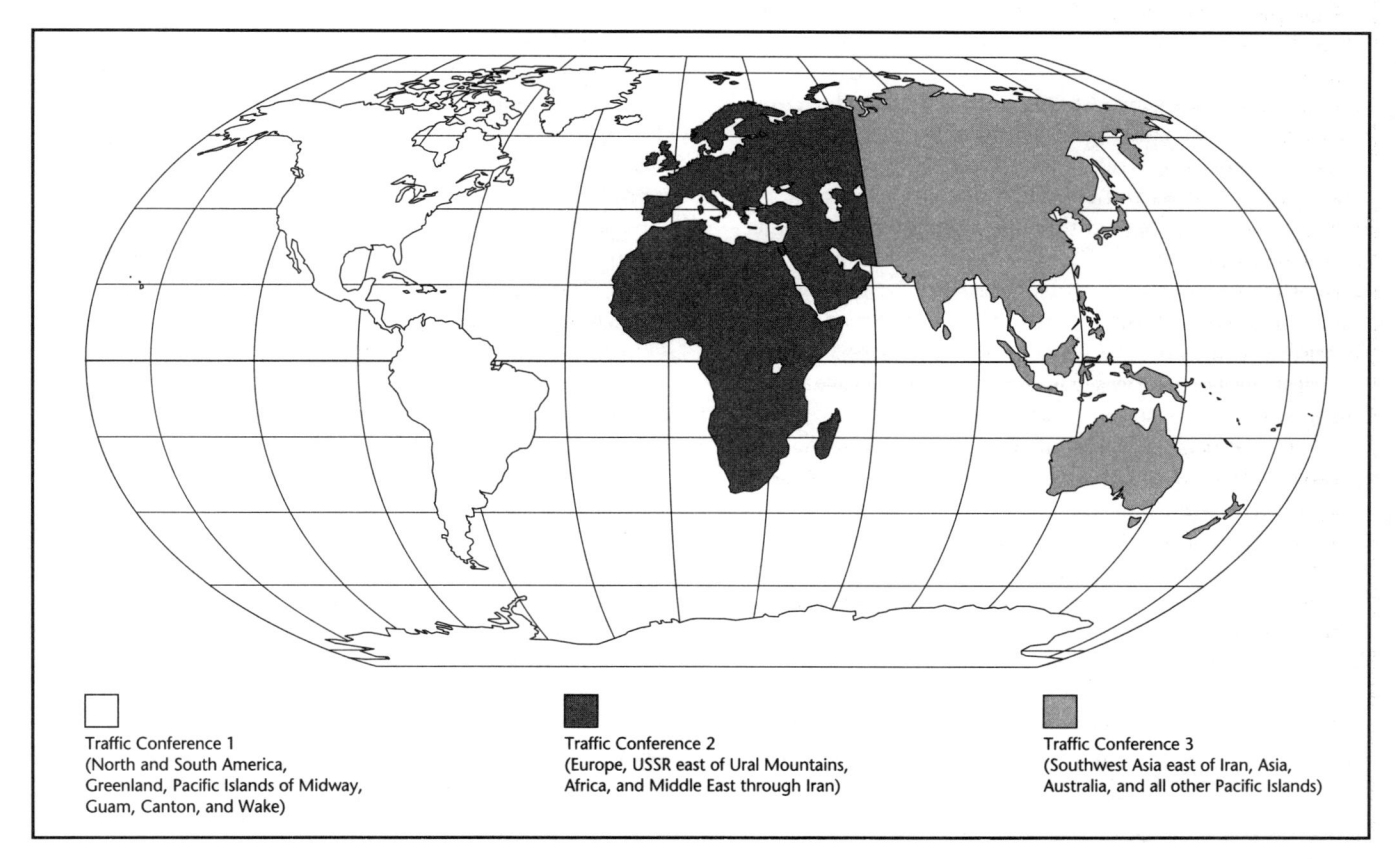

☐ Traffic Conference 1
(North and South America, Greenland, Pacific Islands of Midway, Guam, Canton, and Wake)

■ Traffic Conference 2
(Europe, USSR east of Ural Mountains, Africa, and Middle East through Iran)

▨ Traffic Conference 3
(Southwest Asia east of Iran, Asia, Australia, and all other Pacific Islands)

FIGURE 4-5
The World Traffic Conferences

count package tours by wholesalers. Both nonscheduled airlines and wholesale distributors are outside the international regulatory framework. A third force was overcapacity in some parts of the world. With more wide-bodied jets in use and more airlines offering long-distance services, there were often too many seats and not enough passengers. To fill the seats, a few airlines were bending the rules. Because of these regulatory problems, some critics have suggested that IATA—and bilateral agreements—be dismantled so that the world's airlines can be free to become more competitive.

Regulating Domestic Service — Canada and the United States

This section will examine the regulation of domestic service in both Canada and the United States. The airline industry in these two countries has long been different from the industry in most other countries because of the emphasis on private ownership.

Domestic Service—Canada The federal government extended regulation to the aviation industry by passing the Aeronautics Act of 1919. This created an Air Board to hear requests from applicants wishing to start an air service. In 1937, airline regulation was transferred to the newly created Department of Transport. The development of the Canadian airline industry from the 1930s to the 1990s was traced in Figure 4-2.

The Canadian government was concerned about the proximity of a developing trunk line system in the United States, since it threatened to divert Canadian east-west airline traffic into the United States through feeder services drawing on Canadian cities. The two major railways were approached in 1937 to jointly establish a government-guaranteed air carrier. The CPR did not want government representatives on the board of directors, so it refused to participate. A government-owned carrier, Trans-Canada Airlines (TCA), now Air Canada, was established as a subsidiary of the CNR. TCA was given a Canadian monopoly on transcontinental and international routes.

TCA's monopoly was broken after World War II. Canadian Pacific Airlines (CP Air), now Canadian Airlines, formed from several smaller carriers in the early 1940s, was awarded international routes to Asia, Australia, and South America. However, it was not until 1958 that CP Air was allowed to compete on the transcontinental route, in the form of one flight per day on the Vancouver–Winnipeg–Toronto–Montreal route. Recognition was given to CP Air's need for a domestic system that would link Canadian travellers to its international routes. A royal commission on transportation was established in 1958 to study both passenger and freight service in Canada. Its report (the MacPherson Report), tabled in 1961, led to the National Transportation Act of 1967.

The strong competitive nature of transportation—in particular, between air and rail services, and rail and bus services—was now obvious to all. Domestically, the air carriers were capturing much of the railway passenger market. Internationally, the airline industry had captured most of the steamship passenger market, especially on transatlantic routes. However, among the airlines themselves, competition was not so apparent in the bilateral air service agreement reached between Canada and the United States in 1966. Air Canada was awarded the majority of new routes to cities in the United States.

The Regional Air Policy of 1966 allowed second-level carriers to compete with the main-line trunk carriers. One carrier in each of five regions of Canada was designated as the preferred regional carrier. Eastern Provincial Airways (EPA) was the designated carrier for the Atlantic provinces and in 1968 was awarded a Charlottetown–Montreal route. In 1970 it was awarded a Halifax–St. John's route to compete with Air Canada. Previously it had flown Halifax–Sydney–Deer Lake–Gander–St. John's. During the late 1960s, the regional carriers switched from propeller aircraft to jet airliners, which reduced travel times and further heated competition with the major carriers, Air Canada and CP Air. In 1967, CP Air was allowed additional transcontinental flights (in time for Expo 67 in Montreal); in 1970 it was allowed 25 percent of traffic to compete with Air Canada and the regional carriers.

The Period of Regulated Competition After the mid-1970s, regulated competition was encouraged by the Canadian Transport Commission (CTC), which was established by the National Transportation Act of 1967. More liberal charter regulations were introduced gradually after 1974. However, at the insistence of the scheduled carriers, the regulators required that the new lower-fare services not impinge upon the profitability of scheduled services. The charter carriers, such as Wardair based in Edmonton, helped expand the tourism market for Canadians by providing inexpensive flights to foreign destinations not served by regular carriers. The scheduled carriers also began operating charters themselves, especially to southern resort destinations in the winter, when east-west traffic was in its low period.

By 1980, the equivalent of three airlines—Air Canada, CP Air, and Pacific Western–Eastern Provincial—were competing on transcontinental routes. It had taken more than 40 years since the formation of the air system in Canada, and 22 years since the breaking of the TCA transcontinental monopoly, for Canada's airline industry to achieve this level of competition and consumer choice. Meanwhile, the United States had deregulated its airline industry in 1978.

The number of actual competitors in Canada was reduced as the regional carriers encountered difficulties: Transair was taken over by Pacific Western in 1977; Air Canada purchased a controlling interest in Nordair in 1978; Quebecair was being propped up by the Quebec government; and CP Air and Eastern Provincial, which were competing on the Halifax–Toronto route, began sharing equipment and personnel through a cooperative services arrangement in the spring of 1983. The affiliation of regional carriers with trunk-line carriers was a forerunner of the process that later saw developing commuter and regional carriers associating themselves with major carriers.

The recession of the early 1980s was partly responsible for two major changes in the airline industry in the Atlantic provinces: Eastern Provincial established Air Maritime as a lower-cost commuter division to operate short routes such as the Halifax–Charlottetown "spoke." Then CP Air purchased EPA, reducing competition.

Regulatory Reform While the Canadian airline industry was in a period of retrenchment, the American airline industry was seeing new entrants, new routes, new services, and lower airfares under deregulation. Some Canadians were travelling to American border cities to take advantage of the lower fares. Realizing changes were needed, the Liberal government in Ottawa announced its "New Canadian Air Policy" in May 1984.

This policy, announced six years after airline deregulation in the United States, represented the first phase of regulatory reform for the Canadian airline industry. Major objectives of the policy were to:

1. Provide consumers with a wider range of price and service options.
2. Invigorate the industry and provide a stimulus to growth.
3. Promote national integration through increased domestic travel.
4. Improve the airline industry's efficiency and productivity and encourage innovation.
5. Counter the seepage of passenger traffic via American gateways just across the border.

The Conservatives, who replaced the Liberals in 1984, released a White Paper in 1985, *Freedom to Move*, which put forward a framework for regulatory reform in transportation. It recognized that with the vast distances separating the population, it was essential that Canada have an efficient and competitive air industry capable of moving people and goods quickly and efficiently. By minimizing economic regulation, air regulatory reform proved even more ambitious in scope than the Liberals had planned. The Conservatives' objectives were these:

1. Improvement or expansion of services to the travelling public.
2. Reasonable opportunities for all sizes and types of carriers to compete in the domestic market.
3. Removal of all unnecessary expense and paperwork for both industry and government.
4. Encouragement of a pricing regime to provide travellers and shippers with a competitive product.

The mid-1980s saw the emergence of new low-cost regional and commuter airlines operating mainly propeller aircraft. Most of the new entrants were, or became, affiliates of the major carriers. In the Atlantic region, Air Nova was the Air Canada affiliate, and Air Atlantic was the CP Air affiliate. The major carriers reduced or vacated the shorter routes that had been served by jet aircraft. The regional affiliates took over these shorter routes, typically on a hub-and-spoke basis. Some communities were upset about losing direct jet service to major centres. However, most communities now had more flights per day to the hub, and usually service provided by more than one airline.

The major problem—what to do with federally owned Air Canada—was recognized in air regulatory reform. Air Canada was the dominant airline in the Canadian airline industry, with more than a 50 percent share domestically, most of the transborder routes to cities in the United States, and many of the international routes to other countries. With access to the public purse, Air Canada was able to engage in uneconomic practices.

The National Transportation Act of 1987 The new National Transportation Act of 1987, effective January 1, 1988, replaced the National Transportation Act of 1967. It recognized that a safe, economic, efficient, adequate network of transportation is essential to serve the needs of shippers and travellers, and to maintain the economic well-being and growth of Canada and its regions. A new regulatory body, the National Transportation Agency, replaced the Canadian Transport Commission. The NTA of 1967 emphasized competition between modes. The stated objective of the NTA of 1987 was to increase competition *within* modes as well.

Air Canada was privatized, putting it on the same playing field as the other private carriers. This was to ensure fairer competition, even though Air Canada was still dominant. The other major carriers decided to compete with Air Canada by making mergers. First, Pacific Western took over CP Air to form Canadian Airlines. Soon after, Pacific Western also took over Wardair, which had by that time expanded into a scheduled carrier serving western and central Canada.

The Canadian Airline Industry in the 1990s The net effect of air regulatory reform in Canada is less competition. The airline industry essentially consists of the two major carriers, Air Canada and Canadian Airlines, with their associated regional and commuter airlines.

Air Canada affiliates include Air Alliance (Quebec, Ottawa, and Boston); AirBC (western Canada, Seattle, and Portland); Air Nova (Atlantic Canada, Quebec City, Boston, and New York City); Air Ontario (Ontario, Montreal, Winnipeg, and the northeastern United States); and NWT Air (the Northwest Territories, Edmonton, and Winnipeg).

Canadian Airlines is owned 100 percent by the holding company PWA Corporation. Its affiliated carriers are Canadian regional (with routes in Ontario and the four western provinces, and to Seattle and Minneapolis); Calm Air (with routes north from Winnipeg to northern Manitoba and Ontario and the eastern Northwest Territories); Inter-Canadian (with routes in Quebec and to Ottawa from Montreal); Air Alma (Montreal to northern Quebec); Air Atlantic (Atlantic Canada with routes to Montreal and Boston); and Air St. Pierre (from the French colony of St. Pierre to Nova Scotia and Montreal).

Both airlines were in financial difficulty in the early 1990s, reflecting the prolonged recession and the inevitable pain of restructuring. The operating statistics, including passenger kilometres flown, load factors, and employment, were down from the late 1980s. Two major airline policy issues unfolding in the mid-1990s are airline restructuring and "Open Skies."

Airline Restructuring The two major airlines are continuing to restructure in their efforts to survive domestically and position themselves internationally. Domestically, both airlines are reducing their payrolls, modifying their routes, and changing the number and type of aircraft they use.

More than half of Air Canada's and Canadian Airlines' revenues come from international travel. In future years this will become an increasingly price-competitive market because of the evolution of international megacarriers through strategic alliances. The Canadian carriers have already made initial advances toward global integration. Canadian Airlines has cooperative arrangements with Qantas, Air New Zealand, and Lufthansa. Air Canada has agreements with Air India, Sabena, and Swissair in Europe, and with USAir, and United Airlines. It has also bought an interest in Continental, an American carrier. Canadian Airlines recently negotiated to sell 25 percent of itself to American Airlines.

Open Skies Open Skies refers to the bilateral air negotiations now being conducted between Canada and the United States. The previous agreement was negotiated in 1966 and amended in 1974. Open Skies is analogous to negotiating a free trade agreement in airline service. At present, airlines have to obtain the approval of both countries before they can offer services between a Canadian city and an American city. An Open Skies agreement would allow carriers of either country to fly on any routes they think would be profitable.

The implications for trade and for business and tourist travel are considerable. Free trade may be creating business opportunities between Canada and the United States, but this is not clear from a look at airline schedules. Under the existing 1974 agreement, of the 238 potential connections between major cities on both sides of the border, only about one-quarter have nonstop or one-stop service. Only about 26 cities offer a choice between directly competing carriers. One problem is the shift in economic activity to the growing cities in the American Sunbelt. It is difficult for business and tourist travellers to fly between Canada and the Sunbelt without stops, and possibly plane changes, along the way.

The lack of transborder air service is of major concern for tourism in Canada. More tourists are taking shorter three- and four-day trips. They do not want to spend half their time travelling or waiting in air terminals for a connecting flight. A successful Open Skies treaty should open up more transborder routes, alleviating the existing problem.

Domestic Service — United States

Although airlines in the United States are privately owned, they are subject to regulation by the federal government. The primary justification for this control is that the airlines use federal airways and engage in interstate commerce.

Federal regulation of the airlines began in 1925 with the Kelly Act, which awarded contracts for airmail delivery to private carriers. Since then, regulations have been enacted primarily in the areas of economics and safety.

Economic Regulation: the Civil Aeronautics Board To regulate the economics involved in airline service, the government decided which routes airlines could operate, when they could schedule flights, and how much they could charge for their services.

The Civil Aeronautics Act of 1938 was the most influential piece of legislation in establishing economic regulation. The act led to the creation of the Civil Aeronautics Board (CAB), a five-member board with the following powers:

- Granting route authorizations.
- Establishing a uniform system of rates and fares.
- Ruling on mergers and acquisitions.
- Ruling on unfair competition.

In exercising its authority, the CAB established the system of trunk lines and feeders, which lasted 40 years, from 1938 to 1978.

Deregulation With the growth of the airline industry, a new generation of lawmakers began to re-evaluate government policy on economic regulation. Proponents of **deregulation** argued that the CAB had become too powerful and that airlines should have the right to choose new markets and abandon unprofitable ones. A free marketplace would promote better air service, a wider selection of flights through an expanded route system, and lower airfares.

For the most part, economic regulation ended with the passage of the Airline Deregulation Act of 1978. This legislation allows air carriers freedom to enter and leave the marketplace, that is, they can establish service wherever they want to and drop it wherever they want to.

The Airline Deregulation Act also provided for the gradual phasing out of the CAB and the orderly transfer of remaining federal authority to other agencies, such as the Department of Transportation and the Department of Justice. By virtue of the "sunset clause," the CAB ceased operations at midnight on December 31, 1984.

The New-Entrant Carriers With the almost immediate access to the marketplace provided by the new law, more than 150 carriers have chosen to compete with the established scheduled airlines. These **new-entrant carriers** are classified into four types:

- *Interstate carriers.* Airlines formerly operating within a state, such as Air California, became interstate carriers by expanding their routes across state lines.
- *Supplemental carriers.* Companies such as Transamerica Airlines, which had been offering domestic all-charter flights, began to provide scheduled services.
- *Commuter carriers.* Deregulation, and new rules permitting commuter carriers to fly larger airplanes, brought about enormous growth in this sector. Many nonscheduled air taxi operators chose to leave general aviation and compete as scheduled commuter carriers.
- *Brand-new entrants.* These airlines did not exist in any form prior to 1978. By offering cut-rate prices as a means of entering the marketplace, the brand-new entrants have had a great impact on the travel industry. They were able to charge less by operating used aircraft, employing nonunion workers, and offering "no-frills" flights.

Effects of Deregulation Deregulation means that airlines now compete with each other for passengers. With the new-entrant carriers, competition has become even more fierce, frequently resulting in price wars. In some instances, an airline ticket has been cheaper than a bus ticket to the same destination. In their attempts to get ahead of the competition, airlines have looked for new places to sell tickets, new ways to advertise them, and new ways to package them.

Some airlines have entered into code-sharing partnerships. In a **code-sharing** agreement, a small regional airline flies under the code of a major airline. That way, the major airline can serve the smaller cities that generate too little traffic to fill its own larger planes. For example, Continental Airlines has a code-sharing agreement with Rocky Mountain Air. Travellers who book onto a Continental flight to Aspen, Colorado, may find that they have to transfer to Rocky Mountain Air for the last part of the journey. This often involves transferring from a large jet to a small turboprop. About 50 regional/commuter airlines have entered into code-sharing arrangements.

Deregulation has benefited the public by providing, for the most part, reduced airfares and expanded routes. More airplanes are flying now than ever before. Critics of deregulation say that this growth has created congested airports and airways and increased the likelihood of accidents. The increase in cancelled flights has resulted in stern warnings to the airlines from the federal government. So has the airline industry's increasingly deplorable on-time performance. Critics also point to the reduction of services on many low-traffic routes. Several carriers have abandoned unprofitable routes to and from smaller communities to concentrate on flights in the high-density corridors. As a result, some communities now have fewer flights than before deregulation.

Many airlines, among them some of the oldest and most established companies, have experienced severe economic turbulence in the deregulation marketplace. Eastern and Braniff, for example, have declared bankruptcy and ceased all flight operations; many more companies have merged with other airlines.

Safety Regulation: Federal Aviation Administration While economic regulation has largely ceased, federal regulation of aircraft safety continues. The 1938 Civil Aeronautics Act also strengthened the government's power to regulate air safety. This legislation created the Air Safety Board and authorized it to grant certificates of airworthiness. In 1958 the Air Safety Board was superseded by the Federal Aviation Agency, an independent agency in charge of air safety. When the Department of Transportation was created in 1966, this Agency was made a part of it and renamed the Federal Aviation Administration (FAA).

The primary responsibility of the FAA is to direct air traffic in the federal airways so that accidents do not occur. The federal airway system covers 560 000 kilometres. From ground level, the airways extend almost 23 000 metres above the earth's surface. All aircraft flying between 5500 and 23 000 metres are constantly monitored by ground-based radar control. Aircraft flying below 5500 metres usually fly by a system of visual rules and are not necessarily monitored by the FAA.

Other responsibilities of the FAA include these:

- Establishing and enforcing safety standards.
- Certifying and monitoring the skills and health of pilots.
- Certifying the safety of aircraft.
- Investigating accidents (along with the National Transportation Safety Board).
- Setting standards for designing and building new aircraft and equipment.

Industry Regulation Both the scheduled air carriers and the regional and commuter air carriers are represented by associations located in Washington, D.C. The scheduled air carriers of the United States are represented by the Air Transport Association (ATA). The ATA lobbies the federal and local governments on behalf of the scheduled airlines and actively promotes airline travel. The nation's regional and commuter air carriers are represented in a similar way by the Regional Airlines Association (RAA).

The Airlines Reporting Corporation (ARC) was established by the ATA in 1984. ARC serves as a link between the American airlines that belong to the ATA and the 37 000 retail travel agencies that are accredited to sell the airlines' tickets. The role of ARC, as well as that of the International Airline Travel Agency Network (IATAN), which is the international counterpart of ARC, will be discussed in greater detail in Chapter 13.

> **CHECK YOUR PRODUCT KNOWLEDGE**
>
> 1. What are the three main channels for regulating the international air system?
> 2. Why are the Flying Freedoms important?
> 3. Name two organizations that help to regulate the international airline industry.
> 4. Why was the American airline industry deregulated in 1978? What were the results?
> 5. Why did the Canadian airline industry undergo regulatory reform in the 1980s? What were the results?
> 6. What are the responsibilities of Transport Canada and the FAA?

THE PRODUCT

Every industry has a product. The product of the airline industry is a flight on an airplane. A travel professional must determine the motivations, needs, and expectations (MNEs) of travellers and then sell them the right product.

Factors Affecting the Price of the Product

Matching each traveller with the right product at the right price is not always easy, especially since deregulation. In the deregulated marketplace, there may be several different types of airfares for a trip from Toronto to Vancouver. In some instances, it is less expensive to fly from coast to coast than to a city 2000 kilometres away. The price of a ticket is no longer based solely on the distance of the trip. Instead, the type of journey, the type of flight, the type of service, and whether or not the flight is restricted all influence the airfare.

Type of Journey There are four types of journey. A **one-way trip** begins in an originating city and ends in a destination city (e.g., Winnipeg to Vancouver). A one-way journey can be made on more than one flight, as in Winnipeg via Edmonton to Vancouver.

A **round trip** begins in an originating city, goes to a destination city, and returns to the originating city. The routing must be the same in both directions. Such a trip might be Halifax to Toronto to Halifax. Buying a round-trip ticket is often cheaper than buying two one-way tickets.

A **circle trip** is similar to a round trip, with an important difference: the outbound journey differs from the return journey, either in terms of the routing or the class of service. Routing: Montreal via Toronto to Vancouver, returning from Vancouver to Montreal nonstop. Class of service: Montreal to Vancouver first-class, return trip economy-class.

An **open-jaw trip** is interrupted by surface travel. A traveller may, for example, proceed from Toronto to Vancouver by air; then from Vancouver to Winnipeg by rail; then from Winnipeg to Toronto by air. An open-jaw trip can also be a journey with a return destination other than the originating city. Such a trip may take a traveller from Edmonton to Vancouver, then from Vancouver to Calgary.

Type of Flight There are four types of flights. One type is *nonstop* service with no scheduled stopovers en route.

A second type is *direct* or *through* service. There can be one or more intermediate stops en route, but the passenger remains aboard the same plane.

A third type is a *connecting* flight. With an **on-line connection,** the passenger changes airplanes but remains with the same airline. Air Canada, for example, can offer a flight from Vancouver to Toronto connecting with another Air Canada flight from Toronto to Halifax. An airline can change planes for any number of reasons, including mechanical difficulties and seating considerations. With an **interline connection,** the passenger changes both airplanes and airlines. A passenger can fly Air Canada from Halifax to Boston, and United Airlines from Boston to Washington.

Agreements among airlines to honour the tickets of other carriers make interline connections, or **interlining,** possible. Rather than having a separate ticket for each flight, interlining permits the use of one standard ticket; the system also enables baggage to be checked through to its final destination. Interlining is an international as well as a domestic practice. Some new entrants and regional commuters in the American market, however, do not participate in interlining agreements.

ILLUSTRATION 4-7
Flight attendants provide for the safety as well as the comfort of passengers and must be qualified to handle any emergency.
SOURCE: Courtesy Canadian Airlines International Ltd.

Intermodal ticketing, which simplifies the coordination of different modes of travel, has become another popular travel product. In a system similar to interlining, the passenger buys one ticket for through travel using (for example) an airplane and a bus, or an airplane and a cruise ship, or an airplane and a rental car.

A fourth type of flight is the **stopover.** In a stopover, the passenger requests a deliberate interruption of a trip at some intermediate point for 12 or more hours. A passenger can choose to fly from Toronto to Saskatoon on Monday, remain in Saskatoon until Wednesday evening, then fly on to Vancouver.

Type of Service Forty years ago, in-flight service on a domestic airliner consisted of a cold box lunch and a pack of chewing gum to relieve pressure on the eardrums. Today, passengers eat hot meals, drink cocktails, listen to music, and watch movies.

The type of service passengers receive depends on where they sit in the cabin of the plane, and they often pay accordingly. The most common **configuration,** or seating arrangement, consists of a first-class ("F class") cabin and a coach or economy-class cabin, but an airplane could have all coach seats or, less frequently, all first-class seats. Large jets can have several coach cabins. Aircraft cabins are further classified as narrow-body (one aisle) and wide-body (two aisles).

The most expensive class of service, "R class," is available on Concorde flights only. This is an example of an all-first-class configuration; there are no coach seats on the Concorde. R-class tickets cost 20 percent more than the first-class fare. Some airlines are experimenting with business- or executive-class ("Y class"); halfway between first-class and coach in amenities, business-class was developed for people who want a quiet place to work and who expect greater service than those passengers flying with discounted tickets.

Passengers in first class receive elaborate meals served on fine china, complimentary alcoholic beverages and movies, and individualized service. They also ride in more comfort. First-class seats are at the front of the plane, farther away from the engine noise. They are also wide and have plenty of leg room (that is, greater pitch, which is the distance between the knees and seatback). Coach seats are closer together and narrower, and vary in comfort depending on their location in the cabin. Although coach passengers often receive complimentary meals, they may have to pay extra for alcoholic beverages, and for headsets in order to listen to music or watch in-flight movies.

Airlines usually provide in-flight services for passengers with special needs. Flight attendants are trained to assist challenged travellers in boarding and to take particular care of children travelling alone. Airlines will also cater to passengers with special dietary needs (for example, those who require vegetarian or kosher meals) if they are given advance notice. The provision of such special services does not affect the airfare.

Unrestricted and Restricted Airfares With an unrestricted airfare, also called a nondiscounted airfare or normal airfare, a passenger can board any plane going to his or her destination that has an available seat. People must pay extra for the convenience of an unrestricted airfare.

A restricted airfare—also called promotional, discounted, or excursion airfare—is the airlines' version of a sale or a bargain. The less expensive the airfare, the greater the restrictions, which can include some or all of the following:

- Advance purchase requirement (up to a month prior to departure).
- Minimum/maximum length of stay at destination.
- Fixed itinerary and departure times (no last-minute changes).
- Limited departure dates (good only on certain days of the week).
- Nonrefundable cancellation penalty.
- Capacity control (only a limited number of seats available on any given flight at the discounted fare).
- Nontransferable ticket (i.e., one airline may not honour certain excursion fare tickets from another airline).

Because they generally have more flexible schedules, vacation travellers or those visiting friends and relatives (except in emergency situations) are more likely to purchase restricted airfares than are business travellers.

Since deregulation, airlines have found themselves promoting discounted tickets in order to fill seats that would otherwise remain empty; the philosophy is that half a fare is better than no fare. The result is that the passengers in the coach cabin on any flight will have spent varying amounts of money for the same type of seat and service, depending on whether or not they purchased a restricted ticket. Restricted airfares have in effect done away with the two-tier pricing system and replaced it with a three-tier system: first-class, economy, and excursion fares.

Financial penalties for cancellations have been introduced by a number of airlines in an effort to combat no-shows. **No-shows** are people who make reservations but, for whatever reason, fail to use them. There are always more no-shows when no penalty is involved. Another way airlines protect themselves against no-shows (and, consequently, too many unsold seats) is to **overbook,** or sell more seats than they actually have. However, when an airline overbooks and no one cancels, the airline is liable and must compensate the passengers who are denied boarding. This compensation is often a cash settlement plus transportation on the next available flight, or a free upgrade in class of service.

International Airfares IATA members hold conferences to discuss international airfares. On the basis of rules and principles developed by the organization, IATA decides on rates for city-pair combinations throughout the world. To reduce the complexity of calculating airfares in different currencies, all international airfares are expressed in fare construction units (FCUs). A formula converts FCUs into a specific currency for actual transactions.

As with domestic airfares in Canada and the United States, IATA calculates the price of a ticket on the basis of distance flown, type of service, and whether the fare is restricted or unrestricted. Many IATA airfares are based on distance flown. The actual distance flown between destinations is measured and then compared with a maximum allowable number of kilometres, which is usually about 20 percent greater than the actual number. The "bonus" distance enables the passenger to make stopovers at intermediate cities along the route of travel. This process of computing international airfares is called **fare construction.**

The cost of an international airline ticket, then, is usually directly related to the number of kilometres flown. This means that a trip from Washington, D.C., to Paris (6100 kilometres) should cost more than a trip from Washington, D.C., to Caracas (3300 kilometres). However, various factors in the marketplace can actually make a longer trip less expensive. More people want to fly to Paris than to Caracas. There is also more competition on the Washington–Paris route. In addition, the French government may have authorized a lower promotional airfare in order to encourage travel and tourism. As a result, an airline ticket from Washington, D.C., to Paris will generally cost less than a ticket to Caracas, even though the distance flown is greater.

Marketing in the Jet Age

Prior to the Airline Deregulation Act of 1978 in the United States, and airline regulatory reform in Canada in 1984 and 1988, airline marketing focused on service. To lure passengers, airlines promoted in-flight amenities and friendly skies. There were even drawings for free car rentals, shows by magicians and guitarists, and wine-tasting parties. Following deregulation, marketing centred on pricing. Discounted advance-purchase airfares, such as the Super Apex, made people realize that they could travel greater distances at reasonable prices. In 1982, approximately 75 percent of American passengers flew cut-rate. In recent years, however, there have been some signs of a return to service-oriented marketing. Business-class service and all-first-class service are examples of this trend.

CHECK YOUR PRODUCT KNOWLEDGE

1. Describe the four types of journeys.
2. How does seat location influence the airfare?
3. List five typical restrictions on a discounted airfare.
4. How do airlines protect themselves against no-shows?

CAREER OPPORTUNITIES IN THE AIRLINE INDUSTRY

The air carrier industry employs thousands of people in a wide variety of jobs requiring different levels of education, training, and experience. Airline pilots and flight attendants are the most visible employees, but there are many others working behind the scenes. Delta, one of the largest employers, with a payroll of 64 000, estimates that it takes an average of 156 employees to put one of their planes in the air. Air Canada employed an average of 20 600 people in 1991, down from a high of 23 200 in 1989.

Positions are available both in the private sector (i.e., with the individual airline companies) and in the public sector (i.e., with the local, provincial, and federal governments, which own and operate the larger airports and regulate the airways system).

Employees in the international airline industry can work at a gateway airport in Canada or the United States or at an airport station in a foreign country. (Note: Canadian and American citizens often find it extremely difficult to obtain employment as pilots or flight attendants with foreign airlines because of visa restrictions.) International airline employees, especially those in direct contact with the public, may need to be bilingual or multilingual. Those working for an international airline should be well informed about and accepting of different cultures.

Jobs in the airline industry can be placed in two main categories: flight crew and ground crew. The flight crew includes the people who operate the airplane and provide in-flight service; the ground crew or staff includes those who keep the plane airworthy and fill it with passengers.

Flight Crew

The flight crew can be separated into two groups. The pilots who fly the airplane make up the flight deck crew or cockpit crew, and the attendants who provide in-flight service and passenger safety make up the cabin crew.

Flight Deck Crew There are usually either two or three pilots, the exact number depending upon the type of aircraft. In larger aircraft that use three pilots, the cockpit crew generally consists of the captain, or senior pilot, who makes flight plans, operates the airplane, and supervises other crew members; the first officer, or co-pilot, who assists the captain, charts the airplane's route, and computes flying time; and the second officer, or flight engineer, who inspects the airplane before it takes off and after it lands, monitors all instruments and gauges during flight, and calculates the amount of fuel needed. The latest models of aircraft are designed for two-person crews, with the second officer no longer required.

As nearly all airlines are unionized, a pilot's career is influenced by the seniority system, which determines promotions. New pilots for large airlines begin as second officers; in

A DAY IN THE LIFE OF

A Flight Attendant

People think of my job—a flight attendant for an international airline—as glamorous and exciting. And it is. I get to travel to other countries and to meet interesting people. But it's a lot of hard work, too. Flight attendants are the airline employees passengers see the most of. That means they are often the employees passengers remember most clearly. I think of myself as an ambassador of goodwill for the airline. If I do my job well, people will travel with our airline again.

Most of what I do falls into one of two categories: safety and service. I think the most ignored speech in the world is the one I give at the beginning of each flight when I point out the emergency exits, explain the use of the oxygen masks, and tell people where the life jackets are found. Flying is so safe today that most people take an uneventful flight for granted. In fact, I've never been in an accident myself. Still, simulators train us for emergencies. We learn how to evacuate passengers quickly, safely, and calmly. A flight attendant has to stay calm—especially when passengers are panicking.

I'm also trained in simple first-aid procedures. I have a friend who actually attended at a birth on a flight. Fortunately, there happened to be a doctor on board who did the actual delivery. One time, a passenger on my flight had a heart attack—and there was no physician aboard. I was able to help that person until we could make an emergency landing.

Service is the other major part of a flight attendant's job. Service involves everything from serving meals and drinks to calming nervous fliers to coping with belligerent passengers. Basically, I have to be "people conscious"—often I can sense a passenger's need before he or she voices it.

Some of the neediest passengers are children who are alone on a flight. Frequently, parents will see a child onto the plane and arrange for someone—say, a grandparent—to meet the flight at the destination. The airline I work for treats these small passengers with extra care. They get a special badge, and the flight attendants keep an eye on them during the whole trip. Sometimes a child is frightened or lonely, and I'm sort of a friend, nurse, and parent all rolled into one. I especially feel like a parent when someone asks me for the twentieth time, "Are we there yet?" But part of my job is to answer the question politely and with a smile—every time.

As I said earlier, the airline I work for flies international as well as domestic flights. I speak French fluently—a real advantage for me on overseas flights. Most of the other attendants speak either French, Spanish, or German in addition to English. On a flight several weeks ago, a French businessman broke his only pair of reading glasses during the flight. He was so upset that even though he spoke English well, he wasn't able to communicate in it at the time. In French, I assured him that on landing we could guide him to an optometrist who would replace his glasses.

A second language also helps during layovers—the nights and days I spend away from my home base in Montreal. On international flights, layovers are at least 12 hours, sometimes as long as 36 hours. I may be away from home for a week or so at a time when we lay over in several European cities in a row. During a layover, my food, lodging, and transportation are paid for by the airline. Layovers are forced R&R—rest and relaxation. I sightsee, visit friends I've made on previous flights, or just relax.

On my last flight we had a two-day layover in Paris. I'd already seen the Eiffel Tower, Notre Dame, and all the other Paris sights. This time I rented a car and visited the château region along the Loire River. It's an easy day's drive from Paris. The two days left me refreshed and ready to give "service with a smile" on the way back to Canada.

Of course, during my real vacation time I can take advantage of the low-cost flights offered by my airline or by others we have reciprocal agreements with. Then I sit back and enjoy being the passenger. Believe it or not, I even listen to the flight attendant's speech about oxygen masks and life jackets—you can never know too much in an emergency!

five to ten years they might become first officers. It sometimes takes 20 years to reach the rank of captain. With the new-entrant carriers, promotions tend to come faster, since these companies are largely nonunionized.

The employment outlook for pilots is mixed. With the growth of air traffic and the expansion of airline fleets, especially among the regional and commuter airlines, more pilots are needed. However, the major carriers are reducing their need for pilots. There are excellent opportunities for pilots to fly aircraft owned by private corporations and air taxi services. In particular, airlines are looking to hire more women as pilots.

Cabin Crew While there are usually three people in the cockpit crew on a long-distance flight, there can be as many as 16 in-flight attendants, the actual number depending on the size of the airplane and the proportion of first-class to coach passengers. Flight attendants provide for the comfort and safety of the passengers. Among other duties, they serve in-flight meals and beverages, demonstrate safety equipment, check seat belts, and cope with medical emergencies. Flight attendants personally represent the airline and, in a sense, personify the product. The employment outlook for flight attendants should remain good.

Cross-Training In some nonunion airlines, members of the flight crew also perform the duties of the ground crew. For example, flight attendants work in customer service, and flight officers have scheduling and dispatching duties. Cross-training is more common among the new entrants.

Ground Crew or Staff

A commercial airplane flight would not be possible without the work of the hundreds of people in the ground crew. Jobs on the ground are found in the areas of reservations, passenger services, aircraft and building maintenance, safety regulation and airline security, in-flight and freight services, and management and sales.

Reservations An airline reservations agent is usually the first contact a prospective passenger has with the airline. At the request of customers, airline reservations agents answer questions about flight schedules, check the availability of flights, and book passengers. As the reservations system becomes more automated, fewer agents are likely to be needed.

Passenger Services This group of employees works mainly in the terminal building. Airline ticket agents sell tickets and keep records, tag luggage, assign seats, announce flight arrivals and departures, and board passengers. Customer service agents deal with passengers with special needs, such as challenged travellers and children travelling alone. Ramp agents see that the passengers' baggage is loaded on the correct flight.

Maintenance Maintenance employees work either for a specific airline or for the local governmental authority that runs the airport. Plumbers, carpenters, electricians, and painters maintain airport buildings. Other maintenance workers plough snow and clear debris from the runways.

Probably the most important maintenance workers are the mechanics and engine specialists who service and repair airplanes. As safety standards tighten and airplane traffic increases, there will be more jobs for mechanics.

Other Personnel Airline dispatchers schedule flights for an airline and are responsible for ensuring that Transport Canada regulations are enforced. Airports that allow general aviation aircraft to use their facilities can employ a fixed-base operator (FBO), who provides small-aircraft operators with flight information, fuel, and hangar space.

Security officials inspect baggage and electronically search passengers. Most uniformed security personnel are employed by private security companies hired by the airport authority.

Flight kitchen or catering personnel prepare passenger meals. Aircraft cleaners supply the airplane with items such as clean towels, fresh water, and magazines. Freight handlers process cargo and air freight and load and unload it.

Transport Canada Employees Air traffic controllers coordinate the flights of airplanes to prevent accidents and minimize delays in accordance with Transport Canada rules and regulations. Some controllers give pilots permission to take off and land (airport traffic controllers); others instruct pilots en route between airports (air-route traffic controllers). With airspace becoming more congested and with the rapid turnover among controllers, opportunities for employment should remain high.

Station Manager Every airline operating a scheduled service has a station at the airport, which is run by a station manager. It is his or her responsibility to see that flights are coordinated and that the weight, balance, and load of each departing flight is calculated. The station manager is employed by the airline.

Airport Manager Every airport has a manager who deals with the airlines, oversees maintenance of the buildings and runways, monitors businesses operating in the airport, handles public relations, and makes sure that Transport Canada regulations are enforced. The airport manager is employed by the governmental authority that runs the airport.

There may be assistant managers in charge of specific areas, such as cargo services. Although the number of airports is growing, airport management is a relatively small field and openings are limited.

General Office (GO) Every major airline maintains a general office that serves as the corporate headquarters. Air Canada, for example, has its general office in Montreal; USAir's is in Arlington, Virginia. The GO is the centre for administrative and technical departments, major maintenance, and training. Most public relations and advertising work is also carried out at the general office.

Sales Offices Most airlines operate sales offices. These should not be confused with city ticket offices or airport ticket counters. Very few passengers buy their tickets from an airline sales office. Rather, the sales representatives who work out of these offices are responsible for calling on the intermediaries and decision-makers, such as travel agencies and business travel departments.

Summary

- The airplane evolved as the result of experimentation with lighter-than-air and heavier-than-air craft.
- Domestic and international airline industries began to grow rapidly following World War II. The development of bigger, faster, and more comfortable planes increased the popularity of air travel.
- Modern aircraft either have jet engines or are propeller-driven.
- Civilian air services are divided into air carrier aviation and general aviation. Air carrier aviation specializes in carrying passengers and/or cargo on a large scale.
- Major airports are publicly owned and require large amounts of land. General aviation airports are privately owned.
- Airlines plan their routes for maximum efficiency, by either the linear concept or the hub-and-spoke concept.

FIGURE 4-8
The airline reservations agent is the first contact a potential passenger has with an airline.
SOURCE: Courtesy Canadian Airlines International Ltd.

- International aviation is more complex than domestic aviation because governments must negotiate the use of sovereign airspace.
- Multilateral agreements reached at worldwide conferences have helped define the use of airspace.
- Bilateral agreements are used to work out the specific details of traffic rights between two nations.
- The International Air Transport Association (IATA) helps to regulate the international air system.
- Until 1978 in the United States, the government controlled the routes, schedules, and rates of domestic carriers. Economic regulation ended with the Airline Deregulation Act. Safety regulation continues under the Federal Aviation Administration (FAA).
- Factors influencing the price of an airline ticket include the distance flown, type of journey, type of flight, and level of service.
- Air travellers can buy reduced-price tickets if they are willing to accept various restrictions.
- Thousands of airline employees, both flight crews and ground crews, are involved in the transportation of passengers and cargo.
- The Canadian airline industry has seen several distinct stages:
  1. The establishment of a Crown corporation, Trans-Canada Airlines (now Air Canada), which operated as a sanctioned monopoly on transcontinental routes from 1937 to 1958.
  2. The emergence of stronger regional carriers under the 1966 Regional Air Policy.
  3. A period of regulated competition as a result of the National Transportation Act of 1967.
  4. The regulatory reform period of the 1980s, which resulted in a duopoly of Air Canada and Canadian Airlines, with affiliated carriers.
  5. A period of uncertainty in the 1990s, characterized by operating losses, international alliances, negotiations between carriers in Canada and the United States, and Open Skies negotiations.

Key Terms

pressurization
common carrier
scheduled airline
supplemental airline
charter airline
fixed-base operator (FBO)
cargo terminal
control tower
hangar
runway
loading apron
taxiway
linear route
hub-and-spoke route

gateway airport
flag carrier
foreign flag
deregulation
open skies
frequent flier
regional airline
new-entrant carrier
code sharing
one-way trip
round trip
circle trip
open-jaw trip
on-line connection
interline connection
interlining
stopover
configuration
no-show
overbook
fare construction

What Do You Think?

1. What might happen if airlines owned airports?
2. Do you think the Canadian and American governments should subsidize airline companies to make them more competitive in international markets? Explain your point of view.
3. How might increased security against international terrorism damage the airline industry?
4. Has deregulation had positive or negative effects on the domestic airline industry? Explain your point of view.
5. Do you think that Canada should advocate a policy of open skies, as opposed to sovereign skies? Explain your point of view.
6. Compared with other means of transportation, what are the advantages and disadvantages of airplanes for transporting passengers and cargo?
7. What would be the advantages and disadvantages of having just one type of in-flight passenger service?

Dealing with Product

How fair are airfares? Consider the following scenario. Flight 123 is scheduled to leave Calgary at 7:30 A.M. and to fly nonstop to Toronto, where it will land at 12:30 P.M. Mr. Blue, Ms. Green, and Dr. Brown have been assigned to seats 3A, 3B, and 3C. Each of these travellers will be served an identical complimentary breakfast, and each passenger has checked two pieces of baggage on to Toronto. In other words, each of these passengers will receive exactly the same service as his or her seatmates.

Somewhere above Thunder Bay, at 10 600 metres, the seatmates compare their airfares. Mr. Blue paid $600 for his round-trip ticket, while Ms. Green paid only $499 for her flights to and from Toronto. Imagine their reaction when Dr. Brown announces that he paid only $299 for his passage.

Each passenger has bought what seems to be a similar product—a ticket from Calgary to Toronto and return. Why do you think the fares varied so much? Do you think the airlines are justified in having many different fare structures? Why or why not? What methods can you think of for simplifying airfares?

Dealing with People

You are a newly hired employee with a major airline. You have just completed four weeks of training, and today is your first day on the job. You have been assigned to the ticket counter, and the first voice you hear is not a pleasant one. Your supervisor is busy with a conference call and the senior agent has just gone to lunch, so you are all alone with a very irate passenger.

It seems that this passenger has just arrived from Toronto, but his baggage did not. Furthermore, he is doubly furious because he arrived at Yourtown airport aboard a code-sharing regional aircraft. He is threatening to sue you and your airline not once but twice—first for losing his baggage and ruining his trip, and a second time for false advertising. He thought that because his ticket was issued on your airline and he left Toronto on a large jet, he would fly all the way to Yourtown on a "big bird." Instead, he flew the last leg of his journey in a 19-passenger turboprop. How can you help solve this passenger's problems and convert him into a frequent flier?

CHAPTER 4: The Airline Industry   Name: _____

WORKSHEET 4-1 Airport Codes

Every major airport worldwide is designated by a code that is recognized internationally. This code is used to identify the airport on tickets, baggage, freight packages, and so on. Use the appropriate *Official Airline Guide* (see Chapter 3) or a similar reference guide to obtain the codes for the airports in the cities listed below. If there is more than one airport in a city, give the codes for all the airports.

Toronto, Ont. _____

Saint John, N.B. _____

St. John's, Nfld. _____

Vancouver, B.C. _____

Iqaluit, N.W.T. _____

Quebec City, P.Q. _____

Edmonton, Alta. _____

Charlottetown, P.E.I. _____

Windsor, Ont. _____

Winnipeg, Man. _____

Halifax, N.S. _____

Regina, Sask. _____

Prince Rupert, B.C. _____

Montreal, P.Q. _____

The Pas, Man. _____

Ottawa, Ont. _____

New York, NY _____

Atlanta, GA _____

Boston, MA _____

Newark, NJ _____

Philadelphia, PA _____

Miami, FL _____

Montgomery, AL _____

New Orleans, LA _____

Chicago, IL _____

Detroit, MI _____

Minneapolis, MN _____

Cleveland, OH _____

Washington, DC _____

Richmond, VA _____

Houston, TX _____

Lincoln, NE _____

Denver, CO _____

Phoenix, AZ _____

Salt Lake City, UT _____

Tulsa, OK _____

Albuquerque, NM _____

Boise, ID _____

Las Vegas, NV _____

Los Angeles, CA _____

Seattle, WA _____

Portland, OR _____

San Francisco, CA _____

Anchorage, AK _____

Honolulu, HI _____

CHAPTER 4: The Airline Industry   Name: _____

WORKSHEET 4-2 Yourtown Airport

Find out the following information about an air carrier airport in or near Yourtown. Write your findings in the space provided.

Name of airport

Location

Number of hectares

Ownership/governing body

Number of air carriers currently using facilities

Names of air carriers

Annual volume of air traffic

   In some communities, citizen groups monitor the environmental impact of local airports. Find out if such a group exists in Yourtown. In the space below, describe the activities of the group (e.g., lobbying against airplane noise).

   Imagine you are a travel agent. You have just sold B. P. Walter a round-trip airline ticket on one of the major carriers that serves Yourtown airport. Mr. Walter is new to Yourtown and has never been to Yourtown airport. In the space below, provide Mr. Walter with information about how to get to the airport, where to park, where to check in, where to find his gate, and so on. Obtain a map of the layout of Yourtown airport to help you with your explanation.

CHAPTER 4: The Airline Industry   Name: _____

WORKSHEET 4-3 Travel Arrangements

You are a travel agent. What travel arrangements and airfares can you offer the following customers? Use nonautomated information systems to arrange their travel.

1. A university professor in Kingston, Ontario, wants to attend an international conference in Sydney, Australia. The conference will be held in six months. The university will pay for the professor's trip, but funds are limited.

   _____
   _____

2. A couple is planning their honeymoon, which is three months away. They want to fly from Winnipeg, Manitoba, to Miami. They want to stay for a few days, then board a ship to cruise the Caribbean for ten days. They will fly from Miami to St. Louis the same day the ship returns. The trip is a wedding present from the bride's wealthy father, so money is not a major factor.

   _____
   _____

3. A 60-member high school marching band from Red Deer, Alberta, wants to tour several cities in Germany this summer. The group wants to begin and end its tour in Frankfurt. Although the band members have been working for months to raise money for the trip, they must travel as inexpensively as possible.

   _____
   _____

4. A businessman must fly out of Toronto tomorrow morning to arrive as early as possible in Ottawa. He wants to return to Toronto as soon as possible after 8 P.M.

   _____
   _____

5. Two Ottawa parents and their two pre-school-age children want to visit family in St. John's for Christmas. It is now mid-October. They are flexible about when they fly. They plan to stay about two weeks and want to fly back to Ottawa from St. John's. They would prefer not to change planes, but flying as cheaply as possible is their priority.

   _____
   _____

6. An 80-year-old woman wants to go from Halifax to Vancouver two weeks from now. It is difficult for her to walk, so she does not want to change planes. She wants to travel first-class.

   _____
   _____

CHAPTER 4: The Airline Industry   Name: _____

WORKSHEET 4-4 Special Needs

Providing services to passengers with special needs is important for an airline's success. Contact two major airlines that service the city nearest to Yourtown and find out what services are available for the passengers listed below.

Airline

A physically challenged traveller   _____   _____
                                     _____   _____
                                     _____   _____

A passenger who does not speak English   _____   _____
                                          _____   _____
                                          _____   _____

A child flying alone   _____   _____
                        _____   _____
                        _____   _____

A passenger travelling with an infant   _____   _____
                                         _____   _____
                                         _____   _____

A passenger requiring a low-salt diet   _____   _____
                                         _____   _____
                                         _____   _____

What additional services can the airlines offer?

What other kinds of passengers might require special attention? What services would help them?

CHAPTER 5

The Surface Travel Industries

"I am neither a prophet, nor the son of a prophet, yet.... I believe that many in this room will live to hear the whistle of a steam engine in the passes of the Rocky Mountains and to make the journey from Halifax to the Pacific in five or six days."

Joseph Howe, Halifax, May 15, 1851

OBJECTIVES

When you have completed this chapter, you should be able to do the following:

- Trace the rise and decline of the railway passenger industry in Canada and the United States.
- Describe the government's role in revitalizing passenger rail service through VIA Rail Canada and Amtrak.
- Describe the different types of accommodations and services offered by VIA Rail Canada and Amtrak.
- Compare the importance of the passenger train in Canada and the United States with that of trains in other nations.
- Give reasons for the growth of the charter and tour business in the motorcoach industry.
- Discuss the effects of deregulation on the motorcoach industry.
- List and describe the types of motorcoach tours now available.
- Describe the close connection between the car rental and airline industries.
- Explain why it is easier to enter the car rental industry than other sectors of the surface transportation industry.
- Describe the various urban public transportation systems, the needs they fulfil, and the problems they alleviate.

Despite the advent of air transportation, travel by land is still the major way to get from here to there. The various sectors of the surface travel industry—railways, motorcoaches, car rentals, and mass transit—all play a vital role in modern transportation, in Canada, the United States, and abroad. With the exception of the car rental industry, however, all have experienced periods of decline in Canada and the United States in the postwar period. They have lost passengers to the airlines and, more importantly, to the private automobile. (Car transportation now accounts for almost 85 percent of all intercity passenger miles travelled in Canada and the United States.) Still, the Canadian and American passenger rail services have managed to stay alive through reorganization, and the motorcoach industry has turned to the charter and tour business to offset the decline in its own scheduled services. Clearly, both railway and motorcoach companies are adjusting to supply the needs of travellers in a changing world.

THE RAILWAY INDUSTRY

For many people in Canada and the United States, trains are an important mode of transportation. Some people use them every day to get to work. Businesspeople take high-speed trains, such as the Metroliner between New York and Washington, because they are a fast, comfortable, and easy way to travel from one city centre to another. Canada has studied the feasibility of high-speed trains (HSTs) in the Windsor–Quebec City corridor. Families travel on special family-excursion fares to visit relatives. College students take the train to go home during school break. Retirees planning to spend the worst of the winter in Florida travel south in Auto Trains, which transport passengers and their cars. Trains, then, can satisfy the motivations, needs, and expectations (MNEs) of many kinds of travellers.

Canadian and American trains may not be as glamorous as they once were, but they are still a useful way to travel. In addition, there are many people who are attracted to the special mystique of train travel. Travelling by air may be fast, but there is little to see on the way. The leisurely pace of rail travel gives passengers time to sit back and enjoy the passing scenery. For many, a train trip is more than a matter of reaching a destination promptly; "getting there" is part of the experience.

As a travel professional, you will need to know how to obtain information about train routes and schedules for Canadian, American, and foreign trains. You will also need to know how to make reservations.

In this section, you will learn something about railways past and present—their proud history and their problems today. You will also learn about railways in other countries and about the great trains of the world.

A Brief History of the Railways

The history of railways goes back a long time. As early as the 16th century, primitive railways powered by horses were being used to haul coal and iron ore on wooden tracks. But the real ancestors of the modern railways appeared in the early 1800s, following the invention of the steam engine. In 1804, the world's first successful steam-powered locomotive chugged along a 14-kilometre track in England at a speed of 8 kilometres an hour—little faster than a person could walk.

The idea of steam locomotion crossed the Atlantic, and work on the South Carolina Canal and Railroad started in 1829. This railway, the first scheduled passenger line in the United States, ran from Charleston, South Carolina, to Hamburg, Georgia, a distance of 217 kilometres. It was the wonder of the day.

Canada's first railway opened in 1836, 31 years before Confederation. Backed by John Molson and other Montreal merchants, the 20-kilometre Champlain and Saint Lawrence Railroad connected Laprairie on the St. Lawrence River, across from the Island of Montreal, to St.-Jean-sur-Richelieu. It was constructed as a portage railway to provide a shortcut for New York–Montreal river traffic. Passenger traffic was hauled by the Dorchester, Canada's first steam locomotive, which made the trip in 41 minutes. There are several replicas of the Dorchester in Canada, and a full-size, operational replica of the locomotive John Molson can be seen at the Canadian Railway Museum in Delson, Quebec.

Though few people believed that railways could compete successfully with canal transportation, far-sighted entrepreneurs proceeded to build and then expand them. The Maritimes' first railway, the Albion Railway, opened in 1838 to move coal ten kilometres to Pictou Harbour, Nova Scotia. Two railways from Montreal to the ice-free port of Portland, Maine, opened in 1852: the St. Lawrence and Atlantic Railway in Canada, and the Atlantic and St. Lawrence Railway in the United States. The Great Western Railway between Niagara Falls and Windsor was completed in 1854. The most ambitious railway project proposed was the Grand Trunk Railway, conceived by the Imperial government in England as a means to bind and unite the colonies of British North America. The original proposal was to build it from Halifax to the western boundary of Canada West.

The Grand Trunk Railway, incorporated in 1852, attempted to buy existing railways and to fill in the gaps between Portland, Maine, and Sarnia, Ontario, with provisions for a line to New Brunswick to connect with the proposed Intercolonial Railway to Halifax. The Toronto–Oshawa main line and the Richmond–Levis section of the Maritime connection were opened in the fall of 1855; the Toronto–Sarnia main line was opened as far as Guelph in the summer of 1856; and in October 1856 a seven-car passenger train began operating on the Toronto–Montreal route.

In 1850 the United States government began offering land to the states for railway development. The states in turn distributed the land to local railway companies, which sold some of it to settlers to pay for railway construction. Lines were extended into unsettled areas in the West, and wherever tracks were built, new communities sprang up. This westward expansion in the United States raised concerns in British North America about how to retain control of western Canada.

Confederation in 1867, under the leadership of Sir John A. Macdonald and George Étienne Cartier, brought four provinces into the Dominion of Canada: New Brunswick, Nova Scotia, Ontario, and Quebec. Clause 145 of the Constitution Act promised construction of the Intercolonial Railway, which would link the Maritime provinces with the rest of the Dominion.

Transcontinental Line—United States On May 10, 1869, at Promontory Point, Utah, a crowd of dignitaries and railway workers cheered as the governor of California hammered in a golden spike to mark the joining of the Union Pacific and Central Pacific rail lines. The transcontinental

ILLUSTRATION 5-1
VIA Rail passenger service offers a comfortable way to travel from one city centre to another.
SOURCE VIA Rail Canada

CHAPTER 5: The Surface Travel Industries

railway was completed. Now it was possible to travel from New York to San Francisco by rail in six days—a journey that used to take months. By the end of the century, four more lines stretched across the country, linking the east and west coasts and bringing isolated communities into the national transportation network.

Transcontinental Line—Canada Manitoba entered Confederation in 1870. British Columbia entered in 1871 after being promised that a transcontinental railway would be built within ten years. Prince Edward Island entered in 1873 on the condition that the Dominion would take over and operate its partially completed railway. (The Island government had agreed to pay contractors by length of track laid and in return received a railway that meandered across the province.)

Construction of the Canadian Pacific Railway from Montreal to Vancouver began in 1881. The line was completed at Craigellachie, British Columbia, on November 7, 1885. On Monday, June 28, 1886, CPR train No. 1, the "Pacific Express," left Montreal for the West Coast; 139 hours and 4600 kilometres later, the 4-4-0-type engine (No. 371) eased the train into the CPR station at Port Moody, just east of Vancouver. The Dominion of Canada was bound from sea to sea; the prophecy of Joseph Howe was fulfilled.

Other transcontinental lines were constructed in Canada in the first two decades of the 20th century, including the Canadian Northern, the Grand Trunk Pacific, and the National Transcontinental. These lines and others ran into financial difficulties, particularly when immigration to the Prairies declined during World War I. In 1923 they were amalgamated as the government-owned Canadian National Railways.

The Golden Age of Railways In the years following the completion of the early transcontinental lines, trains became safer, faster, and more comfortable. Some were luxurious. By 1900, railways could offer all the amenities of modern living, including electric lighting and steam heat, sleeping cars, dining cars, and washroom facilities. Train travel was no longer a matter of getting from point A to point B. It had become a distinctly pleasurable experience. Famous trains in Canada had names such as the Imperial Limited, the Trans-Canada Limited, the Continental, and the Ocean Limited. Famous trains in the United States were the Twentieth Century Limited, the Super Chief, and the Empire Builder. There were several trains between Canada and the United States: the Alouette (Montreal–Boston), the International Limited (Chicago–Toronto–Montreal), and the Maple Leaf (Detroit–Montreal). Passengers were pampered as they were carried to their destinations.

Competition Though the railway industry enjoyed a period of relative prosperity in the 1920s, it also faced serious competition from other forms of transportation. The growth in automobile ownership and the development of intercity bus services cut into the railways' passenger business. At the same time, the trucking industry challenged the railways' monopoly of freight traffic. During the Depression, railways lost huge sums of money, and several companies in the United States went out of business. World War II brought a temporary upturn, but in the years since then the railway industry has faced hard times.

Industry in Decline In the 1950s and 1960s, intercity passenger services on railways declined dramatically in both Canada and the United States. By 1980 the railways' share

ILLUSTRATION 5-2
A Canrail pass allows unlimited travel on VIA Rail trains in designated areas.
SOURCE VIA Rail Canada

of passenger kilometres (including those travelled by car) had fallen below 5 percent. During the same period, the number of passenger trains in operation plummeted.

The major factor in the decline of rail travel has been, undoubtedly, the increase in car ownership. In 1929, one in five Canadians owned a car. Today the figure is one in two.

Another important factor in the railways' decline has been the continued growth of the airline industry. After long-distance air routes came into service, it was much quicker and sometimes less expensive to travel by plane than by train. Only in the heavily travelled Windsor–Quebec City corridor in Canada, and in the Northeast Corridor between Boston and Washington, D.C., and on a few other medium-distance routes, could train travel remain competitive.

A third factor in the decline of the railway industry has been its financial structure. The fixed costs of railways are much higher than for other surface transportation industries. Railways have to spend large sums on equipment, maintenance, and labour. Political conflict over the roles government and private enterprise should play in the industry has also been a problem.

Faced with heavy annual losses, many railway companies in the United States went out of business in the 1950s and 1960s. Others survived only by dropping unprofitable services, which in most cases meant passenger routes. Pessimists predicted the end of all passenger service by the 1970s. It was plain that something had to be done to save the passenger train.

There were those who believed that the U.S. government should **nationalize,** or take control of, the railway industry. Opponents of this plan pointed to the heavy losses that had been sustained by nationalized railways in other countries. In the end, there was a compromise.

Canadian Passenger Railway Service

The Canadian government issued a report in 1976 on the future of the Canadian rail passenger service. (A chronology of recent rail passenger service in Canada, emphasizing important dates in VIA Rail history, is shown in Figure 5-1.) It recommended the creation of VIA Rail Canada to take over passenger service from Canadian National and Canadian Pacific. An analysis of VIA Rail reveals five distinct periods:

- transition (1976–78)
- retrenchment (1979–84)
- steady state (1985–89)
- amputation (1990)
- the present

Transition (1976–78) This period saw the establishment of VIA Rail. The name and colours of VIA Rail were introduced in 1976, as was a combined CN/CP timetable. In 1977, VIA Rail was established as a Crown corporation by order-in-council and began the marketing of passenger service for the two major Canadian railways. However, it was not until 1978 that VIA Rail took over equipment from CN and CP and began the direct management and operation of trains. It is important to note that VIA Rail was not directly controlled by Parliament; rather, it was a Crown corporation operating trains on contract from the Ministry of Transport. Government subsidies were provided for VIA Rail operations.

Retrenchment (1979–84) When the railways operated passenger trains, no route could not be abandoned without a hearing before the regulatory authority, the Canadian Transport Commission. Now that VIA Rail was established, the transport minister could shut down routes. Some restructuring occurred in 1979, particularly in the Maritime provinces, but the major cutbacks happened in 1981, when 20 percent of the VIA system was terminated. Notable trains discontinued included the Super Continental (Vancouver–Montreal through Jasper, Edmonton, Saskatoon, and Winnipeg), and the Atlantic Limited

1940s — Rail passenger traffic substantial.

1950s — Decline in rail passenger share of traffic.
— 1954—Introduction of rail diesel cars (RDCs) on short routes.
— 1955—Introduction of streamlined passenger trains (Super Continental on CN; Canadian on CP).

1960s — Continued demise of rail passenger service.
— 1961—MacPherson Royal Commission on Transportation Report.
— 1967—National Transportation Act (emphasis on intermodal competition; subsidized service in national interest).

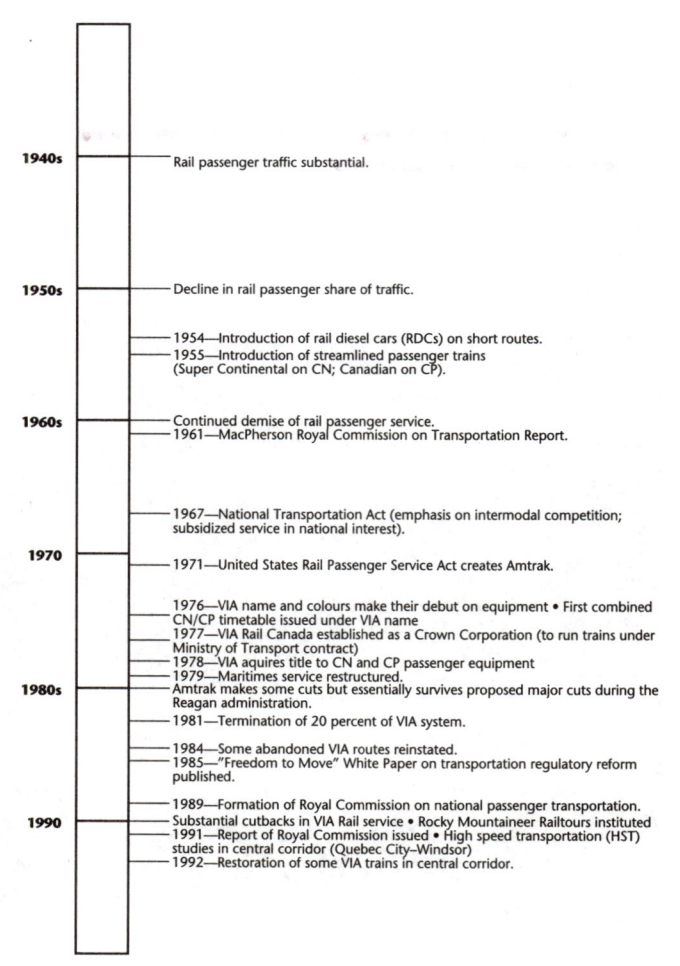

1970 — 1971—United States Rail Passenger Service Act creates Amtrak.
— 1976—VIA name and colours make their debut on equipment • First combined CN/CP timetable issued under VIA name
— 1977—VIA Rail Canada established as a Crown Corporation (to run trains under Ministry of Transport contract)
— 1978—VIA aquires title to CN and CP passenger equipment
— 1979—Maritimes service restructured.

1980s — Amtrak makes some cuts but essentially survives proposed major cuts during the Reagan administration.
— 1981—Termination of 20 percent of VIA system.
— 1984—Some abandoned VIA routes reinstated.
— 1985—"Freedom to Move" White Paper on transportation regulatory reform published.
— 1989—Formation of Royal Commission on national passenger transportation.

1990 — Substantial cutbacks in VIA Rail service • Rocky Mountaineer Railtours instituted
— 1991—Report of Royal Commission issued • High speed transportation (HST) studies in central corridor (Quebec City–Windsor)
— 1992—Restoration of some VIA trains in central corridor.

FIGURE 5-1
Canadian Rail Passenger Chronology

(Montreal–Halifax through Maine and Saint John). Residents of Jasper were upset at the prospect of losing tourists, including thousands from Japan who travelled through the Rockies by rail. The Canadian was still available on the Canadian Pacific route through Banff and Calgary.

Steady State (1985–89) Some abandoned routes were restored, including the Atlantic from Montreal to Halifax and the Super Continental through Jasper. However, the steady state period did see regulatory and funding changes. In 1985 the Conservative government released *Freedom to Move*, a White Paper on transportation regulatory reform. A new National Transportation Act, in effect on January 1, 1988, emphasized both intermodal and intramodal competition. The government wanted to reduce the deficit and expected VIA Rail to find new ways to attract customers, operate more efficiently, and reduce its government subsidy. The Royal Commission on National Passenger Transportation was announced in 1989. Its mandate was to inquire into and report on a national integrated intercity passenger system to meet the needs of Canadians in the 21st century.

Amputation (January 1990) On January 15, 1990, Canada's rail passenger system was basically cut in half: from 810 trains weekly to 396; from 33 routes to 14; and from 6700 employees to 4000. The rationale for this was a diminished budget for VIA Rail. Subsidies from the federal government, running at about $550 million in 1989, were to be cut in stages to $350 million by 1992.

The effect of the cuts was to reduce passenger carriage on CP tracks. Only one route through Northern Ontario and the Atlantic route across Maine remained. The biggest cut was the route of the Canadian from Toronto to Vancouver through Calgary and Banff. The Super Continental on the CN route through Jasper survived, but on a reduced thrice-weekly basis.

The Present (1990 to Date) The focus of VIA Rail is on the central corridor between Quebec City and Windsor/Sarnia. Some trains that were cut in 1990 were restored in 1992. The corridor services provide an integrated network of intercity trains that offer LRC (light, rapid, comfortable) equipment, convenient schedules, VIA 1 first-class service, and a limited number of stops. The VIA 1 is promoted as the most comprehensive concept in first-class travel ever offered in the corridor and features:

- Special early check-in and boarding.
- No lineups and no waiting at the VIA 1 check-in counters.
- Complimentary newspapers and magazines.
- Complete hot meals for breakfast, lunch, and dinner, with complimentary beverages.
- Spacious comfort for relaxing, working, and dining.
- Complete non-smoking cars.
- A consistently high level of personal service.

Clearly, the types of marketing that have been used for decades in the airline industry are now being applied to first-class rail travel in the central corridor. Western and eastern transcontinental services have been rather sparse since the 1990 cutbacks. The Canadian, the former CP flagship train, operates three days a week on the CN route from Toronto to Vancouver through Winnipeg, Saskatoon, Edmonton, and Jasper. The Skeena operates three days a week between Jasper and Prince Rupert. Additional services operate on Vancouver Island and on the Hudson Bay route between Churchill and Winnipeg.

Eastern transcontinental services include the Atlantic (three days a week between Halifax and Montreal through Saint John, the state of Maine, and Sherbrooke); the Ocean (three days a week between Halifax and Montreal through Campbellton and Mont-Joli); and the Chaleur (three days a week between Gaspé and Montreal). There are bus and ferry connections from Yarmouth to Halifax, Charlottetown to Moncton, and Truro to points in Newfoundland.

Stainless-steel passenger cars were restored to transcontinental service in 1993 after an investment of $200 million. This equipment was originally brought into service on the Canadian and the Dominion in 1955 by CP, complete with Canadian artwork featuring the Group of Seven. Five main types of cars are part of this restored fleet: coach cars, Skyline dome lounge cars, sleeping cars (with showers), dining cars with white linen service, and Park cars with their "bullet" observation lounges. The artwork on these trains includes original murals by contemporary Canadian artists.

The routes of VIA Rail and Amtrak connect at various points, providing north-south rail service between Canada and the United States. Amtrak trains such as the Adirondack and the Montrealer start in New York City, cross the border, and carry passengers directly to Montreal. Passengers from Toronto can travel to Chicago on the International and to New York on the Maple Leaf. A Canrailpass allows unlimited travel on VIA trains in designated areas—all Canada, Winnipeg and eastern Canada, Winnipeg and western Canada, or the Quebec City–Windsor/Sarnia corridor—for a fixed rate for periods of 8, 15, 22, or 30 days.

Federal Regulation The National Transportation Act of 1987 created the National Transportation Agency (NTA) to regulate the railways and railway services, including VIA Rail. All passenger fares and conditions are regulated by the NTA. The NTA replaced the Canadian Transport Commission, which had been created by the National Transportation Act of 1967.

United States Passenger Railways Today

When the U.S. government created the semi-public, federally subsidized National Railroad Passenger Corporation* in

---

* "Railroads" is the American word for what Canadians call railways. This book follows the Canadian style, except for proper names.

1970, American railways got a new lease on life. The corporation, better known as Amtrak, was to be financed jointly by payments from participating railways and by federal subsidies. The goal was to restore public confidence in rail travel by improving service and eliminating unprofitable routes.

Amtrak Amtrak took over almost all of the American intercity passenger networks in 1971. Eighteen of the 22 largest passenger railways joined the corporation when it started operations. (The other four joined in 1983.) As a first step, routes and services were cut in half. Service was concentrated along high-density corridors such as Boston–New York–Washington, Los Angeles–San Diego, and Miami–Orlando–Tampa.

Initially, the outlook for the new corporation was not very promising. But Amtrak began an ambitious modernization program. It ordered new locomotives and improved tracks. It also introduced a national reservations system. In the mid-1970s, Amtrak and passenger rail lines in general received a boost from the gasoline crisis. As the price of gas went up, increasing numbers of American motorists decided to travel by train. In the first ten years of Amtrak's operation, passenger kilometres travelled went up 60 percent, and total revenues increased by more than 300 percent.

Despite the impressive rise in passenger use, Amtrak still depends on federal subsidies for 28 percent of its total operating budget. While government subsidies have been cut back—from $896 million in 1981 to $635 million in 1990—plans to eliminate all federal financing seem optimistic. Despite its problems, Amtrak has been able to expand some of its routes in California, Texas, and Florida. And in 1989 it introduced daily rail service between Philadelphia and Atlantic City. It has proposed extending the Portland–Seattle service to Vancouver (to begin in 1995).

As a travel professional, you will need to know about the different types of Amtrak trains and the services they offer:

- Standard coaches are used for day travel on Superliners, Metroliners, and Turboliners across the United States.
- Metroliners are high-speed, first-class, all-reserved trains that travel between New York and Washington, D.C.
- Club service offers extra space, reserved cars, and personalized service on many trains in the northeast corridor.
- Custom-class, available on Empire Service trains, offers reserved seating and reclining seats.
- Superliners provide luxurious long-distance service in double-decker cars between Chicago and New Orleans and the West Coast.
- The Heritage coach cars, equipped for overnight travel, are used for long-distance routes in the East.
- The Vista-Dome Car offers panoramic views on eastern, midwestern, and southwestern long-distance trains.
- The Auto Train carries travellers and their cars between the Washington, D.C., area and Florida.

ILLUSTRATION 5-3
The Japanese bullet train cruises at 200 kilometres an hour or more
Source: Suminoto Metal America Inc.

Federal Regulation In 1887, the U.S. Congress established the Interstate Commerce Commission (ICC) to regulate competition between railways and to ensure reasonable passenger and freight rates. The ICC still oversees the railway industry today, but its powers have been sharply reduced—first by the Regional Rail Reorganization Act of 1973 and then by the Staggers Rail Act of 1980. These laws have allowed railway companies greater freedom to set their own fares and to abandon unprofitable lines. Through deregulation, the U.S. government hoped to help the railways operate at a profit, thus ending the need for government subsidies.

The U.S. Department of Transportation (DOT) is also involved in the railway regulatory process. The DOT and Amtrak work with Congress and local governments to make decisions about routes and the number of trains per route. The Federal Railroad Administration, a division of the DOT, sets safety standards for the industry and inspects rolling stock (locomotives and cars), tracks, and signal systems.

Foreign Railways

In many countries beyond Canada and the United States, railways are still a major form of transportation. Most of these railways are owned and operated by governments.

Europe While the rail passenger industry has been struggling to survive in Canada and the United States, the passenger train has remained a vital mode of transportation in Europe. Most European railways are government-owned and -operated, and although few make a profit, European governments consider efficient and extensive passenger railways an essential service.

There are other factors besides government subsidies that account for the survival of the passenger train in Europe:

PROFILE

The Chunnel

It is now possible to board a train in London and arrive in Paris—about 480 kilometres away—in less than three hours. In 1994, workers completed a 50-kilometre train tunnel under the English Channel, creating the longest undersea tunnel in the world. The channel tunnel connects the British Isles to the rest of Europe for the first time since the last Ice Age. On November 14, 1994, the first successful run was completed from London to Paris in two hours and 57 minutes.

The channel tunnel, or Chunnel as it has been nicknamed, is the fulfilment of a 200-year-old dream dating back to the Napoleonic Wars. At that time, the French Emperor Napoleon talked of digging a tunnel under the channel so that his army could invade England. In the 19th and 20th centuries, others envisioned and even attempted to dig a channel tunnel for commercial travel, but all their attempts were unsuccessful.

In 1986, a group of British and French investors started a new company, Eurotunnel, to raise money and begin work on a new attempt to dig a channel tunnel. Eurotunnel sold more than $2 billion in stock in the company and took out another $10 billion in loans, making the Chunnel the most expensive privately financed construction project in the world. By the time it is finished, it will have cost more than $20 billion due to delays and cost overruns.

The Chunnel is also one of the most ambitious building projects in the world. It consists of three tunnels—two rail tunnels and a middle service tunnel. As work proceeds, huge, 1500-tonne boring machines chewed out millions of cubic metres of chalk from the bed of the English Channel.

Although the tunnel will not be ready for full service until 1995, it is already a reality. At the end of 1990, French and English workers cut through to one another in the central service tunnel and happily shook hands. The boring machines that had started out from England and France were a mere 50 centimetres out of alignment when they met near the centre of the channel.

Once the Chunnel goes into full operation, trains will depart from Folkestone, England, and Calais, France, every 10 to 15 minutes. Train passengers will ride all the way from London to Paris, and their travel time will be cut from twelve hours to less than three. Motorists and truckers will drive to Folkestone or Calais and then put their vehicles aboard double-decker shuttles for the journey across the channel. (Bombardier Inc. of Montreal built most of the Chunnel's single- and double-decker shuttle cars.) The trains and vehicle shuttles will travel at 120 kilometres an hour and will take about half an hour to make the under-channel crossing. It is expected that by the year 2003, the Chunnel will carry more than 120 000 passengers a day across the English Channel.

As construction winds down on the Chunnel, it is proceeding on several other rail lines throughout Europe. France is constructing a high-speed train line between Paris and Brussels, Belgium, while Spain is completing a high-speed rail line between Madrid and Seville. Germany already operates a 240-kilometre-an-hour bullet train between Hanover and Wurzburg. In the meantime, Denmark, Sweden, and Germany are building a multibillion-dollar system of tunnels and bridges to link up train service in those three countries. Great Britain is planning a new high-speed line from London to Folkestone, to be completed by the end of the decade.

These rail lines will provide the European Community (EC) with the finest high-speed train system in the world. For tourists, the new rail system will enable travellers to see more of Europe in much less time. They will be able to enjoy travelling in some of the fastest and most modern trains in the world. The Chunnel will also enable travellers who prefer to drive to get around Great Britain and Europe much more easily.

The year 1992 marked the time when the 12 nations of the European Community became one big, borderless nation for purposes of travel and trade. The Chunnel is an important symbol of that unity.

- *Private car ownership.* Although the number of Europeans owning cars has increased in recent years, it is still well below the level in Canada and the United States.
- *Price of gasoline.* Gasoline is much more expensive in Europe than in Canada and the United States.
- *Proximity of major cities in Europe.* Few Western European capitals are as far apart as the major population centres in Canada and the United States. It takes about the same amount of time, for example, to travel from Geneva to Paris by train as it does to fly. In general, train travel in Europe is more comfortable than air travel, less expensive, and less subject to traffic or weather delays. It is also more convenient in that it goes from one city centre to another.
- *Reliability of rail services.* Throughout Europe, trains almost always depart and arrive on schedule.
- *Price of air travel.* In Europe, it is almost always much less expensive to take a train than a plane.

There is a great deal of cooperation and coordination between European railways. The national systems of each country are integrated into the International Inter City network (formerly the Trans-European Express network), which provides first-class rail travel through nine Western European nations. The opening of the English Channel tunnel in 1994 was a milestone in the history of European railways. The "Chunnel" enables people to travel by rail between England and France.

Another example of cooperation among the railways of Europe is the **Eurailpass.** First introduced in 1959 to promote train travel by non-European tourists, the Eurailpass is good for unlimited first-class travel throughout the 16 participating countries: Austria, Belgium, Denmark, Finland, France, Germany, Greece, Ireland, Italy, Luxembourg, the Netherlands, Norway, Portugal, Spain, Sweden, and Switzerland.

The Eurailpass can also be used on certain ferry and intercity bus services. Eurailpasses are valid for 15 or 21 days, or for one, two, or three months. They are sold only outside Europe, and people living in Europe are not eligible to use them. Eurail Youthpasses are available to people under the age of 26 at a reduced rate.

Great Britain does not participate in the Eurailpass program. It offers a separate **BritRail pass** for rail travel in the British Isles. The BritRail Seapass, an extension of the BritRail pass, allows holders to sail from Britain to Ireland or to continental Europe, where they can connect with the Eurail system. Both the Eurailpass and the BritRail pass have been big successes. Every year, thousands of people from Canada and the United States take advantage of the reduced rates to see Europe by train.

European trains differ from North American trains in several ways. To begin with, most European trains are divided into first- and second-class sections. The differences between the two classes involve price and comfort—there is more room in first-class, and there are generally fewer passengers. Another distinctive feature of European trains is that many railway cars are divided into compartments with six or eight places. On long trips it is possible to reserve a seat in advance for either first- or second-class for a small surcharge. For overnight trips there are a number of options. Passengers can sleep in the regular seats, or they can reserve (by paying a supplement) a **couchette,** which is a bunk in a second-class compartment. **Wagons-lits** are coaches containing private sleeping compartments for one or two persons.

Overnight train travel offers a number of advantages. For example, John Kelly, a Canadian tourist in France, can enjoy dinner in Paris and then board an overnight train to the Riviera. He can sleep in a couchette, wake up in Nice in time for breakfast, and then spend the day at the beach or exploring the countryside. Kelly has saved money by travelling by train instead of plane and by spending the night in a couchette instead of a hotel. And instead of wasting the better part of a vacation day travelling, he can enjoy the sights at his destination.

Most long-distance trains in Europe travel considerably faster than their North American counterparts. The French **TGV** (train grande vitesse), the fastest, cruises at speeds of 260 kilometres per hour. The TGV makes the trip from Paris to Lyons, for example, a distance of 420 kilometres, in a mere 2 hours and forty minutes. The new French TGV Atlantique is even faster, travelling at an amazing 300 kilometres an hour.

The French TGV has inspired an American counterpart. The state of Texas is currently developing the first rapid rail in the United States—the Texas TGV. The new train will travel at speeds similar to those of the French TGV and is expected to make the trip between Dallas and Houston in 90 minutes.

Canadian studies for a high-speed transportation (HST) service in the central corridor began in 1990. HST service is defined as ground transportation, using either a rail system or magnetic levitation (Maglev), that travels at 250 kilometres an hour and above. The Montreal–Toronto route would be covered in less than three hours.

Other Foreign Railways Railways are an important form of passenger transportation in Latin America, Asia, Africa, and Australia. As in Europe, most of the railways are government-owned and -operated. Few, however, are as advanced as the European system.

The ex-Soviet Union has the largest rail system in the world and is one of the few industrialized regions that is still building railways. Russian railways carry about 50 percent of intercity passenger traffic and as much as 75 percent of the country's freight.

The government-owned Japanese National Railways operates most passenger services in Japan, but Japan also has some private railway companies. Experts consider the Japanese passenger train system to be the finest in the world. Service is so fast, comfortable, and reliable that domestic airlines have made little headway.

CHAPTER 5: The Surface Travel Industries

The Shinkansen bullet trains, introduced in 1964, cross that densely populated nation at speeds in excess of 200 kilometres an hour. Japanese engineers are currently working on a new type of high-speed train called the Maglev. In test runs, it has reached speeds of 480 kilometres an hour. The Maglev uses electromagnetism to glide over a single rail. If it becomes operational, the Maglev promises to revolutionize the rail industry in Japan and in the rest of the world.

Great Trains of the World Most people have heard of the fabled Orient Express. Called "the Train of Kings, the King of Trains," it is perhaps the most famous train in the world. In its day, it was the epitome of luxury, and it still stands for the ultimate romantic travel experience. Inaugurated in 1833, the Orient Express carried the rich and powerful from Paris to Istanbul over a spectacularly scenic route. The trip took four days, but in the elegant setting, and with food fit for royalty and service to match, the time passed quickly.

In 1977 the Orient Express—a shabby, forgotten shadow of the old train—made its last run. But five years later, the Venice–Simplon Orient Express was inaugurated, featuring many of the train's original 1920s coaches restored to their former splendour. Orient Express passengers today can start their journey in London or Paris. After crossing France, the train winds through the Swiss and Austrian Alps, cuts through the Brenner Pass to Italy, and arrives in Venice in time for cocktails and dinner.

Here are some other glamorous trains:

- The Trans-Siberian Special, which makes a leisurely 19-day journey from Moscow to Mongolia.
- The Blue Train, which provides a 24-hour luxury trip from Cape Town to Pretoria, South Africa.
- The Royal Scotsman, which meanders through the Scottish Highlands pulling renovated Victorian and Edwardian railway cars. The staff, of course, wear kilts.

Channels of Distribution

In the Golden Age of Rail, the railways did not have to worry too much about promoting and selling themselves. Nowadays, however, VIA Rail and Amtrak have to work hard to promote themselves against stiff competition from the airlines. With catchy slogans, such as "All Aboard Amtrak," "America's Getting into Training," and "Discover the Magic—Amtrak," Amtrak is trying to convince the public that trains are once again a good way to get around the country. VIA Rail has used the slogan "Taking the Train with VIA—It's the Ideal Way to Travel." A new theme, "Take a Look at the Train Today," reflects the modernization of VIA equipment. Both Amtrak and VIA Rail have also modernized their reservations and ticketing systems.

The Reservations System Reserving tickets on VIA Rail and Amtrak has never been easier. Both inherited antiquated reservations systems when they took over passenger services in the 1970s. Since then, their systems have been completely computerized. They now have nationwide reservations and information networks that passengers can telephone to book seats directly.

Amtrak has encouraged the sale of tickets through travel agencies, which now account for about 39 percent of its sales. Amtrak's reservations system is linked to airline CRSs and to ARC standard ticket stock, and almost all travel agencies are now equipped to sell and issue Amtrak tickets by computer.

VIA Rail reservations can be made either directly or through travel agents. Information about VIA trains is available nationwide through toll-free numbers, which can also be used to make reservations. VIA tickets can also be purchased at Amtrak stations in the United States. Eurail and BritRail passes can be reserved through travel agents using airline CRSs.

ILLUSTRATION 5-4
The domestic motorcoach tour is a vacation alternative.
SOURCE: Courtesy of Brewster Transportation and Tours

Types of Fares Both VIA Rail and Amtrak have tried to lure passengers back to trains by offering competitive fares. As a travel professional, you will need to know about their fare structures. The basic fare covers what they call coach service. Special service and accommodations—club cars, slumber coaches, roomettes, and bedrooms, and so on—are available on some routes at additional cost.

Amtrak also offers group and family discount fares, short-term promotional fares, and a U.S.A. rail pass that allows unlimited travel throughout the country for a fixed period of time. Amtrak has entered the tour market as well. Tour packages include hotel accommodations as well as train travel. Some packages also include a car rental, or bus tours and sightseeing. In addition, Amtrak offers **rail/sail packages,** which are vacation packages that include both train fare and a cruise ticket. Train travellers can set sail from several ports, including New York and Miami.

VIA Rail offers a variety of discount fares to encourage travel:

- A 40 percent savings for off-peak discount days.
- A 10 percent discount for seniors and students (which can be combined with the 40 percent discount days).
- Free travel for children under the age of 2.
- Half-fare for children between the ages of 2 and 11.
- Special rates for groups of 20 or more.
- The Canrailpass.

Add-on packages are also available.

Publications Detailed information on the fares, schedules, and services of railways in Canada, the United States, and the rest of the world can be found in a number of publications. For information about Canadian and American trains, the *Official Railway Guide* (ORG) is invaluable. This guide, which appears eight times a year, contains information on both Amtrak and the commuter rail services operated by transit authorities in major cities of the United States. In addition, the guide includes schedules for VIA Rail and a selection of important international routes.

The *Rail Traveler's City Planner* is a useful guide for the traveller in the United States, as it contains information about each Amtrak station and about the connecting transportation and car rental services available.

A number of publications provide information about international rail services. The *Thomas Cook Continental Timetable* and *Thomas Cook Overseas Timetable* both contain exhaustive listings of routes and schedules. They also offer country maps, with train routes, as well as information about visa requirements, time zones, and so on. *The Eurail Guide: How to Travel Europe and All the World by Train* includes a description of recommended excursions from cities around the world. Fodor's *Railways of the World* is a comprehensive tourist guide to travel by train.

CHECK YOUR PRODUCT KNOWLEDGE

1. What effect has increased car ownership had on the North American railway industry?
2. How did the federal governments act to save rail passenger service in Canada and the United States in the 1970s?
3. What role does the Interstate Commerce Commission play in the railway industry in the United States? What does the National Transportation Agency do in Canada?
4. Why has the rail passenger industry been able to survive in Europe?
5. Describe how VIA Rail and Amtrak are trying to encourage more people to ride trains.

THE MOTORCOACH INDUSTRY

The motorcoach, more commonly known as the bus, has played a major role in the surface travel industry throughout the world. In both Canada and the United States, the motorcoach is the most widespread and the least expensive form of public transportation. Covering a vast network of intercity and urban routes, motorcoaches carry more people and serve more communities than do either trains or planes.

Travellers use motorcoach services for a variety of reasons, depending on their MNEs. A business traveller staying at an airport hotel in Toronto might take a chartered motorcoach to a trade show at the Copps Coliseum in Hamilton. In this way she could avoid the bother of riding the train and then switching to a bus or taxi. A college student on summer vacation who wants to see something of Canada without spending too much money might take a cross-country motorcoach tour. An elderly man who doesn't like to fly or drive a car could travel by bus to a small town in Alberta for a family reunion.

Because buses travel over many highways and secondary roads in this country, the bus industry is well-equipped to serve the needs of travellers heading for remote areas or small towns. It is also the most fuel-efficient form of intercity travel.

The Origin of Motorcoaches

The motorcoach, which first appeared in the 1890s, is really a descendant of the horse-drawn stagecoach. Stagecoaches began passenger service in Europe in the 17th century (ser-

ILLUSTRATION 5-5
The Montreal subway system is quiet, clean, and efficient.
SOURCE Phototeque Steum

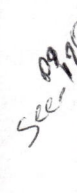

CHAPTER 5: The Surface Travel Industries

vice between London and Edinburgh started in 1670) and in Canada and the United States in the 18th century. The name *stagecoach* came from the fact that the coaches travelled in stages, stopping at scheduled places along the route to change horses.

Horse-drawn coaches were used for intercity travel in Europe and North America until the 1890s, when the gasoline engine was developed. The first gasoline-powered buses were built in Germany. By the early 1900s, urban bus services had started in London and New York. Self-propelled bus service in Canada began in 1892 in Hamilton, Ontario. Motorcoaches were also used for intercity travel. Bus transportation through the countryside developed as a replacement for horse transportation firms. Companies such as Brewster Transport (Alberta and British Columbia) and Penetang–Midland (Ontario) operated both types of services in the early 20th century. The first intercity service in the United States was started in Oregon.

The intercity network expanded rapidly with improvements in road conditions and in bus design. Transcontinental bus service began in the United States in 1928, and by the 1930s, buses were a common sight on highways around the country. The earliest motorcoaches carried about 20 passengers on hard bench seats. The buses ran on solid tires and often had no springs. After 1920, a number of refinements were made. These included more comfortable seats, air-filled tires for a smoother ride, improved brakes, engines, and transmissions, and a lower floor that made it easier for passengers to get on and off the bus.

Such improvements encouraged more people to ride buses. By the 1930s the bus industry was challenging the railways' monopoly of public passenger transportation in the United States. This did not happen in Canada until the 1950s, because of the slower development of the road system.

The Motorcoach Industry Today

The motorcoach is still the most accessible form of transportation in Canada and the United States. Intercity buses carry more passengers and serve far more communities than do airplanes and trains combined. For thousands of communities, buses provide the only form of public transportation. In Canada, buses serve about 3000 communities, while rail and air each serve about 500.

The pattern of bus use has changed dramatically in recent decades, however. Since the end of World War II, there have been two major trends in the motorcoach industry: regularly scheduled passenger services have declined, and the bus charter and tour business has expanded.

Scheduled Services Canada has 35 intercity bus companies, according to the Royal Commission on National Passenger Transportation. The industry has been dominated traditionally by the "Big 10" carriers of scheduled service: Acadian Lines, Canada Coach, Gray Coach, Grey Goose, Greyhound Lines of Canada, Pacific Coach Lines, SMT Eastern, Saskatchewan Transportation, Terra Transport (Canadian National in Newfoundland), and Voyageur. Ridership declined from 34 million passengers in 1975 to 15.9 million in 1991.

In the United States, scheduled intercity bus travel has declined every year since 1945. The number of operating intercity bus companies in the United States had plummeted to around 1000 by the early 1970s. The gas crisis of 1973–74 provided a temporary reprieve for the industry, when people rediscovered the bus as the economical alternative to their cars. But when gas prices fell, many returned to private transportation. In 1977, 325 million passengers rode the intercity buses, the lowest number since 1939. In just five years, scheduled route service had declined 54 percent. As with rail travel, the boom in automobile ownership in the postwar years contributed to this decrease. So did increasing competition from the airline industry, especially on long-distance routes.

Charters and Tours The one bright spot for the motorcoach industry in recent years has been the dramatic growth of the charter and tour business. Although motorcoach tours have been in operation since 1926, they had little impact on the travel market before World War II. In 1939, charters accounted for only 3.4 percent of all bus revenues.

In recent years, many new bus companies have been formed (there were about 2800 in the United States in 1990), and the vast majority of these have entered the charter and tour field. This increase is due mostly to deregulation (discussed in the following section) and to a change in the vacation patterns of the public. Until the first gas crisis, many Canadians and Americans scorned the idea of taking a vacation by bus. They preferred to travel abroad on package tours. But in 1974, travel to Europe and other overseas destinations became too expensive for many Canadians and Americans, and the domestic bus tour emerged as a vacation

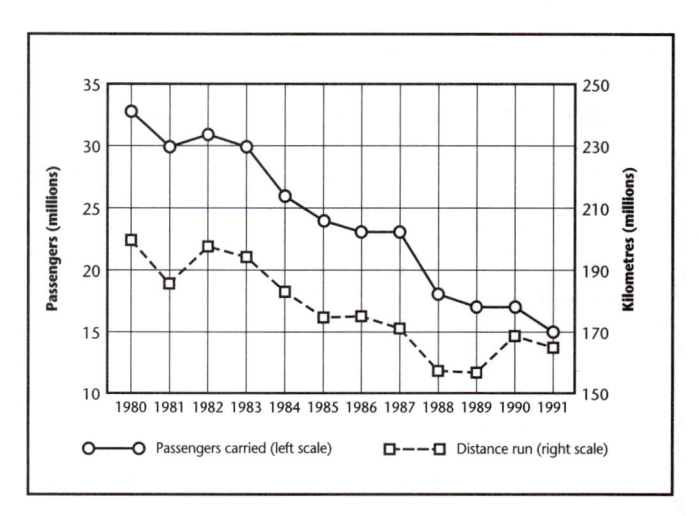

FIGURE 5-2
Intercity Passenger Bus Establishments
SOURCE: Statistics Canada, Passenger Bus and Urban Transit Statistics, Catalogue No. 53–003, May 1994, Figure 5

PROFILE

Henry Ford

Henry Ford, the founder of one of the world's largest automobile companies, was born in 1863 on a farm near Dearborn, Michigan. The oldest of six children, he showed an early interest in machinery, claiming later that the sight of a steam-powered wagon cemented his destiny at the age of 13.

When he was 15, Ford dropped out of school and became a machinist's apprentice in Detroit. Ford's father had wanted him to run the family farm, but his son had no intention of becoming a farmer. After completing his apprenticeship, Ford began working as an engineer for the Edison Illuminating Company in Detroit. He spent his spare time tinkering, trying to build an automobile with an internal combustion engine. He succeeded in 1896.

Ford left the Edison company to form the Detroit Automobile Company. This was the first auto company to be established in the city whose name would become synonymous with auto manufacturing. Unfortunately, Ford's company folded in a little over a year. After that, Ford achieved some renown as a manufacturer of racing cars.

In those days, automobiles were playthings of the wealthy. Ford dreamed of changing that. He wanted to produce a low-priced car that most people in the United States could afford. With that aim in mind, he founded the Ford Motor Company in 1903. He began production with the Model A, followed by Models B through S, and received a favourable response from the public.

In 1908 the Model T appeared. Dubbed "the Tin Lizzie," it was durable and easy to operate. What's more, it was economically priced, at $825. At the time, it came in only one colour—black. (Other colours came later.) The Model T's popularity convinced Ford to limit his production to that one model. This allowed him to standardize production and make one of his most far-reaching contributions to modern industry—the moving assembly line. Instead of having employees go to their work, Ford had their work come to them on a conveyor belt.

By 1914, Ford was producing over 250 000 cars each year and the price of the Model T was down to $440. (It was to go even lower during the Depression.) Ford surprised the auto industry by raising his workers' wages to $5 a day, almost double the average industry wage. However, this was partly to increase his workers' spending power so that they would buy more cars—Model Ts, of course.

Ford became the sole owner of the Ford Motor Company in 1919. In the early 1920s the Model T was unchallenged by rivals, commanding an impressive 57 percent of the automobile market. Later in the decade, however, advances by Ford's competitors caused the Model T to become outmoded. Bowing to pressure, he brought out the Model A in 1927—with huge success. The Depression, however, caused the automobile market to collapse in the 1930s.

Ford's final years were ones of frustration. Never an easy man to work with, he ran the company in an increasingly dictatorial manner. He distrusted his son Edsel's handling of the company and undermined his authority. He also fought bitterly against the unionization of his plants. Although a pacifist when World War II began, he later threw his company's energies into the production of war materials such as aircraft engines. As the company's health improved, however, Ford's declined. He died in 1947 at the age of 83.

Ford's contributions were not so much to the development of the automobile as to its methods of production and promotion. Ford's assembly line brought the purchase of an automobile within the reach of middle-class Americans and opened up isolated rural areas that were inaccessible by train. More cars created a demand for more and better roads, and this led to the excellent highway system we enjoy today. And more travel contributed to the growth of the domestic travel industry. Through his innovations, Henry Ford was instrumental in the creation of a new system of transportation that changed the lives of millions.

CHAPTER 5: The Surface Travel Industries

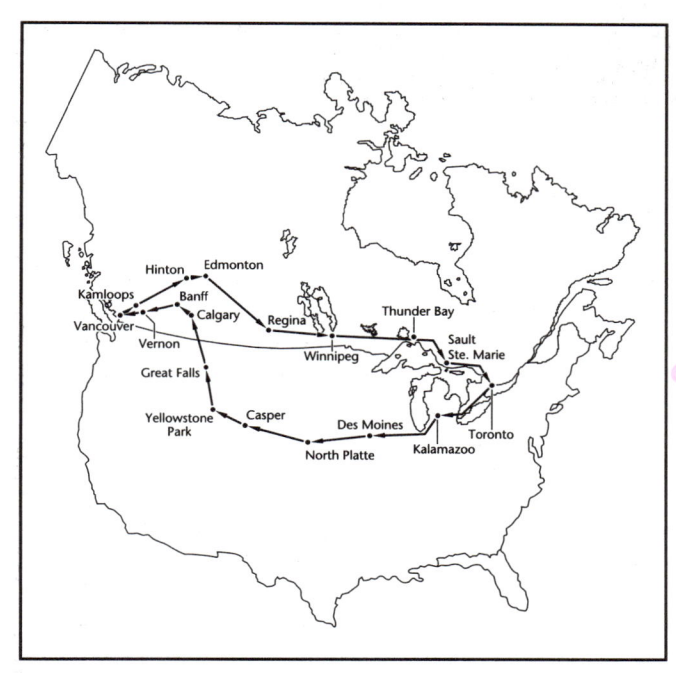

Day 1. Depart from Toronto to Kalamazoo, Michigan
Day 4. The Oregon Trail and Boot Hill, Wyoming
Day 5. Yellowstone Park, Wyoming
Day 7. Calgary, Alberta
Day 9. Banff, Alberta
Day 12. Okanagan Valley and Vancouver, B.C.
Day 13. Ferry ride across the Strait of Georgia to Victoria, B.C.
Day 16. Jaspar National Park, Alberta
Day 17. Edmonton, Alberta
Day 20. RCMP Historical Museum, Regina, Saskatchewan
Day 21. Kenora Lake region and Lake Superior

FIGURE 5-3
A Typical Trentway Wagar Motorcoach Tour
Western Canada & USA   23 Days
SOURCE: Courtesy of Trentway Tours Inc.

alternative. Even when foreign vacations again became affordable, bus charters and tours continued to attract customers. In 1974 the motorcoach industry carried 131 million chartered passengers; fifteen years later, the figure had risen to 300 million.

Regulation The roadways have always been important in Canada. The Highways Act of 1793, passed by the first Parliament of Upper Canada, compelled all men to work on the roads from 3 to 12 days a year, using their own tools.

Before 1954 the federal government left the regulation of the bus industry to the provinces. A Supreme Court of Canada decision in that year gave the federal government responsibility for road transportation companies conducting business outside their home province. Later the same year, Parliament passed the Motor Vehicle Transport Act, which empowered the provinces to exercise federal responsibilities and charged them to treat carriers from outside the province as they did local ones. A revised Motor Vehicle Transport Act was passed by the federal government in 1987.

In the provinces, the bus industry is governed by motor vehicle acts. Under these acts, the provinces exercise full authority over all intercity bus services except in Newfoundland, for the Roadcruiser bus service. The acts control the following:

- market entry and exit
- fare and route regulations
- licensing of drivers
- registration of buses
- the safety of buses

Deregulation in the United States Government regulation of the bus industry in the United States was introduced with the passage of the Motor Carrier Act of 1935, which gave the ICC control over all motor carriers. At first, the industry was tightly controlled: the ICC set motorcoach fares and told companies which routes they were required to operate. This practice often meant that companies had to continue unprofitable routes. New companies could not break into the intercity market unless they could show a public need for the services they proposed.

Regulation was relaxed somewhat in later years, and then was eliminated completely with the passage of the Bus Regulatory Reform Act. When President Ronald Reagan signed the act into law in September 1982, with little opposition and no fanfare, he opened up the industry to competition and to the possibility of expansion. Unlike the Airline Deregulation Act, no one hailed the Bus Regulatory Reform Act as a milestone, but it changed the motorcoach industry dramatically.

Since deregulation, bus companies have had much greater freedom. They can set their own fares and decide which routes they want to operate. These changes have

ILLUSTRATION 5-6
The double-decker bus is a familiar sight on London streets and is a great favourite among tourists.

resulted in a general reduction in bus fares. Deregulation has also made it easier for new companies to enter the bus market and for existing companies to extend their operating authority. Hundreds of new charter and tour companies have come into existence since 1982. Many of these new tour operators cannot afford to buy a whole fleet of buses, which can cost more than $150 000 each. Instead, they lease buses for about $500 a day. Leasing means that a new company does not necessarily need a huge initial capital outlay to go into business.

The inevitable result of the rise in the number of companies has been increased competition. Many of the new companies have adopted aggressive marketing and advertising programs to sell their charters and tours. Some of the older companies have been unable to adjust to the new conditions of the highly competitive market and have gone out of business. There is also the problem of insurance, the skyrocketing cost of which has threatened the future of many bus companies, both old and new. Many smaller companies have been forced out of business by high insurance premiums.

Greyhound and Trailways The two giants in the scheduled intercity bus travel industry merged to become Greyhound and Trailways Lines. The company operates 3900 buses and serves all 48 contiguous states and Canada.

In addition to Greyhound and Trailways, there are thousands of smaller companies that provide local scheduled intercity service, or charter and tour service, or both. Greyhound and Trailways has also been offering charters in recent years in an attempt to survive in the competitive industry.

The future of Greyhound and Trailways is uncertain. In 1990 the company filed for bankruptcy in an effort to prevent its creditors from seizing some of its buses. The bankruptcy was due in large part to losses the company suffered from a drivers' strike that lasted for three months.

Sightseeing Companies Gray Line, the world's largest sightseeing company, offers about 1500 excursions daily. Gray Line is an association of about 200 independently owned and operated companies, with offices throughout the United States and Canada and in major cities overseas.

American Sightseeing International is the number-two sightseeing company, with representation in about 50 cities in the United States and in about 50 cities in other countries.

Both companies have grown impressively in the past 35 years. Together, they account for a large percentage of the sightseeing market. In addition to offering long-distance and local sightseeing tours, both have expanded their services to include charters, limousine service, and transfer transportation.

Information about the services of the two companies can be found in the *Gray Line Sales and Tour Guide*, the *American Sightseeing International World Tariff*, and *Master Key*, published by the World Association of Travel Agents (WATA).

Bus Services in Other Countries Intercity services in most foreign countries are provided by government-owned bus lines as well as by independent companies. Government-run buses often operate in conjunction with the national railways.

Motorcoach as Product

The motorcoach industry in Canada and the United States earns billions of dollars each year carrying travellers to out-of-the-way places and over short distances. For many people, bus service is the only available form of public transportation. For some, it is indispensable.

In recent years the motorcoach industry has focused on the development of tour programs.

Types of Tours To attract more passengers, many bus companies offer package tours and chartered motorcoach services. Several types of tours are available:

- **Charter tours.** A charter tour is a tour taken by a club, organization, school party, or other preformed group. Any group can charter, or hire, a bus from a charter operator for a day trip to a sports event, museum, shopping centre, or casino, among other places. Holiday packages lasting a week or more are also available. These usually include accommodations, meals, and sightseeing trips in addition to the bus ride. A tour escort does not accompany the group on a charter trip.
- **Escorted tours.** These are scheduled group tours that travel from major cities in the United States and Canada to tourist destinations throughout North America. Popular destinations include national parks, the Rocky Mountains, New England, the Gaspé Peninsula, and the California and Nova Scotia coastlines. Many companies also offer escorted tours in Europe. Escorted tours, which can last anywhere from five days to four weeks, include quality hotel accommodations and most meals. A trained tour escort travels with the group for the entire trip.
- **Independent package tours.** These tours visit several cities or places of interest on regular scheduled buses. Hotel accommodations and sightseeing are included.
- **City package tours.** These are similar to independent package tours, but visit only one city.
- **Intermodal tours.** A recent trend in the industry has been the development of motorcoach tours that tie in with other forms of transportation. The idea for intermodal tours began in 1974 with a ticketing agreement between Greyhound and Amtrak to connect nine of Greyhound's routes with Amtrak services. Trailways and TWA later introduced air–motorcoach tours within the United States and abroad. Cruise–motorcoach tours have also become popular. Such a tour might feature a one-week motorcoach tour from New York to Florida, and then a one-week Caribbean cruise. A fly–motor-

CHAPTER 5: The Surface Travel Industries

coach tour in Canada might combine air travel from Toronto to Calgary with a one-week tour by bus of national parks that ends in Vancouver.

Buses as Transfer Transportation The term *transfer* refers to any change in transportation in the course of a journey. Buses are used extensively to provide transfers for passengers between airports and hotels or city centres. There are many companies offering this service in Canada and the United States, either as independent operators or as divisions of larger transportation companies. Many companies also provide van service to small towns and rural areas. In addition, hotels and motels may offer their own complimentary bus service to and from the airport.

The Motorcoach Versus Other Modes of Travel The major attraction of the motorcoach has long been its low cost in comparison with other forms of public transportation. However, while the bus is still generally cheaper than the train, airlines have reduced their fares sufficiently in recent years to compete with bus companies, especially on trips of more than 500 miles. Rather than continue to compete for passengers with the airlines, several bus companies have decided to join them by offering intermodal tickets. An airline, for example, might offer a ticket that combines air passage to a major airport with bus service for passengers travelling from the airport to a more remote destination.

Many people are reluctant to travel any significant distance by bus because they believe that buses are uncomfortable. Modern long-distance buses, however, are much more luxurious than earlier models. Air conditioning and restroom facilities are standard features. Many buses now have wider seats, soundproofing, improved lighting, and large picture windows for sightseeing. Some even offer video screens on seatbacks for viewing television and movies.

In an attempt to lure travellers away from airplanes, many bus companies have stepped up their promotion efforts. Some bus lines offer passes that enable a passenger to tour the country at a discount price. Many of these tours are only promoted overseas to attract inbound tourism, while others have been advertised in Canada and the United States to attract domestic tourism.

Channels of Distribution

Bus tickets can be obtained through several channels of distribution. Many short-distance passengers buy their tickets at the bus station just before boarding or from the bus driver. However, travellers who plan to take a long trip or who are going on a tour offered by the bus line can purchase their tickets in advance from the bus company. Many bus companies subscribe to a computer reservations system and can accept reservations and issue tickets before the departure date. Travellers can also purchase tickets for bus trips, escorted tours, charter tours, package tours, and intermodal tours from travel agents. Tours can be booked through a tour broker as well.

Motorcoach tour information can be found in tour brochures, tariffs, guides, and the like. Detailed information on fares, schedules, and other aspects of motorcoach tours is given in *Russell's Official National Motor Coach Guide* and in *Russell's Official Canada Bus Guide*.

Associations

In Canada the Canadian Bus Association represents the motorcoach industry. In the United States there is the American Bus Association (ABA), a national organization of bus-operating companies, to represent the intercity bus industry. The United Bus Owners of America (UBOA) is the largest trade association serving intercity bus owners. It offers programs in safety, credit, insurance, lobbying, and computer services.

Because bus companies and tour operators often work together on tours and charters, the National Tour Association (NTA) and UBOA agreed, in 1984, to exchange certain membership benefits.

CHECK YOUR PRODUCT KNOWLEDGE

1. How have the patterns of bus use changed in recent decades?
2. In what way is the intercity bus a more essential form of transportation than either the train or the airplane?
3. What have been the main results of deregulation of the bus industry?
4. What are the five main types of tours offered by bus companies?

THE CAR RENTAL INDUSTRY

A business traveller flies from Edmonton to Toronto for a four-day sales trip. He rents a car to make numerous sales calls at companies in the area. A family flies from Vancouver to Halifax for a two-week vacation. They rent a car and drive up the coast to Cape Breton, stopping to admire the scenery and visit the tourist attractions along the way. A retired couple flies from Victoria to Montreal to see their grandchildren, who live just outside the city. They rent a car to explore the Montreal area and to visit the Eastern Townships.

These examples illustrate how the car rental industry meets the MNEs of all types of travellers. The car rental industry is different from other transportation industries in that it allows travellers complete control over their schedules and itineraries. Travellers are free to venture to a remote destination that can't be reached by public transportation, to find a quaint, out-of-the-way country inn, or to make a spontaneous change in travel plans.

A Brief History

The car rental industry is almost as old as the automobile itself. It began back in 1916, when the Saunders brothers of Omaha, Nebraska, borrowed a car when their own broke down. The brothers reasoned that there must be others who sometimes needed a car for a limited period of time, so they bought another car and went into the rental business. They charged 10 cents a mile with a three-mile minimum. Business grew; they bought more cars; and by the time they had merged with another firm in 1925, the company had offices in 21 states. Hertz—today's largest car rental firm—started in 1918. Avis began in 1946, and National in 1947. Tilden, a major Canadian firm, began in Montreal in 1924.

The car rental industry really began to prosper when the first commercial jet airliners came into service in 1958. As the volume of air travel increased, more and more people—especially businesspeople—needed a rental car when they arrived at their airport destination. A car provides business travellers with the mobility they need to conduct business, and ensures that they don't have to rely on taxis and other forms of public transportation.

The idea of operating car rental desks at airports was pioneered by Warren E. Avis, the founder of Avis. Since the late 1940s, the car rental business has been closely connected with the airline industry. By the late 1950s, rental counters could be found at all the major airports.

The Car Rental Industry Today

The car rental industry has expanded impressively, in terms of both revenue and the number of rental cars on the road. In 1989, Hertz and Avis were still dominant in the United States, with National number three and Budget number four. Currently, Tilden has about 365 locations in Canada, Avis about 185, Hertz about 200, and Budget about 388. There are over 5000 companies operating in Canada and the United States today. This number is growing every year. Aggressive companies, such as Tilden in Canada and Dollar, Alamo, and Thrifty in the United States, have won a greater share of the market in recent years.

The economics of the car rental industry are quite different from those of other sectors of the transportation industry. Small companies can enter the market with relative ease. No large initial capital investment is needed. Individuals with good credit can obtain financing for the cars from banks, and can lease rental counter space and garage facilities. Most companies starting out in the car rental business become part of a chain. They give a percentage of their income to the chain in exchange for the benefits of the chain's name and backup services. Rental firms can respond to the demands of the market by selling cars when business is slack and buying more when it picks up.

The car rental industry is still heavily oriented toward the business traveller, but the leisure market is expanding rapidly, from 10 percent of rentals in 1971 to about 35 percent in 1989. The growing popularity of **fly/drive packages,** which are vacation packages that include both airfare and a rental car, has been a major factor in this growth. The popularity of these packages has been stimulated by lower airfares and cut-rate rental prices. **Train/drive packages,** which are similar to fly/drive packages but include train fare instead of airfare, are also now available. It is predicted that the leisure market will continue to be the major growth area in the car rental industry.

Car Rental Companies

The car rental industry has always been highly competitive. With the arrival of many new companies during the 1980s, this competition has intensified. The larger companies have been forced to reduce prices and offer other promotional inducements in an attempt to hold their share of the market.

Types of Companies Car rental companies have two main types of operations: corporate and licensee. Most of the larger firms, including Hertz, Avis, and National, have mostly corporate operations. They purchase the cars and rent them to consumers. After the cars have been driven 30 000 to 40 000 kilometres, these companies resell them at used-car prices, either directly to consumers or to used-car dealers. However, under the more recent "buy back" programs, the used cars revert to the original manufacturer instead of being resold. Licensees are usually part of a chain. They often lease the cars from larger companies rather than purchase and resell them.

Location The large car-rental firms have both in-town and suburban locations, but most business is still conducted at airports. In the late 1980s in the United States, Hertz accounted for about 32 percent of airport business, Avis for 28 percent, National for 17.5 percent, and Budget for 17.5 percent. A car rental company's location affects its rental rates and the convenience with which renters can pick up their cars.

Car rental companies with counters at airports must figure into their rates the often steep cost of leasing airport space. This means that their rental rates are usually higher than those of companies without airport locations. The consumer, however, benefits from the convenience of being able to step off the plane and right up to the rental counter. Most of the larger car rental companies, including Hertz, Avis, and National, have rental locations or facilities at almost all major airports.

CHAPTER 5: The Surface Travel Industries

In the past, many of the smaller car rental companies kept their costs down by not having airport counters and by keeping their cars at off-airport locations. Most of these companies provided free transportation from the airport to their location. Clients were compensated for the slight inconvenience by the lower rental rates that these companies charged. This is beginning to change, however, because many airports now charge the off-airport companies for the right to enter the airport to pick up customers.

Advertising Advertising has had a remarkable effect on the car rental market. Back in the 1960s, Avis launched its "We Try Harder" campaign in an attempt to challenge Hertz's domination of the industry. Hertz responded with its "We're #1" slogan, and now most companies spend heavily on national advertising. A few years ago, Hertz used golf star Arnold Palmer in its "Superstar in Rental Car" campaign. Thrifty has used Wayne Gretzky in its advertising.

Clubs Many car rental companies offer free club memberships to car renters in an attempt to promote customer loyalty. These clubs, such as the Hertz #1 Club, Wizard of Avis, and National's Privilege Club, are also computerized information systems that help car rental companies keep track of the names and preferences of frequent renters. Club members enjoy faster, more efficient service. Some clubs provide express service, which allows members to avoid the rental counter and go directly to the courtesy bus for the short trip to their car.

The Rental Process

As a travel professional, you should know all aspects of the car rental process so that you can better assist travellers. Travellers should be aware that there are certain qualifications they must meet before renting a car. They should also know about the various rental rates, the makes and models of cars available, and the extra charges that they may incur.

Qualifications Car rental is quite different from most other transportation services. Planes, trains, and buses are operated by trained employees of transportation companies. Rental cars, however, are operated directly by travellers. The moment the car rental company hands over the car keys, it surrenders control of the vehicle. It is not surprising, then, that car rental companies place strict requirements on those who rent their cars. Usually, to qualify to rent a car, a client must meet these criteria:

- *Have a valid driver's licence.* Some foreign countries require an international driver's licence, which can be obtained from an automobile club.
- *Be of a certain age.* In Canada the minimum age depends on the car rental firm and its insurance policy; it is usually at least 21 and may be as high as 25. In some countries there is a minimum and maximum age; the minimum is usually 25, and the maximum may be 65.
- *Have a major credit card.* A traveller who does not have a credit card must be cash qualified; in other words, he or she must put down a cash deposit equal to the expected rental amount plus a specified percentage.
- *Be personally responsible.* A traveller who does not have a major credit card must be able to offer an address and name of employer.

Rates Several years ago, companies charged a flat-rate daily fee with an additional charge for the number of kilometres driven. As competition between companies increased, many firms began to offer **unlimited kilometres** plans that allowed clients to travel as far as they wanted for a flat fee within the allotted rental period. Not long ago, with rental rates declining, the four major companies started placing kilometre caps on car rentals in an effort to cover their costs. With a **kilometre cap**, clients are allowed a certain number of free kilometres each day and then charged from 20 to 30 cents extra for each additional kilometre driven. Most of the smaller companies continued to offer unlimited kilometre plans so that they could compete with the larger firms. In 1989, the leading companies returned to offering unlimited kilometre plans in an effort to grab a larger portion of the leisure market.

Rates vary according to the size of the car and do not include gasoline, taxes, or charges for extra services. Many companies offer the following types of rates:

- *Regular rate.* A standard charge for the day, usually with an added amount for kilometres driven.
- *Special rate.* A discount rate for weekends or holidays. A special rate can also include an unlimited kilometre plan.
- *Corporate rate.* A discount rate for employees of companies with a high rental volume.

Makes and Models Thirty-five years ago, each rental company concentrated on cars from just one North American manufacturer, such as General Motors or Ford. Usually, only three or four models were offered to customers. Today the choice is much greater. Although some car rental firms still supply cars from only one manufacturer, many different models are available, as are vans, trucks, and even chauffeur-driven limousines. Other car rental companies offer both foreign and domestic models. Travellers with special requirements, such as physically challenged drivers who need cars with hand controls or other special equipment, and those who need wagons or recreational vehicles, can be accommodated by many rental car firms.

Many rental firms provide charts showing which cars are available within each class. The following are the four basic classes of rental cars and examples of each:

- *Subcompact.* A small car. Examples: Ford Escort, Dodge Shadow, Nissan Sentra.

- *Compact.* An average-size car. Examples: Chevrolet Cavalier, Ford Tempo, Toyota Corolla.
- *Standard.* A full-size car. Examples: Ford Thunderbird, Chrysler Le Baron, Subaru Legacy.
- *Deluxe.* A large luxury car that usually comes equipped with many extras. Examples: Lincoln Town Car, Cadillac Sedan de Ville, Buick Century.

If a customer has a reservation but no car in the requested class is available, most companies will provide an upgrade to the next higher class at no extra charge.

Charges Most car rental companies charge fees not included in their regular rates for any extra services that they provide, including the following:

- *Drop-off.* It is not always convenient for a renter to drop off a car at the place where it was rented. Many companies allow clients to drop off their cars at any location owned by the same company. However, there is usually an additional **drop-off charge** for this service.
- *Gas.* Car rental firms usually charge clients for gasoline when cars are returned with less than a full tank. The prices are much higher than those charged at most gas stations, so clients usually save money by filling the tank before returning the car.
- *Insurance.* Clients are liable for a specified initial amount of damage to the car. Car rental firms offer clients a **loss/damage waiver (LDW)** for a fee of about $13 per day. An LDW is not insurance, but it relieves clients of their liability for this initial amount of damage. It also provides coverage for loss of the use of the rental car should an accident occur. For an additional fee, car rental firms also offer **personal accident insurance (PAI)**, which provides coverage in case of bodily injury to the client. The charges for LDW and PAI are a means by which car rental firms create additional revenue. LDWs are quite controversial, however, and some jurisdictions no longer allow car rental companies to sell them.
- *Lost keys.* A fee is charged if the client loses the keys to the rental car.

North American Companies Abroad

The 1950s witnessed a period of rapid growth in the car rental industry throughout the world. American companies began to enter the overseas market in the 1960s and are now represented almost everywhere, even in China and the former Soviet Union. Many countries also have their own car rental companies.

Hertz, with offices in over 120 countries, dominates the world market. Many other large North American companies also have offices abroad. Even so, the American car rental market is still larger than that of the rest of the world combined.

Tilden of Canada is affiliated with National in the United States and Europcar in Europe.

Foreign Companies In addition to the American companies operating abroad, there are foreign car rental firms that serve travellers overseas. These car rental companies include Europcar, Auto Europe, and Europa Rent-a-Car. Some of these firms offer both American and foreign-made cars.

Driving Abroad Travellers who rent cars abroad should be aware of the different driving conditions and practices in some countries. For instance, in Great Britain, the Bahamas, and a few other countries, driving on the left side of the road is standard. The steering wheel is on the right side of the car, and shifting must be done with the left hand instead of the right. In most countries abroad, cars tend to be smaller than those in Canada and the United States. In Europe, most rental cars have manual transmissions. Travellers who want a car with an automatic transmission must request it specifically and usually pay more.

Speed limits abroad are usually posted in kilometres, which is convenient for Canadians, although Americans may need a conversion chart or a knowledge of the metric system. Canadians travelling in the United States will have to become used to (or remember) the imperial system, which uses miles. Speed limits vary from country to country but tend to be higher in foreign countries than in Canada and the United States. For example, the speed limit on many roads in France is 110 kilometres an hour. The expressways (Autobahns) in Germany have no real speed limit, and some cars race along at speeds of 120 to 160 kilometres an hour.

Channels of Distribution

Several channels of distribution are used in the car rental industry. These include travel agencies, business travel departments (BTDs), and car rental central reservations offices. Recently, travel agents have begun to play an increasing role in the car rental business. Rentals through travel agents were negligible 25 years ago; now they account for about 50 percent of the car rental business. Reservations for employees of large companies are often made through BTDs; these clients usually receive the car rental firm's corporate rate.

Because most travel agents depend on airline CRSs for current information on car rental availability, smaller car rental companies that don't appear on the computer screen may suffer by not being as accessible. Travel agents often make car rental reservations on the CRS as part of a package that includes an airline ticket and a hotel room. Reservations can also be made by calling the toll-free number of the car rental company's central reservations office. Travel agents earn commissions from car rental firms, just as they do from other travel and tourism suppliers.

CHAPTER 5: The Surface Travel Industries

> **CHECK YOUR PRODUCT KNOWLEDGE**
>
> 1. What has been the major factor in the success and growth of the car rental industry?
> 2. How have Hertz and Avis responded to competition from smaller, highly aggressive car rental companies?
> 3. How does the location of a car rental firm affect the rate charged for the rental car?
> 4. What qualifications are required of a person who wants to rent a car?

MASS TRANSIT SYSTEMS

The term **public transportation** refers to any organized passenger service available to the general public within a small geographic area. Commuter buses, trains, and subways are the most important components of public transportation systems. They carry millions of people back and forth to work each day, either within a city or between a city and its suburbs. Public transportation systems are an essential service for people living in urban areas. Most systems are heavily subsidized by local, provincial or state, and federal governments in some combination. The term **mass transit** refers more specifically to the movement of people in large metropolitan areas. The most important forms of mass transit are urban buses, subways, and taxis.

As a travel professional, you may be called on to provide information on mass transit in Canada, the United States, and foreign cities. You may be asked the best way to get from the Brussels airport to the central railway station in downtown Brussels, or how to travel on the Metro in Montreal, or how to reserve a limousine in Dallas.

In this section you will learn about the history of urban mass transit, about getting around in cities in Canada and the United States, and about the transportation systems in some key cities of the world.

The Development of Mass Transit

In 1662 the French philosopher and mathematician Blaise Pascal was instrumental in starting a horse-drawn coach service in Paris. This may or may not have been the first urban transportation system in the world. In any case, it seems to have suffered a fate shared by many such systems. When the fares were raised (in this case from no charge to a charge), ridership dropped sharply, and eventually the service was discontinued.

Urban mass transit really got started in New York, London, and Paris in the early part of the 19th century. Horse-drawn coaches, known as omnibuses, picked up and discharged passengers along set routes. In 1836 the first subway system was opened in London. Built to ease the congestion caused by horse-drawn surface traffic, the six-kilometre underground line was an instant success. New York City built its first subway line in 1870, but it lost money and was soon abandoned. In 1897, Boston opened its first subway line; the present New York subway system was inaugurated in 1904. The first subway in Canada opened in Toronto in 1954. The first part of the Metro system in Montreal began service in 1966, just in time for Expo 67. Montreal has one of the most modern subway systems in the world. The trains run on rubber tires, which provide a quiet, comfortable ride.

In the late 19th century, electric streetcars, or **trolleys**, came into their own. They ran on tracks, which were often laid down the middle of the street, and were powered by overhead wires. Trolleys were introduced in many cities in Canada, the United States, and abroad. Canada was a leader in the introduction of streetcar systems because of its role in the development of electric power. The first system was installed in St. Catharines, Ontario, in 1887. Others followed quickly in Vancouver (1890) and Winnipeg (1891). By World War II, 48 Canadian cities and towns had streetcar systems.

The development of the gasoline engine brought in the urban bus. The early buses were elongated automobiles that seated 12 to 20 people. Regular urban bus service began in London in 1904 and in New York City a year later.

Urban Buses and Trolleys

Today, buses are the primary form of urban mass transit. An **urban bus** is one that operates over short distances within a city. Of the cities in Canada and the United States with some form of public transportation, the majority have bus service only.

In the 1970s, federal programs for planning, financing, and operating public transportation gave urban bus service a new lease on life. Recognizing that buses are a much more energy-efficient form of transportation than cars, several cities have reserved special traffic lanes for buses in downtown areas. The point of this is to speed up bus service, and thereby encourage car owners to leave their cars at home.

In many metropolitan areas, privately operated buses or vans or extended cars, often called **airport limousines,** provide passenger service between the airport and the city centre. Airport limousine service usually operates at fixed intervals and is regulated by the airport. In many cities, large hotels have their own cars or vans to take guests to and from the airport. Some local city buses also provide this service.

A growing number of cities are bringing back trolleys, formally known today as **light-rail transit** (LRT) vehicles. LRTs carry some 500 000 passengers a day in such cities as Boston, Buffalo, Philadelphia, New Orleans, Los Angeles, and San Francisco. Edmonton opened the first new LRT system in North America in 1978. Calgary followed in 1981, and Vancouver in 1986. Trolleys are more reliable than buses and, since they run on their own tracks on the side of the street, can bypass a lot of city traffic. They are also nonpolluting. City planners in Los Angeles have great hopes for trolleys as a means to break through that city's gridlock.

The famous cable cars of San Francisco were recently overhauled and once again carry passengers up and down the city's steep streets. This picturesque but practical form of transportation is on the must-see list of every tourist who visits San Francisco.

To cope with traffic congestion in downtown areas, a few cities have even tried the **monorail,** an elevated urban transit system that runs on one rail. Miami opened a monorail called the Metromover in 1986. The following summer, Detroit inaugurated the People Mover, a 4.7-kilometre monorail that runs six metres above the ground.

Subways

A **subway** is a rail transportation system that provides local rapid-transit passenger service either wholly or partially underground. Subway systems are in operation in Montreal, Toronto, New York, Boston, Philadelphia, Chicago, Atlanta, San Francisco, and Washington, D.C. Baltimore recently opened a subway as well.

Subways provide a way of moving many people around town quickly, inexpensively, and without polluting the atmosphere. The most recently built lines are clean, quiet, and efficient. Many travellers find subways the fastest and easiest way to get around a city, once they overcome their reluctance to figure out the system.

A number of cities in the United States have developed subway or rail links from the airport to the city centre. New York inaugurated its JFK Express connection in the 1970s; Philadelphia and Cleveland also have direct rail connections to their airports.

Taxicabs and Limousines

Taxis and, to a lesser extent, limousines play an important part in public transportation in most cities. Known as **on-demand public transportation,** this kind of service does not keep regular schedules. Passengers arrange individually for service. In most areas, you can get a taxi by hailing it in the street or at a cab stand. In other areas, the taxi must be summoned by phone.

Limousines are privately owned and operated chauffeur-driven cars, often hired for special occasions or for business purposes. Limousines are ordinarily reserved by phone. Fees can be calculated on a per-hour basis or on distance travelled.

In most cities, cab fares are indicated on a meter and calculated according to distance travelled. But fares may also be calculated by zone.

For tourists and business travellers unfamiliar with a city, taxis are an extremely convenient way to get around. They also provide an essential link between the railway station or airport and the traveller's destination in the city.

Taxis and limousines form an integral part of the service systems at airports and railway stations. For the traveller who has just gotten off a plane, a taxi provides the transfer to the city centre. The plane–taxi combination is yet another example of intermodal transportation.

Mass Transit in Foreign Cities

One of the first things a traveller arriving in a foreign city has to find out is how to get around that city. Will a taxi be the fastest and easiest way to go from the hotel to the trade show on the outskirts of town? Or is there a subway line that makes the trip without too much bother and avoids the rush-hour traffic?

Transportation facilities, conditions, customs, and relative costs vary a great deal among the cities of the world. For example, buses in Switzerland operate more or less on the honour system. Passengers board the bus with tickets they have punched in a machine at the bus stop. Occasionally, a conductor comes through the bus to check tickets.

Following are some highlights of mass transit systems in cities around the world:

- *London.* The legendary cabbies of London have to pass a test to demonstrate their knowledge of the city's streets. Most London cabbies still drive ancient-looking black taxis that offer old-fashioned comfort with lots of headroom. The London Underground, known locally as "the Tube," has a reputation for dependability, cleanliness, and civility. A line now runs directly to Heathrow Airport. Last, but not least, are the famous red double-decker buses. A double-decker may not get to the destination faster, but the view from its upper level makes bus travel in London a tourist's delight.
- *Paris.* The Paris Metro, built in 1900, is considered by many to be the finest subway system in the world. It is certainly the fastest, with trains averaging over 100 kilometres an hour on its newest line. Its subway cars, which run on rubber tires, are divided into first- and second-class sections. The main stations have Metro maps, which light up when you push a button to show the best route to your destination.
- *Moscow.* Moscow takes the prize for the world's grandest subway. Marble columns, glittering chandeliers, and paintings adorn the subway's stations. The subway also runs meticulously on schedule.
- *Tokyo.* Tokyo's subway qualifies as the most heavily used in the world. To pack as many riders as possible into each car during rush hour, the subway employs white-gloved "pushers."

Channels of Distribution

Tickets and tokens for mass transit are usually sold directly at the point of departure. The traveller to New York City buys subway tokens at a subway station on arrival in the city, but may have obtained a subway map ahead of time. In this case, the channels of distribution serve as sources of information rather than of reservations or tickets.

Information about a city's mass transit system is usually available from the local tourist office or chamber of commerce. Subway maps, information on bus routes, and tips on using taxis can also be found in guidebooks to the particular destination, be it Paris, Mexico City, or Washington, D.C.

> **CHECK YOUR PRODUCT KNOWLEDGE**
> 1. What forms of mass transit carry travellers between an airport and its city's centre?
> 2. Explain why many cities are building LRTs today.
> 3. Which Canadian and American cities have subway systems? What advantages does a subway system offer?

CAREER OPPORTUNITIES

Career opportunities in the surface transportation industries are varied. Many require mechanical expertise or driving skills. Others involve a knack for sales and promotion.

Careers in the Railway Industry

Probably the best-known jobs in the railway industry are those of engineer (train driver) and conductor. Engineers are responsible for the safe operation of the train, while conductors oversee the safety of the passengers. Other occupations in railway operations include brake operator, signaller, signal maintainer, and track worker.

Some careers in the railway industry involve public contact, or sales and service, or both. These include reservations clerk, sales representative, and station agent (the railway's representative with the public). There is also a wide range of clerical positions.

Railway employment has fallen enormously throughout the 20th century. This sharp decrease can be attributed to a general decline in the industry and to the increasing use of automation on the train, in the yard, and in the office. At the present time, career opportunities in the railway industry are limited.

Careers in the Motorcoach Industry

Bus operators include intercity drivers (city to city), local transit drivers (public transportation within cities), and special-service drivers (charters, tours, and sightseeing). Dispatchers assign drivers to buses and coordinate the movement of buses in and out of the bus terminal.

Careers involving public contact and sales and service include ticket agent, tour manager, tour representative, and sales representative. Clerical and general office positions are also available.

Employment prospects in the charter, tour, and sightseeing sectors of this industry have improved in recent years.

Careers in the Car Rental Industry

Preparing the car for the customer is an important part of the car rental service. Maintenance and service workers and mechanics make sure that each car is clean and in good working order.

Other careers in the car rental industry, such as reservations agent and customer service representative, involve contact with the public. Station managers run rental offices and supervise rental representatives; sales representatives sell the services of their company to airlines, travel agents, and businesses.

The number of car rental companies increases each year, so career opportunities in this industry are expected to remain good.

Careers in Mass Transit

Many careers in mass transit involve driving taxicabs, limousines, urban buses, trolleys, subways, and so on. Subway operators open and close subway doors and announce the stops. Dispatchers regulate the flow of bus and subway traffic. Attendants in subway stations sell tokens or tickets to the public.

Summary

- The first public railways came into service in England and the United States in the early 19th century. Railways in Canada came into service in the mid-19th century.
- Private automobiles, intercity buses, and airlines began to challenge the railways in the 1920s. After World War II the American railway industry declined rapidly.
- Amtrak, a semi-public railway corporation, took over and revamped the intercity railway passenger network in the United States in 1971. VIA Rail, a Crown corporation,

A DAY IN THE LIFE OF

A Car Rental Agent

Some people think my job as a car rental agent is routine and easy. In some ways, I guess it is, but I help provide a very important service to many travellers and I am proud of my work. The car rental agency I work for has a desk in the baggage claim area of a large airport. When people know they are coming to my city and will need to rent a car, they usually reserve one over the telephone. I also receive many calls from travel agents who want to reserve cars for their clients. When customers arrive at the airport, they pick up their luggage and then simply walk over to my counter to get the car they have reserved.

It is my job to process the necessary forms for people who are renting cars from my agency. I explain the rental terms to the customers and have them sign a rental agreement. I also tell them about the types of insurance that are offered. Customers must either leave a cash deposit, or provide a credit card so I can bill the rental to their credit card account. Most customers use credit cards rather than cash.

I must make sure that the car the customer has ordered is clean, filled with gas, and available for use. Some car rental agencies charge just a flat daily fee for the use of their automobiles. Other companies, like mine, charge that fee plus an additional amount per kilometre. When a customer rents a car, part of my job is to verify the kilometres driven so that the agency will know exactly how much to charge when the car is returned.

I also check in cars when they are returned. This involves checking the distance driven and the condition of the car and computing the customer's bill. Since most people pay by credit card, I process the credit card charge and provide the customer with a receipt. Many customers rent automobiles while on business trips, and they need the receipts to get reimbursement from their companies.

My job is an entry-level job, the kind that is the first many people take in a particular business or industry. I have been a car rental clerk for a year. I hope to be promoted to station manager in another year or two. A station manager directs all operations at a car rental office or at a rental station in an airport, bus depot, or train station. The station manager is in charge of supervising the employees, running the desk or building, and managing the cars assigned to his or her station. I could also be promoted to customer service representative. In that position, I would handle customers' problems or complaints.

In order to get this job, I had to be a high school graduate. After I was hired, I took a four-week training course. I learned how to fill out forms, process credit cards, take reservations, greet the public, and so on. Car rental agencies strive to be very professional. The company I work for provides its employees with attractive, businesslike uniforms and makes sure that all employees treat customers with great courtesy and respect.

You may not think my job requires many skills, but there are several things that I need to do well. I need a good command of English, of course, since I work at a Canadian airport. Sometimes I wish I spoke a second language, since many of our foreign visitors aren't fluent in English. Some of my co-workers can speak French, Spanish, or German. They are very handy to have around when I have difficulty communicating with a foreign customer.

I need to be able to operate a computer so that I can take reservations and fill out forms. I must also be able to write legibly and spell accurately, since other people will be following my handwritten work orders. Most of all, I must have excellent math skills and be able to use a calculator, because I spend a good deal of time working with figures. Much of my work involves adding up bills and calculating distance charges.

I got my job by answering an advertisement in my local newspaper. Some of my co-workers applied directly to the agency, some through a school placement office. Many new car rental agencies have started up in recent years, so there are a lot of new jobs in the field. Also, jobs as rental agents open up all the time as people are promoted or change jobs. A car rental agent doesn't earn a big salary, but there are plenty of opportunities for advancement to better-paying jobs.

CHAPTER 5: The Surface Travel Industries

took over the intercity railway passenger network in Canada in stages between 1976 and 1978.
- Railway systems in Europe and throughout the world continue to provide extensive service.
- The first motor buses appeared at the start of the 20th century. By the 1930s in the United States and the 1950s in Canada, buses were a common sight on highways.
- Scheduled motorcoach passenger service declined after World War II as car ownership and air travel increased.
- The deregulation of the American motorcoach industry in 1982 resulted in the entry of many new companies in the growing charter and tour business. In Canada, the provinces are responsible for regulating the motorcoach industry.
- The car rental industry began to grow rapidly during the late 1950s, a boom that continues today.
- The success of the car rental industry is closely related to the growth of air travel—in particular, business air travel.
- Mass transit systems are an essential part of life in urban areas, helping to ease traffic congestion and air pollution.

Key Terms

nationalize
Eurailpass
BritRail pass
couchette
wagon-lit
TGV
rail/sail package
charter tour
escorted tour
independent package tour
city package tour
transfer
fly/drive package
unlimited kilometres
kilometre cap
subcompact
compact
standard
deluxe
drop-off charge
loss/damage waiver (LDW)
personal accident insurance (PAI)
public transportation
mass transit
trolley
urban bus
airport limousine
light-rail transit (LRT)
monorail
subway
on-demand public transportation
limousine

What Do You Think?

1. How important do you think it is to maintain intercity rail passenger service in Canada and the United States? Give reasons for your answer.
2. Should motorcoaches and trains compete for the same intercity routes? What would be the advantages of competition? What would be the disadvantages?
3. Has deregulation had a beneficial effect on the motorcoach industry? Why or why not?
4. If someone asked you to recommend a car rental company, how would you go about choosing one?
5. What steps might be taken by mass transit systems to encourage more people to use their services?

Dealing with Product

VIA Rail is one of the most controversial components of the Canadian travel industry. Many people mistakenly believe that the government in Ottawa directly owns and operates VIA Rail. In fact, VIA Rail is a Crown corporation that the federal government only monitors and for which it sets guidelines and subsidizes operations.

Imagine that you have been appointed to lead a task force looking into Canada's railway system. You are to examine and report on the need for a national rail-passenger system. Is there a need for one in Canada? Should Parliament be involved in funding and running the system? Should VIA Rail be treated differently from the way other modes of transportation are treated?

Dealing with People

You are a travel counsellor with a dilemma. It seems you have just sold four students from Yourtown Community College a tour to Fort Lauderdale for the spring vacation. The package includes round-trip airfare, a shared room at a beachfront motel, and transfers to and from Fort Lauderdale's airport. So far, so good.

Now for the challenge. The students have requested that you also reserve a rental car for seven days. You know that none of them is old enough to rent a car legally, and you also doubt whether they can meet the other criteria for car rental. When you raise the question of age, one of the students tells you not to worry, because he plans to borrow some identification from his older brother. What will you do? What are your responsibilities as a professional travel counsellor? What will you do if the students threaten to cancel their trip and take their business elsewhere?

CHAPTER 5: The Surface Travel Industries   Name: _____

WORKSHEET 5-1 Railways

Select a country that has at least a small railway system. Use Fodor's *Railways of the World,* Thomas Cook's *Timetable* books, or other tour or source books to get the following information:

Overview

Kilometres of track

Number of scheduled trains

Passenger capacity

Yearly passenger load

Speeds reached

Dependability

Plan A Trip On This Railway System

Departure (place/time)

Arrival (place/time)

Number of kilometres travelled

CHAPTER 5: The Surface Travel Industries   Name: _____

WORKSHEET 5-2 Individual Bus Tour

Pick a region of Canada or the United States and plan a two- or three-week bus tour of it. Decide where you will **stop over, for how long,** and what you will see and do. Be sure there is bus service all along your route. Estimate travel time and cost.

Region _____

Bus line(s) _____
_____

Bus route/itinerary _____
_____
_____
_____

Kilometres travelled (each part) _____
_____
_____
_____

Cost of ticket (each part) _____
_____
_____
_____

Other expenses _____
_____
_____
_____
_____

Stopovers (where and how long) _____
_____
_____
_____

Kind of accommodations (each stopover) _____
_____
_____
_____

Expenses (each stopover) _____
_____
_____
_____

Attractions or activities (each stopover) _____
_____
_____
_____
_____

CHAPTER 5: The Surface Travel Industries   Name: _____

WORKSHEET 5-3 Ground Transportation And Sightseeing

For each of the following cities, use the OAG *Travel Planner Hotel and Motel Redbook* or a similar publication to describe the various ways to get from the airport to the city's downtown area. If there is more than one airport near any city, select one and identify it.

Austin, TX _____

Chicago, IL_____

Lincoln, NE _____

Los Angeles, CA _____

Miami, FL_____

Quebec City, P.Q. _____

Vancouver, B.C._____

For each of the following cities, use the *Gray Line Sales and Tour Guide, American Sightseeing International World Tariff,* or a similar publication to select a sightseeing tour. Describe it briefly below. Include highlights, duration, and cost.

Austin _____

_____

Chicago _____

_____

London, Ont._____

_____

Los Angeles _____

_____

Miami _____

_____

Milwaukee _____

_____

Toronto _____

_____

129

CHAPTER 5: The Surface Travel Industries Name: _____

WORKSHEET 5-4 Renting A Car

You are a travel agent. You have just finished arranging a round-trip flight from Yourtown to San Francisco for Rosalind Burton. While in California, Burton plans to rent a car and tour the redwood forests in the northern part of the state. She would like to drive a compact car with automatic transmission. She has never rented a car before and is somewhat apprehensive about the rental process.

    Reserve a rental car for Burton. Choose a car rental company and find out the rates and charges for the type of car she wants. Also, find out the company's procedures for renting a car. Record your findings on the form below.

Name of car rental company _____

Information needed before renting a car _____
_____

Rates _____

Makes and models available in compact size _____
_____

Charges _____

Insurance price and information _____
_____

Where to pick up car _____

What to do in case of mechanical failure or accident _____
_____

What to do before dropping off car _____
_____

Where and how to drop off car _____
_____

130

CHAPTER 6

The Cruise and Steamship Industry

"I must down to the seas again,
To the lonely sea and the sky,
And all I ask is a tall ship,
And a star to steer her by."

John Masefield

OBJECTIVES

When you have completed this chapter, you should be able to do the following:

- List the highlights in the history of sailing ships and steamships.
- Give reasons for the decline of point-to-point passenger service and the rise of the cruise industry.
- Give examples of theme cruises.
- Explain the differences between freighter cruises and standard liner cruises.
- Describe some key marketing techniques used by contemporary cruise companies.
- Evaluate the fly/cruise and land/cruise packages.
- Discuss the concept of the cruise ship as a floating hotel.
- Describe the layout of a cruise ship.
- Identify the factors that affect the price of a cruise.
- Outline the regulations affecting cruises.

The cruise is widely regarded as the most glamorous of all travel products. *Romance, excitement,* and *adventure* are all words that spring to mind when we think about cruising.

The romance of the seas is nothing new, of course, but the cruise industry is. The rich and famous have been taking cruises since the 1920s, but mass-market cruises have been available only since the early 1960s. Shipping companies developed the concept of the contemporary cruise in response to the decline in passenger traffic following the advent of the jet age. The contemporary cruise was a remarkable marketing achievement. The ship was no longer simply a means of transportation but a destination in itself. Cruising became a total vacation experience.

The success of the young cruise industry has been phenomenal. Between 1980 and 1990, the number of people taking cruises each year nearly tripled. The cruise industry is also the fastest-growing segment in travel and tourism. Cruises are offered on oceans and waterways throughout the world, on ships ranging in size from luxury liners that carry 2 000 passengers to small yachts carrying just a dozen.

In this chapter, you will learn about the development of the cruise industry and about the different types of cruises that are available. You will read about cruise programs and about the physical layout of cruise ships. You will also learn how cruise companies have successfully broadened the appeal of cruises through aggressive marketing techniques.

THE ORIGINS OF THE CRUISE INDUSTRY

Ships have played an important role in human history ever since the Egyptians invented the sail about 3200 B.C. Greeks, Romans, and other early seafarers made various technological advances in shipbuilding, improving the seaworthiness of sailing ships and increasing their speed. They did little, however, to make the vessels more comfortable for the people on board. Early sailing ships were used primarily for trade and warfare, not for transporting passengers.

With the development of the compass and navigation charts in the 12th century, ships began to venture out to sea on longer ocean voyages. The invention of the rudder made it easier to steer a ship and allowed for the construction of heavier, sturdier vessels. The period between 1400 and the late 1800s was one of constant improvement in sailing ship design. This was the age of overseas expansion, when sea routes were opened up from Europe to the Far East and across the Atlantic Ocean to the New World. Trade was still the driving force behind the shipping industry, but passenger transportation began to increase in importance (see Figure 6-1).

Small sailing ships were being built in Nova Scotia by the early 1700s for local use. Larger vessels were soon being constructed for trade with Britain, the West Indies, and the American colonies. Canadian seaports such as Halifax and Saint John were established in the late 1700s and soon prospered. Samuel Cunard, a merchant-exporter of Halifax, created a substantial shipping business in the 1820s and 1830s that sailed the triangular route connecting Britain, Nova Scotia, and the West Indies.

Regularly scheduled transatlantic passenger service was introduced in 1818 by the Black Ball Line of the United States. As the pace of immigration quickened, other American lines began to offer scheduled service between England and the United States. Rival companies competed with each other to reduce passage times. By the 1840s, the crossing time between Liverpool and New York was about three weeks. Competition also led to some improvements in passenger comfort, though accommodations were still far from luxurious.

Passengers and cargo were carried on longer routes by the legendary clipper ships, introduced in the mid-19th century and designed for maximum speed. Clippers carried gold prospectors from the eastern United States around the tip of South America to the California goldfields on the famous "round the Horn" journey. They reached their destination in three to four months—half the time it would have taken by the overland route. By the late 1860s, however, clippers were obsolete. The steamship had appeared.

The Age of Steam

The use of steam engines on ships marked the greatest revolution in water transportation since the invention of the sail. Robert Fulton's *Clermont* made its maiden voyage up the Hudson River from New York to Albany in 1807. Within a few years, hundreds of steamboats were carrying passengers on inland waterways throughout North America.

Steamships were soon introduced on transatlantic routes. In 1819 the *Savannah* became the first steamship to cross the Atlantic. In 1840, Cunard of Halifax, with associates in Glasgow and Liverpool, established the British and North American Royal Mail Steam Packet Company, the first company to offer scheduled steamship service across the Atlantic. This company would evolve into the Cunard Line. The paddle steamer *Britannia* crossed from Liverpool to Halifax and Boston in 14 days. Cunard, White Star, and other British lines were the leaders in transatlantic passenger service in the early years. Germany's North German Lloyd and Hamburg-American lines were providing stiff competition by the 1870s. By the end of the century, French and Dutch companies had also entered the transatlantic passenger race. The United States turned its attention to the Pacific, and the Pacific Mail Steamship Company began passenger service in 1867.

As the rivalry among the European shipping companies intensified, each line tried to outdo the others with larger ships, faster crossings, and more luxurious accommodations. Cunard was forced by competition to drop Halifax as a regular port of call on the Liverpool–New York route.

In spite of the improvements in comfort, most passengers continued to travel in steerage, the lowest class on board. Steerage passengers occupied cramped, communal quarters on the lowest deck, near the ship's engines. The low price of steerage-class travel encouraged millions of Europeans to emigrate to North America. A typical steamship of the period might carry 50 cabin passengers, but ten times that number in steerage. Separate cabins with plush interiors, ventilation, and steam heat were only for the privileged few who could afford them. Already, you can see the different motivations, needs, and expectations (MNEs) of different travellers. The rich travelled for pleasure and expected luxury. Steerage passengers travelled to get to their

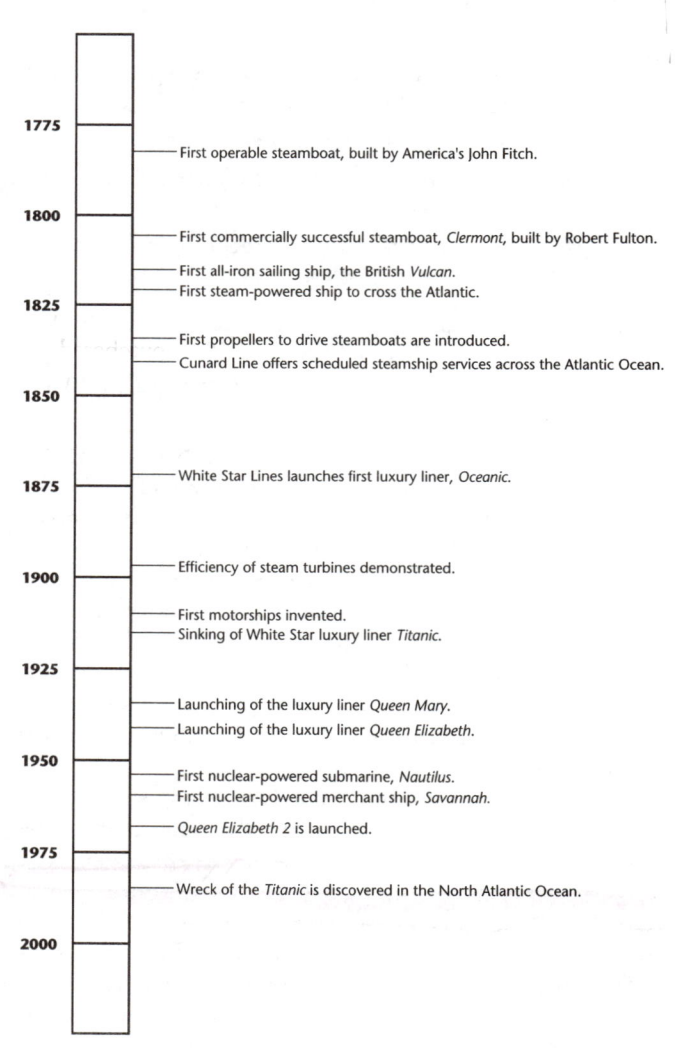

1775 — First operable steamboat, built by America's John Fitch.
1800 — First commercially successful steamboat, *Clermont*, built by Robert Fulton.
— First all-iron sailing ship, the British *Vulcan*.
— First steam-powered ship to cross the Atlantic.
1825 — First propellers to drive steamboats are introduced.
— Cunard Line offers scheduled steamship services across the Atlantic Ocean.
1850
1875 — White Star Lines launches first luxury liner, *Oceanic*.
1900 — Efficiency of steam turbines demonstrated.
— First motorships invented.
— Sinking of White Star luxury liner *Titanic*.
1925 — Launching of the luxury liner *Queen Mary*.
— Launching of the luxury liner *Queen Elizabeth*.
1950 — First nuclear-powered submarine, *Nautilus*.
— First nuclear-powered merchant ship, *Savannah*.
— *Queen Elizabeth 2* is launched.
1975 — Wreck of the *Titanic* is discovered in the North Atlantic Ocean.
2000

FIGURE 6-1
Milestones in Maritime History

destination, could only afford inexpensive accommodations, and had limited expectations.

Significant advances continued to be made in shipbuilding. Iron hulls replaced wooden hulls, propellers replaced paddle wheels, and steam turbines and later diesel engines replaced steam engines. Two of the most important maritime advances occurred on land: the opening of the Suez Canal (1869) and the Panama Canal (1914), both of which saved thousands of miles and dozens of days at sea.

The Age of the Ocean Liners

The late 19th century and first half of the 20th century comprised the great age of the ocean liners. A **liner** is an ocean-going passenger vessel that runs over a fixed route on a fixed schedule. The term is generally applied to those large luxury ships that came into transatlantic service about 1885. Liners also sailed on other routes throughout the world, but the largest and fastest were those built for passenger service between the United States and Europe. They included such great names as the *City of Paris*, the *City of New York*, the *Mauretania*, the *Lusitania*, and the *Titanic*.

The Canadian Pacific Railway started regular rail service from Montreal to Vancouver in 1886. It soon chartered sailing vessels to bring tea and silk from Japan. By 1889 the CPR had secured a contract to carry the Imperial mails from Britain to Hong Kong via Canada. Three CPR vessels entered service in 1891: the *Empress of India*, *Empress of Japan*, and *Empress of China*. They were the first of the famous Empress ships that were to sail the seas for the next 80 years flying the famous red and white checkerboard that was the CPR's house flag. In 1903 the CPR purchased the Beaver Line and opened service on the North Atlantic; in 1914 it purchased the Allan Line and organized Canadian Pacific Steamships. Montreal and Quebec City were that company's regular ports of call, with Saint John being used in the winter.

By the early 20th century the luxury of on-board accommodations had been raised to an extremely high level. In fact, many of the ocean liners had all the comforts of a five-star resort hotel, with hot and cold running water, private baths, sumptuous meals, and lavish public rooms. The emphasis on luxury was meant to appeal to the growing number of wealthy Americans travelling to Europe either on business or for pleasure. By the early 1920s, 80 percent of all steamship passengers were American. Steerage traffic was on the decline, and there was a new breed of passenger—the tourist. A new class—tourist third-class—was created to accommodate the thousands of Americans who were eager to see the wonders of Europe. The number of passengers crossing the Atlantic rose sharply, from 200 000 in 1902 to more than one million in 1929.

Before World War I, the Cunard Line resumed service to Canada, using Montreal as its regular port of call and Halifax as a winter port.

During the 1920s, some shipping companies began to offer world cruises, and winter cruises in the warm waters of the Caribbean and the Mediterranean. During the summer they returned to regular scheduled passenger service.

The rivalry among the shipping lines continued through the 1920s and into the early 1930s. The size of ocean liners continued to increase, reaching its peak during the 1930s with the French Line's *Normandie* and the Cunard's *Queen Mary*. Both could carry over 2000 passengers and were capable of 30 knots. Crossing times were reduced to just over four days. At the end of the decade, the *Queen Elizabeth*, the largest liner ever built, was launched by Cunard.

ILLUSTRATION 6-1
The *QE2* provides point-to-point sailings and warm-water cruises.
SOURCE: Cunard Lines Ltd.

World War II interrupted ocean liner service. Most vessels were pressed into service for the war effort. They served as troopships, armed merchant cruisers, prisoner-of-war carriers, and passenger liners. Six Empresses, four Duchesses, and five other ships from the CP fleet were involved in the war effort; by the end of the war, 11 of these 15 ships had been lost, nine by enemy action and two by marine accident. In the grim autumn of 1940, three ships were lost within 36 days: the *Empress of Britain* was torpedoed and sunk while serving as a troop carrier; the freighter *Beaverford*, with one four-inch and one three-inch gun, engaged the pocket battleship *Admiral Scheer* for five hours before going down with all hands; and the liner *Montrose* was torpedoed while serving in the seas north of Scotland.

The Modern Age

The passenger ship business continued to thrive for 13 years after World War II, largely because of the boom in tourism. Immigrants, business executives, and the wealthy continued to use the service, but the largest group of travellers consisted of American tourists. By 1958 there were 25 companies and 70 ships operating on transatlantic routes.

Although most of the passengers were American, most of the shipping lines were European; by the late 1950s the United States had priced itself out of the passenger market because of high labour costs. American crew members demanded much higher wages than their foreign counterparts. The same problem has continued to plague American cruise companies to the present day. This explains why so many ships are foreign-flag vessels: by registering in a foreign country, American shipowners can pay wages lower than those required by unions in the United States.

Some American lines have survived, however. These include the United States Line (serving Europe), Matson Lines (Hawaii, the South Pacific, Australia, and New Zealand), Moore-McCormack (South America), and American President Lines (the Orient).

Canadian Pacific placed three new Empress ships into service just as the transatlantic service peaked: the *Empress of Britain* (1956), *Empress of England* (1957), and *Empress of Canada* (1961). They maintained the traditional weekly service between Montreal and Liverpool for a seven-month summer season. This service ended in 1971. Fewer than 24 000 passengers had travelled between Canada and Britain in 1970, compared with 98 000 in 1960. The Cunard Line had ended its Canadian service in 1967, the year of Canada's Centennial.

The Birth of the Cruise Ship

The first nonstop flight of a commercial jet airliner across the Atlantic was made in 1958. That event marked the beginning of the end for the passenger ship industry. The airlines had been carrying an increasing number of passengers since the late 1940s. By 1958, as many people were crossing the Atlantic by air as by sea. Just one year later, 63 percent of all transatlantic passengers travelled by air. It was a dramatic turnaround. Only 15 years earlier, virtually all transatlantic passengers had crossed by sea.

Shipping lines tried to hold on to their share of the passenger market by emphasizing that "getting there is half the fun." But travellers didn't agree. It was understandable that business travellers would prefer to cross the ocean in eight hours by plane rather than in four or five days by ship. What is interesting is that vacationers, and travellers visiting friends and relatives, also chose to fly. Evidently, they placed more importance on spending time at their destination than on having fun getting there. The jet overtook the liner because it could better satisfy the MNEs of all types of travellers.

As the volume of air traffic increased, a number of the great liners had to withdraw from passenger service. They could not afford to operate half-empty. Some were junked for scrap; others began new lives as freight carriers; a few were docked as tourist attractions; but most significantly, many were converted into cruise ships.

The development of the modern cruise is a classic example of necessity being the mother of invention. If the shipping companies could not compete with the airlines, they would compete with the resort hotels by offering the cruise as a complete vacation. "Getting there is half the fun" gave way to "Being here is *all* the fun."

Earlier cruises had catered to a small, rich élite. The "contemporary" cruise that was developed in the early 1960s was targeted at a much larger segment of society—the tourist market. To widen the appeal of the cruise, the traditional three-class division (first, cabin, and tourist) was abandoned in favour of a single, high-class accommodation.

Shipping companies began converting their passenger liners into tropical cruise ships in the early 1960s. Some could be transferred to the cruise trade with comparative ease. Others were sold, modernized, and renamed, then reborn as cruise ships. The *France*, for example, became the *Norway*, flagship of Norwegian Cruise Line (NCL). Not all of the older superliners could be adapted for the cruise business. Giants such as the *Queen Mary*, *Queen Elizabeth*, and *United States* proved uneconomical to operate and were withdrawn from service by 1970. The new Empress ships of Canadian Pacific, while intended for winter cruising, were essentially tourist-class ships and could not meet the requirements of cruising.

The established companies continued to build luxury superliners throughout the 1960s, but these were to serve a dual purpose. During the summer they served as **point-to-point** liners, that is, they took passengers from one destination to another. During the winter they served as warm-water cruise ships. Cunard's *Queen Elizabeth 2*, which made its maiden voyage in 1969, was the most notable example. Built as a replacement for the *Queen Elizabeth*, the 65 000-ton liner reflected the demands of the new cruise market. Its on-board facilities included four swimming pools;

bars, lounges, and shops; a nightclub; and a children's playroom. All cabins were fitted with air conditioning and a private bath or shower. The *QE2* had a passenger capacity of 1700 and a crew of 900. This 2:1 passenger-to-crew ratio was to become standard on most cruise ships.

The next phase was the development of the year-round cruise. In this, NCL was a pioneer, packaging the first mass-market, year-round cruises from Miami to the Bahamas in 1966. With the Caribbean becoming the major cruising area, Miami was rapidly replacing New York as the number-one port in the United States. New companies such as Royal Viking Line and Royal Caribbean Cruise Line introduced fleets of ships specifically designed for Caribbean cruising.

The focus of technological improvements in earlier times had been on increased speed and increased ship size. With the development of the cruise ship, the emphasis shifted to fuel efficiency, low operating costs, and continued improvements in passenger comfort. The use of aluminum for a ship's superstructure (that part of the ship above the main hull) meant that the new cruise ships were considerably lighter than the earlier liners. As a result, they consumed less fuel. (The use of aluminum also made possible the addition of more decks.) Fuel costs were further reduced by the widespread use of diesel engines.

Passenger comfort was greatly increased by the introduction of **stabilizers**, which minimize the effects of a ship's side-to-side roll. The development of radar meant that ships could steer clear of the worst storms. As more and more vessels were built for cruising, on-board amenities greatly improved. Cabins were standardized, with private bathrooms and air conditioning throughout. More space was given over to public rooms and outdoor open decks. Dining rooms were located higher in the ship so that passengers could view the sea while dining.

CHECK YOUR PRODUCT KNOWLEDGE

1. List five important technological improvements made in shipbuilding in the past 1000 years.
2. What new kind of passenger appeared during the 1920s? How did this kind differ from earlier kinds of ocean travellers?
3. What effect did transatlantic jet travel have on the passenger ship industry?
4. How do modern cruise ships differ from the luxury ocean liners?

CRUISES OF TODAY

The cruise industry had established itself as a major force in the tourist industry by the early 1970s and has continued to grow to the present day. By the mid-1970s, existing cruise ships were operating at maximum capacity and more were being built. Between 1980 and 1986, $3 billion was spent on cruise ship construction, doubling the world's cruise fleet. New ships were built and old ones were modernized—some by being cut in half and then welded back together with a larger midsection. In 1990, several cruise lines, including Carnival and Chandris Fantasy Cruises, introduced new, larger ships to their fleets.

The rise in the number of passengers taking cruises has been equally spectacular—from 1.4 million in 1980 to near 4 million in 1991. About 70 percent of all passengers are from North America. In just 15 years, Carnival, a leader in the Caribbean with nine ships, has seen its business increase from 100 000 to nearly one million passengers a year.

A few of the older shipping companies (most notably Cunard, Holland America, and P&O) have successfully made the transition from point-to-point service to the cruise trade. But most cruise lines have been in operation for less than 25 years. Today, there are about 50 companies offering a wide variety of cruises on about 190 passenger vessels. More than half the lines belong to the Cruise Lines International Association (CLIA), a regulatory and promotional organization founded in 1975. Figure 6-2 shows the increase in passengers carried by CLIA member ships between 1970 and 1993 (estimated). (CLIA is discussed in detail later in this chapter.)

The number of cruise lines in operation has increased considerably in the past decade. Some of the new lines are owned and operated by American companies, but the majority are in European hands. Greek, Italian, Norwegian, Dutch, and British lines dominate the industry. Russian companies have been growing in recent years and have succeeded in penetrating the Western market by offering cheaper rates than European and American lines.

You can't always tell who owns a ship by the flag it is flying. A number of cruise ships fly what is known as **a flag of convenience.** This flag signifies that a ship of one nation is registered under the flag of another. For example, Carnival's ships, though American-owned, sail under the Liberian flag. You read earlier that foreign registry enables shipping lines to

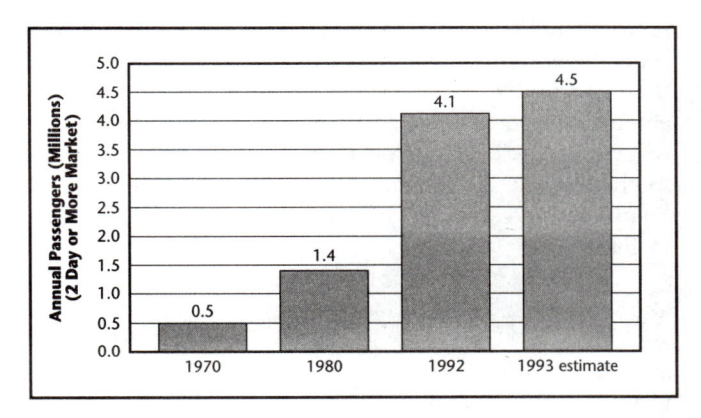

FIGURE 6-2
Cruise Line Passengers
SOURCE: Cruise Lines International Association

cut labour costs. It also allows them to avoid the strict controls and high taxes imposed in their country of origin.

A Wide Array of Cruises

The cruise industry has responded to the varying MNEs of travellers by offering a wide variety of cruise types and cruise destinations. Cruise lines sail to every conceivable maritime location, from the spectacular coast of Alaska to the icy waters of Antarctica. There are cruises to fit every need and pocketbook, and of almost any time length. Possible are weekend jaunts to the Bahamas, six-day journeys along the rivers of Europe, two-week cruises of the Mediterranean, six-week navigations of South America, and, of course, three-month world cruises. Table 6–1 shows the growth of the North American cruise market since 1980.

World Cruises

A world cruise is the ultimate journey, the vacation of a lifetime for those who can afford the time and the expense. For three months, passengers are pampered with first-rate personal service, superb cuisine, international entertainment, and shore excursions to exotic ports of call. The cost can be staggering, beginning at about $35,000 and rising to over $175,000 for a deluxe suite on the *QE2*. At those prices, it's hardly surprising that the market for world cruises is relatively limited.

Cunard offered the first official world cruise, aboard the *Laconia* in the winter of 1922–23. The ultradeluxe *QE2* and the smaller *Sagafjord* maintain the Cunard tradition on today's world cruise circuit. World cruises are also offered by another well-established shipping company—Britain's P&O Line, which has over 100 years of experience as a passenger carrier. P&O's *Canberra*, which sails from Southampton, England, was originally designed as a transoceanic liner but has been converted to the cruise trade.

World cruises usually begin during the first week of January and end in early April. Some call at as many as 30 ports on the way. All ships travel in an east-west direction, generally entering the Pacific through the Panama Canal, then continuing on to Asia and the Indian Ocean, then entering the Mediterranean through the Suez Canal before returning to the North Atlantic. A few take a more southerly route, sailing around the tip of South America and South Africa. *Sagafjord*'s 1992 world cruise itinerary is shown in Table 6–2.

Cruise lines sell not only the complete world cruise but also segments of it. In this way, they cater to travellers who want to savour the luxury and excitement of a world cruise but cannot afford the whole trip. Once again, the supplier identifies a customer need and markets a product to satisfy that need. Typical segments include New York to Los Angeles, Los Angeles to Singapore, Hong Kong to Singapore, Singapore to Rio de Janeiro, and Southampton to Barbados. To encourage travellers to sign up for portions of world cruises, cruise lines offer generous credits for air travel to the port of **embarkation** (the boarding of passengers onto a ship) and back from the port of disembarkation.

	Annual Passenger Growth	
	Actual (Millions)	% Growth
1980	1.4	+13.5%
1981	1.5	+1.7%
1982	1.5	+1.2%
1983	1.8	+15.2%
1984	1.9	+9.9%
1985	2.2	+13.4%
1986	2.6	+13.8%
1987	2.9	+11.0%
1988	3.2	+9.5%
1989	3.3	+2.4%
1990	3.6	+13.5%
1991	4.0	+9.5%
1992	4.1	+4.6%
1993	4.5	+8.8%
Average growth rate 1980–93		+10.0%

TABLE 6-1
Growth of the North American Cruise Market Since 1980
SOURCE: Cruise Lines International Association

Depart from FORT LAUDERDALE — January 6, 1992	
LIMA, PERU	BANGKOK
BUENOS AIRES	HONG KONG
RIO DE JANEIRO	SHANGHAI
DURBAN, SOUTH AFRICA	TOKYO
MOMBASA, KENYA	HONOLULU
MADRAS, INDIA	ACAPULCO
SINGAPORE	ARUBA
Arrive in FORT LAUDERDALE — April 22, 1992	
Fare: $30,340 per person, double occupancy	

TABLE 6-2
Cunard's *Sagafjord* World Cruise Itinerary, 1992
SOURCE: Cunard Line

PROFILE

S. S. Norway

The *S.S. Norway* is one of the largest passenger ships in the world. Built as a transatlantic ocean liner, it now plies the waters of the Caribbean as a cruise ship carrying more than 2000 passengers a week from Miami to the Virgin Islands and back. The *Norway* is owned by the Norwegian Cruise Line (NCL), which also operates four smaller cruise ships in the Caribbean and one in California.

The *S.S. Norway* started life as the *S.S. France*. It was built in the late 1950s to carry passengers across the Atlantic just as people began to desert ocean liners for air travel between Europe and North America. The *France* was one of the last big luxury ocean liners ever built. Its silhouette, with two stately winged smokestacks, became very familiar on travel posters and in travel magazines in the 1960s. Although ocean liner travel was declining, the *France* continued to carry passengers from the United States to France and back until the early 1970s, when the French government took it out of service.

The Norwegian Cruise Line purchased the *France* and renamed it the *Norway* in 1979. The liner had to be refurbished and converted from an enclosed ship, suitable for sailing the frigid North Atlantic, to an outdoor ship, open to the balmy breezes of the Caribbean. NCL altered the *Norway*'s classic lines by adding two huge davits, or cranes, on the foredeck to hold two large tenders, each capable of carrying 400 passengers between ship and shore. It also added two large "Norway" signs between the smokestacks.

In recent years the *Norway* has been assigned to seven-day cruises from Miami to St. Maarten, St. John, and St. Thomas in the West Indies. It also stops for one day at Pleasure Island, which is owned by NCL. The *Norway*'s passengers can enjoy a day of snorkelling, swimming, beachcombing, sunbathing, and beach games on the island.

The sheer size of the *Norway* is one of its most fascinating features. It weighs about 75 000 tonnes. It has 12 decks and about 20 000 metres of sundecks and walkways. Its engine room is almost 250 metres long and seven stories high. It would take more than an hour to descend by stairs from the top to the bottom of the ship. In order to help passengers find their way around, NCL has painted the forward areas of the ship turquoise and the aft areas pink.

Because it is so large, the *Norway* can offer passengers an enormous variety of shipboard activities. The ship's facilities include two pools, a huge Roman spa, a health and fitness centre, two large dining rooms, a gambling casino, a video games room, a library, a nursery, a children's activity room, several shops, and many nightclubs and bars.

On board, passengers can enjoy a wide variety of sports, such as basketball, racquetball, volleyball, and shuffleboard. They can take classes in aerobics, swimnastics, and cooking. They can learn ice carving, attend a fashion show, participate in a wine tasting, practise golf on the ship's driving range, or try their hand at trapshooting. In the evening, they can choose between concerts, dancing, a comedy revue, or a Broadway-type show.

The *Norway* has something for everyone, including children. Some of the many supervised activities for them include ice cream and cookie parties, movies, story times, and crafts. Children can even take their own guided shore trips while their parents are off shopping and seeing the sights.

Since 1983, the *Norway* has been host to an annual floating jazz festival each fall. The festival brings together jazz fans and many leading jazz performers for a week of music and sun. NCL has added several other theme cruises to the *Norway*'s schedule, including a comedy cruise, a country-and-western cruise, a magic cruise, and a Big Band cruise.

NCL also offers a series of sports cruises on the *Norway*. These are intended to bring fans together with big names in professional sports. In recent years, NCL sports cruises have featured football star Larry Csonka, basketball great Michael Jordan, hockey player Brad Park, and baseball player Joe Morgan.

Shorter Sea Cruises

Shorter sea cruises are the mainstay of the cruise industry, accounting for by far the largest number of passengers. Warm-water cruises, with the emphasis on "fun and sun," are the most popular. The Alaskan cruise routes are, however, becoming increasingly well travelled.

The Caribbean The Caribbean became the first area developed for modern cruising during the 1960s, and it has remained the most popular region for Canadian and American tourists. It offers a wealth of tropical islands within a small geographic area. As many as five or six islands can be visited during a one-week cruise. A typical Caribbean cruise is shown in Figure 6-3.

The Caribbean cruise appeals primarily to the traveller who wants to relax in the sun en route, and then experience a little local culture at the destinations. Although the Caribbean offers exotic attractions, it is still familiar and "safe" enough for the traveller who does not want to experience a totally foreign culture.

The islands of the western Caribbean are within a day or two's sailing of Florida ports such as Miami, Fort Everglades/Fort Lauderdale, and Tampa. Nassau, in the Bahamas, is one of the most common destinations. San Juan, Puerto Rico, serves as a base for cruises to the Virgin Islands, Guadeloupe, Martinique, Barbados, and other eastern Caribbean islands.

Another popular cruise destination is the island of Bermuda. One-week cruises to Bermuda, with three days of sailing and four days in port, leave from New York City. Bermuda cruises are so popular that Bermuda's government has placed strict limits on the number of ships allowed to come to the island. This is a means of minimizing the negative effects of tourism on the environment.

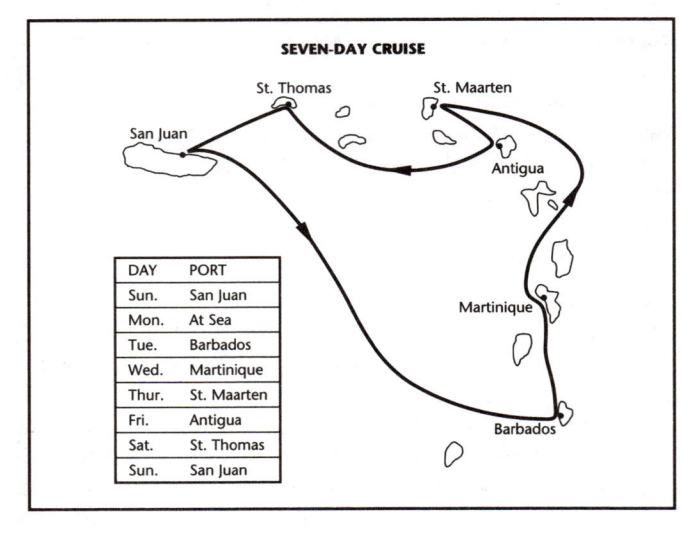

FIGURE 6-3
A Typical Caribbean Cruise Route
SOURCE: Norwegian Cruise Line

In the early days, cruise ships sailed to the Caribbean only during the winter months, generally on seven-day voyages. The winter season is still the busiest, but many Caribbean lines now operate year-round, offering cruises that vary in length from 2 to 14 days. Three- and four-day trips have become increasingly popular in recent years.

More than 30 cruise lines operate in the Caribbean. Carnival, established in 1973, is one of the most aggressive companies in the Caribbean. The company bills itself as "the most popular cruise line in the world." With its casual atmosphere and action-filled on-board program, the emphasis on a Carnival cruise is unmistakably on recreation. (Its nine ships are even billed as " the Fun Ships.")

In 1994, Princess Cruises announced that the world's first 100 000 tonne cruise ship, to be built in Italy, would enter service in 1997 in the Caribbean. It will be capable of carrying 2600 passengers, and will feature a virtual-reality theatre, three show lounges, three main dining rooms, 750 cabins with verandas, and five pools.

The Mexican Riviera The Mexican Riviera is the most popular destination for cruises from West Coast ports, and has been one of the fastest growing areas in the cruise trade in recent years. More than a dozen lines now run there regularly, offering fun in the sun with the added attraction of ports such as Mazatlan, Puerto Vallarta, and Acapulco. Most cruises last seven days or longer and depart from Los Angeles in winter and spring.

Trans-Canal A number of cruise lines offer both the Mexican Riviera and the Caribbean on the same cruise. As well as experiencing two popular cruise areas, passengers also get to pass through the Panama Canal (hence the name trans-Canal cruises). Typical cruises last about ten days and sail between Los Angeles or Acapulco and Fort Lauderdale. Longer cruises terminate or begin at Vancouver.

Alaska Ships that sail south from Los Angeles during the winter season often head north to Alaska in summer. Alaska cruises are currently the fastest growing sector of the cruise market. They are targeted at a different market from the "fun in the sun" cruises. The passenger list may include naturalists, whale watchers, and other adventurers for whom natural wonders are more important than sun.

Seven-day cruises from Vancouver sail up the protected waters of the Inside Passage to the spectacular Glacier Bay National Monument, calling at far northern ports such as Ketchikan, Skagway, Juneau, and Sitka. Fourteen-day Alaska cruises depart from Los Angeles and San Francisco.

The cruise ship terminal in Vancouver is Canada Place, which was built as the Canadian Pavilion for Expo 86. This complex includes a 500-room hotel, a convention centre, and the cruise ship terminal. Its roof—ten peaks that resemble a cluster of unfurled sails—dominates the waterfront.

CHAPTER 6: The Cruise and Steamship Industry

ILLUSTRATION 6-2
Spectacular scenery such as this makes Alaska cruises the fastest-growing sector of the cruise market.
SOURCE: Royal Viking Line

The Hawaiian Islands At present, there are no round-trip cruises from the mainland United States to Hawaii. Honolulu, however, is often a port of call on long South Pacific trips departing from Los Angeles or San Francisco.

American Hawaii Cruises, launched in 1979, operates year-round seven-day cruises of the Hawaiian Islands, calling at all the major ports. The line offers air/cruise packages to encourage people to fly out to Honolulu, the port of departure and return.

The Eastern United States and Canada The coastal waters of New England and the Atlantic provinces have attracted many people, particularly senior citizens. The cruise ships operating in this area are small, with a maximum capacity of 1000. Their size enables them to get in and out of ports that are too small for larger vessels. Coastal cruise ships are generally quieter than the luxury liners that cruise the Caribbean and the Mexican Riviera. They have a greater proportion of elderly passengers on board, and there is little demand for lively entertainment such as discos provide. As always, different travellers have different MNEs.

Seasonal cruises operate along the entire eastern seaboard from Newfoundland to the Florida Keys. A complete cruise along the length of the East Coast takes two or three weeks. The focus is on scenery and historic coastal towns. Shorter cruises of the Atlantic provinces, New England, Chesapeake Bay, the Intracoastal Waterway between Baltimore and Savannah, and the Florida coast are also available. Many of the vessels that serve the East Coast in summer go south to the Caribbean in winter.

The Mediterranean The Mediterranean is the major cruising area in Europe and the most popular destination after the Caribbean. Cruise lines usually concentrate on either the eastern or the western Mediterranean. A few lines operate cruises throughout the region.

The eastern Mediterranean offers attractions similar to those of the Caribbean: plenty of sun and a rich diversity of islands grouped closely together. The area is also steeped in history. Culture can be as strong a motivator as lying in the sun for travellers on Mediterranean cruises.

Piraeus, the port of Athens, is the major point of departure for the Greek cruise lines that dominate the eastern Mediterranean. As in the Caribbean, cruise companies have begun offering more three- and four-day sailings in an attempt to attract first-time cruise passengers.

Western Mediterranean cruises usually depart from Genoa and call at Barcelona, Majorca, Minorca, Gibraltar, and ports on the North African coast.

Northern Europe Norway's North Cape is to Europe what Alaska is to the United States. As in Alaska, the main attraction is the scenery—in this case, the spectacular fjords of Norway's western coast. Cruises lasting 7, 10, or 14 days leave from ports such as Copenhagen, Hamburg, Bergen, and Bremerhaven during the short June–August season. Ships sail up the Norwegian coast as far north as Tromsö and Hammerfest. Some cruises continue even farther north into the Barents Sea.

Copenhagen and Hamburg are also departure points for cruises into the Baltic Sea. Here the emphasis is less on scenery and more on the ports visited, which include St. Petersberg, Helsinki, and Stockholm.

Repositioning Cruises A final type of sea cruise worth noting is the **repositioning cruise**. Because of the seasonal nature of the cruise industry, many cruise lines transfer ships from one cruising area to another between seasons. A line may have a ship that cruises in the Caribbean in winter and in the Mediterranean or northern Europe in summer. Rather than running an empty ship across the Atlantic at the end of the winter, the repositioning voyage is marketed as a special short cruise. Repositioning cruises are also common between the Mexican Riviera and Alaska, and between the Caribbean and the East Coast.

Theme Cruises and Special Interest Cruises

Many of the larger cruise companies try to vary their cruise programs by occasionally offering cruises structured around a particular theme. French-owned Croisières Paquet pioneered the theme cruise in 1968 with the first of its many classical music festivals at sea. Other lines were quick to see the value of theme cruises as a marketing tool and began to develop cruises to fit a wide range of special interests.

Theme cruises can be broken down into several categories, each reflecting the different motivations of different travellers:

- recreation (sports, backgammon, bridge)
- culture (classical music, opera, Big Band music, film, theatre)
- education (history lectures, professional study programs, financial planning)
- health (diet and exercise)
- hobbies (stamp collecting, photography, gourmet cuisine, wine tasting, murder mysteries)

Most of the lines try to hire top-name celebrities to lecture and perform on theme cruises. Paquet, for example, featured renowned international performers, including violinist Isaac Stern and flutist Jean-Pierre Rampal, on its 35th music festival cruise in 1991.

Some smaller companies run nothing but adventure and academic cruises. The emphasis is on exploration, study, or both. Guest scholars lecture on history, zoology, botany, archaeology, anthropology, and related topics. Instructors can even require their student-passengers to complete homework assignments. This is quite a contrast to "fun in the sun"! Clearly, these highly specialized cruises are targeted at a completely different market than are the warm-water cruises.

Ships for adventure and academic cruises usually accommodate fewer than 150 passengers and are designed to reach out-of-the-way areas not served by the larger cruise liners. A number of American companies have stepped into the market and operate a variety of cruises to exotic locations. These companies include Society Expeditions and Special Expeditions.

Freighter Cruises

The world cruise fleet is supplemented by about 80 freighters that provide accommodations for a limited number of passengers on worldwide itineraries. As the name suggests, freighters are principally engaged in cargo transportation, but passengers can be an important source of additional income.

Freighter cruises are an alternative for those travellers who prefer to avoid the crowds of people on large cruise liners. Freighters usually carry a maximum of 12 passengers. (If they carry more, they are required to have a doctor on board.) These cruises last anywhere from one to four months. Travellers who cannot spare that much time can purchase segments of longer cruises. A major attraction of freighter cruises is that they often put in at ports not usually visited by the scheduled cruise lines.

Freighter cabins are as large and as comfortable as those found on cruise ships and are often more moderately priced. On the negative side, on-board entertainment and amenities are extremely limited. Also, schedules and itineraries are subject to change at short notice. While every effort is made to make the cruise as enjoyable as possible, the ship's major business is carrying freight, not pampering guests. For these reasons, freighter cruises are only for the more adventurous travellers, those with different MNEs than, for example, Caribbean cruise passengers.

River Cruises

The river cruise has much in common with the coastal cruise that you read about earlier. On both types of cruise, the vessel never leaves sight of shore. There is always something for the passenger to see, which means that on-board distractions don't have to be as numerous as on ocean-going cruises. The river cruise, like the coastal cruise, tends to appeal more to the over-55 age group.

The Mississippi is the most popular river for cruising in North America. At the height of the steamboat age, thousands of paddlewheelers plied the Mississippi. Today, the two best-known riverboats in service are the *Delta Queen*, last of the old-time steamboats, and its modern sister ship, the *Mississippi Queen*. Both are operated by the Delta Queen Steamboat Company, which offers year-round (excluding January) 3- to 12-night cruises of the Mississippi and Ohio rivers. Shorter cruises depart from New Orleans and call at ante-bellum mansions and at the historic riverboat towns of the lower Mississippi, including Baton Rouge, Natchez, and Vicksburg. Longer cruises may include stops at other cities, such as Memphis, St. Louis, and St. Paul on the Mississippi, and Cincinnati and Pittsburgh on the Ohio.

Recently, some Illinois and Iowa cities along the Mississippi River have revived riverboat gambling on board several "floating casinos."

Seasonal cruises are also offered on the Hudson and the St. Lawrence rivers, and on the rivers of the Pacific Northwest. A new service began on Great Slave Lake in the Northwest Territories in the summer of 1994. This is the M.S. *Norweta*, a small Mackenzie River passenger vessel. The week-long expedition offers day trips for hiking and for observing the summer nesting grounds of over 200 species of birds and waterfowl, as well as a visit to the Dene community of Snowdrift.

The waterways of Europe are well travelled by cruise vessels between April and October. Luxury liners carrying up to 200 passengers cruise the Rhine, Moselle, Danube, Volga, and Don rivers. Tiny barges chug along the smaller rivers and canals of England and France.

More exotic riverboat cruises are available in Egypt and South America. These appeal to the same type of traveller who takes ocean-going adventure cruises. Hilton International has year-round sailings up the Nile, where the tombs and temples of the pharaohs are the major attractions. The Sun Line's 620-passenger *Stella Solaris* sails to one of the most exotic of all cruise destinations—the Amazon.

Yacht Charters

Yachts can be chartered either with or without a crew. In the first category, the people chartering the yacht decide the itinerary but leave the actual task of sailing to a professional crew. However, passengers are sometimes given sailing lessons. In the second category, the yacht is chartered by a group of experienced sailors who operate the vessel themselves.

The Caribbean is the main area for charters. Yachts can also be chartered in the Greek Islands and off the New England coast. The Charter Yacht Brokers' Association represents yacht owners in the United States and abroad and acts as a wholesaler of charters.

Tall Ships

The visit of an armada of "tall ships"—classic sailing ships and training vessels for naval cadets—from various nations to cities such as New York in 1976 and Halifax and Quebec City in 1984 created a new interest in travelling on them. Tourists can now sail on a variety of tall ships. On some of them, they can help crew.

Point-to-Point Crossings

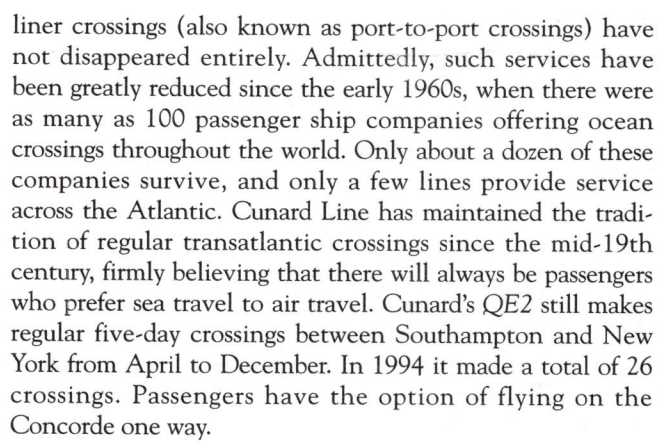

The cruise trade has clearly been the major growth area for the shipping industry in the last 25 years. But point-to-point liner crossings (also known as port-to-port crossings) have not disappeared entirely. Admittedly, such services have been greatly reduced since the early 1960s, when there were as many as 100 passenger ship companies offering ocean crossings throughout the world. Only about a dozen of these companies survive, and only a few lines provide service across the Atlantic. Cunard Line has maintained the tradition of regular transatlantic crossings since the mid-19th century, firmly believing that there will always be passengers who prefer sea travel to air travel. Cunard's *QE2* still makes regular five-day crossings between Southampton and New York from April to December. In 1994 it made a total of 26 crossings. Passengers have the option of flying on the Concorde one way.

It remains to be seen whether long-distance, point-to-point passenger crossings will disappear entirely. Although air travel is much faster than sea travel, point-to-point crossings still offer a number of distinct advantages. At the simplest level, they are the only alternative on transoceanic routes for people who don't like to fly. Also, passengers are free to take much more baggage by sea than by air—an important consideration for those planning an extended stay at their destination. (Even large items such as cars and furniture can accompany the passenger by sea.) And for those who have the time, the crossing is a mini-vacation in itself. The cost of a transatlantic crossing is not much more than first-class airfare, which is quite a bargain when you bear in mind that all meals and accommodations are included.

Ferries Ferry boat service is the one form of point-to-point water transportation that has been largely unaffected by the increase in air traffic. One reason is that ferry routes tend to be short and comparatively inexpensive. Another reason is that ferries often operate on routes that are poorly served by air. Some destinations are only accessible by ferry. Not all ferry routes are short, however. Some ferries steam for several hours and offer cabins, restaurants, and recreation rooms. In spite of these creature comforts, ferry companies do not pretend to be in the cruise business; their priority is transportation from point A to point B.

Some ferries are intermodal. In addition to passengers, they carry cars, trucks, and even railway cars. Intermodal ferries can be as large as cruise ships.

Ferries are in operation throughout the world. They connect, for example, Alaska and the western United States; the Atlantic provinces of Canada; Vancouver Island and mainland British Columbia; the Japanese islands; and Great Britain and continental Europe. Currently, the English Channel is one of the busiest ferry crossings in the world. A staggering 50 million passengers a year cross between southern England and northern Europe. Of course, the opening of the English Channel tunnel in 1994 will decrease the number of ferry passengers. Nonetheless, the ferry business is an extremely important segment of the passenger shipping industry.

Canada's west and east coasts have extensive ferry services. Most routes in British Columbia are between the

ILLUSTRATION 6-3
The *Delta Queen* and the *Mississippi Queen* are pieces of living history that still ply the waters of the Mississippi River.
SOURCE: Delta Queen Steamboat Company

lower mainland and Vancouver Island. A new, $137 million jumbo S-class ferry, the *Spirit of B.C.*, entered service on the Tsawwassen–Swartz Bay route in 1993. Other routes include Vancouver–Nanaimo and Horseshoe Bay–Nanaimo. In summer, a combined boat–train day tour takes passengers from Vancouver to Squamish on the *Britannia* and returns them on the historic Royal Hudson steam train along Howe Sound.

Ferry services on the East Coast operate between various provinces and between Nova Scotia and New England. Marine Atlantic operates routes between Saint John, New Brunswick, and Digby, Nova Scotia, across the Bay of Fundy; between Borden, Prince Edward Island, and Cape Tormentine, New Brunswick, across the Northumberland Strait; between North Sydney, Nova Scotia, and Port aux Basques, Newfoundland, across the Gulf of St. Lawrence; and between Yarmouth, Nova Scotia, and Bar Harbor, Maine. Other routes are summer only: Caribou, Nova Scotia, to Wood Islands, Prince Edward Island, and Yarmouth, Nova Scotia, to Portland, Maine. The international routes have gambling on board while the ferry is in international waters.

CHECK YOUR PRODUCT KNOWLEDGE

1. Why are the Caribbean and Mediterranean such popular cruise areas?
2. Name three cold-water cruise areas.
3. Give two advantages and two disadvantages of cruising by freighter.
4. What are some of the attractions of a point-to-point crossing?

CRUISE MARKETING

Although the number of people taking cruises has increased significantly over the 30 years of the modern cruise industry's existence, only about 4 percent of Canadians and Americans have taken a cruise. This means that there are almost 270 million people in those two countries who are ready to become first-time cruisers! In this section, you will read about how the cruise industry is trying to tap this vast potential market.

Broadening the Appeal of Cruises

There are two main reasons why the cruise industry has not been able to capture a larger share of the travel market:

- Lack of public awareness about the range of cruise products available.
- Misconceptions about cruising.

Individual cruise companies and the Cruise Lines International Association (CLIA) have addressed the first problem by aiming major advertising campaigns and other promotional efforts at potential cruisers.

To understand the misconceptions that exist about cruising, we must return to the distinction between traditional and contemporary cruises. Far too many people in Canada and the United States still think of cruises in terms of traditional cruises—that they are only for the rich and the elderly, that they last for several weeks, and that they are expensive, upscale, and formal. A few modern cruises can still be characterized this way, but by far the greater number are now contemporary cruises, that is, shorter, less expensive, and organized to appeal to a much wider market.

A key marketing tool used by contemporary cruise companies is the three- and four-day cruise. By introducing shorter vacations, cruise lines have been able to attract many first-time passengers who otherwise might not have thought of taking a cruise. About 90 percent of all passengers on three- and four-day cruises are first-timers. Once passengers have experienced and enjoyed a shorter cruise, they are more likely to take longer cruises with the company in the future (see Table 6–3). Some cruise lines even promote one-day cruises to nowhere to give people a taste of cruising.

The three- and four-day cruises have proved particularly popular with the under-40 age group. Carnival Cruise Lines caters heavily to the younger market with activities such as singles parties. Other lines attract young married couples with honeymoon cruises. Families with young children can take advantage of baby-sitting services, and many lines now offer programs for young children and teenagers. Substantially reduced rates for children sharing their parents' accommodations are also an incentive. All these measures have served to lower the average age of cruise passengers. Today, there are almost as many passengers in the 25–40 age group as in the 60-and-older category. More than 40 percent of all first-time passengers are under 40.

Length of Cruise	Passengers (000's) 1980	1993	% Growth
2–5 days	347	1,642	+373
6–8 days	846	2,426	+187
9–17 days	221	408	+84
18+ days	17	16	(6)
Total	1431	4491	+214

TABLE 6-3
Growth by Length of Cruise
SOURCE: Cruise Lines International Association

Cruise companies have begun to develop theme and special-interest cruises. The theory is that people are more likely to take a cruise if it is focused on something that strongly interests them. Lovers of classical music, for example, may be more inclined to take a cruise if there is a program of on-board concerts.

Many cruise companies are also pursuing commercial business. Several ships are now equipped with facilities to handle meetings and conventions, and cruises are being used increasingly as incentives. (Incentive travel is discussed in detail in Chapter 12.)

Fly/Cruise Packages

Cruise lines are also marketing cruises over a wider geographic area. In the early days of cruising, Caribbean cruises sailing from Florida ports were marketed only in the Southeast. West Coast cruises departing from Los Angeles were marketed only in California. This meant that if you lived in Regina, Saskatchewan, you probably didn't think of going on a cruise.

All that has changed, and cruises of all types and to all destinations are now marketed throughout Canada and the United States. What has made this possible is the introduction of the fly/cruise concept. **Fly/cruise packages** (or air/sea packages, as they are sometimes known), now readily available, fly passengers to and from the port of embarkation, wherever they live in North America. The airfare is often included in the package price and can be greatly reduced. Cruise lines arrange air transportation on scheduled or chartered airlines. As an alternative, they may issue passengers an air travel credit; passengers then make their own travel arrangements. The credit is deducted from the cruise fare.

As the market becomes more competitive, particularly in the Caribbean, the fly/cruise package is becoming increasingly important as a promotional tool for the cruise lines. Fly/cruise packages now account for almost 75 percent of all cruise bookings. Fly/cruise options have proved very successful in attracting first-time passengers, especially those who live far from the major cruising ports. That resident of Regina is now much more likely to consider a cruise as a vacation option.

Fly/cruise packages are most often used to transport passengers to warm-water ports like Miami, Fort Lauderdale, and Los Angeles. The advantage for passengers is that they spend their whole vacation at sea in warm weather. On the most practical level, it means that they need only bring one wardrobe instead of two. Imagine, by contrast, a December sailing from New York to St. Thomas. The passenger has to endure two days of cold weather and rough seas on the southbound journey to the Caribbean, and more of the same on the way back. The alternative is a flight of less than three hours to Miami and almost four extra days at sea in the sun.

The fly/cruise concept also has another application. This is the "fly one way, cruise the other" package. This type of package was first introduced on transatlantic routes in the early 1960s. Cunard and British Airways have maintained the tradition with an outward journey from New York on the QE2 and a return flight from Europe by Concorde. The chief advantage of this type of package is that it reduces point-to-point travel time, allowing passengers to custom-tailor their vacation. For example, a passenger may wish to cruise from Los Angeles to Acapulco. The complete round-trip cruise, including shore excursions, will take about two weeks. A passenger who has only one week to spend can cruise to Acapulco, then fly back to Los Angeles.

Land/Cruise Packages The **land/cruise package** is another marketing tool that has been developed by many contemporary cruise lines. The land section of the package typically involves a short stay in a hotel at or near the port of embarkation. It can be taken either immediately before the cruise begins, or after it is over. American Hawaii Cruises, for example, gives passengers booking their seven-day Hawaiian Islands cruise the option of a three-day/two-night vacation at an island hotel.

In Canada, Atlas Tours has an Alaska–Yukon–Canadian Rockies tour that combines travel by cruise ship, motorcoach, rail, and air. And Globus's "Heart of the Canadian Rockies" tour combines travel by motorcoach and snowmobile (on the Columbia Icefields) with a cruise through the Gulf Islands.

It was a stroke of marketing genius that packaged a four-night Bahamas cruise with a three-day Disney World vacation. Premier Cruise Lines—"The Official Cruise Line of Walt Disney World"—pioneered this concept. It has become one of the most popular of all land/cruise options. The Disney World segment typically includes accommodations at an Orlando hotel; admission to the Magic Kingdom, EPCOT Center, and Disney–MGM Studios; a tour of the Kennedy Space Center; and the use of a rental car.

Cruise Pricing

Cruise ships have the highest overheads in the travel industry. To cover operating costs, cruise lines must achieve 80 to 90 percent occupancy rates. (In contrast, airlines can break even at 60 to 65 percent, and hotels at 55 to 60 percent.)

Pricing is the key to making sure that a cruise ship leaves port as full as possible. All cruise lines offer tiered pricing to attract passengers across a wide range of income levels. There can be more than a dozen price categories on a single cruise. The most expensive category (deluxe) can cost twice as much as the least expensive (economy). For the extra money, the cruise passenger gets a better cabin.

Cruise lines also offer discount fares as passenger incentives. Many lines have off-season rates, and reduced rates for clients who book well in advance. Others offer discounts for repeat cruisers. Another promotional pricing technique is to accommodate the third or fourth person in a cabin at a reduced rate.

PROFILE

Robert Dickinson

When Bob Dickinson joined Carnival Cruise Lines in 1973, the company owned only one ship and was on the edge of bankruptcy. Dickinson was hired to direct the floundering company's sales and marketing division, something he admitted he knew little about. Nevertheless, Dickinson's sales and marketing ideas have transformed the cruise industry and helped make Carnival the largest and most popular cruise line in the world.

Dickinson graduated from John Carroll University in Ohio in 1965 and studied two years for a master's degree in business administration at Duquesne University in Pittsburgh, Pennsylvania. Before joining Carnival, he worked for the Ford Motor Company and for RCA. Then he joined the American International Travel Service (AITS), which was then the parent company of Carnival Cruise Lines. In all those jobs, Dickinson's work focused on finance, not on sales and marketing.

When it came to selling cruises, Dickinson once said, "I had no perspective and no experience." Not only did he learn how to sell cruises, he practically reinvented the cruise industry. When he started out with Carnival, the modern cruise industry was in its infancy. The people who then took cruises were mainly older, wealthy people who saw cruising as a quiet, elegant way to travel to a vacation destination.

One of Dickinson's first innovations was to develop the "Fun Ship" concept—the idea that a cruise was not just a way to get from port to port but an entire vacation in itself. The "Fun Ship" concept was also a way to let people know that cruises were not just for older travellers but for families, young couples, and singles looking for romance. Dickinson also sought to change the image of cruises as too expensive for the average vacationer. His idea was to promote the cruise as an entire vacation package at a price that was competitive with any other type of vacation or tour package.

Dickinson's strategies worked so brilliantly that within three years, Carnival had earned enough profit to purchase a second ship, the *Empress of Britain,* which was renamed the *Carnivale.* In 1978, Carnival added a third ship to its fleet—the *Festivale.* These three ships made week-long round-trip cruises from Miami to various Caribbean ports.

In the mid-1980s the company began building new cruise ships (the first to be built in 30 years). In 1979, Dickinson was named Carnival's senior vice-president for sales and marketing. In 1992, he became president of the company.

Early on, Dickinson recognized the value of using travel agents to market Carnival cruises. Here was a ready-made, in-place sales force with thousands of locations throughout the United States. At the time, many travel agencies were little more than ticket offices—places where customers went to buy airline tickets and pick up vacation brochures. Many agencies were uninviting offices whose employees were not necessarily interested in trying to *sell* anything.

Dickinson believed that the best way for Carnival to sell its cruises was to change the way travel agents did business. He envisioned travel agencies as vacation stores where people could go and shop for a vacation, just as they shopped for any other goods and services. He wanted travel agents to sell cruises, but not through high-pressure sales tactics. Instead, he wanted them to learn to match the customers' needs and expectations with the products that Carnival had to offer.

To help travel agents learn how to sell cruises, Dickinson's department developed a staff of sales representatives who, by the early 1990s, numbered more than 75. Each sales representative now serves more than 500 travel agents a year, providing help, suggestions, and information on new products and services. The department also produced a series of short, entertaining videotapes to help educate travel agents and motivate them to sell Carnival cruises. In addition, the company has established a firm policy of supporting travel agents by not participating in any discount programs that might separate travel agents from their commissions.

Coupled with an extensive TV advertising campaign to attract consumers, Dickinson's marketing strategies have paid off handsomely. Carnival's bookings and profits have grown steadily each year. The Carnival fleet has grown to nine "Fun Ships," and the company also owns two other cruise lines. While other cruise companies have sought to duplicate Dickinson's formula, his rivals concede that he is still the man to beat when it comes to selling cruises.

CHAPTER 6: The Cruise and Steamship Industry

> **CHECK YOUR PRODUCT KNOWLEDGE**
>
> 1. What are three image problems that contemporary cruise companies face? What measures have the lines taken to address these problems?
> 2. Explain how the fly/cruise concept works. What are two advantages of fly/cruise packages?
> 3. What pricing techniques do cruise lines use to achieve high occupancy rates?

THE CRUISE AS PRODUCT

The cruise is a unique travel product, one that combines both transportation and destination. This section will focus on the cruise ship as destination. You will read how the ship functions as a "floating hotel" and how the cruise program is structured. You will also look at the physical layout of a cruise ship and at the factors that affect the price of a cruise.

The Ship as Hotel

Almost every cruise ship calls at one or more ports during its journey. This represents the transportation element of the cruise product. Yet on most cruises, the ship itself is the main attraction. A headline in a recent Costa Lines cruise brochure made the point very well: "Even if she never left home port, the *Carla Costa* would be a fabulous vacation destination by herself." In the same brochure, the *Costa Riviera* was referred to as "a floating European island."

A "floating island" may be stretching the point a little far, but a cruise ship is certainly a "floating hotel." For the vacation traveller, the ship must combine all the services of a resort hotel with the amenities of a vacation on dry land. For the business traveller, the cruise ship must be able to offer all the facilities of a convention hotel or convention/conference centre. (Note that cruise ships have limited appeal for our third type of traveller—the person who is visiting friends and relatives. This type of traveller usually travels by air or by land. An exception would be if his or her friends and relatives were travelling on the same cruise.)

Meeting Passengers' MNEs Because passengers cannot leave the ship while it is at sea, the cruise line must ensure that everything they might need or want is on board. A passenger's most basic needs, of course, are for food and a place to sleep. Many will require the services of a laundry and a hairstylist. Others may expect to find a gymnasium or health centre on board. Some will want to attend religious services. Business executives may need to keep in touch with the outside world by telephone or fax machine. They may also want access to a computer while on board. In short, the ship must provide a wide array of services, particularly on longer voyages.

Then there is the question of how to amuse the passengers while they are on board. A few will be content to laze in the sun all day. But most will expect a variety of on-board activities and nightly entertainment.

It is hardly surprising, then, that most ships are so heavily staffed. There is a division between the ship's crew, or ship's company, and the hotel crew, or staff. The ship's crew includes these:

- the captain
- first, second, and third officers (or "mates")
- engineering officers
- radio officers
- medical officers
- pursers
- ordinary and able seamen

The hotel crew includes these:

- the hotel manager
- the cruise (or social) director
- stewards (including cabin stewards, dining room stewards, wine stewards, night stewards, and deck stewards)
- the kitchen and galley staff
- bartenders
- service workers (including barbers, hairstylists, launderers, librarians, masseurs, photographers, printers, and shop assistants)
- entertainers, instructors, and lecturers

ILLUSTRATION 6-4
Royal Caribbean Cruise Line passengers enjoying an early morning workout on sports deck, one of 13 exercise activities offered in the line's Shipshape program.
SOURCE: Royal Caribbean Cruise Line

Cruise guides and manuals often indicate the ratio between the total number of passengers and the number of hotel-crew members. Many cruise ships have one crew member for every two passengers. In general, the higher the crew ratio, the better the level of passenger service.

Physically Challenged Passengers The physically challenged cruise passenger has special needs. He or she may require individualized attention and supervision, as well as special facilities. Some cruise ships are fitted with ramps, elevators, and other devices that circumvent obstacles. There may be one or two cabins on board that have been modified for wheelchair-bound passengers. Not all cruise lines, however, have the facilities to accommodate the physically challenged traveller. Many state in their brochures that they "reserve the right to refuse passengers who require treatment, care, or attention beyond that which on-board facilities can provide, or whose mental or physical condition may make them incapable of an ocean voyage."

The Cruise as Vacation at Sea

A cruise program typically comprises four main elements:

- meals
- activities
- entertainment
- time on shore

The balance of the various components will differ depending on the type of cruise. A warm-water cruise, for example, is likely to stress on-board activities and entertainment. An adventure cruise, on the other hand, is more likely to place the emphasis on time ashore. Even on a theme cruise, where everyone shares a common interest, the elements must be flexible enough to suit the needs and expectations of different kinds of passengers. Some passengers may expect to be served North American–style meals; others may want to try ethnic cuisine. Some passengers will want to spend their free time aboard ship playing backgammon; others will want to attend lectures. What follows is a typical vacation program for a contemporary mass-market cruise.

Meals Eating ranks as one of the most popular activities on most cruises. All cruise lines excel in the quality and quantity of their food. The cuisine can be international or feature ethnic dishes. Many of the foreign-owned lines offer a taste of their home country or port of registry. The Norwegian Cruise Line features such exotic specialties as reindeer pâté.

Activities Cruise directors schedule a full program of daytime activities while the ship is at sea. Exercise classes are popular with many passengers. On most of the larger liners, instructors are on hand to give lessons in golf, tennis, dancing, photography, painting, flower arranging, foreign languages, and even ukulele playing (on Hawaiian cruises). Guest lecturers often give talks on the history and local culture of islands to be visited. There can also be swimming pool games and deck activities, a daily bingo session, as well as tournaments in shuffleboard, ping-pong, chess, backgammon, bridge, and other games.

Entertainment After dinner, many passengers head to the main lounge for the nightly musical variety show. Cabaret singers and piano players perform in the more intimate lounges and bars on board. On many cruises, there is often a masquerade party and talent night for the ship's passengers. Most liners have at least one ballroom, where passengers can dance to the music of an orchestra. Discos and nightclubs have become standard features on many ships, as have casinos. First-run movies and classic favourites are shown in the ship's movie theatre.

Shore Excursions Shore excursions are an important part of almost every cruise. They can sometimes be the main attraction, especially on adventure or academic cruises. When booking a cruise, passengers do not have to commit themselves to shore excursions, which can be purchased individually or as a package from the shore excursion desk on board.

A cruise ship isn't always able to tie up to a pier when it reaches a port; the ship may be too big to use the normal docking facilities. In such cases, the ship rides at anchor in the harbour, and passengers are shipped ashore in small boats called **tenders** or **lighters.**

On three- and four-day cruises, the stay in port is limited to a few hours, giving passengers just enough time to do some sightseeing and shopping, and maybe take in some local entertainment. A few cruise lines have purchased islands or stretches of beach in the Caribbean for the exclusive use of their passengers during shore excursions.

On longer cruises, passengers can spend as long as two or three days at a destination. Occasionally, the ship will move to another port, where the passengers will rejoin it after an escorted overland tour. More and more companies are now selling packages that combine a sea or river cruise with a land tour.

What Is and Is Not Included One of the greatest attractions of a cruise is that it is essentially an all-inclusive vacation. In this respect, it has much in common with the tour package. Most major expenses are prepaid, so passengers don't have to carry large sums of money.

Included in the cruise price are these:

- ocean or river transportation
- shipboard accommodations
- all meals
- on-board entertainment and activities
- most services
- transfers from ship to shore when in port

CHAPTER 6: The Cruise and Steamship Industry

Transportation to the port of embarkation may also be included.

Costs not included in the price are those which reflect personal choice:

- shore excursions
- port taxes
- medical expenses
- laundry (or valet), sauna, and other personal services
- expenditures in shops on board
- gambling chips in the casino
- beer, wine, and spirits
- tips

Port taxes must be paid by every passenger on disembarkation at any port during the cruise. They vary greatly but are usually in the region of $15 to $20 per person at each port.

Tipping can be a cause of considerable confusion, since passengers are not always sure who or how much they should tip. Individual cruise lines usually issue recommendations for tipping hotel and dining room personnel.

Factors Affecting the Price of a Cruise

There are four major factors that determine the cruise price:

- duration of cruise
- season
- cabin location and size
- ship profile

Duration as a factor should be fairly obvious: a two-week cruise is likely to cost more than a seven-day cruise. Costs are usually figured out on a per diem or daily basis. For example, the per diem for an $800, four-day cruise would be $200. Per diems make it easier to compare costs for different cabins or for different cruises.

Cruise prices can vary considerably depending on the time of year when the ship sails. Prices are highest during the peak or high season (winter in the Caribbean, summer in Alaska) and lowest during the off or low season.

The Physical Layout of the Ship

Larger liners can have as many as ten decks. Passenger accommodations are usually concentrated in the lower decks, with the upper decks reserved for public rooms, swimming pools, and activity areas. Meeting rooms are typically located away from the noisiest parts of the ship. Liners designed for warm-water cruising have larger areas of open sun deck on board than ships sailing to Alaska or northern Europe. Some ships are fitted with all-weather sliding roofs, called **magrodomes**, which can be closed in bad weather.

Cabins, or staterooms as they are sometimes known, are either **outside cabins** or **inside cabins**. Outside cabins have portholes or windows and a view of the ocean; inside cabins have no access to natural light and face onto a central passageway. Today, most cruise lines design their vessels with the maximum possible number of outside cabins.

Most cabins are designed to accommodate two passengers, usually in twin beds but sometimes in a double. The beds on some ships are fixed to the floor; on others, they convert from sofas, or must be pulled down from the wall. Regardless of the type of bed, all sleeping places in a cabin are referred to as **berths**.

Smaller cabins designed for singles or two economy-minded passengers have an upper and lower berth. Larger cabins can accommodate up to four passengers and are suitable for families or for young people who want to save money by sharing. The two extra passengers sleep in upper berths above the twin beds. The largest and most comfortable cabins are the suites and minisuites, which usually feature fixed double beds, separate dressing and sitting areas, and a bath as well as a shower.

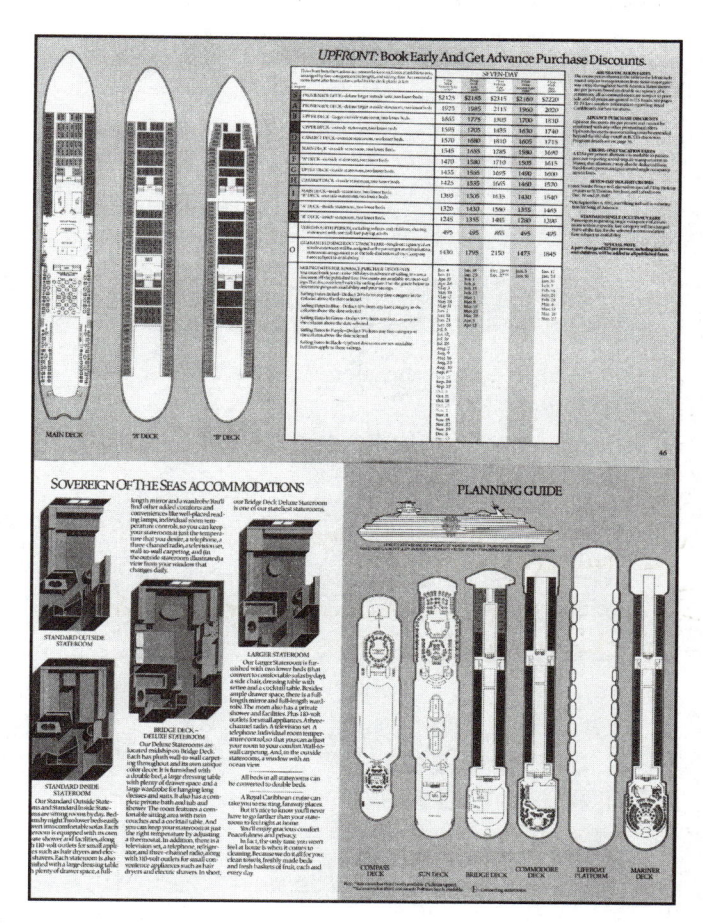

ILLUSTRATION 6-5

On large liners, passenger accommodations are usually concentrated in the lower decks. The cabins are either outside or inside cabins.

SOURCE: Royal Caribbean Cruise Lines

The location of the cabin is the major factor influencing the cruise price. As a general rule, the higher above the water, the more expensive the cabin will be, because higher cabins afford passengers a better view and are usually closer to public areas. And cabins located amidships are more expensive than cabins either forward or aft, because any side-to-side movement (roll) or up-and-down movement (pitch) is less pronounced amidships. Also, outside cabins are more expensive than inside cabins. In fact, an outside cabin on even the lowest deck invariably costs more than an inside cabin on the highest. As well as location, cabin size is a cost determinant, as is the number of passengers in the cabin. In shared cabins, the third and fourth occupants usually travel at a reduced rate. At the other extreme, single occupants have to pay a single supplement. It should be pointed out that even though there are many different cabin price categories, all passengers are entitled to the same high level of service. A passenger travelling in the least expensive inside cabin enjoys the same menu, the same entertainment, the same activities, and the same choice of shore excursions as does a passenger in a deluxe suite.

The final factor affecting the price of the cruise is the ship profile, or type of ship. Some of the older vessels that have been converted from point-to-point service tend to command higher prices than do the newer cruise ships. This is partly because the older ships are more spacious, with lower passenger densities. The space ratio for a ship can be calculated by comparing the **gross registered tonnage (GRT)** to the number of passengers carried. The GRT represents the amount of enclosed space on the ship.

> **CHECK YOUR PRODUCT KNOWLEDGE**
>
> 1. What is the difference between the ship's crew and the hotel crew?
> 2. What are the four components of the cruise program?
> 3. What costs are usually not included in the price of a cruise?
> 4. List the four factors that affect the price of a cruise.

THE CHANNELS OF DISTRIBUTION

In the old days, tickets for point-to-point service were sold through direct sales outlets. The modern cruise passenger, however, almost never buys a ticket from a cruise line's sales office. Over 95 percent of passengers book their cruises through travel agents. This makes the cruise industry more dependent on travel agents than any other segment of the travel industry.

Selecting the Cruise

Selecting and selling a cruise is one of the quickest and least complicated of all travel agency transactions. It is also one of the most lucrative. Agency commissions on cruises are considerably higher than on other travel products. The travel agency gets a commission on every component of the cruise product—transportation, accommodations, meals, entertainment, and sightseeing—and all from a single supplier.

Probably the hardest task for the travel professional is matching the MNEs of different types of travellers to the different types of cruises. Few clients who come into a travel agency have a fixed idea of the specific ship they want to cruise on. Some may not even know what geographic area they want to visit. It is the travel agent's job to find the right ship for each potential passenger. The agent must first establish the MNEs of the client. Is this man looking for a ship with lots of entertainment and opportunities to socialize? Does this woman prefer a quiet atmosphere, formal dining, and older passengers?

After gaining some idea of the client's MNEs, the travel agent can start to narrow down the choice of ships and itineraries. There are a number of reference works to help with this:

- The *Official Steamship Guide International* (*OSGI*) provides up-to-date listings of cruise schedules throughout the world, as well as information on cruise lines and featured ports of call.
- The *OAG Worldwide Cruise and Shipline Guide* offers much the same information as the *OSGI*, as well as information on port taxes and staff/passenger ratios. Also, maps.
- The *OHG Cruise Directory* is similar to the *OSGI*, but includes deck plans and ship profiles.
- *Ford's International Cruise Guide* provides extensive information about individual cruise ships.
- *Ford's Freighter Travel Guide* lists freighter cruises, river cruises, and yacht charters.
- *Ford's Deck Plan Guide* has plans of over 130 ships.
- The *CLIA Cruise Manual*, published by CLIA, has profiles of ships and CLIA cruise lines, maps of ports, detailed descriptions of on-board cruise programs, and information on reservations procedures.
- *Garth's Profile of Ships* contains descriptions of about 200 vessels.

The agent will also show the client some cruise brochures. Once a particular ship has been chosen, the next stage is to analyze deck plans and decide on a cabin category and a specific cabin.

The Reservation Process

Many cruise reservations are still made manually, that is, the travel agent calls a toll-free number to reach the cruise com-

CHAPTER 6: The Cruise and Steamship Industry

pany. Computer availability is, however, increasing. Several of the airline reservations systems used by travel agencies now have the capacity to offer cruise information and bookings. A number of cruise lines have set up links with Cruisematch, a reservations system owned by Royal Caribbean Cruise Lines.

Reservations for cruises are required well in advance, especially for longer cruises. They can be booked as far ahead as two years before sailing time. When the reservation is made, the cruise line gives an option date by which a deposit must be made to confirm the reservation. Final payment is normally required between a month and two months before the cruise begins. Tickets are issued by the cruise line about 30 days before departure.

A client who decides to cancel a reservation is usually charged a cancellation penalty, which gets progressively higher the closer to departure the client cancels. Details of the company's cancellation policy are spelled out in the contract that appears on the back of the cruise brochure. According to the contract, cruise lines guarantee to provide a full refund if a sailing is cancelled. They also reserve the right to change the itinerary or substitute another ship.

CHECK YOUR PRODUCT KNOWLEDGE

1. By what distribution channel are cruises usually sold?
2. What is the normal procedure for paying for a cruise?

THE REGULATION AND PROMOTION OF CRUISES

The cruise industry is one of the least regulated sectors of the travel industry. While not totally free of government intervention, cruise lines are largely free to choose their own itineraries, change their schedules, and set their own prices. The industry also benefits from government promotion.

Government Promotion and Regulation

The main way that the government promotes the cruise industry is by building and maintaining ports, port facilities, and harbours. In the United States, just as airports are owned and operated by local governments, so too are seaports. In Canada most airports and seaports are owned and operated by the Ministry of Transport. Harbour and port authorities regulate the industry by charging port taxes.

In Canada, the Canadian Coast Guard is responsible for safety. In the United States, the U.S. Coast Guard acts as harbour master and enforcer of government safety requirements. Construction plans for each new ship must be approved by the Coast Guard. Once in active service, all vessels are regularly checked to make sure they meet current safety regulations. Canadian and American maritime safety standards are among the strictest in the world—this is a benefit, in that Canadian and American ships are exceptionally safe. At the same time, these standards also mean that Canadian and American ships are much more costly to build and operate than foreign ships.

All cruise ships that call at North American ports, regardless of their country of registry, must meet not only Canadian and American but also international safety standards. The latter are set by the Safety of Life at Sea (SOLAS) Convention.

Cruise ships picking up passengers at American ports must put up a bond with the Federal Maritime Association. In the past, foreign flagships were restricted in the number of American ports where they could call. Federal restrictions were greatly reduced in 1985, so any foreign vessel can now call at any number of American ports during a cruise, provided that the vessel also visits at least one foreign port.

One final federal regulatory agency in the United States is the U.S. Public Health Service. Agents regularly inspect the galleys and dining rooms of all ships calling at American ports. They set standards of hygiene and overall sanitation.

Cruise Lines International Association

CLIA is a trade association of cruise lines that promotes cruises in North America. Since its founding in 1975, CLIA has devoted itself to promoting the cruise as a desirable vacation experience and to improving the industry's public relations. A recent CLIA program promoted February as National Cruise Vacation Month.

CLIA also functions as a regulatory body that sets rules and standards for travel agents who sell CLIA cruises. Agent training is a major CLIA priority. The association trains agents through its Agency Training Program (ATP) and a video training course. CLIA promotes agency cruise sales by encouraging vacationers to see member travel agents for cruise counselling.

CHECK YOUR PRODUCT KNOWLEDGE

1. In what ways do governments promote and regulate the cruise industry?
2. What is the role of CLIA?

CAREER OPPORTUNITIES

The cruise industry employs about 10 000 North Americans, most of them American because of the number of departures from ports in the United States. This makes it one of the smallest employers in the travel business. The problem is that most cruise ships are of foreign registry and usually hire their crews overseas. The few exceptions to this are the positions of purser, social director, entertainer, lecturer, and, occasionally, medical officer.

On Board

The two basic categories of employment on board a cruise ship are ship's crew and hotel crew (or staff). Ship's crew members responsible for the mechanical operation of the ship are, of course, found on all types of vessels. Hotel crew members are specific to cruise ships and perform duties similar to those of a resort hotel staff.

Ship's Crew The captain is the most important person on board. He or she is in charge of the whole ship and is responsible for its operation and for the safety of its passengers and crew. The captain is assisted by a staff of officers. First, second, and third officers direct the navigation of the ship and the maintenance of the deck and hull.

Engineers operate and maintain the engines and other mechanical equipment on board. The chief engineer supervises the engine department. Radio officers maintain contact with the shore and other ships through voice transmissions and Morse code. They also receive and record weather information, maintain the ship's radio equipment, and arrange ship-to-shore telephone connections for passengers on board.

The purser is in charge of the ship's paperwork and handles monetary transactions. He or she assists the ship's passengers by, for example, exchanging traveller's cheques, providing customs and immigration information, and selling shore excursions. On the larger cruise liners, there will also be a number of assistant pursers.

Able seamen are responsible for much of the deck equipment. They handle the ship's mooring lines when docking and departing and steer the ship according to officers' instructions. Ordinary seamen assist the able seamen and clean and maintain the ship's deck equipment and personnel quarters.

Hotel Crew The hotel crew heavily outnumbers the ship's crew on most cruise ships, especially on those that offer a wide array of services and activities.

A cruise ship will often have a hotel manager who is responsible for the smooth running of all hotel services on board. The cruise director arranges and supervises social and recreational activities for the passengers; this is very similar to what a tour escort does on dry land. He or she will invariably be helped by a large staff of assistants.

The steward department has more employees than either the deck or the engine department on most cruise ships. Room (or cabin) stewards have the same duties as hotel room cleaners: they clean cabins, change beds, and so on. Dining room stewards act as servers under the watchful eye of the captain of the dining room. Wine stewards serve wine at tables; night stewards provide room service; and deck stewards hand out deck chairs, serve drinks on deck, and otherwise see to the passengers' comfort. There is always, of course, a large kitchen staff, including a number of chefs. Food and beverage managers arrange and cater private parties on board. Butchers and bakers are present on all but the shortest cruises.

Depending on the size of the ship and the length of the cruise, many other service jobs must also be filled. Most cruise ships require launderers, hairstylists, shop assistants, bartenders, athletic instructors, photographers, entertainers, lecturers, librarians, and so on. Any ship that carries more than 12 passengers is required to have a doctor on board. The larger ships will have more than one, as well as a staff of nurses.

Ashore

A cruise line's general office ashore is divided into several departments:

- sales and marketing
- individual reservations
- group reservations and sales
- fly/cruise sales
- ticketing
- accounting
- management information
- data processing
- systems analysis

Entry-level positions ashore are primarily in reservations and telephone sales. The reservations and group sales departments of many cruise lines are almost identical to those at airline and tour companies. Cruise lines also have professional, regionally based sales forces. Sales representatives target travel agencies, group and tour organizers, and other intermediaries. They do not sell directly to the public.

From entry-level positions in reservations and sales, employees can move to supervisory positions in the sales, group, or fly/cruise departments, or to the marketing department.

Summary

- The history of ships goes back at least 5000 years. However, scheduled passenger service by ship was not introduced until the early 19th century.
- A major steamship line was founded by Sir Samuel Cunard of Halifax.

- Mechanical improvements paved the way for the first superliners at the beginning of the 20th century.
- The first half of the 20th century was the great age for ocean liners. The comfort of passengers became a vital consideration for shipping lines, which competed with each other by providing ever-more-luxurious accommodations.
- The advent of the jet age in 1958 signalled the decline of point-to-point passenger services.
- With the birth of the modern cruise industry in the early 1960s, the ship itself became the destination. Cruise lines, most of which are European owned and operated, began to offer a wider variety of cruises.
- The availability of shorter cruises, special-interest cruises, fly/cruise packages, and land/cruise packages has broadened the industry's appeal, attracting younger passengers and more first-time clients.
- Large luxury liners serve the popular Caribbean, Mediterranean, and Mexican Riviera cruising areas. Other popular areas are Alaska, the Hawaiian Islands, the eastern United States and Atlantic provinces, and northern Europe. Smaller vessels cruise along inland waterways and to more exotic locations. Ferries provide point-to-point transportation over short distances.
- A cruise ship functions as a floating hotel, offering passengers a wealth of services, activities, and entertainment. Often, there is a crew member for every two passengers.
- The price of a cruise is determined by voyage duration, season, cabin location and size, and type of ship.
- The most desirable accommodations are outside cabins located amidships, high above the water, where the view is at a maximum and the motion of the ship is at a minimum.
- Almost all cruises are booked by travel agents.
- Federal governments regulate the cruise industry by setting various health and safety requirements. Governments also promote cruising, as does the Cruise Lines International Association (CLIA).

Key Terms

steerage
liner
point-to-point
stabilizers
flag of convenience
embarkation
repositioning cruise
fly/cruise package
land/cruise package
tender
lighter
port tax
magrodome
outside cabin
inside cabin
berth
gross registered tonnage (GRT)

What Do You Think?

1. Bearing in mind the availability of worldwide air services, is there still a need for point-to-point liner service in the modern age?
2. Why is the cruise industry dominated by European companies?
3. Which is more important to the cruise industry, the first-time or the repeat passenger? Why?
4. More and more young people are taking cruises. On which types of cruises do older people still make up the majority of passengers?
5. Why are the vast majority of cruises booked through travel agents rather than directly?
6. What will happen to the cruise industry in the future?

Dealing with Product

Somehow the message is not getting through. Despite the publicity and the promotion, fewer than 5 percent of all Canadians and Americans have ever booked a cruise. Does that mean that all the rest are secretly afraid of becoming seasick? Or is it possible that most of us really don't understand the cruise product? What do you understand the cruise product to be? How does this product compare with other travel products? What measures might persuade more people to book cruises?

Dealing with People

A person's perception of a product—that is, the way a person thinks a product will be—is often quite different from reality. Such is the case in the cruise industry. Many travellers have a false perception of a holiday at sea. Travel professionals often have to change a client's perceptions about cruises. They also need to avoid making wrong assumptions about a client's perceptions.

What follows is a series of two-part puzzles. First, can you guess how the following travellers perceive a cruise? Second, what type of cruise would you recommend for these clients?

1. A high school teacher, his wife (a secretary), and their two children (ages 7 and 9). They are planning a one-week spring vacation together.

A DAY IN THE LIFE OF

A Purser

I am a purser for a large cruise ship. My ship takes people on seven-day cruises of the Caribbean. It sails each Sunday from Miami and returns the following Saturday. I have many duties aboard ship, but my main job is to look after the passengers in much the same way that a hotel desk clerk helps hotel guests.

We are beginning a new cruise today so I will go to the airport and greet our cruise passengers. Our vans pick up the passengers and their belongings and drive them to the ship. On the ship, I will collect the passengers' return air tickets and lock the tickets in our office for safekeeping until the end of the cruise.

My fellow pursers and I will help the passengers find their cabins, check their valuables, and cash their traveller's cheques. On the first day, passengers always have lots of questions, and it is part of our job to answer them. Most people ask first about where and when they will be eating their meals and about where various shops and recreation facilities are located.

Including me, there are eight pursers on the cruise ship. Since we staff the purser's office 24 hours a day, we work different shifts. We also have different duties. I work primarily with the passengers. Other pursers are in charge of the financial aspects of operating a cruise ship. They collect and count the revenues from the ship's shops and services. These include our shore excursions, casino, diving expeditions, hair salon, restaurants, and bars.

My boss is the chief purser. He supervises all of the pursers and several of the other cruise personnel. The chief purser is personally responsible for all of the ship's revenues and the passengers' valuables. He must also make sure that the ship and its passengers obey all laws and regulations in foreign ports.

My boss always says that to be a good purser you have to like people—and I do. Cruise passengers are on vacation, and they expect to be pampered. One of my main tasks is to make sure they enjoy themselves as much as possible. I must also be able to get along with my fellow crew members. I have to share a cabin with another person, and I have to work closely with others for a week at a time.

A purser has to be able to react calmly and capably if there is a crisis. A passenger may become seriously ill or have to leave the ship suddenly because of a personal emergency. I am the one who arranges for an ambulance or emergency transportation in those instances. Pursers must also enjoy being problem solvers. If passengers have complaints, they often come to me first, and it is my job to try to resolve their problems.

My job as a purser was not an easy one to get, nor are other cruise ship jobs. Hundreds of people apply for each position. The best way to prepare yourself for a purser's job is to learn a foreign language and some office skills such as typing, accounting, and computer operations. Many cruise lines will not hire a purser who cannot speak at least one foreign language. Most pursers have business training or have already worked as travel agents or hotel desk clerks.

I started out as a reservations clerk at a resort hotel. Then I applied for jobs with small cruise lines that took people on lake and river cruises. My first shipboard job was as a cook on a Mississippi paddleboat. Then I just kept applying to all of the Caribbean cruise lines until I finally landed this job. If you want a job on a cruise ship, you have to be very persistent.

Most people think a job like mine is very glamorous. For the most part, it is. I get to live on a beautiful ship and travel around the Caribbean from November to April, when the weather is very cold in the north. On the other hand, I have to be away from my family for five months at a time, and I am often too busy to really enjoy the ports we visit. Still, the pay is good, and the work is very enjoyable. I will probably look for a job on land in another three or four years. Meanwhile, I plan to keep on cruising.

2. A retired couple in their mid-sixties. They are inexperienced travellers who recently sold their vacation cabin at the lake.
3. A surgeon (age 45) and her husband, an accountant (age 46). They have no children.
4. Room-mates. One is 23 and a dental hygienist, the other is 22 and a registered nurse.
5. An outdoor enthusiast in his mid-thirties. He is a freelance photographer and an avid hiker and cross-country skier.
6. A marketing researcher in her early thirties, who has been recently promoted and is recently divorced. She has travelled often, studied and worked overseas, and doesn't like crowds.

CHAPTER 6: The Cruise and Steamship Industry Name: Orville McDermott

WORKSHEET 6-1 Cruise Marketing

You are a travel professional specializing in cruise products. Many people who have never experienced a modern cruise still have misconceptions about cruises. Tell how you would answer each of the following questions asked by potential cruise vacationers.

1. Isn't a cruise vacation expensive?
   no.
   not for what you are getting

2. Are there different classes of service on cruise ships?
   yes

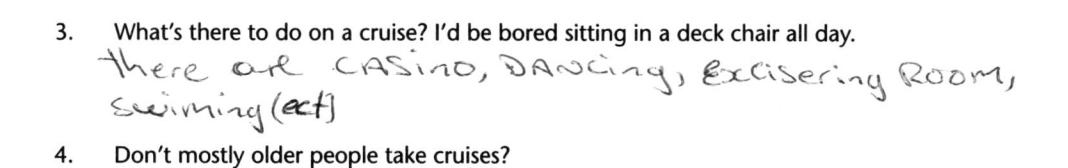

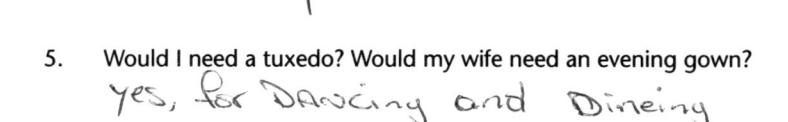

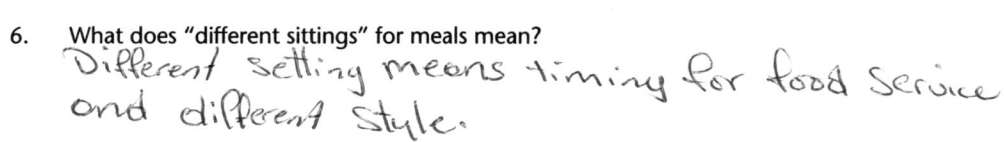

3. What's there to do on a cruise? I'd be bored sitting in a deck chair all day.
   there are casino, dancing, excisering room, swimming (ect)

4. Don't mostly older people take cruises?
   not really

5. Would I need a tuxedo? Would my wife need an evening gown?
   yes, for dancing and dineing

6. What does "different sittings" for meals mean?
   Different setting means timing for food service and different style.

7. What if I don't like the people I'm seated with for dinner?
   you could sit somewere else.

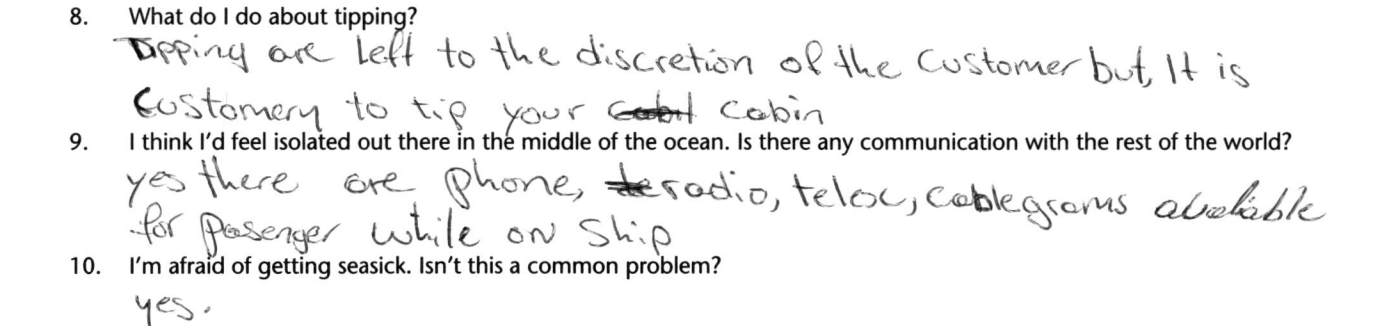

8. What do I do about tipping?
   Tipping are left to the discretion of the customer but, It is customery to tip your cabin

9. I think I'd feel isolated out there in the middle of the ocean. Is there any communication with the rest of the world?
   yes there are phone, radio, telox, cablegrams available for pasenger while on ship

10. I'm afraid of getting seasick. Isn't this a common problem?
    yes.

CHAPTER 6: The Cruise and Steamship Industry   Name: _____

WORKSHEET 6-2 Brochure Information

Get brochures from two cruise lines and compare them.

Cruise line   Royal Caribbean_____   _____

Number of ships in line   _____   _____

Registry   _____   _____

Geographic areas offered   _____   _____
                                   _____   _____
                                   _____   _____
                                   _____   _____

Special features   _____   _____
                                   _____   _____
                                   _____   _____
                                   _____   _____
                                   _____   _____

Deposit and payment schedule   _____   _____
                                   _____   _____
                                   _____   _____
                                   _____   _____

Cancellation policy   _____   _____
                                   _____   _____
                                   _____   _____
                                   _____   _____

Select one cruise from each brochure and compare them.

Cruise   _____   _____

Destination and duration   _____   _____
                                   _____   _____

Accommodation you would choose   _____   _____

Cost   _____   _____

Ports of call   _____   _____
                                   _____   _____
                                   _____   _____
                                   _____   _____

Airfare tie-in (one example)   _____   _____
                                   _____   _____
                                   _____   _____

Special features   _____   _____
                                   _____   _____
                                   _____   _____
                                   _____   _____

CHAPTER 6: The Cruise and Steamship Industry   Name: __Joan Phillips__

WORKSHEET 6-3 Choosing A Cruise

You are a travel agent. A family consisting of <u>two adults</u> in their <u>mid-forties</u>, <u>two children (10 and 14)</u>, and <u>a grandmother in her late sixties</u> wants to cruise the <u>Caribbean for one week</u>. They are <u>not on a restricted budget</u> for this trip, but they <u>do not want luxurious accommodations</u>. They will be <u>flying from and returning to Calgary</u>. Use newspapers, magazines, and brochures to narrow the possible cruises down to two. Then compare them on the following points.

Handwritten calculations in left margin:
adults 2(2689 + 62) = 5502
children 2(1449 + 62) = 3022
gran (2139 + 62) = 2201
to share $1350

Ship	Monarch of the Seas	
Cruise line	Royal Caribbean International	
Ship registry	Norway	
Passenger capacity	2,354	
Chosen accommodations	Outside / Inside / Commodore / Bridge	
Cost Nov 10 – 16	$12 075	
Transportation to (from) port of embarkation (disembarkation)	$1350	
Cost of transportation		
Dates	Nov. 10 '97 – Nov. 16 '97	
Itinerary		
Ports of call	San Juan, St. Thomas, Martinique, Barbados, Antigua, St. Maarten, San Juan	
Activities	Swimming, Jogging Track, Sports, Golf, Fitness, Library, Children's playroom, Teen centre, Casino	
Entertainment	Dancin Lounge, Nightclub, April in Paris Lounge, Piano Bar, Show Lounge	
Medical services		
Facilities for children and teens	Children's playroom, Library, Teen centre	
Facilities for older people	Whirlpools, Library, Sauna, Massage, Boutiques	

157

CHAPTER 6: The Cruise and Steamship Industry   Name: _____

WORKSHEET 6-4 Reading A Deck Plan

Get a brochure from a cruise line. Choose one of the ships and study the deck plan. Then answer the following questions.

Name of ship and cruise line

1. How many decks does the ship have?

   9

2. What is the space ratio? (GRT : number of passengers)

   The average cabin size is 153 sq ft.

3. How many categories of cabins does the ship have?

   14

4. Where are the most expensive cabins located? The least expensive?

5. What is the difference in accommodations between the most expensive and the least expensive cabins?

6. Where are the dining rooms?

7. Where are the gift shops?

8. How many lounges does the ship have?

9. Does the ship have a health and fitness centre?

10. What other entertainment areas does the ship feature?

CHAPTER 7

The Hospitality Industry

"Whoe'er has travelled life's dull round,
Whate'er his various tour has been,
May sigh to think how oft he found
His warmest welcome at an inn."

William Shenstone

OBJECTIVES

When you have completed this chapter, you should be able to do the following:

- **Describe the role played by religion in the early history of the hospitality industry.**
- **Give reasons for the growth of the hotel industry in the 19th century.**
- **Distinguish between motels and motor hotels. Outline the development of resort hotels.**
- **Describe the changes in hotel architecture in the last 25 years.**
- **Classify hotels by form of ownership.**
- **Explain what is meant by market segmentation.**
- **Distinguish between transient and residential hotels.**
- **Classify hotels by function, location, and scale.**
- **Identify the factors that affect the price of a hotel room.**
- **Describe the organizational structure of a hotel.**
- **List the hotel reference books and specify the type of information that each contains.**

Ever since the first lodging houses were built to accommodate travellers in ancient lands, people have been making a living by providing rooms for travellers. Today, of course, hotels offer far more than just a room for the night. Many hotels provide meeting rooms, restaurants, bars, and other facilities to attract business. Some cater to a particular segment of the travel market, such as the business traveller, the convention delegate, or the vacationer. Others offer basic, no-frills service to all guests.

Today in Canada, there are about 300 000 rooms available in more than 7600 hotels and motels. Lodging places range in size from inns with just a few rooms to huge hotels that can accommodate up to 2800 guests. With about 160 000 workers, the accommodation sector is one of the larger employers in the travel industry, ranking third after the food and beverage sector (596 000) and the transportation sector (275 000). The lodging industry is constantly evolving to meet the changing needs of travellers, and this makes it an exciting and dynamic industry.

In this chapter, you'll learn how this giant industry developed, and how it is structured today. You'll also learn about the many decisions that go into the running of a successful hotel, motel, or resort, and about the many kinds of jobs offered by the industry.

A BRIEF HISTORY OF HOSPITALITY

Religion played an important role in the early history of hospitality. There were large numbers of priests, pilgrims, and missionaries journeying to temples and other holy places throughout the eastern Mediterranean region. Many of the first inns came into being because people wanted to open their homes to these religious travellers. These people believed that by so doing they would in some way ensure their own spiritual well-being.

The demand for lodging places increased significantly with the development of an extensive highway system during the Roman era. Roadside inns and taverns throughout Europe provided shelter for travelling merchants and scholars as well as for the growing number of travellers on military, political, and diplomatic missions. Accommodations in these *mansiones* were primitive: quite often there would be stables for the horses but no private rooms for the travellers themselves.

The most elegant inns of the period were developed by the Persians along caravan routes. These *yams*, as they were known, provided travellers with not only accommodations but also food and fresh horses. The explorer Marco Polo estimated that there were as many as 10 000 yams at the time of his journey to the Far East (1275–92).

During the Middle Ages, hospitality was considered a Christian duty. Many monasteries and other religious institutions functioned as inns, offering free accommodations and food for pilgrims and other travellers. One of the largest and most famous lodging places of the period was founded in A.D. 961 by Augustinian monks in the Great Saint Bernard Pass in the Swiss Alps.

An important turning point in the history of hospitality occurred in 1282, when a group of innkeepers in Florence, Italy, was incorporated as a guild and licensed to sell wine. This meant that hospitality was no longer offered as an act of charity. It had become a business venture. The concept spread, and by the early 14th century there were licensed inns throughout Italy.

From Stopping Place to Meeting Place

Few improvements were made in the quality of accommodations until the advent of long-distance stagecoach travel in the 17th century. Journeys by stagecoach over dirt roads were long and arduous. Passengers (most of whom were wealthy) came to expect a warm bed and a hearty meal on their overnight stops. English inns and taverns gained a reputation for cleanliness and comfort and set the standard for accommodations in other parts of Europe.

A typical inn had a dining room in which food and drink were served, a number of private rooms with beds for individual travellers, a large communal room for stagecoach drivers and the staff of the inn, and stables for the horses, all arranged around a central courtyard. These inns were not only for travellers; they quickly became popular meeting places for local nobles, clergy, politicians, and others.

Hotels, which were larger and more luxurious than inns or taverns, first began to appear in France in the late 1700s. The Hotel de Henri IV, built in Nantes in 1788 with beds for 60 guests, was a particularly fine early example.

The first inns in North America were established in seaport towns rather than along stagecoach routes. Stages were ten miles apart. This was the distance a team of horses could run flat out before a change was needed. Villages, and later, inns sprang up at these ten-mile intervals. The first inn in the United States was built in Jamestown on the Virginia coast in 1607. As the population moved inland, inns and taverns began to appear along rivers, canals, and post roads (over which mail was carried). The first inns in Nova Scotia developed along the stagecoach road from Halifax to Windsor. Two early Ontario inns, Willard's (1795) and Cook's Tavern (1822), are preserved at Upper Canada Village. They were built as stopping places for travellers on the King's Highway in Williamsburg Township.

As in England, the New World inns provided travellers with a bed and food, and with stables for their horses. The food was generally excellent and plentiful—meals of up to 15 courses were not uncommon. Accommodations, on the other hand, left much to be desired. There was little privacy, and travellers were expected to share a bed if the inn was crowded. The concept of reservations was, as yet, unheard of.

Canadian and American inns and taverns played an important role in community life as meeting places for local citizens. In the United States, this was especially true during the Revolutionary War. Local residents would meet at the inns to plan strategy, and passing travellers would provide news of developments in other parts of the country. In Canada, the Fathers of Confederation met in a tavern in Charlottetown in 1867 to forge a new country uniting some of the colonies in eastern British North America.

The atmosphere in a typical North American inn of the period was much more informal than in a European lodging place. Meals were served family-style at a communal table, and guests from all walks of life mingled freely with one another. In Europe, by contrast, only the wealthy could afford to travel and stay at inns; once they had arrived, travellers kept to themselves for the most part.

The more democratic spirit of North American inns was also reflected in the special status conferred on innkeepers. In Europe, innkeepers were regarded as servants. In colonial North America, on the other hand, innkeeping was an honourable profession. An innkeeper could be entrusted with information, and his opinions were respected.

Early Hotels in the United States and Canada

The early 19th century was a period of transition for the hospitality industry in North America. The new trend was away from inns and taverns toward hotels, which were based on a French concept and considered more elegant. The 73-room City Hotel, which opened in New York City in 1794, was the first establishment specifically designed as a hotel. Symmes Inn opened in Aylmer, Quebec, in 1831, at a boat landing on the Ottawa River. Rasco's Hotel in Montreal opened in 1836; the building that housed this early hotel is still standing.

Thus, small roadside inns gradually gave way to larger, more elegant city hotels that offered a much wider range of amenities. Boston's 170-room Tremont House, which opened in 1829, was the first modern first-class hotel. It was the largest building in the United States at the time. Among the features it introduced were private single and double rooms with locks, free soap, French cuisine, room service, bellstaff, and workers trained to provide polite service. Similar hotels soon appeared in other eastern cities, with each city competing to build larger and more luxurious lodging places. All of these hotels became important social centres for local citizens.

The western expansion of the railway system in Canada and the United States had an enormous impact on the hotel industry. New towns sprang up along the tracks, and in each of them a hotel was usually one of the first buildings to be erected. In the largest new towns, a few hotels were as elaborate as the grand hotels back east. Most, however, were smaller and less glamorous. They catered to the growing number of business travellers—in particular, to travelling salespeople.

With the invention of the elevator in 1853, hotels began to expand upward. A typical city hotel of the second half of the 19th century was five or six stories high and had as many as 200 guest rooms. Public rooms, such as dining and reading rooms, were now a feature of most hotels. Both men and women were welcome at all hotels, but it was not appropriate for the sexes to mingle in public areas. Women were provided with separate entrances and sitting rooms, and they dined apart from the men.

As cities grew and the volume of train travel increased, hotels in the major cities became still larger and more elaborate. San Francisco's Palace Hotel, built in 1875, was the epitome of grandeur. It had 800 rooms, a central marble courtyard, and a glass-domed roof. Other notable hotels of the period were the Brown Palace Hotel (1892) in Denver, the Netherlands Hotel (1894) in New York City (the first to have in-room telephones), and the Waldorf-Astoria (1896), also in New York City.

The Canadian Pacific Railway became a major hotel owner. Its hotel system came into existence because Sir William Van Horne did not want to have trains hauling heavy dining cars up mountain grades. Consequently, meal stops were substituted at strategic locations in the western mountains. These restaurants developed into small hotels at three locations in British Columbia: Fraser Canyon House at North Bend, Glacier House at Rogers Pass, and Mount Stephen House at Field. Van Horne felt it essential that the new terminal city of Vancouver, as an entry point from the Orient, have a first-class hotel. The original Hotel Vancouver was opened in 1887.

From Boom to Bust

At the opposite extreme to the luxury city hotels were the smaller hotels built close to railway stations. These were inexpensive but often lacking in cleanliness, comfort, and service. Few commercial travellers at the beginning of the 20th century could afford to stay in the luxury hotels, yet many found the smaller hotels near the stations unsatisfactory.

Ellsworth Statler, the father of the modern commercial hotel industry, realized that there was a considerable market for moderately priced hotels for the business traveller. He opened his first hotel, the Buffalo Statler, in 1908. Its 300 rooms were clean, comfortable, and, at $1.50 a night, affordable. Each had a private bath along with such other innovative features as full-length mirrors, built-in closets, and in-room telephones and radios. The hotel was an immediate success, and Statler was encouraged to build more middle-class hotels in other parts of the country. In doing so, he originated the hotel-chain concept that has come to dominate the modern hotel industry. The Statler chain was later bought by Conrad Hilton, founder of one of the most famous hotel chains of all.

Hotel construction reached an all-time peak in the 1920s. Giant hotels were built, such as the 3000-room Stevens Hotel (1927) in Chicago. CP opened the Royal York in Toronto in 1929. After the success of its first season, an addition was built that increased its size to 1156 rooms, making it the largest hotel in the British Commonwealth. Hundreds of smaller hotels opened in cities and towns across Canada and the United States. This boom ended with the Depression, which had a devastating effect on all sectors of the travel industry, including the hotel business. Because fewer people could afford to travel, there was a decline in the demand for accommodations. Between 1930 and 1935, almost 85 percent of American hotels went bankrupt.

> **CHECK YOUR PRODUCT KNOWLEDGE**
>
> 1. In what ways did religion influence the growth of the hospitality industry?
> 2. How did early North American inns differ from 17th-century English inns?
> 3. What effect did the building of the railways in Canada and the United States have on the hotel business?

MODERN HOTELS AND MOTELS

The hotel industry rebounded during and immediately after World War II as the volume of travel increased. It also changed drastically. The automobile and the jet plane had a radical effect on travel patterns and led to the development of different types of hotels. Motels, motor hotels, resort hotels, and convention hotels have evolved to cater to the varied needs of today's travelling public. At the same time, hotel chains have established themselves as the dominant force in the industry, both in North America and abroad.

Canada's largest privately owned hotel company, Delta Hotels, began with a small motor inn in Richmond, British Columbia. Today the company owns 39 hotels and resorts with 11 000 rooms in Canada, the United States, Cuba, and Asia.

We shall look at these important postwar developments in the sections that follow.

Motels and Motor Hotels

Motels evolved from the roadside tourist cabins and tourist courts that were first introduced in the early 1900s in response to the increase in automobile travel. Tourist cabins were usually built and operated by farm families who owned land adjacent to a main road. Most catered exclusively to travelling salespeople. They provided a bed for the night, and a place to park a car, but little else in the way of services or amenities. But they were also inexpensive and saved the motorist the inconvenience of having to leave the main road to find a hotel in town.

Tourist courts differed from tourist cabins in that they were operated as full-time businesses rather than as sidelines for farmers. They usually consisted of between 10 and 20 detached cottages grouped around a central parking place. Services were still extremely limited, though most cottages did have private baths.

As the automobile began to replace the train as the primary means of travel in Canada and the United States, the demand increased for roadside accommodations. The first **motels** began to appear in the 1920s. They were usually one-storey buildings with 25 or so units, or rooms, arranged lengthwise on either side of a central office. (The term **unit** is used throughout the hospitality industry to refer to a guest bedroom or suite.) Since the units opened onto the parking lot, there was no need for a lobby.

Motels really came of age during the 1950s. Two main factors contributed to the boom in motel construction. One was the development of the interstate highway system in the United States and the Trans-Canada Highway across Canada, which encouraged more and more travellers to take to the roads on long-distance journeys. The other was the rise of motel chains. Motels increased in size and, for the first time, added a number of services. Restaurants, swimming pools, and in-room TV became standard features. Motels began to attract growing numbers of vacationers in addition to commercial travellers.

The next step in the development of the motel industry was the move away from highway locations into the downtown areas of larger cities. Many motels began to offer all the facilities that would be found in a downtown hotel and came to be known as **motor hotels** or **motor inns**. The only difference was that they still catered to the travelling motorist and continued to provide free parking for overnight guests. With the increase in air travel, motor hotels also began to move out to the airports.

An interesting reaction to the development of luxury motor hotels has been the recent rebirth of low-cost, no-frills motels. Chains such as Holiday Inn and Ramada Inns, which were originally conceived as providers of budget accommodations, have gradually raised prices as they have added more and more hotel services. Days Inn, Motel 6, Journey's End, and other budget operators have entered the market and returned to the original concept of the motel—that is, they offer clean, comfortable rooms with a minimum of service at low cost. Journey's End merged with the American-based Choice Hotels in 1993 and is now the largest motel operator in Canada, with 120 properties.

Resort Hotels

A **resort hotel** is one that people visit for relaxation, recreation, and/or entertainment in some combination. With the rise in mass tourism in the last 35 years, they have been established in great numbers at destinations throughout the world.

Resorts have existed since ancient times. Wealthy Romans used to escape the cities during the hot summer months and spend the season by the sea, in the mountains, or at spa resorts. The idea of the resort hotel was born in 18th- and 19th-century Europe. Palatial hotels were built along the French Riviera, in the Swiss Alps, and at various mineral springs throughout the continent.

Resort hotels in Canada and the United States developed with the expansion of the railways in the second half of the 19th century. Fashionable early resorts included the first Banff Springs Hotel, which opened in 1888; St. Andrews-By-The-Sea, in New Brunswick; and Greenbrier at White Sulphur Springs, West Virginia. All catered exclusively to the rich and to the upper middle-class. Families stayed for two or three months and returned to the same hotel year after year.

Some of these luxury resort hotels have survived, but today they are heavily outnumbered by resort hotels that cater to ordinary working people who stay from three days to two weeks. With increased leisure time and higher wages, most people now take at least one vacation away from home each year. The jet airplane has opened up areas of the world that were previously inaccessible to the vacationer. Resort hotel construction has boomed in tropical areas such as Mexico, Hawaii, and the Caribbean.

Within Canada, resort hotels are found in various regions; however, most are located near mountains, or water, or both. Examples include the Delta at Whistler, British Columbia, Jasper Park Lodge in Alberta, the Gray Rock's Inn in the Laurentians, and the Pines Resort at Digby, Nova Scotia. In the United States, resort hotels in Florida, California, and Colorado attract millions of vacationers each year. Some of these resorts are seasonal, but many have developed into year-round operations.

Convention Hotels

A **convention hotel** is one that caters to large group gatherings. The rise of convention hotels has been one of the most recent developments in the hotel industry, and conventioneers now account for almost 20 percent of all hotel guests. Many downtown hotels saw occupancy levels drop during the 1950s and early 1960s as motels and motor hotels captured a larger segment of the market. In response, some hotels began to add facilities for conventions and other group gatherings. At first, conventions were scheduled for off-peak periods, but as the volume of convention business increased, they began to be scheduled year-round.

Large hotels that cater exclusively to convention groups began going up in the major cities in the late 1960s. All feature a wide variety of restaurants, banquet rooms, meeting rooms, and convention and exhibition halls. Some can accommodate up to 4000 guests at a single convention. Resort hotels, motels, and airport hotels have also begun to offer convention facilities. Much of this business is generated by industrial conventions and trade shows, though conventions held by political, civic, fraternal, religious, and social organizations are also important sources of income.

The New Architecture

The arrival of the jet age led to the second major hotel-building phase of the 20th century, which lasted from 1958 to 1974. In the early part of this period, the hotel chains' main goals in planning new properties were economy, efficiency, and standardization of design. A Sheraton hotel in Miami, for example, might be almost identical to one nearly 3000 miles away in Los Angeles, even in such minor details as the colour of the drapes.

By the late 1960s, however, there was a reaction against this uniformity of design, and a new hotel architecture was born. The breakthrough came in 1967 with the opening of the Hyatt Regency in Atlanta. John Portman, the hotel's architect, reintroduced the concept of the **atrium**—a roof-high central lobby courtyard. This style had been used in San Francisco's Palace Hotel and Denver's Brown Palace Hotel at the end of the 19th century. The opening of the Atlanta Hyatt marked a return to the grandeur of the old luxury hotels. Portman's other innovations included scenic elevators, fountains, waterfalls, trees, huge sculptures, and bars and cafés in the atrium. The lobby was no longer just a place for registration and check-out; now it was also the main eating, drinking, and meeting area. Even the guest rooms opened onto the central lobby, rather than onto dimly lit corridors as in earlier hotels.

The success of the Atlanta Hyatt Regency led to the building of similar atrium hotels in cities and resorts throughout the world during the 1970s and 1980s. Many are part of complexes that combine commercial, office, and hotel facilities with sporting and recreational facilities.

A related development has been the renovation of grand hotels in downtown areas. Many have undergone total restoration, including Toronto's Royal York, Ottawa's Chateau Laurier, Los Angeles's Biltmore, Philadelphia's Bellevue Stratford, and New York's Commodore. The new atrium hotels and the restored grand hotels function at the opposite end of the scale to the budget motels, offering excellence in architectural and interior design and the ultimate in services and amenities.

CP Hotels now refers to its recently renovated grand properties as its heritage collection. CP is the largest real estate owner/operator of hotels in North America.

Country Inns

The small country inn is one type of lodging place that has not had to survive by offering increased services and facilities. In fact, many shun such modern conveniences as in-room televisions, radios, and telephones. Instead, they offer the attraction of Old World charm and coziness in a scenic or historic setting. Guests can expect to find working fireplaces in their rooms, handmade quilts on their beds, and antique furniture throughout the inn.

Many of the inns are direct descendants of the old inns and taverns that flourished along stagecoach routes 200 years ago. Some even occupy the same building. The smaller country inns—some have as few as three or four rooms—are usually run by friendly couples who pride themselves on the comfort and cleanliness of their accommodations and the quality of the food they serve.

The use of the word "inn" by some of the larger chains (e.g., Holiday Inn, Ramada Inns) is a testament to the appeal of the inn. Motor inns, however, should not be confused with country inns. The chains use the word to suggest a feeling of warmth and friendliness, though their properties are quite different from the more intimate country inns. In the hospitality industry, the term **property** refers to a hotel, motel, or any other kind of lodging facility.

The Growth of Hotel Chains

As you have read, the first chain operation in the United States was started by Ellsworth Statler in the early 1900s. The success of Statler's hotels encouraged the formation of other chains, including Hilton Hotels, which opened its first property in Dallas in 1925. The Depression, which forced so many individually owned hotels out of business, proved to be a bonanza for the chains, since they were able to buy bankrupt properties at low prices.

Chains such as Hilton and Sheraton established themselves before World War II. By the 1950s, they were being joined by scores of others. The introduction of franchising (described in detail later in this chapter) served as a tremendous stimulus to the growth of hotel and motel chains, and by the early 1970s there were almost 200 in operation. Hundreds of independent city hotels and family-run motels were forced into bankruptcy by their inability to meet rising costs and to compete with the chains. Today, over 50 percent of the rooms in Canadian and American hotels are provided by chains.

Holiday Inn is the largest lodging chain in the world, with more than 360 000 units in about 1900 properties. (Table 7–1 lists the 20 largest hotel and motel chains in the world in 1988.) It was launched in 1952 when entrepreneur Kemmons Wilson opened the first "Holiday Inn Hotel Court" on the outskirts of Memphis, Tennessee. Wilson had been dissatisfied with the motel accommodations he encountered on a family vacation trip. He decided to start

Rank	Name of chain	Country	Number of rooms	Number of hotels/motels
1	Holiday Corp.	USA	360 958	1868
2	Sheraton Corp.	USA	135 000	465
3	Ramada Inc.	USA	130 932	769
4	Marriott Corp.	USA	118 000	450
5	Quality International	USA	112 810	978
6	Days Inn Of America Inc.	USA	104 625	775
7	Hilton Hotels Corp.	USA	95 862	271
8	Trusthouse Forte Pic	England	89 546	893
9	Accor	France	80 034	700
10	Club Méditerranée	France	61 860	249
11	Balkantourist	Bulgaria	56 250	386
12	Howard Johnson	USA	54 757	444
13	Motel 6	USA	51 572	452
14	Hyatt Hotels Corp.	USA	50 797	92
15	Raddison Hotel Corp.	USA	46 600	191
16	Ladbroke Group Pic	England	45 630	139
17	Saison Group	Japan	38 921	99
18	Econo Lodges of America	USA	37 984	467
19	Super 8 Motels, Inc.	USA	35 991	574
20	Sol Hotels	Spain	35 994	140

TABLE 7-1
World's Largest Hotel and Motel Chains, 1988
SOURCE: *Hotels,* formerly *Hotels and Restaurants International*

his own chain, one that would offer a full range of services at low to moderate prices.

Holiday Inn offered services that were revolutionary for the times but later became standard for chain operations. These included a swimming pool and restaurant on the premises, air conditioning throughout, a television and telephone in every room, baby-sitters on call, and free accommodations for children under 12 sharing a room with their parents. In 1965, the company installed the hotel industry's first nationwide computerized reservations system.

Over the years, Holiday Inn has evolved from a chain of economy motor courts into a multibillion-dollar-a-year network of lodging places serving multiple markets. It is now a major presence in the North American resort and convention industries as well as in overseas markets.

The international growth of the big American chains has been one of the major developments in the hospitality industry in the last 35 years. A few chains gained an early foothold on the overseas market—Intercontinental in Latin America (1946), Hilton International in Puerto Rico (1949), Sheraton in Canada (1949)—but the greatest period of expansion came after the commercial debut of the jet airplane. Chains moved into the Caribbean and Europe and later into the Middle East, Africa, the Far East, and the Pacific. Holiday Inn is the international leader, with properties in more than 50 countries outside the United States, followed by Sheraton, Ramada, and Marriott. Other big names on the international scene include Quality International, Days Inn, and Hilton.

More recently, foreign chains have been moving into the United States. Trusthouse Forte (United Kingdom),

ILLUSTRATION 7-1
Delta Hotels, in striving to eliminate barriers between its guests and employees, has introduced PODS, multi-functional guest-reception podiums, to replace the traditional front desk (Delta Ottawa Hotel & Suites, Ottawa, Ontario).
SOURCE: Courtesy of Delta Hotels & Resorts

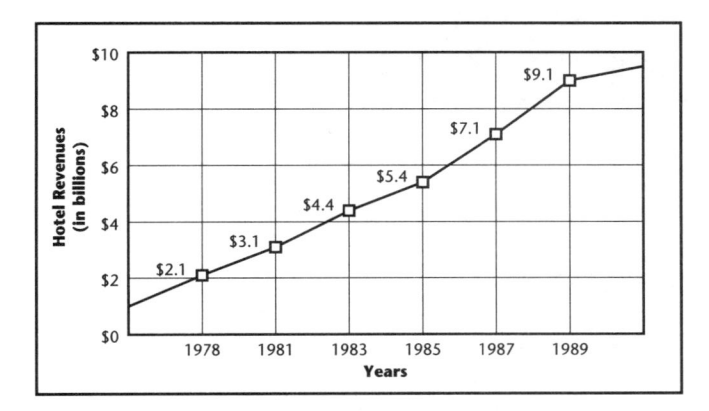

FIGURE 7-1
International Hotel Revenues
SOURCE: Louis Harris and Associates, *Travel Weekly*

ILLUSTRATION 7-2
From its first hotel on Jarvis Street in Toronto, Four Seasons Regent Hotels and Resorts has grown into one of the world's largest luxury hotel chains.
SOURCE: Courtesy of Four Seasons Hotels and Resorts

Meridien (France), Four Seasons (Canada), Regent International (Hong Kong), and Accor (France) are all well established in the United States. Total domestic and international hotel revenues are shown in Figure 7-1.

Overbuilding and Future Trends

In 1986, more new properties were being built than at any time since the late 1950s. In fact, many cities and destinations are now overbuilt with hotels. This means that there are more rooms than the market can fill. The current oversupply of rooms suggests that certain sectors of the hotel industry will experience difficult times in the near future.

The luxury segment of the market is a case in point. It has shown dramatic growth in recent years, largely because so many chains have upgraded their accommodations, added amenities, and moved into the luxury market. Room supply now exceeds demand, and it is unlikely that this segment of the industry will be able to expand much more in the immediate future.

No hotel can afford to operate below its **break-even point,** which is the point at which total revenues equal total operating costs. A break-even analysis determines the percentage of occupancy that a hotel must attain to cover expenses. The break-even point for American hotels in recent years has averaged about 68 percent.

When its costs increase, a hotel must either raise its room rates or attract more occupants. In the current overbuilt market, it is difficult for hotels to raise their rates and still remain competitive, so many have adopted aggressive marketing techniques to try to increase occupancy. The result has been a proliferation of incentive deals, such as weekend packages and special events. A similar development in the cruise industry was discussed in Chapter 6.

Hotel construction in Canada and the United States was beginning to slow down in the early 1990s. In the future, builders will most likely focus less on giant convention hotels and more on smaller properties aimed at specific markets. The outlook is brightest for economy-priced and all-suite hotels (described later in this chapter). So far, economy and all-suite hotels have been showing strong growth without a resulting oversupply of rooms. There should also be fairly consistent growth for resort hotels and airport hotels. The trend toward chain operations will continue, and American chains can be expected to expand overseas in greater numbers as new destinations are opened up. Holiday Inn and Marriott have already opened properties in Poland, and both Ramada and Sheraton are constructing hotels in Russia.

CHECK YOUR PRODUCT KNOWLEDGE

1. Why did motels become so popular during the 1950s?
2. What are the main differences between a resort hotel and a convention hotel?
3. List some of the architectural features that have been included in modern hotels.
4. What were some of the innovations introduced by Holiday Inn?

HOTEL OWNERSHIP

Until the 20th century, almost all hotels were individually owned and operated. With the development of hotel and motel chains, however, a number of new forms of ownership have evolved, such as the lease, the joint venture, and, more importantly in recent years, the franchise and the management contract.

PROFILE

J. Willard Marriott, Sr.

In 1927, J. Willard Marriott borrowed $3,000 and opened an A&W root beer stand in Washington, D.C. The stand had nine stools and occupied half of a bakery shop. From that modest beginning, Marriott, the son of a poor Mormon sheepherder, built his business into the fifth-largest service company in America, with sales of more than $8 billion a year.

Marriott was born and raised in Utah. He began to learn about business at 14, when his father sent him on his own to San Francisco to sell a flock of sheep. Marriott graduated from Weber State College in Ogden, Utah, in 1926, and taught there for a year. While he was there, two inventors named Allen and Wright developed a new formula for root beer and opened their first stand in Salt Lake City. Marriott liked the new root beer and thought it would sell well in Washington, D.C., because of the city's hot, humid climate.

He purchased a franchise from A&W, packed up his belongings, and headed east with his bride, Alice. The root beer stand prospered until the weather turned cold, at which point sales began to decline. Then, cleverly, Marriott put a barbecue machine in the window, changed the name of the stand to the Hot Shoppe, and went into the business of selling hot food along with the root beer.

While Alice Marriott cooked chili and barbecued beef for hungry diners, J. Willard Marriott set about promoting his new restaurant with such gimmicks as coupons for free beverages. The Marriotts did so well that by 1932, they had opened six more Hot Shoppes. By then, the country was in the depths of the Depression and many fancier, higher-priced restaurants were going out of business because people could no longer afford expensive meals. Marriott's Hot Shoppes survived because they were unpretentious family restaurants that offered good food at low prices.

The Hot Shoppes were the foundation of Marriott's business empire. In 1937 he went into the business of supplying meals to airlines after he noticed that many people stopped by one of his Hot Shoppes to purchase meals to eat during plane flights. His restaurants and airline catering service grew steadily into the 1950s, when he decided to branch out into hotels. He opened his first Marriott Motor Hotel on the outskirts of Washington in 1957.

By 1972 the Marriott Corporation owned or operated 20 hotels and nearly 1000 restaurants, including cafeterias, turnpike rest stops, and the Hot Shoppe, Big Boy, and Roy Rogers restaurant chains. Meanwhile, its airline food services had become the largest independently owned airline catering business in the world. Marriott also branched into another very profitable food business, operating cafeterias and restaurants in schools, hospitals, and corporate offices.

Today, the Marriott Corporation operates more than 80 000 hotel rooms and serves nearly 5 million meals a day. As the business grew, Marriott involved more and more of his family members in it, including his three brothers. He turned over the day-to-day operations of the corporation to his son Bill Jr. in 1964, but remained chairman of the board until he died in 1985 at the age of 85. Bill Jr. currently serves as chief operating officer and chairman of the board. Marriott's other son, Richard, is vice-chairman, and Alice Marriott has long served as a member of the board. Now a new generation of Marriotts is being groomed for corporate leadership. Two of Bill Jr.'s sons and a son-in-law work in Marriott hotels.

Marriott believed in treating his employees well. He began share-purchasing and profit-sharing programs for his employees in 1971. He also established incentive bonuses, management training, and career advancement programs to develop competent managers and promote company loyalty.

Marriott was a staunch Mormon and a political conservative all his life. He believed in the basic American values of family and hard work. Today, his name is seen on hotels, restaurants, and other businesses in 27 countries around the world.

CHAPTER 7: The Hospitality Industry

Individual Ownership

About 50 percent of all hotels in Canada and the United States operate as individual proprietorships. The majority of these—the family-owned establishments with fewer than 100 rooms—still make up the backbone of the hotel industry. They include mom-and-pop motels, small hotels, and country inns. The term "individually owned" also applies to individual properties owned by the large corporations that have been investing in the industry since the mid-1960s. These individual ownerships include giant city hotels and deluxe resort properties.

The chief benefits of individual ownership are that the owner enjoys complete control of policies and operating procedures, and gets to keep all profits from the property. An obvious disadvantage is that the owner also assumes full risk.

Chain Ownership

Many chains with multiple properties own and operate a number of hotels directly. The chain owns the building and staffs it with its own employees. This form of ownership offers all the benefits of individual ownership. Expansion of the chain is limited, however, by the amount of capital available. Chains wishing to expand rapidly often do so by franchising and management contracts (explained later in this chapter) rather than by direct ownership.

Leases and Joint Ventures

An individual or a chain can operate a hotel without owning it by entering into a lease arrangement. Under a straight lease, the tenant pays a fixed monthly rent to the landlord for the complete use of the hotel. Profit-sharing leases, whereby the owner of the hotel participates in its profits, are more common.

A **joint venture** can be a partnership between two companies, two individuals, or a company and an individual. Joint ventures have been used in the development of motels, and less frequently in major hotel projects. Most are formed between an individual proprietor or developer who makes a large capital investment, and an established motel chain that contributes management and development know-how.

Franchises

Under a **franchise** system, a hotel owner contracts with an established chain to operate the property under the chain's name. The owner of the hotel, or "franchisee," pays an initial development fee (which can be as much as $50,000, depending on the property) and a monthly franchise fee of between 3 and 6 percent of gross room sales. In addition, the franchisee agrees to abide by the management policies of the chain. In return, the chain, or "franchisor," provides assistance in staff selection and training, and in marketing, sales, and advertising. It also provides access to a central computer reservations system. Perhaps most importantly, the franchisor provides a recognizable image and the familiarity of the chain's name.

Franchises are the most common form of hotel organization after individual ownership. Hotel and motel chains began to resort to franchising during the late 1950s and early 1960s, as a way to expand without substantial capital investment. Kemmons Wilson of Holiday Inn was an early pioneer of franchising. In its first two years of operation, Holiday Inn had been able to build only four motels. Wilson realized that his chain would never grow fast enough if it relied on direct ownership. Franchising was the most viable alternative, and within five years the company was operating 100 franchises. Many other chains were quick to enter the franchising field as well.

Management Contracts

Under the franchise system, an individual or a company owns and operates a hotel, with support from a chain. Under a **management contract** agreement, one company owns the property and another (the chain) operates it. The owner enjoys all the benefits of the franchise system without having to become involved in the operation of the hotel. The chain receives a managerial fee from the owner and has complete control of the operation of the property. Management contracts allow chains to expand with little or no capital investment; the owner, not the chain, is the investor.

The management contract was developed in the 1950s as a way for chains based in the United States to expand overseas. It enabled them to open hotels in countries where foreign ownership laws or political conditions prevented ownership by outside companies. Overseas hotel developers who wanted the managing and marketing expertise of American chains began to invest in properties and to contract American hotel companies to operate them.

Four Seasons manages 38 hotels internationally (with seven more in development and equity stakes in some of these). Over the last decade the company has concentrated more and more on management, at which it has been eminently successful.

CHECK YOUR PRODUCT KNOWLEDGE

1. What percentage of hotels in Canada and the United States are individually owned? What are the chief benefits of individual ownership?
2. What is the difference between a franchise and a management contract?
3. Why would an overseas hotel developer want to enter into a management contract with a hotel chain based in Canada or the United States?

THE HOTEL/MOTEL/RESORT AS A PRODUCT

Thirty-five years ago, many hotels were built and operated with little concern about the different needs of specific groups of visitors. Today, there is a much greater awareness of the motivations, needs, and expectations (MNEs) of different kinds of travellers, including physically challenged ones.

Through market research, hotels can define who their customers will be, anticipate their needs, and modify their services accordingly. Properties are no longer built to serve the "general" traveller. Instead, they are aimed at specific groups, such as business travellers, convention groups, vacationers, weekenders, the affluent, the economy-minded, and so on. The practice of developing different products for different groups of people is known as market segmentation.

Market segmentation has brought great changes to the hospitality industry, but one thing that it has not altered is the principle that there are two basic types of properties: transient hotels and residential hotels.

Most hotels are **transient hotels,** which cater to guests who stay for a limited time—a night, a week, or a month—for business or for pleasure. A transient hotel can be a commercial hotel, a motel, a motor hotel, a convention hotel, an inn, a resort hotel, in fact, any hotel that provides temporary accommodations for its guests.

Residential hotels are apartment houses that offer hotel services. They differ from transient hotels in that they cater to guests who reside on the premises *permanently*. Most residential hotels are luxury hotels that provide wealthy residents with suites, dining rooms, room service, and maid and valet service. Examples include the Pierre and the Sherry-Netherlands in New York City. Some companies maintain suites in residential hotels for the use of executives who are in town on business. At the lower end of the market, there are a number of residential properties that function essentially as rooming houses for moderate- and lower-income city dwellers.

Few residential hotels cater exclusively to permanent residents; most supplement their income by offering a number of rooms to transient guests. Likewise, some transient hotels also have rooms for permanent residents.

Hotels are classified not only by type, but also by function (or level of service), location, and scale.

Function

The primary function of any lodging place is to provide clean, comfortable accommodations. At the very minimum, overnight guests expect to find a bed with fresh linen, a private bath or shower, and fresh towels and soap. A number of low-cost, no-frills chains (Motel 6, for example) offer nothing more than this basic service. Most of them operate highway motels that cater to transient guests who just want a bed for the night before resuming their journey the next morning. All motels offering basic services provide free parking for their guests. Some also offer breakfast, though the vast majority do not have a restaurant on the premises.

Many of the smaller, individually owned properties in downtown areas offer similar basic services. As with the economy motels, their main attraction is their low cost. Guests neither need nor expect a high level of service. These guests may be commercial travellers, tourists on sightseeing trips, or people visiting friends or relatives in the area. Country inns generally provide basic services only, but their accommodations are usually more luxurious than those of the budget motels and small city hotels.

Most hotels in Canada and the United States offer considerably more than this basic level of service. Standard services include in-room telephones, radios, and colour televisions (often with cable); parking facilities; coffee shops, dining rooms, and cocktail lounges; room service; laundry, valet, bellstaff, and baggage service; and front desk service (including cashiers, mail clerks, and information clerks). A service that was once considered a luxury can become a standard requirement as the MNEs of the travelling public change. For example, recreational facilities, such as exercise rooms, saunas, and pools, are now considered a standard feature by many of the major chains. Another feature that is becoming standard is the availability of special rooms, such as no-smoking rooms and rooms with accessibility for physically challenged travellers. Motor hotels, airport hotels, and mid-sized city hotels all offer standard services that cater mainly to the business traveller but also to individuals and families travelling for pleasure. Holiday Inn is a good example of a chain operation providing standard services.

Moving up the scale, we come next to those hotels that offer more complex services. These include properties catering to executive business travellers, convention groups, and the leisure and vacation market. Many business travellers need and expect more amenities than can be provided in a standard-service hotel. They may require more spacious accommodations, with room to work and to hold meetings. Some may need to use computers, fax machines, typewriters, dictation machines, telex and photocopying services, and so on; a few may require the services of a secretary, translator, or notary public. Business hotels operating at the upper end of the market must be able to provide all these services and sometimes more.

The widest range of services is provided by the enormous downtown convention hotels. Properties cannot schedule large-scale conventions and conferences unless they have numerous meeting, conference, and banquet rooms, at least one convention hall, exhibition space, and a wide range of audio-visual equipment. The Sheraton Centre Toronto, for example, has 36 meeting rooms ranging in capacity from 20 to 2800, including a convention room that can hold 2800. It also has a banquet room seating 2000, 1865 net square metres of exhibition space, and 1398 double rooms.

Convention hotels also cater to conventioneers' needs between and after meetings. Almost always available are the following facilities and services:

- recreational facilities (swimming pools, gymnasiums, health centres, indoor games)
- shopping facilities
- evening entertainment
- medical services
- banking services
- transportation assistance (e.g., in-hotel car rental desks)

Guests staying in luxury resort hotels expect a similar array of services and amenities. This is especially true of resort hotels that function as self-contained units and must satisfy all their guests' needs and desires. In many ways, such hotels resemble luxury cruise ships in level and complexity of service. Even more complex are those resort hotels that cater not only to vacationers but also to convention groups. These hotels are at the opposite end of the spectrum from the limited-service motels discussed at the beginning of this section.

Location

There is a close relationship between the location of a hotel and the types of accommodations and services it offers. Downtown areas of large cities—the commercial, financial, and cultural centres—attract the most people, for both business and pleasure. It is only to be expected, therefore, that downtown hotels offer the greatest variety. They range in size from small hotels with fewer than 50 units to giant convention hotels such as the Westin Harbour Castle in Toronto, which has 980 double rooms; they range in type from motor hotels to residential hotels; they offer basic, standard, or complex services according to the needs of the guests they serve. Location within the downtown area is an important factor in determining the type of accommodations offered. Hotels in fashionable neighbourhoods thrive as luxury hotels; those in marginal and slum districts cannot attract wealthy guests and often degenerate into run-down rooming houses.

A recent trend has been the development of hotels (motor hotels in particular) in suburban locations. There are two major reasons for this trend. One is economic—real estate prices in downtown areas have risen to prohibitively high levels. The other reason is practical—suburban hotels offer easy access to the new corporate headquarters and industrial parks that have been built in city suburbs. Suburban hotels provide not only standard services for transient guests, but also facilities such as restaurants, banquet rooms, and meeting rooms. All these things attract local residents and business groups.

Many of the hotels in small and medium-sized cities and towns in Canada and the United States were built near railway stations at a time when rail travel was at its peak. Now that most people travel by car or airplane, many of these small-city hotels are being bypassed by all but a few business travellers, and occupancy levels have consequently dropped. These hotels make up for the loss in room revenue by promoting social functions for local residents. Much of their income is now generated by the restaurants, bars, and banquet rooms on the premises.

ILLUSTRATION 7-3.
Hotels are classified by the number and quality of the facilities they offer. Luxury resort and convention hotels (above) offer complex services and amenities not available in hotels providing standard service (below).
SOURCE: Hyatt Regency-Atlanta and Holiday Inn, Inc.

The development of hotels at or near airports is an excellent example of the hotel industry responding to the needs of the traveller. A few limited-service motor inns had been established at airports in the pre-jet age, but with the growth of the airline industry in the late 1950s, there was a much greater demand for airport accommodations. Almost all airports are far from the city centre. It is often more convenient for passengers travelling by air to stay at a hotel or motel near the airport rather than downtown. Travellers with early-morning flights can avoid the morning rush-hour traffic by checking in at an airport hotel the night before. Travellers with connecting flights are saved the inconvenience of a trip in and out of the city. Airport hotels often provide free transportation to and from passenger terminals.

The airport hotel at Terminal 3 at Pearson International Airport in Toronto opened as a Swissotel but became a Sheraton in 1994. There are more than 6000 guest rooms on the "airport strip" surrounding Pearson, which is Canada's busiest airport.

Business travellers account for much of the airport hotel business, but chain operations have begun to actively promote their airport properties among conventioneers, local residents, and even vacationers. They have added conference rooms, meeting rooms, banquet rooms, and a full range of recreational facilities. Airport properties have evolved from being small, limited-service motor inns in the 1950s to 1000-room luxury hotels providing complex services.

Resort hotels are usually located at or near natural recreation areas, such as national parks, lakes, and ski slopes, and the seaside. The resort area itself is the main attraction and offers its own recreational activities, though the hotel usually supplements these with swimming pools, tennis courts, and sometimes golf courses. The resort property must also provide restaurants, bars, and entertainment, as well as convention services if it caters to the convention market.

Casino hotels are found in legalized gambling areas, such as Las Vegas and Atlantic City. The largest hotels in the world are located in Las Vegas. In 1993, the MGM Grand became the largest of these, with 5000 rooms.

Resort hotels that function as self-contained destinations rather than as bases for activities in natural areas must necessarily offer a wider range of services. The hotel itself is the major attraction. Club Med resorts are probably the best example of self-contained vacation destinations. Each Club Med "village" offers sports and recreational facilities as well as food and accommodations. The Nottawasaga Inn, north of Toronto and within an hour's drive of the airport, is a resort hotel that promotes conventions with 27 meeting rooms, five boardrooms, and three ballrooms. It can accommodate groups of up to 500.

Scale

The three basic price tiers in the hotel industry are budget/economy (e.g., Journey's End, Days Inn, and Motel 6), moderate/standard (e.g., Delta, Holiday Inn, and Ramada Inns), and deluxe/quality (e.g., Four Seasons, Sheraton, and CP Hotels). In general, the price category reflects the level of service: budget motels and hotels offer basic services, and standard and deluxe properties offer progressively more complex services.

A recent phenomenon has been the upward movement of budget chains into the standard tier. Holiday Inn, for example, started out as a low-cost, limited-service chain, then moved up as it gained a greater share of the market. The primary reason for this trend has been the rise in per-room construction costs. Ten years ago, an average hotel room cost about $30,000 to build. Today, construction costs for that same room can be as high as $100,000. As a result, it makes economic sense to build for the upscale market in order to command higher room rates. Budget chains that have not "segmented upward" have survived by resorting to less expensive modular-type construction and by limiting services to the bare essentials.

Another example of upward movement is the development of **all-suite hotels** by some of the big chains. Two all-suite hotel chains are Embassy Suites and Residence Inns. All accommodations in such hotels include a living room and kitchen facilities as well as a bedroom. There is no need for restaurants or meeting rooms on the premises, since guests can make their own meals, and the living rooms double as meeting rooms. The all-suite concept has proved popular with business travellers who need the additional space for working and for meeting with clients and associates. All-suite hotels are expected to become one of the fastest growing segments of the hotel industry.

Rating Systems

There are many different hotel classification systems worldwide, but no international standard that allows for country-to-country comparisons. Many countries use a rating system established by the national government. Properties can be rated by a star system, or a code system, or by name (e.g., economy, standard, first-class, deluxe). The variety of rating systems has obvious drawbacks: a property rated as "five-star" by one country may be little better than "standard" in the eyes of a visitor from another country.

There is no official rating system in Canada or the United States, though hotels are rated by automobile clubs, guidebooks, hotel associations, and hotel critics. The *Mobil Travel Guide*'s rating system, which uses stars, is the one most widely used by hotel and motel reference books. It has the following ratings:

☆	Good, better than average
☆☆	Very good
☆☆☆	Excellent
☆☆☆☆	Outstanding—worth a special effort to reach
☆☆☆☆☆	One of the best in the country

The Canadian Automobile Association (CAA), through its sister organization, the Automobile Association of America (AAA), has a similar five-scale rating system,

CHAPTER 7: The Hospitality Industry

- **Hotel Mercure Paris Vaugirard** 91 Rooms B-4
  69 Blvd Victor POST CODE: F-75015 PHONE: (1)45-33-74-63 CABLE: Hipari TELEX: 260844 F FAX: (1)48-28-22-11 MGR: J.C. Droal, G.M. **REPS:** UIL
  First Class - Motor Hotel (1976) located across from Palais des Exhibitions on the Left Bank, 10 minutes from the Eiffel Tower - 5 km from Montparnasse Train Station and 15 km from Orly Int'l Airport - Soundproof rooms with climate control, private bath, phone, radio, color TV (movies) and minibar - Rooms for nonsmokers - Wheelchair accessibility - Restaurant and Bar - Meeting facilities to 150 - Car Rental - Renovations in 1988 - Government rated 4* - Formerly Holiday Inn-Porte de Versailles
  RATES: EP SWB 690-1020 (138.83-205.23) D/TWB 770-1140 (154.93-229.38) EAP 180 (36.22) - PP-CP +54 (10.87) BB +72 (14.49) - SC & VAT incl COMM: R-08A CREDIT CARDS: AE AIR DC EC JCB MC VISA

- **Mercure Paris-Porte d'Orleans** 192 Rooms
  13 Rue Francois Ory, Montrouge POST CODE: F-92120 PHONE: (1)46-57-11-26 TELEX: 202528 F FAX: (1)47-35-47-61 MGR: M. Fiston, G.M. **REPS:** RSN
  Superior Tourist Class - Hotel (1977) located in South Paris, 3½ miles from city center or Montparnasse Train Station - 15 km from Orly Int'l Airport - Air-conditioned rooms with private bath, phone, radio, color TV and minibar - 6 Suites - Wheelchair accessibility - Room Service - Restaurant - Bar - Meeting facilities to 200 - Renovations in 1989 - Government rated 3*
  RATES: EP SWB 450-750/480-780 (90.54-150.91/96.58-156.94) DWB 450-780/480-810 (90.54-156.94/96.58-162.98) Ste 600-900/650-950 (120.72-181.09/130.78-191.15) EAP 50 (10.06) - Max rates Jul 1-Dec 31 - SC & VAT incl COMM: R-08B CREDIT CARDS: AE DC EC MC VISA

- **Meridien Montparnasse Paris** 950 Rooms C-4/34
  19 Rue Commandant Mouchotte POST CODE: F-75014 PHONE: (1)43-20-15-51 TELEX: 200135 F FAX: (1)43-20-61-03 MGR: Michel Sabot, G.M. **REPS:** MER UIL
  First Class - Multistory Convention-oriented Hotel (1974) located near St. Germain des Pres - 16 miles from Charles de Gaulle Airport - Soundproof, air-conditioned rooms with private bath, phone, radio, color cable TV and minibar - 33 Suites - Wheelchair accessibility - Restaurant - Coffee Shop - Piano Lounge - Lobby Bar - Convention facilities to 2000 - Guest Laundry - Babysitting Service - Shopping Mall - Renovations in 1989 - Government rated 3*
  RATES: EP SWB 990-1200 (199.20-241.45) DWB 1100-1350 (221.33-271.63) - SC & VAT incl - Ste rates on request COMM: R-08B CREDIT CARDS: AE DC JCB MC VISA

- **le Meridien Paris Etoile** 1027 Rooms B-2/54
  81 Blvd Gouvion-Saint Cyr POST CODE: F-75017 PHONE: (1)40-68-34-34 TELEX: 290952 F FAX: (1)47-57-60-70 MGR: J. Pierre Waldbauer, G.M. **REPS:** LRI MER UIL
  Superior First Class - Convention-oriented Hotel located at Porte Maillot, opposite the Convention Center and overlooking the Bois de Boulogne Park - 30 minutes from Charles de Gaulle Airport - Soundproof, air-conditioned rooms with private bath, phone, radio, color TV (videos) and minibar - Room Service - 3 Restaurants - Bar - Nightclub - Meeting facilities to 1600; audiovisual equipment available - Beauty Salon - Renovations in 1986 - Government rated 4*
  RATES: EP S/DWB 1250-1850 (251.51-372.23) - SC & VAT incl COMM: R-10 CREDIT CARDS: AE BC DC EC MC VISA

- **Hotel Meurice** 184 Rooms D-2/13
  228 Rue de Rivoli POST CODE: F-75001 PHONE: (1)42-60-38-60 CABLE: Meurisotel Paris TELEX: 230673 F FAX: (1)49-27-98-06 MGR: Philippe Roche, G.M. **REPS:** UIL
  Deluxe - Elite, Palace Hotel (1815) facing the Tuileries Gardens, near Place Vendome and Rue de la Paix - 10 minutes from Orly Int'l Airport - Classical-style rooms with marble bath, hair dryer, bathrobes, phone, color TV and minibar; some with VCR - 30 Suites - Wheelchair accessibility - Room Service - Gourmet Restaurant - Cocktail Lounge - Bar - Meeting facilities to 600 - Shops and Services - Renovations in 1989 - Government rated 4*L
  RATES: EP SWB 1950-2250 (392.35-452.72) D/TWB 2250-2650 (452.72-533.20) Ste 7500 (1509.05) EAP 350 (70.42) - PP-CP +120 (24.14) BB +180 (36.22) - SC & VAT incl COMM: R-20B CREDIT CARDS: AE DC VISA TRADE DISCOUNT: Inquire direct

- **Hotel Mont Royal** 105 Rooms G-4
  la Chapelle en Serval POST CODE: F-60520 PHONE: (1)45-57-85-25 FAX: (1)44-60-63-63 MGR: Jacques d'Hoir, Dir. **REPS:** RSN
  New Castle-style Hotel (1990) situated in a 300-acre park, convenient to downtown Paris - 10 km from Chantilly and 15 km from Charles de Gaulle Airport - Rooms and suites with private bath, phone and color TV - Terrace Restaurant - Cocktail Bar - Piano Bar - Meeting facilities to 150 - Outdoor Swimming Pool - Sauna - 2 Tennis Courts - Squash Courts - Golf nearby
  RATES: EP S/D/TWB 1100-1250 (221.33-251.51) - SC & VAT incl COMM: R-08 CREDIT CARDS: AE CB DC MC VISA

- **Mont-Thabor Hotel** 118 Rooms D-3
  4 Rue du Mont-Thabor POST CODE: F-75001 PHONE: (1)42-60-32-77 TELEX: 670596 F THABOR FAX: (1)40-20-09-60 MGR: Mr. Ishizuka, G.M.
  Tourist Class - Older Hotel located near Tuileries Gardens - Rooms with private bath or shower, phone and minibar - 2 Restaurants - Bar - Elevator - Renovations in 1989 - Government rated 3*
  RATES: EP SWB 437-677 (87.93-136.22) D/TWB 724-784 (145.67-157.75) - SC & VAT incl COMM: R-08D CREDIT CARDS: AE DC EC JCB MC VISA TRADE DISCOUNT: 8%

- **Montalembert Hotel** 60 Rooms D-3
  3 Rue Montalembert POST CODE: F-75007 PHONE: (1)45-48-68-11 CABLE: Hotemontal TELEX: 200132 F MONTAL FAX: (1)42-22-58-19 MGR: Jean Michel Desnos, G.M. **REPS:** ATH JDL
  Moderate First Class - Hotel (1926) located on Left Bank near Pont Royal and the Louvre Museum in the publishing quarter - Traditional French-style rooms with phone, color TV, VCR and minibar; some with private bath or shower - 5 Suites - Air conditioning available - Cafe - Bar - Meeting Room to 40 - Renovations in 1990 - Government rated 4*

RATES: EP SWB 1350 (271.63) DWB 1550 (311.87) Ste 1800-2800 (362.1 563.38) - PP-CP +80 (16.10) - SC & VAT incl COMM: R-08A CREDIT CARDS: AE CB I MC VISA TRADE DISCOUNT: 25% (TA)

- **Napoleon Hotel** 102 Rooms
  40 Av de Friedland POST CODE: F-75008 PHONE: (1)47-66-02-02 CABLE: Otenapol-Pa TELEX: 640609 F OTENAPO FAX: (1)47-66-82-33 MGR: J.M. Bollack, G.M. **REPS:** CDU L UIL
  First Class - Mid-rise Hotel (1928) located near Etoile - Rooms with phone, radio, color and minibar; most with private bath or shower - 2 Suites - Wheelchair accessibility Restaurant and Bar - Meeting Room to 100 - Renovations in 1986 - Government rated
  RATES: EP SWB 700-1250 (140.85-251.51) D/TWB 1150-1850 (231.39-372.23) 3750-4500 (754.53-905.43) EAP 350 (70.42) - PP-CP +60 (12.07) BB +85 (17.10 SC & VAT incl COMM: R-08B CREDIT CARDS: AE CB DC EC ENR MC VISA

- **New Roblin Hotel** 77 Rooms
  6 Rue Chauveau-Lagarde POST CODE: F-75008 PHONE: (1)42-65-57-00 CABI Hotelroblin TELEX: 640154 F ROBLIN FAX: (1)42-65-19-49 MGR: Joseph Ghannam, G. **REPS:** JDL UIL
  Moderate First Class - Traditional Hotel (1886) located in the Madeleine district, n shopping and the Opera - ½ mile from Saint Lazare Train Station and 16 miles fr airport - Rooms in period and modern styles, all with private bath, hair dryer, phone, rad color TV and minibar - 7 Suites - Restaurant and Bar - Lounges - Meeting Room to 4(Renovations in 1990
  RATES: EP SWB 540-570/570-600 (108.65-114.69/114.69-120.72) DWB 64 670/670-700 (128.77-134.81/134.81-140.85) Ste 1200-1500/1500-1750 (241. 301.81/301.81-352.11) EAP 130/150 (26.16/30.18) - PP-CP +50 (10.06) - N rates Sep-Feb - SC & VAT incl COMM: R-08D or E CREDIT CARDS: ACC AE AIR BC DC ENR JCB MC VISA TRADE DISCOUNT: 20%

- **Hotel Nikko de Paris** 779 Rooms B-3/
  61 Quai de Grenelle POST CODE: F-75015 PHONE: (1)40-58-20-00 CABLE: Nikc TELEX: 260012 F FAX: (1)45-75-42-35 MGR: J.L. Ory, G.M. **REPS:** KEY LRI NHI l
  Superior First Class - Towering Hotel (1976) located directly on the Seine, minutes from Eiffel Tower and Champs-Elysees - Soundproof, air-conditioned rooms with private ba phone, radio, color TV and minibar - 11 Suites - 6 Executive Floors - Room Service - Frer Restaurant - Brasserie - Japanese Restaurant - Bar - Tea Lounge - Meeting facilities - Ind Swimming Pool - Sauna - Massage - Solarium - Shopping Center - Car Rental - Concierg Renovations in 1985 - Government rated 3*
  RATES: EP SWB 1050-1580 (211.27-317.91) D/TWB 1240-1760 (249.50-354.12 SC & VAT incl - Ste rates on request COMM: R-7.5 CREDIT CARDS: AE BC CB DC EC MC VI

- **NORMANDY HOTEL**

128 Rooms	General Manager: Jean Francois Richomme	D-3/5(
First Class	COMMISSION R-08D	PHONE (1)42 60 30 21
ADDRESS 7 Rue de l'Echelle (F-75001)	TELEX 213 015	TELEFAX (1)42 60 45 81
AFFILIATIONS ---	RES/REPS * FEE KEY LRI SRS TBI UIL	CABLE ---

Inviting Hotel (1877) located between the Louvre & Tuileries Gardens; a 5-minute walk to l'Opera & the best shopping areas — 12 km from Orly Airport — Rooms & suites in French Traditional style, all with private bath, phone, cable TV & minibar - Attractive Restaurant & American Bar — Meetings for up to 70 — Renovations in 1981 — Gov't rated 4*
Rates: EP SWB 870-995 (175.05-200.20) TWB 1220-1420 (245.47-285.71) — SC & VAT incl — Ste & group rates avail — Credit Cards: AE CB DC EC ENR JCB MC VISA — *Res: In USA 1(800)44-UTELL or 1(800)SRS-5848 — Apollo (SR 21538), Datas II, Pars (SH PARNO) Sabre (SR 13044), Sahara & SystemOne (PARNOR)

- **Novotel Bercy** 129 Rooms
  85 Rue de Bercy POST CODE: F-75012 PHONE: (1)43-42-30-00 TELEX: 218332 F F/ (1)43-45-30-60 MGR: Patrick Herain, G.M. **REPS:** RSN
  Moderate First Class - Downtown Hotel (1987) located along the banks of the Seine, acrc from the Paris-Bercy Omnisports Centre - 10 km from Orly Int'l Airport - Air-condition rooms with private bath, radio, color TV and minibar - 1 Suite - Wheelchair accessibility Grill Restaurant - Meeting facilities to 230 - Gardens - Government rated
  RATES: EP SWB 580-600 (116.70-120.72) D/TWB 615-630 (123.74-126.76) - SC VAT incl - Ste rates on request COMM: R-08A CREDIT CARDS: ACC AE DC MC VI:

- **Novotel Paris les Halles** 271 Rooms E-3/:
  Place Marguerite de Navarre POST CODE: F-75001 PHONE: (1)42-21-31-31 TELE 216389 F FAX: (1)40-26-05-79 MGR: Jacques Chenet, G.M. **REPS:** RSN
  First Class - Six-story Hotel (1985) located in the renovated old Les Halles marketpla area, opposite the Church of St. Eustache and Forum Shopping Center - 12 km from O Int'l Airport - Rooms with climate control, bath, phone, color TV and minibar - 5 Suites Wheelchair accessibility - Restaurant and Bar - Meeting facilities to 150 - Renovations 1990 - Government rated 3*
  RATES: EP SWB 725 (145.88) DWB 785 (157.95) Jr Ste 1050 (211.27) Ste 14((281.69) EAP 70 (14.08) - PP-BB +52 (10.46) - SC & VAT incl COMM: R-08B CRED CARDS: AE BC DC EC MC VISA TRADE DISCOUNT: 8% (TA)

ILLUSTRATION 7-4

The *Official Hotel Guide* ranks hotels according to a unique ten-level classification system.

SOURCE: Reprinted with permission of *Official Hotel Guide*. *Official Hotel Guide* is a trademark of Reed Publishing (Netherlands) B.V., used under licence by Reed Travel Group.

which uses five diamonds as the highest ranking instead of five stars. The *Official Hotel Guide* uses a rating system with ten categories ranging from "moderate tourist class" to "superior deluxe." It is interesting to note that, in 1990, only eight hotels in the United States were awarded a five-star rating in the *Mobil Travel Guide*. According to Mobil, there were no five-star hotels in Canada.

Factors Affecting the Price of a Room

Most hotels have a standard day rate for a room, which is known as the **rack rate**. Rack rates vary enormously, from under $20 a night in limited-service budget motels to over $2000 a night in luxury resort or convention hotels. A number of factors determine the price of a room.

Hotel Location This is the single most important factor affecting the price of a room. A deluxe resort hotel overlooking a golden expanse of beach will clearly command higher room rates than a resort hotel on a major highway five miles from the same beach. Rooms in the hotel will be even more expensive if there are no other lodging places in the area. In cities, hotels that are convenient to commercial centres, sightseeing attractions, and fashionable shopping areas are more expensive than those in more marginal urban locations.

Room Location The location of a room within a hotel also has a direct bearing on price. This is particularly true of resort hotels, where the rooms with the best views (usually those on the upper floors) are the most expensive. In most hotels, the rooms farthest from noisy public areas (e.g., restaurants, swimming pools, discothèques) also tend to command higher prices.

Room Size and Fixtures Some of the chains at the budget end of the market operate hotels with rooms of a single, standard size, but most hotels offer rooms of different sizes—for example, single rooms (with one twin bed), twins (with two twin beds), doubles (with one large double bed), twin doubles (with two double beds), suites (with one or more bedrooms and a living room), and, at the top of the price scale, penthouse suites (with access to the roof, swimming pool, and tennis court). (Table 7-2 lists these and other commonly used hotel and motel terms, with their definitions.) It should be noted that the number of people occupying a room does not necessarily affect the price—a single room can sometimes cost as much as a twin or double. Children under a certain age may be able to share their parents' room at no extra cost.

Fixtures are fairly standard in Canadian and American motels and hotels and usually include toilet, bath/shower, and air conditioning. A telephone, radio, and television are

ILLUSTRATION 7-5
Suites, such as this one in the Delta Place (Vancouver, B.C.), offer the extra space that many business travellers need.
SOURCE: Courtesy of Delta Hotels Resorts

standard in all but the no-frills budget motels. In many parts of the world, such in-room fixtures are considered luxuries and are only available in the more expensive rooms. Bathrooms, for example, may be located at the end of a corridor rather than in each room.

Length of Stay and Season Some hotels, particularly in Europe, offer special weekly rates, whereby a guest can stay for seven days more cheaply than for four or five days at the rack rate. Weekend rates offered by commercial hotels in Canada and the United States are also lower than rack rates.

The time of year can have a significant bearing on the room rates offered by resort hotels. For example, at ski resorts the summer rates are considerably lower than the winter rates. The same is true for resort hotels in warm-weather destinations. In both cases, winter is the high season and summer the low season.

Meals Some hotels in Canada and the United States include meals in their room rates, though this practice is more common overseas, particularly in resort areas. Meals are, however, often included in the price of a package tour, both in North America and overseas. Foreign hotels include different kinds of meal plans in their room rates:

- **European plan (EP):** room only, no meals
- **Continental plan (CP):** continental breakfast (juice, coffee, roll or pastry)
- **Modified American plan (MAP):** continental or full breakfast and dinner
- **American plan (AP):** continental or full breakfast, lunch, and dinner

The AP room rate will clearly be more expensive than the EP rate.

TABLE 7-2
Hotel Terminology

Single	Room with one twin bed.
Twin	Room with two twin beds.
Double	Room with one large double bed.
Twin double	Room with two double beds.
Suite	Room with one or more bedrooms and a living room.
Penthouse suite	Suite with access to the roof, swimming pool, and tennis court.
Weekly rate	Discount rate charged for a stay of a week or more.
Rack rate	Standard day rate.
Weekend rate	Discount rate charged for weekend stay.
Run-of-the-house rate	Discount rate for block bookings.
Corporate rate	Discount rate for employees of large companies.
Continental breakfast	Light breakfast usually including coffee, juice, and a roll or pastry.
Full breakfast	Cooked breakfast often including eggs, bacon, toast, etc.
EP	European plan. A hotel rate that includes the room only and no meals.
CP	Continental plan. A hotel rate that includes continental breakfast.
MAP	Modified American plan. A hotel rate that includes continental or full breakfast and dinner.
AP	American plan. A hotel rate that includes continental or full breakfast, lunch, and dinner.
Family plan	Special family rate that allows children to share their parents' room at no additional charge.

Special Features The availability of special features, such as recreational facilities, in-room cable television, and 24-hour room service, also affects the price of a room. The high cost of building and maintaining swimming pools, tennis courts, health centres, golf courses, and other sports amenities has to be reflected in higher room rates. Use of these facilities may be "free," but the guest is paying for them in the price of the room.

If a hotel is of historical or architectural significance, room rates will tend to be higher. A guest can expect to pay more, for example, at a country inn which can boast that "Sir John A. slept here."

Special Rates People who stay in a hotel as part of a group can usually expect to pay less for their accommodations than guests who book individually. The rate charged for block bookings is known as the **run-of-the-house rate.** Most hotels also offer a **corporate rate** for employees of large companies. The largest discount of all is given to overnight guests attending conventions and meetings at the hotel. Many chain operations have special family rates—known as **family plan** rates—that allow children to share their parents' room at no additional charge.

Other Lodging Places

In discussing the hotel as product, we have largely concentrated on properties operated by North American chains. A number of other lodging places, found particularly in Europe, also deserve mention.

Youth hostels provide younger travellers with overnight lodgings at rock-bottom prices. Facilities are extremely basic—guests have to provide their own bedding, share a communal washroom, and prepare their own meals—yet youth hostels remain popular with students and other travellers on limited budgets. The idea has been slow to catch on in the United States and Canada. Of the 5000 youth hostels worldwide, only about 225 are in North America.

Pensions are private homes that have been converted into guest houses. They offer meals and lodging in an informal family atmosphere. Found primarily in Europe and Latin America, they are usually less expensive than hotels of comparable quality.

Bed-and-breakfast accommodations are available throughout the British Isles and have been steadily gaining popularity in the United States and Canada as well. Bed-and-breakfast guests can expect a full breakfast, a comfortable room, and often an ambiance quite unlike what is found in most modern hotels.

Paradors in Spain and **posadas** in Portugal are castles and other historic buildings that have been converted into

ILLUSTRATION 7-6
Bed-and-breakfast accommodation, such as is available in the mid-nineteenth century Kiely House at Niagara-on-the-Lake, offers unique surroundings and a welcome change from the modern hotel.
SOURCE: Courtesy of Heather and Ray Pettit

PROFILE

Bed-and-Breakfast

A ranch in Alberta. A heritage inn in Ontario. A summer home on the ocean in Nova Scotia. A century farmhouse in Quebec. These are just a sample of the wide variety of bed-and-breakfasts found in Canada. A bed-and-breakfast, or B&B, is a small, family-owned hotel, or private home whose owners rent out bedrooms and provide meals to travellers. There are bed-and-breakfasts in every province in Canada.

At B&Bs you won't find a vending machine down the hall from your room. You won't find an elevator. You may not even find a bath in your room. What you will find are attractive homes, some decorated with antiques and period furniture. You'll find cozy, comfortable bedrooms, perhaps with quilts and lace curtains. You'll also find friendly, courteous hosts who will give you breakfast and maybe even afternoon tea.

Some Canadians who are familiar with bed-and-breakfasts may have first encountered them while travelling in Europe. B&Bs are very popular in many European countries, such as France, Great Britain, Italy, Spain, and the Scandinavian countries. For travellers in Europe, a bed-and-breakfast is often cheaper than a hotel; more importantly, it allows them to experience firsthand the culture of the country they are visiting. Imagine the excitement of staying in a French château, a Spanish castle, or a 500-year-old English farmhouse. In the same way, foreign visitors to Canada can experience our culture at bed-and-breakfasts in this country.

There have always been bed-and-breakfasts in Canada, but until recently, they were usually known by other names, such as tourist homes or guest houses. These homes were identified by signs in the front yard reading GUESTS or TOURISTS. During the Depression, struggling families often rented their spare rooms to travellers passing by on their way to find work. The arrangement suited both the hosts, who needed the extra $2 a night a room would fetch, and the many travellers who could not afford more expensive accommodations.

In resort areas, guest houses were and still are a popular alternative to hotels. Staying at a bed-and-breakfast or guest house may be the only way a family of modest means can afford to spend a week at the seashore or in the mountains. But price is not the only reason why people choose to stay at a B&B. Although a guest house may lack a private bath in each room, and a swimming pool, many people feel that the charm and family atmosphere of a bed-and-breakfast easily compensate for the lack of amenities.

For example, the Kiely House in Niagara-on-the-Lake was built in 1832 and has been used as a private summer home as well as an inn over the last two centuries. The setting (wide lawns backing on a golf course) is on the edge of the town that holds the internationally respected Shaw Festival each summer. The 13 guest rooms are finished with period furniture and decorations. The comfortable, restorative environment is completed by Heather and Ray Pettit, who as hosts are both convivial and professional.

Today, it is possible to walk into your local library or bookstore and find dozens of guidebooks to bed-and-breakfasts all over America as well as Europe. Travellers who want to stay at bed-and-breakfasts should obtain one of these guidebooks to learn beforehand what kind of accommodations to expect. Some B&Bs will accept children and pets; others will not. Some take credit cards; others do not. Some require reservations far in advance, while others can accommodate guests without notice.

Facilities vary widely from one bed-and-breakfast to another. Some are small hotels with single and double rooms, televisions and private baths in each room, and a dining room serving three meals a day. Many, however, are private homes where the accommodations are simply a spare bedroom, a shared bath, and a television in the owner's living room.

Each bed-and-breakfast is unique. Regardless of the differences among them, however, there is a common thread throughout: they are operated by hosts who love to meet people and welcome them into their homes. What guests seem to remember most from their stay at a bed-and-breakfast is the personal service and warmth of the host family. In fact, many bed-and-breakfast owners have a large collection of thank you notes from pleased guests.

hotels by the government. They cater primarily to vacationers, offer full meal plans, and are reasonably priced. More luxurious castle accommodations are available in France (châteaux) and in Germany and Austria (Schlösser).

Resort condominiums, a comparatively recent addition to the industry's product line, offer an alternative to hotel accommodations in British Columbia, Colorado, Florida, Hawaii, Quebec, and other popular vacation areas. Condominiums are individually owned residential units under common management within a multi-unit project. Owners often use them for vacations and rent them out the rest of the year. Condominiums provide apartment-style accommodations, with kitchen facilities, as well as recreational amenities either on-site or nearby.

The concept of time sharing was introduced first in Europe, then spread to North America in the mid-1970s. In this case, the individual shares ownership of a unit with several other people. Each owner buys a vacation segment (usually two weeks) for a guaranteed number of years. The segments are scheduled so that only one owner uses the property at a time. Some time-sharing companies allow clients to exchange their segments with people who own time-sharing units in other resort areas.

Attracting Different Kinds of Customers

As noted earlier, a major development in the hospitality industry in the last 35 years has been the increasing segmentation of the hotel product. In today's highly competitive market, hotels compete to attract business from different groups of customers by offering more specialized services, extra amenities, and incentive rates.

Hotels are particularly keen to attract business travellers because they constitute the largest guest category in nonresort properties. Many hotels offer discounts and travel bonuses for frequent visitors. Delta's "Delta Privilege" program, for example, offers room rate reductions, gift shop discounts, express reservations, and cheque-cashing privileges. Delta is the first North American hotel chain to guarantee service performance (on approximately ten criteria) or the room is free. Some major hotels designate executive floors for the exclusive use of business guests. Special features may include extra-luxurious rooms, libraries with business publications and international newspapers, private lounges for meeting and entertaining clients, and business centres with fax machines and secretarial, telex, and translation services.

A number of properties at the upper end of the market have introduced special features in response to the increasingly sophisticated needs of their guests. The idea of concierge service has been imported from Europe. A professional concierge (or "guest services person") handles travel arrangements, makes restaurant reservations, obtains theatre tickets, arranges sightseeing tours, and handles other details to make the guest's stay more enjoyable. Valet parking and hotel–airport transportation are other services that many customers have come to expect. Responding to the physical fitness trend, quality Canadian and American hotels are installing health centres with exercise equipment, and offering special menus featuring healthier foods.

A problem for hotels that cater primarily to the business traveller is how to fill rooms on weekends. Many hotels promote special weekend packages for the vacation and leisure traveller, sometimes with tie-ins to local attractions and amusements. Theme weekends—for example, music weekends, western weekends, and mystery weekends (with the guests participating to solve a mystery)—are becoming increasingly popular. You read about a similar development in the cruise industry in the last chapter.

A large percentage of a hotel's guests are out-of-towners, but hotels are also developing facilities so that they can function as centres of activity for local residents. This is particularly true of hotels (and motels) in suburban and airport locations. Meeting rooms and banquet rooms are available for local business groups and for social functions; restaurants and entertainment features also attract local residents. In this way, hotels appeal to three distinct markets: guests travelling for business or pleasure; local businesspeople; and local residents.

The Organization of a Hotel

Small, individually owned hotels without food and beverage and other services are able to operate with a small staff, possibly with just the owners themselves and a maid or two to clean guest rooms. Most hotels, however, require a much more complex organizational structure involving six main departments.

Certain aspects of hotel organization are clearly visible to guests—the lobby, the front desk, the bellstaff, and the like. These are often called the "front of the house." The "back of the house" includes equally important but less noticeable aspects—the kitchen, storage areas, administration, engineering, security, and so on.

Administration Every hotel needs a manager, assistant managers, and a group of people to handle the business aspects of the hotel's operations. The people who work in the administration department include bookkeepers and other financial staff, and purchasing, sales, and marketing personnel. An important function of the administration department is to interview and select the hotel's employees.

Front Office The front office is the most visible department in all hotels and motels. These employees are in direct contact with the public; they handle reservations, room assignments, mail, and baggage, and provide information about activities in the hotel and surrounding area. A well-organized front office is essential to the smooth running of any lodging place.

Housekeeping Guest comfort is a top priority here. Most hotels employ a large housekeeping (or rooms) staff to ensure the cleanliness and neat appearance of guest rooms and public areas.

Food and Beverage Services As you know, the hospitality industry is an integral part of the travel industry. Hotels and motels depend on the travel industry to bring in their guests; as travel increases, the hospitality industry grows. With the growth of the airline industry, hotels have become more complex, as they tailor their services to meet the needs of business travellers, conventioneers, and vacationers. The hotel has evolved from the small wayside inn of earlier times to the giant resort and convention hotel of today. Some lodging places are not merely places to stop, but destinations in themselves.

Methods of Making Reservations

Until recent times, there were no advanced reservations systems; guests simply arrived at a lodging place and hoped there was a room available for the night. Motels still rely on "walk-ins" for much of their business, but most rooms at other properties are now booked in advance.

Travellers can make reservations themselves or through a travel agency. There has been some friction between hotels and travel agencies in the past, chiefly over the question of commissions. Hotel–agency relations have improved in recent years, however, and most hotels now see travel agents as an important extension of their sales force. Figure 7-2 shows the methods travel agents use to make hotel bookings.

As you learned in Chapter 3, the reservations process has become increasingly automated in the last 25 years, and almost all chains now have centralized computer reservations systems linking their properties worldwide. For example, with Holiday Inn's Holidex 2000 systems, clients can make advance reservations at any Holiday Inn property in the world just by calling a toll-free number.

Hotel reservations can also be made through airline CRSs. Airlines that own hotels will obviously try to sell their own accommodations. Even so, many of the large hotel chains also subscribe to the airline CRS systems, which are particularly convenient for clients making airline and hotel bookings at the same time.

Another alternative is to book accommodations through a hotel representative company. A number of chains appoint a single such company to handle reservations for all their properties.

A fourth method is to make reservations by direct contact (i.e., by letter, telephone, fax, telex, or cable). Direct contact may be the only way to book rooms at many small, individually owned properties that are not linked to a reservations system, or that do not have a hotel representative. This is particularly true for overseas properties.

Reservations can also be made through a tour operator or wholesaler if the hotel accommodation is bought as part of a tour package.

References

Several useful reference books are available for travel professionals and travellers. Many contain both objective information (such as factual descriptions of hotel facilities) and subjective comments (evaluations of individual properties in terms of service, atmosphere, and so on).

Hotel and Travel Index (HTI), published quarterly by Reed Travel, is the world's largest one-volume hotel directory. It lists over 45 000 properties worldwide. Although limited information is given for each property, *HTI* is full of advertisements that provide detailed information on over 10 000 hotels and motels. *HTI* also includes listings of hotel representatives and reservations systems, city information (including availability of rental cars and scheduled air service), and city and area maps showing where hotels and corporate headquarters are located. The *Hotel and Travel Index/ABC International Edition (HTI/ABC)* is similar to *HTI* but geared toward the international traveller.

The *Official Hotel Guide (OHG)*, also published by Reed Travel, comprises three volumes. Volume I covers the United States (Alabama–Nebraska). Volume II covers the rest of the United States, along with the Caribbean, Mexico, and Central and South America. Volume III covers Europe, the Middle East, Africa, Asia, and the Pacific region. Properties are described in greater detail than in *HTI* and are rated according to the *OHG*'s own classification system. The guide makes heavy use of maps and contains descriptions of attractions in individual cities.

The quarterly *OAG Business Travel Planner Hotel and Motel Redbook* is available in North American, European, and Pacific–Asia editions. The North American edition has listings of properties in Canada and the United States and for resort areas (including Alaska, Canada, the Caribbean, Hawaii, and Mexico). The same edition incorporates the *Mobil Travel Guide* ratings. The European edition is particularly strong on travel-related services (i.e., airline, rail, and car rental services) and general travel information for visitors to Europe. The European guide includes government ratings for hotels, and incorporates the Automobile Association (UK) ratings for hotels which don't have government rat-

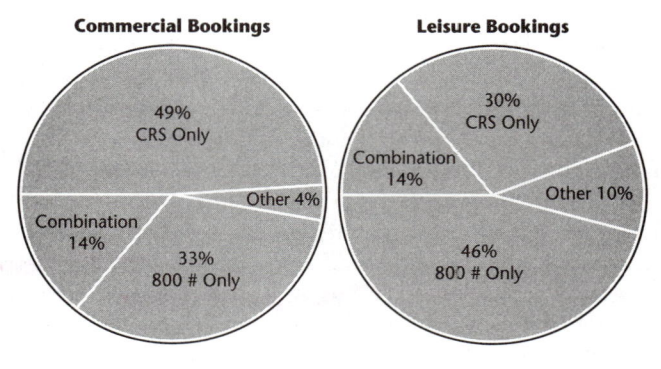

Commercial Bookings
- 49% CRS Only
- 33% 800 # Only
- Combination 14%
- Other 4%

Leisure Bookings
- 30% CRS Only
- 46% 800 # Only
- Combination 14%
- Other 10%

FIGURE 7-2

Methods Used by Travel Agents to Complete Hotel Bookings
SOURCE: Plog Research, *Hotel and Travel Index, Hotel Line*

ings. The Pacific–Asia edition provides extensive general travel information and hotel and motel listings for 50 countries in that region.

The STAR SERVICE, published by Reed Travel, is probably the most subjective guide. It is updated quarterly, with revisions that can be inserted into a three-ring binder. It provides detailed reviews of more than 10 000 hotels worldwide.

In addition to these standard reference guides, there are several consumer guides that provide subjective information about selected properties in different areas and countries. These include Frommer's Dollar-Wise and $20-A-Day guides, Fielding's series of travel guides, and Fodor guides. Hotels are listed and rated in guides such as Michelin's Red Guide series and the Mobil Travel Guide series.

> **CHECK YOUR PRODUCT KNOWLEDGE**
>
> 1. What are the five ways that hotel reservations can be made?
> 2. What is the difference between objective information and subjective information in a reference book?
> 3. Name two multivolume hotel reference guides.

CAREER OPPORTUNITIES

The accommodation sector in Canada employed about 160 000 people in tourism-related employment for 1991, as shown in Table 1-1. This sector employed far more people (138 000) than any other in the travel industry. The industry is expected to undergo stable growth of about 2.4 percent per year in the 1990s, and the employment outlook should remain generally good for most hotel occupations. The positions discussed below exist in the larger hotels. In smaller properties, individual workers often have multiple duties.

Front Office

The front staff comprises two separate departments: the service department and the front desk. Service workers include doorkeepers, bellstaff (who show guests to their rooms, run errands, and sometimes perform room-service duties), baggage porters, and elevator operators. These are all entry-level positions. A superintendent of service is often appointed to supervise this department.

Front desk positions are clerical and include reservations clerks (who handle advance reservations), room clerks (who assign guests their rooms and handle registration procedures), rack clerks (who keep records of room assignments), mail clerks (who handle guests' mail and telegrams), and information clerks (who tell guests about local places of interest). With the increasing automation of the registration and reservations process, a hotel may need only one or two front desk clerks to perform all of these duties. The front office manager supervises all front office staff and operations; he or she may have an assistant. Also part of the front office is the night auditor, whose job involves updating the guests' bills each night.

The security department is sometimes considered to be part of the front office. A chief of security supervises a staff of house officers and patrol personnel. These employees may also deal with guest queries.

ILLUSTRATION 7-7
The North American Edition of the *OAG Travel Planner Hotel and Motel Redbook* lists properties in the United States and in resort areas.
SOURCE: Reprinted by special permission from the June–August 1991 issue of the *OAG Business Travel Planner—North American Edition.* Copyright © 1991, Official Airlines Guides. All rights reserved.

Housekeeping/Rooms

Entry-level housekeeping positions include room cleaner, seamstress, upholsterer, linen room attendant, laundry worker, and valet. The position of executive housekeeper (in charge of all housekeeping operations) is essentially administrative, although in smaller hotels, executive housekeepers may perform cleaning and other duties themselves. In the largest properties, assistant housekeepers and floor housekeepers are sometimes appointed to ease the executive housekeeper's workload.

Food and Beverage

This department has the most complex organization. In the larger hotels, it may be subdivided into three separate departments: food and beverage, restaurant, and banquet. A food and beverage manager oversees the work of all three departments and supervises all food service operations, including the purchasing of food.

Entry-level positions include dishwasher, salad or sandwich maker, kitchen helper, dining room attendant, and server. A chief steward is responsible for all the food served in the hotel and for general kitchen operations. He or she may be assisted by a pantry supervisor, who trains and supervises the kitchen helpers. An executive chef is in charge of the food preparation and supervises the team of cooks and chefs. This team may include a roast chef, salad chef, fry cook, vegetable cook, short-order cook, pastry cook, and butcher.

Restaurant department personnel include restaurant managers, assistant managers, hostesses or maîtres d'hôtel, servers, and dining room attendants.

Hotels that schedule large-scale banquets usually employ a banquet staff, which may operate from a separate kitchen. A banquet manager oversees all banquet operations and also functions as part of the sales team. Many of the positions in this department are almost identical to those in the food-and-beverage and restaurant departments; they include banquet chef, banquet server, and banquet kitchen staff. Two positions unique to this department are decorator (responsible for the eye-catching appearance of the banquet table) and banquet housekeeper (responsible for setting up furniture, bars, and so on, in the banquet room).

Sales and Other Positions

Most larger hotels employ a sales staff to market their product. A sales manager supervises a team of sales representatives who solicit business from travel agencies, tour operators, airlines, business firms, clubs, and social, political, and professional organizations. Group and convention sales are the major source of income; large convention hotels may appoint convention specialists (e.g., planners, consultants, and managers) to handle this lucrative market.

Mention should also be made of the accounts, engineering, and personnel departments. A controller, or chief accountant, heads a large staff of cashiers, night auditors, credit assistants, and payroll clerks, all of whom are responsible for the financial operations of the hotel. Assistant engineers, maintenance engineers, painters, carpenters, electricians, plumbers, and locksmiths work in the hotel under the supervision of a chief engineer. Personnel department staff are responsible for hiring employees and overseeing benefit and training programs. There is usually a personnel director, who oversees secretaries, personnel assistants, interviewers, clerks, and typists.

Summary

- The hospitality industry is an integral part of the travel industry.
- Early lodging places developed along trade and travel routes.
- By the early 19th century, buildings were being designed specifically as hotels.

ILLUSTRATION 7-8
The food and beverage department of any hotel demands a high degree of organizational and management skills.
SOURCE: Courtesy of Delta Hotels & Resorts

A DAY IN THE LIFE OF

A Front Desk Manager

I am a front desk manager at a large resort hotel. My work is often demanding, but I enjoy the challenge. I supervise a staff of dozens of employees, and I must deal with such daily crises as overbooked rooms and missing luggage. I am the person guests come to with their complaints, questions, and comments. If I serve guests well, they will form a good impression of my hotel and they will come back again. Despite its demands, I love my work. I like supervising people and working as part of a team with the other managers in the hotel.

I didn't start out as a front desk manager, of course. My first hotel job was waiting tables in a hotel restaurant during summer vacations from college. After graduation, I took a job as a front desk clerk. When I started out in my first hotel job, my manager told me, "Do every task to the best of your ability because managers are always looking for ambitious, capable people to promote to better jobs." She turned out to be right, because I have been promoted three times since then. Most hotels promote their managers from within.

Some hotel managers that I know started working in hotels right after high school. They took entry-level jobs and learned the business as they progressed up the management ladder. However, many hotels prefer to hire people who took hotel and restaurant management courses at a community college. Many colleges in Canada offer courses in hotel and restaurant management. While in college, I took courses in accounting, hotel management, food and beverage control, business administration, and business finance.

Of course, after I started my first hotel job, I received a lot of on-the-job training. This was very important, because some tasks you can learn only by actually performing them. I have to be able to do any of the jobs of the people I supervise—who include cashiers, bellstaff, reservations clerks, desk clerks, and telephone operators.

People sometimes ask me what special qualities a person needs to be a good front desk manager. I think that it is especially important that you like people and enjoy serving the public. In fact, sometimes I am as much a public relations expert as I am a front desk manager. Because I am one of the first employees that guests meet when they arrive here, I have to be friendly and helpful so they will carry away a good opinion of the hotel and its employees. That way, they will stay at the hotel again when they are in the area, and they will recommend the hotel to friends and colleagues.

Front desk managers must be patient, tactful, and skilful not only in dealing with guests but also in directing other employees. I want the employees I supervise to enjoy their jobs and work well with each other, because they reflect their feelings and attitudes when dealing with guests. It is also part of my job to coordinate the front desk operations with those of other departments, such as housekeeping and food services. If I checked in guests to rooms that had not been cleaned, or overbooked reservations in the hotel's restaurants, it would annoy both the guests and my fellow employees.

Front desk managers must be calm and capable in the face of emergencies. They must be able to make decisions and solve problems quickly. I have to deal with many different kinds of problems every day. Some are minor, such as when one of our magnetic keys fails to open a room door or the television in a room doesn't work. Others can be serious or very aggravating. Just this morning, I had to deal with a family of six whose rooms had been accidentally booked to other travellers. Since my hotel was full, I had to find them accommodations at another hotel and arrange transportation for them.

There are several advantages to my job that you won't find in many other jobs. Among them are that I get to meet people from all over the world, and I live all year round in a comfortable hotel at a beautiful, sunny beach resort. I eat in the hotel restaurant and can use its pool and other facilities whenever I am off-duty. Also, my pay is comparable to other kinds of management jobs.

One disadvantage to my job is that the front desk operates 24 hours a day, so I sometimes have to work a second or third shift. Since I live in the hotel, I am on call around the clock, seven days a week. For me, though, the advantages greatly outweigh the disadvantages. I plan to stay in this field for a long time.

- The hotel industry grew tremendously with the expansion of the North American railway network.
- Luxury hotels were built in the major cities; smaller, less elaborate hotels appeared along the railway lines.
- The first chain operations appeared in the early 20th century.
- The automobile and the airline industry have had an enormous impact on the hospitality industry in modern times, in that they have fostered the development of motels, resort hotels, convention hotels, and airport hotels.
- Forms of hotel ownership include individual ownership, chain ownership, franchise, and management contract.
- Hotels can be classified by type, function, location, and scale.
- Hotel location, room location, room size, length and season of stay, and availability of special services and facilities are the main factors affecting the price of a room.
- Market segmentation has been a major development in the last 35 years.
- Hotels market their products to specific groups of customers, including business travellers, convention groups, vacationers, weekenders, and local residents.
- Hotels are organized into six main departments: administration, front office, housekeeping, food and beverage, engineering, and security.
- Hotel reservations can be made through central reservations offices, airline CRSs, or hotel representative companies, or by direct contact.

Key Terms

tourist cabin
tourist court
motel
unit
motor hotel
motor inn
resort hotel
convention hotel
atrium
property
break-even point
"mom-and-pop" ownership
joint venture
franchise
management contract
transient hotel
residential hotel
all-suite
rack rate
European plan (EP)
Continental plan (CP)
Modified American Plan (MAP)
American plan (AP)
run-of-the-house rate
corporate rate
family plan
youth hostel
pension
bed-and-breakfast
parador
posada
resort condominium
time-sharing
concierge

What Do You Think?

1. What effects might a sharp rise in airline fares have on the hospitality industry?
2. The hospitality industry has become increasingly specialized in recent years. Is there potential for further specialization? If so, in what areas?
3. What impact might the continued development of resort condominiums and time-sharing units have on the hospitality industry?
4. Why might a guest prefer to stay at a well-known chain hotel (e.g., a Holiday Inn) rather than in a small, family-owned hotel in the same neighbourhood?
5. What future do you see for the no-frills budget motels?
6. In recent years, hotels have been developing increasingly sophisticated services to attract different kinds of customers. What further services might they introduce to attract (a) business travellers, (b) convention groups, and (c) vacationers?

Dealing with Product

You have just been promoted to director of sales for a brand-new 300-unit property across the highway from the entrance to Yourtown International Airport. The grand opening of this property is less than a week away.

Your first order of business is to design and implement a marketing plan. Your property includes a restaurant, a coffee shop, a cocktail lounge, and an indoor swimming pool with a sauna and an exercise area, as well as ten function rooms that can be used for meetings and banquets. What types of travellers do you hope to have as guests? What can you do to keep the occupancy rate near 100 percent and the owners happy?

Dealing with People

In the airline industry, it is called "to bump"; in the hospitality industry, it is called "to walk." In either case, the traveller is denied service because the airline or hotel overbooked. Invariably, the traveller is less than thrilled to learn that his or her reservation will not be honoured.

Tonight is your night to learn all about irate travellers. It's 7 P.M., and you are the front desk manager at a 200-unit hotel in downtown Yourtown. You have a full house; there is no room at the inn tonight. Before you stands a weary traveller with a suitcase in one hand and a confirmation slip in the other. He has just been told that because he did not have a guaranteed reservation, the hotel cancelled his reservation when he failed to check in by the 6 P.M. cutoff time. In fact, this weary traveller is the third person that you will have "walked" tonight.

What do you think of your hotel's policy of cancelling reservations at 6 P.M.? What will you say and do to convert this very angry traveller into a repeat customer?

CHAPTER 7: The Hospitality Industry   Name: _____

WORKSHEET 7-1 Choosing Facilities

You are a travel agent. Use the *Official Hotel Guide* or a similar publication to find appropriate hotels, motels, or resorts for the following customers. Narrow down the possibilities to two and describe them in the space provided. Include location, cost, facilities, services, proximity to tourist attractions, number of rooms, and so on.

1. A married couple from Ontario plan to visit friends living in Budapest, Hungary. Since their friends do not have room for guests in their apartment, the couple must stay at a hotel. The couple would prefer a moderately priced, older hotel in the centre of the city.

2. A tired, overworked executive is looking forward to a two-week vacation. Since she travels a great deal for her job, the last thing she wants to do is spend her vacation travelling. A large resort sounds appealing. The executive imagines herself basking in the sun and being pampered by an attentive hotel staff.

3. A man from Vancouver must travel to Hong Kong on business. He wants a suite in a Western-style hotel, preferably an American chain hotel. The hotel must provide a full array of business services, including a fax machine and a translator. The businessman would also like to be near the airport, if possible.

4. A family consisting of two adults and three children (ages 14, 11, and 7) plan to visit Boston and the surrounding area during the first week in July. They would like to stay in a motel in a northern suburb. The motel should be close to a subway station so they don't have to drive into the city. The children want the motel to have a swimming pool.

CHAPTER 7: The Hospitality Industry   Name: _____

WORKSHEET 7–2 Hotel Market Segmentation

As you read in Chapter 7, today's hotels are built to meet the MNEs of different kinds of travellers. Find a newspaper or magazine ad for each type of hotel listed in the boxes below. Use information in the ads to complete each box.

Budget motel
Name: _____
Location: _____
Price range: _____
Market segment: _____
Facilities/services/amenities: _____
_____
_____
_____
_____
_____
_____
_____

Resort
Name: _____
Location: _____
Price range: _____
Market segment: _____
Facilities/services/amenities: _____
_____
_____
_____
_____
_____
_____
_____

Business convention hotel
Name: _____
Location: _____
Price range: _____
Market segment: _____
Facilities/services/amenities: _____
_____
_____
_____
_____
_____
_____
_____

Bed-and-Breakfast
Name: _____
Location: _____
Price range: _____
Market segment: _____
Facilities/services/amenities: _____
_____
_____
_____
_____
_____
_____
_____

CHAPTER 7: The Hospitality Industry   Name: Orville,

WORKSHEET 7–3 Selling the Hospitality Product

You have read about the increasing segmentation of the hospitality industry. For each of the following groups, list facilities, services, or amenities that might attract travellers to one hotel over another.

Travelling salespeople for struggling companies

Vacationing families with children

Affluent young singles

Physically challenged businesspeople

College students on limited budgets touring Canada

Hotels that cater primarily to business travellers must make special efforts to attract weekend guests. For example, a hotel in Toronto might offer a weekend package with reduced room rates, along with prearranged theatre tickets and dinner in a well-known restaurant. What special weekend packages might the following facilities offer?

A medium-sized deluxe resort in the Muskoka area

A large, moderately priced hotel in Edmonton

A small, moderately priced beachfront motel on Lake Ontario

A moderately priced hotel near Montreal's Dorval Airport

A resort in Victoria, British Columbia

CHAPTER 7: The Hospitality Industry   Name: _____

WORKSHEET 7–4 Employment in the Hospitality Industry

You are a personnel manager at a new hotel and conference centre. You have job openings in all six of the hotel's main departments (administration, front office, housekeeping, food and beverage, engineering, and security). You have interviewed the applicants listed below and would like to offer each of them a job. What specific job would you offer each applicant? What are the opportunities for advancement?

A man with two years of college has worked summers on the bellstaff of a large city hotel. He has a friendly, attractive personality and enjoys dealing with people.

A college graduate, major in home economics, is very organized and has experience supervising other workers.

A graduate of a vocational high school has worked summers for a fast food chain and wants eventually to be a chef.

A community college graduate has taken business, advertising, and marketing courses. She is aggressive and motivated.

A former peacekeeper with the Canadian Armed Forces, now a night watchman for a large office building, would like to have more contact with people.

A former travel agent who specialized in convention planning has a college degree in hotel administration and experience in public relations.

A skilled mechanic who has worked both as an electrician and as a carpenter prefers not to work with the public.

A college graduate with a major in accounting has worked summers in the administration office of a large hotel chain.

A high school graduate has worked in the laundry room of a large nursing home.

PART 3

Tourism Systems and Services

CHAPTER 8
Destination Development

CHAPTER 9
The Recreation and Leisure System

CHAPTER 10
Tours and Charters

CHAPTER 8

Destination Development

"All travel has its advantages. If the traveller visits better countries, he may learn to improve his own; and if fortune carries him to worse, he may learn to enjoy his own."

Samuel Johnson

OBJECTIVES

When you have completed this chapter, you should be able to do the following:

- Determine what attracts travellers to different destinations.
- List and describe each of the five steps involved in the planning stage of destination development.
- Define carrying capacity.
- Evaluate the role of different levels of government in destination development.
- Describe the development of a major tourist destination.
- Identify the four stages of the product life cycle and apply them to a specific case.
- Distinguish between the multiplier effect and revenue leakage.
- Discuss the social impact of tourism.
- Define and give examples of the demonstration effect.
- Give reasons why local residents may resent tourists.
- Explain how tourism can help preserve a local culture.
- Identify the possible negative effects of destination development on a local environment.

In earlier chapters, you read about the different modes of transportation that travellers use to get to destinations throughout the world. In this chapter, we will focus on the destinations themselves and, in particular, on the topic of destination development.

Some destinations have existed for hundreds, even thousands, of years. They were not originally created as tourist destinations, but over the years, they have become important centres of tourism. Obvious examples include cities such as London and Paris and natural attractions such as Niagara Falls and the Grand Canyon. Other destinations have been developed specifically to attract visitors. These include Caribbean resorts as well as theme parks such as Disneyland, Busch Gardens, and Canada's Wonderland.

Most Canadians know that Whistler has been developed as a destination; others may be aware of the additional development now taking place at Mont Tremblant in the Laurentians. Both developments are owned by the same Canadian company, Intrawest Developments. However, few Canadians are aware that a European-style spa is being developed near Lunenburg, Nova Scotia. How many realize developers are planning more than $2.3 billion in resort and residential projects over the next two decades in and around Canmore, in the heart of the Bow River Valley between Calgary and Banff?

In this chapter, you'll learn about the complex planning involved in the development of a tourist destination. You'll also read about the role of government in developing and controlling destinations. Finally, you'll learn about the economic, social, cultural, and environmental impact that destination development can have on the people and resources of a region.

DESTINATIONS DEFINED

Every decision to travel is a response to one of two questions: "Where do I want to go?" or "Where do I have to be?" Tourists and vacationers ask the first question. Business travellers and those who plan to visit friends or relatives ask the second. In both cases, the **destination** is a location that travellers choose to visit and where they spend time, no matter what their motivations, needs, and expectations (MNEs).

A destination can be as small as a single building or as large as an entire continent. A student might be inspired to spend an afternoon at the McMichael Collection in Kleinburg, Ontario, after reading a book about the Group of

CHAPTER 8: Destination Development   189

Seven. At the other extreme, a traveller with enough money and time might decide to visit Australia on a four-week tour.

No matter what the destination, adequate facilities and services must be available to satisfy the needs of visitors. To accommodate visitors to Lunenburg, for example, restaurants, shops, parking facilities, and places to stay overnight were added. Larger areas that are created as tourist destinations—such as resorts and theme parks—require a much greater degree of human intervention. In addition to hotels and restaurants, recreational, entertainment, and transportation facilities must be provided. Support services such as fire departments, police stations, and hospitals or clinics are also needed. Even natural attractions require the building of facilities and services. Human intervention may also be necessary to make these locations accessible and to maintain them as attractive destinations.

What Attracts Travellers to Different Locations?

People choose a particular destination according to their motives for travelling. A vacationer who simply wants to lie in the sun for a week, for example, will probably choose a warm seaside resort. A traveller who wants to learn about Italian art might decide to visit museums in Rome, Florence, and Venice. Figure 8–1 identifies nine motivators that can influence a traveller's choice of destination.

Recreation People who travel for recreation might choose to relax on the beach at Cavendish, Prince Edward Island, or go surfing in southern California, or play golf at Banff, or go skiing in the Eastern Townships. They are attracted to the destination by the climate, the natural resources (beach or mountain), and the recreational facilities. Recreational travel can also be for the purpose of shopping (for example, in Hong Kong), gambling (Montreal, Las Vegas, Atlantic City), or socializing (dancing in a nightclub). And, of course, a vacationer might be attracted to a destination because it offers a wide range of activities. At a Club Med resort in the Caribbean, for example, vacationers can sunbathe, play tennis, water-ski, socialize, shop, and amuse themselves in countless other ways.

Culture Historic sites, museums, art galleries, and theatres are all cultural attractions. Some people travel to experience an earlier way of life (Upper Canada Village, Colonial Williamsburg), to learn about European art and culture (the Louvre in Paris), or to enjoy live theatre (London's West End). For many travellers, the local people themselves are a cultural attraction. Some cultural destinations can be exotic, for example, Inuit villages in the Northwest Territories, pre-Columbian sites in Central America, or the Polynesian Culture Center in Hawaii. The common denominator is that people travel to these destinations in order to enrich their cultural perspectives.

Nature Many people travel to experience the great outdoors. They are attracted to natural wonders such as the Grand Canyon, Death Valley, the Canadian Rockies, and the high tides of the Bay of Fundy. The desire to "get back to nature" often encourages vacationers to forgo the conveniences that hotels offer. They stay instead at campsites, lodges, and trailer parks.

Education Some travellers choose a destination for its educational value. A student might, for example, stay with a family in Quebec in order to become fluent in French, or take a summer course at Oxford University, or go on a study tour with an expert guide.

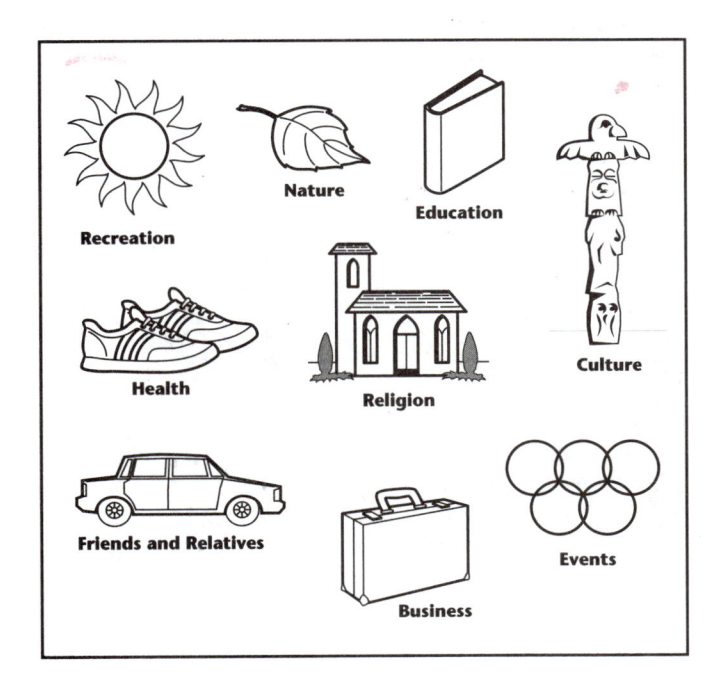

FIGURE 8-1
Motivators for Travel

ILLUSTRATION 8-1
A destination can be as small as a single building or as large as an entire continent.
SOURCE: Karen O'Neill

Events People sometimes plan a vacation around a special event. It can be a sporting event (the Olympics, the Grey Cup, the Kentucky Derby), a celebration (Edmonton's Klondike Days, the Carnival in Rio), a concert or play (the Shaw Festival at Niagara-on-the-Lake), or a parade (the Tournament of Roses parade in Pasadena, California). The event itself is the attraction rather than the city in which it is held. Most people who attend the Indianapolis 500, for example, do so because they want to watch a car race, not necessarily because they want to spend time in Indianapolis. If the race were held in Des Moines, they would go there instead.

Health Many people are motivated by a desire to improve their health and physical fitness. Some travel great distances to visit a health spa or weight-loss camp for an extended time. These latter destinations are popular not only because of the facilities available but also because they are usually attractively set, for example, in the mountains or by the ocean.

Religion Religion has been a prime motivator for travel for hundreds of years. Chaucer's 14th-century pilgrims in *The Canterbury Tales* were on their way to a religious shrine in southern England. Modern-day pilgrims travel to such religious sites as the Vatican, Lourdes, Jerusalem, Mecca, and Ste.-Anne-de-Beaupré, P.Q.

Friends and Relatives Many people travel to a destination because they have friends or relatives who live there. As with event-oriented travel, the destination is of less importance than the motivation for travelling. (Vacationers may choose to visit friends or relatives in a destination that they also want to visit for other reasons, such as recreation, a cultural experience, or business.)

Business Business or professional travellers go to a destination to make sales calls, act as consultants, or attend conventions, conferences, seminars, or other types of meetings. They go to the destination simply because it is where they have to be. Meeting planners do, however, try to schedule meetings at appealing destinations so that those attending can combine business and pleasure. A conference, for example, can be held at a resort that has facilities for golf, tennis, swimming, and other recreational activities. Business travellers might also turn a business trip into a mini-vacation by tacking on a few nonwork days at the beginning or end of the trip. (For a more lengthy discussion of business travel, see Chapters 11 and 12.)

It should be clear that the categories outlined above are not mutually exclusive. A traveller need not visit a destination solely for its recreational attractions or its educational value. He or she may want to lie in the sun, learn how to windsurf, lose weight, participate in an educational seminar, and experience the local culture all at a single destination.

This traveller will be attracted to the destination that can best satisfy all of these motivations.

Other factors also affect the choice of destination. These include ease of access, price, and suitability of accommodations. However attractive a destination may seem, many people won't go there if it is hard to reach or if accommodations are priced beyond their budget. One final factor to consider is the attitude of the local people. Various surveys show that friendly people rank high on the list of what travellers consider important in a destination. Travellers are more likely to return to a destination where they are made to feel welcome than to one where they're not wanted.

> **CHECK YOUR PRODUCT KNOWLEDGE**
>
> 1. How would you define the word *destination* as it is used in the travel industry?
> 2. What kinds of facilities are needed at almost all destinations?
> 3. List six motivations that can influence a traveller's choice of destination.

DESTINATION DEVELOPMENT

Developing a destination for tourism means much more than looking at a lagoon and thinking it would be a good idea to put a hotel on the beach. Considerable research and planning must be done long before a shovelful of earth is turned or a building is designed.

Destination development begins with an idea and with the selection of a site. The idea can come from the government of a developing nation that sees tourism as a way to increase the flow of foreign currency into the country. Or the

ILLUSTRATION 8-2
People travel to historic sites in order to enrich their cultural perspective (Abu Simbel, Egypt).
SOURCE: Karen O'Neill

idea can come from an entrepreneur who sees the opportunity to make a profit, perhaps by converting an unspoiled island into a vacation resort.

Regardless of who has the idea for development, the next stage is planning. Tourism has a tremendous impact on the economy, environment, and social and cultural life of an area. This is particularly true in developing countries. With careful planning, the negatives can be minimized and the positives maximized. Developers must take into account both the needs of the potential visitors and the effects that the development will have on the host community. Benefits must be weighed against costs.

The Planning Stage

Destination planning can be broken down into five main components: market analysis, site assessment, financial studies, environmental impact studies, and social impact studies (See Figure 8-2).

Market Analysis Market analysis involves studying travel trends and travel preferences in order to determine the feasibility of a planned development. Unless it is shown that there is a market for the destination—that is, a sufficient number of potential visitors—there is little point in going ahead with the development. Market analysis can also suggest what type of development might be most successful. Surveys may reveal, for example, that travel for cultural reasons is on the increase. Or they may identify a trend toward more luxurious accommodations, or toward the combining of business trips with vacations. Such findings would influence the types of visitor facilities and amenities to be provided at the destination.

Site Assessment The assessment of the site involves two main questions: "What do we have?" and "What else do we need?" If existing attractions include a long, sandy beach, clear, blue water, and plenty of sunshine, developers may well conclude that they need a golf course and marina to attract more visitors.

The site assessment must note the availability of a local labour force. If the local population isn't large enough to supply the necessary labour, workers will have to be brought in from outside to build and staff hotels, restaurants, and other visitor facilities.

Assessment of the **infrastructure** will determine whether local roads, water and electricity, supplies, sewage systems, and related services are adequate to handle the influx of tourists. Questions that might be raised include these: Do we need to build new roads or can we improve existing ones? Is there adequate drinking water? How do we dispose of garbage? What is the time for snow removal on routes to ski hills?

The assessment must also address superstructure needs. The term **superstructure** refers to all the buildings and other structures that are needed at the destination. The superstructure includes hotels, restaurants, convention centres, recreation facilities, shops, and other visitor amenities. In many developing regions, the superstructure has to be built from scratch.

Finally, the site assessment must study present and future transportation needs. The destination must be made accessible to major markets. New roads and railways may have to be built. Airports and ports may have to be expanded.

Financial Studies At an early stage in the planning process, developers must estimate the cost of the project. They must also determine where and how they are going to get the necessary capital. Financing can come from private investors or, in the case of developing nations, from an international agency such as the United Nations Development Bank.

A good financial study must determine project costs at each stage of development. Also at each stage, the most favourable terms for borrowing capital must be arranged. Developers will, of course, want to make a profit. But they must also consider the likely economic impact of the development on the host community. The financial study might be required to project, for example, the effect of the development on local property values and on local employment patterns. A successful development will be one that minimizes the negative economic impact and maximizes the positive.

Environmental Impact Studies At some point in the planning process, decision-makers must consider the physical effects that a sudden influx of visitors will have on the local environment. An environmental impact study asks such questions as these: How many visitors can our beaches handle and still remain clean? How many highrise hotels can we build before our destination loses its appeal? The term *carrying capacity* refers to the amount of tourism a destination can handle. A destination's carrying capacity is the maximum number of people that can use the site without causing an unacceptable deterioration in the physical environment and

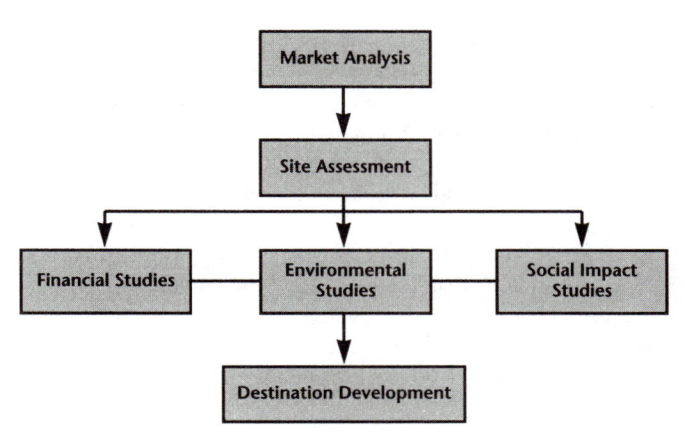

FIGURE 8-2
How a Destination Is Developed

without an unacceptable decline in the quality of the visitor's experience. Canada has four mountain national parks: Banff, Jasper, Kootenay, and Yoho. Amendments to the National Parks Act were made in 1988. A management plan for the four was created in 1989, with a five-year review. In 1994, through an advertisement in various newspapers, the public was asked to participate in this review. As a result of that participation, the proposed developments in Banff National Park, particularly in the Bow Valley, were halted for two years as of the spring of 1994. Parks Canada announced that no new development would be approved until an ecological study of the Bow Valley was completed.

Social Impact Studies Equally important are studies of the likely impact of tourists on the residents of the host community. Local people may well resent the presence of large numbers of affluent tourists. In developing countries, the introduction of foreign cultures with different social standards has the potential to compromise local customs and value systems. Social impact studies aim to minimize this negative impact and to create a healthy relationship between local residents and tourists. With careful planning, the positive social effects on the host community can outweigh the negative ones.

Domestic Destination Development Although many of the examples cited in this chapter involve destinations abroad, especially in underdeveloped countries, the development of a destination for domestic tourism will also have a major impact on the local people and on their environment. Most of the problems created by the influx of visitors will be the same. For example, the development of a new ski resort in the Banff area would have far-reaching repercussions on the economy, social fabric, and environment of the communities involved.

The Role of Government Tourism can be an important source of revenue for a country, province (or state), region, or city. For this reason, governments at all levels are playing an active role in destination development. Public sector tourist organizations are concerned mainly with promoting and regulating tourism. Sometimes, however, they also become involved in the planning of destinations.

Canmore and the Bow Valley corridor in which it is located are critical to Alberta's economic plan, which seeks to develop tourism as a means of diversifying the economy. Consulting reports indicate that substantial growth is possible, especially in overseas markets, including the Pacific Rim, Britain, and France. The number of tourists from Japan could triple in the next ten years; the number from Britain and France could double.

World Tourism Organization At the international level, the World Tourism Organization (WTO), headquartered in Madrid, Spain, represents all national and official tourist interests. As a consultative agency to the United Nations, its main objective is to promote tourism, not only as a source of revenue for tourist destinations, but also as a way to break down barriers between citizens of different nations. The organization views international tourism as a means of fostering peace, understanding, health, and prosperity throughout the world.

Two other WTO objectives are to improve people's access to education and culture through travel, and to raise standards of living in developing countries by promoting tourism in these areas.

The WTO provides a forum for addressing problems that affect tourists everywhere, such as the problem of international terrorism. It also attempts to increase tourism worldwide by encouraging governments to ease restrictions on international travel.

The WTO also conducts research. It studies international tourism trends and devises standards, measurements, forecasts, and marketing strategies. Thus, it can provide valuable information to tourism promotion agencies in individual countries.

National Tourism Organizations National tourism organizations (NTOs) promote their countries as tourist destinations. There are more than 170 official NTOs throughout the world, more than 100 of which belong to the WTO. These NTOs vary widely in structure and organization. Some are independent government ministries. Others are government agencies or bureaus within larger departments. Still others are quasi-public tourism authorities. However they are organized, most have these functions:

- To promote inbound tourism through publicity and advertising campaigns.
- To conduct research into tourism.
- To draft tourism development plans (both national and regional).
- To license and regulate hotels, travel agencies, tour guides, interpreters, and the like.
- To train hotel staff, tour guides, interpreters, and the like.
- To operate resort facilities.

An NTO's goals and policies can range from simply attracting as many visitors as possible to protecting a nation's cultural heritage. Egypt's National Tourist Board, for example, vetoed a major resort proposed by a Saudi financier because of concerns over possible damage to the Pyramids. In Canada, the NTO is Tourism Canada, a branch of Industry Canada.

In the United States, the National Tourism Policy Act of 1981 established the United States Travel and Tourism Administration (USTTA). This increased federal involvement in the promotion of inbound tourism. The USTTA promotes the entire United States as a destination. Individual regions, states, and cities are promoted by state and local agencies and by private tourist organizations.

Many NTOs have progressed beyond promotional and marketing activities to assume greater responsibility in the planning process. This is especially true in countries such as Mexico, Thailand, and South Korea, where planned destination areas are being developed. Governments develop these destinations in cooperation with domestic and foreign private companies. For example, Mexico's government helped to develop and fund the resort areas of Cancun and Hualulco.

For decades, government involvement in tourism was most pronounced in Eastern European countries. NTOs such as Intourist in the former Soviet Union and Cedok in the former Czechoslovakia used to have complete control over tourism in their respective countries. They even functioned as tour operators, selling travel arrangements to foreign visitors. This is quickly changing. Although the NTOs remain dominant, private companies are allowed to compete with them and have begun to take a share of the tourism market.

Provincial and Local Tourism Organizations Provinces and cities promote tourism for the same reasons that national governments do: to obtain tourist revenues and to encourage economic development. Tourism is among the largest retail industries in Canada. It is an important source of revenue in every province. Every province and territory has an official agency responsible for travel promotion and development. Tourist offices (TOs) develop and distribute promotional literature, entertain travel writers, and even try to lure film crews to their province in the hope that the resulting movie will generate favourable publicity. Following the lead of major cities, most provinces have also begun to promote themselves as convention sites.

Tourist promotion is just one aspect of the work performed by provincial and local TOs. Many are also involved in the long-range planning and day-to-day monitoring of existing tourist facilities. Provincial and local TOs are now helping to establish policies on land use, assess infrastructure needs, and perform environmental impact studies. They examine and attempt to improve attitudes toward tourists and tourism. TOs have graduated from doing "Visit scenic…" promotions to examining the long-term results of tourism.

The Need for Greater Government Involvement The trend toward greater government involvement at all levels in tourism development is a positive one. In underdeveloped countries in particular, governments need to formulate policies to ensure that destination development suits the country and its residents. Developing nations cannot afford to rush headlong into destination development without considering the possible negative effects. If they do, they may be sacrificing their future in exchange for today's tourist dollars.

With a carefully planned and well-managed program of tourism development, governments can reap positive benefits, both economic and intangible. The latter often include an improvement in the country's image both at home and abroad, a widening of educational and cultural horizons, and a general improvement in the quality of life.

Before we move on to examine the positives and negatives of destination development, let's take a look at a specific example of development.

A Destination Developed: Walt Disney World

The development of Walt Disney World near Orlando in central Florida offers a textbook example of how to develop a destination for tourism.

The seeds for Disney World were planted almost 5000 kilometres to the west, in California's Orange County. There, in the mid-1950s, Walt Disney built a family-oriented amusement park called Disneyland. Based on characters and events from Disney's popular movies, its 98 hectares offered everything from a ride in the Mad Hatter's giant teacups to a fairy tale castle.

The only "mistake" Disney and his staff made was in underestimating just how popular Disneyland would become. Millions of people flocked there. They spent money, of course, inside the amusement park. But right outside the park, they gave their money for food, lodging, and recreation to independent businesses whose only reason for existence and success was their proximity to Disneyland. Every business in Anaheim, where the park is located, rode Disneyland's coattails to prosperity.

WED Enterprise, the corporation that developed the second Disney park, learned from what happened at Disneyland. Disney World, almost ten times as large as Disneyland, was planned as a self-contained resort. Hotels, restaurants, shops, and recreational facilities would all be located within the park, giving Disney total control over the

ILLUSTRATION 8-3
Based on characters and events from Disney's popular movies, Walt Disney World offers a textbook example of how to develop a destination for tourism.
SOURCE: Karen O'Neill

Disney World environment. The Disney staff were no longer merely providing an amusement park; they were also hoteliers, restaurateurs, and real estate developers.

Florida offered a number of natural advantages as the site for Disney World. Its climate allowed year-round operation and construction. Its East Coast location meant that Disney World would not be competing with Disneyland. The Florida state government, aware of the potential revenue, passed statutes that gave Disney World virtual independence.

The development of Disney World took place in stages. The first stage involved the building of the theme park (Main Street, U.S.A.; Fantasyland; Tomorrowland; Adventureland; Frontierland; and Liberty Square), three Disney hotels, and basic conservation projects. Subsequent stages added more hotels (not owned by Disney but paying rent for the privilege of their Disney World location), restaurants, shops, golf courses, swimming pools, and lakes. Later additions included the Walt Disney World Village and the Experimental Prototype Community of Tomorrow (EPCOT) Center. In 1989 the Disney–MGM Studios Park opened. The Disney complex continues to grow.

The Disney staff have had complete control over the whole project. Existing operations provided a source of capital for every phase of development. Planners and architects gained experience with each successive stage. Lessons they had learned in the development of the theme park, for example, were applied in the planning and building of EPCOT. Because they have had total control over the environment at Disney World, they have been able to test solutions to urban planning problems.

The Disney World tourism complex has not been without its critics. Criticism has focused largely on what might be called the unreality of the venture—the fact that Disney World is a fantasy world in which real city problems are not allowed to exist. While some of this commentary is valid, it also misses the point. Disney World is a corporate venture: its business is to make a profit, not to improve the world. It does exactly what it sets out to do, and does so very successfully.

Other Disney Worlds Disney World later opened a successful theme park in Japan. The overall success of the various theme parks was tempered by the problems of Euro Disney, 49 percent owned by Disney, which opened in 1992 outside Paris.

In its first two years it was hurt by a crippling debt structure and weak spending by visitors. It faced various criticisms relating to the location (would a warmer location on the Riviera have been better?), the food (most Europeans want to be able to drink wine with their meals), and the dress code (some potential employees did not agree with it). In 1994 a Saudi prince offered to buy a portion of Disney World's share in Euro Disney for the purpose of building a convention centre.

Walt Disney World proposed in 1994 a heritage theme park for Manassas, Virginia, about 80 kilometres southwest of Washington, D.C., which is a major tourist destination. Many high school seniors in the United States make a trip to their nation's capital in their graduating year. Colonial Williamsburg is also in Virginia. The proposed heritage theme park would draw on the large number of tourists already visiting these popular destinations. However, there is much opposition to the proposed theme park at Manassas: there are several Civil War battlefields in the vicinity; highways to the theme park would have to be improved; the unemployment rate in Prince William County is extremely low (2.4 percent), so employees would have to be brought in; and many rural Virginians have a "Not In My Back Yard" (NIMBY) attitude.

The Life Cycle of Destinations

Disney World has been in operation for more than two decades. As yet, there is no indication of a decline in its popularity. Not all tourist destinations, however, are as fortunate as Disney World. Some, like rock bands and hairstyles, rise from obscurity to the height of popularity and then fall back into obscurity in a short space of time. Others go in and out of fashion cyclically. The Côte d'Azur in southern France, for example, has gone through several phases of popularity and decline since its initial development as a health spa for the wealthy at the end of the 19th century.

To understand how destinations rise and fall in popularity, we can look at the **product life cycle** theory, a standard marketing concept (see Figure 8–3). The theory identifies four stages in the life cycle of a product:

- inception
- growth
- maturity
- decline

During the inception stage, the destination is discovered, usually by a few allocentric travellers who don't like to go where everyone else goes. The host community usually welcomes this first wave of tourists—as well as investors—

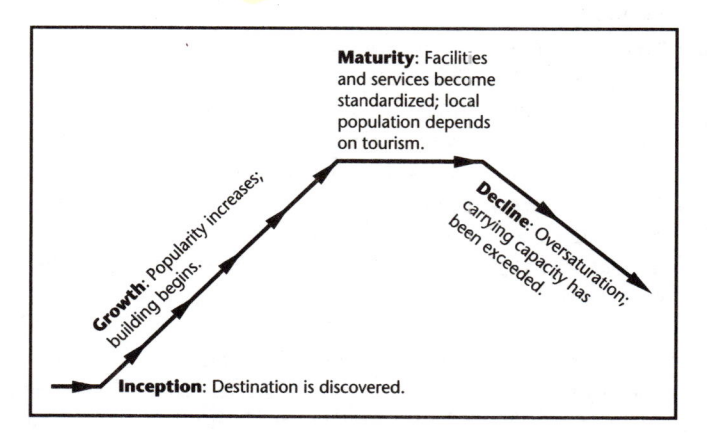

FIGURE 8-3
Life Cycle of a Destination

and there is considerable personal contact between visitors and residents. As word spreads, this "unknown" spot increases in popularity and enters the growth stage. Hotels, restaurants, and other tourist-oriented facilities are built by the local residents, though typically without any well-thought-out plan. Toward the end of the growth stage, relations between tourists and residents tend to become more personal.

As advertising campaigns attract more and more visitors, the destination reaches the maturity stage. At this point, local residents begin to lose control over the development of tourism. Big hotels and restaurant chains move into the area, and facilities and services become standardized. A significant part of the local population comes to depend on tourism for its living. Employment patterns and social standards are altered. By the end of the maturity stage, the local people have begun to resent the growing number of tourists and the loss of their own cultural identity.

The final stage—decline—is reached when the destination becomes oversaturated with tourists. The site has exceeded its carrying capacity—a term you will remember from the discussion of the planning stages of destination development. For the local population, the negative effects of tourism now outweigh the benefits. For the visitors, the destination's attractions have lost their appeal. Beaches have become overcrowded, the site is commercialized, and the natives are no longer friendly.

Carrying capacity can be measured in three different ways. If local residents are squeezed out of local activities, then a destination's *economic* carrying capacity has been reached. If the beaches become contaminated, or historic buildings are damaged, the *physical* carrying capacity has been exceeded. If local residents' tolerance of tourists has reached its limits, then the destination has surpassed its *social* carrying capacity.

Since carrying capacity is based on two intangibles—the characteristics of the tourists and the characteristics of the destination and its population—it is difficult to determine a destination's carrying capacity. Destination planning should, however, always include a reasonable estimate of carrying capacity. Keeping the carrying capacity in mind can help ensure that the destination remains in the maturity stage of its life cycle for as long as possible.

Not all destinations pass through every stage outlined here. A few never progress beyond the inception stage. This is especially true for remote destinations. Others go straight from discovery to maturity, bypassing the growth stage. The Fiji Islands and Guam offer good examples of this. And some, such as Disney World and the resort area of Cancun in Mexico, move directly to maturity without passing through either of the two early stages.

Some destinations lose their appeal as tourist attractions before they ever reach their carrying capacity. This can be the result of unpredictable factors. Political events, for example, have often changed tourists' minds on the desirability of a destination. Cuba was once a very popular vacation spot, especially for residents of the eastern United States and Canada. It was inexpensive, warm, and had magnificent ocean fishing and legalized gambling. When Fidel Castro overthrew the ruling government in 1959 and declared Cuba a communist country, North American tourists stopped going to the island. Civil unrest has had similar effects on tourism in Lebanon and Northern Ireland.

Unfavourable changes in currency rates can also discourage tourists from visiting a foreign country. (The reverse is also true, of course: Mexico became a very popular destination for Canadians and Americans when the peso fell against the dollar.)

Another way in which a tourist destination can decline in popularity is through the loss of the natural resources that made it attractive to begin with. A lake or river may run dry; a beach may be polluted by an oil spill. Finally, the growth of rival destinations can have a negative effect on existing destinations. Each new theme park, for example, draws travellers away from the others.

Sometimes an unpredictable factor can cause a destination to become more popular. When the television show "WKRP in Cincinnati" was on the air, for example, local hotel owners noticed a marked increase in tourism in Cincinnati, Ohio. The *Crocodile Dundee* movies had a similar impact on the number of people who visited Australia. Similarly, the "Anne of Green Gables" series has increased tourism in Prince Edward Island. People in Japan have been reading the Anne books, on which the series was based, for several decades. Now P.E.I. has become such a popular destination for Japanese tourists visiting North America that some tourist publications there are trilingual: English, French, and Japanese. Can the impact of the "Love Boat" series on cruise vacations be measured?

CHECK YOUR PRODUCT KNOWLEDGE

1. What are the five major steps involved in the planning stage of destination development?
2. How do the goals of the World Tourism Organization differ from those of national tourism organizations?
3. What are the four stages of the product life cycle?
4. What unpredictable factors can cause a tourist destination to lose its popularity?

THE ECONOMIC IMPACT OF DESTINATION DEVELOPMENT

When a destination is developed for tourism, the influx of tourists has a tremendous impact on the local and national economy. Regardless of their reasons for travelling, all tourists spend money during their stay at a destination.

PROFILE

Club Med

Club Méditerranée, more commonly known as Club Med, promotes itself as "the Antidote for Civilization." The Club Med concept, played out in more than 100 vacation villages in 33 countries of the world, is simple. Club Med offers an all-inclusive vacation package in an exotic locale with an emphasis on recreation and relaxation. Guests are free to do anything and everything or nothing at all. This concept has enabled Club Med to become the largest vacation-village operator in the world.

The Club Med of today is a far cry from its humble beginnings. In 1950, it was an austere nonprofit sports association with a "resort" in Majorca, Spain. There, guests prepared their own meals and stayed in army surplus tents. In 1954 Gilbert Trigano, who has since been credited with an "uncanny ability to see major trends before anyone else," joined the staff of Club Med. Though the company experienced some financial difficulties in the early 1960s, by 1967 it was on its way to becoming the place to be for the young, the elegant, and the trendy.

All Club Med villages are set up along similar lines. Each is run by a group of *gentils organisateurs,* or GOs. Guests are known as GMs, for *gentils membres.* GOs are the most casual of social directors, acquainting GMs with the village and helping them to enjoy it fully. Entertainment includes plenty of opportunities for fun in the sun; nonstop sports activities; classes, races, and tournaments; special excursions; and nightlife. Meals and almost everything else are included in the package price. Only items like drinks at the bar are extra, and they are paid for not with money (guests lock their valuables in safety deposit boxes in their rooms) but with plastic pop-it beads that can be worn as campy jewels. The formula obviously works, because 50 percent of Club Med guests return.

Club Med's most astounding accomplishment, however, is its continuing ability to adjust its focus to reflect changes in society. In the 1960s and 1970s, Club Med was a singles' paradise—its appeal was to the young, uninhibited, and unattached. In the late 1970s, however, Trigano predicted the demise of "mindless sunbathing" and began to add features that would attract an older, married, more family- and career-oriented clientele. About 40 percent of today's Club Med guests are married couples, and more than 70 percent are between 25 and 44 years of age. Many guests participate in the wide variety of sports programs offered, including golf, horseback riding, tennis, and scuba diving.

Not that Trigano has excluded his original target market: the Buccaneer's Creek village in Martinique and Playa Blanca in Mexico still have a singles' focus. Rather, he has broadened his market to include families. Families enjoy the Mini Clubs, where adults can engage in grown-up pursuits while their children participate in sports and creative activities all day. There are even Baby Clubs that allow new parents to enjoy athletic activities or just sit and read on the beach while their infants are cared for by a specially trained staff.

Computer workshops for both adults and children are available at six European Club Med villages. They enable novices to "get their feet wet" amid balmy breezes while more advanced computer users hone their skills. Club Med also welcomes corporate clients, hoping that companies will take over villages for conferences and offer Club Med vacations as sales incentives. Companies such as Xerox, Air France, Allstate Insurance, and Colgate Palmolive have done just this.

What does the future hold for Club Med? A profitable chunk of the vacation market, without a doubt. Besides opening Club Med villages on the French Riviera and in Ireland, Trigano has been working on a Club Med village on the island of San Salvador in the Bahamas. In 1990, Club Med entered the cruise business by launching its first sailing ship, *Club Med 1.* Its sister ship, *Club Med 2,* sailed at the end of 1992. Trigano is no doubt bursting with other ideas as well. His plans seem certain to capture the trends of the future.

ILLUSTRATION 8–4
During the inception stage of a destination's life cycle, the destination is discovered and patronized by a small number of adventurous visitors.
SOURCE: The Province of British Columbia (Skiing at Blackcomb)

Visitor spending provides income and profit for businesses as diverse as hotels, trailer parks, restaurants, gas stations, golf courses, grocery stores, and souvenir shops. Local, provincial, and national governments receive revenues from sales taxes, occupancy taxes, and alcohol and gasoline taxes, and from user fees for campgrounds, parks, ski slopes, highways, and other amenities. Perhaps most important of all, tourist dollars generate employment for local residents.

A few figures will show just how large a contribution tourism can make to the economy. Tourism spending by Canadians and visitors in 1993 was $26 billion, according to the Tourism Industry Association of Canada; tourism-related industries employed 1.2 million people. In one recent year, American residents and foreign visitors spent an estimated $579 billion on travel in the United States. In the same year, tourism generated more than 8 million jobs for Americans and about $68 billion in federal, state, and local taxes. Figures for other nations are not as high as these, but that is not to say that the economic impact of tourism is any smaller. In fact, in many developing countries it is considerably greater. Tourism can be virtually the only source of export income in countries that lack the agricultural and industrial resources needed to develop a more diversified economy, such as Mexico. The North American Free Trade Agreement should help Mexico. Canada ranked ninth in 1990 in receiving international tourism dollars (see Chapter 2, Table 2–1). Unfortunately, Canada continues to have a negative balance in international tourism. The top four countries—the United States, France, Italy, and Spain—account for 40 percent of the world's tourism receipts. It is interesting to note that two of the world's leading industrial countries, Germany and Japan, had substantial negative balances. Spain had a very positive balance.

Before we move on to consider the effect that destination development can have on a nation's balance of payments, we will first look at what happens to the money that enters a local economy from tourist expenditures.

Tourism Dollars and the Multiplier Effect

The flow of tourism dollars into a local economy is a complicated process. Let's look at an example to see how the money spent by a single tourist at a Caribbean resort is distributed.

Mary Hobbes spends $1,000 during her vacation at Montego Bay, Jamaica. We can break her expenditures down like this: $400 for a hotel room, $200 for restaurant meals, $125 for a rental car, $175 for recreation and entertainment, and $100 for souvenirs and miscellaneous items. These expenditures represent **direct spending**, that is, money that goes directly from the traveller into the economy. It would seem simple to deduce that the local economy has $1,000 more than it would have had if Hobbes had decided to vacation elsewhere. In fact, that $1,000 means considerably more to the economy, because of what economists call the multiplier effect (see Figure 8-4).

Hobbes's $1,000 does not stop working once it has reached the hotelier and the owners of the other tourist facilities. The money is respent several times, generating more income and further employment. The Montego Bay restaurants, for example, must buy food and beverages from local suppliers, who in turn must make purchases from local farmers. Part of Hobbes's $1,000 will also go to pay wages to the employees who work in the hotel, the restaurants, and other tourist businesses. The workers in turn will pay rent, buy groceries, and so on. These successive rounds of spending generated by the initial tourist expenditures are known as **indirect spending** which is defined as money that is respent and generates more money and more employment.

The Tourism Multiplier It can be seen that the total of all income is far greater than the initial $1,000 spent by Hobbes. The actual amount by which the country's income will increase can be worked out using a formula called the **tourism multiplier.** Direct and indirect tourist expenditures affect more than income; multipliers can also be estimated for sales, output, employment, and payroll.

The Concept of Leakage In the example of Hobbes, we assumed that the whole of her $1,000 flowed into the Montego Bay economy. In reality, not all of that money will stay in the local economy. Many of the goods and services that are needed to satisfy tourist desires have to be imported. Hobbes, for example, enjoys a glass of wine with her evening meal. Wine is not produced locally, so it has to be imported. Part of her $1,000 will leave the local economy as payments to overseas wine growers.

Money that flows out of the economy to purchase outside resources is known in economic terms as **leakage.** The more imports that are necessary, the higher will be the leakage; and the less money that stays and is circulated within the local economy, the lower will be the tourism multiplier. Many of the resorts in the Caribbean have to import most goods for tourists. Consequently, they have a relatively low

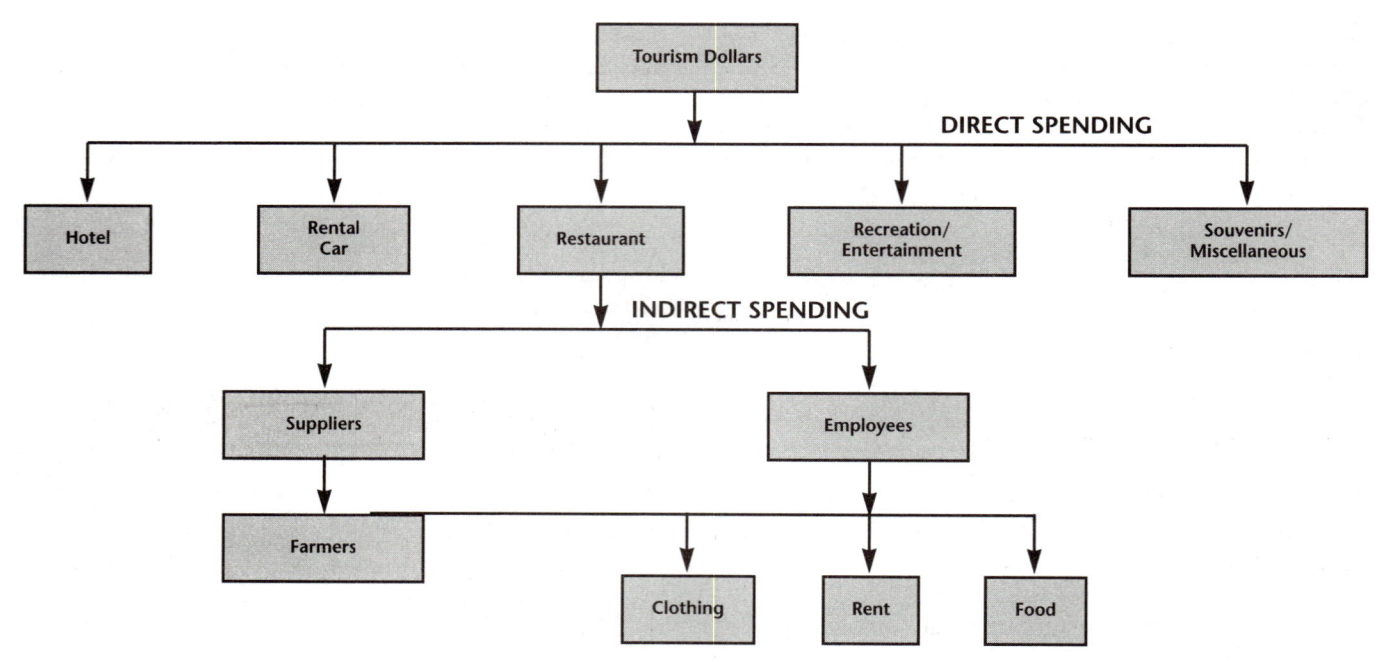

FIGURE 8-4
Tourism Dollars and the Multiplier Effect

multiplier. Hobbes's $1,000 may in fact only contribute $500 to the local economy. If, on the other hand, an area has sufficient resources to produce all the necessary goods and services, tourist expenditures will remain in the area in their full amount and the multiplier will be high. Clearly, the more developed the local economy, the higher the multiplier.

Tourism and the Balance of Payments

Countries develop tourist destinations in order to earn foreign currency and to reduce their balance of payments deficits. A country's balance of payments is the difference between payments for imports and receipts from exports. (Remember that tourism is an export industry.) Unfortunately, many of the developing nations that have the most to gain from tourism are the ones that suffer from the highest leakages. Foreign exchange receipts are substantially reduced because a large proportion of tourist expenditures and profits flow out of the country to foreign investors and foreign suppliers. As a result, tourism rarely eliminates large balance of payments deficits.

Canada traditionally runs a negative balance in its tourism account. The challenge for Canada is to attract more visitors from other countries, and to encourage more Canadians to travel within their own country and spend more dollars here than they do outside this country. The new tourist phenomenon of this decade, which has Canadians taking more trips of one or more nights to the United States than to other provinces, makes the challenge even more daunting.

Where the Money Goes You have already read that money can leak out of the economy to pay for imported goods and services. Our example showed how wine had to be imported into Jamaica. Other destinations may have to import meat, vegetables, and even water to cater to tourists. Tourism can also create an increased demand for imported goods on the part of local residents. With the influx of affluent foreign tourists, residents of developing countries are exposed to new consumer goods. And with higher incomes as a result of tourism development, they can now afford to buy them.

Payment for imported consumer goods and services is just one of many ways that tourist revenues can leak out of the economy. Raw materials may also have to be imported to meet increased demand, especially for utilities such as electricity and gas. Before a destination is developed for tourism, local raw materials may be sufficient to meet the resident population's needs. But with the influx of thousands of tourists, coal may have to be imported to generate the additional electricity required. Similarly, propane gas may have to be imported to fuel hotel and restaurant kitchens.

A significant proportion of tourist revenues may have to be used to pay for imported materials and equipment. If construction materials, for example, are not available in sufficient quantity in the host country, they will have to be purchased elsewhere. Countries with no domestic automobile industry will have to import cars and buses to satisfy tourist transportation needs. Even hotel equipment may have to be brought in from other countries—not just beds and bathroom fixtures, but also elevators and air conditioners.

Income earned by foreign investors is another factor that reduces a country's tourism revenues. The early stages of destination development require a massive investment of capital. Developing countries cannot afford to finance large-scale infrastructural and superstructural projects, so they are forced to seek financial assistance abroad. Without foreign investment, the destinations could not be developed for tourism. But the price the developing countries have to pay is high. They must spend years repaying loans and paying interest on the investments.

The emergence of multinational corporations has also affected tourism revenues in host countries. International hotel and restaurant chains have opened properties in resort destinations throughout the world. Because they are foreign-owned, much of the revenue from their ventures is transferred out of the host country. The payment of airfares to foreign-owned airlines is another way in which countries lose potential tourist revenues. (Few developing nations can afford to operate their own airlines.)

An example will illustrate how large amounts of money can leak out of the host economy. A couple from Saskatchewan decides to vacation in the Bahamas. They make air and hotel reservations through a travel agency in Regina. They are booked on a Canadian air carrier, Air Canada flying through Toronto to Nassau, they stay in a hotel that is part of an American chain, and they eat at an American-owned restaurant. They hire a Hertz rental car for a couple of days. The rest of their time they spend lying on the hotel beach drinking soft drinks bottled in the United States. The only money that remains in the host country is a few dollars for souvenirs and the wages paid to local employees.

Payments may also be due abroad for management fees. Many local hotels that are not part of a chain are managed by foreign corporations that are paid a fee for their services. If the local labour force is not big enough, foreign workers may have to be imported to fill jobs in hotels, restaurants, and other tourist-oriented businesses. Salaries may have to be paid to foreign entertainers who perform in the local nightclubs, to visiting sports professionals who give golf and tennis lessons, and to other nonlocal employees. In all these ways, money is further drained from the host country's economy.

Necessary Leakage One final expense is the cost of promoting the destination abroad. This can be viewed as "necessary leakage": it really can't be avoided if the destination is going to attract tourists. In the competitive Caribbean market, for example, each island resort has to advertise to convince potential customers that it is more appealing than all the other resorts. National tourist organizations promote their destinations by advertising in foreign media and by offering FAM trips to foreign travel agents and travel writers.

This discussion of leakage may make you wonder how any destination manages to make a profit from tourism. But many do, not only in developed nations (where leakages tend to be lower) but also in developing countries. As we stressed earlier in this chapter, planning is the key to success. Developing countries can, for example, minimize the loss of tourist revenues by implementing plans aimed at reducing imports of tourism-related items. One way is by supporting local industries. Another is by offering incentives to local hoteliers, thereby reducing foreign control of the hospitality industry. The number of foreign employees in managerial and professional positions can be reduced if local residents are educated and trained in relevant disciplines.

All these measures will help to ensure that a greater percentage of tourism revenues stays in the host country, and that the economic benefits of destination development—employment, income, and tax revenue—will outweigh possible negative effects.

> **CHECK YOUR PRODUCT KNOWLEDGE**
> 1. What is meant by the multiplier effect?
> 2. What is leakage, in the context of tourism?
> 3. List five ways in which tourist revenues can flow out of a country.

THE SOCIAL IMPACT OF TOURISM

The success of destination development is most commonly measured in economic terms. However, we should not overlook the social, cultural, and environmental implications of tourism. The residents of Canmore, Alberta, fear that their town may lose its "rustic charm" if the pace of development quickens. The director of planning and economic development for the town, Paul Bates, does not want the town to become another Whistler. The thrust of Canmore's strategy is to get the economy and the environment to work together.

It is now widely recognized that destination development brings about social change, which has both positive and negative effects. The social effects of destination development tend to be less significant in developed countries. Less developed nations are more likely to experience the negative social effects of tourism. When tourism replaces other economic activities, or when a destination is developed too rapidly or too intensively, the social impact can be particularly damaging. Here again, intelligent planning is extremely important. With conservative scheduling, good management, and an understanding of local needs, the negative social impact of destination development can be minimized.

Socioeconomic Impact

The economic impact of destination development can have social implications. The most obvious socioeconomic effects relate to population growth, changing employment patterns, increased incomes, and rising property values. In the early stages of destination development, labourers must be hired to build new hotels and restaurants and to upgrade the local infrastructure. Once the destination has opened to tourists, people will be needed to staff the facilities. In developing countries, the local population is rarely large enough to provide the necessary labour force. Workers must therefore be brought in from outside. The migrant workers will require housing, perhaps new schools for their children, and other amenities.

A rapid influx of foreign workers can cause serious social problems. The new workers may find it difficult to fit into the community. The local residents may resent their presence and actively discriminate against the newcomers.

Another negative implication of destination development is the problem of what to do with the construction workers when the development boom is over. Some of the migrant workers may stay on to work in the tourist facilities, but others will have to return home. People who worked steadily during the construction phase may be faced with unemployment. A similar problem arises in destinations where tourism is strictly seasonal. What happens to the local workers during the off-season? Some may return to traditional economic activities, such as farming or fishing, but this in turn can lead to other types of social strain.

Changing Employment Patterns Many local residents will find their social status in the community altered after they take tourism-related employment. Again, this can be positive or negative, or both.

Many women enter the job market for the first time when tourism development occurs. On the positive side, this may contribute to increased family incomes, greater self-esteem for the women, and expanded awareness of the outside world. But it can also disrupt the existing social structure, particularly in countries where men have traditionally been the only wage earners. A husband may have difficulty accepting the fact that his wife can earn more money working in a tourist hotel than he can from fishing or farming. Divorce rates may rise, as may incidents of juvenile delinquency. Also, women working in tourist-oriented jobs may decide to postpone marriage and childbearing.

Traditional relationships between the young and the old may change as young people find work in tourism. Established local industries, such as agriculture and fishing, may suffer as workers are drawn toward tourism. A farmer, for example, may decide that there's a better living to be made as a cook's assistant in a restaurant than by scratching out a crop of corn from a rocky field. Or a young man whose father and grandfather both fished for a living may decide that instead of following the family tradition, he would rather earn more money waiting tables at a dockside tourist restaurant.

Increased Income The increase in incomes that employment in tourism brings can have a radical effect on local lifestyles. The area's residents will be able to afford consumer goods, many of them imported, that were previously beyond their purchasing power. This change in lifestyle may also lead to demands for better housing and recreational facilities, as well as to changes in dress and eating habits. People who once worked the land or the sea for their living may readily come to appreciate the benefits of a steady paycheque. If tourists stop coming to the destination, however, local residents will have to either return to their traditional occupations—and spartan lifestyle—or leave the community. In either case, the social consequences can be serious.

Rising Property Values Destination development can also affect local property values. If there is an increased demand for land for tourist facilities, property values can rise dramatically. Local buyers may be priced out of the market. Local renters may find that they have no place to live if low-priced rental properties are demolished to make way for luxury hotels. Small businesses may be forced to close if they can no longer afford to pay the increased rents.

Such effects can be particularly devastating in communities that have large numbers of fixed-income senior citizens or low-income families. When gambling was legalized in Atlantic City, for example, working-class residents were faced with the choice of paying high rents or moving out of the area.

Resentment tends to be most pronounced in those destinations where tourism is the community's main source of income. As you read earlier, tourists are typically welcomed in the early stages of development. But by late maturity, when all activities have become geared to accommodating tourist demands, the limits of local tolerance have usually been reached. By this stage, the mere physical presence of large numbers of tourists may create resentment. Congestion may have become a problem, and local residents will now be tired of sharing overcrowded facilities and overtaxed services with visitors. They may see vacationers living in comfort and luxury while their basic needs go unmet. An extreme example of this clash between affluence and poverty occurred in the Ivory Coast in West Africa. There, a resort hotel was using 150 gallons of water per room per day, while local villagers did not yet have running water in their homes.

Foreign ownership and employment is a further cause of resentment. This is especially true when foreign employees occupy managerial positions and earn high salaries, while the low-paid menial jobs are left to local residents. Additional anger may stem from the perception that tourists are causing a decline in moral standards. Crime, gambling, and prostitution have all been known to increase in areas that become tourist destinations.

Cultural Effects

An influx of tourists from other cultures can have profound effects on a local culture. One of the most common results of tourism is that the host community adopts the social and

PROFILE

Banff National Park

Written by Don MacLaurin

Ellesmere Island in the Northwest Territories has an extreme climate; the mountainous north of the island is blanketed in ice 2000 metres thick. About 4000 kilometres to the south, the tiny peninsula of Point Pelee on Lake Erie is a mix of wetlands, beaches, and dense forests filled with thousands of birds. Point Pelee is the southernmost tip of Canada, Ellesmere the northernmost. So what do they have in common? They are both national parks, part of the world's largest land area set aside for preservation and for the enjoyment of generations of visitors.

Canada's present system of 36 national parks hosts more than 13 million visitors a year. The most popular parks are in the Canadian Rockies; the least visited are in remote locations such as Ellesmere Island. Two-thirds of the parks are easily accessible by automobile or other transportation. They are administered by Parks Canada, a division of the federal Department of Canadian Heritage. Parks Canada also manages 114 national historic sites, as well as national marine parks, heritage rivers, and historic canals.

The oldest and most popular national park is Banff with over 4 million visitors in 1994. Banff is one of four national parks strung together along the Alberta–British Columbia border (which follows the continental divide). The other parks are Jasper, Kootenay, and Yoho, which together with Banff form the largest continuous land area of mountain national parks in the world—over 12 000 square kilometres. By comparison, the oldest and largest national park in the continental United States, Yellowstone, is smaller than Jasper and less than half the combined size of Canada's four mountain parks.

Banff began in 1883. Two construction workers toiling on the Canadian Pacific (CPR) transcontinental railway saw steam rising from the base of nearby Sulphur Mountain. The men staked a claim to the hot springs and erected crude bathing facilities, which they rented out. The Canadian government wanted the natural features preserved for all Canadians, and in 1885, set aside a 10-acre (4 hectare) preserve around the Cave and Basin Springs. In 1887 the preserved area was enlarged to 400 square kilometres and named Rocky Mountain National Park. The name was later changed to Banff in honour of George Stephen, a native of Banffshire, Scotland, and the first president of the CPR. The park was later expanded to its present size of about 4000 square kilometres.

Banff's history and development is tied to the CPR (now CP Rail and CP Hotels). The original Banff Springs Hotel was built by the railway in 1888 to lure passengers to the new transcontinental rail service. Classic hotels were opened as destination resorts along the railway line, and soon became known to well-heeled travellers from around the world. The names Banff Springs, Chateau Lake Louise, and Jasper Park Lodge are today as well known in the upscale streets of Tokyo as they are in upscale Toronto.

The lure of Banff touches people of all ages and interests. Young people come to challenge the winter powder at the three major ski areas and to partake in the summer thrills of mountain biking, kayaking, and hiking. Older visitors stay in world-class hotels and travel by chauffeured luxury motorcoaches with animated tours. International visitors marvel at the stunning scenery and sample the recreational opportunities in the spacious surroundings. Thousands of Canadian tourism and hospitality students migrate to Banff each year to gain valuable experience in an unparalleled setting for work and fun.

Banff is well positioned to take advantage of the two largest global travel trends of the 1990s—adventure travel and ecotourism. Adventure travellers seek opportunities for high-energy, high-risk, high-reward activities. Banff obliges with whitewater rafting, mountaineering, high-altitude skiing, and gruelling mountain-bike and hiking trails. Ecotourists live by the travel motto, "Take Nothing But Pictures, Leave Nothing But Footprints." They enjoy activities such as catch-and-release fly fishing, bird and animal watching, tree and plant studies, and other activities that are perceived as ecologically correct.

Any Canadian needing an additional reason to be proud of this country should plan a visit to Banff. Of specific interest and pride is the Cave and Base restoration that was completed in honour of the 100th anniversary of Canada's national park system in 1985. The interpretive centre contains an original CPR steam locomotive, with a lifelike mannequin of Prime Minister Sir John A. Macdonald and his wife riding on the front cowcatcher to prove that travel on the new train was safe for all users. The determined jut of Sir John's jaw only partly suggests the wisdom and vision of the man who brought Canada together by building the first transcontinental railway in North America and commissioning a national park system that is now the envy of visitors the world over.

cultural values of the visiting tourists. Because most people who can afford to travel abroad are from Canada, the United States, and Western Europe, it is primarily Western values that are spread throughout the world in this way. Critics argue that, as a result, many local cultures are in danger of disappearing as the world becomes westernized. Others contend that the adoption process works both ways. Local residents may adopt tourist values, but at the same time tourists also adopt the values of the countries they visit. (This is known as **cross-adoption**.) The North American interest in foreign cuisines, for example, has grown in part because so many Canadian and American tourists enjoyed eating local foods while abroad.

There is also some disagreement about the effects that tourism development has on traditional arts and crafts. Some people say that local artistic standards suffer when cheap reproductions of native crafts are mass-produced for tourist consumption. They also claim that commercialization has a negative effect on local religious and social customs. In some places, for example, ceremonial dances that were once performed for religious purposes are now being staged to entertain tourists.

On the positive side, tourism has been credited with helping traditional arts and crafts to survive. There is ample evidence to support this claim. In the southwestern United States, for example, the interest tourists have shown in native cultures has greatly increased the demand for local pottery, jewellery, weaving, and so on. The native people of the Southwest have resisted the temptation to turn out mass-produced imitations, so the quality of their products has remained high. A similar picture emerges in parts of Canada, where the demand for souvenirs has kept alive the Inuit craft of soapstone carving.

Tourism does not just help sustain native art forms; it may also contribute to ethnic preservation. For example, the assimilation of the Cajun population of Louisiana into the general population began in the 1930s, and by the 1950s this group had almost lost its unique identity.

The term "Cajun" is derived from Acadian. Three-quarters of the Acadian population of the Maritimes was deported between 1755 and 1763. Some of these deportees settled in Louisiana, as immortalized in Longfellow's *Evangeline*. When Cajun Louisiana was developed as a tourist destination in the 1950s, local residents began to take pride in their cultural origins. Tourists from all over the nation expressed their appreciation for the hot, spicy Cajun food and the distinctive Cajun music, and took an interest in the Creole language. In this way, tourism helped the Cajuns preserve their cultural heritage and retain a separate ethnic identity. (Incidentally, the Cajuns present a good example of the cross-adoption discussed earlier. Local residents adopt the values of visitors from other parts of North America, while the tourists adopt certain Cajun habits, as evidenced by the popularity of Cajun-style foods in restaurants throughout the United States.)

Similarly, Acadian culture in the Maritimes has been strengthened through destination development. Examples include Fortress Louisbourg, the largest ongoing restoration project in Canada, which showcases about 50 buildings as they appeared in 1744; Port-Royal in Nova Scotia, a reconstruction of the *habitation* established by Champlain in 1605; and historic villages at Mont-Carmel, Quebec, and Caraquet, New Brunswick. Acadians comprise about 40 percent of the population in New Brunswick, 10 percent in Nova Scotia, and 14 percent in Prince Edward Island.

An influx of tourists from different cultures can, unfortunately, have less desirable consequences. The Pennsylvania Amish had lived in quiet obscurity for hundreds of years until they were "discovered" as a tourist attraction. The Amish had no desire to make a profit from tourism; they just wanted to be left in peace. Others, however, had different ideas. They built motels, restaurants, golf courses, souvenir shops, and gas stations to cater to the growing bands of tourists. Today, the Amish are subjected to prying stares from busloads of visitors. They are photographed like freaks in a sideshow. Tourism has disrupted their way of life.

To end this discussion of the cultural effects of tourism on a positive note, the development of a destination can often pay cultural dividends to the residents of the host community. Entertainment and recreational facilities developed for incoming tourists—including cinemas and theatres, cultural centres, sports stadiums, golf courses, and ski slopes—can also be used by the local residents. Cultural events such as the Charlottetown Festival and the Montreal Film Festival are not merely tourist attractions—they also enhance the cultural lives of the local population.

The Environmental Impact of Destination Development

One final aspect of destination development is the impact on the host environment. This is easier to assess than the cultural effects. Measurements can be taken of air, water, and soil quality. Traffic patterns can be charted. The local flora and fauna can be studied, and protected if necessary. Property values can be assessed.

In both developed and underdeveloped countries, the emphasis must be on a controlled rate of development that minimizes harmful effects on the natural environment. Farsighted planning can reduce the conflicts over land use that can arise between local residents and developers. If a destination is developed too rapidly, irreparable damage may be done. In developed countries, destination development can strain the existing infrastructure, causing pollution and overcrowding. Even natural resources may be threatened. In certain national parks, for example, traffic congestion and littering are constant problems. If the natural beauty of a site is ruined by commercialization and the local lake is teaming with tourists and pop cans, the residents will naturally resent the tourist intrusion. However attractive tourism development may seem, developers must always bear in mind the needs and feelings of the local people.

A DAY IN THE LIFE OF

A Provincial Tourism Bureau Worker

What I like best about my job as a tourism training specialist is that there is always something different to do every day. I work for a provincial tourism bureau. My main assignment is to organize conferences and workshops for the travel and tourism industry. I am also involved in helping the colleges and universities in my province develop courses for people training for careers in the travel industry.

Yesterday, I conducted a workshop for several dozen employees of a city convention and visitors' bureau to help them develop their communication skills so they can deal more effectively with the public. I had to give a short lecture, show a 20-minute film developed by my office, then lead the participants in role-playing exercises. In one such exercise, some of the participants pretend to be angry tourists whose hotel reservations have been cancelled, and others pretend to be hotel managers who try to find ways to help the travellers.

I give dozens of similar workshops each year to employees of hotels, restaurants, tourist attractions, and tour boats. My aim is to train tourism workers to be helpful and attentive to their customers so that visitors will form a good impression of our province and will want to come back. In addition to leading these workshops, it is my job to organize them, invite the participants, and solve any problems that arise. One minor problem at yesterday's workshop, for example, was that there was no outlet to plug in the film projector, so I had to bring an extension cord.

I also serve on a committee sponsored by the Ministry of Education to develop a Grade 8 career course. The course is intended to provide an overview of the many different kinds of careers students can choose after they graduate from high school, college, or university. My role is to make certain that travel and tourism careers are included in the course, because tourism is the second-largest industry in our province.

In addition to serving on several similar education committees, I send hundreds of information packets each year to high school and community college guidance counsellors throughout the province so they can advise students about travel careers. I have also developed a speakers' bureau so that those schools and colleges can invite people in the industry to come and talk to the students about travel and tourism careers.

Another part of my job is to field complaints from tourists and pass them on to the hotels, restaurants, and attractions that are the subjects of the complaints. Most complaints have to do with cancelled reservations, sold-out shows, long waits in line, and similar problems. As a provincial employee, I can't do anything about the complaints, but I try to impress on the restaurant, theatre, or hotel how important it is to make guests feel wanted and appreciated. I try to convince them that it is worth their while to send a letter of apology.

I had to pass a very difficult interview to qualify for this job. At one point, I had to give a mock marketing presentation for a panel of judges. Since the main part of my job involves making presentations to groups of people, I had to show the interviewers that I was able to do that. Fortunately, I have worked as a teacher, a travel agent, and a chief flight attendant, so I have had a lot of experience in talking to groups of people.

I was hired for a very specific job, but there are other jobs in tourism bureaus that require less training and experience. For example, several people in my office answer calls on our provincial tourism hotline. These operators send out information packets, take complaints, and answer questions about such things as highway routes, attractions, ski conditions, and the weather. The main requirement for their job is the ability to be fast, accurate, and courteous. Hotline operators who can speak a foreign language are especially useful, because more and more foreign visitors come to our province every year.

Our office is small, like most provincial tourism offices. We employ only about 30 people. The advantage is that we are friendlier and more like a family than a big, impersonal office. The drawback is that because our office is so small, there is little room for advancement or promotion. Still, I enjoy my job so much that I can't imagine doing anything else.

Destination development can also have positive environmental effects. In an underdeveloped area, it can upgrade an inadequate infrastructure. If done right, development leads to improved water supplies, better sewage facilities, and better roads. In Africa, some wildlife species have been saved from extinction by conservation efforts. Governments realized that if they allowed native animals to die out, they would lose a natural resource that attracted thousands of tourists. Developers in other countries have enhanced the natural beauty of certain destinations by devoting part of their investment capital to conservation projects. As we have seen time and time again in this chapter, planning is vital to the proper development of any tourist destination.

Synergism in Destination Development

Synergism is what exists when the sum of the parts is greater than the whole of the parts, as in "two plus two equals five." Potential examples in tourism development are seen when an attraction is developed within a destination, and when a business capitalizes on tourism in its home city.

If the city or region is already a tourist destination, there are probably opportunities to develop new businesses or attractions, such as a bake shop, a bookstore, or a rental shop for bikes or camping gear.

The slogans "Tourism Is Everybody's Business" and "Be Kind to Our Tourists; They're Good for Us" are familiar. However, many sales are lost because of indifference and ignorance at the counters of many small businesses in tourist towns in Canada. Training in service and sales techniques is needed. So is a knowledge of the other activities available for tourists. A salesperson who directs tourists to other events in the community is encouraging additional spending in that community, and perhaps a longer stay by the tourist. The main objective of the Sea Sell program in the Atlantic provinces is to promote the region to vacationers from New England and the Eastern Seaboard states. A useful by-product is that tourist operators in that region are becoming more familiar with attractions and events throughout Atlantic Canada.

CHECK YOUR PRODUCT KNOWLEDGE

1. How do employment patterns change as a result of destination development?
2. What is the demonstration effect?
3. What are two positive effects of destination development on local culture? What are two negative effects?
4. How does the environmental impact of destination development differ between developed and underdeveloped countries?

CAREER OPPORTUNITIES

If you are thinking of a career in the tourism industry, you may not have considered the opportunities that are available in the field of destination development. As you learned in this chapter, destination development is a complex process that requires the creative energies of a wide variety of experts. Most positions carry a great deal of responsibility and require a high level of education. Many workers in this field are hired on a consulting basis.

Careers in destination development involve much more than scheduling, ticketing, and financing. While they may not bring the usual "perks" of the travel industry, they may ultimately be the careers most important to the future of tourism. Representative careers include planner, market researcher, architect, interior designer, landscape architect, anthropologist, and sociologist.

ILLUSTRATION 8-5
The summer Shaw Festival at Niagara-on-the-Lake is an example of the benefits to be gained by a community when development has been carefully thought out.

Planner

The first step in destination development is planning. A planner is responsible for examining each stage of development. He or she takes data from market researchers, land use specialists, architects, and others, and attempts to draw conclusions from it.

The planner develops a master plan for the destination and looks for ways to finance it. He or she must make sure there is sufficient funding available for each stage of the plan.

Market Researcher

Market researchers help a developer decide if there is a market for the planned destination. They work for private developers and for tourist organizations. Most provincial tourist organizations have research staff that help them spot market trends and plan developments.

Architect/Interior Designer/ Landscape Architect

Once it has been determined that there is a market for the destination, and once funding has been approved, architects, interior designers, and landscape architects can begin to submit blueprints for the development. In the case of a resort, for example, the architect is responsible for the design of all the buildings in the complex. He or she may choose a common theme and try to blend the buildings into the natural environment. The interior designer plans the interior of individual buildings, choosing furnishings and other fixtures. The landscape architect is responsible for designing the grounds around the hotels, restaurants, and other facilities. He or she may add lawns, trees, and bushes to make the site more attractive, and design walkways and access roads.

Architects, interior designers, and landscape architects must usually work together at each stage of development.

Sociologists and Anthropologists

Because the development of a tourist destination can have such tremendous social and cultural consequences, it is imperative that sociologists and anthropologists be consulted to assess this impact and, especially, to suggest ways in which negative outcomes can be minimized. Sociologists are especially helpful in assessing the effects of tourism on developed areas. Anthropologists usually study tourism's impact on destinations in undeveloped areas.

Planning and research take much of the guesswork out of development; sociology and anthropology, in a sense, put some of that guesswork back. Statistics might show, for example, that resort development in a Third World country is bringing economic prosperity to a local group. Sociologists and anthropologists may show that the price paid in social conflict for that economic prosperity is too high to justify further development.

The earlier that social scientists are engaged in the planning process, the better the chances are for a fully successful development.

Summary

- A destination is a location that travellers choose to visit and where they spend time.
- People choose different destinations according to their motivations for travel. Motivators include recreation, culture, health, friends and relatives, and business.
- The five main steps in the planning stage of destination development are market analysis, site assessment, financial studies, environmental impact studies, and social impact studies.
- National, regional, and local tourism organizations promote travel to individual countries, regions, and cities. They are also involved in the planning process.
- Destinations can rise and fall in popularity. The product life cycle theory identifies four stages of destination development: inception, growth, maturity, and decline.
- Political changes, the loss of natural resources, and the growth of rival destinations can contribute to a destination's decline in popularity.
- Economic benefits of destination development include increased employment, tax revenue, and personal income.
- Tourist dollars are respent several times within a local community (the multiplier effect).
- Tourist dollars flow out of the local economy when imported goods and services are purchased (leakage).
- Destination development is an instrument for social change. It leads to population growth, changing employment patterns, and increased incomes in the destination developed.
- The presence of affluent tourists can cause resentment in the host community.
- Destination development can revitalize cultural traditions, but it can also place stresses on the local culture.
- The negative environmental effects of destination development can be minimized with careful planning.

Key Terms

destination
infrastructure
superstructure
carrying capacity
product life cycle
direct spending
indirect spending

tourism multiplier
leakage
demonstration effect
cross-adoption

What Do You Think?

1. Of the nine motivators for travel listed in this chapter, which are likely to become more important? Which are likely to become less important? Why? Can you think of any other motivators that are likely to develop?
2. What destinations in your area would appeal to people who travel for culture? education? events? health?
3. Market analysts study travel trends and travel preferences. What trends and preferences have emerged in the last two or three years? What trends are likely to develop in the next few years?
4. If you were asked to plan a new tourist destination for your area, what sort of destination would you choose? How would you prepare local residents for this development?
5. What are the advantages of having multinational corporations develop tourist destinations in underdeveloped countries? What are the disadvantages?

Dealing with Product

Casino gambling is among the most controversial categories of tourism development. During the 1990s casinos have opened in Winnipeg, Montreal, and Windsor. Other provinces have proposed developments. Those who favour casino gambling argue that it will generate millions of dollars in revenues, wages, and taxes. The opponents of casino gambling are equally convinced that the costs to society are far greater than the gains.

What is the casino gambling product? How might this product affect other travel and tourism products? What do you think the economic, social, and environmental impacts would be if Yourtown voted to approve casino gambling? Are you in favour of casino gambling or do you oppose it? Why?

Dealing with People

You are the Vice-President of North American Operations for a multinational tourism development company with headquarters in Japan. Your firm has successfully developed resorts in Africa and Europe, and you are in charge of the first project in Canada.

Your company has been buying up farmland and forests for several months, and you are now ready to announce your plans to build a vast theme park and resort in Apple Valley. At tonight's open meeting of the local town council, you are going to present Phase One of your plan and explain to the community how tourism will help the economy. You will probably have a lot of hard questions to answer. The local paper has learned of your plans, and today's headline charges that FOREIGNERS BUY UP ALL OF APPLE VALLEY!!

What can you tell the good citizens of Apple Valley? Are their worst fears justified? How will a huge theme park and resort affect this sleepy rural community? As director of this project, what steps can you take to ensure that you and your guests will be welcome?

CHAPTER 8: Destination Development Name: _____

WORKSHEET 8-1 Provincial Travel Organizations

What does your province do to promote itself as a tourist destination? Obtain promotional material from your province's travel organization and look through newspapers and magazines. For each of the motivations for travel listed below, briefly describe the attractions your province offers.

Recreation

_____

_____

_____

Health

_____

_____

_____

Culture

_____

_____

_____

Religion

_____

_____

_____

Nature

_____

_____

_____

Events

_____

_____

_____

Education

_____

_____

_____

Business

_____

_____

_____

Can you think of any attractions in your province or territory that are not promoted but should be?

CHAPTER 8: Destination Development

Name: _____

WORKSHEET 8-2 Creating Destinations

What kinds of destinations not currently available do you think would be valuable to society or profitable to the travel industry? Create and describe one destination for each of the categories listed below. Locate your destination anywhere in the world. Explain your choices.

A museum

_____

_____

_____

A resort

_____

_____

_____

A shopping mall

_____

_____

_____

A historical monument

_____

_____

_____

A theme park

_____

_____

_____

Other

_____

_____

_____

A model culture or restoration

_____

_____

_____

CHAPTER 9

The Recreation and Leisure System

"He that travels much knows much."
Thomas Fuller

OBJECTIVES

When you have completed this chapter, you should be able to do the following:

- Explain the difference between public and commercial recreation and leisure systems.
- Describe the national park system and list some of the facilities offered by national parks.
- Give examples of national parks, provincial parks, and local parks.
- Describe the nature and function of public museums, zoos, aquariums, fairs, and festivals.
- Give examples of public recreation facilities in other countries.
- List and describe the kinds of facilities provided by the commercial recreation sector.
- Explain how the travel industry packages and sells recreation.
- List career opportunities in public and commercial recreation and leisure systems.

Canada is the second-largest country in the world. This affects how we see ourselves, and the way visitors see us. Even though in most provinces most people reside in one or two metropolitan areas, Canadians think of their country as one of wide open spaces, forests and lakes, and a vast Far North. Most Canadians living in cities are within an hour's drive of the countryside, whether it is the cottage country north of Montreal or Toronto or Winnipeg, the foothills west of Calgary, or the farms of the lower Fraser Valley, east of Vancouver.

This vision of Canada affects our international tourism, for the better and for the worse. Many visitors come to Canada—and perhaps more importantly, many non-visitors do *not* come to Canada—because of the preconceived notion that this country has "mountains, mounties, and moose" to offer, and little else. Canada does in fact have much more to offer, and these other features need to be marketed properly to the appropriate target markets.

Canadians and visitors have long valued this country's leisure and recreation system, in both the cities and the countryside. The focus of this chapter is on such systems. Examples in both Canada and the United States will be used, given the extensive amounts of cross-border travel. A limited number of overseas examples will also be given. Leisure is the time that people use to do the things they want to do rather than the things they have to do. For most people, leisure time includes evenings, weekends, and vacations. People need leisure time to add pleasure to their lives and to refresh their minds and bodies.

The activities that people pursue in their leisure time are referred to as their recreation. **Recreation** can take many forms. It can be active or passive, close to home or far away, exciting or relaxing, inexpensive or costly. Recreation often involves attractions or events. **Attractions** are either natural or man-made. Examples of natural attractions are the Grand Canyon, Niagara Falls, the seashore, lakes, and forests. Examples of man-made attractions are the Great Wall of China, the Eiffel Tower, and the CN Tower. **Events** range from one-time occurrences, such as a rock concert or boxing match, to regularly scheduled occurrences, such as the Grey Cup, the Super Bowl, or the Academy Awards.

Canada has entertained the world extensively during the past 30 years: Expo 67 in Montreal celebrated 100 years of Confederation; the 1976 Summer Olympics were held in Montreal; Expo 86 was held in Vancouver, with transportation as a theme; and the 1988 Winter Olympics were held in Calgary.

Attractions and events are the magnets that draw people to participate in recreational activities. In general terms, the recreation business has two sectors: public and commercial.

TYPES OF RECREATION SYSTEMS

You might spend your leisure time at home reading a book or working in your garden. On the other hand, you might go to a recreational facility or attend an event sponsored by a public or commercial recreation system.

Public Recreation Systems

The **public recreation system** refers to recreational opportunities operated by federal, provincial, and local governments or by nonprofit organizations. Parks, museums, zoos, fairs, and festivals are examples of facilities and events financed by the public sector. In some cases, legislation sets up the facility and establishes guidelines for its use. Because they are funded by tax dollars, public recreational facilities are generally free or charge nominal entrance or user fees.

Public recreation facilities do not exist to make money. In fact, their primary purpose may not even be to provide recreation. Many public recreation facilities exist to preserve the natural and historic resources of the country. For example, the main function of most national parks is to preserve the beauty of a wilderness area. The opportunities for hiking, horseback riding, and picnicking are secondary to this.

Commercial Recreation Systems

The **commercial recreational system** refers to privately owned small businesses or large corporations that create products, services, and facilities for recreational use. Public and commercial recreation and leisure systems are not absolutely separate. In some cases, they overlap. Golf courses, for example, can be public or private. In other cases, they are interdependent. Private businesses operate the cabins, lodges, and other accommodations that enable people to visit national parks. These private businesses are known as **concessions**. In still other cases, the public and private sectors work together. In Niagara-on-the-Lake, Ontario, the local government, nonprofit organizations, and private businesses teamed up to preserve and promote historic sites and attractions relating to the War of 1812. Together, they provide a recreational experience that would not have been possible without such cooperation.

Recreation and the Travel Industry

Public and commercial recreation and leisure systems provide attractions that encourage people to travel during their leisure time. The travel industry builds tour packages based on skiing, shopping, attending sports events, theatregoing, and many other recreational opportunities. Public and commercial systems provide additional recreational opportunities once travellers have reached their destinations. For example, people who travel to Montreal for gambling can also enjoy the city's night life, take a tour of the Laurentians, or see a hockey game (if tickets are available).

Public and commercial recreation and leisure systems generate millions of tourist dollars and employ thousands of people.

CHECK YOUR PRODUCT KNOWLEDGE

1. What is leisure? What is recreation?
2. What is the difference between public and commercial recreation?
3. What is the relationship between the travel industry and the recreation and leisure systems?

THE PUBLIC RECREATION AND LEISURE SYSTEM

Canada has a vast and growing array of public facilities that entertain and provide recreation for millions of people every year. These facilities offer a wide range of activities that cater to many interests and tastes. First among these facilities in sheer size is the national park system. Canada's national parks, battlefields, monuments, historic sites, recreation areas, and seashores have a total area of almost 130 000 square kilometres, which is almost the size of England and about 1.3 percent of Canada's land area. Provincial parks add more. National, provincial, and local museums are permanent showcases of art, science, history, and culture. Government-supported zoos and aquariums have introduced generations of visitors to the animals and sea creatures of the world. Public festivals and fairs are held annually to commemorate significant events and to exhibit agricultural or trade products, and arts and crafts.

National Parks — Canada

Canada started its national park system in 1885, when an area of approximately 26 square kilometres on the north slope of Sulphur Mountain in Alberta was set aside for public use. This area, including the hot springs, was the beginning of what is now Banff National Park. Five reserves of land in the mountains were set aside between 1887 and 1895, and these became the following parks: Yoho, Kootenay, Glacier, Mount Revelstoke, and Waterton Lakes.

Early in the 20th century, Canada began to develop national parks in eastern Canada. The first of these was St. Lawrence Islands National Park in 1904. The world's first distinct bureau of national parks, the Dominion Parks Branch, was formed in 1911 under the authority of the Department of the Interior. This was five years before the United States organized its National Park Service.

Today, the national parks of Canada are administered by Parks Canada, which is part of Canadian Heritage (formerly a part of Environment Canada). In 1979, Parks Canada's policy stated that the national parks are designed "to protect for all time representative natural areas of Canadian significance in a system of national parks, and to encourage public understanding, appreciation, and enjoyment of this natural heritage so as to leave it unimpaired for future generations."

The government of Canada has designated 67 natural regions—39 terrestrial and 28 marine—and plans to establish a park in each region. At present, about half of Canada's regions contain national parks.

National Parks — United States

The national park system was conceived in the United States in 1872, when Congress voted to make Yellowstone that country's first national park as a way of ensuring that the region's spectacular natural beauty would be preserved for future generations. In subsequent years, other areas of publicly owned land were similarly converted into national parks: Yosemite and Sequoia in 1890, Mount Rainier in 1899, Crater Lake in 1902, and Glacier in 1910. In 1919, the first eastern park area was established—Acadia, on the coast of Maine. The purpose of national parks was soon broadened to include not only the conservation of natural wonders but also the preservation of historic and cultural sites. By 1916, Congress had created 37 parks and monuments and placed them under the administration of the National Park Service, a new agency of the Department of the Interior.

Today, the National Park Service in the United States is responsible for administering more than 350 sites. These sites are classified according to type: parks, mountains, preserves, seashores, rivers and waterways, historic parks, memorials, parkways, and recreational areas.

Park Facilities The kinds of facilities offered in a national park vary widely depending on the location and nature of the park. Some large or remote parks offer hotels, cabins, and campgrounds as well as service stations, general stores, gift shops, and restaurants. Sites located in or near cities or major highways may offer only a visitors' centre and gift shop, since food and accommodations are readily available nearby.

Visitors usually have to pay a small entry fee or camping fee at each park. Campsites at the largest and most popular parks have to be reserved. Some parks belong to a computer reservations system that enables visitors to reserve accommodations or campsites by phone, by mail, or through Ticketron. In other cases, reservations must be made directly with the parks, usually by mail.

Depending on their location and climate, the national parks offer a wide variety of recreational possibilities, including hiking, swimming, boating, fishing, horseback riding, skiing, bicycling, and scuba diving.

National parks have paved roads, scenic overlooks, and, in some cases, shuttle bus service to take visitors from one site to another. One of the functions of the park service is interpretation. The term refers to the process of educating, informing, and even entertaining visitors by offering marked trails, signs, demonstrations, lectures, pictures, and so on. The park service is committed to providing facilities for physically challenged people. Several parks have ramps and paths for people in wheelchairs. Some have tactile exhibits, audio tapes, and Braille and large-type signs for visually challenged visitors, as well as captioned films and slides, sign-language interpreters, and written materials for the hearing challenged.

ILLUSTRATION 9-1
Parks Canada has established a monitoring system to protect our sometimes fragile heritage. Kejimkujik (top) and Fundy National Parks.
SOURCE Photo Services of Parks Canada for Kejimkujik and Barrett and Mackay for Fundy

Modern Problems Since the 1970s, park managers, naturalists, environmentalists, and legislators have been addressing the problems of pollution, vandalism, and environmental stress that have been created by increasingly heavy use (see Figure 9-1). Should the parks be preserved primarily as wilderness sanctuaries or, in response to demands for new recreational uses, should they be allowed to become public playgrounds? In an attempt to balance the two objectives, the park service is experimenting with programs to restrict the number of visitors, to encourage off-peak seasonal use, and to promote patronage of some of the lesser-known parks. Other problems include the following: protecting visitors from bears; maintaining fish stocks; preventing forest fires; reducing accidents from high-risk activities, such as mountaineering, canoeing, and winter camping; and dealing with new technologies, such as snowmobiles, hang gliders, and mountain bikes.

International Role Canada's national park system is part of a global network of more than 2000 protected areas in 120 countries. Canada is a member of the International Union for the Conservation of Nature and Natural Resources (IUCN). Also, Parks Canada is the primary agency responsible for fulfilling Canada's obligations to the United Nations Education, Scientific and Cultural Organization (UNESCO). That group holds all nations responsible for protecting places of unique natural and cultural value that are considered part of the heritage of all mankind. For example, Head-Smashed-In Buffalo Jump, near Fort MacLeod, Alberta, was declared a World Heritage Site by UNESCO in 1981. That highly important site shows the techniques that native people used for 6000 years to stampede buffalo as a means of hunting them.

Provincial and Local Parks

National parks are not the only places in Canada where you can enjoy nature and outdoor recreation. Each province has its own network of provincial parks that offer many of the same facilities as national parks. And almost every city and town has one or more public parks. Municipal swimming pools, tennis courts, and golf courses are common in urban and suburban areas.

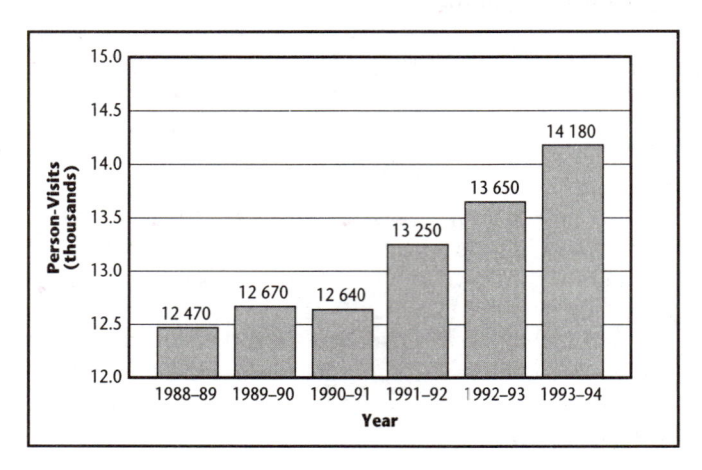

FIGURE 9-1
Person-Visits to Canadian National Parks, 1988–1994

Name	Setting	Classification	Activities
Gros Morne	Newfoundland, the shores of the Atlantic: flat-topped mountains and boggy plains, fjords and lakes, beaches	A World Heritage Site	hiking, backpacking, nature programs, camping, canoeing, swimming, boat tours, fishing, cross-country skiing, winter camping
Banff, Jasper, Yoho, Kootenay	The Rockies (Alberta and British Columbia)	A World Heritage Site	skiing, hiking, climbing, kayaking, rafting, riding, fishing, visiting glaciers
Wood Buffalo	Northern Alberta and the Northwest Territories: bogs, forests, streams, rivers, muskeg	Biggest national park in Canada	nature programs (buffalo sanctuary, whooping crane sanctuary), skiing, snowshoeing, canoeing
Northern Yukon	The Canadian Arctic: mountains, rivers, forest, tundra, Arctic seacoast	Wildlife habitat	hiking and rafting, nature programs (caribou, snow geese, grizzly and polar bears, wolves, foxes, lynx)

TABLE 9-1
Canada's National Parks — a Sampling

CHAPTER 9: The Recreation and Leisure System 215

Provincial Parks Canada has more than 1100 provincial parks. They have been created for the same reasons as national parks—to conserve wilderness areas, preserve historic sites, and provide recreation and enjoyment. They offer areas of uncrowded beaches (on Prince Edward Island), wooded hills (in Saskatchewan), and northern rivers (in Ontario); also, picnic areas, such as the parkway from Fort Erie to Niagara-on-the-Lake, which is administered by the Niagara Commission.

Most provinces have a parks department, a forestry board, and a fish and game commission to regulate hunting and fishing on provincially owned lands. Also, there may be a historical society that oversees the province's historic sites. Some popular parks suffer from overcrowding and must sometimes restrict the number of visitors or campers.

Local Parks To city dwellers hemmed in by concrete and steel, city parks offer welcome relief. City parks have picnic areas and paths for walking, jogging, and bicycling. Many parks are equipped with tennis courts, basketball courts, and other sports facilities.

Some city parks have become tourist attractions in themselves. Stanley Park in Vancouver, one of 138 in the city, is probably this country's most famous urban park. Mount Royal dominates the Montreal cityscape. Halifax has Point Pleasant Park.

Museums

Museums are storehouses and display centres for objects considered worthy of preservation because of their artistic, historic, or scientific value. Almost anything, from prehistoric peoples to antique cars to television sets, can be the subject of a museum exhibit. Visiting museums is an important part of many travellers' itineraries.

Until the 17th and 18th centuries, the pleasures of collecting and displaying works of art and curiosities of nature were reserved for the upper classes. As education spread to the middle classes, the concept of public museums took root and grew rapidly. The first museum in North America, a natural history museum, opened in Charleston, South Carolina, in 1773.

At present, there are about 12 000 museums in the United States and Canada. Many are owned and operated by governments—federal, provincial or state, and local—and are largely financed by tax revenues. Others are owned by nonprofit associations. These museums may be supported by admission fees, private donations, government grants, and corporate contributions. Some museums, such as the Peabody Museum of Archaeology and Ethnology in Salem, Massachusetts, the Fogg Art Museum at Harvard, and the Redpath Museum at McGill University in Montreal, are supported and operated by universities.

Of the many different types of museums, art museums and historical museums are the most popular. Table 9–2 lists and briefly describes the major types of museums.

Today's museums are centres of learning and culture and places for recreation and entertainment. An art museum, for example, may offer courses in and lectures on painting and art appreciation, provide trained guides to talk about the artists whose works are represented, and provide tape players

ILLUSTRATION 9–2
Almost any object with artistic, historic, or scientific value can be found in a museum (BMW Museum: Munich, Germany).
SOURCE: Karen O'Neill

Type	Characteristics	Example
Historical museums	Show collections or buildings of historical interest.	Maritime Museum of the Atlantic (Halifax, Nova Scotia)
Art museums	Show collections of paintings, sculpture, or other art.	The Louvre (Paris, France)
Science and technology museums	Illustrate principles, uses, and history of science.	Ontario Science Centre (Toronto, Ontario)
Natural history museums	Show animals, fish, and aboriginal people in their natural habitat.	Natural History Museum (London, England)
Encyclopedic or general museums	Exhibit a wide range of objects.	Royal British Columbia Museum (Victoria, British Columbia)
Special-interest museums	Focus on a single subject.	Hockey Hall of Fame (Toronto, Ontario)
Children's museums	Specialize in exhibits that explain how things work.	Nashville Children's Museum (Nashville, Tennessee)

TABLE 9-2
Museums

and cassettes to visitors. It may also hold film festivals, concerts, and similar events to educate and entertain its patrons.

Zoos and Aquariums

The word *zoo* is short for zoological garden or park. A zoo is a place set aside for the study and display of wild animals. Aquariums are special zoos for fish and other aquatic animals, such as dolphins and seals. In effect, zoos and aquariums are special museums that collect and exhibit living creatures rather than inanimate artworks or artifacts. The various types of zoos and aquariums are shown in Table 9–3.

In many respects, zoos perform functions similar to museums and parks. They entertain and educate visitors and care for the wildlife in their charge. Zoos also serve as centres for scientific research in all areas of zoology and biology. Many zoos are involved in efforts to rescue endangered species through carefully controlled breeding programs.

Like the earliest museums, the first zoos were set up by monarchs and nobles for their own amusement but were, in time, opened to the public. Other public zoos were founded by government agencies or associations of scientists and animal lovers. The Metropolitan Toronto Zoo has more than 4000 animals living in outdoor settings and glass-roofed pavilions designed to reflect their natural environment. Visitors walk on trails or ride a monorail to see the animals.

Aquariums are not a modern invention. The Sumerians built the first known aquariums 4500 years ago, and in ancient China, ornamental goldfish were bred in artificial ponds.

The first public aquariums were established in the 1850s in London and in New York City. These aquariums were long halls with exhibition tanks built into the walls. In 1938, Marineland, near St. Augustine, Florida, opened an outdoor aquarium featuring large tanks, ramps, and viewing windows. Visitors were able to observe large aquatic animals, such as sharks and porpoises, from above and below the waterline. Marineland proved so popular that many other aquariums around the country adopted the same basic design. Aquariums that specialize in saltwater animals are called oceanariums. Many of these feature shows by trained seals and dolphins, along with more formal exhibits and educational programs.

The Vancouver Public Aquarium, next to the Stanley Park Zoo, displays some 9000 freshwater and saltwater marine animals. Visitors can walk through a humid Amazon rainforest gallery, and see displays of the underwater life of coastal British Columbia, the Canadian Arctic, and other areas of the world.

Fairs and Festivals

Although closely identified with agriculture and commerce, fairs have also been a form of recreation since the Middle Ages. People enjoy strolling from exhibit to exhibit, comparing products, admiring handicrafts, or learning about the latest technological innovations. To attract larger crowds, many fairs offer food and entertainment. World's fairs began when various industries arranged to display their products on an international scale. Canada has the world's largest yearly exhibition, the Canadian National Exhibition in Toronto. It features food displays, grandstand shows with international entertainers, education, fashion, and science exhibits, and sports events. The Pacific National Exhibit, the largest fair in western Canada, is held in Vancouver every August.

ILLUSTRATION 9-3
Marineland visitors enjoying an aquatic show.
SOURCE: Courtesy of Marineland of Canada, Inc.

Type	Characteristics	Examples
Municipal Zoos	Animals are maintained for public display, mostly in large, natural enclosures	Toronto Zoo (Toronto, Ontario)
Wild Animal Parks	Animals roam freely in natural settings.	San Diego Wild Animal Park
Children's Zoos	Allow young people to see and touch various animals	Philadelphia Children's Zoo
Inland Aquariums	Exhibit freshwater fish and animals.	John G. Shedd Aquarium (Chicago)
Oceanariums	Maintain sharks, whales, dolphins, and other marine life in saltwater tanks.	Vancouver Aquarium (Vancouver B. C.)

TABLE 9-3
Zoos and Aquariums

The earliest festivals were usually religious in nature, but people have found many other reasons to hold festivals. Recognizing the enormous economic benefits that festivals can bring to an area, both governments and private groups develop and promote them. Sometimes a parade is part of the festival, or even the main event.

The Calgary Stampede is a ten-day festival in July featuring a parade, chuckwagon races, rodeo events, and exhibits. Oil-company and bank executives flip flapjacks in the streets for breakfast. The principal types of fairs and festivals are listed and described in Table 9-4.

Public Recreation and Leisure Systems Abroad

Every nation and continent has its own culture, history, climate, and natural resources, all of which determine the attractions that can be offered to leisure travellers. Nations with great natural beauty and a pleasant climate emphasize sports and recreational opportunities. The islands of the Caribbean, for example, attract vacationers with their sun, sandy beaches, and tropical waters. Countries with long histories, such as Greece, concentrate on preserving, displaying, and promoting the structures and artifacts of their national heritage.

The attitudes and values of a nation also do much to determine what attractions and facilities it develops and promotes. For example, Mexico and the other nations of Latin America have museums and archaeological sites that highlight their pre-Columbian past. And the conservation of wildlife and other natural resources has become a priority in most parts of the world, so national parks and nature reserves are found in many countries.

National Parks Around the World The United States originated the concept of national parks, and the U.S. National Park Service has been very active in helping other countries establish them. Today, there are approximately 3500 national parks or similarly protected areas in more than 130 nations throughout the world.

The largest national park systems, by area, are in North America (the United States and Canada) and Africa. Parks vary widely in the accommodations they offer travellers, and many are open only during certain seasons of the year. In Asia, for example, the parks may close during the summer monsoons.

The national parks of Africa serve primarily as large game reserves. Two of the best-known wildlife sanctuaries are Kruger National Park in the Transvaal, South Africa, and Nairobi National Park in Kenya. Even though most countries in Asia are densely populated, that continent has many national parks and wildlife sanctuaries. Perhaps the most famous is Fuji-Hakone-Izu National Park in Japan, where Mount Fuji is located.

Zoos Around the World Zoos vary widely in size and in the quality of their settings. Some zoos still follow the 19th-century model, with small, square cages housing bored, lethargic animals. Other zoos have made an effort to create natural, open settings that are more pleasant for animals and onlookers alike. London's Regent's Park Zoo, which opened in 1931, was one of the first to use the concept of open surroundings and concealed barriers to display animals. The Basel Zoo in Switzerland pioneered efforts to make zoo habitats more like the natural surroundings of each species.

Some zoos are noted for the number and kinds of animals they contain. The Taronga Zoo, just across the harbour from Sydney, Australia, has a collection of more than 5000 animals and birds. On the outskirts of Tokyo, the Tama Zoological Park features an insect pavilion.

Museums Around the World The history, resources, and culture of a region or a nation largely determine the kinds of museums that are developed there. Thus, nations such as Egypt and Israel have museums that feature antiquities. The Museum of Egyptian Antiquities in Cairo contains treasures

Type	Characteristics	Examples
Agricultural Fairs	Feature livestock and agricultural products, along with carnival midways and rides (weather permitting)	Royal Ontario Winter Fair (Toronto)
Trade Fairs	Let companies display the latest developments or products in a particular industry	Frankfurt Book Fair (Germany)
Historic Fairs	Recreate food and entertainment of the great fairs of medieval and Renaissance Europe	Renaissance Fairs
World's Fairs	Feature nation-by-nation exhibits of industry and culture	1992 World's Fair in Seville (Spain)
Festivals	Offer seasonal celebrations, cultural events, or commemorations	Mardi Gras (Rio de Janeiro); Winter Carnival (Quebec City)
Parades	Display marching bands, floats, and celebrities	Tournament of Roses Parade (Pasadena, California)

TABLE 9-4
Fairs and Festivals

from the tomb of King Tutankhamen, and the Israel Museum in Jerusalem displays many of the Dead Sea Scrolls.

Visitors on a tour of Europe can expect to spend a great deal of time in art and history museums, such as the National Gallery in London, the Louvre in Paris, and the Uffizi Gallery in Florence. The nations of Europe have also turned hundreds of castles and churches into museums.

The countries of Africa, Asia, and Latin America abound with anthropological and archaeological museums that celebrate their precolonial heritage. At the National Museum of Anthropology in Mexico City, visitors can view a vast collection of the art and artifacts of Mexico's first peoples.

The museums of newer nations settled by northern Europeans, such as Canada, the United States, and Australia, are more likely to emphasize art, science, natural history, and colonial history. The Australian Museum in Sydney, for example, focuses on the exotic animal and plant life of Australia and on the history and culture of the continent's aborigines.

CHECK YOUR PRODUCT KNOWLEDGE

1. For what reasons did governments begin creating national parks?
2. What is the major problem confronting national and provincial parks and forests?
3. List the three main functions of museums.
4. How do zoos and aquariums differ from other kinds of museums?
5. How do the attitudes and values of a nation's citizens influence the kinds of attractions it provides?

ILLUSTRATION 9-4
The Museum of Egyptian Antiquities in Cairo contains treasures of great beauty as well as historical value.
SOURCE: Karen O'Neill

COMMERCIAL RECREATION

The commercial sector provides something for everyone. Theme parks, model cultures, restorations, special museums, and industrial tours educate as well as entertain. Millions of sports fans travel to large metropolitan areas to cheer for their favourite professional teams. For those who prefer to be more active, the commercial sector offers ski resorts, golf resorts, and many other recreational sports. Visitors can also enjoy recreational shopping in enormous malls, and see and hear live entertainment in the form of concerts, opera, dance, and theatre. Gambling casinos and racetracks are also provided by the commercial sector.

Theme Parks

In 1955, Walt Disney opened Disneyland near Anaheim, California. Based on themes and characters from Disney movies, the park was designed to be an exciting environment for family entertainment. As the nation's first major theme park, Disneyland was an immediate success. It has inspired the development of many other theme parks.

Canada's Wonderland is a world-class theme park with 150 hectares featuring various activities such as amusement rides, lifelike cartoon characters, and aquatic shows. In 1989 the top 40 theme parks entertained 122 million visitors.

The Themes Most tourist attractions have their roots in the natural or historical environment in which they are located. The theme park is an exception. By establishing a theme and then having all exhibits, rides, shops, and restaurants relate to it, the theme park creates its own environment. The visitor enters Disney's Fantasyland, for instance, through Sleeping Beauty's castle; meets Captain Hook, Cinderella, and Peter Pan on the streets; and takes an aerial journey in Dumbo the Flying Elephant. Everything is familiar and comfortable, but exciting.

Themes derived from history, animal life, and cartoons have been particularly popular for theme parks. Some parks hold to a strong central theme. Busch Gardens—The Dark Continent (Tampa, Florida) revolves around an African theme. The three Sea World parks (Orlando, San Diego, and Aurora, Ohio) are devoted to marine life. Other parks can have a variety of themes. Rivertown, Wild Animal Safari, Oktoberfest, and Coney Island are theme areas at Kings Island in Cincinnati.

Canada has only a few theme parks. Among them are Frontierland, south of Whitehorse, Yukon; Kinsmen Park in Saskatoon, Saskatchewan; Marineland and Maple Leaf Village Amusement Park, both in Niagara Falls, Ontario; Aqua Park in Montreal; and Magic Mountain at Moncton, New Brunswick.

Characteristics of Theme Parks Before the family automobile became commonplace, amusement parks were built at

PROFILE

Canadian Initiatives in Tourism: Part 2

Manitou Springs Mineral Spa

In its first ten months, Manitou Springs Mineral Spa of Watrous, Saskatchewan, generated about $93,000 in profit and paid for about three-quarters of its $1.9 million facility. No one had expected its instant success as a tourist attraction that would soon be bringing in daily bus tours. "We were hoping to break even the first year," says spa manager Lionel Sproule. "Our success came as a pleasant surprise, and we continue to do well."

In 1989, more than 70 000 visitors from across the continent came to float effortlessly in the spa's salty mineral water, which is said to be healing for arthritis and minor skin complaints. The visitors have had a very healthy effect on local businesses: sales are up 10 to 15 percent, and local hotels are enjoying almost year-round occupancy. Manitou Springs Mineral Spa has been expanded: a $3 million, 60-room hotel–conference centre and mall were built. Both opened for business in 1991.

Oak Bay Marine Group

The Oak Bay Marine Group began humbly, 32 years ago, as a small marina. It is now a diversified company with 17 operations covering a wide range of activities, from tourist services to sport fishing trips. Today, this Victoria, B.C., company is the largest sports-fishing operation in North America, with revenues of $20 million. Under the direction of its founder and president, Bob Wright, the group operates five resorts, a 71 metre steamship, a fleet of offshore boats, and two luxury resort yachts.

Oak Bay has worked hard to maintain a personal, friendly image, and has made use of many innovative promotional tools. Accessibility is a key part of its very effective marketing strategy: a telephone sales department is on duty twelve hours a day, seven days a week.

Arctic Edge

In 1983 a guide and resource manager named David Loeks established Arctic Edge, an adventure travel and outfitting business based in Whitehorse, Yukon. After a slow and sometimes rocky start, Loeks decided to refine both his business activities and his marketing program. In that regard, he began to focus on providing adventure travel experiences for upscale North American and European travellers. He also expanded his product line while phasing out his outfitting service. A multipage, full-colour brochure marked another major step forward. Today, Arctic Edge has become one of the leading northern-based adventure travel companies. The range of activities it offers includes canoeing, rafting, skiing, backpacking, wildlife viewing, and dogsledding in the Yukon, Alaska, and the western Northwest Territories.

SOURCE: Information Canada. Reproduced with permission of the Minister of Supply and Services Canada, 1990

Theme parks are large-scale enterprises employing thousands of people and requiring millions of dollars in operating funds. Sophisticated computer technology is used to operate many of the rides and other attractions. Every detail is carefully managed. Grounds and rest rooms are immaculate, and employees wear informal but spotlessly clean uniforms. At Disneyland, even the brass rails on the merry-go-round receive a daily polishing.

Variations on a Theme In recent years, variations of the major theme parks have developed. Mini-theme parks, such as Crystal Palace in Moncton, New Brunswick, are smaller entertainment facilities, geared mainly toward young children. There are theme rooms in the hotel. At theme restaurants, patrons play electronic games and watch animated shows while waiting for their food. There is also a science fair to attract schoolchildren on bus trips. Cross-marketing with Magic Mountain, outside Moncton at Magnetic Hill, provides an additional incentive to visit the Moncton area.

The most significant variation, however, is the participatory theme park. Rather than being passively strapped into a ride or seated in a theatre, visitors actively participate in events such as grass skiing, Grand Prix racing on a miniature track, and kamikaze sliding into a pool that makes its own waves. At the Vernon Valley Action Park in McAfee, New Jersey—the largest action park in the United States—patrons drive military-style tanks around a pen and shoot tennis balls at other tanks. Participatory areas are now being added to the established theme parks.

Amusement Parks, Carnivals, and Circuses

For past generations, circuses, carnivals, and amusement parks were great places to spend a Saturday afternoon. In recent years, these old stand-bys have been overshadowed by theme parks, television spectaculars, and other more trendy forms of entertainment. But circuses, carnivals, and amusement parks are still around, and popular with young people and families.

Amusement Parks Coney Island was established in the 1880s on six miles of beach in New York City. It became the model for the gaudy amusement parks of the 20th century. In addition to a midway, with its rides, freak shows, cotton candy, and penny arcade, traditional amusement parks had tables and benches for family picnics. Those with waterfront settings offered a beach for swimming. Crystal Beach, Ontario, on Lake Erie, was a popular Canadian amusement park.

Amusement parks typically charged a low admission fee, but an additional fee for every ride or event. Theme park developers have reversed this, charging a high fee at the gate that includes all the rides and events inside.

Because of the overwhelming popularity of theme parks, the number of amusement parks has decreased considerably

ILLUSTRATION 9-5
Theme parks create their own environment, such as Cullen Gardens miniature village in Ontario.
SOURCE: Cullen Gardens and Miniature Village, Whitby, Ontario.

the end of a streetcar line, as Belmont Park was in Montreal. Their customers came primarily from the immediate community. They hopped on the streetcar, stayed a few hours at the park, and then took the streetcar home again. Today's theme parks are located on the outskirts of major urban areas, cover vast tracts of land, and offer a wide range of recreational activities and events: roller coaster rides, theatrical performances, exhibits, tours, movies, and celebrity appearances, all of which can be entertaining and educational. People drive or fly for miles to get to these parks; having arrived, they tend to stay longer and spend more money.

By advertising in newspapers and magazines and on national television, theme parks attempt to draw tourists from all over the country. Because a visit to a theme park is now likely to be part of a vacation trip—or the destination itself—hotels, restaurants, and other entertainment facilities have sprung up around theme parks to serve the needs of travellers. The building of Disneyland, for instance, was followed by the construction of 7000 hotel and motel rooms, a convention centre, and an American League baseball park in Anaheim, California.

ILLUSTRATION 9-6
The popularity of recreational sports continues to grow along with Canadians' passion for physical fitness.
SOURCE Tourism Nova Scotia

over the years. La Ronde, a summer amusement park on Île Ste-Hélène opposite Montreal Harbour, is one of the most popular amusement parks, with clean, modern, and safe facilities.

Carnivals A carnival is a travelling amusement park. In the late 1890s, newly developed technology allowed entire midways—rides, refreshment and souvenir stands, and shows—to be transported from city to city. Today's carnivals are not as elaborate as earlier carnivals. They usually travel from small town to small town, and set up their rides in the parking lot of a shopping mall.

Circuses With daring and skilled performers, trained animal acts, and clowns, circuses offer audiences a wonderful spectacle. In the golden age of the circus, about ten major circuses travelled the continent, and the arrival of the circus was the major event of the summer. Today, the Ringling Brothers and Barnum & Bailey Circus is the only major circus. But a number of small local circuses still delight children across North America.

Model Cultures and Restorations

In a model culture or restoration, visitors learn about the material culture (houses, vehicles, artifacts) and performing arts of a historical age or a different nation. Buildings have been constructed or restored so that they resemble an actual town, village, or fort. Costumed employees serve as guides and demonstrate the arts, crafts, and daily practices of the time or culture. Kings Landing Historical Settlement, north of Fredericton, New Brunswick, in the Saint John Valley, re-creates New Brunswick rural life between 1820 and 1890. Fort Steele re-creates life in southeastern British Columbia at the turn of the century. Restorations in Ontario include Upper Canada Village and Ste. Marie Among the Hurons.

Museums

The commercial sector also operates museums. Most of these are small, and devoted to one type of collection, such as dolls or automobiles.

Nostalgia for the golden age of the railways has led to the establishing of many railway museums across the continent. These display passenger and freight locomotives, coaches, boxcars, cabooses, and other railway paraphernalia. The largest one in Canada is the Canadian Railway Museum at Delson, Quebec, just south of Montreal. Trolleys are featured at the Ontario Electric Railway Museum at Rockwood, northwest of Burlington, Ontario. Many of these museums offer excursions on the old-time railways. There is a summer excursion with Royal Hudson steam engine 2860 from North Vancouver to Squamish, in British Columbia.

Sometimes a museum is the result of one community's special interest or collection—for example, the town of Springhill, Nova Scotia, built Anne Murray Centre to honour its most famous citizen.

Spectator Sports

Armed with peanuts, hot dogs, and soft drinks, more than 50 million fans of professional baseball get out to the ballpark each year and root for their favourite team. Canadians and Americans are avid sports spectators. They take delight in analyzing the skills of the players and second-guessing the coaches. Spectator sports are also a wonderful way to vent emotions. Joe Carter's bottom-of-the-ninth home run that won a second straight World Series for the Toronto Blue Jays will long be remembered on both sides of the border.

Along with baseball, Canadians like to see hockey, football, basketball, boxing, tennis, golf, and racing (car, thoroughbred, harness, and greyhound). The most popular spectator sport in the United States is pari-mutuel racing, which draws nearly 100 million people each year.

The Toronto Blue Jays were the first baseball team to attract 4 000 000 in attendance (their record was broken by the Colorado Rockies in 1993). The Olympic Games are the world's largest single spectator event. Montreal hosted the 1976 Summer Games, and Calgary hosted the 1988 Winter Games.

Most professional sports teams are privately owned; some are owned by the community. Professional sports is a serious business in which the owners do everything possible to produce a winning team and keep the fans in the stands. In recent years, owners have launched a variety of promotions to boost fan interest and attendance.

Spectator sports bring profits to the community as well as to the owners. As with other recreational events, people attending sporting events spend money at concession booths, and for transportation and parking. Many patronize local stores and restaurants before and after the event. Fans from out of town spend money on hotels and entertainment. Amateur sporting events also bring profits. By hosting the

PROFILE

Cavendish Resort Community

Written by Mary Lee White

Centrally located along the north shore of Canada's smallest province rests the famous resort community of Cavendish, Prince Edward Island. This area is noted for its warm community spirit, quaint homes, scenic drives, and broad, sandy beaches. Cavendish is best known for its beloved Anne, the fictional heroine created by Lucy Maud Montgomery in her famous Canadian novel, *Anne of Green Gables*.

Cavendish is a resort municipality that follows the north shore of the island for approximately 13.5 kilometres. This community has three distinct areas: the national park and national park beaches, "Anne's Land," and private development areas. Cavendish is the third-most-visited spot on Prince Edward Island and receives approximately 330 000 visitors a year, most of them during the tourist season, between May and October.

Tourism began in Cavendish in the early 1920s when homeowners began renting out rooms to guests who wished to enjoy the area's white, sandy beaches. These were the first B&B style accommodations in Cavendish. In the 1930s vendors began selling ice cream on the beaches. When they tried to do this on Sunday, they created an uproar among the residents of the community. The founding of Prince Edward Island National Park on April 24, 1937, marked the beginning of the tourism boom in the area. The first golf course opened in 1939 and attracted still more visitors. The next 20 years saw development with little or no organization. It wasn't until the 1960s that systematic development began. Over a four-year period, private and public development proceeded very quickly, and Cavendish became a full-fledged resort area. Development continues to this day.

The two major tourist areas of Cavendish are "Anne's Land" and the National Park. Anne's Land is home to the original 1890s homestead that L. M. Montgomery used as the setting for her novel, *Anne of Green Gables*. The National Park features sand dunes, beaches, red sandstone cliffs, salt marshes, freshwater ponds, woodlands, and wildlife. Facilities are available for camping, swimming, hiking, cycling, picnicking, golf, tennis, and bird watching. Other nearby attractions include water theme parks, a wax museum, amusement parks, museums, craft shops, adventure parks, a marine aquarium, lobster suppers, and a number of family-style restaurants.

On July 2 of every year, an important event occurs in Cavendish: Anne's Land reenacts the arrival of Anne, who arrives in a horse-drawn cart at Green Gables dressed in an 1890s costume. During the next two months, this fiery redhead lives the life of Anne at Green Gables and is available to tourists for conversation and photo opportunities. The other festival of note occurs in mid-August, when the Lucy Maud Montgomery Festival is held. There, tourists can enjoy poetry readings, period games, and a fish fest. In winter, tourists can participate in cross-country skiing and bird watching in the National Park. Within 30 kilometres of Cavendish you can visit Woodleigh Replicas, a 13-hectare country garden in which painstakingly accurate models of many of Europe's famous castles and cathedrals have been built to scale. Deep-sea fishing is available along the coast.

A variety of accommodations are available to travellers. They include many modern motels, country inns, farm tourist homes, bed-and-breakfasts, cottages, and campgrounds. Tourists can make reservations by calling Prince Edward Island Tourism's 800 number.

Cavendish is a unique resort area because it reflects the spirit of "Anne," who is loved by millions around the world. All who come can experience her magic in the morning, bask in the summer sun and swim in the warm waters of the Gulf of St. Lawrence in the afternoon, and savour the island seafood in the evening. Come to Cavendish!

CHAPTER 9: The Recreation and Leisure System   223

1980 Winter Olympics, Lake Placid, New York, re-established itself as a major winter resort. The 1996 Summer Games will have a huge economic impact on Atlanta, Georgia, their host city.

Because of the economic impact, cities vie with each other to host major events such as the Grey Cup or Super Bowl. They also compete for major league franchises. National Basketball League franchises have recently been awarded to Toronto and Vancouver; both teams will commence play in 1995. To win a franchise in any sport, a city must be able to offer a first-class arena or stadium, or show that it will soon build one. In recent years, many cities have built gigantic sports facilities in the hope of attracting more business to the area. The 60 000-seat B.C. Place enclosed stadium in Vancouver could host a major-league baseball team.

Enormously expensive to build and maintain, these facilities are designed to serve many purposes. When a facility has several uses, more events can be held, and more operating revenue is generated. The Skydome, home of the Toronto Argonauts and Blue Jays, also hosts the Vanier Cup for university football, as well as rock concerts, religious gatherings, and other events.

The travel industry, of course, also profits from spectator sports. For some time, it has been building package tours around major sporting events such as the World Series, Grey Cup, Kentucky Derby, and Indy 500. But now a new phenomenon is beginning to appear: when the home team goes on the road, the fans, instead of staying at home and watching on television, are going on the road, too. Blue Jay fans from the Lakehead and Manitoba now travel to Minneapolis, Milwaukee, and Chicago to watch regular season games. And for the most avid sports fans—those who can't wait until the baseball season opens—there are package tours to Florida that enable them to watch their team in spring training.

RECREATIONAL SPORTS

While millions of Canadians are sitting at spectator events, millions of other Canadians are actively participating in recreational sports, both indoors and outdoors. This increased interest in active sports reflects the public's rising awareness of the importance of physical fitness.

Canadians' interest in traditional recreational sports such as bicycling, curling, swimming, and hiking remains high. At the same time, the popularity of newer sports such as jogging, exercise walking, racquetball, and white-water rafting continues to grow. There has also been a renewed interest in roller-skating, thanks, in large part, to the development of in-line skates. For the more adventurous, hang-gliding, parasailing, and bungee-jumping are gaining in popularity. In bungee-jumping, a long elastic cord is attached to the jumper, who leaps off a high place such as a tower, crane, or bridge. The cord acts like a huge rubber band, causing the jumper to rise back up before hitting the ground or water.

The sports people engage in are a function of where they live. Skiing and scuba diving, for example, can only be done in certain parts of the country. On the other hand, tennis courts and golf courses exist nearly everywhere. Bowling is the number-one recreational sport in Canada and the United States because there are bowling alleys in almost every neighbourhood.

Recreational sports provide a good illustration of how the public and commercial sectors can overlap. For instance, almost every city park provides tennis courts. Privately owned businesses also operate tennis courts. The difference is that private tennis clubs—for a fee—offer more amenities, such as a clubhouse, reserved court times, saunas, locker rooms, and refreshments.

Nowadays, people are taking up sports at an earlier age. This is because more families have double incomes; parents are more health conscious; and most people have more leisure time. Most children who take up a sport will keep playing it well into adulthood. This is yet another indication that recreational sports are more important than ever in Canada. In making travel decisions, parents will consider the availability of recreational facilities for the family.

Facilities   As mentioned earlier, national and provincial parks provide facilities for many recreational sports. These sports, however, have been classified as part of the commercial sector because of the potential for private enterprise to make a profit in them. Sporting goods stores provide all sorts of equipment—running shoes, cross-country skis, guns, racquets. Some businesses, called **outfitters**, provide services, such as fishing and hunting guides or white-water rafting equipment, while others stage events for recreational enthusiasts. Each year, the Boston Marathon generates enormous revenue for the city in travel services, hotel accommodations, and food. The bicycle rally in Montreal provides revenue for that city.

The commercial sector also provides and operates facilities for recreational sports—skating rinks, marinas, fishing resorts, fitness centres. For tennis players who are very serious about improving their game, there are privately operated tennis camps where they can spend their vacations.

Some types of facilities, such as ski resorts, require more financial investment and are riskier to operate than others. If the weather is too warm and there is not enough snow, ski resorts lose money. If the weather is too cold, skiers stay at home. Operating costs are high. During the summer months, expensive ski lifts sit idle. To generate off-season income, many ski resorts have developed year-round programs; for example, they offer scenic chair lifts and convention facilities during the summer months. By clustering their facilities, resorts in the Laurentians, north of Montreal, have been able to concentrate more nightlife, restaurants, and shopping in one area. This tends to draw more patrons than would a string of isolated resorts.

The travel industry, of course, is mainly interested in those recreational sports, like skiing, that require most people to journey some distance from home. It also likes to advertise recreational sports as features that round out the attractiveness of a particular destination.

Recreational Vehicles One type of recreational facility that has grown tremendously is the private campground. Kampgrounds of America (KOA), North America's largest privately owned campground franchise, had seven facilities in 1964. By the early 1990s, there were more than 650.

This growth does not mean that more people are pitching tents and building bonfires. Rather, it is related to the rise in popularity of recreational vehicles (RVs) for travel. Campgrounds cater to these homes on wheels by providing them with a parking spot, electricity, running water, and sewer access. Some campgrounds have even installed swimming pools, golf courses, kennels, restaurants, and cocktail lounges.

The recreational vehicle represents a new way of travelling that has contributed to the tourism boom. However, because they take their beds and kitchens with them, RV owners do not make much use of hotels and motels, or restaurants. Convention and entertainment centres seek to capitalize on RV traffic by establishing nearby campsites.

The RV industry hopes to install RV rentals in the channels of distribution used for other travel products. Thus, like a car rental, travellers could rent an RV at an airport or as part of a fly/drive package arranged through a travel agency. Some computer reservations systems have already begun to list RV rental companies among their subscribers.

Recreational Shopping

Visitors to the CN Tower usually purchase a souvenir to remind them of their trip (and to prove to friends back home that they were really in Toronto). Travellers to the American Southwest often buy Navaho blankets and jewellery because similar merchandise is not available back home.

Shopping has long been a by-product of travelling. Recently, however, shopping itself has become a reason for travelling. The development of three types of facilities—the megamall, the waterfront shopping complex, and the factory outlet centre—has greatly increased recreational shopping. These facilities are promoted as tourist attractions. Chartered buses and planes bring thousands of tourists to them each year.

Megamalls Megamalls are gigantic indoor shopping and entertainment complexes—a shopper's paradise. Under one roof, shoppers can find department stores, hundreds of shops, restaurants, theatres, banks, health clubs, and art galleries. Sculptures, fountains, and tropical gardens add to the luxurious atmosphere.

The West Edmonton Mall is listed in *The Guinness Book of Records* as the largest mall in the world. It is eight city blocks long and three wide—about the size of 85 football fields. The total cost of construction was $1.1 billion. An estimated 60 000 people visit the mall every day, including 26 000 tourists from outside Alberta. The mall contains 900 stores, 110 eating places, and 10 feature attractions, including a swimming pool, an ice skating rink, an amusement park, and a reproduction of Bourbon Street in New Orleans.

Another megamall, part of which has opened, is being built in Bloomington, Minnesota. When construction is completed in the late 1990s, it will cover 32 hectares and have its own indoor amusement park, miniature golf course, and nightclubs.

By attracting out-of-town visitors, megamalls have helped to restore vitality to the downtown areas of several big cities. Downtown St. Louis, for example, was practically deserted until developers converted an old train station into a shopping mall, hotel, and restaurant complex. Now the city centre is alive again. With enclosed malls, northern cities can attract visitors year-round, instead of only in the warm summer months.

Waterfront Marketplaces Waterfront marketplaces are shopping and entertainment complexes built along a river or bay. The architecture of the complex gives visitors a pleasant view of the waterfront. A waterfront marketplace is usually part of an effort to restore the historic section of a city; in this capacity, it becomes the scene of civic events and festivals. The success of waterfront marketplaces in Halifax, Saint John, Toronto, Boston, New York City, and Baltimore has stimulated similar developments elsewhere.

Factory Outlet Centres A factory outlet centre comprises several stores that sell name-brand merchandise at cut-rate prices. Discounts can be as high as 50 percent. Whereas megamalls and waterfront developments have been an economic boon to large cities, factory outlet centres have revitalized once-dying small towns. Not many years ago, the retail shops along the main street in Boaz, Alabama, were empty. Then a shopping centre for factory outlet stores was opened nearby. Busloads of bargain hunters now pour into Boaz every weekend. Their zest for shopping has spilled over, so that the stores on the main street have reopened for business.

Another area that has become a prime location for factory outlet centres is along the border between the United States and Canada. The Niagara Factory Outlet Mall in Niagara Falls, New York, is a popular destination for Canadian shoppers looking for good buys. Prices for many items in the outlet stores are much lower than in Canada.

Celebrity and Industrial Tours

Recognizing the public's fascination with the lives of famous people, the commercial recreation sector has been quick to turn the homes of celebrities into tourist attractions. For example, in Beverly Hills, California, visitors can buy a map that directs them to the homes of movie stars. When Jimmy Carter was president, tour buses regularly drove through his home town of Plains, Georgia. Graceland in Memphis, Tennessee, has become a shrine to thousands of devoted Elvis Presley fans.

Factories, processing plants, and breweries around the country have also become tourist attractions. People enjoy seeing how various products, from breakfast foods to jet planes, are made. The company often provides a guided tour through its plant, and explains its products through an exhibit or a video.

Since companies generally do not charge admission, industrial tours are nonprofit ventures for the commercial sector. However, companies find these tours a very useful exercise in public relations. Alberta's visitors' guide provides a listing of industrial tours.

Live Entertainment

Despite the popularity of television and movies, many people enjoy the sense of involvement they get from live entertainment. Stage, ballet, and opera companies, and symphony orchestras, can be public or private; rock concerts and night-club shows are almost always commercial ventures—and enormously lucrative for some performers.

The audiences for live entertainment tend to be specialized. That is, people go to events they understand. If you're unfamiliar with ballet, you probably won't appreciate the skill of the dancers. Likewise, a rock concert can be ear-shattering clatter if you're not a fan of the performers and their music.

Live entertainment is sometimes the main attraction for a vacation trip. For instance, people travel to Nashville just to hear country and western music at the Grand Ol' Opry. Opryland USA—Nashville's theme park—and other area attractions are spin-offs of the Grand Ol' Opry. A theatre tour to see Broadway plays is another example of live entertainment as the main attraction for a trip. Most often, however, live entertainment adds to the recreational activities available at a particular destination and increases the likelihood that tourists will visit that destination.

In the past, only a few cities—notably Montreal, Toronto, New York, Boston, Chicago, and Los Angeles—offered top-quality live entertainment. Now, however, opportunities to attend excellent performances are available throughout Canada and the United States. There are symphony orchestras in most provinces. Regional theatres, such as the Neptune in Halifax and the Stratford Festival in Ontario, provide outstanding productions. Regional ballet and modern dance associations flourish in many provinces. Also, countless schools and community groups offer concerts and plays.

Sometimes, people attend a concert or a play just to see the hall. Place des Arts in Montreal, New York City's Carnegie Hall, and Toronto's Pantages Theatre are all famous in their own right.

Gambling and Gaming

North Americans spend more money on gambling than on movie tickets—billions of dollars every year. Gambling (also known as gaming) has been a leisure activity for centuries. There are four types of gambling: pari-mutuel wagering, lotteries, the activities of nonprofit organizations (mainly bingos and raffles), and casino gambling. The first three types have existed in most parts of Canada for years. Any new traveller on a Nova Scotia–Maine ferry has probably been surprised, if not shocked, at how busy the slot machines become once the vessel enters international waters.

Casino gambling is very limited in Canada; however, more jurisdictions are considering opening casinos to generate employment and tax revenue. The Crystal Casino in Winnipeg's historic Fort Garry was the first, but very small. The first large casino in Canada opened in Montreal in the fall of 1993. It averages between 10 000 and 12 000 visitors on weekdays and 15 000 on weekends. Ontario opened a casino in Windsor in 1994. More may follow, in other provinces.

In the United States today, gambling is a popular though also controversial form of recreation. No state has legalized all forms of gambling, and only a few states have any form of legalized gambling. More states, however, are looking into gambling as a way of raising revenue. Many Canadians travel to Las Vegas, Reno, and Atlantic City specifically to gamble.

Since lotteries, bingo, and raffles are geared toward the residents of a particular area, the travel industry is primarily interested in casino gambling and pari-mutuel wagering.

Casino Gambling Casino gambling consists of playing either slot machines or table games such as roulette, craps (dice), blackjack (twenty-one), baccarat, and poker. Casinos are either free-standing or part of a large hotel–entertainment complex. They are privately owned by independent businesspeople or by corporations. For instance, the Tropicana in Las Vegas is a casino hotel operated by the Ramada Corporation.

Nevada, New Jersey, Colorado, and South Dakota were the first states to allow regular casino gambling. Some states have recently begun to allow casino gambling on riverboats. The major casino concentrations are in Las Vegas, Reno–Sparks, and Lake Tahoe (Nevada), and Atlantic City (New Jersey). The more than 200 casinos in Nevada make gambling the basis for that state's most important industry—

tourism. Colorado has permitted gambling in Cripple Creek and Central City, two old Rocky Mountain mining towns. South Dakota just recently began to allow limited gambling in Deadwood, an old gold-rush town. The state plans to use the gambling profits to restore the town's many historic buildings in the hope of bringing more tourists to the area.

Travel for the purpose of casino gambling has increased. In 1970, casino revenues were only $6 million; in 1990, they were more than $8 billion. The slot machines bring in more money than all the table games together. The first "cashless" casino opened in Australia recently. Its slot machines take debit cards—which are similar to credit cards—rather than quarters, dimes, and nickels. This system is expected to come to North America as well and further increase the haul of the one-armed bandits.

Atlantic City, where casino gambling has been legal since 1978, is trying to challenge Las Vegas as the casino capital of the United States. Located in a densely populated area, Atlantic City draws 70 percent of its business from people who live within a 300-mile radius. Las Vegas depends on tourists from all over the country.

Pari-Mutuel Betting This is the kind of betting people do at dog or horse races. People bet on the first-, second-, and/or third-place finishers; the winners then share the total amount bet, less a percentage for the track. In the United States, Florida has the largest number of pari-mutuel activities.

More people attend thoroughbred racing than any other racing event. There are over 100 thoroughbred tracks in Canada and the United States, many of them located in Ontario, New York, and California.

Harness racing, in which the driver sits behind the horse in a small, two-wheeled cart, is especially popular in southern Ontario, Montreal, and the Maritimes; also, around Chicago and in Delaware, upstate New York, and Michigan.

Quarter horse racing is popular in the West and Northwest, and usually takes place at regional and county fairs. As the name implies, the quarter horses run a quarter of a mile.

In dog races, greyhounds chase a mechanical hare around the track. There are well-attended dog tracks in Revere, Massachusetts; St. Petersburg, Florida; and West Memphis, Arkansas. In Florida, betting is also legal in jaialai, a ball-and-racquet game.

Commercial Recreation and Leisure Abroad

Outside Canada and the United States, there are many recreational activities sponsored by privately owned businesses. Most of these exist in the countries of Europe, which have well-established tourist routes as well as the economic resources to develop and support commercial attractions. Even more recreational opportunities will become available as new destinations in South America, the Orient, and Australia are developed. Only a glimpse of the possibilities for commercial recreation abroad can be given here. Table 9-5 lists some of the highlights.

CHECK YOUR PRODUCT KNOWLEDGE

1. What are the characteristics of theme parks?
2. What important service do model cultures and restorations provide?
3. What is the difference between a spectator sport and a recreational sport?
4. As it relates to the travel industry, how has the importance of shopping changed?
5. What are four types of gambling?
6. Why are the attractions of Europe more familiar to Canadians and Americans than those of Asia and South America?

Type	Examples
Amusement/Theme Parks	■ Tivoli Gardens, Copenhagen, features outdoor cafés, flower gardens, midway, and specialty shops ■ Tokyo Disneyland, Japan Euro Disneyland, France
Restorations	■ Fort Louisbourg, Nova Scotia, reconstructed eighteenth-century French fort
Sports	■ Wimbledon tennis tournament, London. ■ The 1994 World Cup hosted by the United States
Shopping	■ Indian Craft Market, Mexico City ■ Cloth Alley, Hong Kong ■ Edmonton Mall, a giant shopping entertainment complex with over 800 shops
Industrial tours	■ Perfume factories in France ■ Diamond cutting in Amsterdam ■ Cheese making in Switzerland
Casino gambling	■ Casinos of Monte Carlo, Estoril, and the Caribbean
Live Entertainment	■ Classical music—symphony orchestras; opera—Berlin, London, Milan, Paris, Vienna. ■ Theatre in London, Stratford-upon-Avon ■ Nightclubs—Folies Bergère in Paris, native gaucho music in Buenos Aires, Kabuki theatre in Japan

TABLE 9-5
Commercial Recreation and Leisure

RECREATION AS PRODUCT

To the travel industry, recreation is a product—something that must be created, packaged, and sold in the same way as other products.

The Package Tour

To make travel more appealing and convenient, as well as less expensive, the travel industry groups its products into packages. For example, transportation and accommodations products are often packaged together. Package tours are discussed in detail in Chapter 10.

Some travel packages are built around specific recreational attractions. To enhance the attraction, the package generally includes transportation and accommodations. Extra features, such as meals or free baggage-handling, can be included to make the package more enticing. Recreational package tours, which can be put together by hotels, airlines, travel agencies, wholesale operators, or the attraction itself, are becoming increasingly popular. There is an infinite variety of packages, depending on the options selected, the length of stay, the quality of accommodations, and the number of people participating. Here are a few examples that focus on commercial recreation:

- *Gambling junkets*. Bargains for gamblers are available in package tours to casinos. Typical packages include bus fare or airfare, accommodations, a supply of poker chips, tickets to nightclub shows, and a discount coupon book. Big-spending gamblers are sometimes offered an all-expenses-paid trip, known as a *junket*, to a casino hotel in the Caribbean. Junkets are by invitation.
- *Theme park vacations*. Walt Disney World Travel Agency has a variety of package tours to Disney World. These include transfers between airport, hotel, and Disney World; accommodations; admission to Disney World; and additional sightseeing.
- *Adventure tours*. Many companies now offer guided rafting tours in Canada and the United States. A typical package might include a two-day white-water expedition, with all the necessary gear, an experienced guide, transportation to and from the river, one night's accommodations at the company campground, breakfast, and box lunches for two days.
- *History and art tours*. Sometimes a tour package is planned around a number of related attractions. Someone interested in English history and architecture might take a 15-day motorcoach tour of the castles of Great Britain. This would most likely include accommodations; most meals; visits to castles and great houses in England, Scotland, and Wales; and the services of a professional guide.

Channels of Distribution

Traditionally, the public sector has done little to promote and sell its recreation and leisure products. As the interest in travel and tourism grows, however, so does the public sector's awareness of the need to compete. Many museums, zoos, aquariums, and other attractions have established marketing and public relations departments that advertise, offering group discounts, annual memberships, and cooperative tie-ins. Admission and entrance fees are often included in tour packages. Kentucky's was the first state tourist department to acknowledge the importance of retail travel agencies as generators of visitors, and the first to pay commission to agencies for bookings in its state park system. More public-sector sites are now considering using mass distribution systems like Ticketron to sell their products.

With the growth in travel and tourism have come problems of overcrowding and congestion. To keep the crowds within bounds, public facilities will need to go to automated reservations systems. The days of first-come, first-served may soon be a thing of the past at many attractions.

The situation is also changing in the private sector, which consists of hundreds of large companies and thousands of mom-and-pop operations. In the past, few of the latter were willing to pay a commission to a travel agency or offer a discounted price to a tour operator. This, too, is changing as travel and tourism continues to grow and the number of visitors increases. The theme park, a comparatively new product, has had a tremendous impact on the methods of marketing and promoting commercial attractions.

Each year, more and more travellers make long trips to visit and enjoy new recreation and leisure attractions. As more public and private sector operators realize that their visitors are just as likely to come from across the nation—or from across the ocean—as from across town, these systems will develop methods to place their products in the channels of distribution.

CHECK YOUR PRODUCT KNOWLEDGE

1. What does a tour package based on a recreational attraction generally include?
2. Why are public sector recreation facilities taking a greater interest in promoting their products?
3. Why is the first-come, first-served system in our national parks likely to change?
4. What effect is the growth in tourism likely to have on mom-and-pop recreation operations?

CAREER OPPORTUNITIES

Public and commercial recreation and leisure systems offer interesting career opportunities. Many of these involve managing a recreational facility, such as a golf resort or nightclub. Others involve helping people enjoy their leisure time.

Public and commercial recreation systems employ more part-time and temporary workers than most components of the travel industry. These workers are needed to handle crowds during peak seasons or one-time events. The public sector also relies on volunteer workers to help with fundraising or routine clerical work, or to serve as guides. Part-time or volunteer work in the public sector can be an excellent introduction to a full-time career in recreation.

In 1991, 50 100 Canadians were employed in the adventure tourism and recreation sector, and 90 700 more were employed in the attractions sector.

Parks and Forests

National and provincial parks and forests employ many different kinds of specialists, such as botanists, ecologists, and wildlife biologists. However, the worker you are probably most familiar with is the park ranger.

Some park rangers work primarily with people, enforcing federal and provincial laws, issuing permits, providing information, and giving tours. Others work alone, patrolling isolated wilderness areas and keeping an eye on park conditions. Many park rangers are directly involved in environmental management, such as fighting fires and planning recreational facilities.

Park rangers need to be strong and healthy because they work outdoors in all kinds of weather. Job applicants are usually required to have a college or university degree, but high school graduates can sometimes become rangers. Eventually, park rangers can work their way up to supervisory and administrative jobs.

Museums

To fulfil their functions as collectors, educators, and entertainers, museums employ specialists in many different fields. A new and high-growth career is that of curator.

Museum curators locate, acquire, and display the works of art and artifacts that museums exhibit. They are also responsible for protecting, preserving, and repairing museum collections and for supervising assistants and technical experts. Clearly, the curator of any museum must be very highly educated.

Museums also employ conservators (who preserve the objects on display); taxidermists (who prepare animal specimens for exhibit); and designers (who plan and prepare the display cases and exhibits where objects are shown). Finally, there is the museum director, who administers the entire museum.

Zoos

Zoos require several types of highly educated administrators. A zoo director generally holds a doctorate in some branch of zoology. He or she supervises the staff, manages the budget, establishes priorities, and serves as the link between the government and the zoo board. Animal curators, who must have a Master's degree in zoology, decide on the best locations for the animals, study their behaviour, and encourage breeding. Zoo veterinarians, who require six years of post-university training, monitor the animals' diets, watch for parasites, and run routine tests.

Zoos also require a great many keepers. These workers feed, exercise, and clean up after the animals. The educational demands for keepers are less stringent, but the competition for places is much more intense.

Theme Parks

Theme parks provide thousands of job opportunities. Disney World, the single largest employer in Florida, has about 32 000 people on its payroll. It also offers a college internship program in which students work at the park while receiving classroom instruction.

Seasonal workers at theme parks are usually high school, college, or university students who learn their responsibilities on the job. They can be food service workers, game attendants, souvenir and gift shop clerks, guides, maintenance and sanitation workers, ride operators, or security personnel. These unskilled positions offer a behind-the-scenes view of the inner workings of a theme park. Many theme parks will not hire anyone for a professional staff position who has not at some time worked as a seasonal employee or an intern.

A variety of managerial or executive positions are available at a theme park—food service manager, ride superintendent, entertainment director, director of group sales, operations manager, and so on. People with degrees in tourism and hospitality management, food services, business management, liberal arts, merchandising, and other related areas can expect to find positions to match their training.

Since theme parks are constantly adding new features to attract visitors, creative people who can design show productions, exhibits, rides, festivals, and other attractions are needed. Also, with the increasing interest in participatory recreation, theme parks are seeking people who are skilled in recreational programming. Many participatory facilities are being designed with the needs of the challenged in mind, and this means there are strong employment opportunities for recreational therapists.

Stadiums

The growing number of stadiums (and stadium events) means employment opportunities for many people. Racetracks, arenas, and theatres provide similar opportunities.

Stadiums have a regular staff of office and maintenance personnel. One of the most important positions is that of groundskeeper. Groundskeepers mow the grass or maintain the artificial turf, plough and smooth baseball diamonds, and convert the playing field from one sport to another.

For stadium events, platoons of workers are brought in—ushers, security guards, concession workers, ticket takers, parking lot attendants. Many people are needed to sweep up after an event. Generally, part-time stadium workers are employed through an agency under contract to provide services to the stadium.

Overseeing all activities and personnel is the stadium manager, who also promotes the stadium's use and negotiates contracts with organizations that rent it. This position generally requires a degree in business administration or public relations, as well as experience in managing a small athletic field, or in helping to manage a large stadium.

Resorts

Ski resorts and tennis camps hire instructors to help guests improve their skills. Other resorts offering sports facilities may provide tennis pros and golf pros. In addition to demonstrating skill in a certain sport, these instructors need to know about equipment, physical fitness, and safety. A university degree is not necessary, but the instructor should have a record of varsity or professional experience. In fact, a well-known instructor lends prestige to a resort.

Hunting and fishing lodges employ guides to go on expeditions with guests. These guides must know the wildlife of the area, be familiar with the territory, and know conservation laws. Besides knowing the best places to catch trout or shoot deer, guides prepare campsites and help clean, skin, or preserve the animals.

Resorts also hire lifeguards, fitness instructors, and various attendants. Since resorts usually operate on a seasonal basis, these jobs are also seasonal. Instructors, guides, and recreation workers need to find alternative employment for the off-season.

Casinos

Many employees are needed in order for a casino to operate smoothly. A single game of craps, for instance, requires a crew of four. Besides knowing their game extremely well, dealers must be able to handle bets and payouts efficiently and keep the game moving. Dealers must also be courteous and pleasant.

All business operators worry about making profits. But, since casinos have very high operating expenses, the worries of casino operators are especially great. If the volume of gamblers is low or if too many high rollers hit hot streaks, the casino's profit margin may suffer.

Summary

- Recreation refers to the activities that people pursue in their leisure time.
- Recreational facilities and services can be public or commercial.
- The public sector includes government funded and operated facilities—primarily national and provincial parks, zoos and aquariums, museums, and fairs and festivals. These are not intended to make a profit, but to preserve the country's natural and historic heritage.
- The commercial sector includes recreational facilities operated by private businesses. Theme parks, stadiums, resorts, shopping malls, theatres, and casinos are generally part of the commercial sector. The purpose of these facilities is to make money for their owners.
- The public and commercial sectors often overlap and are often interdependent.
- National and provincial parks provide recreational areas for millions of Canadians. Both types of parks face problems of overcrowding and pollution.
- Museums serve as repositories for valued objects, centres of learning and culture, and places of recreation and entertainment. Museums reflect the culture, history, and resources of the nations in which they are found.
- Zoos and aquariums are museums that display live animals and marine life and provide education and entertainment for visitors.
- The theme park—for example, Disneyland—is the outstanding example of a commercial venture in recreation.
- Model cultures and restorations demonstrate how people of another time or culture lived.
- Spectator sports are an example of passive recreation. Recreational sports are an active form. Both provide the commercial sector with millions of dollars in profits.
- Megamalls, waterfront shopping complexes, and factory outlet centres have turned shopping into an important tourist activity.
- The travel industry is primarily interested in recreational opportunities that entice people to travel or that make a particular destination more appealing. The industry builds tour packages around recreational attractions and advertises them in the media.
- The public and commercial recreation and leisure systems provide interesting career opportunities, particularly in management. This component of the travel industry also requires thousands of part-time and temporary employees.

Key Terms

leisure
recreation
attraction
event

public recreation system
commercial recreation system
concession
interpretation
oceanarium
model culture
outfitter
megamall
pari-mutuel betting
junket

What Do You Think?

1. Should Canada's national parks be preserved mainly as wilderness sanctuaries or be developed as public playgrounds? Why?
2. With so many of Africa's people starving, should time and money be spent on trying to save the continent's wildlife? Why or why not?
3. Should gambling be legalized throughout Canada? Explain.
4. How does the economy of a country influence the development of commercial recreation?
5. Do Canadians depend too much on commercial recreation to fill their leisure time? Explain.

Dealing with Product

You have just taken over a private golf course and campground next to Shady Acres Provincial Park and the Big Bear Wildlife Preserve. A quick look through the financial records shows clearly that your property has a seasonality problem. Business is booming in the late spring, the summer, and the early autumn. However, there has been no business whatsoever from late fall to early spring, and no wonder—who wants to play golf in the snow or camp out when it's 20 degrees below zero?

What can you do? Is it best to shut down the park each Labour Day and reopen the following Victoria Day weekend? Is there any way to turn those snowstorms into money-making attractions and events? What about creating some cross-country ski trails? Would a snowmobile course be a good way to make money each winter? What other ideas can you think of?

Dealing with People

You have just been appointed the Director of Parks and Recreation in Yourtown. Unfortunately, the city newspaper does not share your enthusiasm for recreation and leisure. In fact, in today's editorial, the newspaper has charged that public parks and recreation programs are a waste of the taxpayers' money and a luxury that Yourtown can no longer afford. The editorial urges the city council to cut your budget by two-thirds and to spend the money on the school system and on expanding the police and fire departments. The mayor has just ordered you to prepare a speech defending your department, which you must deliver next Monday at the city council meeting. What will you say?

A DAY IN THE LIFE OF

A National Park Interpreter

I just spent the summer working as a student interpreter in Banff National Park. It was a wonderful experience. I got to work outdoors all day, make new friends, and meet people from all over the world who came to visit the park.

I was hired last spring and spent two weekends in May being trained for the job. The main part of my job was to be an "interpreter." An interpreter at a park does not work with languages but instead "interprets" the sights and sounds of the park for visitors. I gave many talks to groups of visitors about the park's history, wildlife, plant life, and geology. Some summer interns in Canada's national parks work in the visitors' centres answering questions about park attractions, giving directions, and taking reservations. Other interpreters do clerical work in the park offices. A few of us even dress up in pioneer costumes and give presentations about early settlers at the park's pioneer history centre.

My job really began in mid-June. At that time, my fellow student interpreters and I received another week's training. During the training session, our instructors took us around the park so we could become familiar with all of its attractions and facilities. After the training period, we were assigned to a specific area of the park and given room-mates for the summer.

I was assigned to a part of the park that is made up of a large area of Alpine meadows and woodland trails. Those of us assigned to this area lived in tent cabins. These are large, tent-sided, wooden platforms containing a wood stove for heat and cooking, cold running water, and electricity. Bath and toilet facilities were in a separate building.

Most days we woke up early and reported for work by 8 a.m. Some of us worked repairing trails, picnic areas, and other facilities, or taking people hiking. My favourite assignment was to lead groups of children on junior ranger hikes. Usually I would teach the children how to spot animals and animal signs, such as tracks and nests. I liked to show the children how animals survive by adapting to their environment.

At night the interpreters took turns leading the campfire talks. I enjoyed that activity because it reminded me of nights around the campfire at summer camp when I was younger. I've taken geology courses in university, so I sometimes gave presentations about the special geology of Banff and the surrounding mountains.

The national parks try to choose student interpreters who have had some part-time work experience and who are studying in a related field. They also look for students who have had some experience in public speaking—such as student teaching—because so many summer jobs involve giving talks and presentations to park visitors.

Usually the student interpreter gets paid a uniform allowance, a small salary, and, if needed, a travel allowance to get to the park and back home again. Being a summer interpreter is a very popular job. Not only is it fun, but we also gain valuable work experience.

Students learn how to manage natural resources and work with tourists. In addition, this job is a great way to get your foot in the door if you are aiming for a career in conservation management or tourism.

I made several good friends and had a lot of fun working as an intern at Banff. During our off-duty hours, we were able to hike, rock-climb, canoe, ride horses, swim, and camp throughout the park. All in all, working as a student interpreter there was the best summer vacation I ever had.

CHAPTER 9: The Recreation and Leisure System   Name: _____

WORKSHEET 9-1 Yourtown Recreation Facilities

List the recreational facilities and services found in Yourtown. Indicate which are public and which are commercial. If there is an entrance charge, note it.

Parks and forests

_____
_____
_____

Zoos and aquariums

_____
_____
_____

Theme parks, amusement parks

_____
_____
_____

Celebrity attractions

_____
_____
_____

Spectator sports

_____
_____
_____

Model cultures and historical restorations

_____
_____
_____

Museums

_____
_____
_____

Fairs and festivals

_____
_____
_____

Historic sites

_____
_____
_____

Industrial tours

_____
_____
_____

Recreational sports

_____
_____
_____

Live entertainment

_____
_____
_____

Gambling

_____
_____
_____

CHAPTER 9: The Recreation and Leisure System   Name: _____

WORKSHEET 9-2 National Park Service

Parks Canada administers scores of separate sites. For each of the kinds of national parks below, locate the ones closest to Yourtown (or your province). Describe the facilities offered. If two or more are equally close, choose the one you prefer.

National park   National monument
_____   _____
_____   _____
_____   _____

National preserve   National seashore
_____   _____
_____   _____
_____   _____

National lakeshore   National river or riverway
_____   _____
_____   _____
_____   _____

National historical park   National memorial
_____   _____
_____   _____
_____   _____

National recreational area   National parkway
_____   _____
_____   _____
_____   _____

National cemetery   Performing arts centre
_____   _____
_____   _____
_____   _____

CHAPTER 9: The Recreation and Leisure System   Name: _____

WORKSHEET 9-3 Recreation and Leisure Abroad

Governments and private companies throughout the world provide opportunities for recreation and leisure. The chart below lists just a few examples. Use travel guides and encyclopedias to help you locate and describe each attraction.

Legoland Park

Location: _____

Description: _____

_____

_____

_____

La Scala

Location: _____

Description: _____

_____

_____

_____

Serengeti Plain

Location: _____

Description: _____

_____

_____

_____

The Ginza

Location: _____

Description: _____

_____

_____

_____

The Hermitage

Location: _____

Description: _____

_____

_____

_____

Great Barrier Reef National Park

Location: _____

Description: _____

_____

_____

_____

Upper Canada Village

Location: _____

Description: _____

_____

_____

_____

Carnival

Location: _____

Description: _____

_____

_____

_____

CHAPTER 9: The Recreation and Leisure System   Name: _____

WORKSHEET 9-4 Recreational Vehicles

You have read something about how the popularity of recreational vehicles has affected the travel industry. Read some recent newspaper and travel magazine articles to get more specific information.

Statistics (for example, number of RVs owned by individuals, cost of an average RV, number of RVs rented yearly)

Advantages (for example, freedom of travel)

Drawbacks (for example, awkward to drive and park in cities)

Travel components that have benefited (for example, campgrounds)

Travel components that have suffered (for example, motels, restaurants)

Modifications that have been made in travel components (for example, campgrounds provide electricity, water, sewer access; RV rentals)

Outlook for the future (for example, more or fewer, cheaper or more expensive)

Factors that determine the future (for example, price of gas, condition of highways)

CHAPTER 10

Tours and Charters

"Travelling is almost like talking with men of other centuries."

René Descartes

OBJECTIVES

When you have completed this chapter, you should be able to do the following:

- Describe the development of the package tour.
- List the components of a package tour.
- Discuss the role of the tour operator.
- Summarize the benefits of package travel.
- Distinguish between independent, hosted, and escorted tours.
- Classify tours according to destination and purpose.
- Explain why age is an important factor in defining the traveller.
- Describe the work of a tour manager.
- Explain how tours are regulated.
- Show how a package tour is put together.
- Give reasons for the popularity of charter travel.
- Distinguish between private and public charters.
- Diagram the distribution channels of the tour industry.
- List the career opportunities in the package tour industry.

It's one thing to decide to go on a tour, but quite another to organize the trip. Many people don't have the time or the inclination to plan a tour for themselves. They prefer to have somebody else make the decisions and the arrangements. For this reason, among others, the tour package came into being. Tour packages offer travellers prearranged transportation, accommodations, meals, and other vacation preparations—all at a predetermined price. They take some of the aggravation out of travel and usually provide significant cost savings as well.

Canadians are turning on to package tours in a big way. Today, the package tour industry is one of the fastest growing segments of the travel industry. In this chapter, you'll learn about the many different kinds of tours, discover some reasons for their popularity, and read about the career opportunities that the package tour industry presents.

A BRIEF HISTORY OF THE PACKAGE TOUR

As you have learned, the concept of travel is an ancient one. But package travel, which combines arrangements for transportation, accommodations, sightseeing, and so on, is a comparatively recent development. We can trace its origins to the grand tour. This extended journey through continental Europe was traditionally undertaken by the sons (and later the daughters) of the British aristocracy during the 17th and 18th centuries.

The primary purpose of the grand tour was to educate. Indeed, no education was considered complete without it. While he was abroad, the young nobleman was expected to enrich his knowledge of the classical past, acquire antiques and works of art, learn foreign languages, and develop socially desirable skills and manners. France and Italy—the cities of Paris, Rome, and Naples in particular—were the main destinations. Some itineraries also included stays in Germany, the Low Countries, Austria, and Switzerland.

Travel through Europe by stagecoach and riverboat was dangerous and arduous, and the grand tour could last as long as three years. (By contrast, a comparable modern tour of Europe takes about three weeks.) There were no travel agencies, tour operators, or tour escorts in those days. The individual traveller might carry letters of introduction to aristocratic European families, who would provide him with lodging and entertainment. But for the most part, he was on his own.

The development of railways and hotels in the 19th century encouraged more middle-class travellers to embark on tours of Europe. With this middle-class "invasion" came a change in the reasons for foreign travel. The emphasis moved away from education and culture and toward recreation and pleasure. This was the beginning of mass tourism.

The Pioneer of the Package Tour

Thomas Cook, a Baptist missionary and an Englishman, invented the organized package tour. In 1841, he chartered a train to carry 570 people to a temperance meeting in Leicester. This first tour featured a number of components that were to become standard for later package tours: transportation (a 40-mile round-trip rail journey); meals (a picnic lunch and afternoon tea); entertainment (a band playing hymns); an event (the temperance meeting); and the services of a tour escort (Cook himself).

The success of this and subsequent excursions encouraged Cook to form the world's first travel agency and to branch out into overseas travel. In 1856, Cook led the first conducted grand tour of Europe. By the late 1860s, his agency was offering Nile cruises, rail trips to India, and guided tours of Canada and the United States. Cook also invented the travel brochure, the passenger itinerary, and the travel voucher.

The Evolution of Tour Formats

While personally conducted group tours were an important service offered by early travel agencies, the bulk of their business involved making travel and hotel arrangements for independent travellers. An American planning a grand tour of Europe, for example, would consult a travel agent to arrange his or her personalized itinerary. The travel agent would then organize the traveller's steamship passage across the Atlantic, rail travel within Europe, accommodations, and sightseeing. Such custom-made tours—known either as **foreign independent tours (FITs)** or **domestic independent tours (DITs)**—were the norm for the vast majority of vacation travellers right up until the early 1960s.

The breakthrough for the prearranged package tour arrived with the jet age in 1958. Transatlantic crossing times were cut to seven hours (from 18 hours by propeller aircraft, or four days by ocean liner). Time savings, together with increased prosperity and cheaper airfares, brought overseas travel within reach of ordinary working Canadians. International travel was no longer exclusively for the wealthy few.

Tour operators developed a variety of packages to cater to the new class of travellers. The packages offered bargain prices, convenience, and reliability. Taking advantage of charters, reduced excursion fares, and all-inclusive tour packages, the number of North Americans visiting Europe rose from under 700 000 in 1958 to almost 7 million in 1989. In 1991, there were 1.25 million person-trips by Canadians to Europe. About half visited continental Europe only, one-third visited the United Kingdom only, and about one-sixth visited both the United Kingdom and continental Europe.

Not only have package tours become more accessible in the jet age; they have also become more flexible in terms of length. In the days when overseas travel entailed a journey by steamship, tours were necessarily longer, commonly lasting two or three months. A few tour operators still offer lengthy packages: Globus–Gateway, for example, offers a 38-day "Super European." But most have scaled down their multi-nation European tours to around 22 days (which is about as much vacation time as most Canadians enjoy). As a result, tours are less leisurely than they used to be, and less time is spent at each destination. Shorter tours, featuring only two or three destinations, have also been developed.

CHECK YOUR PRODUCT KNOWLEDGE

1. What was the grand tour?
2. What role did Thomas Cook play in the history of tourism?
3. What effect did the jet airplane have on the package tour?

THE MODERN TOUR

A **package tour** consists of several travel components provided by different suppliers. These are combined by the tour company and then sold to the consumer as a single product at a single price. The package tour typically includes two or more of the following components:

- One or more forms of transportation (including fly/drive, fly/cruise, motorcoach tour, and rail tour packages).
- Accommodations.
- Meals.
- Attractions and events (including sightseeing and admission to natural and commercial attractions, entertainment, recreation, and a variety of special events).
- Extras (including transfers and baggage handling, tips and taxes, the services of a professional tour manager and tour guides, travel bags, and discount coupons for restaurants and shops).

Package tours vary in complexity from the **two-component package** (for example, air transportation and limited sightseeing, or hotel accommodations and rental car) to the **multicomponent**, all-inclusive package. With the popular **all-inclusive package**, the traveller pays one price that covers just about all trip expenses, including transportation, accommodations, meals, sightseeing, and so on. When a tour involves air travel to the destination or point of departure, the components are usually separated into air arrangements and land arrangements. Land arrangements include surface transportation while on the tour, accommodations, meals, sightseeing, and other activities. Some tour companies quote an all-inclusive price for both air and land arrangements. Others quote air and land rates separately. When the rates are given separately, clients can opt to buy just the land package and make their own arrangements to get to the starting point of the tour.

The Role of the Tour Operator

A tour operator or tour wholesaler contracts with hotels, transportation companies, and other suppliers to create a tour package to sell to the consumer. By buying hotel bednights, airline seats, and admission tickets in bulk, the tour operator can get lower rates than would be offered to an individual traveller. The savings are passed on to the consumer (after allowance for business overheads, profit, and any commission to the seller).

The terms tour operator and tour wholesaler are often used interchangeably, although the former more commonly sells packages directly to the consumer, while the latter sells the package through a retail travel agency. For the purposes of this discussion, we will use the general term tour operator throughout.

There are four different categories of tour operators. The first is the independent tour operator. This can be an individual or a multinational corporation. American Express is an example of the latter. The second category is the travel agency that functions as a tour operator. Such an agency packages tours, which it sells to its clients or wholesales to other travel agencies. In-house tour operators make up the third category. These are owned and operated by air carriers (Canadian Holidays, a wholly owned subsidiary of PWA Corporation; Air Canada Vacations; United Airlines; and Qantas are examples). The fourth category consists of travel clubs and incentive travel companies, which do not sell their products to the public.

All tour operators take risks when they put together a package tour. They must make block reservations far in advance, with no guarantee that their tours will sell in the competitive market. (In reality, many will not.) Suppliers are willing to reserve their products for the tour operator if they are given a deposit. However, the percentage of the deposit that will be refunded decreases as the departure time nears.

Canadian tour operators will have different types of tours for the different seasons: fall foliage tours in the autumn; tours to Canadian ski destinations, as well as fun-in-the-sun tours, in the winter; country music excursions to Nashville and Branson in the spring; and eco-tours in the summer.

The Popularity of Tours

The package tour industry is one of the fastest growing sectors of the travel industry. Package tours represent an important share of domestic tourism and an even more significant portion of overseas tourism. Why have package tours become so popular? The main reason is that they offer a variety of practical benefits that independent travel cannot provide.

Known Costs Because all package tours are prepaid, the client can fairly accurately calculate the total cost of the tour in advance. This is especially true with an all-inclusive package. Accommodations, meals, sightseeing, entertainment, transfers, and taxes will all have been prepaid before departure. The only additional expense, therefore, is for personal items such as souvenirs, gifts, and drinks.

Bargain Prices The single greatest attraction of the package tour is its relatively low cost. Because they buy in bulk from suppliers, tour operators can offer packages at a much lower price than the sum of the individual components bought separately. Just as an institutional-sized can of beans costs less per ounce than a single-serving can, so a block reservation of hotel rooms costs less per room than a single room reservation. Tour operators who provide a guaranteed high volume of bookings to a hotel chain can pay as little as 50 percent of the standard rack rate. Even after the markup and the standard (10 percent) travel agent commission, the room is still less expensive than it would be for an individual. Volume discounts allow similar savings on other components of the package.

Guaranteed Arrangements When travellers buy a package, they are also buying peace of mind. Independent travellers may have to cope with unpleasant surprises en route, such as being bumped off a flight or finding that a hotel has no record of their reservation. A package tour takes the anxiety out of travelling, because all arrangements have been made in advance by the tour operator. In addition, group

ILLUSTRATION 10-1

Tours of the great vinyards of France can be an educational as well as an aesthetic experience (Pauillac, France).
SOURCE: Karen O'Neill

reservations are invariably honoured, because suppliers rely heavily on the business generated by tour operators.

Guaranteed Entrance It is often easier to get into a special event as a member of a tour than as an individual. This is because tour operators make block ticket purchases to ensure entrance to tour participants. For example, it's almost impossible to attend the Oberammergau Passion Play, staged every ten years in Germany, unless you are part of a tour. There are even some countries that will permit access to certain places only to visitors who are part of a tour group.

Tried-and-True Sightseeing Tour operators have the experience to know which attractions are worth a special trip. They know which local nightspots offer the best entertainment, and which restaurants can be recommended. Unlike the individual traveller, tour members don't have to worry about winding up at a second-rate museum or at a restaurant with inedible food.

Time Savings On a package tour, the traveller doesn't have to spend time looking for accommodations, arranging transfers, or getting tickets for a show. Group travel can also lead to time savings at theatres and other attractions. Tour participants often don't have to wait in line; they can enter and exit more easily than individuals.

CHECK YOUR PRODUCT KNOWLEDGE

1. What are the typical components of a package tour?
2. What is meant by the term land arrangements?
3. What are the benefits of package tours over independent travel?
4. Why are tour operators able to offer reduced prices for tour components?

TOURS, TOURS, TOURS

The common image of a package tour is of a group of senior citizens travelling through Europe aboard a motorcoach under the watchful eye of a uniformed tour escort. Such tours do indeed exist, but recent years have seen a rapid increase in the number and variety of tours to virtually every corner of the world.

Wholesalers have developed tours to fulfil the needs of an increasingly sophisticated travelling public. They cater both to the mass market and to specific segments of that market. There are tours tailored to attract young singles, families, middle-aged couples, senior citizens, and physically challenged people. Some tours are designed for people who prefer to relax on their vacation, while others cater to those who want to find adventure, or to learn as they travel. There are one-day sightseeing tours, weekend escape packages, two-week special-interest tours, and one-month cultural packages. A sample package tour is shown in Figure 10-1.

People can sign up for all-inclusive tours or for independent tours, for leisurely tours or fast-paced tours, for budget tours or deluxe tours. These tours are not limited to tourists. Travellers visiting friends and relatives (VFR), for example, can purchase a package for the bargain price and then use only part of it, such as the airfare and the car. In such cases, the tour is called a "throwaway."

All tours can be categorized by the package format, by destination, or by purpose.

Basic Package Formats

Deciding to go on a package tour is just the beginning. The traveller then has to decide what kind of package he or she wants. Tour packages come in many different formats.

Independent The independent package tour is the least structured of all formats. It offers participants the benefits of package savings but allows them the flexibility and freedom of travelling alone. An independent package features a minimum of components. Typically, it includes hotel accommodations as well as one other land arrangement (for example, round-trip transfers, use of a rental car, a daily continental breakfast, or a half-day sightseeing tour).

When booking an independent tour, participants can choose their departure and return dates. They can also choose from a variety of different-priced hotels, and extend their stay by adding a fixed extra-night rate for each additional night. A fly/drive package is a good example of an independent tour. Popular destinations for independent tours include resort areas (for example, Hawaii and Cancun). Canadian Holidays featured a one-night package tour to see a Blue Jays game that involved flying to Toronto on Canadian Airlines and staying in a room overlooking the playing field at the Skydome Hotel.

Independent tours should not be confused with foreign independent tours (FITs) and domestic independent tours (DITs), which are custom-made for clients by travel agencies. FITs and DITs have become less common in recent years because they are much more expensive than package tours and far more time-consuming for the travel agent.

Hosted On a hosted tour, a host is on hand at the hotel to arrange optional excursions, answer questions, and help people plan their free time. The host is not an escort and does not accompany the group on sightseeing tours or on overland journeys. If the tour visits more than one destination, a different host will be available at each hotel on the itinerary.

Hosted tours are ideal for vacationers who wish to strike a balance between organized events and free time. Aside

CHAPTER 10: Tours and Charters

from scheduled sightseeing and entertainment, participants are free to arrange their time as they please. As with independent tours, they have the freedom to choose their departure date, level of accommodations, and length of stay.

Escorted The escorted tour is the most structured of all formats. It offers participants accommodations at a number of destinations, as well as meals, point-to-point transportation, and a full program of organized activities. A professional tour manager or escort accompanies the group for the duration of the tour. In recent years, there has been a rise in the number of escorted tours, partly because of an increase in the number of tours to Eastern European countries. On these tours, participants need a bilingual escort to ease the language problem.

Escorted tours appeal to travellers who want their entire vacation to be planned in advance. For this privilege, they sacrifice the flexibility and independence that travellers on other tours enjoy. Participants travel as a group at all times, and have limited free time to branch out on their own. They must begin and end the tour according to schedule and stay in the hotels selected by the tour operator. The 8 days/7 nights Canadian Mountain Discovery tour (a fly/motorcoach tour) is an example of an escorted tour.

Special Tour Formats There are a number of types of packages that are not available to the general public:

- *Incentive tours* are offered by companies as a reward to employees for achieving corporate objectives, such as sales targets.
- *Convention tours* are packaged for sale to members of an association or group attending gatherings such as conventions, conferences, exhibitions, or trade shows.
- *Special-interest group tours* are arranged for clubs, societies, and organizations whose members share a common interest such as photography, bird-watching, or opera.

All three special tour formats are developed jointly by the tour operator, the travel agent, and the company, association, or club. Tours designed primarily for the business or professional traveller are discussed in greater detail in Chapter 12.

Incoming Tours An incoming tour is one that originates in a foreign country and has Canada as its destination. The product is essentially the same as an outgoing tour, but with the itinerary reversed (for example, Tokyo–Banff–Tokyo instead of Banff–Tokyo–Banff). Foreign visitors are of great importance to Canada (as they are to other nations). They generate jobs and increase incomes and tax revenues.

Algonquin Park

Seven-Day Canoe Trips

7 Days/7 Nights

MAY 28 – JUN 04
JUN 04 – JUN 11
JUN 11 – JUN 18
JUN 18 – JUN 25
JUN 25 – JUL 02
JUL 02 – JUL 09
JUL 09 – JUL 16
JUL 16 – JUL 23
JUL 23 – JUL 30
JUL 30 – AUG 06
AUG 06 – AUG 13
AUG 13 – AUG 20
AUG 20 – AUG 27
AUG 27 – SEP 03
SEP 03 – SEP 10
SEP 10 – SEP 17
SEP 17 – SEP 24

Departs 7pm Saturdays Returns 7pm Saturdays

Mid Week Canoe Trips

5 Days/4 Nights

JUNE 20 – JUNE 24
AUG 22 – AUG 26
SEP 19 – SEP 23

Departs 10 am Mondays Returns 7pm Fridays

5-Day "Canada Day Weekend" Canoe Trip

5 Days/4 Nights

JUNE 29 – JULY 03

Departs 7 pm Wednesday
Returns 10 pm Sunday

Specialty Canoe Trips

Canoe Trips for Students

7 Days/7 Nights

MAY 07 – MAY 14
AUG 20 – AUG 27

Departs 7pm Saturdays Returns 7pm Saturdays

White Water Canoe Trips

White Water Workshops/Magnetawan River

2 Days/2 Nights

MAY 06 – MAY 08
MAY 13 – MAY 15
MAY 27 – MAY 29

Departs 7pm Fridays Returns 9:30 pm Sundays

3 Days/3 Nights

MAY 20 – MAY 23

Departs 7pm Friday Returns 9:30 pm Monday

French River by Voyageur Canoe

5 Days/4 Nights

MAY 19 – MAY 23
JUN 29 – JUL 03
JUL 20 – JUL 24
JUL 27 – AUG 01
AUG 17 – AUG 21
SEP 01 – SEP 05

Departs 7am on the Wednesday or Thursday
Returns 7pm on the Sunday or Monday

Demoine River

7 Days/7 Nights

JUN 25 – JUL 02
JUL 02 – JUL 09
JUL 09 – JUL 16

Departs 7pm Saturdays Returns 7pm Saturdays

Nahanni River

Raft Trips from Virginia Falls

9 Days/8 Nights

JUL 21 – JUL 29
AUG 04 – AUG 12

12 Days/11 Nights

JUL 04 – JUL 15
AUG 15 – AUG 26

Canoe Trips from Rabbit Kettle Lake (17')

14 Days/13 Nights

JUL 04 – JUL 17
JUL 18 – JUL 31
AUG 01 – AUG 14
AUG 15 – AUG 28

Canoe Trip from the Moose Ponds

21 Days/20 Nights

JUL 02 – JUL 22

Raft Trip from the Moose Ponds

23 Days/22 Nights

JUN 30 – JUL 22

INCLUDED IN ALL SCHEDULED TRIPS

Return transportation from Toronto, all meals while on trip or at base camp, complete equipment outfitting (except sleeping bag), the services of an experienced guide, and use of base camp facilities. The Dumoine River trip also includes a bush flight. Sleeping bags are available for rental.

All trips **DO NOT INCLUDE** personal clothing and gear (a detailed list is forwarded upon registration), hotels, restaurant meals during transportation to and from base camp, and coverage for additional expenses due to safety delays or emergency evacuation, or travel to trip rendezvous in Toronto. Prices do not include the 7% Goods and Services Tax. Trip participants from outside of Canada are eligible for a partial refund of this tax.

FOR NAHANNI RIVER TRIPS INCLUDED IN ALL SCHEDULED TRIPS

Return transportation from Fort Simpson, all meals while out on trip, complete equipment outfitting (except sleeping bag), and the services of a professional guide. A bush flight is also included. The 14 and 21-day Nahanni trips include one night's bed and breakfast accommodation at Blackstone Landing.

All trips **DO NOT INCLUDE** personal clothing and gear (a detailed list is forwarded upon registration), hotels, restaurant meals during transportation to and from the start of the trip, coverage for additional expenses due to safety delays or emergency evacuation, or travel to trip rendezvous in Fort Simpson. Prices do not include the 7% Goods and Services Tax. Trip participants from outside of Canada are eligible for a partial refund of this tax.

FIGURE 10-1

Sample Tours from Canadian Wilderness Trips.

SOURCE: Courtesy Canadian Wilderness Trips

Tours Defined by Destination

Many tours are aimed at providing travellers with the general flavour of particular destinations. This is especially true of escorted tours that cover several countries in a short time. Grand tours of Europe are a prime example—some of them visit 9 countries in 17 days. When tourists spend a maximum of three days in any one country, they can only glimpse the major highlights.

Area tours allow more time in each country, although there is little opportunity for any in-depth appreciation. A 15-day tour of Scandinavia, for example, might include four nights in Denmark, five in Sweden, and five in Norway, with two nights in each capital. Other popular destinations for area tours are Alpine Europe and the British Isles.

Single-country tours are more focused, and enable the traveller to see and do much more than is possible on an area tour. England, France, Italy, Germany, Spain, Israel, Japan, New Zealand, and countless other countries all lend themselves to this kind of tour. Some single-country tours concentrate on a particular area. There are, for example, eight- and ten-day tours of Shakespeare country, of the French château country, and of the Canadian Rockies.

Tours to one or two cities are the most focused of all packages. These are usually independent or hosted. Two-city tours are ideal for travellers who do not want to be tied to a single destination. Equal time is usually spent in each city, with transportation between the two included in the price of the package. The two cities can be in the same country (for example, Rome and Florence, Montreal and Quebec City), or in different countries (for example, London and Paris, Bangkok and Hong Kong). The two-country combination allows tourists to experience more than one culture.

Travellers who really want to get to know their destination might choose a single-city tour. This can be a four-day sightseeing tour, or a more extended visit focusing on the unique attractions of a particular destination (for example, theatre in London or New York, shopping in Hong Kong, art museums in Paris, or opera in Milan).

Tours Defined by Purpose

While the destination itself is often the strongest selling point, other tours are popular because they focus on a specific type of activity. The activity can be as strenuous as white-water rafting or as relaxing as lying on a beach. Tour operators have developed packages to satisfy a wide variety of motivations, needs, and expectations (MNEs).

Relaxation Many people want nothing more from a vacation than the chance to relax, with plenty of sun, a sandy beach, good food, and perhaps some nightly entertainment. Such stay-put resort vacations are available in many parts of the world (for example, the Caribbean, Hawaii, Mexico, and the Mediterranean). These vacations may be combined with some sports and recreation (as in a Club Med package), or shopping, or limited sightseeing. But the main purpose is relaxation.

Scenic Tours for people who want to enjoy spectacular scenery while they are away from home exist in great variety. Most involve a fair amount of travelling, either by motorcoach (New England fall foliage packages, tours throughout Europe), train (trans-Canada packages, national parks of the Canadian West), or ship (Alaska's Inside Passage, Rhine River cruises). They are almost always escorted trips.

Learning Every tour provides a learning experience, but here we refer specifically to those tours taken by people travelling because of their interest in culture, history, science, or education. Some tour operators package these products under the generic term "intelligent travel." Cultural tours come in various formats. Typically, they involve a structured program of visits to museums and art galleries, or attendance at theatre productions, music festivals, and so on. Individual travellers can also arrange to stay with host families, thereby gaining a greater understanding and appreciation of the cultures they experience. Historical tours can entail participation in an archaeological dig or a study of ancient civilizations. Members of a scientific tour might take part in a geological expedition or study the botany of a particular region. Historical and scientific tours usually feature guest lecturers and other experts. The distinction between historical or scientific tours and educational tours is often hazy, but the latter generally focus more on classroom than on field study. All educational tours offer travellers personal enrichment. As an additional bonus, some offer the opportunity to earn college credits.

Religious and Ethnic The pilgrimage has been an important reason for travel since ancient times. Tour operators continue to develop packages to holy sites for members of different religions. Ethnic travel is a related category, covering Canadians who visit the country from which their parents or grandparents came. Recent examples of ethnic travel include black Americans going to West Africa and Italian Canadians visiting Italy.

Adventure Travellers seeking adventure are a rapidly growing segment of the market. Tour operators such as Mountain Travel, Sobek's International Explorers Society, and Society Expeditions Cruises offer a staggering array of escorted packages to exotic destinations. Here's a small sampling of the adventure tours offered:

- Mountaineering in the Himalayas.
- Camel expeditions in the Sahara.
- Dogsledding in the Northwest Territories.
- Trekking in Nepal.
- African safaris.

PROFILE

Brewster Transportation and Tours

Written by Don MacLaurin

In the 1890s, visitors to Banff would step off the Canadian Pacific train, load a horse-drawn conveyance with steamer trunks, and go to the Banff Springs Hotel, the new destination for royalty and wealthy adventurers. A three- or four-week stay was the norm. Activities included horseback riding, fishing, hiking, and mountain climbing in a tangled wilderness of peaks, valleys, and glaciers. Around this time, two young brothers, Jim and Bill Brewster, were appointed by the Banff Springs Hotel to guide guests through the wilderness and cater to their every whim.

Canadian Pacific brought the visitors to Banff; the local people, including the Brewsters, peddled their wares once the guests arrived. By the early 1900s, the Brewster brothers had the concession to transport the visitors from the train station to the hotel. This meant they could solicit visitors directly upon arrival and sell their other services: pack trips, fishing expeditions, and sightseeing by horse-drawn "tally-hos" on the few developed roads.

By the 1920s, these two young entrepreneurs were operating much more than a local outfitting service. They now owned the Mount Royal Hotel and a fleet of touring cars. No longer did they depend solely on CP trains and hotels for a customer base. Around this time, the Brewsters began promoting the Canadian Rockies to travellers everywhere in the world.

By the late 1920s, the Brewster company had joined the Gray Line Association, which was synonymous with sightseeing in North America. For the next four decades, members of the Brewster family moved to Chicago, Florida, New York, and California in the off-season to promote their services for the coming summer season. They held receptions and dinners and made sales calls throughout the United States and Canada until, like CP Hotels, they were synonymous with the Rockies.

By the mid-1960s, Brewster's marketing efforts had extended beyond Canada. In 1968, Don Warner, the reservations manager, made the first sales trip to Australia. By 1990 over 5000 Australians and New Zealanders had participated in Brewster's Royal Glacier Tour. In 1973, Brewster joined Canadian Pacific Airlines and CP Hotels in their sales efforts in Japan. By 1994, over 120 000 Japanese visitors a year were riding Brewster's Columbia Icefield Snocoaches in Jasper National Park. That same year, Brewster Transportation & Tours provided tourism services to over 600 000 visitors to western Canada.

Brewster's Royal Glacier Tour program, created in conjunction with the Gray Line Sightseeing program, offered half-day and full-day sightseeing tours in the Banff, Lake Louise, Jasper, and Calgary areas. This sightseeing program was a perfect opportunity to create independent package tour products by adding hotel accommodation, meals, and various attractions. Added to the Banff–Lake Louise–Jasper–Calgary network were the Royal Glacier Tour, a two-day tour between Banff and Vancouver with an overnight stop at Lac Le Jeune resort near Kamloops, and the Royal Yellowhead Tour, a one-day tour between Jasper and Lac Le Jeune.

All packages are designed for individuals, but offer the economy of travelling with a group. These tours are not escorted, but Brewster's excellent drivers act as guides on all motorcoach segments in the Rockies.

To handle the intricacies of the Royal Glacier Tour program, Brewster has had a special customized computer program designed. In addition to handling reservations, it generates hotel, bus, and train space inventories, passenger lists, and itineraries, as well as various statistical reports to assist with marketing and sales analysis.

Brewster now spends more than $1.5 million annually on sales and marketing for its various services: Gray Line Sightseeing, Brewster's Charter Coach, Brewster Group Tours, Great Canadian Train Vacations/Royal Glacier Independent Package Tours, The Columbia Icefield Snocoach Tours, The Mount Royal Hotel, and the Mount Norquay ski area. The company makes sales calls around the world, and will attend over 70 travel trade shows in 1994, in Australia, New Zealand, Japan, Korea, Great Britain, the United States, Canada, and continental Europe.

Brewster prints over 1.2 million brochures every year to distribute through travel agents, airlines, and wholesalers worldwide. Much of its travel, trade, and consumer advertising around the world is done in conjunction with airlines, other tour operations selling Brewster products, and wholesalers in Great Britain, Australia, New Zealand, Japan, and the United States. Brewster's marketing and sales team, headed by Jim Fraser, is on the road for six to eight months each year, from September to May. Also, every year, Brewster's product managers meet the company's heavy trade show commitments.

- Horseback riding in the Canadian Rockies.
- Hot-air ballooning over Kenyan game preserves.
- Amazon jungle expeditions.
- River rafting in Alaska.

The selection is likely to grow larger as travellers continue to seek something new and exciting.

Soft Adventure This type of tour, which is growing in popularity, allows people to experience adventure travel without discomfort or personal risk. The degree of comfort may vary, for example, some soft adventure tours include lodge accommodation rather than camping, and gourmet food instead of camp food, and walking without carrying any gear. There are also tours that involve walking from town to town, spending nights at different bed-and-breakfasts.

Eco-tourism The ecology movement has not gone unnoticed by the tour industry. Eco-tourism, or nature tourism, is one of the fastest growing sectors in tourism. Tours that take the vacationer to observe unusual ecological systems, and endangered species in their natural habitat, are becoming quite popular. Tourists are flocking to such diverse areas as the lush Amazon rainforest, the Annapurna Massif of Nepal, and Graham Land in Antarctica. Eco-tourists can view harp seals in Canada, white heron colonies in New Zealand, and hawk's-bill turtles on Antigua. There is a 4 days/3 nights Seal Watching Getaway tour to Prince Edward Island.

Sports and Recreation The sports and recreation market has been strong since the early days of package tours and has diversified in recent years. For those who want an active vacation, there are golf, tennis, and ski packages, as well as organized biking and walking tours. There is a 5 days/4 nights Fundy Island Biking Explorer tour of Grand Manan, Deer, and Campobello islands in the Bay of Fundy out of Saint John. Recreational travel can also mean a visit to a theme park (for example, Disney World), or a gambling package (Las Vegas, Atlantic City). The recreational activity can be the sole purpose for the trip, or it can be combined with other features, such as sightseeing, relaxation, or study.

Spectator sports packages feature a special sporting event as the main attraction. Examples include the Grey Cup, the Olympics, the World Series, the Super Bowl, the Kentucky Derby, the Indy 500, and the Masters golf tournament. (Similar tours are also designed around other types of special events, including New Orleans's Mardi Gras, Munich's Oktoberfest, and the Cannes Film Festival.)

Special-Interest Tours These tours have great potential. Tour operators have packaged a wealth of different tours for groups sharing common interests. For example, there are chocolate lovers' tours of Switzerland, bird-watching tours of China, and, in the United States, garden tours of the American South. Some enthusiasts travel with a preformed group, club, or organization. Others buy a special-interest package as individuals.

Weekend Canadians are taking shorter vacations, and taking them more often. This means that cut-price weekend packages are becoming increasingly popular. These can be family packages (with free accommodations for children); second honeymoon packages; recreational, educational, or special interest packages; or theme weekends (for example, a murder mystery package). The common denominator is the "quick fix" escape from the daily routine.

Special Needs Wheelchair-bound travellers clearly have needs different from those of more mobile travellers. Hotels and public buildings must be fitted with ramps, wide doorways, and other features that reduce architectural obstacles. Physically challenged people require specially equipped guest rooms and hydraulic lifts. Special arrangements must also be made for developmentally challenged people and for those whose hearing or sight is impaired. Tour operators have only recently begun to tailor packages for this potentially large market. Those catering exclusively to physically challenged people include Flying Wheels Tours, Evergreen Travel, and New Horizons.

Defining the Traveller

Tour operators develop packages by determining where people want to go (destination) and what they want to do when they get there (purpose). In addition, tours must be designed to fit the MNEs of different kinds of travellers. We can identify a number of basic MNEs:

- Security. Many people do not feel confident about travelling alone—especially overseas, where the language and customs may be unfamiliar. An escorted tour, with an experienced tour manager at the helm, offers these travellers the security that independent tours lack.
- Companionship. Some people are perfectly happy travelling on their own; other people prefer the companion-

ILLUSTRATION 10-2
Ecotours that take vacationers to observe endangered wildlife are becoming popular. Here is whale watching off the coast of Nova Scotia.
SOURCE Tourism Nova Scotia

CHAPTER 10: Tours and Charters   245

ILLUSTRATION 10-3
Public-sector organizations, such as the New York Convention and Visitors Bureau, promote their destinations to tour operators.
SOURCE NY Convention and Visitors Bureau

packages designed with children's interests in mind, such as visits to amusement parks and zoos. Mature travellers tend to have more money and can afford to travel in style. If they are experienced travellers, they may be keen to explore new and exotic places. Senior citizens traditionally favour worry-free tours conducted at a leisurely pace and with plenty of scheduled activities.

Flexibility and Pacing Every tour must be flexible enough to suit the tastes of individual travellers. On a general-interest tour of the capitals of Europe, for example, it would be unwise to schedule three consecutive nights at the opera. Opera lovers might be delighted, but others will want more varied entertainment. Meals have to be varied, too. Some group members may want to experience the exotic local cuisine at every stop. Others would flinch in horror at the sight of a plate of frog legs and will expect more familiar food.

Balance is the key word here. To keep everyone happy, the package must offer a variety of entertainment and a choice of meals. It must also strike a balance between scheduled activities and free time. Not all travellers want their every waking hour filled with organized activities. Many appreciate an occasional quiet night at a hotel, as well as free time for relaxation, sightseeing at leisure, and so on.

The pace of the tour is another consideration. Many tours stop at a different destination virtually every night. This may look appealing in the brochure, but, in reality, a succession of long days on the road can be exhausting, especially for older travellers. A good tour operator will try to schedule a day without travel after a particularly long journey, or after a tiring initial flight.

ship that group tours offer. They may want to share experiences with others on the tour, or they may hope to form long-lasting friendships.
- *Status*. Being first on the block to visit China or some other exotic destination can be an important motivation for travel.
- *Romance*. For many vacationers, "Love Boat" cruises, Club Med singles' packages, and honeymoon packages fulfil a desire for romance.

The Traveller's Age While some tours are designed for people of all ages, others are tailored to specific age groups:

- students
- youths
- families
- mature people
- senior citizens

Each market has its own particular MNEs. Cost is likely to be a major consideration for students. Young people typically demand action, adventure, and entertainment, with free time to go off on their own. Families are attracted to

Price A tour is a product, just like a television set or any other commodity. Not everyone can afford a deluxe colour television with wide screen and stereophonic sound. Similarly, the deluxe, all-inclusive tour package is beyond many people's budgets. Tour operators must offer a range of products at a range of prices. American Express, for example, has European tour packages in four price categories—freelance, value, select, and priceless. Itineraries are often similar in each category, but the number of features included and level of accommodations vary.

CHECK YOUR PRODUCT KNOWLEDGE

1. What is the difference between a hosted tour and an escorted tour?
2. What is an area tour? Give examples of possible area tour destinations.
3. List six different types of tours that focus on a specific activity and explain the purpose of each.
4. Why are flexibility and pacing important on any tour?

THE INGREDIENTS OF A TOUR

To illustrate the many ingredients of a package tour, we have created an imaginary tour. It is an escorted 12-day European package with overnight stops in five countries (England, the Netherlands, Germany, Switzerland, and France) and daytime passage through one other (Belgium). The tour is tailored to the general-interest traveller, and has extensive sightseeing and some entertainment features. A detailed itinerary is given in Table 10–1.

The Human Element

Tours do not magically materialize out of thin air. Someone has to have the original idea for the tour, and then package the product so that it is attractive enough to sell. As you read earlier in this chapter, most tours are put together by a tour operator and sold through travel agents. Our feature tour was created, let's say, by European Horizons, a Toronto-based tour operator, and marketed to travel agents throughout Canada. The 27 tour participants have come from cities all over the country and from a variety of backgrounds.

LONDON, PARIS, AND EUROPEAN HIGHLIGHTS

- First-class hotels throughout—all rooms with private bath or shower.
- Continental breakfast daily.
- Dinners included in Amsterdam, Frankfurt, Lucerne, and Paris.
- Round-trip airport transfers, including baggage handling.
- Touring by luxury, air-conditioned motor-coach.
- Rhine River cruise.
- London theatre reservations.
- Local entertainment.
- Sightseeing in all major cities, including admission charges and guide fees.
- Experienced tour manager.

Day 1	DEPART CANADA. Overnight transatlantic flight.
Day 2	LONDON. Arrival in the British capital, with welcome from our tour manager who sees us settled in our London hotel. Balance of day free to relax—or perhaps to start exploring. Evening cocktail party gives us a chance to get acquainted.
Day 3	LONDON. Morning sightseeing with a professional London guide. See Buckingham Palace, Big Ben, and the Houses of Parliament before our visit to the eleventh-century Westminster Abbey. Free afternoon for independent activities or join an optional excursion to the Tower of London. Tonight, we have reserved seats to a London show.
Day 4	LONDON–AMSTERDAM. Morning drive to Dover on the South Coast. By hovercraft to Calais. Motorcoach through Belgium, then on to Amsterdam, arriving in time for a Dutch dinner party at the hotel.
Day 5	AMSTERDAM–COLOGNE. Morning sightseeing features a visit to a diamond factory and a look at Rembrandt's masterpieces in the Rijksmuseum. After lunch, we head for the German Rhineland and overnight in the cathedral city of Cologne.
Day 6	COLOGNE–FRANKFURT. After a leisurely breakfast, we board an excursion steamer and cruise the romantic Rhine—past castles, terraced vineyards, and medieval towns. Then by motorcoach to Frankfurt, for dinner, complimentary beer, and entertainment provided by a local German band.
Day 7	FRANKFURT–HEIDELBERG–LUCERNE. Morning stop in Heidelberg, for sightseeing in Germany's oldest university town and tour of the castle. Then on through the Black Forest, past the thundering Rhine Falls, and into Switzerland. After the eventful day, a quiet night at our Lucerne hotel at the foot of the Swiss Alps.
Day 8	LUCERNE. Our morning sightseeing takes us around the city walls, over a fourteenth-century wooden bridge, and to the famous Lion Monument. This afternoon, perhaps shop for watches or cuckoo clocks, cruise the lake by paddle steamer, or take an optional cable car ride up Mt. Pilatus for stunning Alpine views. Tonight's Swiss folklore party features fondue dinner, unlimited wine, and yodelling and alpenhorn blowing.
Day 9	LUCERNE–PARIS. Today's drive takes us into France and through the world-renowned vineyards of Burgundy. A photo stop at the Palace of Fontainebleau and then on to Paris.
Day 10	PARIS. Morning sightseeing takes in the French capital's famous landmarks: the Eiffel Tower, Arc de Triomphe, Opera, and more. A special visit to the magnificent Notre Dame Cathedral. Balance of the day at leisure, perhaps to visit the Louvre, cruise on the Seine, or enjoy some shopping. For tonight, why not treat yourself to a gourmet dinner, followed by a lively cabaret show?
Day 11	PARIS. A morning tour to Versailles, then a chance to relax before our gala farewell party at the hotel.
Day 12	RETURN TO CANADA. Jet back home, arriving the same day.

TABLE 10.1
Sample European Tour Itinerary

PROFILE

Tours for the Physically Challenged

Peter would love to travel, but he dreads the hassle of manoeuvring his wheelchair through narrow doorways and worries about how he will get up and down steps in unfamiliar places. Grace, who is blind, enjoys guided tours of museums and historic sites, but she becomes frustrated because many tour guides do not understand her special needs. When Carol travels, she needs to stay in hotels that have visible fire alarm and telephone systems, but few facilities of this type are available for the deaf.

According to the Society for the Advancement of Travel for the Handicapped (SATH), approximately 40 million physically and mentally challenged North Americans would travel if obstacles were removed from their path. Add to that number those family members and friends who might accompany the travellers. This represents an enormous, and largely untapped, market for travel services and products.

Evergreen Travel, in the state of Washington, is one company that specializes in meeting the needs of physically challenged travellers. Company founder Betty J. Hoffman has provided travel services for wheelchair-disabled and sight-impaired clients since the early 1960s.

Hoffman is a retail travel agent and wholesale packager of tours for the physically challenged. She provides packaged and customized vacation tours to almost anywhere in the world. With Evergreen Wings on Wheels Tours, mobility-impaired and wheelchair-disabled clients have visited South America, the South Pacific, and the Far East; two other tours have gone around the world. With Evergreen White Cane Tours, sight-impaired clients have visited the Caribbean, Europe, and North America. The company also arranges adventure, business, and convention travel for its clients.

Hoffman was an industry pioneer in this field of travel. Her company operated the first tour for the blind to Europe in 1966 and printed the first travel brochure in braille. In 1990 it led the first group of wheelchair-disabled travellers on a tour of the former Soviet Union. Nothing daunts this company in its efforts to help clients experience the wonders of the world. It has carried them up the Great Wall of China and constructed ramps that allowed them to ride elephants in India. The company even arranges for quadriplegics to obtain scuba-diving certification.

Evergreen provides complete travel services for all disabled people; other companies specialize in a particular type of disability or a particular type of vacation experience. Flying Wheels Travel in Owatonna, Minnesota, arranges group and independent tours and cruises for wheelchair travellers. The Guided Tour Inc., in Melrose Park, Pennsylvania, serves the developmentally challenged. Another specialized travel company is Unique Reservations, based in Indian Rocks Beach, Florida, which takes kidney dialysis patients on cruises all over the world.

As might be expected, arranging and conducting these tours presents some challenges. All accommodations, restaurants, and attractions must be thoroughly checked ahead of time for accessibility and safety. And, although the number of accessible hotel rooms and cruise cabins is growing, available accommodations are still limited. This further complicates planning.

Arrangements must also be made for properly trained and compassionate escorts to assist the physically challenged on the tour. Some companies employ attendants to accompany the tour group. Evergreen, for example, trains and furnishes one sighted guide for every three blind or sight-impaired clients. Or companies may require that clients provide their own travelling companions. Concerns about insurance liability or industrial injury are a major factor in this segment of the travel industry.

Scheduling arrivals and departures can also be tricky. By necessity, a physically challenged tour group moves at a slower pace than a nonchallenged group. Evergreen has turned this into a positive feature by promoting the "leisurely" nature of its tours.

Companies specializing in travel for the physically challenged need to arrange for, or invest in, special equipment or devices. Motorcoaches need to be equipped with electric lifts, wheelchair tiedowns, and—ideally—on-board wheel-in restroom facilities. For clients who wish to travel independently, Evergreen provides cars and vans with hand controls and other special features.

Accessing this market will become easier as governments continue to mandate accessibility for the physically challenged in public facilities and accommodations, and as the travel industry itself discovers this important consumer group.

Not every tour is the brainchild of a tour operator. Some tours are the idea of a member of an organization or club. For example, a high school French teacher might want to put together a summer study trip to France. In this case, he or she is known as a tour organizer. The organizer likely has little expertise in travel, and will most likely cooperate with a local travel agency and a tour operator, as well as (possibly) an airline representative.

To return to our feature package, a key part of the escorted tour is the tour manager (also known as the tour conductor or tour escort). Our tour manager is Mary DeVries. Mary works for European Horizons, and it is her responsibility to oversee the group for the duration of the tour and to make sure that everything runs smoothly. Her work begins long before the departure day.

Mary has been involved with preparing the package from an early date. She has even negotiated contracts with suppliers at several destinations. Before departure, she will have familiarized herself with the itinerary. She will know about interesting sights en route and will have thought about lunch stops for each of the days the group is on the road. Mary will take with her copies of all contracts and correspondence with the various suppliers, just in case there is a problem with hotel bookings or dinner reservations.

The next stage is the tour itself. Mary will greet the tour members as they arrive at the hotel in London, allocate rooms to them, and briefly describe the scheduled itinerary. She will also discuss the itinerary with the driver to get a fairly exact idea of travel times and suitable rest stops. In preparation for the next night, she may call the theatre to confirm reservations for the show, and possibly the hotel in Amsterdam where the group will stay on Day 4. A tour manager must always be thinking ahead.

On Day 3, Mary will get everyone on the bus for the morning's sightseeing. She will not, however, lead the guided tour of London's landmarks (although she will be on the bus). This will be up to the professional tour guide, who has an in-depth knowledge of the city's attractions. There will be a different tour guide in each city. That night, Mary will accompany the group to the theatre.

The first real travelling begins on Day 4 with the trip to Amsterdam. Mary must make sure that all the baggage gets loaded onto the bus, and later onto the hovercraft. Since this is a day with a lot of travelling, she will try to break up the day with rest stops and, of course, lunch. When they finally arrive at the hotel, Mary will go inside to register while the group waits on the bus.

And that, in outline, is the nature of the tour manager's job. The other days will follow a similar pattern. The tour manager will also be expected to do a lot more. He or she will answer a constant barrage of questions, give advice on how best to spend free time, deal with complaints, help find medical care as necessary, and deal with any visa or other documentation problems. In short, the tour manager needs to have a limitless supply of patience, energy, and good humour.

Transportation

All tours include at least one form of transportation, and many combine several different modes. Our feature tour, for example, involves travel by air (not included in the package price), motorcoach, hovercraft, and cruise ship, as well as airport–hotel transfers in London and Paris. If tour members opt for the Mt. Pilatus excursion on Day 8, they will also experience travel by cable car.

Many other combinations are possible, including transportation by rail, rental car, bicycle, barge, gondola, and even camel or pack mule. All add variety to the tour experience and can be a strong selling point for the package.

Meal Plans

The number of meals included in the package is a key factor in determining the overall price of a tour. If maximum economy is uppermost in the tour operator's mind, a limited number of meals will be provided—probably just a daily continental breakfast, consisting of juice, rolls, and tea or coffee. A more substantial full breakfast (eggs, meat, toast, juice, hot beverage) is traditionally served in England and Ireland.

If the operator provides no meals at all, the package is known as a European plan. At the opposite end of the scale, an American plan includes three full meals a day. A modified American plan involves two meals a day (usually breakfast and dinner). Other combinations are also possible—our feature tour includes a daily continental breakfast, dinner on only four nights, and no lunches.

Deluxe tours tend to offer diners greater choice at each meal. À la carte means that you can choose from the complete menu, regardless of price. Table d'hôte, on the other hand, limits you to a set three-course meal at a fixed price. A dine-around plan gives you the option of eating at any of a variety of restaurants. Tour members are issued vouchers and coupons that they can use at participating restaurants.

There are obvious advantages to buying an American plan package (prepayment, guaranteed reservations); there are also drawbacks. You may grow tired of the hotel meals—especially if the menu is limited—and wish you could eat in a local restaurant once in a while. You are, of course, free to do so, but there are no refunds for missed meals.

Accommodations

Our tour group of 27 consists of eight couples, a family of four, a family of three, and four single people. Almost all tours are based on double occupancy, that is, on two people sharing a room. Accommodations for the eight couples are straightforward enough—each couple will occupy either a twin with bath (TWB) or a double with bath (DWB). The former has two twin beds, the latter one double bed.

CHAPTER 10: Tours and Charters

The family of four will either reserve two separate rooms or perhaps share the same room (a quad). Similarly, the family of three may share a triple room. Quads and triples are not necessarily larger than twins and doubles. A common practice is for hotels to add cots or rollaway beds to a regular room to make a triple or a quad. Under this arrangement, children are sometimes allowed to stay for free. Most tour operators offer a slight price reduction for triple or quad occupants.

Single people, on the other hand, have to pay extra if they want a room to themselves. A single supplement can sometimes add as much as 50 percent to the package price. A hotel may have a few smaller rooms for individual guests, with one twin bed and bath or shower (SWB), but most singles have to occupy a regular double room. Some tour operators get around the single supplement by matching singles and allowing them to share a room. Not everyone wants to share a room with a stranger, however. Many singles prefer to pay the supplement for the sake of privacy. On our tour, two singles have decided to share a room, while the other two have opted for separate rooms.

The Itinerary

Our tour is considered relatively fast-paced, in that participants will stop at several cities in a short space of time. The configuration is 2 1 1 1 2 3 (10 nights spent in 6 cities). A more leisurely tour might have three nights at each destination.

Even though the tour includes a lot of cities, there are only three full days of travelling (Days 4, 6, and 9). Time and distance on the road per day is an important consideration, and few tour operators schedule more than ten hours or 350 miles of travel in any one day. Even fewer have consecutive days of almost nonstop travelling.

Our tour also strikes a fairly good balance between scheduled activities and free time. Although there is no single day when tour participants are free from dawn to dusk, Days 2, 3, 8, 10, and 11 offer free afternoons, and Days 5, 7, and 9 have quiet evenings. Days 4 and 6 are the only two filled with scheduled activities.

Another consideration in fixing the itinerary is the location of the hotel. A central location is preferable, especially on a tour such as ours that has overnight stays in major cities. Participants do not want to have to travel a long distance into the city centre when they have free time to spend.

> **CHECK YOUR PRODUCT KNOWLEDGE**
>
> 1. What is the difference between a tour manager and a tour guide?
> 2. Define each of the following: (a) European plan, (b) American plan, (c) modified American plan.
> 3. Give three considerations involved in planning an itinerary.

SELF-REGULATION AND ETHICS

In Canada, tours and charters and their components are regulated by different jurisdictions and departments. Air and rail travel is regulated by the National Transportation Agency; motorcoach travel is regulated by the public utilities boards or agencies of the provinces. Tour operators are licensed by the provinces. The interests of consumers are protected by Consumer and Corporate Affairs Canada and by provincial departments of consumer affairs. Canadian Holidays, the wholly owned subsidiary of PWA Corporation, is a tour operator licensed in Ontario, British Columbia, and Quebec.

The Alliance of Canadian Travel Associations (ACTA), profiled in Chapter 13, has a two-part code of ethics. The first part relates to dealings between ACTA members and the public, the second part to dealings between ACTA members.

In the United States, the Interstate Commerce Commission's control of the tour industry effectively ended when the bus industry was deregulated in 1982. Federal regulation has been replaced by self-regulation. Two trade associations—the United States Tour Operators Association (USTOA) and the National Tour Association (NTA)—set standards for the tour industry.

USTOA's 39 members include some of the biggest names in tour packaging—American Express, Globus–Gateway, Maupintour, Olson–Travelworld, and Tauck Tours. The association has strict eligibility requirements. Member operators must meet these criteria:

- Have been in business for at least three years.
- Handle a certain volume of business.
- Carry at least $1 million in liability insurance.
- Post an indemnity bond for consumer protection.

In addition, members are pledged to the highest ethical standards in their dealings with consumers and retailers, as described in the USTOA publication, *Ethics in U.S. Tour Operations: Standards for Integrity*.

The NTA is the largest group-travel industry association in North America. Its members include 575 tour operators, who package and sell tours in the United States, Canada, and Mexico, and over 2000 suppliers (including hotels, airlines, bus and sightseeing companies, restaurants, and attractions). In addition, about 750 public sector organizations (including tourism agencies, convention and visitors' bureaus, and chambers of commerce) belong to the NTA.

Since deregulation, the NTA has functioned as a consumer advocate. Like the USTOA, the association demands high standards from its members, who are required to adhere to a strict code of ethics and to carry at least $1 million in insurance for professional liability.

Recent years have seen a greater emphasis on education in the tour industry. The NTA's Certified Tour Professional (CTP) program rewards individuals who successfully complete requirements in academic study and in service to the industry. To be eligible for this program, candidates must have been employed full-time in the tour industry for at least two years.

The International Air Transport Association

IATA plays a primary role in the regulation of tours outside the United States and Canada. It requires the following:

- That the tour include air transportation on the flights of an IATA member (although the airfare can be quoted separately).
- That accommodations be included for the duration of the tour.
- That at least one additional feature be included (for example, sightseeing, entertainment, transfers).
- That the tour price be not less than 20 percent of the airfare (if departure is from the United States).
- That the tour brochure meet IATA standards.

Although these requirements are specifically for overseas tours, many domestic tour operators choose to follow the same guidelines.

Once a tour has been approved, it is registered with an identifying number (**IT number**). American Express's "French Impressions" tour, for example, might appear in the brochure with the IT number IT1AF1AE549. Here's a translation of that number:

IT: inclusive tour
1: 1991 (the year the tour was approved)
AF: Air France, the carrier
1: Area 1 (the Western Hemisphere)—the area in which the tour will be sold
AE549: the identifying number chosen by the tour operator (American Express)

The Performance Bond

As discussed earlier, the tour operator is a speculator and risk taker. Individual suppliers—hotels, motorcoach companies, and sightseeing companies—will insist on a deposit from the tour operator before reserving the product. But the client and travel agent need protection in case the tour operator goes into default or out of business. A performance bond offers such protection. It is a special type of insurance policy that guarantees payment to all parties owed any money—the clients, their travel agents, and all suppliers—in the event that the operator experiences financial difficulties. The tour operator pays a premium and is said to post a bond. Performance bonds are sometimes worth millions of dollars.

Statement of Conditions

All tour operators are required to include in their brochures a statement of terms and conditions. This appears at the back of the tour brochure, usually in fine print. Typically, it includes information on the following:

- What is and is not included in the package.
- Reservations procedures.
- Deposit and payment schedule.
- Travel and health documents required (passports, visas, vaccinations).
- Cancellation and refund policy.
- Status of fares, rates, and itinerary (all may be subject to change).
- The tour operator's limited responsibility and liability.

In this age of lawsuits, it is essential that the travel agent make sure the client understands the statement of conditions.

CHECK YOUR PRODUCT KNOWLEDGE

1. Which two trade associations regulate the tour industry?
2. What is an IT number?
3. List the items that would appear in a tour brochure's statement of conditions.

THE TOUR AS PRODUCT

A package tour, like any other complex product, is the end result of the work of many different people. Putting together a tour product involves a close working relationship between the following sectors:

- Suppliers (hotels, restaurants, airlines, cruise ships, bus companies, sightseeing companies, attractions, resorts, and so on).
- Public sector organizations (provincial and local tourism agencies, convention bureaus, and so on).
- Tour operators.
- Travel agents.

The suppliers are the producers of the various components of the tour product. Their primary aim is to sell their product to the consumer at a profit. Suppliers usually sell to intermediaries rather than to the consumer. What direct contact there is between the sales representatives for the suppliers and prospective tour clients usually takes the form of group presentations, public speeches, or public trade shows.

The sales offices for most suppliers are organized and structured in much the same way as airline sales offices—that is, by city, region, and nation. Locally owned or franchised suppliers, however, seldom have the need for a nationwide sales force.

Public sector organizations (PSOs) promote group travel to particular cities or provinces. They include provincial departments of tourism, local and municipal tourism councils, and convention and visitors' bureaus, all of which market their destinations to tour operators. Popular marketing approaches include direct mail and the devising of catchy slogans ("Beautiful British Columbia," "Halifax Likes Company," and "I Love New York" are good examples). At the NTA's annual fall convention and spring Tour and Travel Exchange, PSO representatives can market their destinations to tour operators.

National tourist offices (NTOs) exist to promote tourism to an entire country. In the United States, the federal government takes a low-key approach to the promotion of incoming tours, through the United States Travel and Tourism Administration (USTTA), a branch of the U.S. Department of Commerce. The governments of some other countries play a much more active role in the promotion of tourism.

Tourism Canada, a branch of Industry Canada, is the federal agency responsible for encouraging and supporting the economic growth, excellence, and international competitiveness of the tourism industry for all of Canada.

Tour operators consolidate the services of suppliers into a marketable tour package that is sold either directly or indirectly to the consumer. In the United States and Canada, tour operators are private businesses. Since deregulation, it has become relatively easy for tour operators to enter the market. The industry is characterized by low initial capital requirements, fast cash flow, and the potential for high return on equity invested. In the nations of Eastern Europe, state-controlled tourist boards used to hold a monopoly on the travel industry. This is changing as the different countries introduce free market economies and encourage free enterprise.

Travel agents are the final link in the chain, handling the actual sale of tour packages to consumers. They represent the outlet for the suppliers' and tour operators' products, and are compensated for their services with a commission (usually 10 percent). The client is not required to pay a fee for the services of the travel agent.

Packaging the Components

The work involved in producing a tour package can be divided into four main stages:

- operations
- costing
- brochure production
- promotions

Operations The operations stage begins with planning. Market research tells the tour operator which tours will sell. (Tours may also be created in response to an offer from a supplier who wants to attract group business, or in response to a suggestion from an organization.) Once the tour destination, approximate dates, and length of tour have been determined, the next stage is to negotiate with the suppliers of transportation and ground services. At around the same time, a detailed itinerary is developed.

Costing An accurate costing of the various components of the package is vital. The package must be offered to the consumer at an attractive price that still allows markup to cover promotional costs, business overheads, commissions, and profit. Costs can be fixed or variable. Fixed costs are those that must be paid regardless of the number of tour participants. If a tour operator books hotel rooms or bus seats in blocks, the cost will be the same whether 15 or 25 people take the tour. Such are the risks of block booking. Variable costs are those charged on the basis of the number of people on the tour. For example, if hotel rooms are not block booked, the tour operator pays the supplier only for the rooms that are used.

Tour operators can vary the cost of a package by omitting or including various features. An all-inclusive tour will cost more than one that features accommodations and transportation only. A tour operator can economize by limiting the number of meals included in the package (and by offering table d'hôte rather than à la carte), by choosing first-class rather than deluxe hotels, and by scheduling more free time and fewer organized activities.

Brochure Production The next stage is the production of a brochure for distribution to travel agents and potential clients. The brochure will typically contain general information on the tour operator and its product, along with listings

ILLUSTRATION 10-4
A tour manager or director is responsible for the day-to-day operation of an escorted tour.
SOURCE: Courtesy of Great Canadian Railtour Company Ltd.

of all available tours (featuring what is included, detailed daily itineraries, prices, maps, and so on) and a statement of conditions. Many of the larger tour operators produce their own brochures. Smaller companies often customize "shells" produced by airlines, hotels, and so on. Shells are brochures that contain full-colour photos and possibly a short generic text. The tour operator then adds details of its own tours. Shell brochures offer considerable savings in time and expense for the tour operator.

Promotions The final stage is the promotion of the tour. Media advertising has long been recognized as an effective means of promotion; it includes advertisements aimed at travel industry professionals (in trade publications such as the NTA's monthly *Courier*, *Travel Weekly*, and *The Travel Agent*) and at potential consumers. Trade advertisements tend to be more informative; consumer advertisements stress the glamour of particular tours. Tour operators also use direct mailing, as well as group sales presentations to retailers who might be interested in selling their tours. Familiarization (FAM) tours, which are offered to travel agents either at a discount or for free, are another common promotional technique.

References

A number of publications listing both domestic and overseas tours are available to the trade. The *Consolidated Tour Manual* (CTM) catalogues tours to destinations in Canada, the United States, Mexico, the Caribbean, and Central and South America. It is published in four editions: All Year, Winter, Spring/Summer/Fall, and Winter Sports. Tour operators pay a fee to be included in the CTM.

The *Official Sightseeing Sales and Tour Guide* is published annually by Gray Line Corporation. This guide lists net rates for sightseeing, transfers, limousine rental, and even shore excursions. Though it focuses on destinations in Canada, the United States, Mexico, and the Caribbean, it also includes many other international destinations.

The Official Tour Directory is published twice a year by Thomas Publishing. It covers tours to destinations in Canada and the United States and around the world. It also provides an alphabetical listing of tour operators.

CHECK YOUR PRODUCT KNOWLEDGE

1. Which four groups of people must work together to produce a package tour?
2. What is the role of the tour operator in the production of the tour package?
3. What are the four main stages in the development of a tour package?

CHARTERS

A **charter** is a travel arrangement in which transportation equipment is leased or rented at a net price. The company (or individual) that charters the airplane, bus, ship, or train is the charterer. Tour operators handle the bulk of the charter business, but travel agents, individuals, and groups can also act as charterers.

Charters present a number of advantages and disadvantages, both for the charterer and the traveller. First, the advantages:

- The greatest attraction for the traveller is the charter price. If the charter is fully occupied or sold out, per-passenger costs can be as low as 40 percent of the regular fare.
- The operator can make a higher per-passenger profit when the charter is fully occupied or sold out.
- Charters can offer greater convenience than scheduled transportation. A charter from Thunder Bay to Fredericton, for example, could fly direct without stopping. Passengers on a scheduled flight would probably have to change planes at least once.
- Charters give a group or an organization a sense of exclusiveness. Group members will refer to the charter vehicle as "our plane" or "our bus."
- Charters can often be customized to meet the MNEs of the passengers.

And now the disadvantages:

- Pricing is based on the assumption that the flight will sell out. If it does not, the cost per seat can be high.
- The operator can lose money if the number of seats sold doesn't cover costs.
- Charter flights have a worse on-time record than scheduled flights. Because the charter flight coming into an airport is usually scheduled to take off again on another charter as soon as it's serviced (this is called back-to-back scheduling), the chances for delay are higher. Charters are also subject to cancellation.
- A charter ticket is nontransferable. If a traveller misses his or her charter flight to Las Vegas because of a flat tire en route to the Vancouver airport, no other carrier will honour the ticket.
- Charter operators can consolidate two or more flights if their charters are not selling well. This can cause last-minute changes in departure times, airports, and even itineraries.
- The charterer may add a last-minute surcharge. An increase in fuel costs, for example, can lead to a sudden fare hike. (Charterers are by law allowed to increase fares by as much as 10 percent up to ten days before departure.)

The charter operator, like a tour operator, is a speculator and risk taker. When arranging a charter with a carrier, the operator must sign a contract and pay a deposit. The cost of the deposit is passed on to the sales intermediaries, or passengers, or both.

Chartering Different Modes of Transportation

Most people think of charters as involving a plane or a bus. However, it is also possible to charter a train or a ship. An entire train can be chartered for a whistle-stop political campaign, or to carry a circus group. Such charters, however, are the exception. More commonly, groups or individuals charter a single railway car and hook it up to a scheduled train. Vessels that are available for charter tend to be small (for example, windjammers, riverboats, and yachts), although it is possible to charter an entire liner.

It is less complicated to charter a school bus than a cruise ship or a DC-10. But, regardless of size and price, all charters require some sort of contractual agreement.

Many charter flights take place on board scheduled carriers; while others are provided by all-charter airlines (known as supplemental carriers), which usually do not have scheduled services. United Airlines is an example of a scheduled carrier that offers charters (for professional football teams, and other groups). When scheduled airlines assign a portion of their fleet to charter service, the plane configuration changes. Almost all charter flights are economy only, with no first-class section.

Airline deregulation in the United States has had a significant effect on the charter market there. Scheduled airlines can now compete in price with the supplemental carriers, and offer equally attractive packages with fewer restrictions and less risk. Several supplemental carriers chose to become scheduled carriers after deregulation. Deregulation of the American motorcoach industry has made it easier for bus companies in that county to obtain a tour broker's licence. This, in turn, has led to a great increase in the number of charter companies.

Canada's airlines were given greater pricing freedom in the 1980s. Edmonton-based Wardair, Canada's major charter airline, developed a regular scheduled service between western and eastern Canadian cities but was unable to compete. It was taken over and eventually folded into Canadian Airlines. Other charter airlines, such as Canada 3000, emerged around that time.

Different Types of Charter

Charters can be private or public. Private charters are not for sale to the general public. Some private charters, known as single-entity charters, are paid for in full by a single source. For example, the Denver Broncos football team will charter a 727 from United Airlines to fly the team and its staff to a game in Miami. Or IBM will charter an Air Canada 767 and fly 250 of its top salespeople and their spouses to Barbados for an incentive holiday. As a rule, the passengers do not pay for their own tickets: these are provided, along with any accommodations, by the company that arranges the charter.

Other private charters are sold through organizations, such as a club or association. These are called affinity charters, indicating some sort of voluntary membership or affinity to an organization. An affinity charter can be announced to the membership through a direct mailing or in some form of publication; each interested member then reimburses the sponsoring organization for the tour. For example, Dalhousie University's alumni association in Halifax may charter a Canadian Airlines 727 for a trip to Bermuda. The charter is promoted and sold by direct mail and in the alumni newsletter. Those who decide to take the tour send their money to the alumni association.

As the name suggests, public charters are sold to the general public either through a travel agency or by a tour or charter operator. There are no restrictions in terms of membership in an organization. The public charter may include transportation only (either one-way or round-trip) or be part of a package (known as a charter tour). Canada 3000 advertises the lowest cost charter flights between selected major Canadian cities, between Toronto and Florida, and to Britain and certain European cities.

Pricing

Charterers determine the price of their product by dividing the total price quoted by the carrier (plus any markup) by the number of seats, berths, or cabins. Most private charters are not marked up, since they require no commissions to sales intermediaries.

As an example, a school charters a 40-seat bus for a trip to the circus. The bus company charges $200 for the bus. If all seats are sold, the price per passenger will be $5 ($200 ÷ 40). Similarly, a seat on a 250-seat 767 that has been chartered for $50,000 will cost each passenger $200 ($50,000 ÷ 250).

Important Charter Terms and Concepts

You will understand better how charters work if you become familiar with the following terms and concepts:

- Charters are priced by the carrier as *wet* or *dry*. Wet means fuel is included; dry means no fuel is included.
- When the carrier provides the crew, this cost is included in the quote.
- If the driver of a motorcoach has to wait for three hours while the group tours an attraction or attends a show, an hourly *wait charge* is figured into the price.
- Most charters base their price on cost per kilometre, or cost per hour, or a combination of these. A one-way charter can, therefore, cost as much as a round-trip

charter, because the operator has to get the vehicle home (unless the operator practises *back-to-back* scheduling, whereby the vehicle returns with a full load).
- When planning multiple charters, operators try to establish a *pattern*. They might organize, for example, one flight per week, May 15–August 31, Toronto–Rome, as well as one flight per week, May 15–August 31, Montreal–Rome. Patterns make consolidation much easier; for example, if the May 30 departures from Toronto and Montreal are both undersold, the operator can stop the Toronto flight in Montreal and proceed to Rome with all passengers in a single plane.
- Consolidation can also involve consolidating dates. A Friday departure and a Sunday departure, for example, can be consolidated into a single Saturday departure.

References

Charters are never listed in the *Official Airline Guide* or other travel schedules. The best source of charter information is *JAX FAX Travel Marketing Magazine,* a monthly directory of air tours published by the Jet Air Transportation Exchange. Other sources include charter operators' programs and brochures.

CHECK YOUR PRODUCT KNOWLEDGE

1. List three advantages and three disadvantages of travelling by charter flight.
2. What is the difference between a scheduled carrier and a supplemental carrier?
3. How are charters priced?
4. What is meant by back-to-back scheduling?

THE CHANNELS OF DISTRIBUTION

All products, including tour packages, must be moved from producer to consumer. The tour industry has its own distribution system, with wide variations, combinations, and interactions. We can identify four main channels of distribution—one direct and three indirect.

With the one-stage, direct-sale system, an individual or group buys the tour product directly from the producer or supplier of tour services. This cuts out all sales intermediaries. An example would be a client who buys an air tour through an airline reservations centre. Some hotels and sightseeing attractions also package tours for direct sale.

The two-stage distribution system involves a single sales intermediary—usually a tour operator who packages the various supplier services into a single tour product. Some travel agents also buy directly from the suppliers, as do incentive travel companies, travel clubs, convention planners, and corporate travel offices.

The three-stage system involves the intervention of a second sales intermediary between the tour operator and the consumer. The additional intermediary is usually a retail travel agent, who is paid a commission for handling the tour operator's products.

The four-stage system is the most complex of all, as it involves three intermediaries. The additional intermediary is normally a specialty channeler, whose role it is to intervene between the consumer and the travel agent. An organization planning a convention for its members, for example, might first consult a convention planner for advice on transportation and accommodations. The convention planner might then make the necessary arrangements with a travel agent, who in turn will contact a tour operator.

The Tour Organizer

A tour that is promoted and sold to a specific group or within a local market often involves a tour organizer, who may be a member of the group (for example, the president of a garden club who leads a tour to the Chelsea Flower Show in London), or a media celebrity who shares an interest with the group (for example, a sportscaster who leads a tour to the Grey Cup).

The tour organizer will be compensated with a free trip if there are enough people on the tour (15 is usually the minimum). The tour organizer may also receive a certain amount of money for each tour participant. The tour operator will either add a pro rata surcharge to each fully paid package or build the cost of the organizer's free trip into each package.

Local and Nationwide Tours

The terms local tour and nationwide tour refer to the marketplace in which the tour is promoted, not to the destination. An example of a local tour is a high school spring trip to Ottawa; such a tour would be marketed only to local high school students. Local tours are often joint efforts involving a tour organizer, a local travel agency, a tour operator, and a transportation representative. Sign-up parties with promotional film shows are sometimes held to attract potential buyers.

Nationwide tours are promoted and sold from coast to coast in Canada and the United States. You can buy the same American Express, Tauck, or other big-name tour in any of the 40 000 travel agencies in the United States and Canada.

> **CHECK YOUR PRODUCT KNOWLEDGE**
>
> 1. Describe how the tour product gets from producer to consumer in a three-stage distribution system. Give an example.
> 2. What is the difference between a local tour and a nationwide tour?

CAREER OPPORTUNITIES

The tour industry is rapidly expanding and offers a wide variety of career opportunities at the entry level, as well as good prospects for advancement. Many people are attracted to the tour sector by the promise of unlimited free travel to glamorous destinations throughout the world. In reality, only a few employees (such as tour managers) get to travel extensively. For the rest, the work involves year-round office work, with only limited opportunities for discount travel.

Careers are available in four main areas:

- the tour operator office
- tour management
- tour sales and promotion
- entrepreneurship

The Tour Operator as Employer

A tour operator's office employs a number of clerical workers and supervisors. Some positions are described below:

Reservationist The main duty of a reservationist is to handle incoming calls from travel agents who are interested in booking the operator's tours. Reservationists also handle computer bookings. Reservations can be confirmed over the phone or in writing. The reservationist must be familiar with all the components of each tour.

Operations Clerk This position requires little or no personal contact with the travel agent or the general public. Operations clerks process information from the reservationists to prepare passenger lists, rooming lists, and updates on the status of tour availability. Other duties can include typing confirmations and mailing them to travel agents, and preparing passenger tour documents.

Reservations Supervisor A reservationist can advance to the position of reservations supervisor and be placed in charge of all reservations staff and procedures. He or she will be responsible for the interviewing, hiring, and training of all new reservationists. Group bookings and major accounts will usually be handled by the supervisor rather than by a less experienced reservationist.

Operations Supervisor This is another supervisory position. This person is responsible for all operational staff and procedures.

Other positions in the tour operator's office include group coordinator (who handles special interest groups booked by travel agencies); accountant; and costing specialist.

Tour Management

As outlined earlier, the tour manager or director is responsible for the day-to-day, even minute-by-minute, operation of the escorted tour. It is a pivotal position: the reputation of a tour operator can hinge on how successfully the tour manager does his or her job.

Tour managers must have strong skills in negotiating, finance, accounting, and planning, as well as a limitless supply of patience and energy. Knowledge of a foreign language (or several foreign languages) is essential for a tour manager who hopes to conduct tours overseas. Opportunities for managers of European tours are extremely limited, since tour operators usually like to employ native Europeans.

Certification through the NTA program is an excellent qualification for a tour manager, as is membership in the International Association of Tour Managers (IATM).

It should be noted that tour management is not only a career field in itself, but also an entry-level step toward managing an entire tour operator company.

There are plenty of opportunities for part-time tour managers, tour guides (who work at local sites and attractions), and tour organizers. These positions are often held by people with full-time jobs (for example, teachers) or by retirees or special-interest enthusiasts. Students are sometimes employed as tour guides if they have an in-depth knowledge of a certain destination or subject.

Tour guides are called travel guides in Canada. In Canada there are about 7000 travel guides. Most are women (63 percent), young (61 percent under the age of 25), part-time (92 percent), and well educated (19 percent have a university degree). Native people are well represented.

Tour Sales and Promotion

The sales representative is the most visible employee in any sales and promotion department. The position involves calling on travel agents and making presentations to various groups. Other positions within the promotional department include publicist and writer. Graphic artists are often employed to design and lay out brochures and other promotional materials.

A DAY IN THE LIFE OF

A Tour Manager

If you have ever taken a tour, you probably already have a good idea of what a tour manager does. I am the person who shepherds the tour group from place to place and makes sure all aspects of the tour run smoothly. I take care of hotel reservations, arrange for meals and transportation, obtain tickets for local attractions, and so on. This allows the members of the group to simply relax and enjoy their vacation.

The first day of the tour, I greet the members of my tour group, make sure they have all of their luggage, and brief them on the schedule for the day. Then we set off to our first destination. Most of the travellers in my tour groups are retired people, and we usually travel by bus. When we arrive at our hotel, I check in for my group and get everyone room assignments. Later, at dinner, I will tell everyone about the next day's schedule.

A lot of people have misconceptions about what tour managers do. Some people think I'm some kind of drill sergeant who bosses people around and tries to fill every minute of the day with organized activities. Nothing could be further from the truth. My job is to take care of the paperwork and headaches involved in travelling so that people can concentrate on doing the fun things they want to do.

It is true that I do organize group activities, because the group expects it and because it is cheaper for people to visit local attractions at a group rate. However, the members of my tour always have the option of joining in the activity, doing something else, or simply relaxing. In addition, on my tours, I always leave plenty of free time in the schedule for people to go off and do things on their own.

Some people think tour managers are experts on the history of the tour area. This is not necessarily true. Many tour managers lead tours of the same routes over and over again and do become experts on the local area. In some cases, however, the tour company provides a sightseeing guide, in addition to the tour manager, to inform the tour members about the history of the area. Sightseeing guides specialize in one specific region, museum, park, or building.

My main job is to act as the liaison between my tour group and the hotels, restaurants, and attractions that my group will visit. I make all the reservations, pay the bills and tips, and stand ready to solve any and all problems that may arise during the course of a tour. I must always be resourceful and calm in the face of a crisis, because no tour ever goes completely smoothly. On a recent tour, our bus broke down. I had to arrange for another bus to pick us up, and then I had to keep the tour members occupied while we waited.

My job requires tact, organizational skills, and leadership ability. Knowledge of more than one language is a major advantage, because so many foreign tourists have started visiting our country in recent years. Some tour managers lead tour groups on wilderness and adventure tours. They may lead tourists on hikes through the foothills of the Himalayas, on white-water rafting trips down the Ottawa River, or on horseback tours of the Rocky Mountains. These guides need strength and stamina as well as all the other attributes of a good tour manager. Some tour managers specialize in archaeology, art history, fine dining, or wine appreciation. These managers need special training in those fields.

When my tour company hired me, it put me through an intensive training course. Then it sent me out in the field with an experienced tour manager. That's how I learned my job. Being a tour manager is not a high-paying job, but it gives me the opportunity to travel and stay at nice resorts for free. Many tour managers work only part-time, with long gaps between tours. Some are freelance, and keep busy by working for several tour operators instead of just one company.

I like being a tour manager because I like people and I like to travel. I think the nicest thing about my job is that I start out with a group of strangers and I help them become a group of friends who are sharing the fun and adventure of a trip together. When that happens, I know I have done my job well.

Entrepreneurship

Since deregulation, tour operators, transportation companies, and charter operators have entered the market in a flood. Those who aspire to own and operate their own business might consider the following:

- a motorcoach and sightseeing company
- a small tour operator company
- a charter company
- a reception service
- freelance tour management

Most people need experience working in the tour industry before they go into business for themselves.

Summary

- The tour has evolved from the grand tour, through the custom-made tour, into the package tour.
- A package tour is a combination of two or more travel components put together by a tour operator and sold to the consumer as a single product at a single price.
- Package tours have become increasingly popular because they offer travellers known costs, bargain prices, and guaranteed arrangements—they are the most worry-free form of travel.
- Tours can be categorized by format, destination, and purpose.
- Independent, hosted, and escorted are the three basic package tour formats.
- Tour operators develop packages to fit the MNEs of different kinds of travellers.
- Flexibility, pacing, and different price ranges are important considerations in developing tours.
- A tour manager accompanies a group for the duration of an escorted tour, making sure that all the ingredients come together as planned.
- Since deregulation, the USTOA and NTA have set financial and ethical standards for the industry.
- All overseas tours are required to conform to IATA regulations.
- The production of the tour product requires a close working relationship between suppliers, public sector organizations, tour operators, and travel agents.
- Operations, costing, brochure production, and promotions are the four main stages in the preparation of a tour package.
- Charters, which can be private or public, offer travellers considerable savings on transportation costs.
- The tour product is channelled from producer to consumer by one of four distribution systems.
- Tours can also be categorized as local or nationwide, depending on the area in which the tour is promoted.

Key Terms

Foreign independent tour (FIT)
Domestic independent tour (DIT)
package tour
all-inclusive tour
tour operator
tour wholesaler
hosted tour
incentive tour
convention tour
special-interest group tour
incoming tour
area tour
single-country tour
two-city tour
single-city tour
eco-tourism
tour organizer
tour manager
tour guide
à la carte
table d'hôte
dine-around plan
double occupancy
quad
triple
single supplement
IT number
charter
private charter
single-entity charter
affinity charter
public charter
local tour
nationwide tour

What Do You Think?

1. What effects might a reintroduction of federal regulation have on the tour industry as a whole?
2. Despite the considerable savings that package travel allows, why do many travellers still prefer to travel independently?
3. What special arrangements could tour operators make for hearing-impaired travellers and sight-impaired travellers?
4. Why do some travel agents make it their policy not to handle charters?
5. Are hotels justified in charging a single supplement for travellers who room alone? Explain.

Dealing with Product

Marketing specialists believe that the secret to successful marketing is finding the right product at the right time for the right person at the right price. Romantics will tell you that "Somewhere, somehow, there is something or someone for everyone."

Try your skills as a "romantic marketing specialist." Recommend a package tour for each of the following clients:

- a garden club
- high school seniors
- an amateur theatre club
- a family of five (three children ages 8, 5, and 2)
- a neighbourhood senior citizens' centre
- honeymooners
- race car fans
- stamp collectors
- a middle-aged widow with no dependent children
- two 25-year-old secretaries who are single

Dealing with People

You are the vice-president of a large retail travel agency. Your board of directors has decided to develop a special tour department and to begin promoting a series of escorted tours for the coming summer season.

Your job is to hire and train the tour managers. Your first order of business is to write a job description. What qualifications should a tour manager have? Are education and experience important? Does "personality" enter the picture? What do you expect each manager to be able to do? Can you train a candidate with lots of enthusiasm but no previous experience?

CHAPTER 10: Tours and Charters   Name: _____

WORKSHEET 10-1 Choosing Tours

You are a travel agent. Use the *Consolidated Tour Manual* or a similar publication to pick tours for the customers listed below. Describe cost, air and land travel arrangements, accommodations, meals, sample itinerary, and additional components.

1. A middle-aged couple wants a leisurely escorted tour of Europe. They want first-class accommodations, and price is not of great concern.

2. A single woman wants a hosted scenic tour of the Canadian Rockies that is moderately priced.

3. Two amateur archaeologists want to participate in a dig on the Yucatán Peninsula. They need an inexpensive tour.

4. A young woman wants to relax in the Caribbean for two weeks. She also wants to do some sightseeing and shopping. She wants nice, but not deluxe, accommodations.

5. A group of hearing-impaired travellers want an escorted historical tour of South America.

6. A family consisting of two adults and two teenagers wants a low-budget adventure tour in the Yukon.

CHAPTER 10: Tours and Charters   Name: _____

WORKSHEET 10-2 Inbound Tourism

You are a receptive tour operator. Your job is to package and promote tours for Japanese visitors to Canada.

A major part of your job is to negotiate contracts with suppliers of transportation, hospitality, and tourism. In addition to basic services, you expect your suppliers to furnish special services and amenities for your Japanese customers. What could each of the following tour components do to help your tour groups feel welcome in this country? (For example, hotels along the tour route might agree to make Japanese newspapers available for guests to read.)

Airlines

_____

_____

Hotels/motels

_____

_____

Restaurants

_____

_____

Stores

_____

_____

Tourist attractions

_____

_____

What would you do to promote your tour package to Japanes consumers? (For example, you might hire an ad agency to create ads for Japanese television.) Create a slogan for your ad campaign.

_____

_____

_____

_____

In addition to packaging and promoting outstanding tour products, you could also encourage the provincial government to promote inbound tourism. What specific things might the government do to encourage more foreigners to visit your province?

_____

_____

_____

_____

CHAPTER 10: Tours and Charters   Name: _____

WORKSHEET 10-3 Terms and Conditions

Get brochures for two tours that are currently available. Compare the terms and conditions.

Tours   _____   _____
                                        _____   _____
                                        _____   _____

What is and is not included   _____   _____
                                        _____   _____
                                        _____   _____

Reservations procedure   _____   _____
                                        _____   _____
                                        _____   _____

Deposit and payment schedule   _____   _____
                                        _____   _____
                                        _____   _____

Travel and health documents required   _____   _____
                                        _____   _____
                                        _____   _____

Cancellation and refund policy   _____   _____
                                        _____   _____
                                        _____   _____

Status of fares, rates, and itinerary   _____   _____
                                        _____   _____
                                        _____   _____

Tour operator's limited responsibility and   _____   _____
liability   _____   _____
                                        _____   _____

CHAPTER 10: Tours and Charters   Name: _____

WORKSHEET 10-4 Eco-Tours

One of the hottest travel trends in the 1990s is eco-tourism. Eco-tours take travellers to various areas of the world to observe wildlife or explore nature. Eco-tourists might hike through the rainforests of Indonesia, trek across the ice of Antarctica, or cruise down the Amazon. In addition to enjoying a great adventure, eco-tourists gain appreciation and concern for the environment.

Select an eco-tour currently being advertised. Find as much information about the tour as you can. Then complete the items below.

Name of tour

Name of eco-tour operator or company

Tour destination

Tour price

Description of tour

Educational element (What makes this trip different from other trips to the area?)

Qualifications of the person leading the trip

Company history (How long has it been in business? How long has it been offering eco-tours?)

Environmental impact (Does the company seem genuinely concerned about the environment? Is it possible the tour could actually damage the environment?)

PART 4

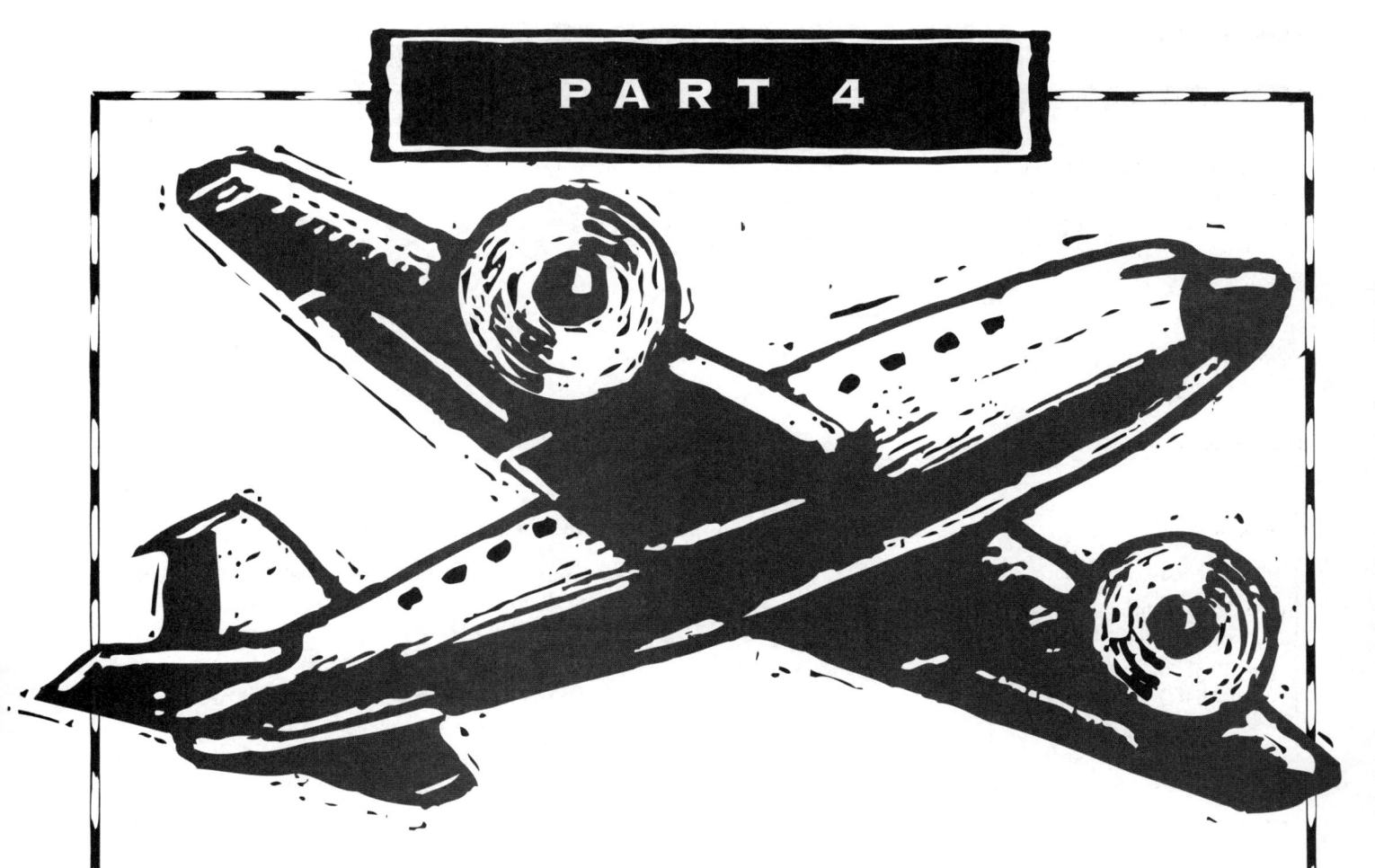

Business and Professional Travel

CHAPTER 11
The Business of Business Travel

CHAPTER 12
Meetings, Conventions, and Incentive Travel

CHAPTER 11

The Business of Business Travel

"Business is like riding a bicycle. Either you keep moving or you fall down."

John David Wright

OBJECTIVES

When you have completed this chapter, you should be able to do the following:

- List reasons for business travel.
- Explain the main differences between business travel and vacation travel.
- Describe the motivations, needs, and expectations (MNEs) of business travellers.
- Tell how airlines compete for the business of the business traveller through business-class service, frequent flier programs, discounts, and rebates.
- Describe the efforts of car rental chains and railways to meet the needs of the business traveller.
- List the special services and facilities that the hotel industry offers business travellers.
- Describe the work of business travel departments (BTDs) and corporate travel agencies.
- Discuss careers related to business travel.

Flight 820 from Toronto to Ottawa is nearly full. Occupying seat 6A, near the window, is Jill Rosendahl. Jill works for a company that produces training materials for *Financial Post* 500 companies. Part of Jill's job is to interview clients to find out what information and skills they want their sales representatives to learn. On this trip, Jill plans to meet with the marketing staff of a software company.

Sitting in seat 6C, on the aisle, is John Wu. Wu is a field engineer for a laboratory equipment manufacturer. He spends 80 percent of his time on the road, helping customers install equipment and trouble-shooting when problems develop.

Across the aisle from Wu, in seat 6D, is Maria Tremblay, who is a microbiologist for the Saskatchewan Department of Health. While in Ottawa, she'll attend the annual meeting of the Canadian Society of Microbiology. When she returns to work, she'll report to her colleagues on what she learned at the meeting.

Frank Delgado has seat 6F. Just a few months ago, he started his own small-tool manufacturing company. At present, Delgado employs ten people. He's going to the Ottawa area to visit manufacturing plants that might be able to use his company's tools in their production processes.

What do these four people have in common? You probably recognize that they are all business travellers. Unlike tourists, who travel for fun and pleasure, business travellers must travel to do their job. Travel is part of their job description.

Business travellers may work for a private company, a government agency, or a nonprofit organization, or they may be self-employed. They travel to buy and sell goods and services, visit branch offices, attend company meetings, or seek new business opportunities. They may also travel to attend conferences and seminars related to their field, although sometimes this type of travel is referred to as professional rather than business travel.

TRAVEL FOR BUSINESS

People who live in New Brunswick may wear jeans manufactured in Manitoba. Their bedroom furniture may have been put together in Quebec, and their cars may have come off the assembly line in Windsor. Canadians can purchase products from all over Canada because businesspeople have negotiated agreements with each other. In most instances, those businesspeople have had to travel in order to accomplish this.

A Brief History of Business Travel

Travel for the purpose of exchanging goods and services has been going on for centuries. In early times, farmers travelled to local markets, where they could trade their vegetables, grain, and eggs for a piece of cloth or pottery. A famous business traveller of the 13th century was Marco Polo of Venice. He travelled to China and brought back silk, tea, and other exotic products. When Europeans began to desire a constant supply of these products, trade routes between Europe and the Far East developed. Inns sprang up along the major routes to provide food and lodging for the merchant caravans.

During the Middle Ages, trade fairs, especially those of England, stimulated business travel. Merchants and craftspeople from all over the country brought their wares to villages and towns such as Winchester and Smithfield. Even then, village officials recognized the economic benefits of travellers coming to the community. In order for a village to host a fair, the king had to grant permission, and there was much competition among villages for this privilege.

Travel for the purpose of developing new business opportunities has also been going on for some time. The early explorers, who searched for precious metals and new lands, were actually business travellers because they were interested in enriching themselves and in expanding the trade and economy of the country that sponsored their voyages. In the 17th century, for example, Henry Hudson was commissioned by the Dutch East India Company to find a northwest waterway to the Far East. Although Hudson didn't find the Northwest Passage, his explorations helped develop the fur-trading business in North America.

North America was originally seen as a treasure trove, with goods to be exported back to the European mother country. Later, colonization took place. Raw materials, such as lumber and fish from the Maritimes, were exported, and finished goods were imported. A trade "triangle" began to thrive connecting Europe, the Caribbean, and the Maritimes and Newfoundland.

In the 19th century, people began to travel to international trade expositions, where they could display new products. The first of these was the Great Exhibition of 1851, held at the Crystal Palace in London. Inventors and entrepreneurs from the United States and Europe displayed new products, such as reapers and dental instruments. When visitors to the exposition became interested in obtaining these products, this encouraged businesses to manufacture and distribute them on a wide scale.

During the late 1850s, free trade existed between the Maritime provinces and New England under the Reciprocity Treaty. Confederation in 1867 shifted trading patterns. The Nationalist Policy used tariffs and customs duties on imported goods to help build canals and railways, and to protect "infant industry," mainly in Ontario and Quebec. Business travel shifted from north-south to east-west.

Following World War II, major corporations expanded their facilities all over Canada, the United States, and the world. They did this to be closer to local markets or to take advantage of lower tax rates or cheaper labour. The need for on-site visits provided another stimulus for business travel. At the same time, worldwide trade markets expanded. Today, Canadians can purchase jeans manufactured in Mexico, television sets made in Japan, and cars assembled in Germany. Likewise, some products made in Canada fill the shelves of stores in other countries.

Business Travel and the Travel Industry

Business travel by Canadians has grown dramatically in recent years, from 1.3 million person-trips for one or more nights abroad in 1982 to 2.4 million in 1991, according to Statistics Canada. Most of these trips, about 1.9 million, were to the United States. This was about 10 percent of person-trips to the United States; however, business travellers spent 14 percent of total travel expenditures, that is, about $1.1 billion of the $7.8 billion total.

A 1994 study by the Travel Services Group of American Express Canada and the Conference Board of Canada stated that Canadian companies increased their business travel by 87 percent between 1987 and 1993, from $6.2 billion to $11.6 billion. This study analyzed business travel by major components, as shown in Figure 11-2.

Similarly, business travel by Americans has also grown in recent years. In 1989, approximately 34 million Americans took almost 170 million business trips. In 1991, about 14 percent of trips by Americans to Canada for one or more nights were for business purposes. That was about 1.6 million trips with a total expenditure of $875 million—about 24 percent of all travel expenditures by Americans in Canada, according to Statistics Canada. The number of business trips is constantly increasing. So is the number of women business travellers; today, more than one-third of business travellers are women. Table 11-1 compares the demographics of women and men business travellers.

The travel industry supplies products and services that make business travel possible. Travel agencies help travellers with the arrangements for their trips by securing airline tickets and making hotel reservations. Airlines and railways provide transportation to the destination. Car rental agencies furnish local transportation. Hotels and motels provide accommodations and, in many instances, are the site for

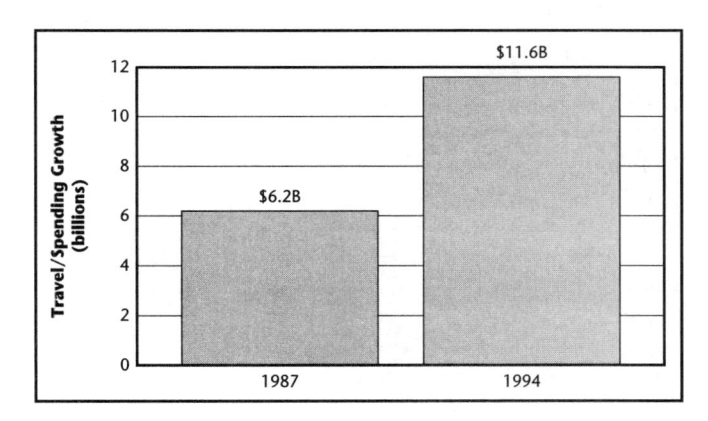

FIGURE 11-1

The Growth of Business Travel and Entertainment Spending in Canada

SOURCE: The American Express Survey of Canadian Business Travel, 1994–95 Edition

business meetings. To relax between appointments or in the evening, business travellers can shop, attend a concert, go to a ball game, or take part in many other events provided by the public and private sectors.

The Business Travel Bonanza To the travel industry, business travellers are a gold mine. Canadian and American firms spend $125 billion a year on business travel. Business travellers fill more than half of all nonresort hotel rooms and domestic airline flights.

There is much competition within the travel industry to win a share of business travel revenues. Airlines compete with other airlines, car rental agencies compete with other car rental agencies, and hotels compete with other hotels. In each case, the goal is to woo the business traveller with the best products and services at the best price.

Characteristics of Business Travel Business travel has other features that make it attractive to the travel industry. Unlike vacation travel — which tends to be heaviest during the summer months and then tapers off during the winter months — business travel is not seasonal. It occurs with the same frequency year-round, and so provides a steady source of income.

Also, business travellers tend to spend money more freely than other travellers. Business-related travel and entertainment expenses are often tax-deductible because they are viewed as a cost of doing business.

Business travel also tends to be inelastic, or inflexible. When a meeting is scheduled out of town or an emergency arises in an out-of-town plant, businesspeople must be there. They can't wait for bargains. Unlike vacation travellers, business travellers often book flights at the last minute and consequently are ineligible for advance-purchase discounts. This usually translates into higher revenues for the travel industry.

If there's an economic recession, the cost of travel goes up and vacation travellers tend to stay home. Business travellers, on the other hand, continue to travel at whatever the going rate happens to be. In fact, a recession may even encourage business travel, because businesspeople feel that they must get out and try even harder to develop their accounts.

Another reason why the travel industry likes business travel is that it can generate revenue for vacation travel. If business travellers are favourably impressed with a destination, they may return to it for a vacation, this time bringing their families along.

For travel agencies, business travel can require less work than vacation travel. Many business travellers visit the same destinations over and over. Thus, once the account has been established, arrangements usually become straightforward and routine. However, many business travellers are notorious for making last-minute changes in their itineraries. This results in extra work under pressure for the travel agent.

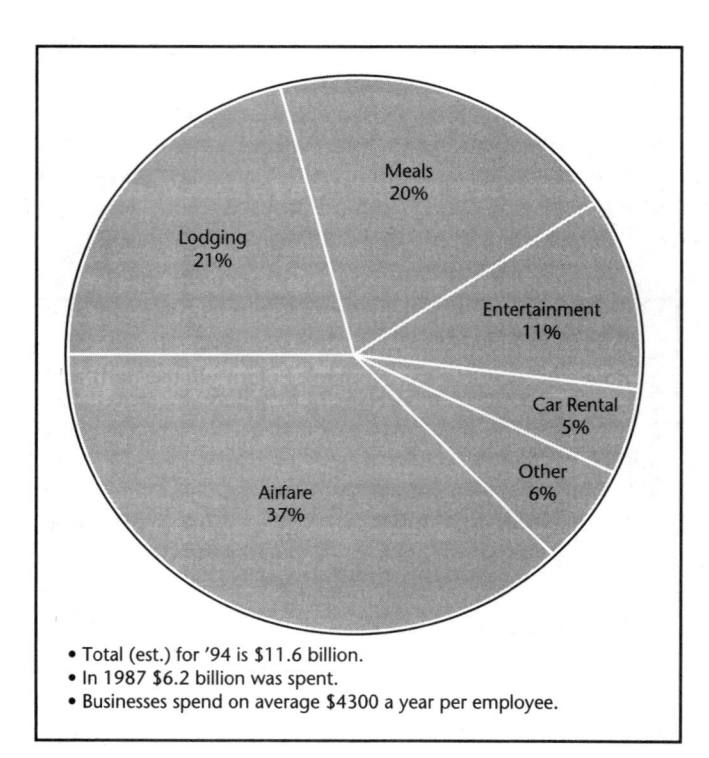

- Total (est.) for '94 is $11.6 billion.
- In 1987 $6.2 billion was spent.
- Businesses spend on average $4300 a year per employee.

FIGURE 11-2
Business Travel: Canadian Domestic Spending Patterns
SOURCE: *The Globe and Mail*, May 26, 1994, p. B-3.

Pie chart values: Lodging 21%, Meals 20%, Entertainment 11%, Car Rental 5%, Other 6%, Airfare 37%.

Category	Women business travellers	Men business travellers
Age		
18–34	37%	42%
35–44	29	27
45 or older	34	31
Education		
Some college or less	63	59
College graduate or more	37	41
Household income		
Less than $40,000	58	50
$40,000–$49,999	15	17
$50,000 or more	27	33
Occupation		
Professional or managerial	21	24
Lower level technical or managerial	31	30
Clerical or sales	18	11
Self-employed	27	30

TABLE 11-1
Demographics of Business Travel
SOURCE: United States Travel Data Center

> **CHECK YOUR PRODUCT KNOWLEDGE**
>
> 1. What is the main difference between a vacation traveller and a business traveller?
> 2. What are some reasons for business travel?
> 3. Why does the travel industry actively seek the business of business travellers?
> 4. Explain how business travel tends to be inelastic, and what this means to the travel industry.

THE FREQUENT BUSINESS TRAVELLER

At age 30, and with degrees in engineering and computer science, John Wu fits the profile of the frequent business traveller. Most frequent business travellers have this profile:

- Between the ages of 25 and 44.
- Well educated.
- Working in a professional, technical, or managerial occupation.
- Upwardly mobile, earning an annual salary of $40,000 or more.

Most areas of the travel industry define frequent business travellers as people who take ten or more trips per year, with each trip averaging four nights. Because of the potential for repeat business, the travel industry is most interested in satisfying the motivations, needs, and expectations (MNEs) of the frequent business traveller.

Motivations, Needs, and Expectations

Frequent business travellers must accomplish a task while they're away from the home office. They have definite needs and expectations relating to getting their work done. Hotels, airlines, car rental agencies, and travel agencies attempt to design products and services to meet these needs.

Business travellers are on tight schedules. They must be at appointments on time. When meetings run longer than expected or the meeting time is changed at the last minute, they must be able to adjust airline and hotel reservations immediately. For business travellers, time is money, and they don't want to waste it through delays, such as waiting in a long line to check out of a hotel, or through mistakes, such as when luggage is lost by an airline. Nor do business travellers want to waste time waiting for flights or for transportation to a hotel. Quick, reliable service is a priority for most travellers, but especially for business travellers.

The business traveller often wants to do paperwork or plan strategy while travelling to a business appointment. Being seated next to a screaming toddler on an airplane would certainly disrupt his or her thought processes. Business travellers also look for prompt, efficient, and courteous service from hotel employees. They want to know that they can check in and out quickly and will be assigned a room that offers the comforts and conveniences that they need. No one wants to hold a business meeting in a room next to a group of high school students celebrating their team's victory in the provincial hockey tournament. Business travellers need quiet to think and relax. Often this means separating them from the mass of travellers.

When travelling abroad, business travellers may have additional needs. They appreciate ease in making international calls to their office or home. If they're not fluent in the language of the country, they may require translation services in order to conduct business.

As you can see, frequent business travellers value efficiency, speed, and comfort. They demand respect and recognition. To get all of this, they are often willing to pay higher airfares and pay more for better accommodations and larger rental cars.

Women Travellers

In the early 1970s, when women began travelling for business in large numbers, the travel industry wasn't quite sure how to treat them. Some travel industry employees couldn't get used to seeing a woman travelling by herself. If a woman was standing behind a man in a hotel check-in line, the desk clerk often assumed that they were together.

Women business travellers have the same MNEs as men business travellers. When surveyed about their needs and wants, women and men give the same responses. Convenience of schedule is the number-one factor in choosing an airline, and convenience of location is the number-one factor in choosing a hotel.

Women also want the same respect and high quality of service that the travel industry offers to men. Travellers like Jill Rosendahl don't want to be called "honey" or "dear" by hotel maids. They don't want to be ogled by desk clerks and bellstaff or treated rudely by flight attendants. And when they dine alone in restaurants, they don't want to be seated in a dark corner by the kitchen. Although attitudes toward women travelling alone have improved greatly, airlines and hotels still need to train employees to treat women travellers with more courtesy.

The Cost Factor

With business travel, the company, not the traveller, usually foots the bill. Although expense may not seem to be as much of a concern for the business traveller as it is for the vacation traveller, business travellers cannot be wildly extravagant. After convenience, the cost of a ticket or of a room is the business traveller's next consideration.

The circumstances of the business traveller also determine how much money he or she will spend. The expectations of a corporate executive with an unlimited expense account will be different from those of a struggling entrepreneur like Frank Delgado. A government employee, such as Maria Tremblay, may be travelling on a per diem allowance. (A **per diem** is the amount of money a business traveller is permitted to spend each day for expenses.)

With changing federal tax laws, and with competition in the airline industry shrinking because of mergers and bankruptcies, travel costs are expected to increase even more. As a result, many companies are making concerted efforts to control their travel expenditures. For example, employees may be asked to take a less convenient flight—a night flight or a flight requiring a stopover—in order to get a lower airfare. Many companies also try to save money by negotiating discounts directly with hotels, airlines, and car rental agencies. In such cases, employees can stay only in certain hotels, and use certain airlines and car rental firms.

Another way companies attempt to control costs is through travel policies. Many of this country's largest companies have written travel policies that specify who may fly first-class and who must fly economy, as well as the type of hotel employees can stay at, and the size of rental car they can obtain. All of this is usually determined by the employee's status in the company or by the distance or duration of the flight.

CHECK YOUR PRODUCT KNOWLEDGE

1. What qualities do business travellers need and expect from travel products and services?
2. What are the MNEs of women business travellers?
3. Why might business travellers spend different amounts of money for travel products and services?
4. What is the purpose of a company travel policy?

TRANSPORTATION SYSTEMS AND BUSINESS TRAVELLERS

When making arrangements for a business trip, travellers can choose to fly, drive, or take a train to their destination. The average distance of a business trip is 2000 kilometres. Driving to the destination might be less expensive in terms of travel costs, but more expensive in terms of time lost for conducting business. Consequently, business travellers are more likely to choose air transportation, and they generally choose the airline with the most convenient flight schedule.

There are situations, however, where taking a train is the best choice. This is particularly true for trips between major cities in densely populated areas, such as along the Washington–Philadelphia–New York City–Boston corridor in the northeastern United States; along the Windsor–Quebec City corridor in Canada; and in parts of Western Europe and Japan.

Once at their destination, travellers need transportation from the airport to their hotel. They may also need transportation to meeting sites or for making scattered sales calls. For local transportation, travellers can choose among taxis, limousines, subways, buses, or rental cars. Since rental cars and taxis provide on-demand transportation (that is, transportation whenever the traveller needs it), business travellers are more likely to choose these means of travel. On-demand transportation is generally more expensive than buses or rapid transit, but for the time-conscious business traveller, the flexibility is well worth the extra cost.

Airline Service

When John Wu arrived at Ottawa's airport, a manager of special services was there to help him and other frequent business travellers make their connecting flights. If there had been time, Wu could have relaxed for a while in a VIP lounge.

As you know, after regulatory reform of the airlines, competition for passengers became very intense. Airlines have tried to attract vacation travellers primarily through discounts; they have tried to attract business travellers primarily through special services. A wide array of products and services now caters to the needs of the business traveller.

Business-Class Service Some airlines have **business-class** sections on their planes, especially those used for international flights. Business-class falls between coach-class and first-class in terms of price and amenities. It aims to satisfy the business traveller's need for comfort, quiet, and special attention. Passengers receive complimentary drinks and headsets, better meal options, and increased service. Since business travellers generally prefer to keep their briefcases and suitcases with them, there is more room for carry-on luggage. The seats are larger and farther apart so that there is more legroom. TWA even has extra-wide seats specifically designed for the frequent business traveller. Called "business loungers," these seats also feature extra padding and automatic footrests. Air Canada introduced Executive Class service on all routes in Canada and the United States in 1992.

Canadian Airlines International went a step further in the late 1980s with a fleet of all-business-class planes. Linen and crystal were used for meal service aboard flights. The airline also provided an exclusive reservation line and departure lounge for business travellers. In the United States, Air One and Air Atlanta also experimented with the all-business-class plane, with mixed results.

For the ultimate in speed, comfort, and prestige—and for $3,200 each way—the international business traveller can fly from New York to London or Paris on the supersonic Concorde. Although not exclusively for business travellers, the Concorde is first-class all the way. Passengers sip champagne from crystal goblets and savour gourmet meals served on bone china. Flying at twice the speed of sound, the executive traveller can cross the Atlantic in less than four hours.

Many airlines are now providing amenities even after the flight is over. The most notable service is free transfers between local airports or from the airport to downtown. For example, Japan Air Lines offers free minibus transfers between LaGuardia Airport and Kennedy Airport in New York City, and British Airways provides limousine service into New York City or London after a Concorde flight.

Canadian Airlines provides an Orient Business Card Service for customers doing business in Japan, Hong Kong, Korea, or Taiwan. They will translate, print, and deliver business cards of business travellers to these destinations, with three weeks' processing time.

Frequent Flier Programs Frequent flier programs were originally designed to pull travellers away from the multitude of low-fare carriers that sprang up after deregulation. The hope was to encourage brand loyalty by awarding bonuses to faithful travellers. It was believed that if travellers had to choose among airlines for a particular flight, they would choose the one with which they had already accumulated distance points.

Since 1981, when American Airlines introduced them, frequent flier programs have become very popular. Every major airline now has its own program, with millions of travellers participating. John Wu belongs to Canadian Plus, the frequent flier program of Canadian Airlines. Every time he flies on Canadian, he earns distance points. When his account reaches 16 000 kilometres, he will be able to cash in for a free upgrade from economy-class to first-class on his next flight. (A **free upgrade** means that the customer does not pay the difference in going from a lower to a higher class of service or product.) Or Wu can let his kilometres accumulate till they reach 160 000. Then he's entitled to two airline tickets to Europe.

Most frequent flier programs have tie-ins with hotels, car rental chains, other airlines, and even cruise lines. Sample tie-ins are shown in Table 11-2. Wu, for example, can also earn distance points in Canadian Plus by flying on American Airlines, staying in a Delta Hotel, or renting a car from Thrifty. Companies participating in a tie-in program benefit from increased patronage; for that reason, they pay the airline for the right to participate in its club.

A question that arises with frequent flier programs is this: Who should be able to keep the business traveller's bonus points? Some companies feel that since they pay for their employees' tickets, the coupons should be turned in to them. Companies can then reduce their travel costs by applying the coupons to trips by other employees. Other companies regard frequent flier points as compensation for having to travel, and allow employees to keep these benefits for their personal use.

Keeping track of points can become quite confusing, especially if the traveller belongs to more than one program. Books, newsletters, and computer software are available to help travellers with record keeping and to inform them about changes in the programs. A company's business travel department or travel agency may keep track of a traveller's points.

Although frequent flier programs have been very successful, there have been some problems. One problem has been overcrowding on flights to popular vacation destinations, such as Hawaii, when travellers are using their bonus vouchers or coupons. On any given flight, it's entirely possible that not one passenger in first-class has paid for his or her ticket! Awarding free seats to frequent fliers, of course, prevents the airlines from selling those seats to cash-paying customers and making a profit on them. Attempts on the part of airlines to raise distance requirements for popular destinations have angered club members, who feel that this is the equivalent of changing the rules in the middle of the game.

Another problem has been with coupon brokers in some countries. These people buy bonus points from frequent fliers. They redeem the points and then turn around and sell the tickets to the public at a discount. Say, for example, that a traveller in the United States has earned enough points for two coach tickets to Europe that would ordinarily cost about $1,200. The traveller may instead sell his points to a coupon broker for $500. The broker then obtains the tickets and sells them to a couple from Des Moines for $750. Everyone except the airline makes money on such deals.

Although coupon brokering is legal, airlines have been battling this practice on the grounds that it deprives them of ticket sales (the couple should have bought the tickets from the airline for $1,200). In addition to lawsuits, airlines have been formulating new rules to curb abuses, such as the requirement that bonus tickets be transferred only to travellers with the same last name.

Because of the problems, some airlines would like to do away with frequent flier programs altogether, but nobody wants to be the first to do so. Certainly, the programs have been very effective marketing tools, and it seems likely that the airlines will continue to use them. Besides encouraging product loyalty, club memberships provide airlines with convenient databases. Instead of paying for expensive advertising time on national television, airlines can market their products and services through direct mailings to frequent fliers—the group most likely to purchase them anyway.

Airport Comforts Airlines provide private lounges where their frequent fliers can relax or work between flights or before an appointment. Canadian Airlines has the Empress Lounge system, which is available to any President's Club Gold or Empress Lounge member, as well as to first- and business-class customers travelling on international and transborder scheduled flights. Airports, too, provide special facilities geared toward business travellers.

At many airports, travellers can take advantage of full-service business centres. The Tele-Trip Company, for example, operates business centres in 19 airports in the United States. These centres provide foreign money exchange as

NORTH AMERICAN PARTNERSHIPS

Airline Program	Partner Airlines	Hotels	Car Rentals	Credit Cards	Other
Air Canada Aeroplan	Continental, United, Air Canada Connectors	The Capri, The Charlottetown, Regina Inn, Hilton International, Holiday Inn, Keddy's, Ocean Pointe Resort, Sheraton, Vista International, Westin, Radisson, Hotel des Gouverneurs	Avis, Budget	CIBC Aerogold Visa, enRoute/Diners Club	Air Canada Vacations, Park n' Fly
Canadian Plus	Air Alma, Air Atlantic, Aloha Airlines, Aloha Island Air, American Airlines/American Eagle, Calm Air, Canadian Regional, Inter Canadien, North-Wright Air, Pem-Air, Ptarmigan Airways	Albatross, Cambridge Suites, CP, Coast, Delta, Doubletree, Explorer Hotel, Frobisher Inn, Glynmill Inn, Inter-Continental, Ramada, Swissôtel-T3, Westcoast, Westmark	National Interrent, Thrifty, Tilden Interrent	Canadian Plus Royal Trust MasterCard, American Express Membership Rewards	AMJ Campbell Van Lines, Brewsters, Canadian Luggage Centres, Park & Jet, YVR Park (Vancouver Int'l Airport), Canadian Holidays
American AAdvantage	American Eagle, TWA, Ultra Air, Canadian Airlines	Hilton, Inter-Continantal, Marriott, ITT Sheraton, Wyndham, Conrad, Forum	Avis, Hertz	Citibank AAdvantage Visa and MasterCard, Diners Club	AMR Teleservice Resources, MCI Calling Card, American Traveller Catalog, Citibank Consumer Banking, American, AAdvantage Money Market Fund, SNET Mobilecom
Continental OnePass	GP Express, BWIA International, Cayman Airways	Camino Real, Aston, Radisson, Doubletree, CP, Marriott	Dollar, National Interrent, Thrifty, Tilden Interrent	American Express, Diners Club, OnePass Marine Midland Gold MasterCard and Visa	TWE Phone Services, SkyCar Limousines
Northwest WorldPerks	America West, Alaska Airlines, USAir, Midwest Express, KLM	Colony, Holiday Inn, Hyatt, Marriott, Radisson, Westin, New Otani	Tilden Interrent, National Interrent, Nippon Interrent (Hawaii only), Hertz, Budget	American Express, Diners Club, WorldPerks Bank One Visa	WorldPerks MCI Calling Card, Dining for Miles
United Mileage Plus	Air Canada, Aloha Airlines	Hilton, Hyatt, Inter-Continental, ITT Sheraton, Westin	Hertz, Alamo, National Interrent	Diners Club, Mileage Plus First Chicago Gold MasterCard and Visa, Mileage Plus First Chicago Visa, United Airlines Travel Card	Holland America Lines, Princess Cruises, Royal Caribbean Cruise Line, Royal Viking Line

TABLE 11-2
Sample Frequent Flier Tie-Ins; North American Partnerships
SOURCE: "Miles Ahead," *Destination: Business Traveller, The Globe and Mail,* May 1993

PROFILE

Frequent Traveller Program

If you fly 100 000 miles (160 000 kilometres) on Continental Airlines, the company will give you two round-trip, first-class tickets to Hawaii or two round-trip, business-class tickets to Europe. The Sheraton Hotel chain awards points for every dollar you spend at one of their hotels, which you can redeem for discounts on gifts and travel expenses. When you rent a car from General Rent-A-Car, you earn credits toward free car rentals, free kilometres, or a vehicle upgrade.

Airlines, hotels, and other suppliers use frequent traveller programs like these to attract, keep, and reward loyal customers. The idea is simple: the more you use the same companies for your travel needs, the more free travel and other discounts you get back.

Most of the major airlines began frequent flier programs in the early 1980s, after they were deregulated and began to compete more aggressively for customers. Since then, these programs have mushroomed into multimillion-dollar giveaways. An estimated 22 million travellers are enrolled in frequent traveller programs, and several hundred thousand people take free trips each year.

The frequent flier programs have been a particular boon to business travellers, who must fly thousands of kilometres each year on company business. Some corporations allow their employees to keep the frequent flier bonuses for their personal use. Many companies, however, require that their employees turn their points over to the company travel department so that other employees can use them for business trips. In this way, the company saves on travel costs.

The airlines have the oldest and most extensive frequent traveller programs, but other travel suppliers have similar plans. Several hotel chains have "frequent stayer" clubs or plans that allow guests to earn points toward free rooms, discounted meals, and other perks. Some chains offer "recognition" to frequent guests in the form of extra services, which can include express check-in and check-out, newsletters, gift certificates, and exclusive weekend packages. One hotel goes so far as to embroider the names of frequent guests on hotel robes.

Many car rental agencies and some cruise lines also offer special programs to repeat customers. A typical car rental program offers a free weekend day with a minimum two-day rental. Most cruise lines work in conjunction with airlines. For example, a flier who has logged 80,000 miles (128 000 kilometres) on USAir can buy a three-day cruise on a Carnival ship and get a second three-day cruise for free. Other cruise lines offer discount rates to frequent fliers.

Commonly, frequent traveller plans are tied into one another. If you are a member of American Airlines's AAdvantage club, you can use your accumulated points to receive discounts on certain foreign airlines, such as Qantas and British Airways. Other options are to rent a car at Avis, stay at a Hilton hotel, or take a cruise on a Royal Viking ship, all at discounted rates.

Travel agents have long been ambivalent about frequent flier clubs. Many do not like the programs because they do not receive commissions on free flights. Other travel agents accept the clubs because free flights often generate commissions from hotel bookings and car rentals. Travel suppliers have had mixed results with their frequent traveller programs. Many hotel chains have tried, then dropped, their point systems in favour of recognition programs, and some car rental agencies have had only modest success with their programs.

For some airlines, the frequent flier clubs are too successful. An airline has to spend just as much to honour a free ticket as one that has been paid for, but free flights generate no income for the company. In the late 1980s, the airlines began to realize that they had given away a lot of free kilometres that had not yet been used. By 1989, according to one analysis, frequent fliers had accumulated $750 million worth of unclaimed free travel.

Fearing a run on free tickets, the airlines began to look for cheaper ways to entice customers to cash in their free kilometres. Some held auctions at which customers could bid accumulated kilometres for such prizes as golden retriever puppies and round-the-world trips. Others issued glossy catalogues in which they offered discounts on the purchase of cars, jewellery, furs, and vacation homes. The auctions and discount purchase programs were only moderately successful. Most frequent fliers, the airlines have found, still want free travel more than anything else as a reward for their loyalty.

ILLUSTRATION 11-1
Business travel has grown enormously during the decades since World War II. Business centres, such as this one at the Delta Toronto Airport Hotel, offer the latest accommodation to business travellers.
SOURCE: Courtesy of Delta Hotels & Resorts

well as postal and notary services and photocopying and fax machines. Also, travellers who find themselves short of cash can obtain emergency funds.

Most major airports have conference rooms that they rent to corporations. Executives from all over the country can fly in, attend a meeting, and fly out again without ever having to leave the airport.

Corporate Discounts Canadian consumers are accustomed to seeing advertisements proclaiming 10 percent off the price of a refrigerator or 25 percent off the price of a sweater. Discounting—selling merchandise at less than the published price—is a standard practice in marketing.

Airlines offer discounts directly to corporations in order to gain their business. By designating an airline as its preferred carrier and promising a certain volume of travellers, the corporation gets dollars off each airfare it purchases.

Airlines offer various types of discounts. A systemwide discount, offered by major carriers with extensive routes, applies to any combination of cities to which the company's employees normally travel. A city-pair discount is offered where there is intense airline competition between two points, such as Toronto to Montreal. A group discount—different from a discount offered to groups for a one-time trip—may be given when a corporation has many employees consistently travelling to the same place. For example, a California movie studio periodically sends production-crew members from Los Angeles to San Francisco for filming. These employees fly at a discounted rate each time they make the trip.

Although discounting is commonplace, the airlines don't advertise the fact that they give corporate discounts. Deals are made behind closed doors and are not discussed publicly. Airlines don't want the specifics of a particular deal revealed, for fear that they would have to make the same deal with every other corporation.

Airlines don't particularly like giving discounts. For one thing, there is no assurance that corporations will remain loyal, so time and effort spent in negotiations may be wasted. Airlines also worry about fighting discounting wars with other airlines, which could drain them financially. Revenues lost to discounting must be recovered either through higher costs to vacation travellers or through reduced services. But these solutions can backfire on an airline if they turn customers away.

Corporate Rebates Another popular sales tool is the **rebate.** Whereas a discount is money off the listed price, a rebate is cash back after the purchase has been made. In a typical rebate offer, a consumer purchases (for example) three packages of light bulbs and sends proof of purchase to the manufacturer. The manufacturer then sends the consumer a check for $1. Offers of cash rebates are commonly used in advertising for new cars and appliances.

Airlines, too, offer rebates. For example, after a corporation has purchased products and services totalling $25,000, the airline might give the corporation a rebate of 4 percent.

Car Rental Service

To compete for the business of business travellers, car rental chains employ tactics similar to those of the airlines. These tactics include corporate discounts and rebates, club memberships with tie-ins to frequent flier and frequent stay programs, and special incentives.

To get a standard discount, corporations contract to do a certain amount of business (say, $10,000 a year) with the car rental agency. Each time an employee rents a car from that agency for business travel, the corporation gets from 10 percent to 30 percent off the regular price. The type of car

ILLUSTRATION 11-2
Travellers can take advantage of car rental kiosks found at today's airports.
SOURCE: Courtesy Tilden Rent-a-Car System Ltd.

PROFILE

P. Lawson Travel and Carlson Wagonlit Travel

Written by Marie Rennie

In 1931, Peter Lawson founded P. Lawson Agencies, the first travel bureau in Alberta. In 1957 the company began a calculated expansion, opening its first branch office in Lethbridge, Alberta. In 1966, the company moved its administrative offices from Calgary to Toronto.

During the 1960s and 1970s P. Lawson established links with Bel-Air Travel and Warnock Hersey International Limited. In 1983 it became a part of the Carlson Marketing Company and assumed responsibility for the John Austin Travel and Ask Mr. Foster Travel offices in Canada. In 1986, the company entered into a partnership with Harvey's Travel Ltd. of St. John's, Newfoundland.

Today, there are about 125 P. Lawson/Bel-Air/Harvey's offices in Canada with about 1000 employees, many of whom have earned long-service awards.

On January 1, 1994, Michael Hannah became president of Lawson Travel. Hannah had joined the company in January 1991, as senior vice-president operations. He is currently national president of the Alliance of Canadian Travel Associations (ACTA) and a director of the board of trustees of the Ontario Travel Compensation Fund.

Carlson Travel Group, the parent company of Lawson Travel, announced in April 1994, that it would launch an associate program in Canada by offering franchise agreements to qualified, independent Canadian travel agencies. The program will be similar to Carlson's successful association program in the United States.

"There is tremendous potential for independent agencies that affiliate with us," said Hannah. New associates will benefit from increased regional presence through cooperative marketing programs, greater buying power, and a wide array of customer and agency services that the agencies would not be able to provide on their own."

Lawson Travel will coordinate the new associate program in Canada and has already begun taking applications from interested agencies. "We anticipate signing at least 30 associate agencies by December 31, 1994, growing to approximately 150 by December 1997," Hannah has said.

Lawson Travel associates will be able to offer leisure and business travellers new benefits, including guaranteed lowest airfares at the time of purchase, reduced rates at major hotels worldwide, for cruise vacations, specially arranged tours, and access to Carlson's 24-hour service centre and international rate desk.

Associate agencies also have access to marketing support, advertising materials, the Associate Consulting Service, and a broad range of training programs; they can also participate in national and international meetings and forums.

Carlson Travel Network was born as Ask Mr. Foster in St. Augustine, Florida, in 1888. In 1979, the company was acquired by international businessman, Curt Carlson, of Minneapolis, Minnesota. In 1993, Carlson and its franchisees had system-wide revenues of more than $6 billion. The network's 2300 offices in 22 countries made it the second-largest American travel company.

Carlson Travel Group is still based in Minneapolis. It is one part of the Carlson Companies empire, which also includes Carlson Marketing Group (one of the world's largest marketing services organizations), and Carlson Hospitality Group, which operates, manages, and franchises Radisson Hotels, T.G.I. Friday's restaurants, Country Lodging, and Country Kitchen.

Wagonlit Travel was founded in 1872 by a Belgian, Georges Nagelmackers. He started out serving overnight travellers on European trains by creating *wagons-lits,* literally, "sleeping cars." His company grew to service all types of travellers. In 1928, full-service Wagonlit travel agencies appeared in rail ticket offices throughout Europe. In 1993, Wagonlit Travel had system-wide revenues of more than $5.2 billion and offices in 125 countries. Its parent company is the Accor Group.

The Accor Group is a $14 billion travel, tourism, and business services company. From its base in Paris, the group operates 2250 hotels, 700 restaurants, and 4500 institutional catering facilities; Accor also rents 3 million cars each year, sells 7 million service vouchers, and serves 7 million rail passengers.

Carlson Travel is joining with Wagonlit to form Carlson Wagonlit Travel, the world's largest business travel management company. This megagroup will have more than 4000 locations in 125 countries and more than 20 000 employees worldwide. In the United States and Canada, by December 1995, all Carlson-owned business travel offices and Lawson, Bel-Air, and Harvey's offices will take the name Carlson Wagonlit Travel.

(i.e., luxury or economy) and distance restrictions (if any) are specified in the contract.

The major car rental chains—including Hertz, Avis, and National—have fairly well saturated the corporate market. They are now competing with second-tier rental companies for small-business customers. By requiring lower volume and offering attractive incentives, lesser known companies such as Alamo, Dollar, and Payless are doing well against the industry giants.

Because of the tie-in with Canadian Airlines's Mileage Plus, John Wu usually rents from Thrifty. As a member of the Thrifty Club, Wu is entitled to express rental service at airports. By calling ahead and reserving a car, he can bypass the rental counter and go directly to the rental lot. When returning the car, all he has to do is leave it in the lot—his company is billed by mail. Avis Express and Budget Rapid Action provide similar services for the business traveller in a hurry.

Many agencies now offer mobile telephones in some cars. (There is a per-minute charge for each call made.) With a mobile phone, a person riding in a car can make calls to and receive calls from almost any regular telephone in the world. This is ideal for businesspeople who must be in constant communication with their home office or with clients. Even when trapped in a traffic jam, they can conduct business via phone.

Car rental agencies are constantly introducing other incentives as well. These include computerized driving directions, 24-hour emergency road service, and destination travel guides.

Rail Service

To go from Montreal to Toronto by air costs about $400 and takes approximately two hours. This includes the cost of a taxi and the time it takes to drive from the airport to downtown. (The actual flight time is usually about one hour.) To go from Montreal to Toronto by rail costs $70 and takes about four hours. The traveller goes from city centre to city centre without having to deal with traffic.

For certain trips, taking the train is easier and cheaper than taking the plane. This is particularly true where the distances between major cities are not great. In Canada, most rail business travel occurs in the Windsor–Quebec City corridor. In the United States, trips between cities in the Northeast Corridor (New York City–Washington, D.C.; New York City–Boston; Washington, D.C.–Philadelphia) lend themselves well to train travel. Los Angeles–San Diego and Milwaukee–Chicago are also convenient train trips. In Europe, where many major cities are only 200 or 300 kilometres apart, travel by train is the rule rather than the exception.

Domestic Rail Service In Canada, the VIA 1 First Class service is available in the corridor on certain trains. It is attractive for many business travellers: advance reservations, seat selection service, pre-boarding privileges, complimentary meals, newspapers, magazines, and beverages, and more spacious seats. Business travellers can park and board trains in convenient suburban locations such as Dorval, on the Montreal lakeshore, and Guildwood, 21 kilometres east of Toronto's Union Station.

American Rail Service Amtrak's Metroliner service between New York City and Washington, D.C., is designed for the business traveller. There are frequent arrivals and departures. Travellers can make reservations by telephone any hour of the day or night. They can pick up their tickets at a special express window shortly before their train leaves.

Once on board, business travellers have room to relax. The club cars have tables so that they can spread out their paperwork. Using Railfone®, they can communicate with clients from coast to coast. They are offered free continental breakfasts and hors d'oeuvres. All of these extras are meant to lure business travellers away from airlines.

The Metroliner is developing a reputation for speed and efficiency. Since there is a high demand for this service, the ticket prices are not discounted.

Foreign Rail Service In Europe, the International Inter City trains are designed for business travel. These modern, clean, and comfortable trains even provide stenographic and photocopying services for their business passengers. Canadian travellers who travel frequently in Europe can purchase various types of passes that allow unlimited travel for a specific time. Some passes, such as the France Vacancespass, are good for one country only, while others, such as the famous Eurailpass, are good for many countries.

ILLUSTRATION 11-3
Some business travellers have found that, for certain trips, taking a train is easier and cheaper than flying.
SOURCE: VIA Rail Canada

In Japan, a nation with short distances between cities, train service has been developed to a high level. Japan, in fact, has some of the fastest, safest, and most punctual trains in the world. A business traveller who needs to get from Tokyo to Osaka (a distance of about 320 kilometres) in a hurry can take the Shinkansen, a train that travels over 400 kilometres an hour. Japanese National Railways (JNR) also boasts the world's most tightly scheduled train service. Canadian travellers to Japan can purchase rail passes through Japan Air Lines.

> **CHECK YOUR PRODUCT KNOWLEDGE**
>
> 1. How does the business-class section of an airplane meet the needs of the business traveller?
> 2. What is the purpose of frequent flier programs?
> 3. What are some services provided to business travellers at airports?
> 4. Name two services provided by car rental agencies that are especially appealing to business travellers.
> 5. In what types of geographic areas can rail service effectively compete with air service?

HOSPITALITY SERVICES AND BUSINESS TRAVELLERS

The hospitality industry provides two types of facilities geared to business travellers—hotels and motels, and conference centres. Convention centres, a third type of facility, are usually built with public funds. The hospitality industry strongly promotes the construction of convention centres. These and conference centres will be described in more detail in Chapter 12.

Hotels and Motels

At 6 a.m., John Wu hears a knock on the door of his hotel room. As he had expected, it's the executive-floor concierge with his morning wake-up call. When Wu opens the door, the concierge greets him with a cheery "good morning" and hands him a cup of coffee and the morning newspaper.

At a roadside motel, a wake-up call might be a phone call from the desk clerk. At a hotel catering to frequent business travellers, services are provided with much more style and flair. Although convenience of location is the main reason for selecting a certain hotel, business travellers look for other features as well. Increased competition among hotels for the business traveller's dollar has brought about a host of special facilities, amenities, and services.

Business-Class Accommodations In response to business travellers' demands to be kept away from tourists, hotels primarily for business travellers have been developed. These hotels, which include luxurious all-suite hotels and more practical budget hotels, offer a more sedate atmosphere.

In an all-suite hotel, each unit has two main rooms—a living room and a bedroom—along with a bathroom. The living room may feature a kitchen area with refrigerator and microwave oven, so that guests can prepare meals or snacks if they wish. All-suite hotels allow business travellers more space and comfort than regular hotels. More importantly, though, the living room of the suite provides business travellers with a suitably professional and private place to meet with clients.

Hotel consultants say that all-suite hotels are now the fastest growing segment of the hospitality industry. In 1991, there were an estimated 96 000 suite units, and that number is expected to keep growing. Embassy Suites and Residence Inns are among the better-known all-suite hotel chains.

Budget hotels provide accommodations for business travellers on a tight budget. Middle-level managers, limited-expense-account travellers, and travellers paying their own expenses are typical guests. A room at a budget hotel generally costs less than $60 per night, which is 20 to 50 percent lower than a suite in an all-suite hotel. There are no bellstaff, ballrooms, or fancy restaurants. Budget hotels do try to provide some amenities, however, such as remote-control television and hair dryers.

Budget hotels have also been a fast-growing segment of the hospitality industry. Days Inn of America, one of the best known of the budget hotel chains, has 540 franchises. In Canada, Country Inn and Journey's End (now Comfort Inn by Journey's End, part of the Choice chain) are examples of rapidly growing budget chains.

Other major hotels may scatter suites among their regular hotel rooms, or they may offer executive floors for business travellers. Executive floors are usually the top floors of the hotel. For still more privacy, guests can often enter the hotel through a separate entrance and ride a separate elevator to their floor. There may also be a special hotel desk to serve business travellers.

The rooms in the executive section generally cost from 5 to 25 percent more than a regular double room. The decor is more elegant, and there are more amenities, such as bathrobes, hair dryers, and coffee makers.

A popular feature found on many executive floors is the common living room, where business travellers can relax after a long day of meetings. There, travellers can find snacks, a wet bar, and books and magazines provided by the hotel. The hotel may also employ a concierge, whose job it is to pamper business travellers. He or she may search for missing luggage, arrange sightseeing tours, sew broken zippers, send flowers, call a taxi, and much more.

Business Facilities Most hotels that cater to business travellers set aside an area where they can work. This area typically contains typewriters, photocopying machines, fax machines, personal computers, and other business equipment. It may also include a business library, with reference books too heavy for a traveller's suitcase, as well as business journals and newspapers. As necessary, the hotel will provide secretaries to help prepare documents for presentation at a meeting or to take care of correspondence.

Some hotels, such as the Waldorf Astoria in New York City, offer a full-service business centre. In addition to supplying office space and equipment, this centre has a receptionist, secretary, and notary public. Translating services are also available.

Other Facilities Hotels can provide other facilities that appeal to business travellers. Health and fitness centres are becoming common. The better ones offer an exercise room, jogging track, swimming pool, tennis and racquetball courts, and a fully equipped spa. These amenities allow guests to release the stress of working and travelling, and to continue their usual exercise regimen. For guests who prefer to exercise in private, the hotel may furnish in-room aerobics on a closed-circuit television channel.

For guests who prefer not to dine alone in a restaurant, hotel room service is available. The quality of room service in most hotels is improving, as management sees another source of profit. Guests can now order gourmet meals late at night. The meals are prepared quickly and served elegantly.

Facilities for Women Jill Rosendahl appreciates the full-length mirrors, skirt hangers, women's magazines, cut flowers, and other amenities that hotels provide to please their women guests.

The rising number of women business travellers has improved hotel service in two important ways: there is now more attention to details and better security. These improvements have benefited all travellers, not just women. For example, hotels have installed better lighting in their bathrooms so that women can see to put on their makeup. However, men also appreciate good lighting when they're shaving—as well as the free toiletries, such as shampoo, and the free use of hair dryers.

Improvements in security decrease the chances that hotel guests will be robbed or attacked. Largely because of women business travellers, many hotels now provide adequate lighting in halls and parking ramps, keyless or deadbolt locks and viewers on guest-room doors, and closed-circuit surveillance in elevators and hallways. On request, hotels will also provide security escorts to and from parking ramps.

Frequent Stay Programs Frequent-stay programs are offered by many hotels. They are similar to frequent flier programs. To encourage repeat business, hotel chains offer incentives, such as room discounts, complimentary cocktails, and express check-in and check-out. After staying a certain number of nights, guests are entitled to bonuses, such as free travel, free rental cars, or free accommodations. Table 11-3 lists some of the benefits offered by some frequent-stay programs.

Because of the tie-ins with Canadian Airlines and Thrifty, John Wu frequently stays at a Canadian Pacific (CP) hotel. He also earns bonus points that can be redeemed for

ILLUSTRATION 11-4
Hotels seek to attract fitness-conscious business travellers by offering a pool and exercise facilities.
SOURCE: Marriott Hotels and Resorts

Hotel chain	Benefits
Holiday Inn	Discounted membership events; travel and merchandise awards; travel bags; staff incentive program.
Hyatt	Check-in by phone; video check-out system; priority reservations; upgrades; newsletter; gifts; reception; concierge service; priority restaurant seating; gift certificates to friends; travel, food, and beverage awards; airline and car rental upgrades.
Marriott	Video check-out system; free travel; bonus points when flying Continental, Northwest, TWA, and USAir, or when renting Hertz; complimentary newspaper; turndown service; cheque cashing; guaranteed reservations; free upgrades when space allows; show tickets; dining discounts; sports bags.
Sheraton	Guests' club with special weekends; points can be supplemented with cash for travel awards and can be transferred for distance credits in the American or Pan Am programs; awards can be used for cash for travel with most air carriers, cruise lines, rail lines, or Sheraton hotels; merchandise catalogues.

TABLE 11-3
Sample Frequent-Stay Benefits

food and beverage awards at CP hotels, and for travel awards. After a certain number of stays, he receives a free upgrade to a more deluxe room.

Wu also patronizes Delta Hotels, where he can earn bonus points for a variety of free travel awards. Since he is always in a hurry, he appreciates Delta's in-room video check-out system. When he presses a code on a box near the television, his bill appears on the screen. He can quickly review it and authorize it for check-out. On his way out of the hotel, he can pick up a printed copy at the desk or arrange to have it mailed to his office.

Conference Centres

When Jill Rosendahl's company underwent a reorganization, the management needed to explain the new structure to the employees and help them establish new working relationships. Rather than trying to do this in an office setting—where there are all sorts of distractions—the management decided to conduct a two-day retreat at a conference centre.

A conference centre is a special facility designed to enhance various types of corporate learning. A company might rent space at a conference centre in order to hold sales meetings, brainstorm new directions, or train employees on new procedures. The centre is like a resort, with sleeping accommodations, dining rooms, and recreational opportunities. But there are also excellent facilities and equipment for meetings. Conference centres are often located in a rural area, such as the woods or the mountains. They provide a quiet setting in which employees can concentrate and gain a fresh outlook. The Chateau Montebello, halfway between Ottawa and Montreal, and said to be the "largest log cabin in the world," opened in 1930 as a resort for executives. It later became an exclusive club; then, in the early 1970s, it was opened to the public. Canada hosted the 1981 world economic summit at the Montebello.

Convention Centres

Every year, millions of North Americans like Maria Tremblay travel for the purpose of attending conventions, conferences, seminars, and workshops. In the early 1990s, annual revenues from meetings and conventions in Canada and the United States totalled approximately $43 billion. Because of the economic benefits that conventions bring to a community, cities compete with each other to attract them. Any city with a convention centre—a huge facility providing exhibition areas and a variety of meeting spaces—has an edge in this competition. Consequently, almost every city with a population of 50 000 or more has already built one or is in the process of doing so. Examples of major convention centres include the Metro Centre in Halifax and the Las Vegas Convention Center.

CHECK YOUR PRODUCT KNOWLEDGE

1. What are three types of hotel accommodations designed to meet the needs of the business traveller?
2. How do hotels meet the business traveller's need to get work done?
3. What changes have hotels made to accommodate women business travellers?
4. How do travellers become members of frequent-stay programs? What are the benefits of belonging?

THE CHANNELS OF DISTRIBUTION

In the days before airline deregulation, making arrangements for a business trip was fairly easy. There were only two or three airlines flying between major city pairs. Each one offered about the same services and charged about the same fares. Most business travellers made their own arrangements or had their secretaries make them.

However, since deregulation of the airline industry in the United States in 1978 and airline regulatory reform in Canada in 1984 and 1988, making travel arrangements has become more complicated. Both countries saw an influx of new airlines, followed by a period of consolidation and contraction. Innumerable products have flooded the marketplace, and prices of products and services are constantly changing. Following airline deregulation came deregulation of the channels of distribution. Businesses other than travel agencies could now sell airline tickets, and this further com-

ILLUSTRATION 11-5
Every year, thousands of Canadians travel to attend conventions and conferences.
SOURCE Montreal Convention Centre

plicated the marketplace. Figure 11-3 shows the methods that are used to arrange business travel.

At present, business travellers depend on two main channels of distribution to help them through the travel maze. They use the services of either a business travel department within the corporation, or a corporate travel agency. A typical corporate travel agency is a regular travel agency that has a specialty service for corporate clients. The corporation usually funnels all its travel business through this agency. Travel managers from both these channels of distribution may choose to belong to the National Business Travel Association (NBTA), a professional organization that seeks to educate and inform both its members and the greater business community about trends and issues in business travel.

Business Travel Departments

A **business travel department (BTD)** is a separate department within a corporation that handles the travel arrangements of the corporation's employees. In some cases, the BTD staff work with a selected commercial travel agency. In other cases, the staff are organized to function like a commercial travel agency. They may have their own supply of air tickets, schedules, and tariffs as well as direct access to a sponsoring airline through a computer reservations system. They look up flights, call airlines, make reservations, and issue tickets. BTD staff also make hotel and motel reservations and arrange for car rentals and other services.

Clearly, companies that have their own BTDs have a large volume of travel, which they feel they can handle more efficiently themselves. Some also feel that they can negotiate better discounts and rebates by dealing directly with the airlines.

BTDs can also provide travellers with detailed information about their destinations. For example, an executive planning a trip to Nigeria can ask the BTD to do research and provide information on the culture and business practices of that country. Travel agencies cannot be expected to conduct thorough political and economic research on every country in the world. BTDs, on the other hand, can gather detailed information on the countries with which their company deals.

In some companies, BTDs also handle personnel relocation and plans for meetings and conventions. If the company has a fleet of cars, the BTD will often be in charge of scheduling and maintenance. If the company operates corporate aircraft, the BTD will coordinate scheduling with the corporate flight department.

More and more companies are installing satellite ticket printers, or STPs (see Chapter 3). At the end of 1989, STPs were being used at approximately 3840 locations, mainly in remote areas. For example, the BTD of a company in Prince George, British Columbia, calls its ticketing agency in Vancouver and says it needs some airline tickets by the next day. Since even an express delivery service might not be able to get the tickets to Prince George so quickly, the travel agency sends the necessary information over the wire and the company's STP prints the tickets.

Corporate Travel Agencies

Aisle seat; low-calorie meals; compact car. These are some of the details in John Wu's computerized client profile. His travel agent keeps this information on file so that she can make arrangements for his trips quickly and accurately. This is just one of the ways the agency seeks to please its corporate clients.

Travel agencies are still the primary channel of distribution for corporations. However, they face a great deal of competition, mainly from business travel departments. As you have learned, BTDs can negotiate discounts and rebates with suppliers. To stay competitive, some travel agents feel compelled to offer their corporate clients similar rebates, which come out of the commissions they receive from their suppliers.

A great deal of competition exists among travel agencies themselves as they bid against each other for corporate contracts. According to one industry consultant, there were 32 500 travel agencies in 1988 in the United States. These agencies had a combined total of $42 billion in air sales. Of that total, 19 percent, or $8 billion, was generated by just 25 agencies. This is obviously a disproportionate share of the travel business. These 25 agencies are the **mega-agencies**—travel agency chains such as Carlson Travel Network and American Express. Mega-agencies bring millions of dollars of business to suppliers and can often receive greater-than-average commissions. As a result, they are willing and able to

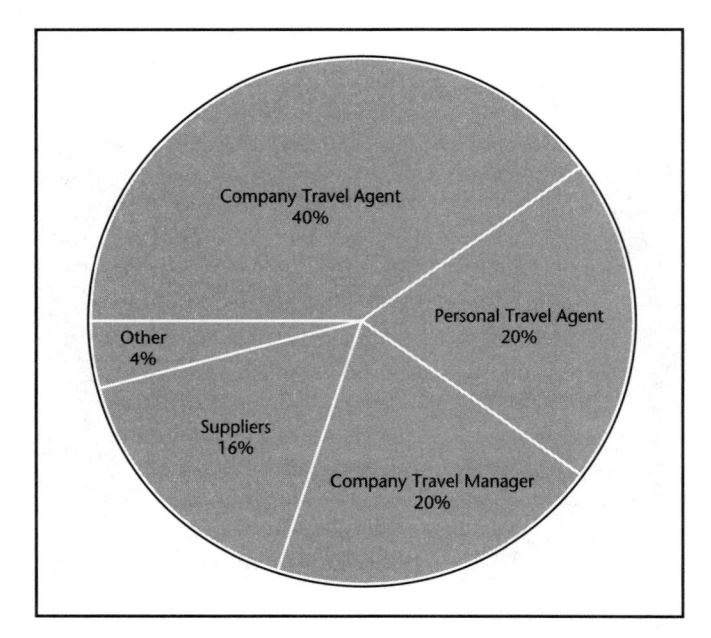

FIGURE 11-3
Methods Used to Arrange Business Travel
SOURCE: Louis Harris Survey, *Business Travel News*

- Company Travel Agent 40%
- Personal Travel Agent 20%
- Company Travel Manager 20%
- Suppliers 16%
- Other 4%

provide rebates and other services demanded by major corporate buyers. Smaller agencies could not offer the same rebates and stay in business.

Travel Management Services Because of airline regulatory reform, travel agencies are no longer just providing basic ticketing and reservations services. To win commercial accounts, travel agencies must offer complete **travel management services**. No longer can they expect to gain a company's business by mailing out a simple brochure. Now they must present a well-prepared proposal in which they demonstrate an understanding of the client's needs and show how the client will save time and money. These are some of the travel management services that clients expect from a corporate travel agency:

- Help in developing and monitoring a travel policy.
- Quarterly and monthly travel management reports.
- Delivery of tickets to the corporate office or to a drop-box at the airport.
- A WATS (wide-area telecommunications service) line so that employees can change arrangements easily while travelling.
- Extended office hours.
- A frequent flier monitoring program.
- Group meeting planning.
- Up-to-date information on changes in the travel industry.

Of course, to provide these services an agency must be fully automated—especially because business travellers tend to make frequent itinerary changes at the last minute. Computer software has been developed to help travel agencies audit a corporation's total travel budget. Some functions of the software include tracking employees' travel and entertainment spending, and reviewing trips to ensure that they meet travel policy requirements.

It's becoming more commonplace for corporations to deal directly with suppliers, particularly with the airlines. Industry analysts believe, however, that most corporations will continue to rely on the expert services of travel agencies to help them sort out a complicated market. Although suppliers may wish to reduce their dependency on travel agencies, they realize that travel agencies can provide a much wider distribution network.

Government Accounts Another result of deregulation in the United States has been that the federal government and many state governments have turned to commercial travel agencies to make travel arrangements for their employees. The federal government has been doing business with travel agencies since 1982.

Federal and state government accounts have opened up a whole new market for travel agencies. In 1990, the government travel market was estimated to be $15 billion. There is even a professional organization for agents who specialize in government travel—the Society of Travel Agents in Government (STAG).

Travel agents have discovered a great deal of difference between working with the federal government and working with state governments. The federal government is easier to work with because there is a centralized authority—the Government Services Administration (GSA). The GSA imposes uniform rules, regulations, and requisites on the contracting of travel agents. State governments are generally more difficult to work with because there is no centralized authority, and procedures vary from state to state and from department to department within a state.

In Canada, governments at both the federal and provincial levels have used both travel agencies and BTDs. With the trend toward privatization, governments are utilizing the services of travel agencies to a greater extent.

CHECK YOUR PRODUCT KNOWLEDGE

1. Give three reasons why a corporation would establish its own business travel department.
2. What advantages does a mega-agency have over a small travel agency?
3. How have travel agencies that handle corporate accounts changed since deregulation? Why have these changes occurred?
4. List the eight travel management services that are designed to meet the needs of the business traveller.
5. What new market has opened up to travel agencies in recent years?

CAREER OPPORTUNITIES

As a future travel professional, you may want to choose a career related to business travel. Two challenging and rewarding careers are corporate travel manager and commercial travel agent. Perhaps the main requirement for each of these careers is flexibility. You must be able to adapt to changes that occur in travellers' itineraries and in available products and services. These changes occur weekly, daily, and sometimes even by the minute!

Corporate Travel Manager

Corporate travel managers establish and monitor a company's travel budget and travel policy. They may serve as a liaison between the company and an outside travel agency, or they may manage a company's in-house travel department. Liaisons are responsible for choosing the agency that will handle the company's account.

Managers of a BTD are responsible for the travel arrangements for executives, salespeople, and other employees who are authorized to travel. Depending on the size of the company, they may make these arrangements themselves or supervise a staff. If the company is very large, a corporate travel manager may also supervise the travel of other divisions of the company.

A BTD manager must also find new and innovative ways to provide business travel services that will benefit the company and its employees. The BTD manager arranges corporate discounts with suppliers and must therefore possess excellent negotiating skills.

As business travel increases and as companies seek to control their travel costs, more and more companies will employ corporate travel managers. In fact, many current positions were created by people who at one time worked in their company's purchasing or accounting department. They saw a need for travel to be handled as a separate function and convinced company executives to let them set up a program.

Because of the need to prepare financial reports, corporate travel managers should have a business background in marketing and accounting. They should also be thoroughly familiar with computer reservations systems. Many corporate travel managers have experience as reservationists with an airline or as travel counsellors with a travel agency.

At present, about 70 percent of corporate travel managers are women. Corporate travel managers can advance by assuming the same position in a larger company.

Commercial Travel Agent

Commercial travel agents work for agencies specializing in making travel arrangements for corporations. Besides being able to look up schedules and rates, make reservations, and write tickets, commercial travel agents must be well acquainted with products and services geared to the business traveller. They must be able to relate this kind of information:

- Special business services and amenities offered by hotels.
- How to qualify for lower airfare.
- The most convenient hotel.
- The best way from the airport to downtown.
- Changes in frequent flier programs.

Agents keep up-to-date files on their business clients. These files state the client's travel preferences so that arrangements can be made quickly and accurately.

Commercial travel agents with more experience may become involved in writing and presenting proposals to gain corporate accounts, and in managing corporate accounts. They need strong negotiating skills for these tasks. They may also be asked to analyze the profitability of accounts. For example, some accounts will offer high volume but result in little profit for the agency because of low-yield tickets and delays in payment.

Post-secondary training is becoming increasingly important for travel agents. Courses in computers, business administration, and accounting are essential for agents working on commercial accounts. If business travellers will be going abroad, agents must know about foreign fares and transportation. They must also know about the culture and customs of an area and about health and visa requirements. Of course, personal travel experience is invaluable.

Commercial travel agents can advance by becoming agency managers or directors. They can even go into business for themselves. As with hotels, there are more opportunities for advancement in an agency with many branch offices. Because of agency mergers and competition, the employment outlook for commercial travel agents is uncertain.

Summary

- Business trips are taken for the purpose of buying and selling goods and services, developing business opportunities, visiting branch offices, and attending business-related meetings.
- Business travellers provide the travel industry with a great deal of income. The travel industry appreciates business travel because it tends to be nonseasonal and inelastic.
- The various components of the travel industry compete with each other for the business of the business traveller. They especially attempt to meet the needs and expectations of the frequent business traveller.
- Business travellers expect speed, efficiency, and comfort from travel products and services. They are willing to pay higher prices to have their needs met, but cost is still a factor in selecting an airline or a hotel.
- The number of women business travellers is increasing. In general, women business travellers have the same MNEs as their male counterparts.
- Airlines attempt to meet business travellers' needs by scheduling frequent flights to major destinations, business-class service, and special airport lounges. They also reward frequent fliers with bonus points, which can be redeemed for free travel and other prizes. Airlines also negotiate discounts and rebates with corporations.
- Car rental chains compete for the business traveller's dollar by offering discounts, special privileges for club members (such as speedy rental procedures), and other incentives (such as free upgrades and phones).
- In densely populated regions, and anywhere the distance between major cities is not great, rail service is often less costly and more efficient than air service for the business traveller.
- Hotels help business travellers relax and get work done by providing all-business-class accommodations and office space. Hotels also offer frequent-stay programs to encourage repeat business.

A DAY IN THE LIFE OF

A Hotel Concierge

As a hotel concierge, my job is to solve problems for the guests in my hotel. I sit at a desk in the lobby where guests can come to ask for information, complain, or seek help. Usually their most pressing problem is where to find a good restaurant or how to get theatre tickets. Sometimes their needs are more difficult to meet, but I take great pride in trying my best to solve every problem.

To many Canadians, a concierge is a doorkeeper at a European hotel or apartment house. *Concierge* is French for "guardian" or "doorkeeper." It can also mean a janitor or building superintendent. In fact, at European hotels, a concierge is more like a private secretary for guests, especially business and professional travellers. The concierge makes the arrangements and performs the tasks that a private secretary might perform, such as making restaurant reservations, booking airplane flights, reserving rental cars, and hiring limousines.

Concierges are very common in European hotels, and they are gaining popularity in North American hotels as well. In some American hotels, the concierge is called the assistant manager for guest relations. Some American hotels consider having a concierge an unaffordable luxury. Others have learned that concierges are very useful because they free the front desk staff to concentrate on making reservations, renting rooms, and preparing bills. In addition, concierges generate much good will for the hotel, thus ensuring return visits.

I am a member of Les Clefs d'Or, which means "the Golden Keys." This is an international association of concierges, which has about 4000 members worldwide. Many concierges wear the concierge's symbol of crossed gold keys on their lapels. Many years ago, the crossed keys meant that the concierge was the person in charge of the hotel's keys. Now, of course, we don't literally keep the keys; still, I like to think we are the key to making sure our guests have a pleasant stay.

Concierges are sometimes asked to do very difficult, if not impossible, tasks. One of my colleagues was once asked to stock a guest's private zoo with 20 pairs of animals. Another arranged a facelift for a client, and still another colleague once organized the purchase of a town house for a guest. More often, however, the problems we solve are less difficult. We find lost luggage and passports, make reservations for guests at nearby restaurants or at hotels in other cities, arrange for baby-sitters, and help foreign guests with language problems.

As a concierge, I must be very resourceful and discreet. Concierges have to know a lot of people, because we have to be able to tap many different sources to obtain hard-to-get items, like tickets for sold-out shows and sporting events. In addition, concierges enjoy the confidence of their clients, even up to the point of helping them out of embarrassing situations. Our clients count on us to keep our mouths shut about their business, and we do.

At the best hotels, the concierge is a high-level employee, sometimes even a member of management rather than of the service staff. Some concierges at large hotels head their own staff of five or six assistant concierges. Concierges usually have to work their way up to their position by serving in lower-level positions such as desk clerk. It usually takes several years on the job for a person to acquire the training and experience necessary to be a first-class concierge.

I was promoted to concierge at my hotel after graduating from a university school in hotel and restaurant management and working at the front desk for five years. Some people learn to be concierges at the International Concierge Institute in Paris, a training school for concierges. In addition to my formal training, I speak French and Spanish as well as English. Knowing at least one foreign language is a must for concierges. Some of the best concierges know several languages.

I love my job because it is so interesting and challenging. I enjoy helping people, and I especially enjoy being confronted with a difficult problem that takes all my ingenuity to solve. That is when I function at my best. I think being a concierge is the perfect job for me.

- Business travel departments and corporate travel agencies help business travellers make arrangements for their trips. To win corporate accounts, travel agencies must propose a program of travel management and offer a wide array of services.

Key Terms

per diem
business-class
frequent flier program
free upgrade
rebate
frequent-stay program
business travel department (BTD)
mega-agency
travel management services

What Do You Think?

1. List as many differences as you can between vacation travellers and business travellers.
2. Should frequent flier awards be taxed like interest on a savings account? Why or why not?
3. What can airlines do to prevent abuses in their frequent flier programs?
4. Should airlines and other suppliers of travel products offer corporate discounts and rebates? Explain.
5. Will advances in technology, such as the satellite ticket printer, make travel agents redundant? Why or why not?
6. Do business travellers spend too much money on travel? Explain your point of view.
7. What factors are likely to stimulate or reduce the amount of business travel in the future?

Dealing with Product

You are the manager of a medium-sized travel agency, the fourth-largest of the 12 retail travel agencies in Yourtown. The largest employer in Yourtown is the Ajax Widget Manufacturing Company, which has three separate plants as well as a large warehouse facility near the airport. You have just learned that Ajax intends to consolidate all of its company travel activities within a single business travel department (BTD), and to award all of its business to a single travel agency. At present, Ajax uses four travel agencies, including yours. It is common knowledge that Ajax spends more than $5 million on corporate travel every year.

Ajax will be entertaining bids. Do you want to be the low bid for this commercial account? Exactly what would you guarantee to do for Ajax in your proposal? What will Ajax expect you to do? How might this commercial account affect your organization?

Dealing with People

By now, you fully recognize that every traveller has a special set of MNEs. Although we seldom think of a business as a "person," most companies also have a set of MNEs when it comes to corporate travel.

You are the manager of a large business travel department. At today's departmental meeting, the treasurer is recommending a new company policy on frequent traveller awards. The present policy allows employees to keep their bonus points, free flights, and other prizes. The treasurer insists that since the company paid for the travel, the company is entitled to all frequent traveller awards. These "freebies" are company property, and the company will save money by using the free trips and travel services for future company travel.

"No way!" says the vice-president of sales, who manages 30 field representatives. These salespeople are on the road and away from home for days, even weeks at a time. They live in an often-hectic world of flight delays and cancellations, rescheduled appointments, and high pressure. She insists that her sales reps should be allowed to keep all the free trips and bonuses that they earn. Furthermore, she believes that taking away these "freebies" would cause a severe morale problem.

You are expected to share your wisdom at today's meeting. What will you say to the treasurer and to the vice-president of sales? What will you recommend to the president?

CHAPTER 11: The Business of Business Travel   Name: _____

WORKSHEET 11-1 Meeting the MNEs of Business Travellers

Contact an airline, a hotel, a car rental agency, and a travel agency in Yourtown. Find out what services and amenities each one offers to meet the MNEs of business travellers. Use the boxes below to record your findings.

Airline _____	Yes	No
Business-class section		
Airport lounge		
Free transfers		
Frequent flier program		
Other:		

Hotel _____	Yes	No
Business-class area		
Office facilities		
Recreational facilities		
Frequent-stay program		
Other:		

Car Rental Agency _____	Yes	No
Express service		
Mobile phones		
Tie-ins		
Emergency road service		
Other:		

Travel Agency _____	Yes	No
Client profiles		
Ticket delivery		
Frequent flier monitoring		
WATS line		
Other:		

CHAPTER 11: The Business of Business Travel   Name: _____

WORKSHEET 11-2 Arranging Business Travel

You work in the business travel department of a large Toronto corporation. What kind of travel and accommodations arrangements will you make for the company employees listed below? Describe the kind of transportation, accommodations, and services you will arrange (in general terms—not specific flights, names, and so on).

1. A vice-president of research and development will tour facilities in Europe, stopping in Munich, Vienna, Budapest, Warsaw, and Berlin. He does not speak a foreign language. He would like to be able to work while travelling from city to city. He would also like to do a little sightseeing.

2. A computer technician will be spending a week in Calgary to help set up satellite facilities. He needs to get to and from several locations by himself at various times of the day and night.

3. A member of the board of directors is meeting with an important potential client in Halifax, Nova Scotia. The board member has been confined to a wheelchair since being injured in a car accident several years ago. He will spend two nights in Halifax and would like to be able to take the potential client to dinner at one of the city's finest restaurants.

4. A company lawyer is spending three days in Tokyo and two days in Osaka, Japan, for intensive contract negotiations. She will need space to meet with clients and will need to have papers typed and copied. She will have to stay in touch with the main office, and will also need access to a fax machine.

5. The 20-member marketing staff is hosting a four-day sales conference for the company's 500 salespeople.

6. The executive vice-president for corporate affairs will be travelling to Ottawa to give the keynote address at the annual meeting of the Chamber of Commerce. Immediately after her speech, she must travel to Montreal for another meeting. After an overnight stay in Montreal, she must be in Quebec City early the next morning.

CHAPTER 11: The Business of Business Travel   Name: _____

WORKSHEET 11-3 Women Business Travellers

The number of women travelling for business is steadily increasing. Consequently, the hospitality industry is increasingly concerned with appealing to this market. A woman business traveller will probably appreciate having a hair dryer in her hotel room, for instance, so that she does not have to pack one. You work in the public relations department of a large, nationwide hotel chain. You are planning a promotional letter to be sent to members of the National Society of Women Executives. What features, facilities, and services can your chain offer women business travellers?

Which of these features would also attract men business travellers?

Besides direct mailings to professional women's organizations, how can your chain promote itself to women business travellers?

CHAPTER 11: The Business of Business Travel   Name: _____

WORKSHEET 11-4 Provincial Government Business Travel

Contact the appropriate government office to determine the travel policy for provincial officials and employees in your province. What are the regulations or guidelines for the following?

Official cars and limousines

Air transportation

Surface transportation

Car rental

Hotel and motel accommodations

Attendance at conferences or special meetings

Expense accounts for travel

Per diem allowances for travel

Frequent flier benefits

CHAPTER 12

Meetings, Conventions, and Incentive Travel

*"There are dancing rooms and dining rooms, listening
rooms and talking rooms ... big rooms, small rooms,
banquet rooms, ballrooms ... pink rooms, red rooms,
blue rooms, bedrooms ... fun rooms, sun rooms ...
old rooms, new rooms—altogether six hundred
and two rooms."*

advertisement for St. Regis Hotel, New York

OBJECTIVES

When you have completed this chapter, you should be able to do the following:

- Explain why the number of meetings held every year has grown dramatically in recent decades.
- Identify the six major types of locations where meetings are held.
- Distinguish between conference centres and convention centres.
- List the different kinds of meetings.
- Name the different categories of associations that hold meetings.
- Determine the needs of the association market.
- Identify the six types of corporate meetings.
- Outline the characteristics of the corporate market.
- Describe the role of the meeting planner.
- Explain the difference between pure incentives and sales incentives.
- Distinguish between trade shows and exhibitions.
- List characteristics of international trade shows.
- Identify the channels by which the meetings product is distributed to the consumer.

Meetings, conventions, and incentive travel have become an important source of income for travel industry suppliers. In the past 35 years, the meetings and conventions business has grown from relative insignificance into a multibillion-dollar-a-year industry. Today, it is estimated that more than 100 000 meetings are held every year in Canada alone, generating almost $4 billion worth of goods and services. Many Canadians also travel to meetings and conventions in the United States. In addition, thousands of corporations have introduced incentive travel programs, on which they spend millions of dollars a year.

THE WHERE, WHAT, AND WHY OF MEETINGS

Until the late 1950s, most meetings were regional. Ford Motor Company might, for example, hold a meeting in Calgary for Alberta Ford dealers, a meeting in Moncton for Maritime dealers, another meeting in Sherbrooke for dealers in Quebec, and so on. National meetings were rare because long-distance travel was impractical. Trans-Canada Airlines (now Air Canada) offered some transcontinental services in the early 1950s, but most long-distance travel was still by rail or by road. Business executives could rarely afford the time to travel to meetings on the other side of the country.

The Growth of Meetings

The breakthrough for the meetings business came with advances in the transportation industry. As you have read so often in this book, the advent of the jet age brought major changes. When Trans-Canada Airlines introduced nonstop passenger jet service between Montreal and Vancouver, coast-to-coast crossing time was cut to five hours. Jet planes made travel to meetings faster, more convenient, and in many cases less expensive. With the extension of domestic jet routes, many destinations became accessible for national meetings. International meetings became possible once daily flights to overseas destinations were introduced. The lower airfares of recent years have further stimulated the growth of the meetings business.

Improvements in ground transportation have also contributed to the expansion of the meetings market. State-of-the-art motorcoaches transport delegates and businesspeople to local meetings in luxury. Car rental fleets have been expanded to accommodate even the largest of meetings crowds.

One final factor in the growth of the meetings market has been the increased automation of the travel industry. Computer reservations systems have made it possible to coordinate meetings of 10 000 or more delegates.

The volume of the meetings business has grown; so, too, has the number of destinations with facilities to handle large meetings. Hub cities—those cities at the centre of an air carrier's route structure—are presenting themselves as ideal meeting sites. They include mid-sized cities such as Halifax, Winnipeg, Calgary, Nashville, Memphis, Denver, Phoenix, Cincinnati, and Charlotte. The 1970s and 1980s were a boom period for the building of convention centres throughout Canada and the United States. Resort locations have also become increasingly attractive as sites for meetings.

The increased demand for meetings has created a corresponding demand for new services, including meeting planning and destination management. You will read about these developments in the sections to come. You will also read about the different kinds of meetings and about the two basic segments of the meetings market.

Locations for Meetings

Off-site meetings—those that do not take place on the premises of the sponsoring company—can be held at any of six main types of location:

- hotels
- resorts
- conference centres
- convention centres
- civic centres
- cruise ships

Hotels Today, meetings generate about 20 percent of total hotel revenues. Some individual properties derive as much as 40 percent of their income from meetings and conventions. Thirty-five years ago, however, few hotels actively solicited meetings business. In fact, many were reluctant to open their doors to convention groups, preferring to rely on individual business travellers and vacationers. What meeting rooms

ILLUSTRATION 12-1
Opened in July 1987, the Vancouver Trade and Convention Centre has 21 meeting rooms and 8700 square metres of column-free exhibition space. It can cater to 7000 banquet guests, or 10 000 for a reception.
SOURCE: Vancouver Trade and Convention Centre

there were in hotels were usually small and designed for weddings, balls, and other social functions.

By the mid-1960s, hoteliers had begun to realize that the growing meetings business could provide a valuable source of income, particularly during off-peak periods. Giant showcase hotels, such as the Hyatt Regency, built in downtown Atlanta in 1967, were specifically designed to cater to the meetings market. They were equipped with spacious assembly rooms and exhibition areas and a full range of audio-visual aids. Convention hotels were also built at airports and in suburban locations. By the 1980s, almost all new commercial hotels featured facilities for meetings.

Resorts Resorts have become increasingly popular as sites for meetings. A resort's secluded, scenic location is a prime attraction for meeting planners; so is the availability of on-site recreational facilities. The history of resorts as sites for meetings mirrors that of hotels. In the early days, resort owners had little interest in attracting group business. Convention-goers were regarded as second-class citizens, inferior to the wealthy upper classes who constituted the bulk of the resort clientele.

However, changing social values in the post-World War II period forced resorts to review their policies. Fashionable resorts such as the Banff Springs Hotel, the Algonquin-by-the-Sea at St. Andrews, New Brunswick (which celebrated its 100th anniversary in 1994), and the Arizona Biltmore in Phoenix changed with the times and added extensive conference facilities. Meetings now account for a large percentage of business at these facilities. Many older resorts have been converted to accommodate the growing meetings market; some new resorts have been built as year-round convention sites.

Conference Centres Conference centres cater almost exclusively to meetings, especially corporate meetings. For this reason, many meeting planners regard conference centres as ideal meeting locations. The emphasis is on a working environment with few outside distractions. Conference rooms are specifically designed for meetings (whereas in many hotels, a conference space often has to double as a banquet room or ballroom). Guest rooms have work areas with ample lighting so that delegates can work at night. A professional meetings staff is on hand to cater to the needs of delegates and planners. The Banff Centre was specifically designed and built for meetings, for both corporate and non-profit groups.

To provide delegates with some relief from work, some conference centres have added resort-type amenities, such as health facilities and tennis courts. These conference centres are not much different from resorts with meetings facilities.

Convention Centres Hotels, resorts, and conference centres can rarely accommodate groups of more than 1000 people. Larger meetings and exhibitions are held in convention centres. In addition to being larger, convention centres differ from conference centres in other ways. For example, they are always located in cities, and they do not have guest rooms on the premises. Also, they are usually built with public funds.

Before 1960, there were only a few sites capable of hosting large national conventions and trade shows. They included the Automotive Building of the Canadian National Exhibition in Toronto, Maple Leaf Gardens (in summer), the National Guard Armory in Washington, D.C., and Madison Square Garden and the Coliseum in New York City. The first convention centres with extensive exhibit areas all on one level were opened in 1960. Detroit's Cobo Hall, with 37 000 square metres of exhibition space, was the largest at the time. Since then, convention centres have been built in cities all over Canada and the United States, and more are on the way.

Canada has several major convention centres with extensive facilities—for example, Vancouver (capacity of 10 795), Edmonton (8000), Winnipeg (7200), Toronto (10 500), and Montreal (11 300). Toronto has announced that it will double the size of the Metro Convention Centre in the next few years. Table 12-1 shows how much the average convention delegate was spending on specific items as of 1990.

Many of the Canadian convention centres were built during the 1970s and 1980s in a rather rare example of the public and private sector working well together. Funding was provided by the three levels of government (federal, provincial, and municipal); the private sector offered advice and did the actual building. Some of the centres, especially those in Montreal and Toronto, were built almost solely to cater to the American convention market. Toronto's Sheraton Hotel, the largest that chain has anywhere, was built in the 1970s to host meetings held by American groups.

Category	1988	1989	1990
Hotel room and incidentals	$264.56	$275.51	$298.38
Hotel restaurants	56.87	59.22	64.14
Other restaurants	59.06	61.53	66.63
Hospitality suites	26.86	27.97	30.29
Entertainment	25.95	27.02	29.27
Retail stores	42.44	44.20	47.87
Local transportation	22.39	23.32	25.25
Other	20.50	21.35	23.12
Total	$518.65	$540.12	$584.95

TABLE 12-1

What the Average Convention Delegate Spends per Stay

SOURCE: International Association of Convention and Visitor Bureaus

Civic Centres Civic centres have much the same function as convention centres. They are used for large regional and national conventions, exhibitions, and trade shows. They are usually located in the city's central business district. Meetings are not necessarily their primary source of income, however. Cultural and sporting events are also held at civic centres. The Halifax Metro Centre (capacity of 10 000) is adjacent to the Halifax World Trade and Convention Centre (1300). Similarly, the Olympic Saddledome (16 700) provides additional capacity for the Calgary Convention Centre (2500).

Cruise Ships Meeting planners looking for more exotic locations began to use cruise ships for offshore meetings in the late 1960s. Foreign-owned cruise ships were popular until 1976 because they offered tax advantages over American ships. In 1976, however, the American government changed the tax laws and took away the advantage previously enjoyed by foreign vessels. American cruise and yacht companies were quick to step into the market, and several now have vessels fully equipped to handle small and medium-sized meetings. Cruise ships are also used for incentive travel programs (discussed later in this chapter).

Kinds of Meetings

So far in this chapter, we have used the general term *meetings* to refer to all types of gatherings. However, meetings can be classified according to the number of participants, the kinds of discussions and presentations involved, the amount of audience participation, and whether the meeting is formal or informal.

One type of meeting is called a **convention**. Conventions typically involve a general group session held in a large auditorium, followed by committee meetings in small breakout rooms. (The term **breakout** is used when a large group "breaks out" into several smaller groups.) Most conventions are held regularly (usually annually) and meet for at least three days. Trade and technical conventions are often held in conjunction with exhibitions. Attendance varies from 100 participants to 30 000 or more.

Conferences are similar to conventions, but they usually deal with specific problems or developments rather than with matters of a general nature. The Canadian Medical Association, for example, might call a conference to discuss a breakthrough in the treatment of a particular disease. Conferences involve much member participation. Attendance varies, though it is rarely as high as at conventions. **Congresses** are similar to conferences. The term is commonly used in Europe to describe international gatherings.

A **forum** involves back-and-forth discussion on a particular issue. It is usually led by panellists or presenters. Audience participation is expected and encouraged. A **symposium** is similar to a forum, though it tends to be more formal and involves less audience participation. **Lectures** are even more formal. An individual expert addresses the audience, usually from a raised platform. The presentation is sometimes followed by a question-and-answer period. Attendance at forums, symposiums, and lectures varies greatly.

Seminars are informal meetings involving face-to-face discussion. Participants share their knowledge and experiences in a particular field under the supervision of a discussion leader. **Workshops** are small group sessions (usually with a maximum of 35 participants) held for a period of intense study or training. The emphasis is on exchanging ideas and demonstrating skills and techniques. **Clinics** offer drills and instruction in specific skills for small groups. An airline reservations agent, for example, might attend a clinic to learn how to operate a computer reservations system. Many people attend clinics when they want to learn a sport, such as golf or tennis. Both clinics and workshops can last for several days.

The **panel** format calls for two or more speakers and a moderator. Panellists present their views on a particular subject. The meeting is then opened for discussion among the speakers, who may also invite comments from the audience.

Exhibitions are used for the display of goods and services by vendors. They are staged as part of a convention or conference. The term *exposition* is used in Europe to describe this same kind of presentation.

Trade shows (or **trade fairs**) feature freestanding vendor displays. Unlike exhibitions, they are not held as part of a convention. Trade shows are typically the largest type of meeting. Attendance at a major show lasting several days can top 500 000.

Teleconferencing is a way of holding one meeting at several locations simultaneously. Participants use advanced communications technology that enables them to see and hear participants at other locations. Teleconferencing is a way of bringing people together without the time and expense of long-distance travel. Several hotel chains, con-

ILLUSTRATION 12-2
Trade shows bring together exhibitors who demonstrate their products to the general public.
SOURCE: Vancouver Trade and Convention Centre

vention centres, and conference centres have introduced teleconferencing facilities in response to growing demand.

The Need for Meetings

Why has the number of meetings held every year grown so dramatically in recent decades? The simplest explanation is that technology has made the world we live in a much more complicated place than it was 35 years ago. As a result, there is a much greater need for communication in the business world. Companies must keep up-to-date with the latest technological advances if they are to remain competitive. Salespeople must be aware of new products coming onto the market. Technicians, scientists, and members of the health professions need to learn about new discoveries and techniques in their respective fields on a regular basis. Employees must be trained to operate sophisticated new machinery.

Face-to-face meetings have proved to be the most effective way of sharing information and knowledge. In addition, they present a valuable opportunity to exchange points of view, resolve problems, and discuss matters of mutual concern.

> **CHECK YOUR PRODUCT KNOWLEDGE**
>
> 1. What have been the major factors in the growth of the meetings business in the last 35 years?
> 2. List the kinds of locations used for off-site meetings.
> 3. What is the difference between a conference centre and a convention centre?
> 4. List six types of meetings that involve a high degree of audience/member participation.

THE MARKETPLACE

The previous section outlined the types of meetings and the various locations at which they are held. In this section, you will read about the different kinds of groups and organizations that hold off-site meetings. The meetings market can be divided into two basic segments: the association market and the corporate market. Each market has different characteristics and different motivations, needs, and expectations (MNEs).

The Association Market

The association market is the better known and more visible segment of the meetings field. There are associations for almost every subject and interest. Of the 80 000 associations in Canada and the United States, about one-third are national or international; the remainder are regional, provincial, or local. Most associations in Canada and the United States hold an annual convention; many have several meetings a year. In addition to holding conventions, associations also sponsor thousands of educational seminars and workshops.

The association market can be divided into these categories:

Trade Associations Almost every trade has at least one national association, as well as several regional and provincial ones. Within a single trade, there may be separate associations for manufacturers, wholesalers and distributors, and retailers. Trade conventions at the national level tend to be large gatherings: in the United States, the National Restaurant Association's annual meeting in Chicago attracts more than 100 000 delegates over a five-day period. Trade conventions are often held in conjunction with exhibits.

Professional Associations Members of professional associations can be individuals, companies, or corporations with similar business needs. Examples include the Canadian Medical Association, the Canadian Bar Association, and the Canadian Bankers' Association. All hold annual national conventions and conferences as well as regional meetings throughout the year. They use exhibits less frequently than do trade associations.

Scientific and Technical Associations Organizations in this category are another lucrative source of meetings business. Representative associations include the Engineering Institute of Canada and the Chemical Institute of Canada. In addition to holding regularly scheduled conventions, such organizations often call special meetings when the need arises to discuss new developments. These meetings tend to be highly technical and often require sophisticated presentation equipment. Social events are typically kept to a minimum so that delegates are not distracted from the business at hand.

Educational Associations National and provincial teachers' associations are the best known of the educational organizations, though this group also includes professional educators in a wide variety of other fields. In the travel industry, for example, the Society of Travel and Tourism Educators and the Council on Hotel, Restaurant and Institutional Education are prominent associations. Educational meetings are often held in the summer months, when schools are closed. This makes them particularly attractive to downtown hotels, because in many cities this is when hotel occupancy levels are at their lowest. Educational conventions tend to be longer than most other kinds, commonly involving a full five-day meeting program.

PROFILE

Darlene Stewart

Written by Don MacLaurin

What can people growing up in small-town Canada do if they want to travel and meet new people? For Darlene Stewart, who grew up in a small town near Cobourg, Ontario, the answer was obvious. In her final year of high school she researched the tourism and travel programs offered by Ontario community colleges. She decided to attend Sir Sandford Fleming College in Peterborough, Ontario; it offers tourism, travel, and hospitality programs.

In 1985, she enrolled in the two-year travel merchandising program. In 1986, a new three-year diploma program in convention management was offered, the first such program at a Canadian school. Stewart was part of the first class to graduate from that program, in 1988. She was a dean's scholar every year and the recipient of three scholarships and awards.

Her education in convention management focused on a comprehensive set of skills, all necessary for success in the meeting, convention, or trade show industry. She completed coursework in meeting planning, convention sales and services, and large-group catering and accommodation. She also completed a four-week work placement at the Ottawa Congress Centre and joined Meeting Planners International (MPI), a 10 000-member professional association. She has kept her membership. She volunteered for several work placements with MPI members and eventually received the Metro Toronto Convention and Visitors' Association "Tourism Superhero" award for her dedication.

Stewart's first job after graduation was food server at Toronto's Westin Harbour Castle Hotel. After three months she was promoted to manager of two hotel food service outlets. The restaurants were open from 6 a.m. to 2 a.m. She was responsible for all aspects of customer service and a staff of 20. She also helped analyze labour costs and make sales projections.

She accepted her first "official" meeting planner position with Base Services Meeting Planners and Association Management in Toronto. This position exposed her to the tasks involved in planning within the context of a smaller, family-operated, business environment.

She then moved to the Holloway Group as a meeting planner and operations coordinator. There, she was responsible for selling meetings and destination services and she gained experience in making cold sales calls (i.e., unannounced visits to potential clients), and with formal, written contracts. She also contracted, coordinated, and supervised tour guides used by client groups. Finally, she sharpened her administration skills in accounting, payroll, tax remittances, and other operations.

In 1991, she moved to her present employer, Odeon Cineplex of Canada. Her mandate was to research, develop, implement, and monitor a full convention-servicing program combining the facilities of 128 Odeon Cineplex cinemas with the professional services of audiovisual and catering suppliers. The company's goal was to generate income during nonfilm hours—to create a business within a business. The uniqueness of the mandate was noted by the media, and a Canadian Press article, with a photo of Darlene, appeared in many newspapers across Canada. Cinema operators around the world are watching this pilot program. Using the facilities for daytime meeting space will enhance revenues for the chain.

In April 1994, Stewart assumed a new role as manager of training and development for all North American Odeon Cineplex operations. Using the latest technology, she will develop and implement fully interactive training programs for all employees. Training will be ongoing and include workshops, videos, worksheets, job aid booklets, and a master operations manual.

Stewart views her latest promotion as the classic career progression for a meeting planner within a corporation: one starts out planning external meetings and, in time and with experience, becomes an integral part of the corporation's in-house meeting and programming needs.

Stewart believes that people educated in the meeting and convention industry today can anticipate positive career opportunities. She notes that the career advertisement for the Odeon position specified an "energetic, organized, responsible, and self-motivated person with a diploma in hospitality education." She says that recent graduates should have confidence in their abilities, but also be humble and diplomatic in their business communications. Networking is essential. Look for mentors, ask lots of questions, volunteer, join professional associations, and commit to continued self-learning.

Darlene's favourite expression is, "All things worth doing, at first seem impossible." Judging by her past, there will likely be many more achievements in her future.

Veterans' and Military Associations Veterans' groups such as the Royal Canadian Legion hold annual reunions for former members of the armed forces. Conventions at the national level attract large numbers of attendees and are mainly social in purpose. Military organizations such as the Air Force Association have conventions for active service personnel.

Fraternal Associations There are probably more fraternal associations in Canada and the United States than any other type of association. They can be divided into three main categories:

- Student fraternities and sororities.
- Service groups, whose members have a common interest or purpose, such as assisting the needy.
- Special-interest associations.

All hold regular conventions. National conventions of service groups, such as the Elks, the Loyal Order of Moose, and Rotary International, are particularly large gatherings. The emphasis is on social events, recreation, and entertainment rather than on technical, business, or professional matters. Examples of special-interest associations are the Royal Philatelic Society of Canada, the American Contract Bridge League, and the Soaring Association of Canada.

Ethnic and Religious Associations Ethnic organizations are similar in general philosophy and purpose to service groups. They place a similar emphasis on comradeship and include such organizations as the Order of the Sons of Italy and the Canadian Association in Support of the Native Peoples. Religious conventions are held both for those people whose vocation is religion (such as priests and ministers) and for the laity. The Canadian Catholic Conference is an example of the former.

Charitable Associations These include such organizations as the Canadian Red Cross and the National Multiple Sclerosis Society. They exist to raise money for charitable causes.

Political Associations and Labour Unions The most visible political conventions are those held by national parties, such as the Progressive Conservatives, the Liberals, and the New Democrats. These can be leadership conventions or policy conventions. Many other political meetings are held at the provincial and local levels. Labour unions such as the Canadian Auto Workers (CAW) also hold national and local meetings. National meetings are usually held in large convention centres and attract thousands of delegates.

Characteristics of the Association Market We have touched on some of these characteristics in describing the different types of associations. The main characteristics can be summarized as follows:

- Large number of participants (especially at national conventions).
- Voluntary attendance—participants often pay for their own travel and accommodations.
- Tourist attraction or resort often chosen as destination.
- Different destination each year.
- Meetings held on a regular cycle (usually annually or semi-annually).
- Annual meetings planned two to five years in advance.
- Three- to five-day average duration (less for smaller meetings and seminars).
- Major conventions often include exhibitions.

The MNEs of the Association Market Destination is a key motivator in attracting participants to an association meeting. Since attendance is voluntary, the organizers must choose a destination that appeals to the maximum number of potential attendees. Delegates often like to combine a business trip with a vacation, so the destination selected must have adequate recreational facilities and access to sightseeing and entertainment attractions. Spouses are more likely to attend if there is something for them to do while their husbands or wives are in a meeting. For these reasons, resorts are popular venues for association meetings. Some destinations are selected because they relate to the particular interests of the association. The Canadian Ski Council, for example, might hold its convention at a ski resort.

Delegates who regularly attend annual conventions do not want to go back to the same destination over and over. For this reason, associations usually choose a new meeting place each year. There is little point, however, in choosing an exotic, faraway location if delegates can't afford to get there (remember that most association members have to pay their own travel expenses). Ease of access is an important consideration in selecting a site, especially for regional meetings. The destination chosen will often be the one that is closest to the greatest number of members.

An association's decision-makers rate availability of suitable meeting rooms as the number-one factor when choosing the meeting site. Depending on the size and scope of the meeting, there may be a need for a large general auditorium as well as smaller spaces for workshops and committee meetings. The availability of exhibit space, meeting support services, and audio-visual equipment may also be crucial. Another very important consideration is the experience and efficiency of the convention centre's management.

Almost all national conventions need overnight accommodations. Hotels must be within the delegates' budgets. Ideally, an association tries to book all attendees into a single property. This isn't always possible if the convention is large. In such cases, a number of hotels in close proximity often cooperate to accommodate all the association's members. The quality of guest rooms (and suites, if necessary) is clearly an important factor in the selection of hotels. Other considerations might be the quality of food service and the efficiency of check-in and check-out procedures.

The Corporate Market

The corporate market is the most rapidly growing segment of the conventions market. As communication becomes ever more essential in the modern business world, the need for meetings as a means for information transfer continues to increase. The corporate market generates a greater volume of meetings business than the association market, yet corporate meetings are less visible to the public. This is because companies generally have no need to publicize off-site meetings. The delegates are required to attend.

The corporate market in Canada and the United States is made up of tens of thousands of businesses and corporations. Meetings are held at all levels of business and industry and can be divided into six main types:

Sales Meetings Sales meetings, which can be regional or national, are the best known kind of company meeting. They can be used as morale builders, or to introduce new products or new company policies, or to teach new sales techniques. Locations for sales meetings vary considerably. Some are conducted at hotels with access to the company's manufacturing plant, so that salespeople can see the product in the production stage. Others are held in major market areas, so that salespeople can make customer contacts between meetings. Average attendance is 60 for regional meetings, 175 for national meetings.

Dealer Meetings These are meetings between a company's sales staff and the dealers and distributors who represent the retail sales outlets. Like sales meetings, they are held to encourage sales performance. Dealer meetings are commonly used for introducing new products and for launching new sales and advertising campaigns. Attendance can vary from less than 20 to 2000 or more, depending on the size of the corporation and the number of retail outlets maintained.

Technical Meetings These meetings are held frequently to update engineers and other technical personnel on the latest technological developments and innovations. The seminar and workshop formats are widely used for technical meetings.

Executive/Management Meetings This category includes both executive conferences and management development seminars. The former vary greatly in attendance; the latter are usually small. As the most prestigious company personnel, executives expect the finest in accommodations and service. Deluxe hotels and conference centres, especially those in isolated resort locations, are suitable venues.

ILLUSTRATION 12-3
Advanced communications technology permits teleconferencing, where companies hold meetings at several locations simultaneously.
SOURCE: Courtesy of ADCOM Electronics Limited and PictureTel Corporation

Training Meetings Training meetings form the largest and fastest growing segment of the corporate meetings market. They are conducted for all levels of personnel, even for top executives. Attendance at workshops and clinics is usually under 50 and can be as low as 10. Isolated resorts with a minimum of outside distractions are popular locations, particularly in the off-season. For shorter training sessions, a location convenient to the company workplace is usually chosen.

Public Meetings Public meetings are those that are open to nonemployees. Shareholder meetings are the most common type. They rarely last longer than a day and therefore require no overnight accommodations.

Characteristics of the Corporate Market The corporate market is different from the association market in a number of respects. Its main characteristics include the following:

- A smaller number of participants per meeting.
- Mandatory attendance—travel and accommodation expenses are paid for by the corporation.
- The destination is sometimes keyed to the location of a company office or factory.
- The same destination may be used year after year.
- Meetings are held as need arises.
- A significantly shorter planning/booking period—often less than one year's notice.
- A slightly shorter average duration—usually about three days.
- Less use of exhibits.

The MNEs of the Corporate Market The selection of an attractive destination is not as important for the corporate market as it is for the association market. Attendance at corporate meetings is mandatory—the choice of destination therefore has no effect on the number of people attending. Corporate meeting planners do not have to "sell" the destination. Nor do they have to vary the meeting site to attract participants. In fact, many companies use the same hotel year after year (especially for training meetings). A hotel with a proven service record is usually guaranteed repeat business. This is a fundamental difference between the corporate and association markets.

Location is an important factor in destination selection. Sites close to the company facility are usually chosen. The more distant and inaccessible the location, the more it will cost the company in travel expenses. Time spent travelling also means time away from the job for company employees, who must be paid while they are attending the meeting.

The emphasis at corporate meetings is on work, with considerably less time for leisure and social activities than is provided at association meetings. Privacy and a distraction-free environment are consequently of more importance in site selection than the availability of recreational facilities and ease of access to entertainment, sightseeing, and shopping.

Corporate decision-makers have similar needs to association decision-makers when it comes to selecting a particular hotel or other venue for the meeting. They look for properties with adequate meeting space, enough guest rooms, and quality service. Because corporate meetings tend to have fewer participants, they can often be held in small and medium-sized hotels. Since many corporate meetings last for less than a day, not all of them require overnight accommodations.

CHECK YOUR PRODUCT KNOWLEDGE

1. What are the nine main types of associations that hold regular meetings?
2. List six ways in which association meetings differ from corporate meetings.
3. What is the difference between a sales meeting and a dealer meeting?
4. In what ways are the MNEs of the corporate and the association markets similar? In what ways do they differ?

THE ROLE OF THE MEETING PLANNER

The meetings market has become larger, more sophisticated, and more specialized. There is today a need for professional decision-makers who can supervise all stages of meeting preparation and presentation. Until recently, meeting planning was one of several functions performed by association and corporate executives. Now it has emerged as a specialized field.

The Meeting Planner Defined

In Canada and the United States, approximately 100 000 people are involved in meeting planning. We can identify three main categories of meeting planners:

- association executives
- corporate meeting planners
- independent meeting planners and consultants

Association Executives These meeting planners are full-time professional administrators employed by the various associations. They are responsible for the planning, coordination, execution, and promotion of annual conventions and smaller association meetings. Association executives are the key decision-makers in the selection of meeting sites. Many belong to the Canadian Society of Association Executives (CSAE), based in Toronto, or to the American Society of Association Executives (ASAE).

Many smaller associations cannot afford to employ a full-time meeting planner. These groups can employ the services of a management company that specializes in planning association meetings.

Corporate Meeting Planners Corporate meeting planning is a comparatively new and rapidly growing field. Until recently, the planning of meetings and conferences was usually up to the director of sales or vice-president of marketing. Today, however, most large corporations and businesses have a full-time meetings department that arranges all meetings. Some companies appoint a training executive to organize group training sessions. (If a company does not have a meetings department, corporate group travel and meetings arrangements are often arranged through the in-house business travel department.)

Meeting planners have FORMED their own professional associations. Meeting Planners International (MPI), founded in 1972, is the most prominent of these. Its 9000 members plan hundreds of thousands of meetings each year. MPI members include corporate meeting planners, association executives, and independent consultants, as well as travel and meeting service suppliers. MPI has local chapters in Canada.

The Association of Conference and Events Directors–International (ACED–I), founded in 1980, is an organization of colleges, universities, and associations. It arranges conferences and other meetings on university campuses.

Independent Meeting Planners Associations and corporations that do not have in-house meetings departments often

A DAY IN THE LIFE OF

A Meeting Planner

I'm a full-time meeting planner for a large corporation. I do just what my title implies: I plan, schedule, and supervise all the elements of the meetings the corporation holds. My goal is simple—to run a successful meeting—but my job is not. Coordinating travel, accommodations, food, and sometimes even entertainment takes a lot of doing. A good meeting planner needs to be aggressive in making deals with hotels, but sensitive in communicating needs. He or she has to be detail-oriented, yet creative. The best way to show how important these qualities are is to go through the steps I usually follow in planning a large meeting.

The first step is to choose where the meeting will take place. I have to consider a number of factors, including the nature of the event (What is its purpose?); the makeup of the attendees (Will spouses attend?); the geographical location of the site (Is it easy to get to?); and so on. I have to investigate a number of things about a hotel, from banquet facilities to the kind of lighting available in meeting rooms. Most of all, I have to learn about the quality of service a place gives. Attendees will remember how they were treated long after they've forgotten what they had for dinner each night.

I always visit and inspect a possible site personally, even if I've booked meetings there before. Mostly, I'm concerned about the meeting facilities. Meeting rooms come in all types. I remember one time, I visited a prospective site that used accordion-type flexible partitions to divide a large room into two smaller rooms. I had been told that the rooms were soundproof, but in fact they let in plenty of noise. I could just imagine a serious discussion being punctuated by bursts of laughter from a sales presentation next door.

Lighting is another important but easily overlooked aspect of a meeting's setting. Early in my career, I booked a meeting in a room with several of those wagon-wheel-type fixtures that have bare bulbs hanging from them. A lot of the people complained about the glare. After that, I paid special attention to lighting.

Once I decide on a site, I sit down with the hotel's convention service manager. I provide the service manager with as many details of the program as I can; the more he or she knows, the better. Then I make my requests for accommodations, meals, meeting rooms, equipment, and so on, and get every guarantee in writing. I'm always wary of people who say things like, "Don't worry, we'll take care of everything." I need written confirmation. At the same time, I try to get every concession I can—like complimentary morning coffee and newspapers for attendees—from the hotel. Little touches like that score points with people.

During the preparation phase, I use lots of checklists. They help me keep track of which things are done and which need to be done. I also negotiate with airlines, car rental firms, and other services to ensure that attendees will get to the meeting and back comfortably.

A couple of days before the meeting, I fly to the site. Once there, I make sure everything is set up. The night before the meeting opens, I check all the equipment and run through any slides in the actual rooms where they'll be used, even if I've been assured that everything was checked "back at the office." One time, a worker had jostled a slide carousel while packing it, dislodging some slides. He put them all back, but some were upside down and out of order. My preliminary run-through saved the speaker an embarrassing moment.

During the meeting, I always assume that Murphy's Law will operate: Everything that can go wrong will go wrong. I'm on hand to figure out how to prevent disaster when emergencies arise. The hotel helps me there, too. I've returned to some hotels partly on the basis of their ability to replace a dead microphone quickly or change a meeting room at the last minute.

Even when the last attendee has gone home, my job isn't done. After the meeting, I get together with hotel representatives for a postmeeting critique. At these face-to-face meetings, I often gain valuable insights into how attendees and meeting planners can make meetings run more smoothly. After a good meeting, I have a feeling of accomplishment. I know that I've planned well, that the company's business needs have been met, and that people's personal and social needs have been met, too.

hire independent consultants on a freelance basis. The number of individuals and companies offering this service is growing rapidly. The Association of Independent Meeting Planners (AIMP) promotes education and communication among planners in this field.

The Meeting Planner's Responsibilities

Whether meeting planners work for associations, corporations, or independent consultancies, their main objective is to run successful meetings. The fundamental responsibilities of the meeting planner include these:

- Establishing meeting objectives.
- Selecting the meeting site.
- Scheduling meetings and meeting rooms.
- Negotiating rates with suppliers.
- Budgeting and controlling expenses.
- Making air and ground transportation arrangements.
- Planning audio-visual and technical details.

It is clear from this list—which could easily be extended—that meeting planners are more than just travel and accommodations organizers. They are involved from the earliest planning stages to the final execution of the meeting. The success of the meeting depends heavily on how well they perform their tasks.

Experienced meeting planners may be certified by the Convention Liaison Council. Certification is awarded to meeting planners who have reached professional standards in their field as measured by experience and examination.

The MNEs of Meeting Planners

The meeting planner must keep his or her employer's needs in mind when selecting destinations, choosing hotels, making travel arrangements, and so on. When negotiating with suppliers, the meeting planner must ensure that the sponsoring organization is getting the best possible deal and the best value for its money. Strong negotiating skills are a key requirement for the meeting planner.

Top priorities in selecting sites for meetings are the quality of service and the availability of meeting room facilities. Meeting planners must ensure that meeting areas are large enough, suitable for both general sessions and breakout meetings, well lighted, soundproof, and so on. Each meeting that a planner organizes will have different requirements Other important priorities are the site's accessibility, the quality of guest rooms, room rates, and the quality of food service. The availability of recreational facilities is usually of lesser importance. So is geographic location.

The Meeting Planner and the Hotel Staff

Meeting planning involves a high degree of cooperation between the meeting planner and the hotel staff. The convention service manager is usually the meeting planner's contact person in the hotel. The relationship between the two is important to the success of the meeting. Both must keep the needs of the meeting participants in mind. The meeting planner wants to secure the best possible services at the lowest possible rates. The convention service manager wants to satisfy the guests so that they will return for subsequent meetings, but he or she must also ensure that the hotel makes a profit.

Meeting planners who use the same hotel time and time again can often negotiate favourable rates, and secure other privileges such as free function rooms. For an especially large or important meeting, the hotel may agree to host a cocktail party for delegates or offer complimentary coffee and breakfast. Using the same hotel over and over again is not always a good idea, however. Meeting planners may find that the hotel's services deteriorate over time, or that other hotels can offer better services at better prices.

> **CHECK YOUR PRODUCT KNOWLEDGE**
>
> 1. What are the three different types of meeting planners?
> 2. What is Meeting Planners International? Who are its members?
> 3. List six important responsibilities of a meeting planner.

INCENTIVE TRAVEL PROGRAMS

Incentive travel programs have become an important segment of the corporate travel market (they are not used in the association market). Major corporations began to use travel as an incentive in the 1950s. Incentive travel programs have since been introduced by thousands of small and medium-sized companies.

Incentive Travel Defined

There is some disagreement within the industry as to how incentive travel should be defined. Purists maintain that the term should be used only to describe incentive trips that are strictly for pleasure. Others include those trips that combine business and pleasure. It is, however, universally accepted that incentive travel is used as a reward for top company producers and achievers.

James E. Jones, former president of MPI, defines incentive travel as "the application of travel as a motivational award for the accomplishment of a business objective." The objective is most commonly a sales target. A company sets a specific quota for its sales staff. Salespeople who meet the quota qualify for the trip. The theory is that the increase in sales more than covers the cost of the trips awarded. Companies run incentive travel programs not only to reward sales performance, but also to achieve new sales goals and to improve morale and reduce employee turnover. Whatever the reasons for incentive travel programs, all involve travel as a motivational tool.

Salespeople, dealers, and distributors are the most popular targets for incentive programs. In recent years, travel has also been used to motivate other types of employees, such as engineers, production personnel, and management. It is anticipated that these will be the prime growth areas for incentive programs in the future.

Incentive travel has proved effective in most business environments. It has been used extensively by food and insurance companies and by automotive, pharmaceutical, and appliance manufacturers (see Table 12-2).

Type of company	Expenditure (in thousands)
Food	$733,021
Insurance	615,012
Tires/batteries/accessories	436,072
Pharmaceuticals	428,950
Auto/boat/air	381,336
Durable goods—wholesale	243,388
Nondurable goods—wholesale	221,136
Books	216,098
Housewares	168,069
Office equipment	146,815

TABLE 12-2
Top Ten Users of Incentive Travel in 1990
SOURCE: *Business & Incentives*

Characteristics of Incentive Travel Programs

Incentive travel programs can be categorized as either pure incentives or sales incentives.

Pure incentives, as the name implies, are strictly for pleasure. No business meetings or sales calls are scheduled during the vacation. Having reached the required performance objective, the employee is rewarded with the prize of a luxury vacation for a job well done. Destination is the key motivator. Workers are more likely to increase production if the reward is a trip to a glamorous location. It might be a big city, a foreign capital, a resort, or a natural attraction. The incentive can also be a cruise. Pure incentives represent about one-third of incentive travel programs.

Sales incentives are combination vacation and business trips that usually include mandatory meetings. As such, the incentive trip is used as a vehicle for meetings. The amount of time spent on business-related activities varies, depending on the objectives of the sponsoring company. There may be a single visit to a company factory or a series of meetings in which participants are introduced to new product lines, shown new sales techniques, and so on. In general, more time is allotted to pleasure than to business. An attractive destination is still the most important factor, but the availability of suitable meeting facilities must also be considered. Sales incentives represent two-thirds of incentive travel programs.

Whether the trip is a pure incentive or a sales incentive, it is always of the highest quality. Winners expect a better class of service than do most other travel clients—accommodations are deluxe and all-inclusive. Employees are often accompanied by their spouses, whose vacation expenses are also paid for by the company.

Incentive travel programs typically last about five days; few are longer than a week. Weekend incentive trips are growing in popularity. Almost all programs involve group rather than individual trips. Incentive programs have been organized for groups as large as 10 000, but between 50 and 100 is a more common size. The greatest growth in recent years has been in the small-group market, with an average of ten participants per trip.

Incentive Travel Planners

Large corporations and businesses that sponsor incentive travel programs sometimes have their own in-house incentive planners. These company employees rarely spend all of their time on incentive travel. They can also be involved in meeting planning, trade shows, public relations, and advertising. Incentive travel planning is often the responsibility of the corporate meeting planner.

There are a small number of companies that do nothing but arrange incentive travel programs. Large, full-service incentive houses include E.F. MacDonald and Maritz Travel. They negotiate with suppliers and create an attractive package in much the same way that a tour operator does. Incentive companies are usually both wholesalers and retailers. Incentive planning typically involves more promotion than does meeting planning. Professional planners are not just involved with the travel aspect of the incentive program; they also help to set the objectives of the program.

Not all companies can afford to use the larger incentive travel companies. They may turn instead to a travel agency that specializes in incentive travel. Incentive travel planning is similar to group travel planning, although it typically means more work, and the agency is involved in the marketing of the incentive program. Like incentive travel companies, travel agencies may also work with the sponsoring company to set objectives for the program.

The Society of Incentive Travel Executives (SITE), which has a membership of 2000, is the most important organization for incentive travel planners. SITE holds numerous trade shows and seminars throughout the year.

> **CHECK YOUR PRODUCT KNOWLEDGE**
>
> 1. What types of organizations use incentive travel programs?
> 2. What is the difference between a pure incentive and a sales incentive?
> 3. What are the three different types of incentive travel planners?

TRADE SHOWS AND EXHIBITIONS

Trade shows and exhibitions are another important segment of the meetings market. A trade show (or trade fair) is an event with free-standing vendor displays that is not connected to a convention. An exhibition, on the other hand, is always staged as part of a convention. In the early 1990s, about 11 000 trade shows were held annually in Canada and the United States.

Trade Shows

For many years, trade shows were used solely to advertise products. Nothing was sold at them. Since the 1950s, however, they have also been used to market and sell products. Today, a significant percentage of purchases in industry and the trades and professions are prompted by visits to trade shows. Vendors rent **booths** to display a wide variety of products, from computer hardware to boats, and often demonstrate those products to potential buyers. Some trade shows, such as auto shows and home and garden shows, are open to the general public. Many more are by invitation only. Companies may participate in both international and domestic trade shows.

International Trade Shows Modern international trade shows came into being after World War II, when efforts were being made to rebuild Europe. Since then, Germany has remained the leading host country for international trade shows.

International trade shows provide an ideal means for companies to test overseas markets. Representatives have the opportunity to meet potential buyers and distributors from all over the world. Buyers come to the seller in one central location, so there is no need to spend time and money on individual sales calls. Even allowing for transportation costs, international trade shows are the most cost-effective way to enter world markets.

International trade shows differ from trade shows in Canada and the United States in several ways. First and foremost, they are more heavily sales-oriented. People go to trade shows to do business, not to attend meetings. Also, attendance is considerably higher at international shows. The Hanover Fair in Germany regularly attracts up to 500 000 attendees over an eight-day period. Many thousands of people also attend the annual Photokina Camera and Optics Trade Show in Cologne, Germany. Individual exhibits at these shows are more elaborate than at North American trade shows. A company may have as many as 1000 employees working a single exhibit. The biggest exhibitors' booths (or **stands**, as they are called in Europe) include several meeting rooms as well as display space. One final difference is the international flavour of overseas shows. Interpreters are on hand to assist visitors from all over the world.

Canada's federal and provincial governments often provide financial help so that small and medium-sized companies can exhibit their products in overseas trade fairs. The point, of course, is to help them penetrate overseas markets. These same governments also encourage foreigners to attend trade shows in Canada.

North American Trade Shows Trade shows in Canada and the United States grew up as an extension of conferences that featured trade booths. These shows generally put more emphasis on attending meetings and are not as sales-oriented as international trade shows. They are also less formal and are attended by fewer people. Even so, domestic trade shows can be an important source of business for hotels in the host city. The largest shows are held in the giant convention centres, such as the Vancouver Trade and Convention Centre, the Metro Toronto Convention Centre, and the Las Vegas Convention Centre. A number of convention hotels have exhibit space for smaller trade shows.

Trade shows generate more than $20 billion in expenditures in North America. There are shows for every conceivable trade, industry, and profession. The Henry Davis Trade Show and the International Travel Industry Expo are examples of shows for the travel industry. At these shows, travel industry suppliers set up booths to showcase their products and services, and travel agents visit the booths to gather information and make contacts.

The Trade Show Bureau is an organization that conducts research into the trade show industry and disseminates information to those involved in trade show planning.

Exhibitions

The number of exhibitions held every year has increased with the growth of the meetings business as a whole. As mentioned earlier, exhibitions differ from trade shows in that they are tied to a convention. They are used more frequently in the association market, particularly by trade, technical, scientific, and professional associations.

Exhibits are important for associations both as a way to attract attendance and as a revenue producer. By allowing exhibitors to promote their wares at the convention, associations make money to offset the expense of staging the meeting. Exhibitors pay for the amount of space they rent to display their products.

Vendor displays and booths vary from simple to elaborate, though they are rarely as elaborate as at trade shows. A vendor will sometimes sponsor a "hospitality suite," offering free food and beverages to delegates. Exhibitors may also agree to sponsor coffee breaks and meals during the convention in exchange for recognition and, possibly, the right to display their products in the coffee area.

Attendance at the exhibition necessarily depends on the number of people attending the convention. Exhibitions are not open to the general public. The duration of the exhibition is tied to the length of the meeting, though most are at least three days long.

The International Exhibitors Association (IEA) is the major organization in the exhibitions field.

> **CHECK YOUR PRODUCT KNOWLEDGE**
>
> 1. What is the difference between a trade show and an exhibition?
> 2. What are four ways in which international trade shows differ from domestic trade shows?
> 3. What types of organizations commonly hold exhibitions?

THE CHANNELS OF DISTRIBUTION

We have established that associations and corporations are the two major types of organizations that hold meetings. They are the *buyers* of group travel, group accommodations, and meetings services. The *sellers* are the hotels, resorts, and conference, convention, and civic centres, and the cruise ships that host meetings. The airlines and ground transportation companies that transport participants to the meetings

ILLUSTRATION 12-4
The Dallas Infomart is the world's largest permanent trade show of computers and computer-related products.
SOURCE: Courtesy Infomart

PROFILE

National Trade Shows, Inc.

How does a person get into the business of putting on travel trade shows? Bill Gardiner did it almost by accident. He was working in the advertising department of a large New Jersey newspaper when a group of travel advertisers asked his paper to sponsor a travel trade show. After running a small annual trade show for the paper for a few years, Gardiner branched out on his own and started National Trade Shows, Inc. Today, NTS stages nearly 70 mini travel trade shows around the United States each year. The company is still a family-owned business, run by Bill and his son, Bill, Jr., in New Jersey.

The Gardiners' mini-shows are very different from a typical travel trade show. A typical show takes place in a large exhibition hall and lasts one or more days. It involves 100 or more exhibitors and attracts thousands of people. Such shows usually feature elaborate displays, tons of literature, and plenty of wining, dining, and entertainment.

Bill, Jr., calls these kinds of trade shows "pipe and drape" shows, after the materials used to construct the exhibition booths. The Gardiners' mini-shows are much less elaborate. Each is just three hours long and takes place in a hotel ballroom. Each show is limited to a maximum of 30 exhibitors and 110 local travel agents. According to Bill, Jr., the mini-shows are actually more efficient than the large trade shows because they cut out the "browsers" who attend the large shows without intending to buy anything.

The exhibitors who participate in the NTS shows include hundreds of hotel chains, resorts, airlines, tour operators, car rental firms, and cruise lines, as well as several government tourist bureaus. The British Tourist Authority, Club Med, Peter Pan Tours, and Alamo Rent-A-Car are among NTS's clients.

The format of the shows is simple. During the first hour, the travel agents visit tables placed around the edge of the ballroom, which are staffed by the exhibitors. The second hour is reserved for a sit-down dinner for the suppliers and agents. Many of the suppliers then spend the third hour speaking informally and handing out door prizes such as free trips, airline tickets, travel bags, and champagne.

National Trade Shows recruits its exhibitors by sending out mailers several times a year announcing the schedules for upcoming mini-shows. Once the suppliers sign up for a specific mini-show or week of shows, they provide NTS with lists of travel agents to invite to the shows. From each agency invited, only two people are permitted to attend. Usually they are the owners or managers of the agency.

According to Bill Gardiner, Sr., the mini-shows serve several purposes. They enable the suppliers to reach 100 travel agents in just three hours. It would take each supplier several weeks to visit the same agents by travelling from office to office. In addition, by limiting the numbers of participants, the suppliers and agents have the time and opportunity to really get to know one another.

The NTS mini-shows are grouped geographically. For example, the Gardiners might stage a week of shows in Florida and another week in Arizona and California. Suppliers pay several hundred dollars to participate in one show and more than $2,000 to participate in a week-long series of shows. Most suppliers sign up for a week's worth of shows. Chartered buses take the suppliers from one show to another during the week.

Despite the high fees, there is usually a waiting list of suppliers and agents who want to participate in each show or week of shows. Bill, Sr., believes that the NTS shows are so successful because they tap a market that the large shows don't reach and that the suppliers can't cover as efficiently any other way. "These shows aren't cheap, yet the same suppliers keep coming back year after year, so we must be doing something right."

are also sellers. As you have read in earlier chapters, the buyer does not always purchase travel products and services directly from the seller. The same is true for the meetings business. The seller uses intermediaries as distribution channels when selling services to the buyer. Intermediaries in the meetings field include tour operators, travel agencies, meeting planners, and incentive travel companies.

In this section, you will read about other companies that intervene between the supplier and the consumer. These include site destination selection companies, destination management companies, convention services and facilities companies, and convention and visitors' bureaus.

Tour Operators

In many ways, the business and convention product is similar to the product that the vacationer buys as a holiday tour package. The product includes transportation, accommodations, activities, and events in some combination. In Chapter 10, you read that it is more convenient (and cheaper) for a vacationer to buy a package of travel products from a single source than to buy each component from individual suppliers. The same is true for the person attending a meeting.

Tour operators are experienced in group travel arrangements. Some tour operators arrange packages for meetings and conventions, especially for the association market. Here's an example. The Kelowna chapter of Kiwanis International (a fraternal association) plans to attend the association's annual convention in Ottawa. A representative of the chapter contacts a local tour operator to make the arrangements. The tour operator makes the necessary flight reservations, arranges transfers, and books rooms for the delegates in a hotel (or hotels) close to the Ottawa Congress Centre. The tour operator may also make car rental reservations for members of the group, schedule group activities (such as sightseeing and entertainment), and so on. Because the tour operator buys in bulk from suppliers, the package will be less expensive than if each Kelowna Kiwani had made his or her own arrangements.

Tour operators don't only sell directly to the consumer. Some will place a deposit on an allotment of rooms for a large, popular trade show and package the rooms for resale through retail travel agencies and business travel departments. In doing so, the tour operator is taking a risk.

Travel Agencies

Travel agencies that have an ongoing relationship with a corporation or company often make travel arrangements for meetings. They are also becoming increasingly involved with incentive travel programs. The companies they work with are often small or medium-sized firms that do not employ a full-time, in-house meeting planner. The meetings and incentive programs that the travel agencies service typically have less than 100 participants.

The work involved in making arrangements for meetings and incentives is more complex than that for group travel. An agency will usually assign this work to its convention department or incentives department. In addition, the agency may staff a service booth at the convention site to handle reconfirmations, complaints, and so on.

Meeting Planning Companies/Incentive Travel Companies

These firms or individual consultants provide full-service planning for businesses and associations for a fee. They are involved not only with travel and accommodations arrangements but also with the promotion and marketing of the meeting or the incentive program. Usually, meeting planning companies and incentive travel companies don't use travel agencies or tour operators: they deal directly with carriers, hotels, and other suppliers.

Airlines, Hotels, and Car Rental Companies

An airline is often designated the "official carrier" for a particular meeting or convention. Canadian Airlines, for example, served as the official carrier for the Tourism Industry Association of Canada's 1993 annual convention in Saint John, New Brunswick. The airline assisted in that group's promotion and marketing efforts and offered a discount for participants. Similarly, a hotel may be appointed as the "official hotel," and a car rental company as the "official car rental agency." This practice is more common in the association market than in the corporate market.

The official carrier may set up a temporary department in its reservations centre. Or it may staff an existing group or convention desk with sales representatives to assist with check-in and arrival. Major carriers have staffs that work full-time on meetings arrangements. They help clients select an appropriate meeting site, secure discounted fares, arrange hotel accommodations, and coordinate car rentals and ground transportation. They may also provide assistance with audio-visual equipment and recommendations for multimedia presentations.

Site Destination Selection Companies

These companies suggest possible meeting sites based on corporate or association needs. Meeting planners and incentive travel planners may consult a **site destination selection company** several years before a meeting or incentive program is scheduled. Destination companies conduct familiarization tours so that planners can inspect and sample hotels and meeting facilities at potential sites. White Glove is one of the larger companies in the field. In the late 1980s, it offered a five-day FAM tour of Atlanta for corporate and association meeting planners, as well as a seven-day tour of Thailand for corporate incentive travel planners. For a nominal registration fee, participants were provided with round-trip air transportation, lodging, ground arrangements, many meals, and special activities.

Destination Management Companies

Destination management companies (DMCs) provide on-the-scene assistance for corporations and associations holding meetings at a particular location. If, for example, a Toronto company is planning a meeting in Las Vegas, it may hire a DMC in that city to handle all the details. The DMC will arrange ground transportation, deal with restaurants, line up local speakers, and perform many other useful services.

Convention Services and Facilities Companies

This group includes a wide variety of independent companies that provide support services that are not available at the convention site. Some of these companies design and install stages, booths, and modular exhibit systems; others are audio-visual specialists, or sound and light specialists. Still others provide temporary personnel, or actors and entertainers for industrial shows, or security staff.

Convention and Visitors' Bureaus

A few years ago, there were only about 300 **convention and visitors' bureaus (CVBs)** in Canada and the United States. Today, there are an estimated 1000. A CVB can be a department within a city's chamber of commerce, or an office of a municipal government, or a completely independent organization. CVBs have two main functions: to promote travel to the city they represent (be it for pleasure, or business, or meetings); and to help service the conventions and trade shows that are held in the city. Their job is to sell the *whole* city: not just convention centres and other meeting sites, but also hotels, restaurants, stores, transportation companies, and other suppliers. A CVB is a nonprofit organization funded by its members. Most of these are suppliers who profit when conventions are held in the city. The International Association of Convention and Visitors' Bureaus (IACVB) represents major CVBs from around the world. You will read more about convention and visitors' bureaus in Chapter 14.

CHECK YOUR PRODUCT KNOWLEDGE

1. Name four intermediaries in the meetings business between supplier and consumer.
2. What role do tour operators play in the distribution of the meetings product?
3. What are (a) site destination selection companies and (b) destination management companies?

CAREER OPPORTUNITIES

The tremendous growth of the meetings business in recent decades has bred a demand for specialists in several fields. Meetings-related careers fall into three main categories:

- Planning jobs, within the organizations that hold meetings or within the travel industry.
- Convention service jobs at the various locations that host meetings (hotels, resorts, convention centres, and so on).
- Entrepreneurial jobs with companies that work independently in the meetings field.

Meeting/Incentive Planners

In an earlier section of this chapter, you read about the work done by people who arrange, manage, and promote meeting activities. The largest employers of meeting planners are the associations and corporations that hold regular conventions and other meetings. These jobs are within the private sector; but you should also be aware of possible openings with government agencies and with a number of United Nations affiliates. Both these sectors hold frequent meetings and employ people to plan them.

Many of the corporations and businesses that hold meetings also sponsor incentive travel programs. Several of these companies employ in-house incentive planners to coordinate their programs.

Meeting planning and incentive travel planning have become important sources of income for retail travel agencies. Many agencies have separate departments for this type of business. So do a number of major airlines.

Meeting planning is rarely an entry-level position. People typically come into the business from the hospitality industry, having gained experience in dealing with meetings and meeting planners. Competition for jobs with associations and corporations is growing tougher. It is often easier to get into a meetings department if you have worked for the organization's support staff. Similarly, travel agencies and airlines also promote from within.

Meeting planners may rise to become heads of their departments in corporations and associations; or they may be promoted to marketing and public relations positions. For some, the job of meeting planner is a stepping stone to a career as an independent consultant.

Convention Service Managers

Convention service managers work in hotels, resorts, conference centres, convention or civic centres, or on cruise ships—that is, at the locations that host meetings. They work on the scene with meeting planners, coordinating all aspects of the meeting.

Almost all hotels involved in the meetings business employ convention service managers. As with meeting planners, promotion is usually from within. An individual is typically promoted to convention service manager after experience in some other hotel department. A background in sales and in food and beverage management is useful.

Convention managers with experience in hotels sometimes advance to positions with conference, convention, or civic centres. Convention centre management is a particularly responsible job, involving extremely complex logistics. Management positions at convention centres include transportation director, security director, public relations director, and events coordinator. The largest convention centres, such as the Metro Toronto Convention Centre and the Las Vegas Convention Centre, may employ as many as 1000 people. In addition to management positions, there are hundreds of blue-collar jobs in convention services, such as equipment mover, electrician, plumber, carpenter, security guard, and so on.

Entrepreneurs

This group includes all those people who work for themselves in the meetings field. Many run their own convention services and facilities companies, and provide various kinds of support to associations and corporations. Other entrepreneurial roles in the meetings business involve trade show management, site destination selection, and destination management. Finally, there are independent freelance meeting planners (who are hired by associations and organizations) and incentive travel companies (who are hired by corporations only).

Summary

- Advances in the transportation industry—the arrival of the passenger jet, in particular—have spurred the growth of the meetings market.
- Off-site meetings are held in hotels, resorts, conference centres, convention centres, and civic centres, and on cruise ships.
- Meetings can be classified as conventions, conferences, forums, seminars, workshops, exhibitions, or trade shows.
- Technological advances have resulted in a greater need for meetings.
- The association market and the corporate market are the two major segments of the meetings market.
- Associations that hold regular meetings include trade, professional, scientific, educational, and fraternal organizations.
- Sales meetings, dealer meetings, technical meetings, executive meetings, training meetings, and public meetings are held by corporations and businesses.
- Association meetings differ from corporate meetings in that they are held on a regular cycle, at a different destination each year, and attract a larger number of participants (who attend voluntarily).
- With the increased demand for meetings expertise, meeting planning has emerged as a profession in its own right.
- Meeting planners work for associations, corporations, or travel agencies, or as independent consultants.
- Incentive travel programs are used as motivational tools for employees by corporations and businesses.
- Trade shows differ from exhibitions in that they are not staged as part of a convention.
- Tour operators package convention travel for sale to associations and corporations, either directly or through retail travel agencies.
- Site destination selection companies, destination management companies, and convention services and facilities companies provide support services for meeting planners.
- Convention and visitors' bureaus promote and service conventions for a particular destination.

Key Terms

off-site meeting
convention
breakout
conference
congress
forum
symposium
lecture
seminar
workshop
clinic
panel
exhibition
trade show
trade fair
teleconferencing
pure incentive
sales incentive

booth
stand
site destination selection company
destination management company (DMC)
convention and visitors' bureau (CVB)

What Do You Think?

1. The number of meetings held every year has grown tremendously in recent decades. What factors might cause a slowdown or halt in the growth of the meetings business?
2. Which segment of the market is more important to the meetings business: the association market or the corporate market? Explain.
3. What problems might a travel agency face in trying to enter the meetings and incentives business?
4. Meetings are currently held at hotels, resorts, and conference, convention, and civic centres, and on cruise ships. What other locations could conceivably be developed as meetings sites?
5. Why are international trade shows more heavily sales-oriented than domestic trade shows?
6. Why might an individual choose to work as an independent meeting planner rather than as an association executive or as a corporate meeting planner?
7. What site features would you stress to attract meetings business if you were the convention service manager (a) at a downtown hotel, (b) at an airport hotel, (c) at a resort, and (d) on a cruise ship?
8. Canada currently has only about 4 percent of the North American meetings industry market share, though it has the potential to achieve 10 percent. What are the major reasons for this shortfall? What should Canada do to increase its market share?

Dealing with Product

You are the meeting planner for a corporation that has a dozen regional sales offices around the country. It is Monday morning and the vice-president of sales expects you to present a plan for the annual sales meeting during this afternoon's departmental meeting. You have nearly completed the rough draft when the vice-president of human resources phones.

It seems that she has just finished reading an article on teleconferencing, which describes how it is now possible for delegates to "meet" through wall-sized television screens that offer two-way communication. She argues that teleconferencing could save the company thousands of dollars. It would reduce the costs of transportation, lodging, meals, and time away from work. Furthermore, she feels that teleconferencing would cut down on the fatigue often associated with business travel.

What will you tell the attendees at today's departmental meeting about the two types of meeting—the traditional sales meeting and teleconferencing? Do you think the former will become obsolete as a result of the latter?

Dealing with People

You are the owner and manager of a 100-unit hotel and resort on the Gaspé Peninsula. Your hotel is a popular vacation destination, but your business is seasonal. The summer and early fall are your busiest months. You have decided to actively seek convention and meetings business in order to "fill the house" throughout the year.

Imagine that you are going to prepare sales presentations for the following decision-makers. What do you think their MNEs will be, and what can you offer to meet them?

- the executive director of a scientific research association
- the president of a trade union local
- the vice-president of marketing for a software manufacturer
- the social director of the local branch of Parents Without Partners
- the president of a chapter of Alliance Canada Travel Associations

CHAPTER 12: Meetings, Conventions, and Incentive Travel   Name: _____

WORKSHEET 12-3 Multiplier Effect and Leakages

You learned about the multiplier effect and leakage in Chapter 8. Think about how these concepts would apply to a large meeting or convention held in Yourtown.

Use the expenditures of one attendee or a group of attendees to demonstrate how tourist dollars are spent and respent.

Describe how part of the tourist income might flow out of Yourtown's economy to purchase goods or services elsewhere.

CHAPTER 12: Meetings, Conventions, and Incentive Travel   Name: _____

WORKSHEET 12-4 Convention and Visitors' Bureau

Locate the convention and visitors' bureau closest to Yourtown and obtain information and promotional materials from it. What facilities does the city offer for the following?

Small to medium-sized meetings _____
_____
_____
_____

Conventions _____
_____
_____
_____

Exhibitions and trade shows _____
_____
_____
_____

Visitors in general _____
_____
_____
_____

How large a convention or meeting could the city accommodate? _____
_____
_____
_____

Are any improvements or expansions planned? If so, what are they? _____
_____
_____
_____

Read the Yourtown newspapers. List the conventions, conferences, trade shows, and exhibitions that will be held in Yourtown in the next six months.
_____
_____
_____
_____
_____

Will any of them be open to the public?
_____
_____
_____
_____
_____

PART 5

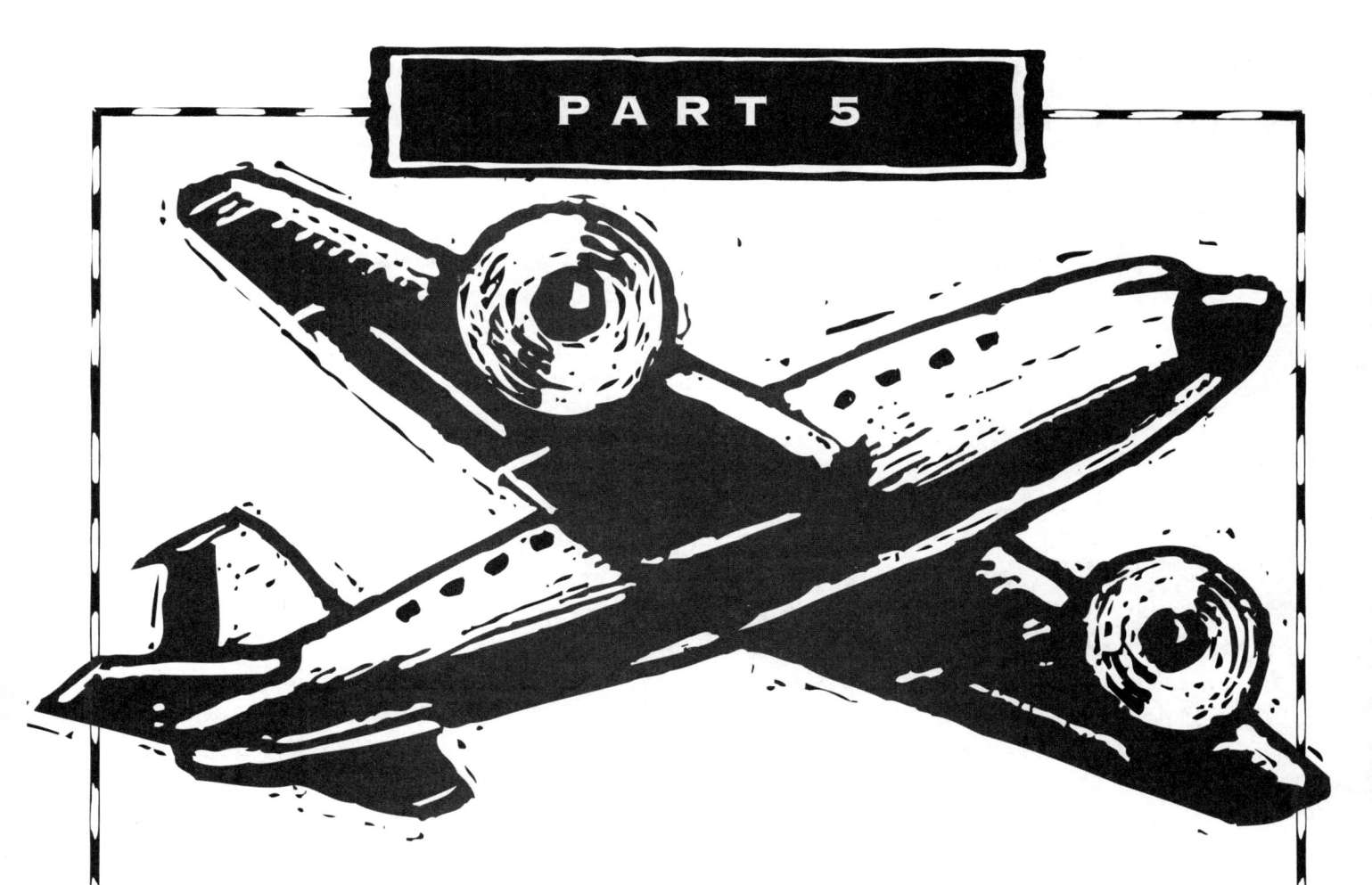

The Travel and Tourism Marketplace

CHAPTER 13
Travel and Tourism Distributors

CHAPTER 14
Promotion and Sales

CHAPTER 15
The Future and You

CHAPTER 13

Travel and Tourism Distributors

*"If you be a traveller, have always two bags very full,
that is one of patience and another of money."*

John Florio

OBJECTIVES

When you have completed this chapter, you should be able to do the following:

- Explain how a travel agency is similar to, and different from, a traditional retail store.
- Discuss how travel agencies are compensated.
- Describe the relationship between the travel agency, the customer, and the supplier.
- List several types of travel agencies.
- Explain how airline regulatory reform, the competitive market decision, and automation have affected travel agencies.
- Describe the trend toward consolidation of travel agencies.
- List the steps involved in opening a retail travel agency.
- Describe how a travel agency functions.
- Identify other travel and tourism distributors.
- Name the main professional associations for travel agents.
- Explain how to become a professional travel agent.

Tim Ayers, a self-employed management consultant, is also his own travel agent. He recently planned the itinerary and made all the arrangements for a trip to Ireland for himself, his wife, and another couple. Tim checked out books on Ireland from the public library and read about places to visit. He also picked up a travel video at his local video store. Months before their departure, he wrote letters to bed-and-breakfast establishments requesting accommodations. To purchase round-trip air tickets from Montreal to Dublin, he drove from his home in the suburbs to a downtown airline ticket office. He then drove to another airline office to purchase tickets for a connecting flight from his hometown to Montreal. And by dialling a special toll-free phone number from his home, he was able to reserve a rental car for ground transportation while in Ireland.

Tim is an exceptional traveller. Most travellers have neither the time nor the know-how to make their own travel arrangements. They're also not interested in sorting through complicated schedules and fares. And they don't want to worry about everything connecting smoothly. Instead, they depend on travel and tourism distributors—travel agencies, business travel departments (BTDs), and travel clubs—to take care of all the arrangements.

In Canada, travel agencies are grouped under the travel trade sector, along with wholesale tour operators. This sector is the smallest of the six tourism-related employment sectors in Canada, with 27 200 employees in 1991 (Mohan and Gisiason, 1992). That is, employment in this sector is only about 2 percent of total tourism-related employment. However, since all employees in this sector are classified as entirely employed in tourism, they comprise about 6 percent of direct tourism employment. There are an estimated 5500 travel agencies in Canada, according to the Alliance of Canadian Travel Associations (ACTA). About 2200 retail travel firms belong to ACTA. This is more than 40 percent of all Canadian travel agencies; however, ACTA members account for an estimated 75 percent of the agency travel volume in Canada.

THE TRAVEL AGENCY AS INTERMEDIARY

In all channels of distribution, as you know by now, there is usually an intermediary, or link, between the supplier and the customer. One type of intermediary is the retail store. Hardware stores, supermarkets, clothes boutiques, drugstores, and many other retail stores provide a convenient place for consumers to purchase a variety of products. Retail stores are also convenient for the suppliers. Without them, suppliers would have to set up their own outlets or send sales representatives all over the country.

A travel agency acts much like a retail store in that it provides suppliers with a link to the public. In this case, the suppliers are airlines, cruise lines, bus companies, railways, hotels and motels, car rental agencies, tourist boards, and wholesale tour operators. The customers include vacation and leisure travellers, business travellers, and travellers visiting friends and relatives (VFRs).

Of all the travel intermediaries, the travel agency is the most important. Retail travel agencies reserve more airline seats, cruise berths, hotel rooms, and package tours than any other intermediary. (See Figure 13-1)

Compensation

Like other retail stores, travel agencies are in business to make money. However, travel agencies do not earn their money in the same way as most other retail outlets.

Most retailers buy goods for a certain price from suppliers and then sell these goods, for a higher price, to customers. Retailers need to stock their store with inventory. The owner of a hardware store, for example, buys nuts and bolts, tools, wood, and other merchandise from a manufacturer or a wholesale dealer. The owner buys these products in bulk and so gets them for a reduced rate. Before selling them to the public, the owner marks up the price of each item. The customer pays for the item at its retail price, and the difference between the wholesale and the retail price—the "markup"—is the owner's compensation.

Travel agencies do not "stock" products in this manner. Rather, the supplier compensates the agency in the form of commissions and overrides. The supplier compensates the agency for the time and money it spends promoting and selling the supplier's products. Customers pay no more for travel products at a travel agency than they would by going to the supplier directly. In fact, travel agents can often save clients money by comparing different products to determine the best value. And travel agents offer free counselling on destinations, routing, transportation, accommodation, and sightseeing.

More than half of travel agency compensation comes from the sale of airline products and services. (See Figure 13-2) Because the airlines have a tremendous influence on travel agencies, much of this chapter focuses on the relationship between airlines and travel agencies.

Commissions A commission is the percentage of the total sale price that is paid to an agency. If an agency (or agent) sells an airline ticket for $1,000 and the airline has agreed to pay a commission of 10 percent, the agency (or agent) receives a commission of $100 ($1,000 x .10 = $100). At 10 percent commission, $1 million in sales will result in $100,000 in commissions, from which operating expenses and corporate taxes must be paid. Since profit margins in the travel industry can be quite low, managers and owners must watch finances carefully.

The standard commission paid by most transportation companies in Canada is as follows: domestic air travel within Canada by the two national carriers, 8.25 percent; transborder travel and travel wholly within the United States, 10 percent; international travel, 9 percent. This means that the average commission is less than 10 percent. (Commission on the sale of tour packages, however, runs between 11 percent and 22 percent.) In 1993, total commissions from airline ticket sales were $718 million.

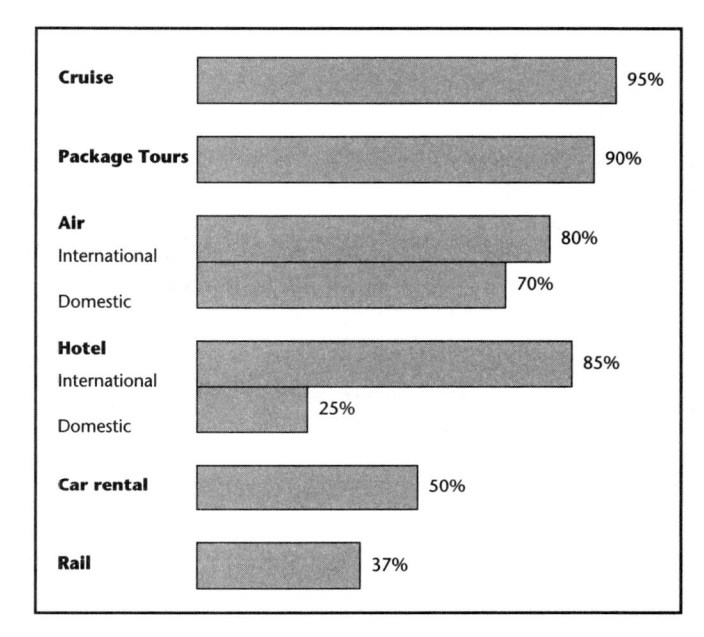

Cruise	95%
Package Tours	90%
Air International	80%
Air Domestic	70%
Hotel International	85%
Hotel Domestic	25%
Car rental	50%
Rail	37%

FIGURE 13-1
Percent of Travel Product Sold by United States Travel Agencies
SOURCE: *Travel Industry World Yearbook*

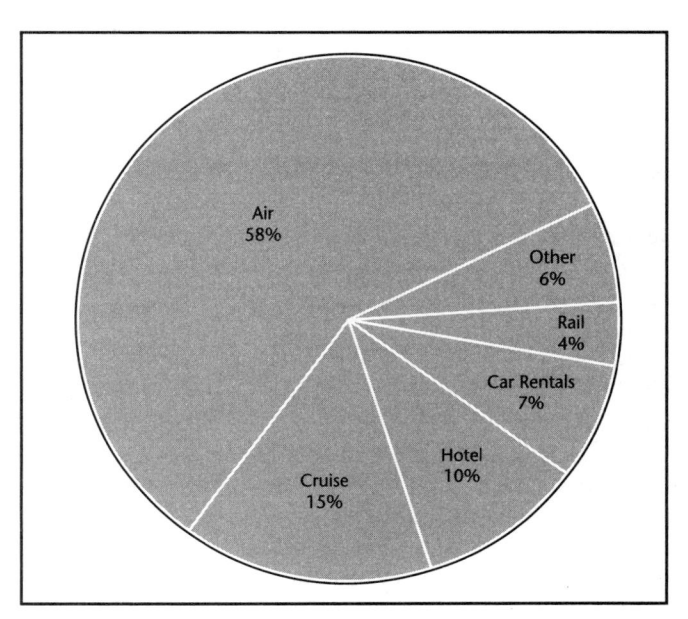

Air	58%
Cruise	15%
Hotel	10%
Car Rentals	7%
Rail	4%
Other	6%

FIGURE 13-2
Sources of Travel Agency Revenue.
SOURCE: Louis Harris and Associates

Overrides Suppliers also compensate travel agencies through overrides. As you learned in Chapter 3, an override is a bonus or extra commission for selling in greater volume. For example, a cruise line might pay a travel agency a commission of 10 percent on the sale of every cruise package. However, after the agency sells $10,000 worth of cruises, the cruise line pays an additional 1 percent commission—a total of 11 percent—for every cruise sold after that.

Some suppliers offer overrides on a graduated scale up to 15 percent. Canadian airlines use overrides to supplement the bare 8.5 percent commission rates. Below is an example of a graduated scale:

Sales	Override
$10,000–14,999	1 percent
$15,000–24,999	2 percent
$25,000–34,999	3 percent
$35,000–44,999	4 percent
$45,000+	5 percent

Overrides are sometimes retroactive once the agency has reached a certain total. For example, when an agency has reached a sales total of $45,000, the supplier may pay a 15 percent commission for all previous sales. Some overrides in Canada are a matter of individual negotiation between the carrier and the agent. Most Canadian suppliers that pay overrides, do so on larger sales volumes than were shown in the previous example.

Rebates As a means of attracting and maintaining customers, some travel agencies share a portion of their commissions and overrides with their clients. This takes the form of rebates, or money back on the price of the ticket. Rebates for airline tickets are commonly given to corporations. In fact, some corporations demand a certain percentage of an agency's commissions before they will contract to do business with the agency. There are rebates in Canada that are arrived at by individual negotiation between the carrier and the agent.

Service Charges These charges are common in the United States, but less so in Canada. To cover their expenses, some travel agencies charge customers for certain services. This is largely because of airline deregulation—with the onslaught of low airfares, travel agencies are earning less in commissions. (A commission of 10 percent on a ticket costing $75 yields less revenue than the same commission on a ticket costing $100.)

Services that some agencies now charge for include preparing a lengthy and involved itinerary, making a non-commissionable hotel reservation, obtaining visas, sending telegrams, and making long-distance telephone calls. Because it is time-consuming to undo arrangements, agencies may also charge for trip cancellations. A consulting fee may be charged if the travel agent spends an hour talking to a customer about a trip and the customer doesn't book. Fees may be waived in certain circumstances. For instance, clients booking a round-the-world cruise would probably not be charged for long-distance telephone calls made in connection with their trip.

Agencies that charge service fees should state this clearly to customers before starting any transactions. Many people feel that charging fees violates the service nature of the travel agency industry; the practice is currently under debate in the United States.

If long-distance charges were to be applied in Canada, the Canadian method would be to either charge time and charges on the call or charge the call to the client's home phone. At present, most Canadian travel agencies are very reluctant to demand service charges.

Relationships

Travel agencies have relationships both with suppliers and with clients. They have agreements, written or implied, to sell the products of their suppliers. They are expected to represent suppliers honourably and faithfully and to avoid dishonest practices. At the same time, agencies depend on suppliers to deliver products and services as promised. Once a trip has started, travel agents have no control over supplier errors, although clients tend to blame the agent when things go wrong. Agencies need to select carefully the suppliers with whom they will do business.

Travel agencies also act on behalf of their clients. Agents have an obligation to provide competent travel planning for clients who are spending money on travel products, which—unlike most other consumer goods—cannot be returned if the buyer is not pleased. Clients expect travel agents to represent suppliers' products truthfully. They also expect travel agents to be knowledgeable about transportation and accommodation and to offer them the most complete and up-to-date information about destinations. Clients would certainly want to know, for example, if there was serious political unrest at their planned destination. Travel agents must be meticulous in seeing to the details of a client's trip. Typing the wrong departure time on a client's itinerary or forgetting to inform that client about visa requirements could ruin a trip and make the agency liable for damages.

Relationships among travel agencies, suppliers, and customers are very complex. As an intermediary, the travel agency must relate well to both supplier and customer. This often means walking a fine line.

Agency and Supplier An automobile dealership generally sells the products of only one manufacturer—perhaps Chrysler, Ford, or Nissan. A travel agency, however, generally represents many suppliers. The fact that a travel agent can show customers a variety of products and help them select the best ones for their needs has long been one of the strongest arguments for purchasing through a travel agency.

ILLUSTRATION 13-1
A travel agent performs the role of travel counsellor, and of sales representative.

> **CHECK YOUR PRODUCT KNOWLEDGE**
>
> 1. Name four intermediaries in the travel industry's channels of distribution. In what way is the travel agency like a retail store?
> 2. Which supplier has had the most influence on the operations of the travel agency?
> 3. Name two ways in which suppliers compensate travel agencies. How are these methods different from those used in most other areas of retailing?
> 4. What are rebates? Why do suppliers and agencies offer them?
> 5. What is the dealership concept of retailing? In what way is the retail travel agency different?

However, certain circumstances may prevent an agency from maintaining a neutral role as a general supplier of travel products. To obtain lucrative overrides, an agency may use one airline for most of its business, even though this may not be in the best interest of the customer. Some suppliers offer other incentives, such as yearly bonuses and free travel, to persuade travel agents to promote their products. An agency that leases the computer reservations system of a certain carrier also tends to favour that carrier.

Agency and Customer Travel agents relate to their clients in three ways: as counsellors who advise clients on trip planning and provide information about destinations; as sales representatives who interest customers in new products and services; and finally, as clerks who make reservations and type itineraries.

Monica Hilber has a good relationship with a travel agency. Monica's agency took the time to learn her motivations, needs, and expectations (MNEs), as a pleasure traveller and as a business traveller. Now, when she needs to arrange a flight and hotel room for a business trip, all she does is place a routine call to the agency, which quickly makes the bookings. This winter, Monica will be taking a vacation trip to Australia. She probably wouldn't have considered Australia, but her travel agent sent her some brochures and articles believing they would whet her curiosity. Monica's company may be sending her on a research trip to Peru, so her travel agent is looking for information about that South American country.

Most travel agents find that counselling clients is the most rewarding aspect of their profession. It presents a challenge and allows them to be creative. In fact, many travel agents feel that the term *agent* no longer gives the full picture of what they do. Instead, they prefer to call themselves "travel consultants" or "travel counsellors."

TYPES OF TRAVEL AGENCIES

To meet the varying needs of consumers, different types of travel agencies offer a variety of travel products and services. There are two main types of travel agencies: general and specialized.

General

Most travel agencies in Canada and the United States offer general services. These agencies are like department stores, and offer a wide variety of products and services to suit a wide variety of customers. These "full-service" agencies handle all types of travel—airplane, rail, cruise, rental car—and all types of accommodation. They book all sorts of tours, from sightseeing trips through Europe's capital cities to 12-day rafting trips on the Tatsheshini River in northwestern British Columbia. Customers can find products to fit almost any budget.

There are some differences between full-service agencies in Canada and those in the United States. There is less business travel in Canada, and it offers a lower commission, so revenue from that source is lower; on the other hand, more package tours and charters are sold in Canada.

Owners of full-service travel agencies believe that a diversity of products and services results in steadier income. Brisk business in one area can offset slow business in another area. The agents must know something about every aspect of travel, and this is a challenge.

Larger travel agencies are usually divided into departments, such as commercial and vacation. These departments may be further divided into international and domestic. Each department is staffed by travel agents with specialized knowledge.

PROFILE

ACTA

The Alliance of Canadian Travel Associations (ACTA), founded in 1977, is the not-for-profit trade association representing the travel industry in Canada. The alliance was formed by seven provincial associations now known as ACTA Atlantic, ACTA Quebec, ACTA Ontario, ACTA Manitoba, ACTA Saskatchewan, ACTA Alberta, and ACTA British Columbia.

ACTA has over 3000 members in two categories: retail/wholesale (travel agencies, tour operators, and travel wholesalers), and supplier/auxiliary (travel service and marketing service suppliers such as airlines, hotels, tourist boards, cruise lines, railways, car rental companies, and CRS vendors).

ACTA's mission is to have dedicated volunteers, supported by the provincial and national staff, work together for the following purposes:

- Promote the goals of the travel industry.
- Improve travelling standards for the public.
- Voice the interests and concerns of its members.
- Represent the interests of its members to the public, suppliers, governments, and other bodies.
- Support and assist members in maximizing their economic objectives.

Each of the seven provincial or regional associations works with a network of volunteers and professional staff, and undertakes a broad range of projects significant to its own members. ACTA National is overseen by an executive board of directors, which is composed of travel professionals elected by their peers and of all the provincial association presidents. The national executive works together to respond to both regional and national issues.

ACTA maintains continuous effective dialogue within the industry (e.g., with the Tourism Industry Association of Canada, and the Air Transportation Association of Canada, and represents its members in front of government bodies on issues of concern and relevance to all ACTA members. These government bodies include Transport Canada, Consumer and Corporate Affairs, External Affairs, the National Transportation Agency, Tourism Canada, Revenue Canada, and Finance Canada. ACTA expresses its members' views on key issues such as consumer and trade protection, air transportation taxes, tariffs, customs, Canadian tourism, regulation of tour operators and travel agents, and regulation of supplier organizations such as airlines.

ACTA contributes to international dialogue in the travel industry through alliances with sister associations in other countries, and through its alliance with the Universal Federation of Travel Agents' Associations (UFTAA).

In order to help provide the public with the highest quality travel services, and to promote the most efficient and amicable dealings with other members, every ACTA member has accepted a two-part code of ethics. The first part applies to relations between ACTA members and the public; the second applies to relations among ACTA members.

Each ACTA provincial association has a yearly conference and trade show. ACTA National also has a conference and trade show, which is sometimes held outside Canada (e.g., Hong Kong in 1995).

ACTA sponsors national and provincial education courses and seminars and is a partner in ACCESS (the ACTA CITC Canadian Educational Standards System) with the Canadian Institute of Travel Counsellors (CITC). In addition, ACTA members can participate in group health and insurance plans, and in a business insurance plan. This is a desirable feature, as many members are categorized as small businesses.

Commercial

A commercial travel agency specializes in the business travel requirements of firms and corporations. Because destinations are determined by the nature of the business, agents do less counselling with business travellers. The emphasis is on making arrangements quickly and efficiently. Commercial travel agencies tend to enjoy consistent year-round business, free from the seasonal or economic fluctuations that are part of vacation and leisure travel. Some commercial agencies branch into leisure travel for their business clients.

Vacation and Leisure

A vacation and leisure agency generally has a more relaxed atmosphere, and agents do more counselling. This type of agency may sell nationally advertised tours—such as Canadian Holidays, Caravan, and Globus–Gateway—or organize its own tours. Vacation and leisure agencies also design foreign and domestic tours for individual clients. Called Foreign Independent Tours (FITs) or Domestic Independent Tours (DITs), these arrangements cost more, but they meet the traveller's personal expectations better. Vacation and leisure agencies may also assist VFR travellers, although travellers driving to familiar locations usually don't require the services of a travel agency.

All-Cruise

Some agencies, with names like "Ship Shop," specialize in vacation cruises. Since only 5 percent of travellers have ever taken a cruise, a tremendous potential for business exists in this area. Also, since cruises represent a complete vacation package (transportation, accommodations, meals, sightseeing), commissions are calculated on the full amount of sale, and the compensation can be quite high. Through workshops and mailings, the National Association of Cruise Only Agents (NACOA) helps agencies promote their sector.

Specialty

While conducting a full-service business, some agencies may have a branch or division that concentrates on one form of travel, or on services to a special group of travellers. These agencies are usually located in metropolitan areas, where there is greater market segmentation. Agencies also tend to specialize when there are many agencies competing in one location. Some specialty agencies reflect the talents and interests of the owner and staff. The following specialty agencies are worth noting:

Adventure Adventure travel is a fast-growing segment of the travel market. Adventure travel agencies specialize in package trips to exotic and difficult-to-reach destinations. Such trips often involve much physical activity. Examples are rafting on Chile's Bio-Bio River, camping on Easter Island, and cross-country skiing in the Arctic.

Seniors Many people say that their dream for retirement is to travel more. Agencies concentrating on seniors' travel help make those dreams come true. Escorted tours for seniors are another fast-growing segment of the travel market. In planning such tours, agencies recognize that many seniors have special needs. For example, travellers whose sense of hearing is diminishing appreciate a guide who speaks clearly and loudly. For travellers who tend to tire easily, no long walks or flights of stairs should be necessary for viewing attractions.

Singles Singles can take advantage of tours and cruises arranged exclusively for them. Some agencies provide matching services to help singles find travel companions. Singleworld, one of the best-known companies in this specialty area, sells its tours through travel agencies.

Ethnic Ethnic travel agencies exist in cities with large ethnic communities. They arrange individual or group travel to the parent country, for example, to Greece, Italy, Poland, Israel, or Japan.

Physically Challenged At present, only a few travel companies offer tours specifically designed for physically challenged people. The companies that do exist have organized trips in North America and abroad for quadriplegics, for visually or hearing challenged people, and for people suffering from emphysema, muscular dystrophy, multiple sclerosis, or renal failure. Other types of travel agencies are willing to adapt travel plans to the needs and abilities of the physically challenged if they are told specifically what is needed.

Student Travel Cuts is the travel company of the Canadian Federation of Students. It has more than 35 offices on campuses across Canada. These specialize in serving Canadian students and have developed an expertise in language courses and work programs in foreign countries.

CHECK YOUR PRODUCT KNOWLEDGE

1. Name four types of travel agencies.
2. What is the difference between a general or full-service travel agency and other types of travel agencies?
3. What factors might induce an agency to offer travel products for a select group of people?

THE GROWTH OF THE TRAVEL AGENCY

In 1841, Thomas Cook arranged for a railway company to transport 570 British working-class people to a temperance convention. This was a 20 kilometre trip. He thus became the first travel agent. As you learned in Chapter 1, the agency of Thomas Cook and Son dominated the early travel industry. Cook conducted tours to Europe and later to the United States and Canada. His agency represented various transportation companies, including several steamship lines.

The idea of organized travel assistance spread to Canada and the United States. By the end of the 19th century, numerous agencies were operating. These included the American Express Company, an offshoot of the famous Wells Fargo Company. Travel agencies at this time specialized in selling steamship tickets and grand tours to the wealthy.

Where there were no agencies, suppliers found other ways to sell their products. Steamship companies sent agents on horseback to small towns across Canada and the United States. These agents sold steamship tickets to people who wanted to bring their relatives from Europe to this country. In the 1920s, railway companies compensated hotel porters for getting train tickets for hotel guests. Early airlines also sold tickets through hotel porters, giving them a 5 percent commission.

Airlines soon realized that travel agencies offered a more efficient way of distributing airplane tickets. In particular, they saw the potential of travel agencies for selling pleasure travel on the popular DC-3s. At the beginning of World War II, over 1000 agencies existed in the United States and Canada. When public acceptance of air transportation increased after the war, the commercial airlines continued to grow, and so did the number of travel agencies.

The Effects of Jet Travel

In the travel industry, 1956 is considered to be the dawn of the modern age of travel. The flight of the first transatlantic passenger jet ushered in an era of pleasure travel for millions of people. Between 1965 and 1988, the number of passengers on Canadian scheduled carriers increased 414 percent, from 7 million to 36 million. In the United States between 1960 and 1980, the number of passengers on scheduled carriers increased 378 percent, from 62 million to 297 million. The growth in travel has been matched by the growth in the number of travel agencies. In 1958, there were about 3000 agencies in Canada and the United States. Today, there are more than 5500 in Canada and 37 000 in the United States.

In 1956, before most people had taken their first jet flight (or any airplane flight, for that matter), travel agencies were quite different from most travel agencies today. The travel agency of the 1950s was usually a part-time business, with a staff of one or two people. It may have been located

ILLUSTRATION 13-2
Ethnic travel agencies exist within ethnic communities and can arrange travel to parent countries.
SOURCE: Karen O'Neill

in a back office of the local bus depot or in a café. Office furnishings were bare, and there were no computer terminals blinking information. Selling bus and railway tickets was often the main business. If a customer wanted to travel to a faraway place, the agent wrote letters to make reservations.

The Travel Agency Today

Of the more than 42 000 travel agencies in Canada and the United States today, about half are located in attractive offices in metropolitan areas. Two-thirds take in revenues of less than $2 million a year. Most agencies are owned by women, and more women than men work in agencies.

In the late 1950s, travel agencies were concerned mainly with pleasure travel; today, business travel accounts for a large percentage of a general agency's bookings. Modern travel agencies offer products that were not dreamed of 40 years ago. At the same time, travellers are more sophisticated and demand more services. The environment in today's agencies is likely to be fast-paced and hectic. Agents receive and send information instantaneously, using sophisticated technology. The work is complex and intense, and made even more so by airline deregulation and competitive marketing.

Deregulation As you have already read, the Airline Deregulation Act of 1978 in the United States and airline regulatory reform in Canada in the 1980s led to an increase in the number of airlines. This, in turn, resulted in a multitude of new routes, schedules, and airfares, all of which were constantly changing. For flights between any two cities, several price alternatives were often available depending on the airline, day, and various restrictions. As airlines scrambled for passengers, price wars broke out. A highly competitive climate developed, with offers of rebates and discounts.

Deregulation had an immediate effect on travel agencies. Before deregulation, routes and airfares followed an orderly, predictable pattern. Agents could practically memorize the information they needed. After deregulation, the system became confusing and difficult to handle. And, as mentioned earlier, lower airfares and negotiable commissions decreased revenue for travel agencies. Many agencies must now deal in volume sales (i.e., sell large quantities of product at reduced prices) to counteract low revenues.

At the same time, most travel agents believe that deregulation has made travel agents even more important. Customers are baffled by the complex airfares and routes and need travel agents to help them through the maze. Suppliers, too, depend on travel agencies to sort things out for the customer. As you can see in Figure 13-3, the total dollar volume of travel agency bookings has increased dramatically since 1978. Table 13-1 shows airline ticket sales by Canadian travel agents in 1993.

Automation To keep up with the rapid changes in airfares and schedules and to increase sales volume, computer reservations systems have become a necessity for almost all travel agencies. Automation also simplifies accounting and facilitates information gathering for managerial purposes.

Most travel agencies in Canada and the United States are now automated. Travel agents need to be familiar with computerized reservation systems (CRSs) such as Galileo (Air Canada) and Sabre (Canadian Airlines).

The Consolidation of Agencies

Another way of categorizing travel agencies is by the amount of business they do annually. The breakdown might be as follows:

- Small—$1 million or less. (The International Air Transport Association has a different financial standard for accreditation for agencies with annual sales of less than $2 million.)

Item	Amount	Change since 1992
Number of tickets sold on scheduled air carriers	8.5 million	(-3%)
Total value of airline tickets sold	$ 5.4 billion	(+6%)
Average value of ticket sold	$ 635.33	(+9%)
Average commission	13.3 percent	(+23%)
Total value of commission on airline tickets	$718.2 million	(+19%)

TABLE 13-1
Airline Ticket Sales by Canadian Travel Agents in 1993
SOURCE: "International Growth Can't Stop Decline in Ticket Demand," *Perspective*, Canadian Travel Press, March 3, 1994, p.2.

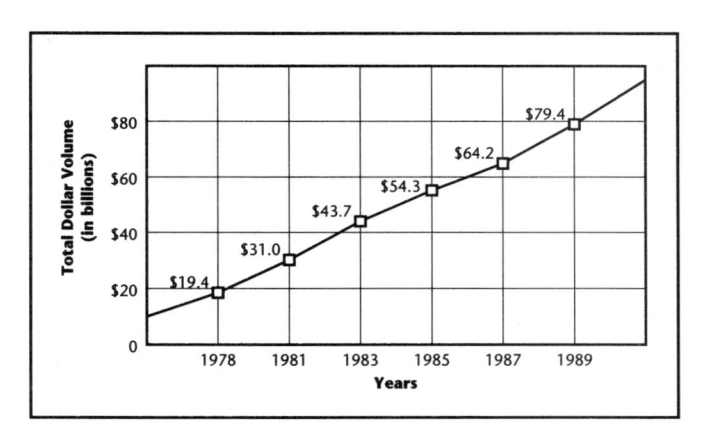

FIGURE 13-3
Total Dollar Volume of Travel Agency Bookings in the United States
SOURCE: Louis Harris and Associates, *Travel Weekly*

- Midsized—$1 million to $1.99 million.
- Large—$2 million to $4.99 million.
- Very large—$5 million and over.

The travel agency industry is overwhelmingly composed of small businesses. However, a small number of very large agencies, or mega-agencies, have a disproportionate share of the business. In 1988, mega-agencies in Canada and the United States made up less than 1 percent of the total number of agencies but had 19 percent of total air sales. Mega-agencies became large and continue to grow by taking over medium-sized and large agencies or by squeezing them out of business.

The Impact of Globalization The globalization of business has had an impact on the travel business. Travel agencies in various countries are associating with each other to meet the needs of multinational firms. These firms want to channel their business through one agency. In 1993, Thomas Cook purchased Marlin Travel, then Canada's largest travel agency. This allowed Thomas Cook to expand in Canada and Marlin to expand globally—something it could not do by itself.

In 1994 a joint-venture worldwide travel firm was proposed by Carlson Travel of Minnesota and Wagon-Lit Travel of Paris. P. Lawson Travel of Canada, owned by Carlson, would become a member of the new group, which would have 4000 locations in 125 countries.

Mega-Agencies Mega-agencies such as the Canadian Automobile Association (which has about 126 locations across Canada), the American Automobile Association (AAA), Liberty Travel, The Carlson Group, Thomas Cook Travel, American Express, and Rosenbluth Travel, are primarily interested in multimillion-dollar corporate accounts. The American Express Travel Service office in Halifax, owned by American Express Canada, Inc., advertises separate telephone numbers for business travel and for leisure travel.

With offices in many cities (and perhaps several offices in a single city), mega-agencies represent the supermarkets and giant discount houses of travel. Because they are so large, they can purchase travel products in bulk. The more volume they do, the more easily they can offer rebates, which cost-conscious corporations earnestly seek. Mega-agencies can offer many services, such as monitoring frequent-flier programs and compiling travel and entertainment expenses; these services may be beyond the capability of smaller agencies.

Consortiums To compete against the mega-agencies, some independent travel agencies have formed consortiums. A **consortium** is a group formed to achieve a goal that is beyond the resources of any one member. Travel agencies pay a fee to become members of a consortium. Membership rules may also specify that an agency must have a certain gross income or a certain level of automation. Not all independent agencies are able to join a consortium.

Consortiums exist for both leisure and business travel. They may be regional or nationwide. Woodside Travel Management Corp., one of the best-known consortiums, specializes in commercial travel. In 1988, Woodside comprised 85 agencies with 1500 locations worldwide. Its revenues from air sales were $6 billion. Other consortiums are Hickory Travel Systems, Associated Travel Network, and Travel Trust International.

Independent agencies benefit greatly from the bargaining power of consortiums, which are able to obtain bulk discounts for their members that would be unavailable to individual agencies. They also provide a forum for information exchange.

Consortiums do have some problems, however. With the help of a consortium, some independent agencies become so successful that they become mega-agencies themselves. If an agency—especially a strong one—leaves the consortium, the entire organization is weakened. Consortiums also tend to raid one another's ranks for members.

A variation of the travel consortium is the **cooperative.** In a cooperative, independent agencies band together temporarily to achieve a goal. Usually, they have a joint interest in promoting a product or an event.

Franchises To combat mega-agencies and consortiums, an independent agency might join a nationwide franchise group such as Ask Mr. Foster Travel, Empress Travel, or Uniglobe. An agency that joins such a group retains its individual ownership. In contrast to the agencies in a consortium, it also adopts a company name and image. Franchises deal mainly with leisure and vacation travel.

To join a franchise group, an agency pays an initial fee and agrees to pay an annual percentage of its gross earnings. In return, it acquires bulk buying power, advertising support, training programs in business development, and brand-name recognition. Agencies may convert to franchises, or they may start out in business as franchises.

Small Agencies Small agencies are the corner grocery stores or the modest boutiques of the travel industry. They may employ only two or three people and have little automation.

Medium-sized and large agencies are in constant danger of being gobbled up; small agencies can often survive if they find the right market. For example, they might specialize in organizing FITs, or in arranging travel for small commercial

Organization	Number of members	Locations
Carlson Travel Wagon-Lit (Paris) (P. Lawson Canada)	4000 locations (127 locations in Canada)	125 countries
GEM	1125 companies; 1375 locations (includes 70 cruise only)	United States
GIANTS	900 companies; 1900 locations	United States and Canada (746)
Hickory	80 companies; 600 locations	Worldwide
Thomas Cook (Marlin Canada)	2000 locations (200 locations in Canada)	International
Travel Trust International	114 companies; 2000 locations	International
Uniglobe	Approx. 775 companies; 800 locations	United States and Canada (plans to expand into other countries)

TABLE 13-2
Comparison of Several Consortiums
SOURCE: ASTA Agency Management (updated)

firms (such as law offices) or for seniors. Locating in a small town or city may also be a key to success.

Small agencies are able to offer personalized service and more thorough trip counselling. When clients return from a trip, small agencies are more likely to call them up and ask how things went. Agents will often write letters expressing regret if a trip is cancelled or if something goes awry. Says one small-agency employee, "If you make yourself valuable enough on a personal level, customers will not be looking around for discounts."

> **CHECK YOUR PRODUCT KNOWLEDGE**
>
> 1. What has been the most important influence on the growth of travel agencies?
> 2. What effect did airline deregulation have on travel agencies?
> 3. What new channels of distribution challenge the travel agency?
> 4. Why has automation become necessary for most travel agencies?
> 5. What has been the effect of the mega-agency on the travel agency sector?

ILLUSTRATION 13-3
Travel agents sell dreams.
SOURCE: Karen O'Neill

OPENING A TRAVEL AGENCY

Suppose you want to enter the retail travel business. Assuming you don't want to purchase a franchise or an existing agency, how would you go about opening your own full-service travel agency? How would you get airlines, cruise lines, and other suppliers to furnish you with tickets and pay you a commission?

An entrepreneur wanting to open a travel agency should become familiar with conference appointments, conference requirements, and provincial requirements.

Conference Appointments

Compared with other retail businesses, the travel agency industry is still highly accessible to entrepreneurs. Of the more than 42 000 travel agencies in Canada and the United States, more than half were started after 1980. Many people become owners of travel agencies as a second career after retirement or as a career change in midlife. The owners must have qualified employees working at the agency.

To open officially, a travel agency must be appointed, or approved, by industry conferences. In this context, a conference is not a meeting but a regulatory body that formulates standards for acceptance, reviews and appoints new agencies, and disciplines existing agencies when necessary.

The Air Transport Association of Canada

The Air Transportation Association of Canada (ATAC) represents commercial aviation in Canada. All the major scheduled and chartered carriers and regional airlines, and many smaller operators, belong to ATAC. ATAC members account for more than 97 percent of commercial aviation revenue earned in Canada.

The ATAC Traffic Conference, a separate entity within ATAC, oversees all matters dealing with interline standards, ticketing, and passenger and baggage processing. It also oversees the Canadian Travel Agency program, which sets the rules that govern domestic and transborder air transportation sales. In 1986, ATAC contracted with the International Air Transport Association (IATA) to operate the Canadian program.

Major Conferences The major conferences in Canada are as follows:

- The Air Transport Association of Canada (ATAC).
- The International Air Transport Association (IATA), headquartered in Montreal—for selling air tickets. (The International Airline Travel Agency Network, or IATAN, is a subsidiary of IATA. It serves as a link between retail travel agencies and IATA.)
- Cruise Lines International Association (CLIA)—for selling cruises.
- VIA Rail, Inc.—for selling domestic rail tickets. VIA is also the Canadian agent for Amtrak.

The four major conferences in the United States are as follows:

PROFILE

American Express Company

The American Express Company, in business for over 140 years, has grown and changed with the times. It started out in the express cargo business and later moved on to a variety of travel-related services. Today, it is becoming well known for its international financial operations.

The original company was founded in 1850. It resulted from the merger of three firms involved in the express transport of goods, valuables, and money between the East Coast and the Midwest. By the mid-1860s, it had 900 offices in ten states. It also had a major competitor called the Merchants Union Express Company. After several years of cutthroat competition, the two rivals merged to become the American Merchants Union Express Company, which was renamed the American Express Company in 1873.

The travel arm of American Express (often referred to as Amex) was brought into being after James Fargo, the son of the original president, took over the company. During Fargo's 33 years of leadership, the American Express money order was introduced (1882), as were American Express traveller's cheques (1891). The latter were designed to replace the more cumbersome letters of credit that were then in use. Amex opened its first European office in Paris in 1895.

In 1918 the American government nationalized the express industry. American Express compensated for the resulting loss of business by focusing more heavily on its travel and banking operations.

Today, Amex is known in four major business areas: travel, insurance, banking, and investment. Travel-related services still account for a large portion of its profits. American Express traveller's cheques are still the most popular ones among travellers. For one thing, they are internationally recognized and accepted. Also, Amex provides several special services. For example, travellers can get emergency refunds 24 hours a day and can obtain cheques in many foreign currencies. Traveller's cheques are profitable for Amex. Most buyers purchase them long before they actually use them. The money they spend on them amounts to an interest-free loan from the customers to Amex. Also, travellers pay a 1 percent fee for purchasing cheques (though much of that fee goes to the issuing agent). Amex puts the cash it receives into high-yield investments. Related services for travellers include travel agencies, tour packages, and motel and car rental reservations services.

Amex was not the first company to introduce the credit card (Diners Club did so in 1950); but the Amex "green card," introduced in 1958, was the best-known card for a number of years. (Since then, "gold" and "platinum" cards have been issued.) After bank cards such as MasterCard and Visa were introduced, Amex faced heavy competition. However, clever marketing has brought many consumers into the Amex fold. First, there was the "Don't Leave Home Without It" campaign, which warned travellers of the dire consequences of forgetting their American Express card (or not having one at all). In the mid-1970s and early 1980s, the "Do You Know Me?" campaign thrived. It spotlighted high achievers, such as designer Bill Blass and writer Stephen King, whose names were better known than their faces. The point was that their Amex card gave them instant recognition. More recently, there has been the "Interesting Lives" campaign, designed to attract women to the card. These 30-second commercials show women in various roles making use of their American Express cards. This, too, has been a huge success.

Although Amex now makes as much money from its banking and investment activities as from its travel services division, many people still think of it as a premier travel service supplier. Amex seems to like it that way. The corporation's executives don't plan anytime soon to phase out the division that made the American Express Company famous. Amex continues to be a money-maker today.

- The Airline Reporting Corporation (ARC)—for selling domestic air tickets.
- IATA—for selling international air tickets.
- CLIA—for selling cruises.
- The National Railroad Passenger Corporation (Amtrak)—for selling domestic rail tickets.

The membership of each conference consists of companies that sell transportation. IATA, for example, is composed of more than 200 airlines from 116 countries. These companies, of course, want the people selling their products to be competent and honest, and the **conference appointment system** is a way of ensuring this. An agency that receives a conference appointment has the right to sell the products of all the conference's members and to receive commissions from them.

Conference Requirements

Each conference establishes requirements, or standards, that an agency must meet in order to be approved. While an agency needs the approval of all conferences, it should concentrate on meeting the airline conference requirements first, because the sale of air tickets forms a major part of any agency's business. Having satisfied the airline conference, the agency is likely to satisfy the other conferences.

IATA provides an accreditation kit for new applicants who want to become approved passenger sales agents. IATA publishes the *Travel Agent's Handbook*, which states in detail the rules and regulations for setting up a travel agency, as well as for many other procedures involved in selling air transportation. These rules and regulations are modified from time to time. Anyone who is planning a career as a travel agent or who is considering opening a travel agency should read this handbook.

ATAC and IATA issued a joint handbook in 1994. To reduce confusion and work toward an international standard, the Canadian air carriers incorporated into the Canadian program almost all IATA resolutions dealing with travel agency rules.

The following are some of the requirements for opening an agency:

Open for Business To apply for IATA and ATAC accreditation, a travel agency must already be open and operating. You might wonder how the agency can sell tickets before it's even been approved. While waiting for approval, it can obtain tickets from the airlines on a cash basis. Once the agency has been accredited, it can apply to receive commissions retroactively to the date of application.

Experience There must be at least two people employed full time at the agency for which the application is made: a qualifying management person, and a qualifying ticketing agent. Each of these people must have experience in their respective fields.

Location The agency must be accessible to the public, and clearly identified as a travel agency by a sign that is visible from the street. (Exceptions are sometimes made for agencies that organize inclusive tours.)

It must be in a location separate from any other travel agency or air carrier, and it must be open for regular business. Also, the location should be such that proper security can be maintained at all times. No unauthorized person should have access to the agency's documents and equipment.

A downtown store with a good display area that can be seen by pedestrians and by people in cars is an ideal location, as is a store in a high-traffic suburban mall.

Finances Careful attention to financial requirements and procedures is essential to anyone wishing to gain and keep IATA accreditation. Current financial statements, prepared in accordance with generally accepted accounting principles and reviewed by an independent accountant, must be submitted on an ongoing basis. Minimum standards for accreditation include $25,000 of working capital and a tangible net worth of $35,000. The *Travel Agent's Handbook* gives precise details about these financial requirements.

Promotion The agency must be actively involved in the promotion of travel. It is encouraged to promote and sell domestic, transborder, and international air transportation in a competitive and efficient manner that is in the interests of the consumer and the industry. It can do this by advertising its products and services in newspaper, television, and radio ads, and through brochures, flyers, and direct mail.

Procedure for Appointment

A travel agency that desires accreditation from IATA (for international flights) and ATAC (for domestic and transborder flights) makes application to IATA/ATAC. Included with this application must be very detailed documentation about the agent and the place where the agency is located. On receiving the application, IATA notifies its member agencies and arranges for an inspection of the agency and its staff.

Once approved, the newly accredited agency becomes linked up with the Bank Settlement Plan, which has been developed over the past several decades. This centralized reporting and remitting system benefits both carriers and agents, as it standardizes and automates travel documents, thereby streamlining services and payments. Details of this plan are available in the *BSP Manual for Agents*, published by IATA.

Once accepted, the accredited agency must, of course, maintain IATA standards at all times.

Provincial Requirements Certain provinces in Canada—for example, Ontario, British Columbia, and Quebec—require a travel agency to be registered with the provincial registrar. In Ontario, travel agencies must follow the rules and regulations stated by the Ontario registrar under the Ontario Travel Industry Act. The Ontario act includes a travel protection section, which requires insurance and bonding to protect the travelling public if a tour operator goes out of business.

CHECK YOUR PRODUCT KNOWLEDGE

1. What are the four major conferences?
2. Why must an agency receive conference appointments?
3. What are the main requirements for receiving accreditation by a conference?
4. List the procedures for obtaining conference approval.

HOW A TRAVEL AGENCY FUNCTIONS

When customers enter most retail stores, they expect to see the merchandise on display. Before purchasing an item, customers want to look it over and learn something about it. They'll try on a new suit or coat to see how it looks and fits. They'll ask the salesperson to demonstrate how to operate a washing machine or a microwave oven. And they would never buy a car without first taking it for a test drive. If, after purchase, the product turns out to be defective or otherwise unsuitable, customers can return it to the store or receive some sort of adjustment to their account.

What's for Sale?

The products sold by a retail travel agency seem quite different. Although some are tangible, most are intangible.

The Travel Product Travel agencies sell products such as a trip on an airplane, a stay in a hotel room, a view of the mountains, or a cruise on a ship. None of these products can be displayed in the retail agency. Nor can they be inspected or tried out before they're purchased. Once customers buy these products, they have them for only a short time. If travel products prove unsatisfactory, they can't be returned—although suppliers and agencies might compensate dissatisfied customers in some way.

Why would anyone buy a product that can't be seen or touched and that doesn't come with a warranty? The reason is that when it sells travel products, the industry doesn't emphasize the technical features of an airplane or the dimensions of a hotel room. Instead, it is promoting the psychological benefits of its products.

Travel agents sell dreams to vacation and leisure travellers. A travel ad might show a beautifully tanned young couple dancing in a moonlit tropical garden. The ad is suggesting that by purchasing certain travel products, travellers will experience glamour, romance, relaxation, pleasure, and excitement. The vacation, long after it is over, will continue to exist as a wonderful memory.

To business and professional travellers, travel agents sell time, convenience, and prestige. A travel ad might show a flight attendant serving a gourmet meal to a distinguished-looking executive, or a chauffeur putting a business traveller's luggage into a limousine. Such ads tell travellers how important they are. By purchasing certain travel products, they will receive the efficient, prompt service they require.

Related Products To make a major purchase more enjoyable, customers often buy accessories or optional items. Travel agencies sell products that make trips safer, easier, and more pleasant. These products include traveller's cheques, passport photos, luggage, sportswear, and travel books.

A related product that has become a significant source of revenue for agencies is travel insurance. Different types of insurance are available, which can be sold separately or in a package.

- Flight insurance.
- Accident and health insurance.
- Insurance for baggage and personal possessions.
- Trip cancellation or interruption insurance.
- Bad weather insurance.

Even though travel insurance seems to emphasize what can go wrong on a trip, it is usually offered to clients as a means of adding to their peace of mind. The major suppliers of travel insurance products in Canada are Voyageur Insurance, Mutual of Omaha (national), Blue Cross Cooperative (Atlantic Canada), and Travellers Rite (western Canada). Out-of-province and out-of-country medical insurance became more important in the 1990s as several provinces cut back on their out-of-province coverage.

A new product that is being combined with travel insurance is travel assistance. Travel assistance not only covers the costs of emergencies during travel but also provides personal counselling and assistance. For example, say that a husband and wife are travelling in Mexico. The husband, who has a history of heart trouble, becomes seriously ill. The wife calls the 24-hour assistance hotline and receives directions to the nearest hospital. The assistance–insurance company also pays the required on-the-spot hospital admission costs and all hospital and doctor bills. In addition, it consults with the man's doctors in Canada regarding his treatment.

The Staff

In a retail travel agency, the number of employees depends on the size of the agency. So does the work those employees do. A mega-agency might be organized like a corporation, with separate departments for sales, personnel, accounting, public relations, and word processing. A small agency may simply have an owner–manager and a handful of travel agents and outside sales representatives.

Manager By assigning duties and work schedules, the manager directs the work of the other employees. He or she trains new employees, or trains current employees in new procedures. The manager is responsible for developing new products, improving the agency's efficiency, and overseeing financial transactions. He or she must also plan the agency's future.

Travel Agents As mentioned earlier, travel agents function as clerks, sales representatives, and counsellors—whichever role is appropriate at the time. As clerks, travel agents use automated systems to secure airline tickets, lease cars, and reserve hotel rooms for customers. As sales representatives, travel agents interest customers in various destinations and types of travel. As counsellors, travel agents help clients get in touch with their dreams, which are usually only partly formed when they come into the agency. Most clients need help in deciding which travel arrangements best suit their values and lifestyle.

Outside Sales Representatives A travel agency frequently has agreements with outside sales representatives, whose work involves arousing people's interest in travelling. They might show slides or movies at a meeting of a social or special-interest group, or arrange meetings with business managers. Wherever they are—in the produce section of the supermarket or on the telephone with their friends—outside sales representatives seek to direct business toward the agency with which they have contracted.

Many outside sales representatives work on commission. If people they introduce to the agency actually make a booking, they get between 25 and 50 percent of the commission, depending on how much work they've done for the sale. For example, if the commission on the sale of an airline ticket is $20, the representative might get $5. All transactions must go through the travel agency office, and transactions must be made under the name of the travel agency, not that of the sales representative.

Outside sales representatives are often homemakers, retirees, or other people who want to work part-time. Aggressive representatives who work full-time, however, can sometimes develop a large clientele, who are often more loyal to them than to any agency.

Money Matters

Travel agencies handle large sums of money. As trustee of both the customer's payments and the supplier's funds, the agency must keep accurate records of monies received and disbursed.

Sending Payment to the Airlines How do agencies forward money to the airlines from the sale of tickets? Does each agency send each airline a payment—say, twice a month? That's the way it used to be done, and the amount of record keeping, reporting, and auditing was staggering for both the agencies and the airlines.

In the mid-1960s, at the same time it introduced standard ticket stock, the Air Traffic Conference in the United States (which was later replaced by the Airline Reporting Corporation), instituted a much more efficient system. Under this system, known as the **Area Settlement Plan (ASP)**, a commercial bank in Louisville, Kentucky, has contracted with the ARC to serve as a clearing house.

In Canada, as mentioned above, payments (as well as record keeping and standard traffic documents) have been simplified for both travel agents and carriers by the development of IATA's Bank Settlement Plan Canada. The first BSP was developed in Japan in 1971; there are now 50 such plans in operation around the world.

Streamlined methods for payment have reduced both paperwork and the time spent on that paperwork. Much of this system is now automated so that agencies report sales electronically to their designated clearing house. Payments are made to a clearing bank, which then settles the agency's accounts with the designated airlines.

Sending Payment to Other Suppliers Since most agencies generally sell fewer products for cruise lines, railway companies, tour operators, and other suppliers, they issue cheques directly to them. Before doing so, they must be sure that the client has paid in full. Agencies deduct their commission before sending payment to the suppliers. A cover letter explains what the cheque is for and how payment was calculated.

The client is given the appropriate tickets and vouchers by the agent. **Vouchers** are coupons and documents that can be exchanged for travel products such as hotel accommodations or sightseeing tours.

CHECK YOUR PRODUCT KNOWLEDGE

1. What is the difference between products sold by retail travel agencies and those sold by other retail stores?
2. What are some related products sold by travel agencies?
3. Name staff positions held by employees in a typical small agency.
4. What is the function of an outside sales representative?
5. What is the Bank Settlement Plan Canada?

OTHER TRAVEL AND TOURISM DISTRIBUTORS

Instead of using travel agencies, some travellers go to other established intermediaries to obtain travel products and to receive help with trip arrangements. These channels of distribution include business travel departments, and travel clubs.

Business Travel Departments

Some business travellers are able to use the services of their company's business travel department. As you learned in Chapter 11, some companies employ their own staff to make travel arrangements for the company's employees. Since BTDs are not open to the public, and since the BTD employees are paid by the company, BTDs are not accredited. Nor do they receive commissions on the sale of airline tickets. Instead, BTDs operate as freelancers. They negotiate with the airlines for the right to sell their products and to receive discounts and rebates.

A variation of the BTD is the in-plant agency. An in-plant agency is a retail travel agency that is located on the premises of a corporation and does business primarily with that corporation. The classification of in-plant agencies is currently a subject of hot debate in the travel agency industry.

Another variation is the out-plant agency. An out-plant agency is an accredited, full-service travel agency located near a corporation's premises. The corporation has its own BTD to handle most travel arrangements, but it depends on the out-plant agency to issue tickets. The out-plant agency splits airline commissions with the BTD.

Travel Club

As you know by now, travel products are extremely perishable. A seat on Canadian Airlines' 2 p.m. flight from Calgary to Toronto on March 23, 1995, exists only for that moment. If it isn't sold, the airline receives absolutely no income from it. Because of the perishability of travel products, travel suppliers, like other retail suppliers, make use of marketing techniques such as clearance sales.

The travel club is the travel industry's version of a clearance sale. Travel clubs specialize in the sale of unsold travel products to vacation and leisure travellers. These products are usually cruises and international flights to Europe. To take advantage of bargain prices (anywhere from 20 to 60 percent off), travellers must belong to the club. They join by paying a nominal annual fee—usually around $50.

There are two main types of travel clubs. One type deals almost exclusively with last-minute bookings. The other is more like a tour operator—it publishes a catalogue of tours that is distributed to all members. Some travel clubs even operate their own aircraft and offer private charter packages that range from weekend gambling junkets to trips around the world.

Here is how travel clubs generally work. At some point before the departure date, suppliers discount unsold inventory. To avoid offending travellers who have paid the full price, suppliers advertise their clearance sales only through travel clubs. Club members find out the latest information on departures by calling a secret hotline. They must keep all information they hear confidential. A member who wishes to purchase a sale item can use a credit-card number to complete the transaction over the telephone. The travel club then receives the commission for the sale.

While travellers can save a lot of money by joining a travel club, the selection they are offered may be quite limited and may not meet their personal MNEs. Members must also have very flexible schedules so that they can leave for a trip on short notice. One Canadian travel club is the Last Minute Club, which advertises a toll-free number across Canada. That company's ads sometimes include a section for French-speaking Canadians, Club Tout D'Suite. The Last Minute Club negotiates special rates with Canada's leading travel companies, buying their unsold inventory of airplane seats, package holidays, and cruises at up to 50 percent off (and sometimes even more).

To promote membership, some travel clubs offer their members additional bargains, such as discounts on car rentals and rebates on tour and hotel bookings. Some clubs have frequent traveller plans. After purchasing $3,000 in air travel, for instance, a member might be entitled to a free week aboard a cruise ship.

CHECK YOUR PRODUCT KNOWLEDGE

1. How is a business travel department different from a commercial travel agency?
2. What is the purpose of travel clubs?

ASSOCIATIONS

The major Canadian travel association is the Alliance of Canadian Travel Associations (ACTA), founded in 1977. It has over 3000 members representing 14 categories of firms and individuals within tourism. There are 2200 travel agencies that belong to ACTA. Two of the association's main purposes are to promote the goals of the travel industry, and improve travelling standards for the public. A detailed profile of ACTA is found in Chapter 15.

The major association in the United States is the American Society of Travel Agents (ASTA), which includes members worldwide. One of its goals is to protect the public from fraud, as shown in this example:

Not too long ago, several hundred people in ten states became the victims of a telemarketing travel scam. Each of these people paid $200 for a travel certificate that, they were led to believe, could be applied toward discount travel. But when they tried to buy round-trip airfare to Hawaii for $29.95, they discovered their certificates were worthless.

Founded in 1931, ASTA's other main goals are to promote and advance the interests of the travel agency industry, and provide a public forum where travel agents can speak out on issues that concern them.

With 21 000 members in 129 countries, ASTA is the world's largest professional association of travel agents and agencies. ASTA's membership also includes airline, steamship, railway, and bus companies, as well as car rental firms, hotels, government tourist offices, and other travel-related organizations.

ASTA provides many services to its members. For example, it publishes a newsletter and magazine and sponsors workshops and seminars. In these ways, ASTA keeps its members informed on current happenings in the industry and helps them develop new skills.

Another professional association for travel agents is the Association of Retail Travel Agents. With about 3500 members, ARTA is smaller than ASTA or ACTA. Unlike ACTA and ASTA, ARTA does not allow travel industry suppliers to be members. ARTA's purposes are similar to ASTA's, although ARTA emphasizes improving the working relationship between the airlines and the agents. ARTA was founded in 1963.

CHECK YOUR PRODUCT KNOWLEDGE

1. Name two professional associations for travel agents.
2. What are the main purposes of professional associations?

BECOMING A TRAVEL AGENT

Do you enjoy helping other people? Are you able to solve problems? Can you work under pressure? Do you pay close attention to details? If you can answer "yes" to these questions, you possess qualities necessary for becoming a travel agent.

The position of professional travel agent is currently a high-growth career. ASTA has predicted that, because of the expansion of the travel industry, several thousand additional agents will be needed each year for the next several years. Growth in Canada between 1991 and 2001 is expected to be about 25 percent (Mohan and Gisiason, 1992).

Some jurisdictions require travel agents to be licensed, but the federal government does not. However, all travel agencies expect their agents to possess a certain body of knowledge and skills and to have completed some specialized training.

General Knowledge and Skills

When hiring new agents, managers try to determine the applicant's knowledge and skills in certain general areas. Foremost among these is a knowledge of geography. Travel agents must know where in the world they're sending their clients. They must be able to locate destinations on a map. Agents must know (or know how to find out) about the climate, culture, and attractions of an area so that they can answer clients' questions about what to wear, how to act, and what to see.

A knowledge of arithmetic is important, since travel agents are constantly computing fares, preparing invoices, reading timetables, and exchanging currency. Much of this is now done on the CRS. For agents who wish to be promoted, a knowledge of accounting is very useful.

Travel agents must demonstrate good communication skills and sales techniques. They must be able to converse pleasantly with their clients, encouraging them to express their MNEs so that appropriate travel products can be suggested. A pleasant telephone manner is also important, because many clients shop by phone to locate bargains.

Since most travel agents must produce their own letters, itineraries, reservation requests, and invoices, keyboarding skills are important. And of course, since almost all agencies are now automated, computer skills are now essential.

Education and Training

In the past, people who wanted to become travel agents started out doing clerical work for an agency. They learned the job by "looking over the shoulder" of an experienced agent. Agencies were even willing to let high school students type invoices, answer phones, and file documents.

This situation has changed in today's travel agency. CRSs have eliminated much of the simpler clerical work. Because of the complexity of modern agencies, managers are very reluctant to allow an inexperienced individual to work on an account. And with their low profit margins, most agencies can't afford to lose accounts because of a trainee's errors. Also, few managers can find any time to train a completely inexperienced person.

All of this means that to break into the industry as a travel agent, a person now must have some specialized schooling or experience. People who have worked as airline reservationists, for example, are in great demand at travel agencies. Applicants who can transfer skills learned in other businesses are also acceptable, especially if they have a network of business contacts to whom the agency can sell products. Outside sales representatives frequently learn enough about an agency's operations to break in as travel agents.

Extensive domestic and foreign travel experience is also valuable for the prospective travel agent.

Specialized Schooling Throughout Canada, courses in travel agency operation and the travel industry are offered in various kinds of schools, such as vocational schools, private business schools, community colleges, adult education centres, and universities. In addition, many of the mega-agencies and franchises have established their own schools. In this way, they can tailor training to match the procedures followed in their particular organization, and recruit new agents from among the best students.

Accreditation of travel counsellors in Canada is conducted through ACCESS (ACTA CITC Canadian Educational Standards System). CITC is the Canadian Institute of Travel Counsellors. ACCESS, IATA-UFTAA also runs travel agents professional training programs worldwide.

Advanced Training Experienced travel agents can take an advanced program offered through ACCESS that leads to the ACCESS Certified Travel Manager (ACTM) designation. The CITC offers a variety of educational programs designed to help travel agents learn new skills and procedures. Membership in the CITC signifies that an agent has professional status.

CAREER OPPORTUNITIES

The career path for travel agents depends on the size of the agency where they work. In a small or medium-sized agency, a person might start out as an agent, advance to an agent specializing in a certain type of travel or destination, and then advance to manager. Many managers go on to become owners of agencies. In a large or mega-agency, there are more levels of management and thus more opportunities for advancement.

People with training and experience as travel agents can work in places other than a retail travel agency. They might become the owner of a travel club, or work for a business travel department, automobile club, or government tourism office. Travel agency experience would also be excellent preparation for work with an airline, cruise line, or other transportation company.

Summary

- The travel agency is the main intermediary in the travel industry's channels of distribution. In many respects, a travel agency is like a retail store, linking suppliers to the public.
- The airlines have had the most influence on the growth and development of agencies.
- Travel agencies are compensated through commissions and overrides. To attract and maintain customers, agencies grant rebates.
- In addition to making arrangements for trips and selling travel products, agents provide information about destinations and legal documents. Counselling clients as to the products best suited to their MNEs is the service that distinguishes the travel agency from other intermediaries.
- Different types of travel agencies exist to meet the needs of various segments of the travel market. These segments include general, commercial, vacation and leisure, all-cruise, and specialty.
- There are now more than 5500 travel agencies in Canada, and the number is growing. Most agencies are operated as small businesses.
- Airline regulatory reform has made the travel agency industry more complex in Canada. Automation has become a necessity for sorting out a multitude of fares and schedules.
- There is a trend toward combining smaller, independent agencies to create larger, more powerful agencies—mega-agencies. Consortiums, cooperatives, and franchises have developed in response to this trend.
- To be able to sell suppliers' products and obtain commissions, an agency must receive conference appointments. Accreditation by the airline conference is the most important. The conference has specific requirements regarding the location, finances, and management of agencies.
- Most of the products sold by travel agencies can't be seen, touched, tested before purchase, or returned. Agencies sell experiences, which yield psychological benefits. As in other retail stores, employees are needed to sell the products.
- Agencies send payment to the airlines following the Bank Settlement Plan.
- Business travel departments and travel clubs are other distributors of travel products.
- The Alliance of Canadian Travel Associations, the American Society of Travel Agents, and the Association of Retail Travel Agents promote the travel industry and uphold the professional standards of their members.
- To become a travel agent, a person needs some specialized schooling or work experience that relates to the travel industry. Job openings for agents are expected to remain ample through the 1990s.

Key Terms

consortium
cooperative
conference appointment system
standard ticket stock
Bank Settlement Plan
voucher

A DAY IN THE LIFE OF

A Travel Agent

In my work as a travel agent, service is top priority. I do a lot of different tasks, but they're all aimed at serving the customer well. Primarily, I'm a counsellor and information provider. I answer the many questions travellers have. People who are making their first trip abroad, for example, often rely on me to advise them about obtaining passports, getting required immunizations, and figuring out exchange rates. I have to have the latest information to serve my customers well. I'm also an intermediary—between clients and airlines, clients and hotels, clients and resorts. The most detailed part of my job comes as I arrange for flights or room reservations or make out itineraries—double-checking facts is important to ensure a smooth trip.

I'm also, at times, a "friend in need." I remember one incident a few years ago, when a honeymoon couple lost their voucher for their prepaid accommodations. The hotel in Puerto Rico refused to let them register unless they paid or came up with the voucher. The couple was frantic by the time they called me. I got on the telephone with the manager and convinced her to locate the copy of the voucher that had been mailed to the hotel and have the couple sign that. A very relieved couple enjoyed the island that day. Efforts like this are part of good service.

The most crucial skill for a travel agent, however, is the ability to size up a client quickly and to translate that client's ideas into tangible plans. If clients don't really know what they want, I ask a few leading questions to get started. Different kinds of people have different needs. Suppose a retired couple walks into my office. I discover through conversation that they want to relax in a warm climate and that they like to be waited on. Money is not an issue. I suggest a cruise on one of the lines that specializes in slow-paced, luxurious trips. They've never been on a cruise before, but they love the idea.

Perhaps an engaged couple comes in to plan a honeymoon. They want some seclusion, but also the possibility of evening entertainment. They're very athletic, and they want to be able to enjoy the outdoors during the trip. And their budget is limited. My suggestion? A hotel in Bermuda that has separate beachfront cottages. The island has plenty of nightlife and lots of opportunities for activity—swimming, hiking, tennis, and so on. And the complete package is value for the money.

The next clients to walk in may be a couple with young children. They want a place the whole family can enjoy. My suggestions to them include Prince Edward Island, with its beaches, family farm vacations, and theatre featuring *Anne of Green Gables*; Disneyland or Walt Disney World; and some of the "club" package vacations that provide activities for both adults and children. Their needs are totally different from those of another typical client—the business traveller, who wants the right flight at the right time and a hotel that is convenient to business contacts. To serve each of these clients well, I have to discover and translate their unique needs.

Other skills are important, too. Travel agents need good math skills, keyboarding ability, a good command of English, a knowledge of geography, and an awareness of what's going on in the world. (I don't want to send someone to an island that is about to experience an armed revolution!) In addition, I need to be able to locate information about schedules and prices quickly, and to be able to react fast in an emergency such as an airline strike or a resort shutdown.

Being a travel agent has some disadvantages. I deal with the public all the time, and some people can be demanding and difficult to please. Business is affected by the season—with overtime one month and layoffs the next—and by the economy. On the other hand, my job allows me to take free or inexpensive trips, and since I love to travel, that's very important. The flip side of putting up with demanding people is being able to serve appreciative ones well. I encourage clients to come back and tell me how their trip went. It's satisfying to know I did a good job, and I get to relive their trips with them. It's a way of travelling without leaving my desk, while learning how best to serve my future clients.

What Do You Think?

1. What are the advantages and disadvantages of negotiable rates of commission for travel agencies?
2. Why is rebating legal for domestic air travel, but not for international air travel?
3. Should travel agents apply service charges? If so, what kinds of services should they charge for? What effects might increased service charges have?
4. If you were to open a travel agency, what type would you choose? Why?
5. In what ways has airline regulatory reform harmed the travel agency industry? In what ways has it helped it?
6. Will the travel agency lose its dominance as the main intermediary? Explain.
7. Travel clubs sell travel products at clearance-sale prices. In what other ways might unsold tickets be sold?
8. In what ways have the education and training requirements of travel agents changed in the past few years?

Dealing with Product

You are a travel counsellor employed by a medium-sized travel agency in Yourtown. Your clients, Mr. and Mrs. West, are inexperienced travellers. In fact, Mrs. West has never flown before. Nevertheless, these recently retired senior citizens have long dreamed of a trip to Europe, and now you have an opportunity to help make their dreams come true.

As a travel professional, you know that there are literally hundreds of seemingly similar products available. How would you decide which products would best suit Mr. and Mrs. West's MNEs? Also, which of the travel insurance products would you recommend, and why?

Dealing with People

You are an outside sales representative employed by a medium-sized travel agency in Yourtown. One of your most productive accounts is Beta Industries, located in the new airport industrial park. Much to your dismay, Mr. Blanc, the manager of Beta's travel department, tells you he has just read an article in the local newspaper about consolidators.

Consolidators are travel intermediaries, not unlike brokers, who buy large quantities of airline tickets for as little as half-price directly from certain airlines, and then distribute these tickets through travel agents. Travel agencies that use a consolidator can often earn 25 to 35 percent commissions as opposed to the traditional 10 percent.

Blanc insists that you use a consolidator for all of Beta's travel, and he expects you to give his company a 15 percent rebate on all airline tickets. He wants an answer by the end of the week. What will you tell your boss at the agency? What do you think you and your boss can do for Blanc?

CHAPTER 13: Travel and Tourism Distributors   Name: _____

WORKSHEET 13-1 Specialized Travel Agency

You want to open a travel agency that specializes in serving physically and mentally challenged people.

What special facilities and services will you require of your transportation suppliers?

What special facilities and services will you require of your accommodations suppliers?

What knowledge, abilities, or qualities will you require of your tour operators?

How will you locate suppliers who are appropriately equipped or are willing to become so?

How will the MNEs of challenged travellers differ from those of nonchallenged travellers? How will they be similar?

How will you find customers?

How might the employees you hire affect your business?

Will you expect special compensation? If so, from whom?

CHAPTER 13: Travel and Tourism Distributors   Name: _____

WORKSHEET 13-2 Owning a Travel Agency

You are interested in having your own business. You see the following ad in the travel section of the Yourtown newspaper and decide to contact the seller for more information. As someone who knows about operating a travel agency, what questions do you need to ask? Write them in the space below.

FOR SALE
TRAVEL AGENCY

Present volume approximately 2 million. Strong growth upside. Good suburban office and staff. Cash with some terms to qualified buyer. Respond to:

45 Main St.
Yourtown, Canada V6J 2L6
555-2626

CHAPTER 13: Travel and Tourism Distributors   Name: _____

WORKSHEET 13-3 Yourtown Travel Agencies

Select six of the travel agencies located in Yourtown or in the closest town or city that supports a large number of agencies. Briefly describe each. Include whether it is conference accredited or awaiting accreditation; its size; whether it is completely independent or a member of a consortium, cooperative, or franchise; the type of product it sells (for example, general, commercial, vacation and leisure, all-cruise, specialty); whether it is computerized and, if so, which system it uses; and any special services it offers or special marketing methods it employs.

1. _____
   _____
   _____

2. _____
   _____
   _____

3. _____
   _____
   _____

4. _____
   _____
   _____

5. _____
   _____
   _____

6. _____
   _____
   _____

Do you think there are travel needs in Yourtown that are not being met by existing travel agencies? If you do, what are they, and how would you meet them?

CHAPTER 13: Travel and Tourism Distributors   Name: _____

WORKSHEET 13-4 Conference Appointments

You have learned in general about the standards a travel agency must meet to receive conference approval. You have also learned in general about the procedures for receiving conference accreditation. Choose one of the major conferences: International Air Transport Association, Cruise Lines International Association, or VIA Rail. Research the conference's requirements and procedures for accreditation. (See Appendix B for conference addresses.) Write your findings in the spaces below.

Name of conference

Requirements for appointment

Procedure for appointment

CHAPTER 14

Promotion and Sales

"In the modern world of business, it is useless to be a creative, original thinker unless you can also sell what you create. Management cannot be expected to recognize a good idea unless it is presented to them by a good salesman."

David MacKenzie Ogilvy

OBJECTIVES

When you have completed this chapter, you should be able to do the following:

- Distinguish between marketing and sales.
- Explain the difference between product-oriented marketing and consumer-oriented marketing.
- Identify the types of advertising used in travel and tourism promotion.
- List the advantages of print media advertising.
- Explain the difference between intrusive advertising and directional advertising.
- Identify the major sales-promotion techniques.
- Show how public relations differs from advertising.
- Describe the role of governments in the promotion of travel and tourism.
- Give examples of public sector promotional campaigns.
- Distinguish between outside sales and inside sales.
- Explain how travel agents sell.

Imagine a tropical island paradise with miles of white-sand beaches, secluded bays, and crystal-clear waters. With such outstanding natural resources, it would be no surprise if the island were developed as a vacation resort. This would surely involve improving the infrastructure by building an airport to handle flights from overseas and by upgrading the port facilities to encourage cruise ships to anchor. Development would also mean expanding the superstructure by building hotels, restaurants, and other amenities to cater to foreign visitors. Golf courses, tennis courts, and a conference centre might be added to increase the destination's appeal.

You might think that our imaginary resort now has all the necessary ingredients to prosper as a tourist destination. Yet one vital ingredient is missing: a promotional campaign to encourage people to visit. After all, few travellers will go to a place unless they know something about it. The same is true for every kind of travel product or service. Flights, rail journeys, car rental services, cruises, hotel rooms, and tour packages all depend for their profitability on effective promotion.

In this chapter, you will learn about the various types of promotions that are used to communicate the benefits of travel products to potential consumers. Special emphasis will be placed on the use of advertising as a promotional tool. Then you will read about the different organizations, in both the public sector and the private sector, that promote travel and tourism.

An effective promotional campaign creates a demand for a product or service. Once the demand has been created, the product must be sold to the consumer. The latter part of this chapter focuses on travel and tourism sales, with specific reference to the ways both suppliers and travel agents sell.

TRAVEL AND TOURISM MARKETING

Before we look at promotion and sales in detail, we must first place them within the broader context of marketing.

The American Marketing Association, which has a number of chapters in Canada, defines **marketing** as "the performance of business activities directed toward ... the flow of goods and services from producer to consumer or user." Many people confuse marketing with sales; they believe that marketing and sales are one and the same. In fact, sales are the culmination of marketing process, and only one aspect of that process. Other elements of marketing include market research, product development, pricing, distribution, and promotion. In short, marketing is the sum of all the activities that bring buyer and seller together.

Marketing Strategies

Until the 1950s, almost all marketing was product-oriented. A product-oriented marketing strategy would typically begin with the question, "What do we want to sell?" The marketing process involved developing a product and hoping that customers would buy it. Modern marketing approaches the process from the consumer's perspective. A consumer-oriented marketing strategy asks the question, "What do our customers want to buy?" Marketing involves determining what customers want or need and then developing a product to meet those needs.

Travel and tourism marketing is heavily oriented toward the consumer. Suppliers and other tourist organizations identify potential customers, or markets, by conducting **market research**. Market research involves gathering and analyzing information about present and potential clients in an attempt to predict what they will want to buy. More specifically, market research involves these processes:

- Surveying clients through questionnaires and personal interviews.
- Reviewing past bookings.
- Analyzing census studies and information from sources such as Tourism Canada's Tourism Reference and Documentation Centre.
- Predicting social and economic trends.

Information obtained from market research allows suppliers to divide the market into different segments. Products can then be developed to match the motivations, needs, and expectations (MNEs) of each target market. Canadian Airlines, for example, introduced its Business Class service on domestic flights to cater to the MNEs of the business traveller. Market research had shown that business travellers were dissatisfied with the existing two-class service. Business travellers complained that seating in economy-class (Canadian Class) was too cramped, while first-class was too expensive. They also preferred an area separate from the noise of children so that they could do their work. The new Business Class gave passengers room to work and a number of first-class perks at a price only a little above economy fare. Similarly, Air Canada has Executive Class service to satisfy the MNEs of the business traveller.

The Four Ps

Once the target market has been identified by market research, the travel supplier develops a marketing strategy. As you learned in Chapter 1, the various elements involved in the marketing process are often referred to as the four Ps:

- product
- price
- place
- promotion

Product The product stage involves selecting and developing the right range of products and services. Suppliers of transportation, such as airlines, railways, and motorcoach companies, must decide which routes to serve and what level of service to offer. Suppliers of accommodations, such as hotels, motels, and resorts, must decide where to locate their properties and what amenities to provide. Cruise lines and tour operators must select destinations and itineraries and decide on the right mix of travel components for their packages. Travel agencies must choose whether to sell a wide range of travel products or to specialize in just a few. All these decisions will be affected by the MNEs of the markets that the travel companies have chosen to serve.

Price Pricing follows logically from product selection. When developing a pricing policy, suppliers must bear in mind not only the MNEs of the target market but also the prices charged by competitors. Suppliers can choose to sell their product at, below, or above the market price.

The **market price** is established by supply and demand and is often an average price. Many travel products are **parity products**—that is, one company's product is very similar to that of another. When companies offer parity products, the competitive forces of the market help establish a market price. A company charging below-market prices bases its pricing policy on no-frills service. A company selling above the market price emphasizes premium service. Some companies use more than one pricing strategy to appeal to different market segments. Choice Hotels International, for example, markets one product for economy-minded guests (Comfort Inns), another for midprice guests (Quality Inns), and yet another for those who are prepared to pay for luxury (Clarion Hotels). The company also markets several products for guests on a tight budget (Sleep Inns, Rodeway Inns, Econo Lodges, and Friendship Inns). Journey's End motels in Canada are under the Comfort label.

Place Place, the third of the four Ps, refers to the channels used to distribute the product. Suppliers may sell directly to the client or through one or more intermediaries (travel agents, tour operators, and so on). Most car rental firms, for example, use direct distribution. Cruise lines, on the other hand, usually distribute their product through travel agencies. The distribution channel chosen will be the one that gets the product to the target market most effectively.

Promotion Promotion is the final stage in the marketing process before the sale of the product. Promotional techniques are used to attract attention, create interest in the product, and prepare prospective clients for the selling

PROFILE

Michael Eisner

When Michael Eisner took over as chairman of the Walt Disney Company in 1984, he told its board of directors that he felt like a kid turned loose in a toy store. "I don't know which toy to take home because they're all fabulous and they all work and I'm so excited I can't sleep at night."

Eisner and Disney turned out to be a perfect match. When Walt Disney died in 1966, his legendary movie, animation, and theme park empire began to go into a slow decline. Company executives were afraid to branch out into new ventures or to change the company image that Disney had established. The Disney Company continued to turn out children's movies and animated features, but children were deserting it by the millions for action-packed thrillers like *Star Wars* and *Raiders of the Lost Ark.*

While the Disney Company declined, Eisner was busy establishing his credentials as a major creative programming talent in television and the movies. He was born in 1942 into an affluent New York City family. He attended the prestigious Lawrenceville Preparatory School in New Jersey, then attended Denison University in Ohio. Eisner graduated with a degree in English literature and theatre in 1964 and went to work as a clerk at the National Broadcasting Company (NBC).

Within a few months Eisner jumped ship and went to the American Broadcasting Company (ABC), where he was put in charge of specials and later Saturday morning children's programming. His experience in children's programming came in very handy when he became head of the Disney operation.

In 1976, Eisner was named president of Paramount Pictures. Applying what he had learned in television, Eisner helped turn the financially ailing company into the top-ranking movie studio in Hollywood. Eisner seemed to have a genius for choosing movie projects that would become big hits with the public. His formula was simple: produce low-cost hit movies and steer clear of big-budget pictures and high-priced stars. Among his most spectacular successes at Paramount were *Beverly Hills Cop, Flashdance, Airplane,* and *Raiders of the Lost Ark.* Eisner also produced two very popular TV series, "Cheers" and "Family Ties," and the syndicated entertainment news show, "Entertainment Tonight."

In 1983, the troubled Walt Disney Company fought off corporate raiders who had intended to break up the company and sell its assets. Walt Disney's nephew, Roy Disney, then persuaded the company's board of directors to hire Eisner to try to revive it. Frank Wells, former vice-president of Warner Brothers, joined Eisner at the Disney Company. Wells became president and chief operating officer. Everyone expected Eisner to take at least two or three years to turn the company around, but he surprised everyone by doing it in a matter of months.

Eisner has been a whirlwind at Disney. Under his direction, the Disney Company and its adult film production company, Touchstone Pictures, have produced one blockbuster hit after another. These films include *Three Men and a Baby; Who Framed Roger Rabbit?; Honey, I Shrunk the Kids; Dick Tracy,* and *Pretty Woman.* The Disney Channel, the company's pay TV network, has grown from a few hundred thousand to nearly 4 million subscribers. In the early 1990s, the Disney Channel's profits were more than $5 million. The company's TV feature, "The Golden Girls," and cartoon shows, "Duck Tales" and "The Adventures of the Gummi Bears," have attracted millions of viewers.

Eisner has also transformed Disney's aging theme parks at Disneyland in Anaheim, California, and Disney World in Orlando, Florida. He has built $500 million worth of new attractions, including the Disney-MGM theme park and a number of hotels at Orlando. A new park, Tokyo Disneyland, is operating in Japan, and Euro Disneyland opened near Paris in 1992. Revenues have skyrocketed under Eisner's aggressive leadership, and in 1990, Disney Company profits approached $824 million.

Eisner takes great pride in being the idea man at the Disney Company. He likes to think up new projects and hire competent executives to develop them. The amiable, six-foot, three-inch tall Eisner became well-known to television watchers during the late 1980s when he served as host for the Disney Sunday Movie.

Eisner, an unabashed family man and father of three, has remained true to Walt Disney's ideal of producing top-quality family entertainment. At the same time, he has managed to wrench the Disney Company from its 1950s time warp and bring it squarely into the 1990s.

message. Promotional activities used to create a demand for travel and tourism products and services can be divided into three main categories:

- advertising
- sales support/sales promotion
- public relations

Promoters of travel and tourism seldom employ just one technique to reach prospective clients, but rather a combination of all three. Determining the right promotional mix is a crucial part of developing an effective marketing strategy.

> **CHECK YOUR PRODUCT KNOWLEDGE**
>
> 1. What is marketing?
> 2. What is the difference between product-oriented and consumer-oriented marketing?
> 3. What are the four Ps of marketing?

ADVERTISING

Advertising is the best known, most visible, and most widely used of the three promotional techniques. It can be defined as the use of paid media space or media time to present a product in such a way as to attract consumers. The three main functions of advertising are to inform, to remind, and to persuade. If the advertising message does these things effectively, it will develop leads that can be followed up with sales. The bridge between advertising and sales is typically provided by a call to action at the end of the message, such as "See your travel agent for details," "Mail this coupon for a free brochure," or "Call our toll-free number for further information."

The major advertising media can be classified as follows:

- print (newspapers, magazines)
- broadcast (television, radio)
- direct mail (letters, brochures)
- out-of-home (billboards, transit signs)

There are also two minor categories: directory advertising and specialty advertising.

Travel organizations spend a great deal of money to advertise their products. Table 14-1 shows how advertising expenditures have increased in recent years. Most travel organizations use at least two media to get their message to the public. The choice of media depends to a large extent on the advertiser's budget and on the market that the advertiser is trying to reach. If the target market is wide (as in the case of a hotel chain promoting all its properties), the advertiser will typically choose media such as network television and national magazines. The message will reach millions of viewers and readers, although only a small percentage of them are likely to be potential customers. This is known as the **shotgun approach.** If the target market is narrow (as in the case of a tour operator promoting a theme package), the promoter will tend to advertise in special-interest magazines and by direct mail. The message will reach far fewer people, but a greater percentage of them are likely to be interested in the product. This is known as the **rifle approach.**

Print Media

Newspapers and magazines are the major print media for advertising. Together, they account for almost half of all travel and tourism advertising expenditures.

Newspapers In considering newspapers as an advertising medium, we must distinguish between mass-circulation dailies and local weeklies. The former serve wide metropolitan areas and include such publications as *The Globe and Mail*. The major advertisers in the dailies tend to be national and international travel organizations, such as airlines and car rental firms, which have broad target markets. Smaller

	Dollar Amount (in thousands)			
Categories	1985	1986	1987	1988
Airlines	$654,883	$719,876	$697,327	$706,228
Cruise lines	126,424	127,384	134,335	167,353
Domestic destinations	80,966	100,791	101,562	130,091
Foreign destinations	64,787	79,623	80,201	99,510
Grand total	$927,060	$1,027,674	$1,013,425	$1,103,182
Annual Percent Change	+9	+11	−1	+9

TABLE 14-1
Trends in Advertising Expenditures in the United States
SOURCE: Ogilvy & Mather

travel companies do, however, advertise in the weekend travel sections that are a feature of most large city newspapers.

Local weekly newspapers have a much smaller circulation, sometimes as low as 5000. They are used as an advertising medium by local travel firms that serve a small geographic market. A suburban travel agency, for example, will reach its target market more effectively, and more economically, if it advertises in a local weekly paper rather than a mass-circulation daily.

All newspapers have distinct advantages over other advertising media:

- Frequency of publication.
- Wide readership. Most people (about 85 percent) look at a newspaper every day.
- Comprehensive coverage of selected geographic markets.
- Relatively low cost, especially for local weeklies. (Note: the greater the circulation, the higher the advertising rates.)
- Short lead time. Advertisements can be placed in most newspapers as late as one day before publication. This allows for flexibility in making changes to ads that run for several days.
- Ease and speed of response. Newspaper ads often have coupons that readers can mail in for further information.

They also have these disadvantages:

- Waste circulation. Newspapers reach a broad cross-section of the population. Many of the people who see the ad will have no interest in the travel product advertised.
- Low print quality, especially for colour reproduction.
- Short life. Most people discard a newspaper soon after they have read it.

Magazines The type of magazine that can be used most effectively by travel and tourism promoters is the specialty magazine. There are literally thousands of these magazines in circulation, appealing to special interests as diverse as motorcycling and stamp collecting. The travel advertiser has a good idea of each magazine's readership and can target specific markets. A tour operator promoting garden tours, for example, will clearly reach more potential clients by advertising in *Flower and Garden* rather than *Sports Illustrated*. Consumer travel magazines like *Travel and Leisure*, *Condé Nast Traveler*, and *Travel/Holiday* are particularly useful for travel advertisers, because their readers are predisposed to travel. Within the travel trade, there are professional magazines such as *Canadian Travel Press*, *Travel Courier*, *Travel Weekly*, *The Travel Agent*, and *ASTA Agency Management*.

General circulation magazines, such as *Maclean's*, *Reader's Digest*, *Time*, and *Newsweek*, tend to attract the same travel advertisers as do the daily newspapers, namely, the major organizations. Canadian, American, and foreign destinations also advertise heavily in the national magazines.

ILLUSTRATION 14-1
Different magazines have different readerships, making it easy for travel advertisers to target specific markets.
SOURCE Karen O'Naill

Some publications have regional editions that allow advertisers to target geographic markets at lower rates.

City and provincial magazines, such as *Toronto Life* and *Beautiful British Columbia*, are popular advertising outlets for local travel organizations.

Magazine advertising has these advantages:

- They are a good way to target special-interest markets. (This is less true for the general circulation magazines, though these have the added advantage of wide readership.)
- Excellent print quality and colour reproduction.
- Long life. People tend to save magazines far longer than they save newspapers. Magazines kept in libraries, waiting rooms, and other public areas reach a large number of secondary readers.
- Prestige. Advertisers benefit by association with well-known magazines. Readers tend to think, "If XYZ Travel

Company is advertising in *Saturday Night*, it must be a reputable outfit."

The disadvantages include these:

- Long lead times. Many magazines require ads as much as three months before publication date. This makes it very difficult to make last-minute changes to advertising copy.
- Infrequency of publication. Weekly magazines appear 52 times a year, monthlies only 12 times a year. (Compare this with daily newspapers, which publish about 315 days a year in Canada.)
- High production costs, particularly for colour ads.

Broadcast Media

Television and radio are the major broadcast media. Of the two, television is more widely used by travel and tourism advertisers. Both media rely heavily on repetition to get messages to the consumer, which means that the same ad may be aired several times a day.

Television Television can be divided into these categories: network, local, and cable. Network advertising is accessible largely to the high-budget travel organizations: airlines, hotel chains, cruise lines, car rental companies, VIA Rail, and destinations. Local television is suited to firms serving a small geographic area. Cable television (which includes sports channels, entertainment channels, and so on) offers advertisers the best opportunity to target markets by interest. However, not all cable channels accept advertising.

The advantages of television as an advertising medium include these:

- Strong audiovisual image. No other medium can match television for its ability to show the product in moving format. This powerful visual element makes television a natural for destination advertising.
- Large audiences. Prime-time programs on network television are watched by millions of viewers.
- Viewer identification with the product, especially if celebrities are used to advertise it.

And on the negative side:

- Very high costs for media time and production. A 30-second commercial on network prime time can cost hundreds of thousands of dollars.
- Time restrictions. Commercials must fit a standard time length, called a **spot**, that usually lasts 15, 30, or 60 seconds.
- Short life. Once a commercial is seen, it is soon forgotten. This is why so many are repeated over and over again.

ILLUSTRATION 14-2
Billboards are a highly visible form of advertising.
SOURCE: Karen O'Neill

- Waste coverage, especially on network television.
- Long lead times. Advertising spots usually have to be booked at least three months in advance.
- Difficulty of response. Viewers are less likely to respond to a phone number given at the end of the message than to mail-in coupons or return envelopes.

Radio Some radio programs are aired nationally, but most reach a fairly small geographic market. Nevertheless, many major travel and tourism companies, especially airlines and hotels, use local radio for advertising. An airline such as Air Nova, for example, might use a local radio station in Halifax, Nova Scotia, to advertise its flights from that city. Because there are various categories of radio stations—all-news, classical, rock, country and western, and so on—it is possible to segment the market both demographically (according to age, income, education, occupation, and so on) and by special interest.

The advantages of radio advertising include these:

- They are a good way to target markets based on geography, demography, and special interests.
- Low cost.
- Short lead times. Radio is much more flexible than other media. It is much easier to change a radio ad at short notice than it is to alter printed copy or visual messages.
- Personal touch. The sound of the human voice makes radio a more intimate medium.

The disadvantages include these:

- Lack of visual appeal.
- Time restrictions.
- Waste coverage on general interest or nationwide broadcasts.
- Difficulty of response.

- Inability to hold the listener's attention. For many people, radio is only a background medium—they may not even hear the commercials.

When selecting a radio time for an advertisement, often the travel company will match the product to the broadcast. A hockey weekend to Montreal would best be advertised at the beginning and end of the sports news for the day. Similarly, a special discount in business fares within Canada would best be slotted on the 6 p.m. and 8 a.m. news for commuters.

Direct Mail

The most widely used form of direct mail advertising is the sales letter sent to past and prospective clients. The letter may be mailed alone or combined with travel catalogues, brochures, fliers, and other materials. Travel agencies, tour operators, and cruise lines are the main travel organizations that advertise by direct mail. The three main sources of direct mail lists are mailing list brokers, local directories, and records of past customers.

Newsletters are another category of direct mail. They are used not only as promotional tools but also to provide information to travel club members, frequent fliers, frequent stayers, regular clients of travel agencies, and other good travel prospects.

The main advantages of direct mail are these:

- They are a good way to reach specific markets. Once a mailing list has been compiled, direct mail pieces can be sent out just to likely customers. There is little waste circulation. No other medium can reach identifiable market segments as effectively.
- Personal touch. Direct mail can be addressed to individual prospects by name.
- Flexible production. There are few restrictions on space or format—direct mail packages can be as large or as small as the advertiser wishes.
- Lack of competition. Newspaper and magazine ads often run ten or more to a page. Television and radio often air five or more commercials in a row. A direct mail ad stands alone, with no other messages competing for attention.
- Ease of response, via coupons, prestamped reply cards, and the like.

There are, of course, disadvantages:

- Some waste coverage. Not everyone will read or even open the packet.
- Poor image. Many people are wary of offers they receive in the mail. If the offer sounds too good to be true, they might think there is a catch.
- High expenses per potential reader. Postage is expensive, as is the cost of obtaining mailing lists, preparing the message, and so on.
- Difficulty of obtaining and maintaining accurate mailing lists.

Out-of-Home Media

Outdoor advertising takes two main forms: billboards and transit signs. Billboards are usually placed along highways and at points of high pedestrian traffic (for example, at airports, railway stations, and bus terminals). Transit signs are displayed on the sides of buses, streetcars, and taxis, and in subway cars. Out-of-home advertising is usually used to supplement print and broadcast advertising.

The advantages of outdoor signs include these:

- They are a good way to target specific geographic markets. The best signs are typically placed close to the tourist attraction advertised—for example, "Holiday Inn: 5 kilometres at Exit 24" or "Visit Magnetic Hill—next exit."
- Eye-catching appeal, because of their physical size and good colour reproduction.
- Relatively low cost.
- Repetitive value. Travellers often see the same sign day after day.

The negatives of outdoor advertising are these:

- Very high waste coverage. Many people will not consciously take in the message. Even if they do, only a few will be potential customers.
- Length of message is restricted. It's no use putting a long message on a sign that people will see for only a few seconds.
- Difficulty of changing copy.
- Restrictions on use (i.e., highway signing laws).

Directional Advertising

Almost every form of advertising you have read about so far can be classified as **intrusive advertising.** This type of advertising forces itself on the reader's, viewer's, or listener's attention with a persuasive message. **Directional advertising**, on the other hand, is informational rather than persuasive; it emphasizes where to buy a product, not what to buy. A key difference is that potential customers seek out directional advertising, whereas intrusive advertising seeks out customers.

The yellow pages in the phone book are the best example of directional advertising. Companies pay an annual fee to be listed, and may also buy ad space. There are other private local telephone directories, as well as city directories, chamber of commerce directories, and various business directories. One advertising medium you read about earlier lends itself to some forms of directional advertising: the travel sections of newspapers, trade journals, and magazines.

Specialty Advertising

Giveaway items bearing a company name are a popular, though minor, form of advertising. Virtually anything can be given away to advertise a travel organization—for example, pens, calendars, T-shirts, hats, key rings, and shoehorns.

Co-op Advertising

Many ads, particularly in the print media, are jointly sponsored by two or more mutually interested companies. This is known as **co-op advertising**. In one of its most common uses, tour operators or other suppliers assemble ad copy, to which a travel agency then adds its name. (For example, Air Canada Vacations and Maritime Marlin Travel may advertise in the weekend travel section of the *Chronicle-Herald* in Halifax, under the name of the Thomas Cook Group.) Suppliers also cooperate with other suppliers in co-op advertising and with government tourist offices. Air France, for example, co-sponsors ads with the French Government Tourist Office for vacation packages to France. Qantas Airlines and the Australian Tourist Commission advertise jointly to promote their country as a tourist destination. There are hundreds of other examples.

CHECK YOUR PRODUCT KNOWLEDGE

1. What are the three main functions of advertising?
2. What are the four main advertising media?
3. List the main advantages of newspaper advertising over other types.
4. What advantages does television offer as an advertising medium?
5. Explain the difference between intrusive advertising and directional advertising.

OTHER TYPES OF PROMOTION

Advertising can do only so much. The two other types of promotion—sales support and promotion, and public relations—fill some of the gaps created by the limitations of advertising.

Sales Support and Promotion

Sales support is an extension of advertising. Ads are limited by space and time in the amount of information they can convey, so they must be supplemented by more detailed sources of information. Sales support materials such as brochures, booklets, slides, films, guides, and maps provide this additional information.

While advertising creates the initial demand for a product or service, sales support can help turn this demand into bookings. Suppliers sometimes mail sales support materials directly to prospective clients, but these are more commonly distributed through travel agencies and other retail intermediaries. Sales support is a vital channel of communications between the supplier and the sales distributor. If agents have specific information in an attractive format to present to the client, they are more likely to be able to sell the supplier's product.

Brochures Brochures are issued by almost every type of travel and tourism organization—by tour operators, cruise lines, and government tourist offices in particular. They may be as simple as a small leaflet promoting a single tourist attraction, or as elaborate as a 200-page, full-colour catalogue featuring a complete program of tours to a number of destinations. Most of the major tour operators put out lengthy catalogues twice a year (summer and winter), with detailed descriptions of itineraries, schedules, accommodations, and prices. The address of each provincial and territorial tourist office is shown in Appendix B.

Travel Videos These take the brochure one step further and show the product in motion. Clients are particularly receptive to videos, since they can actually see the destinations they are thinking about visiting. Videos are produced by government tourist offices and some suppliers and are distributed to travel agencies. Consumers can also rent travel videos—just like movies—at many video rental stores, or borrow them from libraries. Many travel agents lend out travel videos, if a small deposit is made.

Point-of-Purchase Materials This type of sales support includes posters, sales literature racks, and cardboard stands for floor and counter display. Suppliers place the display materials in their sales offices, or in travel agencies, or in both. These materials serve mainly to reinforce the advertising message at the point of purchase.

Promotional Activities Sales promotional activities are one-time events used to stimulate consumer interest. They may be targeted at prospective clients, to encourage them to buy the product promoted, or at travel agents and tour operators, to motivate them to sell the product. Sales promotions directed at the consumer include these:

- Special offers, such as promotional airfares and hotel rates, free gifts with purchase, and free trips offered as prizes in contests.
- Travel fairs and exhibitions. These are particularly effective promotional events, because they allow suppliers to

reach a large number of potential travellers in a single location. Sales literature is distributed at the event.
- Travel nights. Staged by travel agencies and sometimes co-sponsored by suppliers, travel nights are often used to promote tours and cruises. Prizes may be awarded to further stimulate consumer interest.

Popular promotional activities targeted at travel intermediaries are:

- Familiarization trips (or FAM trips). As you learned in Chapter 1, suppliers offer FAM trips to travel agents and tour operators so that they can experience a product firsthand. These inspection and information tours are usually offered free or at minimum cost. They are used by airlines (to promote new routes, new destinations, and new aircraft), by hotels (to promote new properties), and by government tourist offices (to promote cities, regions, or whole countries as tourist destinations). The theory behind FAM trips is that "you cannot sell what you haven't seen."
- Sales contests. These are sponsored by suppliers to reward travel agents who sell a certain number of airline tickets, hotel rooms, cruises, and so on.
- Travel trade shows, travel marts, and travel seminars. Held for members of the trade, these gatherings offer an excellent opportunity for government tourist offices and suppliers to meet face to face with travel agents and other distributors. They are particularly effective for promoting new products and services.

Public Relations

Public relations, the third of the main promotional techniques, is used to reinforce advertising and sales support. It can be defined as the use of planned communications to create a positive image for a company and its products. Unlike the other forms of promotion, it is not directed at prospective clients or travel intermediaries, but rather at journalists, editors, travel writers, and other media representatives. Travel companies target these individuals because they are in a position to influence public opinion.

Typical public relations activities include press releases, press conferences, guest appearances on radio and television, and FAM trips for travel writers.

A **press release**, the most commonly used public relations tool, is a document prepared by a travel or tourism organization and mailed out to newspapers, magazines, and television and radio stations. The release might announce an inaugural flight; the opening of a hotel, travel agency, or government tourist office; the introduction of a new product or service; or some other newsworthy event.

A **press conference** is used to publicize travel-related events. Instead of sending out a press release, the company holding the press conference sends out invitations to reporters from the print and broadcast media. Those attending the press conference are issued a press kit with background information on the company and its new product or service. If the press conference achieves its goal, the event will receive favourable coverage in the news media.

Guest appearances on radio and television talk shows are an excellent opportunity for travel company representatives to promote their products at no cost. All-expense-paid FAM trips for travel writers can also be a very effective way to receive publicity. These can backfire, of course, especially if things go wrong (for example, if a flight connection is missed or a bad hotel is chosen).

Public relations has much in common with advertising in that it aims to promote a product, a service, or a destination. There are, however, important differences between the two:

- Public relations involves the securing of *free* media space or time. No payment is made for the print or broadcast of press releases. For this reason, public relations is sometimes referred to as "free advertising."
- Because it is written or printed by a third party, public relations tends to have more credibility than advertising. People are often sceptical of advertising messages, but they are inclined to believe what they see, hear, or read in the media.
- On the negative side, promoters have far less control over public relations than advertising. A press release, for example, may be edited or not even used at all. In addition, public relations is hard to evaluate because of the difficulty in measuring its cost-effectiveness.

CHECK YOUR PRODUCT KNOWLEDGE

1. Name three types of sales support materials.
2. List five sales promotion activities.
3. What are the main promotional tools used by public relations firms?
4. How does public relations differ from advertising?

THE PROMOTERS

Several references have already been made in this chapter to the various organizations that promote travel and tourism. In this section, we will look more closely at the promoters and give examples of some memorable promotional campaigns.

Travel and tourism organizations fall into two main categories:

- The public sector (government tourist offices).
- The private sector (airlines, railways, and other transportation suppliers; hotels and other accommodations suppliers; attractions; tour operators; and travel agencies).

We can identify a third category that is neither public nor private—the quasi-governmental agencies such as convention and visitors' bureaus (CVBs) and regional tourism organizations.

Government tourist offices and private sector suppliers differ in many ways, but there is one fundamental difference between them: government tourist offices promote but do not sell; suppliers do both. The Italian Government Travel Office, for example, promotes travel to Italy, but the organizations that sell the travel arrangements are the airlines, railways, tour operators, and so on. There are a few exceptions; for example, even now some Eastern European government tourist offices both promote *and* sell travel products.

Public Sector Promoters

Public sector tourism organizations can be national tourist offices (NTOs) or provincial and territorial tourist offices (PTTOs).

National Tourist Offices National tourist offices represent the highest level of government involvement in travel and tourism promotion. Many nations around the world have an NTO, though the NTOs vary considerably in their roles in promoting inbound tourism. Some NTOs are autonomous ministries within the government, such as the Bermuda Department of Tourism. These tend to play a major promotional role. Others are agencies within government departments and play a lesser role. The United States Travel and Tourism Administration (USTTA), an agency within the Department of Commerce, is an example of the latter category.

Tourism Canada, a branch of Industry Canada, is the Canadian agency responsible for encouraging and supporting the economic growth, excellence, and international competitiveness of the tourism industry in all parts of Canada.

The American government has traditionally left the job of tourism promotion to the private sector. As a result, funding for the USTTA is in relative terms lower than in many other nations. The agency may be preparing to play a more active role in tourism. The number of promotional efforts it has recently taken part in with the private sector is an encouraging sign.

The Atlantic and Caribbean nations are considerably more active in tourism promotion. The Bermuda Department of Tourism has already been mentioned. Jamaica launched a major promotional campaign in the late 1970s in an attempt to reverse the decline in tourism brought about by unstable political conditions on the island. The campaign—highlighted by the "Come Back to Jamaica" slogan—has been very effective, and Jamaica is now one of the most popular destinations in the Caribbean. The more recent campaign—"Come to Jamaica and Feel All Right"— has also been successful. In an effort to capture a larger share of the tourist market, Barbados has begun its "Play the Bajan Way" campaign.

Tourism Canada has one of the best tourism promotion campaigns in the world. It aims its efforts at various market targets: Canada (to encourage Canadians to travel within their home country); the United States; the European market; the Asia-Pacific market; and the business travel market. Canada spends more money on advertising in the American media than does any other country (Mexico is second). You've probably seen or heard some of the ads that promote Canada as "The World Next Door." Table 14-2 shows the top ten foreign country advertisers in the United States.

Australia, another big foreign advertiser in the United States, has used two catchy slogans: "Australia. The Wonder Down Under," and more recently, "Come and Say G'day." Aggressive marketing has certainly played a major role in bringing more tourists to Australia, but so too have a couple of unforeseen factors. One was the renewed outbreak of terrorism in Europe in 1986, which encouraged many North American travellers to seek safer destinations for their vacations. The other was the phenomenal success of the Australian movies *Crocodile Dundee* and *Crocodile Dundee II*. Paul Hogan, the star of both movies, appeared in commercials promoting Australia on North American television. The commercials were very well received, which shows the value of using a celebrity to advertise a travel product or destination.

European NTOs promote their countries both individually and as a group within the European Travel Commission (ETC). In the wake of the 1986 terrorism outbreak, the ETC held a series of travel supermarts throughout Canada and the United States in order to revitalize interest in Europe as a destination for Canadians and Americans. The travel marts were targeted at travel agents, but the ETC also took the campaign directly to consumers with "Invitation to Europe" advertising supplements in major American daily newspapers.

Foreign NTOs use a wide variety of promotional techniques, but place particular emphasis on travel industry shows and travel marts, international travel conferences, FAM trips, and, above all, advertising.

Rank	Country	Amount
1.	Canada	$11,193,000
2.	Mexico	10,560,000
3.	Jamaica	9,972,000
4.	Bermuda	9,714,000
5.	Bahamas	4,235,000
6.	France	3,500,000
7.	Australia	3,318,000
8.	Spain	3,011,000
9.	Barbados	2,766,000
10.	Singapore	2,393,000

TABLE 14-2.
Foreign Country Advertising Expenditures in the United States, 1988

Provincial and Territorial Tourist Offices Provincial and territorial tourist offices in Canada play a major role in public sector tourism promotion. PTTOs promote travel and tourism within the province or territory, within Canada as a whole, and overseas. Every province and territory has an official tourist agency. These are listed in Appendix B.

Television advertising is a major promotional tool used by provincial tourist offices. PTTOs also advertise to a lesser extent in magazines, newspapers, and radio. Most PTTOs work closely with the private sector in developing advertising campaigns (this is a good example of co-op advertising). PTTOs also promote tourism by doing the following:

- Producing and distributing travel guides and travel videos.
- Staging travel conferences.
- Participating in travel trade shows.
- Conducting FAM tours for travel writers, tour operators, and travel agents.
- Operating highway information centres.

The Atlantic provinces have operated a Sea Sell promotional venture along the eastern seaboard of the United States using the Yarmouth–Portland ferry *Prince of Fundy* as a floating trade fair. Ports of call have included Boston, Providence, New York, and Baltimore. Both private sector operators and provincial tourism offices participate.

Every province and territory tries to come up with a catchy slogan to give continuity to its promotional campaign. Some of these are used on licence plates as travelling billboards. Here is a sampling of these slogans:

- "Beautiful British Columbia."
- "Canada's Ocean Playground." (Nova Scotia)
- "Look What's Tucked Away in Our Little Corner of the World." (Newfoundland and Labrador)
- "It Feels So Different." (Quebec)
- "Yours To Discover." (Ontario)
- "Where You Belong." (Sakatchewan)
- "Within Reach, Yet Beyond Belief." (Northwest Territories)
- "Alberta, in All Her Majesty" and "Explore and Experience." (Alberta)
- "One of the World's Great Islands." (Prince Edward Island)
- "You'll Love Our Good Nature." (New Brunswick)

Both the Yukon and Manitoba have used the word "friendly" in their slogans, as in "Friendly Yukon" and "Friendly Manitoba." Probably one of the best examples of a promotional campaign was the "I Love New York" campaign. It was dreamed up in 1977 when New York City was on the verge of bankruptcy. Though initially conceived as a way of promoting just the city, it has since been extended to encourage inbound tourism to all parts of the state. Sometimes provinces link up to promote an area of the country, quite often with assistance from the federal government. An example would be the 1991 campaign "A Coast of Difference." It was sponsored by the four Atlantic provinces and the Atlantic Canada Opportunities Agency and was aimed at New Englanders and central Canadians.

Quasi-Governmental Promoters

Quasi-governmental promoters of travel and tourism are private promotional organizations that receive government funding. They include regional tourism organizations and convention and visitors' bureaus.

Regional Tourism Organizations Many provinces promote tourism through regional or area associations within the province. An example would be the South Shore Regional Tourism Association in Nova Scotia. Public sector participation in these organizations is through the various local governments—the counties, cities, villages, and townships. The private sector is represented by travel suppliers.

Convention and Visitors' Bureaus Most major cities in Canada and the United States promote local tourism through convention and visitors' bureaus. There are two main types of CVBs:

- Those that are attached to the local government, either as a department within the chamber of commerce or within the municipal government.
- Those that are independent nonprofit organizations backed by the private sector and funded in part by local government.

A major function of all CVBs is to promote their cities as venues for meetings, conventions, and seminars. (Several CVBs actually own the convention centres in the cities they represent.) To this end, they aim their promotional efforts at corporate and association meeting planners. CVBs also promote pleasure travel, with campaigns directed at tour operators, motorcoach companies, travel agents, and the general public. The Calgary Convention and Visitors' Bureau is an example of a CVB for a major city. Calgary has about 80 hotels and motels with 9500 beds. The Calgary CVB can promote four major halls with varying capacities: the Olympic Saddledome (16 700), the Stampede Corral (6500), the Jubilee Auditorium (2750), and the Convention Centre (2500).

CVBs function as the liaison between potential visitors to the city and the businesses that will host them if they come. In both business and pleasure travel promotion, the key word is *cooperation*. CVBs work to encourage local businesses to work together to promote the entire city as an attractive destination.

PROFILE

I Love New York

By now, just about everyone is familiar with the "I Love New York" tourism promotion and advertising campaign. We've all seen the television commercials in which famous actors, singers, and dancers, and the casts of Broadway shows sing and high-step their way through a rousing chorus of "I Love New York." And we've all seen countless bumper stickers and souvenir T-shirts and mugs with the familiar slogan, with a heart shape taking the place of the word *love*.

Many states have similar tourism advertising and promotion campaigns, but New York's program is one of the largest and most successful. It began in 1977, when the New York State Department of Economic Development launched a major effort to revive the state's sluggish tourism industry.

No one really knows who came up with the "I Love New York" slogan. It was a joint effort by state officials and copywriters at the advertising firm Wells, Rich, and Greene, which had been hired to devise an advertising campaign for the state tourism department. Illustrator Milton Glaser then hit upon using the heart in place of the word *love*, and the slogan was born. Steve Karmen, who is famous for his commercial jingles, wrote the "I Love New York" tune that is used in all of the campaign's TV commercials.

The "I Love New York" campaign is a three-part effort involving advertising, promotion, and cooperation with the travel industry. The advertising component consists of a series of television and print advertisements, all built around the "I Love New York" theme but with two different focuses—New York City and upstate New York. Most of the New York City commercials have had an entertainment or Broadway theme. Over the years, the commercials have featured such famous names as Frank Sinatra, Cher, Kirk Douglas, Elizabeth Taylor, Gregory Peck, Liza Minnelli, Mikhail Baryshnikov, and Shirley MacLaine, as well as cast members from the Broadway shows *Cats* and *La Cage Aux Folles*. The stars in these commercials worked for union scale, a small fraction of what they usually earn.

Commercials about upstate New York usually focus on statewide or regional attractions, resorts, and events. Some of these commercials have featured New York governor Mario Cuomo extolling the virtues of New York state.

The promotion side of the "I Love New York" campaign has been extensive. The state tourism department has produced or sponsored guidebooks, discount coupon books, trade shows, conferences, and familiarization tours for journalists. The state also works with airlines, travel agencies, tour operators, airports, and other travel and tourism businesses. Much of the state's work with the private sector is with travel and tourism businesses in Europe and Japan, two regions that send many free-spending tourists to the United States.

Some of the state's "I Love New York" promotional activities have been tied to specific events. Among these have been the 1980 Winter Olympics in Lake Placid, the 1986 Statue of Liberty Centennial, the opening of the Jacob Javits Convention Center in New York City, and the 1989 Niagara Falls Festival of Lights.

Has all of this hoopla and effort paid off? Spectacularly. Since 1977, New York State has spent about $160 million on its promotional and advertising program. Since then, according to state figures, the campaign has generated more than $8 billion in income for the state's 53 000 travel and tourism businesses and about $1 billion in state and local tax revenues.

The state's tourism department estimates that air passenger traffic and hotel room rentals have nearly doubled since the "I Love New York" campaign began in 1977, and that the amount of money spent on summer vacations in New York state has more than tripled. Over the same time, travel and tourism jobs in the state have increased by more than 100 000. State government budget cuts have reduced the scale of the "I Love New York" campaign in recent years, but it will certainly continue to lure visitors and dollars to the Empire State.

Private Sector Promoters

All private sector travel and tourism associations use promotion as an aid to sales. At one end of the scale, there are the two major airlines, Air Canada and Canadian Airlines, each of which spends millions of dollars a year on advertising. At the opposite extreme are the mom-and-pop motels, minor sightseeing attractions, and local motorcoach companies that can afford only a few hundred dollars a year for promotional activities. Regardless of the size of the organization, all depend to some extent on promotions to motivate consumers to buy their products and services.

In this section, we will summarize the ways in which private sector suppliers promote themselves and their products. Advertising is by far the most common form of promotional activity. In general, the major travel companies advertise in the national media, while smaller companies with limited geographic markets use the local media.

Airlines The airline industry as a whole spends more on advertising than any other segment of the travel industry. Newspaper advertising accounts for almost half the total advertising expenditures of the airlines, followed by television, radio, magazines, and out-of-home media. One of the most successful advertising campaigns of all time has been United's "Come Fly the Friendly Skies." Since deregulation, the skies have become a lot less friendly, with the airlines competing fiercely for market share. Delta's "We Love to Fly and It Shows" and American's "Something Special in the Air" are two slogans that have been used effectively in the airline war of words.

Canadian Airlines has used the themes "The Dawn of Civilized Travel," "We Are Your Global Airline," and "We Bring Canada to the Rest of the World." Canadians short-lived "wing walker" campaign in the early 1990s, showing Air Canada passengers transferring to Canadian by walking across the wings of aircraft flying side by side, was quite controversial.

Air Canada has used themes such as "You're Always a Winner with Air Canada" and "The Choice of Frequent Flyers," in conjunction with its partner airlines.

Foreign airlines, such as British Airways and Lufthansa, also advertise in Canada. For years, Delta has used "One Ticket, One Airline, All of America" in Canada to emphasize that it serves 220 cities in the United States from five cities in Canada.

Car Rental Companies Like the airlines, the car rental companies spend most of their advertising dollars on magazine and newspaper ads and television spots. Because business travellers are the major rental car users, they place many ads in business publications, such as *Canadian Business*, *The Wall Street Journal*, and *Business Week*. Car rental companies often share advertising costs with individual airlines to promote fly/drive packages.

Hertz and Avis are the two big promoters, battling each other with slogans such as "America's Wheels" (Hertz) and "We're Trying Harder Than Ever" (Avis). Budget in Canada has used "The Smart Money Is on Budget." Thrifty has used Wayne Gretzky as a spokesperson.

Railways VIA Rail and Amtrak are in a unique position in that neither has a direct competitor: each is the only passenger railway in its own country. However, each has to compete with other transportation suppliers and with the private automobile. It is interesting to trace the course of Amtrak's successive promotional campaigns since it was founded. In its early years, when it was struggling to survive, Amtrak introduced the slogan "We've Been Working on the Railroad." As train ridership began to pick up, this was replaced by "America's Getting into Training." Most recently, Amtrak has sounded a more positive note with its slogans "All Aboard Amtrak" and "Discover the Magic—Amtrak."

VIA Rail divides its advertising expenditures between the print and broadcast media. It has used the theme "Take a Look at the Train Today" and has emphasized "Silver & Blue Class" to promote its refurbished transcontinental passenger equipment. British Rail and European railway companies also advertise in Canada and the United States, promoting the BritRail Pass and Eurailpass in particular.

Motorcoach Companies Because most motorcoach companies are small, they tend to advertise exclusively in local media. The exceptions are the big names like Greyhound and Trailways Lines and Gray Line, which do run nationwide ad campaigns. Many motorcoach companies have used the theme "Take the Bus and Leave the Driving to Us."

Cruise Lines The glamorous nature of the cruise product seems to lend itself to promotion on television. Until recently, however, surprisingly few cruise lines used television as their major advertising medium. With the success of Carnival Cruise Lines' "Carnival's Got the Fun" and "If My Friends Could See Me Now" campaigns, other cruise lines have realized the importance of television advertising. Royal Caribbean, Norwegian Cruise Line, Holland-American, and Princess Cruises are some of the other major television advertisers. Most cruise lines advertise heavily in the print media as well, and make extensive use of brochures for sales support.

Ferry Lines Marine Atlantic, which serves all four Atlantic provinces and the state of Maine, has used the theme "Great Connections."

Hotels/Motels The chains promote themselves in generic ads on network television and in the large-circulation newspapers and magazines. Individual properties, whether independent or part of a chain, are usually advertised in local media. Holiday Inn ("Stay with Someone You Know"), Ramada ("You're Somebody Special at Ramada"), and Hyatt ("The Hyatt Touch") are some of the major advertisers. Radisson Hotels International ("This Must Be the Place") emphasizes tranquillity within the rush of several Canadian cities.

Tour Operators Tour operators promote their products in much the same way as the cruise lines—mainly through print advertising, brochures, and travel catalogues. They tend, however, to make more use of specialty magazines and direct mail.

Travel Agencies Travel agencies tend to serve small geographic areas, so they spend most of their advertising dollars in the local media and on direct mail campaigns.

In-House Departments vs. Outside Agencies

Most of the major travel suppliers have their own advertising or public relations departments, or both. Smaller organizations, however, tend to hire the services of professional agencies. Typically, an agency is hired to do these things:

- Plan the campaign and think up a campaign theme.
- Conduct market research so the campaign can be targeted at the best prospects.
- Write the ad copy and prepare the layout.
- Buy media time and space for the client.

The agency may also plan and carry out public relations for the client (writing press releases, arranging press conferences and interviews, and so on). Some organizations prefer to hire a separate public relations agency.

Travel Associations

In addition to the individual travel companies, there are a number of national and international travel associations that promote travel and tourism. Some of these represent a single segment of the travel industry, such as the Alliance of Canadian Travel Associations (ACTA), the American Society of Travel Agents (ASTA), the International Association of Tour Managers, and the Caribbean Hotel Association. Others bring together a wide range of private sector travel interests, for example, the Pacific Asia Travel Association, the Africa Travel Association, and the Caribbean Tourism Association.

The Pacific Asia Travel Association (PATA) is one of the most highly regarded travel associations. PATA's members include airlines, cruise lines, hotels, tour operators, and travel agencies from 35 countries; their common goal is to promote travel to the Pacific region. The association's promotional activities include conducting travel marts that bring together buyers and sellers of travel; offering seminars and FAM trips for travel agents; and producing sales support literature.

> **CHECK YOUR PRODUCT KNOWLEDGE**
>
> 1. Give three examples of NTOs that play a major role in tourism promotion.
> 2. What is the European Travel Commission?
> 3. List five ways in which provincial and territorial tourist offices promote tourism.
> 4. How do car rental agencies promote their product?

SALES

Advertising and other forms of promotion stimulate interest in travel products and services, but they cannot complete the sale. This is the function of sales, the final stage of the marketing process. Travel and tourism industry sales can be divided into two categories: supplier sales and travel agency sales.

How the Suppliers Sell

Airlines, car rental companies, hotels, and other travel suppliers typically target their sales efforts at the travel intermediaries, not at individual clients. Sales representatives work both outside the employer's office, making personal calls on prospective accounts (**outside sales**), and inside the office, selling either face to face or over the telephone (**inside sales**).

Outside Sales The size of a supplier's outside, or field, sales force depends to a large extent on the size of the company. In the case of the smaller suppliers—such as bed-and-breakfasts, trailer parks, and local sightseeing companies—a single person (usually the owner) assumes all sales responsibilities. At the opposite end of the scale, a major supplier such as an international airline will have a highly complex outside sales organization, typically structured as follows:

- An international sales force, with a vice-president for each international region.
- A national vice-president of marketing and sales.
- Regional sales forces under regional sales managers.
- District sales forces under district sales managers.

Sales representatives call on travel agents, tour operators, and business travel intermediaries such as business

A DAY IN THE LIFE OF

An Outside Sales Representative

If you walked into the travel agency where I work and saw me sitting at a desk, you would think that I was a travel agent employed by the agency. Actually, I am self-employed. As an outside sales representative, I use the travel agency's office space, literature, and equipment. But I find and serve my own clients, and the income I make depends solely on the amount of business I generate for myself.

Some outside sales representatives (or commissioned sales agents, as we're also called) work full-time, and some work part-time. I used to work as a salaried travel agent for a big agency. I became an outside sales representative at the same agency after I had my first child and I needed to have more flexible work hours. For a while I worked only part-time, but as my list of clients grew, I found I had to work full-time to take care of all of them.

I do all of the same things that a regular travel agent does. I plan vacation packages, book airline and hotel reservations, provide advice, literature, and information, and so on. I spend most of each day on the telephone with clients or doing paperwork, just like a salaried agent. The major difference is that I get no salary or benefits from the agency where I conduct my business. I work strictly on commission, and I share my commissions with the agency in return for being able to use its facilities.

Because I work on commission, I feel that I have to work harder than a salaried travel agent. After all, I am selling exactly the same thing as every other travel agent. My livelihood depends on providing my clients with that extra measure of personal service that they don't get from a regular agent. I will deliver tickets and itineraries, and I will spend hours on the phone trying to find just the right resort or airline flight for a client. If there's any kind of problem, I will do everything I can to solve it.

Another difference between me and a salaried travel agent is that I cannot serve customers who walk into my agency off the street. I have to have my own clientele, but if I left this agency and went to another one, I could take my clients with me. I find my clients through my family, friends, and business contacts. Many of my clients recommend me to their family and friends as well. I also find clients by passing out my cards at church suppers, bar and bat mitzvahs, business dinners, and PTA meetings. I even found a client once while sitting in my dentist's chair having my teeth cleaned!

I usually receive about 50 or 60 percent of the commission that my agency collects for booking a trip. That's because I do virtually all the work. Some outside sales representatives are homemakers, ministers, or retirees who drum up business among their friends and acquaintances. They bring their agencies business but don't do the planning and booking. Those people normally receive a small percentage of the commission, perhaps 10 or 20 percent, as a finder's fee.

You need the same attributes to be an outside sales representative as you do to be a travel agent. You have to like people, be skilful in matching clients to the right vacation destinations, be knowledgeable about geography and world events, and of course be able to operate the agency's computers.

Some travel agencies won't use outside sales representatives; others rely exclusively on them; and still others use a mix of salaried and commissioned agents. My agency is a mix. The owners like my work because I bring in business that they wouldn't get otherwise. Many of my clients are from out of the area. They book trips through my agency instead of a local agency only because they want to do business with me.

I like the flexibility of being an outside sales representative. I can come and go as I please and make my own hours. One part I don't like is that things sometimes go wrong that are out of my control. If a plane was late or the food was lousy, the clients sometimes come back and complain to me. I tend to take these complaints personally, because my clients nearly always become my friends. On the other hand, I often receive postcards and thank you notes from clients who had a wonderful time on their vacation. That makes it all worthwhile.

travel department (BTD) managers, corporate and association meeting planners, and incentive travel planners. There are four main ways that a sales rep can get into the prospect's office to make a sales pitch:

- By following up leads created by promotional activities.
- By telephoning for an appointment.
- By sending a letter and making a follow-up phone call.
- By making **cold calls**, which are personal visits made without any advance warning to the prospect. Sales reps usually make cold calls when they want to canvass several prospects within a single location (such as an office building or an industrial park).

Of the four different methods, the first is the most effective, because the prospect has already expressed interest in the product or service being sold. Cold calls usually have the lowest success rate.

Besides making initial sales, the sales representative must also service existing accounts. This is usually done by arranging seminars and FAM trips and by negotiating deals.

Inside Sales The major airlines, car rental companies, and hotel chains all maintain central reservations offices. Sales representatives working in these offices handle incoming telephone calls from travel agents, tour operators, and other travel intermediaries.

Suppliers sell to the public through sales outlets established in the major urban areas (city ticket offices), and in airports, hotels, convention centres, and elsewhere. Sales outlets are used primarily by airlines and car rental companies. Sales representatives answer telephone calls and respond to inquiries from potential clients who come into the office.

The major difference between inside sales and outside sales is that with the former, the prospect approaches the seller, whereas with the latter, the seller approaches the prospect. Inside salespeople are not, however, mere order takers. If the salesperson can identify the customer's needs, he or she may be able to generate more sales than were initially requested. A client who calls to make a flight reservation, for example, may be persuaded to buy a fly/drive package or to make hotel reservations.

How Travel Agents Sell

Travel agents sell products on behalf of suppliers. The emphasis is on inside sales to individual clients.

Inside Sales Travel consultants sell to the public either over the telephone or, more commonly, in person. Clients who visit a travel agency tend to have a less clear idea of the travel products and services they want to buy than do clients who go directly to the supplier. To turn these half-formed plans into firm travel arrangements—to make the sale—the travel consultant has to perform five tasks:

- Qualify the customer. This typically involves five questions: Where do you want to go? When do you want to go? How many people will be travelling? How long do you plan to stay? What class of service do you require?
- Identify the customer's needs. Find out his or her motivations for travel.
- Recommend a product or service to fill those needs.
- Overcome any objections, such as, "That's more than I expected to pay."
- Persuade the client to make a commitment, which is known as "closing the sale."

Outside Sales Most outside selling involves selling to groups and to corporate accounts. However, a growing number of outside sales representatives also sell to individuals.

Sales representatives selling to groups must identify the needs of the group as a whole. The initial contact is made with a decision-maker representing the group; this is followed by a sales presentation before the entire group.

Sales representatives selling to corporate accounts are usually selling the services of the travel agency rather than a one-time travel product. Their aim is to secure commercial accounts over an indefinite period of time, by persuading corporate decision-makers to use the agency for all its travel arrangements.

Some travel agencies, especially large agencies and those that specialize in commercial travel, maintain professional outside sales representatives. They perform tasks similar to those performed by sales reps employed by airlines, hotels, and car rental companies. In many medium-sized and smaller agencies, the owner or manager assumes responsibility for outside sales. Among smaller agencies, outside sales work is also done by part-time employees.

CAREER OPPORTUNITIES

Marketing career opportunities are available in both the public and the private sector. Public sector positions are all related to promotion (with the exception of convention sales careers at the semi-public CVBs). Private sector careers can involve both promotion and sales.

The Public Sector

There are openings in the public and semi-public sectors at federal, provincial, and territorial tourism offices (NTOs and PTTOs), and at the local level (CVBs).

National Tourist Offices In Canada, the highest level that you can work at in the field of public sector travel promotion is with Tourism Canada, which has four branches: market development, product development, research, and management services and liaison. Market development is concerned with advertising, public relations and promotion, and planning and program development. Product development is concerned with the tourism product and overall federal tourism policy. Research involves conducting studies and surveys and analyzing tourism-related information. Management services and liaison coordinates the activities of the various governments and tourism associations.

Provincial and Territorial Tourism Offices All provinces and territories have tourism offices, with employees who do marketing, research, and public relations.

Convention and Visitors' Bureaus CVBs are not always part of the local government, but it is more appropriate to consider them here than under the private sector. The number of CVBs in operation has increased dramatically in recent years, and CVBs offer excellent opportunities for careers in destination promotion. Typically, CVBs are headed by an executive director and staffed by up to 60 employees. Convention sales is a key area, involving considerable contact with corporate and association meeting planners. A convention sales manager directs the sales effort. Entry-level positions are available in a variety of administrative and marketing areas.

The Private Sector

Most of the larger suppliers have their own promotional and sales departments. Airlines, cruise lines, car rental companies, and hotels are the major employees. VIA Rail and Amtrak also have marketing staff.

Careers are available in advertising, public relations, market research, and sales. The sales force is divided between those who work in the office and those who make sales calls outside the office.

Advertising and Public Relations Agencies A few advertising and public relations agencies specialize in travel promotion, both for travel suppliers and for government tourist offices. Ad agency employees, who must have strong creative skills, may eventually rise to become art directors or senior media planners. Public relations professionals write press releases, handle press inquiries, and arrange interviews and press conferences.

Travel Writing and Travel Photography Travel writers and photographers are employed by the travel trade press (*The Travel Agent*, *Travel Weekly*, and others) and by the consumer press. The latter category includes travel publications such as *Travel and Leisure*, general interest magazines that feature occasional travel articles, and the major newspapers that have weekly travel sections. Travel writers and photographers are employed both full-time and as freelancers. Competition is intense, especially for travel photographers.

Summary

- Marketing is the sum of all the activities designed to bring buyers and consumers together. It involves market research, product development, pricing, distribution, promotion, and sales.
- Products are developed to satisfy the needs of different markets.
- Advertising, the promotional tool used most widely in the travel industry, is the use of paid media space or time to attract customers.
- Newspaper and magazine advertising accounts for almost half of travel advertising expenditures. Other advertising media used include television, radio, direct mail, and billboards. Each has specific advantages and disadvantages.
- Co-op advertising is the sponsoring of advertisements by two or more companies.
- Sales support, an extension of the advertising effort, uses brochures, travel videos, and point-of-purchase displays.
- Sales promotional activities are targeted at prospective clients and travel intermediaries. They include special offers, travel shows, FAM trips, and sales contests.
- Public relations activities, targeted at the media, are staged to create a positive image for a company and its products. Press releases and press conferences are common PR tools.
- Within the public sector, travel and tourism is promoted by national and provincial travel offices. These offices promote destinations, but they do not sell travel products.
- Within the private sector, travel and tourism is promoted and sold by airlines, by hotels and other suppliers, and by tour operators and travel agents.
- Most supplier sales representatives sell to travel intermediaries, not to the general public.
- Outside sales reps work outside the employer's office. Inside sales reps make sales by telephone, or in person with prospective clients who come to the office.
- Travel agents sell products on behalf of the suppliers to individual clients, groups, and corporations.

Key Terms

marketing
market research
market price
parity product
advertising
shotgun approach
rifle approach
spot
intrusive advertising
directional advertising
co-op advertising
press release
press conference

outside sales
inside sales
cold call

What Do You Think?

1. Briefly compare Tourism Canada and the United States Travel and Tourism Administration (USTTA). Should the USTTA play a more active role in promoting travel and tourism? Explain.
2. Why do travel organizations as a whole advertise most heavily in newspapers?
3. Could travel suppliers sell their products without spending so heavily on advertising? Explain.
4. What type of publicity might have negative effects on a tourist product or service?
5. Is it important to have a catchy slogan at the heart of an advertising campaign? Think up an original slogan for (a) Canada, (b) the province where you live, and (c) the city or town where you live.
6. List three ways that the travel professional can access promotional materials.
7. Suggest three sources of information that travel professionals can tap to keep abreast of industry developments, and new products and services.

Dealing with Product

You have been appointed the sales and marketing manager of Yourtown's new convention and visitors' bureau (CVB). The product that you have to promote is the sum of all the attractions and events that Yourtown has to offer, as well as all the travel and tourism services that bring hosts and guests together.

The mayor and city council have promised you a generous budget and their enthusiastic support. However, before the funding can begin, they will need to see a thorough and well-written marketing plan from you.

Design a master marketing plan for Yourtown. What does Yourtown have to offer? What are the various MNEs of the clientele you hope to attract? How will you promote your product?

Dealing with People

"He's a born salesman." "She's a born saleswoman." How many times have you heard such comments? Do you believe some people are born to be successful salespeople, or do you believe that almost anybody can be taught to be a sales pro? Here's your chance to express your beliefs.

Imagine that you have just become the owner of a wholesale tour operation. You plan to offer a dozen different Caribbean tour programs, and you have determined that your initial market will consist of your entire province. What type of sales force do you think you will need? What qualifications will you look for in your salespeople? How important will high school or college transcripts and character references be? Will you be looking for a particular type of personality? If so, what type, and why?

CHAPTER 14: Promotion and Sales   Name: _____

WORKSHEET 14-1 Travel Advertising

The chart below lists various organizations that promote travel and tourism. Find an ad (print, broadcast, direct mail, out-of-home, or directory) sponsored by each promoter. In the appropriate box on the chart, list the promotional slogan or theme used in the ad. Identify the product or service being advertised.

Airlines	Attractions

Railways	Travel Agencies

Motorcoach Companies	Provincial Tourist Offices

Car Rental Companies	Hotels/Motels

Cruise Lines	Other

CHAPTER 14: Promotion and Sales   Name: _____

WORKSHEET 14-2 Promoting the Travel Product

Tell how you would promote each of the following travel products. Choose one advertising technique, one sales support and promotion technique, and one public relations technique. Write your suggestions in the grid below. Be as specific as possible.

Product	Advertising	Support/Promotion	Public Relations
1. A tour of Ottawa, Ontario, for grandparents and their grandchildren.			
2. A bus tour of Scandinavian countries, hosted by a local radio personality.			
3. A 14-day Alaskan cruise.			
4. The opening of a new vacation resort in Mexico.			
5. A wilderness camping trip for physically challenged adults.			
6. New air service to Eastern Europe and the ex-Soviet Union.			
7. A university alumni tour to China.			
8. A budget motel near the Trans-Canada Highway.			
9. Travel insurance.			
10. Vacation travel arranged by a small neighbourhood travel agency.			

CHAPTER 14: Promotion and Sales Name: _____

WORKSHEET 14-3 Selling Travel Products

Study the following conversation between a travel agent and a potential client. Note how the travel agent performs each of the five sales tasks: (1) qualifies the customer, (2) identifies the customer's needs, (3) recommends a product, (4) overcomes objections, and (5) closes the sale. On the lines provided, write the number of the task that is being performed by the travel agent.

Client: Do you sell cruises?

_____ **Agent:** We certainly do. We offer Caribbean cruises, Mediterranean cruises, and cruises to Alaska and Mexico. We even offer cruises to China.

Client: Well, I like to go someplace warm in the winter. I need to rest and unwind. I've gone to Florida the last three years, but I'm getting tired of going there.

_____ **Agent:** It sounds like you're ready for something new and exciting.

Client: Yeah, that's what I've been thinking.

_____ **Agent:** How long do you want to be gone?

Client: Well, I've never been on a cruise before. I don't know if I'd like it.

_____ **Agent:** Does a week sound about right?

Client: Yeah, but it has to be in January. That's when I get my vacation.

_____ **Agent:** Oh, that's no problem. There are cruises leaving all the time. Now, where do you think you'd like to sail?

Client: Gee, I don't know.

_____ **Agent:** Well, tell me. What did you enjoy seeing and doing while you were in Florida?

Client: Well, you know, I'm a real baseball fan. I like watching the pros in spring training.

_____ **Agent:** It sounds like you might enjoy a theme cruise designed for baseball fans. You'd even get to mingle with sports celebrities.

Client: No kidding! I'd love to meet some baseball players. But there's just one thing. I'd be going by myself. Wouldn't I feel out of place on a cruise?

_____ **Agent:** Not at all. It's really easy to meet people on a cruise—especially a theme cruise. You'll have a lot to talk about with other baseball fans. But if you like, I could arrange a double-occupancy cabin for you. That way you'd be sure to meet someone.

Client: Oh, no, that's okay. I'd rather stay by myself. Nothing too fancy either.

_____ **Agent:** Would you prefer an outside cabin or an inside cabin?

Client: I'd want one with a porthole.

_____ **Agent:** Okay. Now how does this sound? Royal American has a seven-day theme cruise to Mexico called "Great Sports Legends." It departs from Los Angeles on January 15. Players from the Oakland A's and California Angels will be on board. I can book you in a single-occupancy outside cabin on B Deck for $1,495.

Client: That sounds great. I'm not sure about the price, though.

_____ **Agent:** A cruise package is a great deal. Remember, the cost includes your transportation, meals, accommodations, and entertainment. And it's all right there on the ship. You don't have to wear yourself out finding a place to stay or eat.

Client: Yeah, I never thought of that.

_____ **Agent:** These cruises fill up fast. I can book you today if you like.

Client: Well, okay. Do you take credit cards?

_____ **Agent:** We sure do.

CHAPTER 14: Promotion and Sales   Name: _____

WORKSHEET 14-4 Selling Travel

You are a travel agent. How would you handle the following situations?

1. A retired couple was planning to pay a deposit on an expensive tour of the Middle East, but a recent outburst of terrorism has caused them to reconsider. What will you do?

2. A young couple has consulted with you repeatedly over the last three weeks. You have spent a lot of time trying to define their motivations, needs, and expectations and to select a perfect travel package. Tomorrow is the last day they can qualify for the reduced airfare you arranged for them. They are still going back and forth in their decision. How do you close the deal?

3. You are trying to book a tour for a specia- interest club with a membership of more than 100. You have had a fair response but are still three people short of the minimum needed for the tour. How do you sign up three or more additional club members?

4. A family of six purchased airline tickets from you for a cross-country flight. Today there was a terrible accident involving the airline they are booked on. The family refuses to fly on that carrier and is considering cancelling the trip. What do you do?

CHAPTER 15

The Future and You

"The way to find the limits of the possible is by going beyond them to the impossible."

Arthur C. Clarke

OBJECTIVES

When you have completed this chapter, you should be able to do the following:

- Explain why the travel and tourism industry will continue to grow.
- Give reasons why the academic community and governments are recognizing the importance of travel and tourism.
- Discuss the future of deregulation.
- Indicate technological advances that will affect the future of travel and tourism.
- List different kinds of automated channels of distribution.
- List situations and events that may curtail or discourage travel and tourism.
- Cite demographic changes that are likely to have an impact on the travel industry.
- Explain why increased education will be important for future travel professionals.

"Without a passport, you're stuck in travellers' limbo. You can't go anywhere." That's the way one travel journalist described the importance of a passport. As you know, this official government document identifies its owner as a citizen of a particular country. Without it, most other countries won't let you in.

We hope that this book, by providing basic information about the travel and tourism industry, will be your passport into a career as a travel professional. The earlier chapters introduced you to the past and present operations of the various components of the travel industry—air, maritime, and ground transportation, the hospitality industry, and the leisure and recreation industry. You have learned about the nature of travel products and services and the motivations, needs, and expectations (MNEs) of travellers, and how the channels of distribution bring them together. You have also read about the many career opportunities available in travel and tourism.

Yet another area to explore before you continue on your journey as a travel professional is the future of travel and tourism. Since you'll be directly involved, you'll certainly want to have some idea of the directions in which the industry is headed. Although no one can predict the future with certainty, this chapter suggests the trends, issues, and developments that are likely to be important for travel and tourism in the last half of the 1990s and the decades beyond.

CONTINUED GROWTH OF TRAVEL AND TOURISM

As you know by now, the international travel and tourism industry has grown tremendously in the last few years. It is now the largest industry worldwide, and accounts for $3.4 trillion in gross output. The potential for job creation in the next ten years is vast.

However, Canada has not shared in this growth in the last few years. The Canadian tourism industry was seriously hurt by the recessions of the early 1980s and early 1990s and by the economic restructuring of the past 15 years. In the rankings of global destinations, Canada dropped from sixth in 1980 to tenth in 1993. Over the same period, Canada's travel deficit increased from about $1.2 billion to $7.7 billion. The latter figure is about one-third of Canada's current account deficit. The challenge for Canadians involved in the tourism industry is to encourage more foreign travellers to visit this country, and more Canadian travellers not to leave it. A Canadian Tourism Authority has been proposed to market this country.

Will the international growth in tourism continue? Will tourism in Canada begin to grow again? Current indications are that travel by all three types of travellers will continue to increase in the years ahead.

Vacation and Leisure Travel

The conditions that gave momentum to the growth of vacation and leisure travel are expected to continue:

- *Increased discretionary incomes.* As long as economic growth remains steady and people feel positive about the future, they will be willing to spend their money on discretionary goods and services.
- *Leisure time.* The number of retirees increases every year as the nation's population ages. These retirees have plenty of leisure time, and more and more of them have the inclination and resources to travel.
- *Higher educational levels and the desire for nonmaterial experiences.* Because they are better educated, people are more aware of and interested in all the things there are to do and see in the world.

In addition, more travel promotion and the creation of new travel products will stimulate interest in travel.

Vacation and leisure travellers will continue to be cost-conscious. Low-cost group travel will characterize pleasure travel in the 1990s. In fact, some analysts predict that the demand for charter flights will be 50 percent higher than for scheduled flights. Travellers have become accustomed to low prices for air travel, and they will demand that such price incentives continue. The travel industry will need to follow the pattern of other industries by regularly selling merchandise at a discount.

Because of its culture and history, Europe will always be a traditional destination for outbound North Americans. However, as these travellers become more experienced, they will also become more adventurous and look for more variety. With the removal of barriers to trade and tourism in the 1990s, the popular destinations will probably include China, the former Soviet Union, and the countries of Eastern Europe. The Pacific Rim region—Hong Kong, Thailand, Singapore, and Japan—is already enjoying tremendous growth in tourism, and this trend is likely to continue. Improved infrastructures and control of costs will make mass travel to these areas possible.

Of course, Canadians and Americans will not be the only people to travel. Analysts predict that worldwide tourism will grow at an annual rate of 7 to 14 percent over the next 20 years. Increased industrialization will provide citizens of developing countries with the time and money to travel, and Canada and the United States should be ready to receive many more visitors. In the future, the number of tourists coming to this continent from Japan may exceed the number of tourists from Western Europe.

Business and Professional Travel

Business travel will continue to grow as the international business community continues to expand. The competitive climate and rising number of acquisitions and mergers have already made travel an integral part of business.

Offices, plants, and sources of supply are being decentralized and internationalized. For example, Northern Telecom, with its corporate headquarters in Mississauga near Toronto, has several manufacturing locations in Canada and the United States and facilities in many foreign countries. The need for managers and executives from different areas to meet or work together on a regular basis has increased the need for travel.

Corporations aren't likely to curtail travel spending drastically, but they will be looking for better value. Administrative control over travel arrangements will continue to increase. Some industry observers foresee a change in the relationship between the airlines and business travel departments that would see BTDs collecting commissions and becoming profit-making departments for the companies to which they belong.

Professional travel will increase, too, as people recognize the need to communicate more with others in their profession and to keep their skills and knowledge up-to-date. The travel industry will continue to develop new marketing techniques to meet the needs of professional travellers.

Travel by Visiting Friends and Relatives

Canada began as a nation of immigrants, and Canadians continue to migrate. To find or maintain employment or to change their lifestyles, people move from the country to the city, from the city to the country, from city to city, or from Atlantic Canada to the West. Today's families are likely to have members scattered in many parts of the country. Most people have friends who have moved to different areas. As the population of Canada continues to grow and the proportion of retired people increases, there will be more people visiting friends and relatives. Visiting friends and relatives (VFR) is already the main reason for travel.

Consider the case of Ruth and Ed Soto. Ed recently retired from his teaching position at a university in Thunder Bay. Because they wanted to live in a warmer climate, he and Ruth moved to Victoria. They can now play golf year-round and make new friends who have similar lifestyles and interests. Ruth and Ed also spend much of their time travelling. They've been to Hawaii and Mexico, and they also make periodic visits to their children. One married daughter lives in Alberta and another lives in Nova Scotia. After graduating from college, their son moved to Peterborough, where he works for a law firm. Whenever they visit their children, Ruth and Ed also try to see friends who live in the area. Every summer, they attend a reunion of Ed's World War II regiment. A highlight in 1994 was a trip overseas to England and France to mark the 50th anniversary of D-Day. Ed went ashore on Juno Beach in Normandy with the 3rd Canadian Division. The Sotos appreciate having the time to keep in personal contact with family and friends.

> **CHECK YOUR PRODUCT KNOWLEDGE**
>
> 1. What changes can be expected in the area of vacation and leisure travel in the next decade?
> 2. What characteristics of modern business make travel a necessity?
> 3. Why is VFR travel likely to increase?

INCREASED RECOGNITION

Until recently, the travel industry was more or less ignored by the academic community, by government, and by other industries. However, with the growing realization of the power of travel and tourism to employ millions of people, to improve international relations, and to help balance foreign trade, the industry is gaining new respect. In addition, the airlines, cruise lines, hotel chains, and other travel components are beginning to appreciate their interconnectedness and to project themselves as a single industry.

Academic Community

People who work in the travel industry need practical job skills. They also must know how to negotiate deals in the commercial sector, where profit is the motive. This type of orientation has not fit the traditional philosophy of colleges and universities in Canada and the United States.

Undergraduate programs at post-secondary institutions have traditionally presented students with a general curriculum, the objective being to acquaint students with many areas of knowledge so that they emerge as well-rounded individuals. Students take courses in arts, literature, history, and science. The development of intellectual skills receives the most emphasis.

In part because of pressure from businesses, this situation is changing. Schools are beginning to focus more on practical skills that have a direct application in the working world. In the area of travel, programs are being introduced to prepare students for careers in the travel and tourism industry.

Canada has long had a number of programs at the community college level, but has lagged behind the United States in programs at the university level. At the present time, there are several programs at the college or university level for training travel professionals. Post-secondary students can now major in these:

- lodging, tourism, and restaurant management
- tourism and travel administration
- transportation, travel, and tourism
- hospitality management
- travel agency management

ILLUSTRATION 15-1
Visiting friends and relatives is the number-one reason for travel.

Students in tourism and related programs are studying for the world's largest industry. In Canada in 1993, over 12 000 students were enrolled in hospitality and tourism programs; 65 000 were enrolled in the United States; 30 000 were enrolled in other countries. Students face global competition when they graduate.

Government

Governments around the world now understand the economic benefits of tourism, especially inbound tourism. To promote tourism and to ensure that it's well planned, countries such as New Zealand, Australia, France, and Indonesia have created tourism ministries. In many countries, the Minister of Tourism is as important as the Minister of Transportation or the Minister of Education. Tourism ministries are generously funded in many foreign countries.

The Financial Post, in an article and editorial in 1994, called for the creation of a Canadian Tourism Authority (CTA) to market tourism, particularly inbound tourism. Currently, there are 22 travel offices in New York City promoting Canadian hotels, airlines, railways, car rental agencies, and destinations. This presents a fragmented image of Canada. Under the CTA, industry resources would be pooled with government funding for marketing, and a more consistent image would be presented.

PROFILE

Dr. Margaret Bateman Ellison

Margaret Bateman Ellison was born on Grand Manan Island, a haven for rock hounds and bird and whale watchers long before eco-tourism was a word. Summers helping her father at boy scout camps, assisting an aunt at a bed-and-breakfast, and being a student dietitian at a hospital introduced her to tourism and hospitality.

Bateman Ellison is an associate professor at Mount Saint Vincent University in Halifax, Nova Scotia. In 1981, after several years of providing facility planning services to the hospitality industry, she joined the planning committee for Atlantic Canada's first degree program in tourism and hospitality management, to be offered at MSVU. She believed that links between academic theory and real-world practice needed to be established.

The four-year cooperative program began at MSVU in 1986. Bateman Ellison helped negotiate agreements with the community colleges in Atlantic Canada. She has taught design and the tourism and hospitality product, facility management, environmental and facility planning, and research methods.

Since 1984, Bateman Ellison has taught several hundred hours on DUET (distance university education via television)—both credit and noncredit courses. "We find people already in the industry do not want to study full-time," she explains, "or cannot take time off, or live too far away to come to campus, so they are able to tape a course and study on their time."

Like many other tourism and hospitality educators, Bateman Ellison's career evolved. After studying institutional management at Mount Allison University, she taught vocational education in Ontario. She earned a B.Ed. in guidance and administration, which included courses related to occupational curriculum development. She then became the first dean of women at the University of Prince Edward Island. Experience in student services, especially managing residence accommodation, served as a catalyst for a consulting practice in facility planning and management.

In the mid-1970s, Margaret, her husband, and two young children went to Tennessee where she returned to graduate school at the University of Tennessee. During her masters and doctoral studies, she supplemented her program in environmental design with studies in food systems administration and urban and regional planning. When one of her advisers had to go on sick leave, she was asked to teach the fourth-year class in food service design for the first class graduating in the tourism, food, and lodging program at UT/Knoxville. She returned to Canada to teach at UPEI and Holland College, and to consult in facility planning, before her appointment at MSVU.

Over the years in her consulting practice, she has worked on various facility planning projects, doing feasibility studies, facility management assessments, and interior design. As a professor, she annually coordinates facility assessment and planning projects with industry partners for 10 to 17 student teams. "I believe there are universal principles in facility management based upon the interrelation of the physical plant, client and front office, human resources, maintenance and housekeeping, and purchasing," she says. "I try to challenge students to apply these principles to understanding actual facilities, from heritage sites to hotels."

In 1993, Bateman Ellison began a research program to assess facility management with respect to quality management processes practised within the hotel sector in meeting internal and external customer expectations. She worked with the Opryland Hotel, Nashville, the Halifax Sheraton, Delta Chelsea, Toronto, and Delta Pacific. "The experience was invaluable and illustrates how willing industry is to be involved in the education process," she says.

Also in 1993, she was a guest lecturer at the Alpina Hotel School in Switzerland, where she delivered the program for the AH & MA certificate in facility management.

Bateman Ellison says her goal is to provide comprehensive and relevant courses that prepare students to meet challenges in an evolving marketplace. "It is not enough to teach the core content and rules for doing something so you can specialize in one area. Educators must facilitate students' abilities to think critically, conceptualize tourism globally, encourage them to continue to learn and develop leadership skills. Then they will be able to pursue a range of opportunities."

Work–study is an integral and mandatory part of the program at MSVU. Industry partnerships are formed for field lab experiences; cooperative education work terms are incorporated into the program. This involves extensive travel to work sites across Canada.

Margaret Bateman Ellison has been active in her profession, serving a term as CHRIE Canada president in 1993–94, as director of the Canadian Tourism Human Resources Council, and on the National Resource Council Building Code Committee for Residential and Small Buildings, 1990–94.

The CTA, which was first proposed in 1992, would be patterned after the Australian Tourism Commission, which is supported financially by both the private and the public sector. Australia has developed a marketing strategy that has encouraged many tourists from Europe and North America to visit. Commercials featuring kangaroos, koalas, Ayers Rock, and the Sydney Opera House have been very successful.

Prime Minister Jean Chrétien, in a speech to the 1994 annual meeting of the Tourism Industry Association of Canada in Vancouver, announced the establishment of a national tourism commision. It will be set up to promote Canada as a tourist destination, with a $50 million budget. The Commission which is to become operational in 1995, will have a board of directors with representatives from the federal and provincial governments, as well as representatives from private businesses involved in tourism. The goal is to create a $100 million marketing fund, with matching funds from the provinces and industry, to reestablish Canada as a force in the global tourism industry.

In the United States, the most recent formal recognition that international travel and tourism is important came with the signing into law of the National Tourism Policy Act in 1981. This legislation, which established the United States Travel and Tourism Administration (USTTA), has 12 broad goals, including the following:

- To increase the American share of international tourism.
- To expand American export earnings through trade in tourism.
- To promote international understanding, peace, and good will.

Nonetheless, the efforts of the American government in the area of travel and tourism have not equalled those of other countries. The USTTA, which is the only federal agency dealing with tourism, is buried within the Department of Commerce and is seriously underfunded. In fact, on at least two occasions in the 1980s, the Reagan Administration attempted to dismantle the USTTA by budget starvation. Only the efforts of Congress and the travel industry rescued it.

Why is the federal government in the United States reluctant to promote tourism? To begin with, many policymakers are uncertain about the government's proper role in the travel and tourism industry. In the spirit of American capitalism, these people believe that government should not intervene in private enterprise. If the government were to promote tourism, they say, travel companies and their shareholders would gain an unfair advantage. Government involvement in travel would also establish a precedent for the government to subsidize other industries.

The relationship between government and the travel and tourism industry will be an interesting area to watch in the coming years. A national tourism policy may soon become an important part of every nation's economic policy.

Continued Deregulation

More than a decade has passed since the beginning of airline regulatory reform in Canada in 1984, following airline deregulation in the United States in 1978. The effects of reform and deregulation are still being debated. Each time there is a midair collision or an airline goes bankrupt, a certain segment of the population cries out for **reregulation.** Indeed, there are signs that deregulation may not be achieving what was intended. Three areas, in particular, concern both advocates and opponents of reform and deregulation:

- The level of service and safety in the airline industry—in an attempt to cut costs, airlines may be tempted to reduce service or take shortcuts that compromise safety.
- The trend toward concentration—just a few large carriers could end up controlling all the business.
- The inequitable spread of savings among travellers—airlines may be tempted to charge higher fares on routes where they have less competition and use the profits to subsidize discounted fares on intensely competitive routes.

ILLUSTRATION 15-2
Governments around the world are recognizing the importance of tourism to their country's economy. This travel poster advertises the island of Madeira.

For the immediate future, airline deregulation, which has achieved lower airfares and improved operating efficiency, will continue. However, if abuses caused by the pressure of competition become too great and steps aren't taken to correct them, there will probably be a swing back toward government regulation.

On a related note, governments abroad are beginning to deregulate airlines and other travel components. (Actually, the word *privatize* would be more accurate than *deregulate*, because overseas foreign governments not only regulate but also own travel enterprises. Governments **privatize** industries when they transfer control or ownership of them from public to private hands.) In 1987, for example, the British government sold British Airways to private investors. By that year the airline had become a severe drain on the public treasury.

CHECK YOUR PRODUCT KNOWLEDGE

1. Why is the travel and tourism industry gaining new respect?
2. In what ways are many foreign governments demonstrating their awareness of the importance of travel and tourism?
3. What is the National Tourism Policy Act in the United States? How successful has it been?
4. What circumstances might lead to reregulation of airlines in Canada and the United States?

ADVANCED TECHNOLOGY

When travellers return from a vacation, one of the first questions they are asked is, "Well, how was the weather on your trip?" The weather has a major influence on how much people enjoy their travels. If it rains for nine out of ten days of a vacation, travellers are sure to be glum.

Meteorologists may soon be able to predict precisely what the weather will be like weeks—perhaps even months—ahead. Travellers will be able to plan their vacations according to weather forecasts. Travel suppliers will offer discounts on products and services during periods when bad weather is expected.

Developments in technology are taking place every day and will continue to do so. Travel planning according to weather forecasts is just one example of how future technology will affect travel and tourism. Some developments will make travel more pleasant, efficient, and comfortable. Others may harm the industry. Three sectors that are bound to feel the impact of technology are transportation, hospitality, and distribution.

Transportation

In late 1986, test pilots Jeana Yeager and Dick Rutan guided their *Voyager* aircraft around the world nonstop without refuelling. This historic flight was possible because the *Voyager* was constructed of a new, composite material—plastic reinforced with graphite fibres—that made the aircraft ultralight, but strong.

Research scientists are always rearranging molecules to create new materials. The most recent of these new materials—known as superstuff—include nonbrittle and heat-resistant ceramics that conduct electricity without losing energy (**superconductors**), extremely strong plastics that can replace steel, and advanced cements that will not crumble. When this technology is applied to the manufacture and operation of airplanes, ships, and trains, it will help get travellers to their destinations more quickly and economically.

Aircraft Present-day jets, which are voracious consumers of fuel, will gradually be taken out of service. The latest models of the Boeing 747 (the 747-400) and 777 (unveiled in 1994), and the McDonnell Douglas DC-10 (the MD-11) are far more fuel-efficient than the earlier models. In addition, the new models are equipped with state-of-the-art technology called **electronic flight information systems (EFISs)**. EFIS is sometimes referred to as "the glass cockpit," because the dials and gauges found in the older planes have been replaced with a large video display. Aircraft equipped with EFISs require only two pilots instead of three.

The big aviation news, however, may be the return of propellers. By the late 1990s, airliners powered by new-technology prop-fan engines may be transporting passengers. These planes will be constructed of lightweight, advanced composite materials and new aluminum-lithium alloys. While capable of flying as fast as present-day jets, the new planes will use from 30 to 50 percent less fuel. The cockpit will look like an electronic office, with computers monitoring all systems.

Innovations can also be expected in passenger areas. The interior of the passenger cabin will be designed so that seating configuration can be changed quickly—for example, from economy- to first-class sleeperettes. And on some planes, rather than craning their necks to see a screen at the front of the cabin, passengers can now view movies on individual seatback screens.

Another expected development is the **hypersonic** transport (HST). Possibly fuelled by hydrogen, the HST will cruise at a speed of 6500 kilometres an hour—six times the speed of sound. (By way of comparison, the **supersonic** Concorde flies at a mere 2500 kilometres an hour.) The HST will be able to fly from New York to London in less than an hour—a trip that now takes about seven hours by conventional jet. This incredible plane will fly at an altitude of 36 500 metres and carry 200 passengers.

Trains Trains will also become faster and more fuel-efficient, and this should encourage more people to return to rail

A DAY IN THE LIFE OF

A Family Hotel Operator

You could say that I was quite literally born into my job. I own a hotel with 35 rooms in the beach town of Cape May, New Jersey. My grandfather bought the hotel in the 1940s, and when he retired 20 years later, my parents took over the business. I've lived in my parents' hotel all my life and began working here when I was about eight or nine.

My first jobs were to turn on the lights at night and put out the silverware in the dining room for lunch and dinner. Later I did all sorts of jobs around the hotel—cleaning rooms, cooking, waiting tables, fixing toilets, patching the roof, manning the front desk. By the time I went to Widener University School of Hotel and Restaurant Management, I was already able to perform every job in my family's hotel.

After I graduated, I went to work for a large hotel chain as an assistant desk manager. It just wasn't the same as working for my own family, though. I soon quit and returned to Cape May to help my father manage our hotel. A couple of years later I met my wife. She had taken a summer job waitressing in our dining room. Today she is our bookkeeper and office manager.

My parents retired five years ago and turned the entire hotel over to me and my wife. Now, we have two sons who are beginning to learn the business. Of course, I hope that when they grow up they will want to continue running the hotel.

During the summer tourist season, my day usually starts in the dining room and kitchen. I supervise the kitchen staff and help the waitresses serve breakfast to our guests. Then I may hold a management meeting with my supervisory staff or spend a couple of hours in the office doing paperwork. In the afternoon, I visit the housekeeping and maintenance staff and check in with the front office to make sure everything is running smoothly. In the evenings, I again help out in the kitchen and dining room. I also spend a lot of time mingling with the guests, getting to know them and listening to their comments and complaints.

During the winter, I plan for the next season, order supplies, and oversee maintenance and repairs. I also attend trade shows and conventions to drum up business for my hotel among travel agents and tour operators. Sometimes I make recruiting trips to schools that offer hotel and restaurant courses to find new employees. Because ours is a seasonal business, we have to hire a new staff each year. Some years, many employees from the year before come back; in other years, most of our employees are new people.

Running a small family hotel like ours is very different from working for a large hotel chain. When you work for a chain, you are just a wage earner. When you run a family hotel, you are the owner of your own business. Chains employ large staffs. You may do only one job or learn only one part of the business. You can take a day off and someone else will be there to do your work. At a small family-owned hotel, you must be able to do every job because if someone takes a day off, there's no one else to step in. You have to roll up your sleeves and pitch in.

Running a family-owned hotel can be very difficult, but it also has special rewards. One of the great pleasures of running my hotel is that I have made a great many friends over the years. Some guests come back year after year. As a child, I played with the children of our guests. Now their children play with mine. I always look forward to a new tourist season because it means I will be able to renew many old friendships.

I am a member of the Society of Family Hoteliers, which is a new group formed a couple of years ago to promote the running of hotels as family businesses. Our group now has more than 100 members. It is a part of the American Hotel and Motel Association, but it is open only to hoteliers who have another family member in the business. Most of our members run small hotels and resorts, but a few own large chains of hotels. The purpose of the group is to try to help members deal with problems that are common to family-owned businesses, such as promoting family members, estate planning, and interesting the next generation in hotel careers.

I love owning my own hotel because I like being my own boss. I really like working with the people—the employees and guests—who come to the hotel each year. Sometimes when the chef calls in sick or a toilet is overflowing, I might wish I were in another line of work, but not really. I love it even then.

transportation. The French National Railroad's TGV trains already travel at 300 kilometres an hour and, at 65 percent occupancy, use four times less energy than private automobiles carrying the same number of people. The private sector and VIA Rail have carried out many studies on high-speed rail in Canada in recent years. The major question is the economic viability of such systems, given the capital investment required and the lack of population density in Canada, even in central Canada. Fourteen million Canadians would have reasonably convenient access to a high-speed rail system in the Quebec City–Windsor corridor; that is 10 000 people per kilometre (or 13 500 between Montreal and Toronto). This compares with 5000 per kilometre in the Edmonton–Calgary corridor, 25 000 per kilometre in the Paris–Lyons corridor, and 60 000 per kilometre in the Osaka–Tokyo corridor.

Scientists are working to develop magnetically levitated trains—trains that don't touch the track but are propelled along a cushion of air. There was a MagLev train exhibition at the Japanese pavilion during Expo 86 in Vancouver. Made possible by advances in superconducting electromagnets, these trains will race along at 480 kilometres an hour—twice as fast as Japan's bullet trains.

Hospitality Industry

Advances in the field of communications, such as interactive computers and video displays, are certain to affect the hospitality industry and may eventually bring additional revenue to hotels and motels from business and professional travellers.

One of these developments—teleconferencing—is already being used throughout Canada. As you learned in Chapter 12, teleconferencing enables people at different locations to meet via satellite-transmitted audio-visual signals. It is particularly useful for introducing a product or piece of equipment not easily moved, for announcing mergers or other major events, and for performing highly technical presentations. By using teleconferencing, huge meetings, such as shareholders' meetings, can be arranged on short notice.

Teleconferencing allows businesses to reduce the time and expense allotted for long-distance travel. Although the cost of a teleconference depends on many things, such as the number of participants, the number of locations, the length of the meeting, and the time of day, it is usually much lower than the cost of travel. The average cost per person for a teleconference runs between $25 and $50, while the average cost per person for a face-to-face business meeting is about $500.

Of course, the significance of this has not been lost on the hospitality industry (or, for that matter, on the airlines). If teleconferencing becomes popular, hotels, motels, and restaurants could lose substantial amounts of revenue. To meet this challenge, Holiday Inn, Hilton, Marriott, and InterContinental have established their own teleconferencing divisions. By arranging meetings and providing the necessary equipment and technical assistance, these hotels are promoting themselves as sites for teleconferences.

Channels of Distribution

As discussed in Chapter 13, the channels of distribution are expanding. Many of the new intermediaries will be machines.

Personal Computers Using a personal computer and the appropriate software or a modem, people have already begun to shop for travel products without leaving their home. Monitors display computerized information about the availability of airline seats, hotel rooms, and other products. A person who is planning a trip to Thunder Bay, for example, might get a listing of the available hotels and their prices. Along with this information might come a full-colour picture of the exterior of each hotel along with pictures of various rooms. The home shopper could then book a room by calling a toll-free number.

Video Kiosks Video kiosks that have been customized for the travel industry are being installed in high-traffic locations, such as shopping malls. Each kiosk contains a video catalogue that displays a number of travel packages. A computerized voice explains the various packages and answers basic questions. For more complicated questions, the customer can use the kiosk phone to call the firm that manages the kiosk. Customers confirm their choice of a travel package

ILLUSTRATION 15-3
Recomm's Automated Travel and Health Centre brings together two of today's largest market segments: health care and travel.
SOURCE: Automated Travel Centre, Toronto

by using a major credit card. Tickets and documents are mailed within 24 hours. These units may eventually be able to issue all documents on the spot. Although video kiosks have appeared in only a few places, industry observers predict that thousands will be installed in the near future.

Automatic Ticketing Machines To help fill half-empty planes, airlines will likely be installing automatic ticketing machines not only in airports, but also in convenience stores, shopping malls, and other high-traffic locations. These machines dispense low-cost tickets for simple point-to-point travel. Because of the perishability of their product (in this case, seats on a particular flight), airlines are anxious to establish additional outlets for selling tickets. Ticketing machines provide a way of reaching new markets.

Service Versus Self-Service Now the question is this: will travellers prefer doing business with machines, or will they want to deal with human beings? Once people can secure reservations through computers, the travel agent's role as a clerk or a ticketing agent may become obsolete.

On the one hand, Canadians have become accustomed to waiting on themselves. What is happening in the travel industry has already occurred in other retail industries. For example, Canadians patronize self-service gas stations, fast-food restaurants, convenience food stores, and one-hour photo finishing shops. Often, their only time for shopping is during their lunch hour or on their way home from work. They want to get in and out of stores in a hurry, and even where salespeople are available to give advice, busy shoppers may not want to take time to listen to it.

On the other hand, the purchase of travel products and services often represents a major investment. Many industry observers believe that most people in the leisure market want personal service, not high-technology equipment. They feel unsure about their plans and want to talk to a human being about their vacation. Human contact is especially important in an industry dealing with intangible products. Furthermore, while a machine may be able to generate a ticket, it can't describe what the driving conditions are like in Ireland or help the customer obtain a passport.

Electronic channels of distribution represent a trend to which travel professionals must adapt. Many are already doing this by promoting their services as travel consultants. In fact, it may become common practice for travel agents to charge fees for their professional services, much as doctors and lawyers do. Other travel agents are finding ways to incorporate the new technology into their businesses. For example, an agency might use video kiosks to market some products. In this way, it could expand without having to establish a full-service branch at every location.

Finally, in the travel industry of the future, the degree of human contact may become the standard for measuring the worth of a travel product. In other words, the more luxurious the product, the more service the traveller will receive from the hotel staff, airline personnel, and other travel professionals.

CHECK YOUR PRODUCT KNOWLEDGE

1. What developments are expected in the design and manufacture of aircraft?
2. How will advances in communications affect the hospitality industry?
3. Name three electronic channels of distribution. What advantages do they have over traditional channels, such as travel agencies?

WORLD PROBLEMS

Although the future of the travel industry appears bright, certain conditions may arise and events may occur to discourage or curtail travel and tourism. In fact, a few pessimistic observers believe that congested and unsafe airways, labour strikes, terrorist hijackings and bombings, and overcrowded and polluted destinations may return travel to its original meaning of *travail*—that is, dangerous and hard work.

Overcrowding and Pollution

A Canadian couple from Calgary recently returned from a trip to Yellowstone National Park in Wyoming with their children. They wanted to see the effects of the major forest fire in 1991. Both adults had visited the park before, as children, and were surprised at the changes, both physical and managerial, in Yellowstone. They recalled that 25 years ago tourists were allowed to park their cars close to the geysers and hot springs. They could throw coins for good luck into Morning Glory Pool. And, from the safety of their cars, they could feed candy and ice-cream cones to bears along the road.

Today, however, Yellowstone operates under a strict management program. Automobile traffic has been diverted from the geysers and hot springs. Visitors must now walk along a boardwalk—sometimes for over half a mile—to view many of the attractions. There are many more park rangers. Besides teaching tourists about the wonders of Yellowstone, the rangers manage and protect its resources. For instance, the park service now confines bears to the back country, where they will not serve as entertainment for tourists.

Such regulatory measures became necessary because overcrowding, with all its accompanying abuses, was threatening to destroy the natural beauty of Yellowstone. Several of the geysers, for example, were plugged up by garbage. Coins and litter had discoloured Morning Glory Pool.

Yellowstone illustrates the dangers that overcrowding and pollution present to many popular attractions and destinations, both natural and man-made. When these problems are not addressed, the attraction begins to lose its appeal and visitors stay away. Canada was one of the first countries to rein in development inside and around parks. Parks Canada is particularly concerned about Canada's Rocky Mountain parks: Banff, Jasper, Kootenay, and Yoho. It has recently established an ecosystem-based approach to park management, the main purpose of which is to preserve the wilderness character and ecological integrity of this country's parks.

An important task for the tourism industry in the years ahead will be to manage attractions carefully. Requiring reservations, limiting the number of visitors, and charging user fees will be some of the management techniques employed. A few countries, believing that the environmental and social damage caused by tourism is not worth the economic benefits, may even develop antitourist policies or restrict the number of visitors allowed.

Availability of Oil

Oil is the lifeblood of the travel and tourism industry. Without it, there would be no travel. An increase in oil prices means an increase in the cost of travel products; and if travel products become too expensive, consumers won't purchase them.

Consequently, oil prices are an ever-present concern to the industry. When Syrian and Egyptian forces invaded Israel in 1973, disrupting oil shipments in the Persian Gulf, a worldwide energy crisis was set off. This seriously curtailed airline and automobile travel. Again in 1979, when Iranian terrorists seized the American embassy in Tehran, the United States cut off oil imports, and another oil crisis resulted.

Oil prices dropped sharply in the early 1980s and then remained stable for several years. But as tensions in the Middle East increased, uncertainty returned and oil prices began to edge up again. The Persian Gulf, an essential transit point, was mined, and the passage of tankers through it was interrupted a number of times. In the summer of 1990, Iraq invaded Kuwait, cutting off a major oil supplier. This act, and the ensuing Persian Gulf War in early 1991, sent oil prices soaring once again.

During 1993 world oil prices dropped substantially and the price of gasoline in Canada declined as well. However, gasoline prices are still much higher in Canada than in the United States. This discourages Americans from travelling by car in Canada and encourages Canadians to travel by car in the United States.

When an energy crisis occurs again, the travel and tourism industry can expect the following developments:

- An increase in package tours and organized tour groups (as opposed to independent travel).
- An increase in travel closer to home.
- A decrease in the number of trips, but increased lengths of stay.

Political Instability

June 1985 was to have been the beginning of the season for global tourism. Instead, it was the beginning of the season for global terrorism:

- At Athens airport, terrorists hijacked a TWA aircraft carrying 145 passengers.
- At Frankfurt airport, a terrorist bomb exploded, killing 3 people and injuring 42.
- At Narita airport in Tokyo, a terrorist bomb exploded as luggage was being removed from a Canadian Pacific aircraft.
- Terrorists hijacked the Italian cruise ship *Achille Lauro*, with many Americans aboard.
- Terrorists gunned down travellers at Vienna and Rome airports.

According to one report, there were over 800 international terrorist incidents in 1985. Because of continued unrest in the Mediterranean region, 1986 was a disastrous summer for European travel. Millions of North Americans decided to stay home or go elsewhere, rather than risk being victims of terrorist attacks. The Persian Gulf War in the early 1990s had a similar effect on travel.

The bombing of an Air India 747, off the coast of Ireland, on a flight from Toronto to Europe in 1986, killed many Canadians, including neighbours of the Canadian author of this textbook.

Terrorism, as well as open warfare in many countries, has become a major deterrent to travel and tourism. Although a traveller's chances of being hijacked are one in a million, many people are still afraid to travel. To deal with the threat, international airports are taking measures to improve security. Books such as *Everything You Need to Know Before You're Hijacked* (by Douglas McKinnon, former chair of the Civil Aeronautics Board) advise travellers on how to minimize the risk of being victimized by terrorists. Even so, terrorism remains an insidious problem that is extremely difficult to control.

Fluctuating Currency Rates

Another important factor in travel and tourism is fluctuating currency rates. The value of a currency has the power to shift travel patterns—sometimes it can make or break a destination. When the exchange rate is favourable at a destination, travellers will go there. When their money buys less at a destination, travellers tend to stay away. The value of the Canadian dollar fluctuated greatly against the American dollar during the early 1990s, from a low of $0.70 up to $0.89 in early 1992, then back down to $0.71 in late 1994. This affected all forms of outbound travel, from one-day cross-border shopping trips to overseas travel to "snowbird" trips by Canadians to the southern United States. It also affected inbound travel.

CHAPTER 15: The Future and You

In recent years, the value of the American dollar has been weak in Japan and in most of the countries of Western Europe. The Canadian dollar, relative to currencies other than American, tends to move in the same direction as the American dollar. Indeed, in the summer of 1991, travellers to Europe were probably more concerned about the value of the dollar than they were about terrorism. At a restaurant in Vienna, for example, travellers paid the equivalent of $63 for dinner for two. A room at a moderately priced hotel in London cost $233, and a litre of gas in Paris topped $1.

Even if the dollar remains weak against many foreign currencies, Canadians will continue to travel abroad. They'll compensate for having less buying power by shortening their trips, settling for lower-cost accommodations, taking package tours with guaranteed prices, and seeking the lowest possible airfares. They'll also switch to destinations where the dollar will buy more—possibly Greece, Brazil, Australia, and China.

While a devalued Canadian dollar makes outbound travel to certain destinations less appealing, it also pulls in more visitors from abroad. Since they're able to buy more Canadian dollars with their currency, travel to Canada has become a bargain for many foreign visitors. Discouraging the export of dollars helps to reduce the federal trade deficit. So does bringing in more foreign exchange. A long-term pattern of growth in inbound tourism can be expected. Table 15-1 shows the exchange rate for the Canadian dollar with the currency of selected countries on a particular day.

Disease and Poverty

Travellers avoid going to areas where they might become seriously ill. If, for example, an outbreak of typhoid occurs at a destination, the tourist business there will certainly drop off.

Tourists also stay away from areas where poverty is widespread. They want to be able to enjoy themselves. Seeing people who live in shacks on top of garbage dumps is too distressing for most tourists. This is the reason why some resorts in the Caribbean and other places are built in secluded areas, away from disease and poverty. Canadians made a total of 1 100 000 visits to the Caribbean in 1991. However, about 46 percent of these were same-day visits, probably by cruise ship or from Florida. This indicates a preference for staying overnight elsewhere.

Africa is an example of a destination that suffers from a poor image. Only about 2 percent of North Americans travelling abroad visit the "Dark Continent." In 1991, there were 84 000 visits by Canadians to Africa. Years of television viewing—especially news coverage of drought, famine, and civil war in Ethiopia—have reinforced the concept that Africa is a land of disease, poverty, and strife. While it's certainly true that parts of Africa have these problems, the continent contains 53 different countries and has a wide variety of cultures, traditions, scenery, and wildlife.

Country	Currency	Cdn. $ per unit	U.S. $ per unit
Fiji	Dollar	0.9600	0.6885
Finland	Markka	0.2631	0.1901
France	Franc	0.2547	0.1841
Greece	Drachma	0.00579	0.00418
Hong Kong	Dollar	0.1790	0.1294
Hungary	Forint	0.01352	0.00977
Iceland	Krona	0.02015	0.01456
India	Rupee	0.04451	0.03217
Indonesia	Rupiah	0.000640	0.000463
Ireland	Punt	2.1084	1.5238
Israel	New Shekel	0.4584	0.3298
Italy	Lira	0.000860	0.000836
Jamaica	Dollar	0.04515	0.03263
Jordan	Dinar	2.0113	1.4535
Lebanon	Pound	0.000823	0.000595
Luxembourg	Franc	0.04240	0.03064
Malaysia	Ringgit	0.5314	0.3840
Mexico	New Peso	0.4086	0.2953
Netherlands	Guilder	0.7787	0.5827
New Zealand	Dollar	0.8210	0.5933
Norway	Krone	0.2006	0.1490
Pakistan	Rupee	0.04521	0.03267
Philippines	Peso	0.05162	0.03730
Poland	Zloty	0.0000619	0.0000447
Portugal	Escudo	0.00849	0.00614
Romania	Leu	0.0008	0.0006
Russia	Ruble	0.000695	0.000502
Saudi Arabia	Riyal	0.3890	0.2686
Singapore	Dollar	0.9084	0.6564
Slovenia	Koruna	0.0437	0.0316
South Africa	Rand	0.3800	0.2746
South Korea	Won	0.001716	0.001240
Spain	Peseta	0.01084	0.00789
Sudan	Dinar	0.0382	0.0283
Sweden	Krona	0.1814	0.1311
Switzerland	Franc	1.0393	0.7510
Taiwan	Dollar	0.0519	0.0375
Thailand	Baht	0.0588	0.0402
Trinidad, Tobago	Dollar	0.2462	0.1794
Turkey	Lira	0.0000444	0.0000321
Venezuela	Bolivar	ERR	ERR
Zambia	Kwacha	0.092113	0.601527
European Currency Unit		1.6715	1.2079
Special Drawing Right		2.0073	1.4506

TABLE 15-1

Foreign Exchange Rates for Canadian Dollar as of June 29, 1994

SOURCE: Adapted from *The Globe and Mail*, June 30, 1994, B8.

> **CHECK YOUR PRODUCT KNOWLEDGE**
>
> 1. What are some of the factors that discourage or curtail travel and tourism?
> 2. What can be done about overcrowding and pollution of tourist attractions?
> 3. Why is fuel efficiency an important concern in the design of new aircraft?
> 4. Why did travel to Europe drop off dramatically in the summer of 1986?
> 5. How does the devalued dollar affect travel and tourism?

CHANGING DEMOGRAPHICS

You'll recall that demographics is statistical information that describes a group of people: how many are male and how many are female, what their ages are, what their occupations are, where they live, how many are married, what religions they belong to, and so on. From these facts, researchers draw conclusions about people's lifestyles. The statistics can also be used to determine any changes in the population. For the travel and tourism industry, certain demographic changes are significant when products and services are being planned and promoted.

Age

Canada is growing older. Fewer babies are being born, and the number of teenagers and young adults is decreasing. People between 25 and 44 comprise the largest group of Canadians, with the number of people 65 or older growing as well. Figure 15-1 shows the changing age distribution of the population.

Age 25 to 44 In 1991, about one-third of Canadians were between the ages of 25 and 44. These people offer excellent prospects for travel. For one thing, they're an affluent group and tend to spend the most money. Most of these people grew up in families that took vacation trips, and they tend to think of travel as a necessary part of life—even as a birthright—rather than as a luxury. Furthermore, they're well educated and appreciate the benefits of travel. From this group come the middle managers who form a large part of the business travel market.

Despite their favourable attitude toward travel, it's sometimes more difficult to sell discretionary pleasure travel to people in the 25–44 group. This is because they have so many other things to pay for: homes, furnishings, automobiles, and other tangible products. Perhaps the approach to take is to emphasize the practical, long-lasting value of travel. Also, the industry might make the point to the parents in this age group that many tourist attractions are a learning experience for children.

Age 65 and Older In the 1980s, people 65 and older—senior citizens—outnumbered teenagers for the first time. In 1921, they were 4.7 percent of the population; by the year 2001, they will form about 13.7 percent of the population. Clearly, Canadians are living longer, and this is important information for the travel industry.

Besides being a growing market segment, senior citizens make good travel prospects because they have the time to travel. Retired from their jobs, they can take long vacations. They're also free to travel any time of the year. Many senior citizens are "snowbirds," who migrate to the American South during the winter months.

Most senior citizens also have the means to travel. The amount of money they need for routine expenses (such as mortgage payments, food and clothing for the family, and school tuition) has decreased, leaving them with more discretionary income. Furthermore, many senior citizens today have had better financial planning for their retirement.

In promoting travel to seniors, the travel industry needs to keep several factors in mind. Although they have the money to travel, many seniors are reluctant to do so because of their values. Having grown up during the Depression and been active in World War II, many tend to look on travel as an extravagance. When they do travel, they may favour budget accommodations.

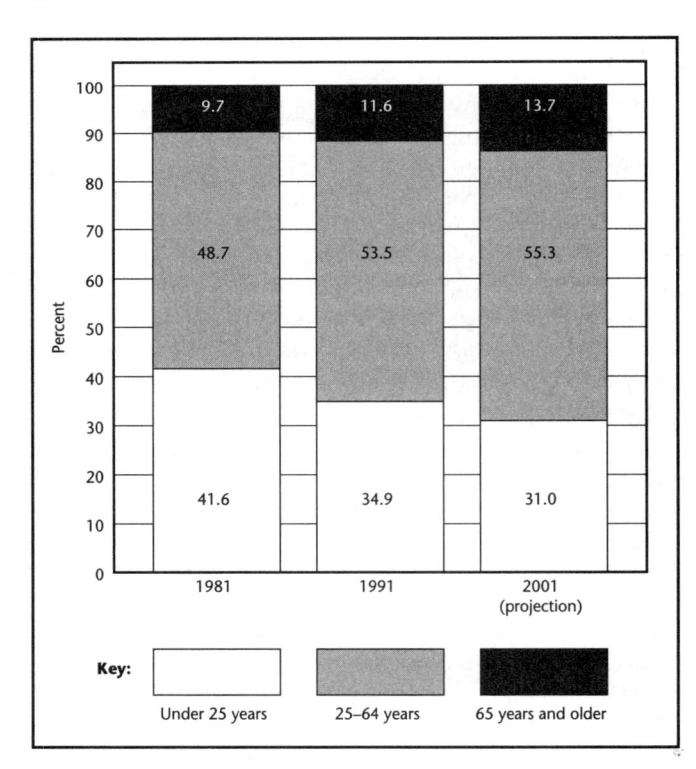

FIGURE 15-1

Canadian Resident Population by Age Distribution
SOURCE: *Statistics Canada, 1991 Census* Data

The travel industry also needs to be more aware that many seniors lack a travelling partner and don't want to travel alone. In 1991, there were 695 000 females over 75 compared with 480 000 males. Seniors are also sensitive to security and safety while travelling. Of course, any products that the industry promotes should be appropriate for the needs and interests of older travellers.

Finding the best way to advertise to the seniors market can be a challenge. The message needs to be delivered without making seniors feel like old fogeys. The Tennessee Office of Tourism, for instance, created an upbeat and lively advertising campaign using "The Senior Class" as its theme.

Work

Changes in the workplace—particularly in work schedules—have a direct impact on vacation and leisure travel. Some employers today are experimenting with the four-day work week, job sharing, flex time, and two vacations per year.

Three-Day Weekends A current trend in pleasure travel—and one that is likely to grow—is the three-day weekend, or "mini" vacation. Rather than taking the traditional two-week vacation, many families and individuals are taking several weekend vacations during the year. According to some surveys, these shorter vacations have surpassed longer vacations in popularity.

Several factors account for this shift in vacation scheduling. Because the modern workplace tends to be fast-paced and hectic, workers feel the need to escape from the pressure. But with two wage earners in a family, it's often difficult to coordinate extended vacation time. It's easier to get away from work for a few days. Shorter, more frequent vacations provide a healthy release throughout the year. For single parents who work, short vacations have two advantages: it's easier to arrange for the care of children at home or to take them along on vacation. Workers in Canada and the United States have an average of 17 vacation days and holidays per year, but they have 104 weekend days. This represents a tremendous potential for pleasure travel, and the travel and tourism industry is now developing products—such as "getaway" weekends at hotels—to take advantage of this market.

The trend toward shorter vacations has been a boon to regional tourism, as travellers look for attractions close to home to visit. In the future—especially with more advanced transportation systems—it may become commonplace for people living in all parts of Canada and the United States to travel to such places as Toronto, Vancouver, Las Vegas, Honolulu, Mexico City, and London for extended weekends.

The travel and tourism industry will need to come up with more and more fresh ideas for weekend excursions. For example, a travel agency in Toronto could organize a tour to a small town for an old-fashioned Victoria Day weekend. The tour would feature a parade down Main Street, a picnic and band concert in the town park, and fireworks.

Increased Leisure Time? While it's generally believed that people have more leisure time today, recent studies indicate that this may not really be the case. For most Canadians, two weeks of vacation a year is still the norm. Manufacturing industries have maintained the same work hours for the past 20 years. In some companies, workers have agreed to work longer hours without additional pay. The executive work week is longer, too, with managers expected to place high priority on their work. In view of these findings, it will become even more important for the travel industry to develop the concept of weekend travel.

Other Trends

The following demographic trends will also have a big impact on the travel and tourism industry:

- By the year 2000, more women will be in the labour force. Many of them will be in executive positions, and travelling a great deal on business.
- The proportion of adults completing additional years of school is increasing. Education not only stimulates people to travel but also makes them more sophisticated and demanding consumers of travel products.
- The number of professional, technical, and managerial workers is growing. People in these occupations tend to travel more.
- Later marriages, fewer children, and more single-parent households will cause shifts in recreational activities, times, and locations.

CHECK YOUR PRODUCT KNOWLEDGE

1. How can the travel industry use demographic information?
2. Why is the travel industry particularly interested in people aged 25 to 44 and in senior citizens?
3. Why has weekend travel become popular?

INCREASED EDUCATION AND PROFESSIONALISM

Doctors, lawyers, and teachers are commonly recognized as professionals. A professional is someone who has mastered a specific body of knowledge and possesses certain skills not readily available to those outside the profession. After completing an approved curriculum at an accredited institution, these people are licensed by the government to practise their profession. They may be required to demonstrate knowledge of their field by passing difficult examinations. To maintain their status, they must keep up-to-date on the latest developments in their field

PROFILE

Global Trends in Tourism

Written by Mary Lee White

Kevin J. Jenkins President and CEO, PWA Corporation and Canadian Airlines International Ltd.

"In many ways, the airline industry is where the manufacturing sector was in the early 1970s, facing global competition and low-cost new entrants. The driving principle in this economy is that customers will continue to hunt for value with their discretionary spending. Whoever provides the best service for the lowest price—that is, whoever gives the best value—will be the winner.

"As globalization progresses, it will become increasingly important for government and business to work together. In particular, government must identify Canada's competitive advantages and champion Canadian businesses which are positioned to build on those advantages. Countries that we are competing with, such as Japan, have been doing this for years."

Jim Smith President, Maritime Marlin Travel

"The role of the retail travel agency is still very strong in the nineties; however, their continued place within the travel industry will depend upon their ability to develop strong affiliations with other travel organizations to globalize their businesses. Technology is changing at a rapid pace, with the use of 'smart terminals,' which offer customized vendor reservation formats, global facsimile services, and enhanced client documentation, all of which are geared to increasing productivity in the agency. The focus of the travel agency in the nineties is to provide staff with the latest technologies, professional development opportunities, incentive plans, and self-management training to help them provide more efficient service to their clients."

Owen Colliss General Manager, Sales, Galileo Canada Distribution Systems Inc.

"The travel and tourism industry, one of the world's largest industries, is one that continues to grow. Complexities permeate every level—from initial product exposure to the travelling public to service delivery—and create the need for automation. We at Galileo Canada provide leading edge technology tools to the travel and tourism industry to address this changing need. The travel industry requires systems that enable travel counsellors to access vast amounts of data, display product detail, make reservations, create necessary documentation, and perform administrative tasks such as accounting. Others are required to provide the service providers with means to make travellers aware of their offerings. We see the relationship between service supplier, service seller, and travellers placing increased demands on CRS providers and the growing importance of automation to all suppliers of travel-related products and services."

Michael Beckley President Commonwealth Hospitality Ltd.

"The hotel industry of the nineties will see little new construction as the market takes time to stabilize. Growth can be expected in the leisure market with the increased demand of international inbound travel, the low Canadian dollar, and the aging population. Business travellers will be more value-conscious than before the recession, demanding a wider variety of facilities and services. The hotel industry will have to provide such upgraded amenities as rooms with work stations, computer link-ups, facsimile machines, and in-room coffee machines.

"A major trend in the hotel industry will be competition by global brands for a clearer identity as they diversify their product and struggle for brand recognition. Rather than new construction, existing properties will be redesigning both interior and exterior areas to strengthen their image of global standardization. The emphasis in human resource development will be on development of programs which give employees *power, information,* and *knowledge,* with a *reward* in recognition of a job well done."

and constantly refine their skills. Professionals are also expected to maintain high ethical standards. Years of experience add to their professional stature.

Throughout this book, the term **travel professional** has been used to describe your career in the travel and tourism industry. While most workers in the industry don't need to be licensed, the concept of professionalism is still important. Increasing competition, the complexity of the industry, and the sophisticated demands of tomorrow's travellers mean that travel and tourism employees will need to be better educated. Education will also help them adapt as required in an industry that is constantly changing. To inspire the confidence of the public, the travel and tourism industry will need to develop a more professional outlook.

Traditional and Continuing Education

Opportunities for industry-related education for the travel professional are expanding. Colleges and universities, trade schools, professional associations, and the industry itself now provide courses of study that help prepare men and women for the field. Experienced professionals can update their knowledge and skills in seminars and workshops, as well as through coursework.

College and Trade School Curricula As mentioned earlier, more community colleges and universities are offering degree and diploma programs specifically related to travel and tourism. General programs in business administration, computer science, and accounting are also useful in many areas of the travel and tourism industry. In addition, private business schools, vocational schools, community education classes, and travel agencies offer courses for the travel professional.

More and more, travel companies are looking for entry-level employees with academic and vocational training. It's no longer practical in this fast-paced, complex industry to train people from the ground up. Furthermore, the industry's vulnerability to consumer liability makes travel managers hesitant to hire workers who have had no exposure to travel and tourism. By showing students what the industry is like, colleges and trade schools tend to weed out students who are looking only for glamour. In doing so, they are able to provide travel companies with employees who will stay on the job. Also, by completing a course of study, students demonstrate their commitment to the industry.

Other Coursework Various components of the travel and tourism industry provide training programs. These courses are designed both for people already in the industry and for those hoping to enter it.

The airlines, in particular, are noted for their training programs. The airlines and computer reservations system (CRS) vendors offer computer training programs for travel agencies who subscribe to their systems. And airlines offer courses in advanced ticketing procedures, sales skills, and fare schedule and tariff interpretation.

A number of professional associations related to travel and tourism have education divisions that offer coursework, complete with textbooks and other learning materials. The Educational Institute of the American Hotel & Motel Association (AHMA), for instance, offers a full range of hotel, motel, and food service management courses. Students receive a certificate for each course or combination of courses they complete. These certificates are recognized throughout the hospitality industry and indicate the recipient's commitment to professionalism.

Organizations devoted exclusively to travel and tourism education also exist. The Council on Hotel, Restaurant and Institutional Education (CHRIE), the Travel and Tourism Research Association (TTRA), and the Society of Travel and Tourism Educators (STTE) publish newsletters, hold education conferences, and foster improved teaching methods.

Canada CHRIE Canadian chapters of CHRIE were formed in the early 1990s. Canada CHRIE held its first meeting in St. Andrews, New Brunswick, in 1993. Canada CHRIE participated in developing the proposal for the National Human Resource Council of Canada. The Canadian Tourism Human Resource Council, based in Ottawa, was created in 1993. This council will set a direction for human resource development in the tourism industry; help develop national standards and certification in tourism occupations; promote a training culture in the field; encourage people to think of tourism as a career destination; and provide the industry with an important link to national and international institutions addressing labour market issues.

Seminars and Workshops Attending seminars and workshops is another way to learn about the travel and tourism industry. Seminars and workshops generally focus on current issues and trends of interest to the profession. They also provide opportunities for professionals from different regions to meet each other and share ideas.

Professional associations and industry groups sponsor seminars and workshops, many of which are designed to acquaint travel professionals with various travel products. One of the best known is Cruisefest, sponsored by the American Society of Travel Agents (ASTA) and the Cruise Lines International Association (CLIA). This three-day seminar, held once a year, provides travel agents and agency owners and managers with information on packaging and selling cruise travel.

Certification Programs A person who has been certified has achieved the highest standards of his or her profession. The public has confidence that this person is competent, knowledgeable, and skilful. The names of travel professionals may also be followed by initials, such as ACTC, ACTM,

CTC, CTP, or CHA. These initials signify that the travel professional has achieved the highest distinction in his or her segment of the industry.

In place of government licensing or academic accreditation of travel professionals, various travel-related institutes and professional associations have set standards of knowledge and skill for travel professionals. Travel professionals achieve these standards by completing a certification program. Certification programs not only recognize excellence in the profession, but also motivate workers in the travel and tourism industry to pursue advanced education, thus increasing their own professionalism and that of the industry.

Each component of the travel and tourism industry has its own certification program. Although the specifics of each program differ, they do share some general characteristics. To apply for certification, candidates must be actively employed in the industry. In many cases, candidates must also have worked in the industry for a certain number of years and have passed an entrance examination. Some programs require that the candidate be at a certain level of employment. To fulfil certification requirements, candidates must complete a number of educational courses and participate in leadership roles in their professional association. They may be required to pass a written examination or write a research paper.

The best-known certification program in Canada is the ACCESS program of the Canadian Institute of Travel Counsellors (CITC), and the Alliance of Canadian Travel Associations (ACTA), profiled in Chapter 13. This program leads to designation as an ACCESS Certified Travel Counsellor (ACTC) or ACCESS Certified Travel Manager (ACTM).

Perhaps the best-known certification program in the American travel industry is that offered by the Institute of Certified Travel Agents (ICTA). ICTA awards the title of Certified Travel Counsellor (CTC) to travel agents who complete its CTC Travel Management Program. To qualify for certification, candidates must complete a series of courses on topics such as marketing, personnel management, and business management. They must then pass four 3-hour examinations and write a research paper. Candidates are allowed three years to complete the certification program. Since 1964, when the institute was formed, more than 13 700 travel professionals have earned the right to place the initials "CTC" after their name.

Other certification programs include the following:

- The National Tour Association awards the designation Certified Tour Professional (CTP) to tour operators, suppliers of tour components, and other people employed in group travel. To remain certified, CTPs must continue to earn education credits.

- The National Business Travel Association offers a certification program leading to the designation Certified Corporate Travel Executive (CCTE). One of the newer programs, the CCTE is for retail travel agents dealing with business travellers or for managers of business travel departments. Candidates must earn a total of 100 points in the areas of education, industry experience, and professional activities. A written thesis is required.

- The Hotel Sales & Marketing Association International administers the Certified Hotel Sales Executive (CHSE) program. Professionals who have worked in the hospitality industry as sales or marketing director, convention service manager, account executive, or hotel manager qualify for this program.

- The American Hotel & Motel Association offers several certification programs. The most advanced and prestigious is that of Certified Hotel Administrator (CHA). To apply, a candidate must be a general manager or corporate executive in the hospitality industry, with at least three years' experience in that position.

> **CHECK YOUR PRODUCT KNOWLEDGE**
>
> 1. What is a professional?
> 2. Why is increased professionalism important to the travel and tourism industry?
> 3. Where can travel professionals find appropriate educational opportunities?
> 4. What is the purpose of certification programs?
> 5. What are some general requirements for being certified as a professional by the travel industry?

CONCLUSION

As the world changes, so will the travel and tourism industry. Technological, social, and geopolitical changes will make the travel market and travel consumer of the future different from what they are today.

As the world becomes smaller through advances in transportation and communications, travel professionals will have an excellent opportunity to help people get to know their world neighbours. As travel increases, the industry will become even more intertwined with the economic health of nations. Countries will be less likely to engage in conflict if it means risking economic benefits. Thus, the travel and tourism industry can play an important part in establishing political stability in travelled regions.

To be successful as a travel professional, you will need to be open to change and flexible in dealing with it. You will also need the knowledge and skills to manage change. The travel and tourism industry itself can be the finest of schools for learning about yourself and others. If you enjoy change and growth, you will find travel and tourism a rewarding career.

Summary

- Travel by all three types of travellers—the vacation and leisure traveller, the business and professional traveller, and the traveller visiting friends and relatives—is likely to increase in the years ahead.
- Colleges and universities are recognizing travel and tourism as a professional career field by creating programs of study.
- Governments around the world are recognizing the importance of travel and tourism by creating tourism ministries and establishing tourism policies.
- Canada established a National Tourism Commission in 1995.
- Airline deregulation, which has been a major influence in the travel industry for the last decade, is likely to continue.
- Technological advances, primarily in the areas of material science and communications, will have a significant impact on the travel and tourism industry. The industry must be able to adapt to these changes.
- Pollution, overcrowding, disease, poverty, political instability, fluctuating currency rates, and changing oil prices are some of the conditions and events that can have a negative impact on travel and tourism. The industry must be prepared to deal with these situations.
- Changes in the way Canadians are living and working will affect the future of travel and tourism. Because people are living longer and retiring earlier, the senior citizens' market will become increasingly important. Another major trend is toward weekend vacations.
- As the travel and tourism industry becomes more complex, the people who work in it will need more education. Post-secondary schools, trade schools, professional associations, and the industry itself are providing a wealth of learning resources. Certification programs recognize the achievements of travel professionals in the various components of the industry.

Key Terms

reregulation
privatize
superconductor
electronic flight information system (EFIS)
hypersonic
video kiosk
travel professional

What Do You Think?

1. What trends and developments do you predict for the travel industry?
2. What is the proper relationship between government and the travel industry?
3. Is deregulation working? Explain.
4. How will teleconferencing affect the business travel market?
5. If you were asked to write a national tourism policy, what would you include in it?

Dealing with Product

Cottage industry is a term used to describe work that takes place in the home rather than in a factory or an office building. Traditional cottage industries, which often involve piecework, have included knitting, weaving, and light manufacturing.

Many futurists predict that our society will soon have an "electronic cottage industry." They forecast that automation will make the traditional office obsolete, and that personal computers, interactive telecommunications, and similar systems will enable tomorrow's clerical and administrative employees to work in their own homes. Obviously, there would be benefits for both the employer and the employee in this electronic evolution, but are there also risks to be considered?

What do you think would happen in Yourtown? How would this new type of cottage industry affect the travel and tourism industry? How many travel and tourism products would be replaced, and how many would be changed? Finally, how would such a major change in the marketplace affect the channels of distribution for travel products?

Dealing with People

This chapter has focused on the process of change in the travel industry. Some changes mentioned here are already happening; others are expected to occur. Many of the changes are the result of new technologies, new products, and new markets. However, one of the most significant changes has taken place in an area as old as business itself—that is, in relations between management and labour.

New working conditions have been established, partly owing to deregulation, unrestricted competition, and a volatile marketplace, and partly as a result of management's search for greater productivity. Labour has been forced to change its stand in three key areas: pay scales, part-time employment, and concessions (also known as "give backs"). The change in pay scales has created two-tiered systems of compensation in which newly hired employees earn less money for doing the same work as more senior employees. Part-time workers seldom receive the same benefits as their full-time counterparts. "Give backs" involve labour giving up concessions it had previously won.

You are the vice-president for human resources at a large resort with a workforce of 600. Your employees are members of an international union. For the third consecutive year, the resort has lost money. Quite frankly, business is bad and not expected to improve in the near future. The general manager has formed a crisis management team, and you have been instructed to develop a personnel plan that will cut costs without damaging the level of service. The union representatives will attend today's meeting, as will the management team. What will you propose? What will you tell your teammates and the union representatives? Is your proposal really fair or just expedient?

CHAPTER 15: The Future and You   Name: _____

WORKSHEET 15-1 Travel Industry Past and Future

Choose an aspect of the travel and tourism industry that you might like to work in.

How has that part of the industry changed in the last ten years?

How do you think it will be different ten years from now?

Are there any ways you prefer the industry as it was in the past compared with what it may be in the future? If so, explain. If not, why not?

CHAPTER 15: The Future and You   Name: _____

WORKSHEET 15-2 Education

Contact community colleges and universities in or near Yourtown. Find out what programs they offer related to travel and tourism. Choose one program and describe it below.

Name of college or university

Title of degree or diploma program

Course requirements

Other requirements

Industry jobs related to program

Placement services available

Contact a vocational school, business school, or travel school. Find out what courses they offer related to travel and tourism. Choose one school and describe its program below.

Name of school

Courses offered

Industry jobs related to coursework

CHAPTER 15: The Future and You   Name: _____

WORKSHEET 15-3 Certification

Select a certification program that interests you and find out its specific requirements.

Certificate

Program offered by

Employment requirements/level of employment

Entrance exam

Educational/course requirements

Experience/leadership requirements

Written exam(s)

Professional activities

Requirements to remain certified

Other

CHAPTER 15: The Future and You   Name: _____

WORKSHEET 15-4 The Future of Travel

Below are several trends that are expected to be important for the travel and tourism industry. For each one, suggest what the Canadian travel industry should do in response to the trend.

Increasing civil rights for physically and mentally challenged Canadians

Evolving European economic unity

An increasing number of single-parent families in Canada

An increased demand for energy conservation and environmental safeguards

Continued tension in the Middle East

An increase in the number of North Americans age 65 or older

Continued advances in technology

An increase in the number of overseas travellers to Canada

APPENDIX A

Commonly Used Abbreviations

AAA	American Automobile Association	GRT	Gross Registered Tonnage
ABA	American Bus Association	HTI	Hotel Travel Index
ACTA	Alliance of Canadian Travel Associations	IACVB	International Association of Convention and Visitors Bureaus
AC	Air Canada		
ACED-I	Association of Conference and Events Directors–International	IAMAT	International Association for Medical Assistance to Travelers
ADS	Agency DataSystems	IATA	International Air Transport Association
AHMA	American Hotel and Motel Association	IATAN	International Airline Travel Agency Network
AIMP	Association of Independent Meeting Planners	IATM	International Association of Tour Managers
AP	American Plan	ICAO	International Civil Aviation Organization
ARC	Airlines Reporting Corporation	ICTA	Institute of Certified Travel Agents
ARTA	Association of Retail Travel Agents	IEA	International Exhibitors Association
ASAE	American Society of Association Executives	MAP	Modified American Plan
ASP	Area Settlement Plan	MNEs	Motivations, Needs, and Expectations
ASTA	American Society of Travel Agents	MPI	Meeting Planners International
ATAC	Air Transport Association of Canada	NACOA	National Association of Cruise Only Agents
ATM	Automated Ticketing Machine	NBTA	National Business Travel Association
ATP	Agency Training Program	NTA	National Transportation Agency
ATPCO	Airline Tariff Publishing Company	NTA	National Tour Association
BSP	Bank Settlement Plan	NTO	National Tourist Office
BTD	Business Travel Department	OAG	*Official Airline Guide*
CAA	Canadian Automobile Association	OHG	*Official Hotel Guide*
CAB	Civil Aeronautics Board	PATA	Pacific Asia Travel Association
CAIL	Canadian Airlines International Ltd.	PC	Personal Computer
CCTE	Certified Corporate Travel Executive	PNR	Passenger Name Record
CHA	Certified Hotel Administrator	PRIT	Pacific Rim Institute of Tourism
CHRIE	Council on Hotel, Restaurant and Institutional Education	PSO	Public Sector Organization
		PWA	Pacific Western Airlines
CHSE	Certified Hotel Sales Executive	RAA	Regional Airlines Association
CITC	Canadian Institute of Travel Counsellors	RV	Recreational Vehicle
CLIA	Cruise Lines International Association	SABRE	Semi-Automated Business Research Environment
CMP	Certified Meeting Professional	SATH	Society for the Advancement of Travel for the Handicapped
CN	Canadian National		
COD	Channel of Distribution	SITA	Societé Internationale de Télécommunications Aéronautique
CP	Canadian Pacific		
CP	Continental Plan	SITE	Society of Incentive Travel Executives
CPU	Central Processing Unit	STO	State Tourist Office
CRS	Computer Reservations System	STP	Satellite Ticket Printer
CTC	Certified Travel Counsellor	STTE	Society of Travel and Tourism Educators
CTM	Consolidated Tour Manual	TC	Tourism Canada
CTP	Certified Tour Professional	TIAC	Tourism Industry Association of Canada
CVB	Convention and Visitors' Bureau	TO	Tourism Organization; Tourist Office
DIT	Domestic Independent Tour	TTRA	Travel and Tourism Research Association
DMC	Destination Management Company	UBOA	United Bus Owners of America
EFIS	Electronic Flight Information System	UFTAA	Universal Federation of Travel Agents' Associations
EP	European Plan		
ETDN	Electronic Ticket Delivery Network	USTOA	United States Tour Operators Association
FAA	Federal Aviation Administration	USTTA	United States Travel and Tourism Administration
FBO	Fixed-Base Operator	VFR	Visiting Friends and Relatives
FCU	Fare Construction Unit	WATA	World Association of Travel Agents
FIT	Foreign Independent Tour	WTO	World Tourism Organization

APPENDIX B

Travel Industry Associations and Organizations

Canadian Provincial and Territorial Tourism Offices

Travel Alberta
3rd Floor, City Centre
10155–102 Street
Edmonton, AB T5J 4L6

Tourism British Columbia
1117 Wharf Street
Victoria, BC V8W 2X2

Travel Manitoba
Dept. 20, 7th Floor
155 Carlton Street
Winnipeg, MB R3C 3H8

Tourism New Brunswick
P.O. Box 12345
Fredericton, NB E3B 5C3

Newfoundland and Labrador Tourism Division
P.O. Box 8730
St. John's, NF A1B 4K2

Travel Arctic
Northwest Territories
P.O. Box 1320
Yellowknife, NT X1A 2L9

Tourism Nova Scotia
P.O. Box 456
Halifax, NS B3J 2R5

Ontario Travel
Queen's Park
Toronto, ON M7A 2E5

Prince Edward Island
Dept. of Tourism and Parks
P.O. Box 940
Charlottetown, PE C1A 7M5

Tourisme Québec
Case Postale 20000
Québec, PQ G1K 7X2

Tourism Saskatchewan
1919 Saskatchewan Drive
Regina, SK S4P 3V7

Tourism Yukon
P.O. Box 2703
Whitehorse, YT Y1A 2C6

Canadian Travel Industry Associations

Tourism Industry Association of Alberta
Horizon Business Centre, #250
2635–37th Avenue N.E.
Calgary, AB T1Y 5V7

Tourism Industry Association of Manitoba
18th Floor, 155 Carlton Street
Winnipeg, MB R3C 3H8

TIANB/Tourism Industry Association
  of New Brunswick
1133 Regent Street, Suite 217
Fredericton, NB E3B 2Z2

Tourism Industry Association of
  Newfoundland and Labrador
P.O. Box 13516
St. John's, NF A1B 4B8

Tourism Industry Association of the
  Northwest Territories
P.O. Box 506
Yellowknife, NT X1A 2N4

Tourism Industry Association of
  Nova Scotia
1800 Argyle Street, Suite 513
Halifax, NS B3J 3N8

Tourism Ontario
49 The Donway West, Suite 420
Don Mills, ON M3C 3M9

APPENDIX B: Travel Industry Associations and Organizations

TIAPEI/Tourism Industry Association
of Prince Edward Island
P.O. Box 2050
Charlottetown, PE C1A 7N7

Les Associations Touristiques
Régionales Associées du Québec
6, rue St–Pierre, #126
Québec, PQ G1K 4A5

Tourism Industry Association of
Saskatchewan
203 Airport Drive, Suite 109–B
Saskatoon, SK S7L 6M5

Tourism Industry Association of
the Yukon
208 Main Street, Suite 203
Whitehorse, YT Y1A 2A9

Other Associations and Organizations

Air Canada
Head Office
P.O. Box 14000
St–Laurent, PQ H4Y 1H4

Air Transport Association of America
1709 New York Avenue NW
Washington, DC 20006–5206

Air Transport Association of Canada
99 Bank Street
Ottawa, ON K1P 6B9

Airline Reporting Corporation
1709 New York Avenue NW
Washington, DC 20006–5206

Airport Ground Transportation Association
901 Scenic Drive
Knoxville, TN 37919

Airport Operators Council International
1220 19th Street NW, Suite 200
Washington, DC 20036

Alliance of Canadian Travel Associations
1729 Bank Street, Suite 201
Ottawa, ON K1V 7Z5

American Association for Leisure and Recreation
1900 Association Drive
Reston, VA 22091

American Association of Airport Executives
4212 King Street
Alexandria, VA 22302

American Association of Retired Persons
1409 K Street NW
Washington, DC 20049

American Automobile Association
8111 Gatehouse Road
Falls Church, VA 22407

American Bed and Breakfast Association
1407 Huguenot Road
Midlothian, VA 23113–2644

American Bus Association
1015 15th Street NW, Suite 250
Washington, DC 20005

American Buyers of Meeting and Incentive Travel
Old Route 17, Box D
Harris, NY 12742

American Car Rental Association
927 15th Street NW, Suite 1000
Washington, DC 20005

American Hotel and Motel Association
1201 New York Avenue NW
Washington, DC 20005–3931

American Park and Recreation Society
1800 Silas Deane Highway #1
Rocky Hill, CT 06067

American Public Transit Association
1201 New York Avenue NW
Washington, DC 20005–3931

American Recreation Coalition
1331 Pennsylvania Avenue NW, Suite 726
Washington, DC 20004

American Sightseeing International
211 East 43rd Street, Suite 1001
New York, NY 10017–4707

American Society of Association Executives
1575 Eye Street NW
Washington, DC 20005–1168

American Society of Travel Agents
1101 King Street, Suite 200
Alexandria, VA 22314

Association of Corporate Travel Executives
P.O. Box 5394
Parsippany, NJ 07054–5394

Association of European Airlines
Avenue Louise 350, Bts 4
1050 Brussels, Belgium

Association of Group Travel Executives
424 Madison Avenue, Suite 707
New York, NY 10017

Association of Retail Travel Agents
1745 Jefferson Davis Highway, Suite 300
Arlington, VA 22202–3402

Association of Travel Marketing Executives
P.O. Box 43563
Washington, DC 20010

British Columbia Ferry Corporation
1112 Fort Street
Victoria, BC V8V 4V2

Canadian Airlines International Limited
Customer Relations
Calgary Administrative Building
615 18th Street S.E.
Calgary, AB T2E 6J5

Canadian Association of Tour Operators
701 University Avenue, Suite 250
Toronto, ON M5J 2M4

Canadian Automobile Association
1175 Courtwood Crescent
Ottawa, ON K2C 3J2

Canadian Bus Association
610 Alden Road, Suite 201
Markham, ON L3R 9Z1

Canadian Business Travel Association
P.O. Box 6021
Station "D"
Calgary, AB T2P 2C7

Canadian Camping Association
1806 Avenue Road, Suite 2
Toronto, ON M5M 3Z1

Canadian Cycling Association
1600 James Naismith Drive
Gloucester, ON K1B 5N4

Canadian Hotel Marketing & Sales Executives
39 Manor Road East
Toronto, ON M4S 1P9

Canadian Institute of Travel Counsellors
55 Eglinton Avenue East, Suite 209
Toronto, ON M4P 1G8

Canadian National Railway
P.O. Box 8100
935 de la Gauchetière Street West
Montreal, PQ H3C 3N4

Canadian Pacific Rail
Windsor Station
Montreal, PQ H3C 3E4

Caribbean Hotel Association
18 Marseilles Street, Suite 1–A
Santurce, PR 00907

Caribbean Tourism Association
20 East 46th Street
New York, NY 10017

Confederation of Latin American Tourist Organizations
Viamonte 640, Piso 8
1053 Buenos Aires, Argentina

Convention Liaison Council
1575 Eye Street NW, Suite 1200
Washington, DC 20005

Council on Hotel, Restaurant and Institutional Education
1200 17th Street NW, 7th Floor
Washington, DC 20036–3097

Cruise Lines International Association
500 Fifth Avenue, Suite 1407
New York, NY 10110

Department of Transportation
400 Seventh Street SW
Washington, DC 20590

European Travel Commission
630 Fifth Avenue
New York, NY 10111

Evergreen Travel Service, Inc.
4114 198th Street SW
Lynnwood, WA 98036–6742

Federal Aviation Administration
800 Independence Avenue SW
Washington, DC 20591

Flying Wheels Tours
143 Bridge Street
Owatonna, MN 55060

APPENDIX B: Travel Industry Associations and Organizations

Gray Line Sightseeing Association
350 Fifth Avenue, Suite 1409
New York, NY 10018

Greater Independent Association of National Travel Services
915 Broadway Avenue
New York, NY 10010

Greyhound Lines of Canada
877 Greyhound Way, SW
Calgary, AB T3C 3VB

The Guided Tour, Inc.
613 West Cheltenham Avenue, Suite 200
Melrose Park, PA 19126–2414

Hotel Association of Canada
1016–130 Albert Street
Ottawa, ON K1P 5G4

Hotel Sales and Marketing Association International
1300 L Street NW, Suite 800
Washington, DC 20005

Incentive Travel Association of Canada
208 Bedford Road
Toronto, ON M5R 2K9

Institute of Certified Travel Agents
P.O. Box 82–56
148 Linden Street
Wellesley, MA 02181–7900

International Air Transport Association
IATA Building, 2000 Peel Street
Montreal, PQ H3A 2R4

International Airline Passengers Association
4341 Lindburg Drive
Dallas, TX 75244

International Association of Amusement Parks and Attractions
4230 King Street
Alexandria, VA 22302

International Association of Conference Centers
900 South Highway Drive
Fenton, MO 63026

International Association of Convention and Visitors Bureaus
P.O. Box 758
Champaign, IL 61824–0758

International Association of Fairs and Expositions
Box 985
Springfield, MO 65801

International Association of Tour Managers
(North American Region)
1646 Chapel Street
New Haven, CT 06511

International Civil Aviation Organization
International Aviation Square
1000 Sherbrooke Street West
Montreal, PQ H3A 2R2

International Exhibitors Association
5501 Backlick Road, Suite 200
Springfield, VA 22151

Marine Atlantic
100 Cameron Street
Moncton, NB E1C 5Y6

Meeting Planners International
Infomart
1950 Stemmons Freeway
Dallas, TX 75207

Minister of State for
  Small Business and Tourism
235 Queen Street
Ottawa, ON K1A 0H5

National Air Carrier Association
1730 M Street NW, Suite 806
Washington, DC 20036

National Air Transportation Association
4226 King Street
Alexandria, VA 22302

National Association of Business Travel Agents
3255 Wilshire Boulevard, Suite 1514
Los Angeles, CA 90010

National Association of Exposition Managers
719 Indiana Avenue, Suite 300
Indianapolis, IN 46202

National Association of Passenger Vessel Owners
1511 K Street NW, Suite 715
Washington, DC 20005

National Association of Railway Passengers
326 Massachusetts Avenue NE, Suite 603
Washington, DC 20002

National Business Travel Association
1650 King Street, Suite 301
Alexandria, VA 22314–2747

National Campground Owners Association
11307 Sunset Hills Road, Suite B–7
Reston, VA 22090

National Caves Association
P.O. Box 106, Route 9
McMinnville, TN 37110–8629

National Park Service
U.S. Department of the Interior
P.O. Box 37127
Washington, DC 20013–7127

National Railroad Passenger Corporation (Amtrak)
60 Massachusetts Avenue NE
Washington, DC 20002

National Recreation and Park Association
3101 Park Center Drive, 12th Floor
Alexandria, VA 22302

National Restaurant Association
1200 17th Street NW
Washington, DC 20036–3097

National Tour Association
P.O. Box 3071
546 East Main Street
Lexington, KY 40596–3071

Pacific Asia Travel Association
One Montgomery Street, Telesis Tower
Suite 1750
San Francisco, CA 94104

Parks Canada/Canadian Heritage
25 Eddy Street, Room 10 G3
Hull, PQ K1A 0M5

Professional Guides Association of America
2416 South Eads Street
Arlington, VA 22202

Recreation Vehicle Industry Association
1896 Preston White Drive
Reston, VA 22090

Regional Airline Association
1101 Connecticut Avenue NW, Suite 700
Washington, DC 20036

Society for the Advancement of Travel for the Handicapped
26 Court Street
Brooklyn, NY 11242

Society of American Travel Writers
1155 Connecticut Avenue NW, Suite 500
Washington, DC 20036

Society of Corporate Meeting Professionals
2600 Garden Road, Suite 208
Monterey, CA 93940

Society of Incentive Travel Executives
21 West 38th Street, 10th Floor
New York, NY 10018

Society of Travel Agents in Government
6935 Wisconsin Avenue, Suite 200
Bethesda, MD 20815

Society of Travel and Tourism Educators
19364 Woodcrest
Harper Woods, MI 48255

Tourism Canada/Industry Canada
235 Queen Street
4th Floor
Ottawa, ON K1A 0H5

Tourism Industry Association of Canada
130 Albert Street, Suite 1016
Ottawa, ON K1P 5G4

Trade Show Bureau
1660 Lincoln Street, Suite 2080
Denver, CO 80264

Trans Canada Trail
837–2nd Avenue S.W.
Calgary, AB T2P 0E6

Travel and Tourism Government Affairs Council
1133 21st Street NW
Washington, DC 20036

Travel and Tourism Research Association
P.O. Box 58066
Salt Lake City, UT 84158–0066

Travel Industry Association of America
Two Lafayette Centre
1133 21st Street NW
Washington, DC 20036

United Bus Owners of America
1300 L Street NW, Suite 1050
Washington, DC 20005

United States Forest Service
P.O. Box 16090
14th Street and Independence Avenue
Washington, DC 20090

APPENDIX B: Travel Industry Associations and Organizations

United States Tour Operators Association
211 East 51st Street, Suite 12B
New York, NY 10022

United States Travel and Tourism Administration
U.S. Department of Commerce
14th Street and Constitution Avenue NW
Washington, DC 20230

United States Travel Data Centre
Two Lafayette Center
1133 21st Street NW
Washington, DC 20036

VIA Rail Canada Inc.
Customer Relations
P. O. Box 8116
Station "A"
Montreal, PQ H3C 3N3

World Tourism Organization
Calle Capitan Haya 42
E–28020 Madrid, Spain

APPENDIX C

Travel and Tourism Publications

BOOKS

Ames, Margaret. *The Travel Agency of DC—A Job Simulation.* Cincinnati, OH: South-Western Publishing Co., 1991.

Ames, Margaret. *The Travel Agency of San Diego.* Cincinnati, OH: South-Western Publishing Co., 1986.

Astroff, Milton T., and Abbey, James R. *Convention Sales and Services,* 2nd ed. Cranbury, NJ: Waterbury Press, 1988.

Bryant, Carl L., Reynolds, Ike, and Poole, Terese. *Travel Selling Skills.* Cincinnati, OH: South-Western Publishing Co., 1992.

Brymer, Robert A. *Introduction to Hotel and Restaurant Management,* 5th ed. Dubuque, IA: Kendall-Hunt, 1987.

Burke, James, and Resnick, Barry. *Marketing and Selling the Travel Product.* Cincinnati, OH: South-Western Publishing Co., 1991.

Butler, Richard, and Pearce, Douglas, eds. *Change in Tourism.* New York: Routledge, 1995.

Byers, Andrew R., ed., *Canadian Book of the Road.* Montreal: The Reader's Digest Association (Canada) Ltd., 1991.

Capwell, Gerald K., Lee, Wendy, and Resnick, Barry P. *SABRER Reservations: Basic and Advanced Training.* Cincinnati, OH: South-Western Publishing Co., 1989.

Cater, E., and Lowman, G. *Ecotourism: A Sustainable Option.* New York: John Wiley and Sons, 1994.

Coltman, Michael M. *Introduction to Travel and Tourism: An International Approach.* New York: Van Nostrand Reinhold, 1989.

Convention Management and Service. East Lansing, MI: The Educational Institute of the American Hotel and Motel Association, 1986.

Coyle, John J., Bardi, Edward J., and Novack, Robert A. *Transportation,* 4th ed. St. Paul: West Publishing Co., 1994.

Davidoff, Philip, and Davidoff, Doris. *Sales and Marketing for Travel and Tourism.* Elmsford, NY: National Publishers of the Black Hills, 1983.

Deland, Antoinette. *Fielding's Worldwide Cruises,* 5th ed. New York: Wm. Morrow, 1990.

Ferguson, Stewart A., and Howell, David W. *Northstar One: United States Destination Geography Using the Microcomputer.* Cincinnati, OH: South-Western Publishing Co., 1989.

Foster, Dennis L. *First Class: An Introduction to Travel and Tourism.* New York: Glencoe/McGraw-Hill, 1990.

Fuson, Robert. *Fundamental Place-Name Geography,* 6th ed. Dubuque, IA: Wm. C. Brown Co., 1988.

Gee, Chuck Y., Choy, Dexter J.L., and Makens, James C. *The Travel Industry,* 2nd ed. New York: Van Nostrand Reinhold, 1988.

Gold, Hal. *The Cruise Book: From Brochure to Bon Voyage.* Albany, NY: Delmar Publishers, Inc., 1990.

Gray, William S., and Liguori, Salvatore C. *Hotel and Motel Management and Operations,* 2nd ed. Englewood Cliffs, NJ: Prentice-Hall, 1990.

Gregory, Aryear. *The Travel Agent—Dealer in Dreams,* 3rd ed. Elmsford, NY: National Publishers of the Black Hills, 1989.

Gunn, Clare A. *Tourism Planning,* 2nd ed. New York: Crane Russiak, 1988.

Harrison, David. *Tourism and the Less Developed Countries.* New York: John Wiley and Sons, 1993.

Howell, David W. *Passport: An Introduction to the Travel and Tourism Industry,* 2nd ed. Cincinnati, OH: South-Western Publishing Co., 1993.

Howell, David W. *Discovering Destinations: Geography for Travel and Tourism,* 2nd ed. Elmsford, NY: National Publishers of the Black Hills, 1987.

Howell, David W. *Principles and Methods of Scheduling Reservations,* 2nd ed. Elmsford, NY: National Publishers of the Black Hills, 1987.

Hudman, Lloyd E., and Jackson, Richard. *Geography of Travel and Tourism,* 2nd ed. Albany, NY: Delmar Publishers Inc., 1994.

Hudman, Lloyd E., and Hawkins, Donald E. *Tourism in Contemporary Society: An Introductory Text.* Englewood Cliffs, NJ: Prentice-Hall, 1989.

Hyndman, Louis D., Chairman. *Getting There* (Interim Report of the Royal Commission on National Passenger Transportation). Ottawa: Ministry of Supply and Services, 1991.

Jedrziewski, David R. *The Complete Guide for the Meeting Planner.* Cincinnati, OH: South-Western Publishing Co., 1991.

Johnson, H. Webster, and Faria, Anthony J. *Creative Selling*, 4th ed. Cincinnati, OH: South-Western Publishing Co., 1987.

Lundberg, Donald E., and Lundberg, Carolyn B., *International Travel and Tourism*, 2nd ed., New York: John Wiley and Sons, 1993.

McIntosh, Robert W., Goeldner, Charles R., and Ritchie, J.R. Brent. *Tourism: Principles, Practices, Philosophies*, 7th ed. New York: John Wiley and Sons, 1994.

Mancini, Marc. *Conducting Tours: A Practical Guide.* Cincinnati, OH: South-Western Publishing Co., 1990.

Mancini, Marc. *Selling Destinations: Geography for the Travel Professional.* Cincinnati, OH: South-Western Publishing Co., 1992.

Mill, Robert Christie. *Tourism: The International Business.* Englewood Cliffs, NJ: Prentice-Hall, 1990.

Mohan, Marilyn, and Gisiason, Gordon. *Tourism-Related Employment in Canada.* Ottawa: Industry, Science and Technology Canada, 1992.

Notturno, Francis, and Russ, Frederick. *Effective Selling*, 8th ed. Cincinnati, OH: South-Western Publishing Co., 1990.

Nykiel, Ronald A. *Marketing in the Hospitality Industry*, 2nd ed. New York: Van Nostrand Reinhold, 1988.

Nylen, David W. *Advertising: Planning, Implementation, and Control*, 3rd ed. Cincinnati, OH: South-Western Publishing Co., 1986.

Page, Stephen. *Urban Tourism.* New York: Routledge, 1995.

Page, Stephen. *Transport for Tourism.* New York: Routledge, 1994.

Pearce, Douglas, and Butler, Richard. *Tourism Research.* New York: Routledge, 1993.

Plog, Stanley. *Leisure Travel: Making It A Growth Market … Again!* New York: John Wiley and Sons, 1991.

Powers, Thomas E. *Introduction to Management in the Hospitality Industry*, 4th ed. New York: John Wiley and Sons, 1992.

Powers, Thomas E. *Introduction to the Hospitality Industry*, 2nd ed. New York: John Wiley and Sons, 1992.

Powers, Thomas E. *Marketing Hospitality.* New York: John Wiley and Sons, 1990.

Prentice, Richard. *Tourism and Heritage Attractions.* New York: Routledge, 1993.

Reilly, Robert T. *Travel and Tourism Marketing Techniques.* Albany, NY: Merton House/Delmar, 1988.

Ritchie, J.R. Brent, and Goeldner, Charles R., eds. *Travel, Tourism, and Hospitality Research.* New York: John Wiley and Sons, 1994.

Rubin, Karen. *Flying High in Travel: A Complete Guide to Careers in the Travel Industry*, rev. ed. New York: John Wiley and Sons, 1992.

Sebo, Roberta. *The Traveler's World: Destination Geography.* Cincinnati, OH: South-Western Publishing Co., 1991.

Smith, Valene L., ed. *Hosts and Guests: The Anthropology of Tourism*, rev. ed. Philadelphia: University of Pennsylvania Press, 1989.

Starr, Nona. *Travel Career Development*, 4th ed. Wellesley, MA: Institute of Certified Travel Agents, 1990.

Tourism's Top Twenty: Fast Facts on Travel and Tourism. Boulder, CO: University of Colorado, 1987.

Travel Industry World Yearbook: The Big Picture. New York: Childs and Waters, Inc., 1990.

Wagner, Paula E. *Communicating with SABRE.* Cincinnati, OH: South-Western Publishing Co., 1988.

Weissinger, Suzanne S. *Hotel/Motel Operations: An Overview.* Cincinnati, OH: South-Western Publishing Co., 1989.

Wells, Alexander T. *Air Transportation: A Management Perspective*, 2nd ed. Belmont, CA: Wadsworth Publishing Co., 1989.

Wheatcroft, Stephen. *Aviation and Tourism Policies: Balancing the Benefits.* New York: Routledge, 1994.

Zedlitz, Robert H. *Getting a Job in the Travel Industry.* Cincinnati, OH: South-Western Publishing Co., 1990.

PERIODICALS

Advertising Age, Crain Communications Inc., 220 East 42nd Street, New York, NY 10017–5806.

Adweek, ASM Communications, 49 East 21st Street, New York, NY 10010.

Agent Canada, 1534 West 2nd Street, Suite 300, Vancouver, BC V6E 2S3.

Airline Executive, Communication Channels Inc., 6255 Barfield Road, Atlanta, GA 30328–4369.

Airport Pocket Guide, A M Data Services, Inc., 67 South Bedford Street, Suite 400W, Burlington, MA 01803.

Amusement Business, Box 24970, 49 Music Square West, Nashville, TN 37202.

Annals of Tourism Research, Pergamon Press (Journals Division), Maxwell House, Fairview Park, Elmsford, NY 10523.

Association Meetings, Laux Co., Inc., 63 Great Road, Maynard, MA 01754.

ASTA Agency Management, American Society of Travel Agents, Yankee Publications, 666 Fifth Avenue, New York, NY 10103.

ASTA Notes, American Society of Travel Agents, 1101 King Street, Alexandria, VA 22314.

Auto Rental News, Bobit Publishing Company, 2512 Artesia Boulevard, Redondo Beach, CA 90278.

Automation News, Grant Publications, 450 Park Avenue, Suite 2702, New York, NY 10022–2605.

Aviation and Aerospace, Baxter Publications, 310 Dupont Street, Toronto, ON M5R 1V9.

Aviation Week and Space Technology, McGraw-Hill, 1221 Avenue of the Americas, New York, NY 10020.

Beautiful British Columbia, 929 Ellery Street, Victoria, BC V9A 7B4.

Business Flyer, Holcon, Box 276, Newton Center, MA 02159.

Business Travel News, CMP Publications Inc., 600 Community Drive, Manhasset, NY 11030.

Business Travel Review, National Business Travel Association, 1650 King Street, Suite 301, Alexandria, VA 22314–2747.

Business Traveler's Airport Hotel Directory, National Association of Business Travel Agents, 3255 Wilshire Boulevard, Suite 1514, Los Angeles, CA 90010.

Business Traveler's Newsletter, Runzheimer International, Runzheimer Park, Rochester, WI 53167.

Bus Ride, Friendship Publications Inc., Box 1472, Spokane, WA 99210–1472.

Canadian Geographic, 39 McArthur Avenue, Vanier, ON K1L 8L7.

Inflight, Inside Guide Magazine Ltd., 300–199 Avenue Road, Toronto, ON M5R 2J3.

Canadian Travel Press, Baxter Publications, 310 Dupont Street, Toronto, ON M5R 1V9.

Canadian Hotel & Restaurant, 777 Bay Street, Toronto, ON M5W 1A7.

Canadian Yachting, Kesswil Publications Ltd., 395 Matheson Boulevard East, Mississauga, ON L4Z 2H2.

Commuter Air Communications Channels Inc., 6255 Barfield Road, Atlanta, GA 30328–4369.

Condé Nast Traveler, Condé Nast Publications, 360 Madison Avenue, New York, NY 10017.

Consumer Reports Travel Letter, Consumers Union of the United States, Inc., 256 Washington Street, Mount Vernon, NY 10553–1017.

Cornell Hotel and Restaurant Quarterly, Cornell University, School of Hotel Administration, Ithaca, NY 14853.

Corporate and Incentive Travel, Coastal Communications Corporation, 488 Madison Avenue, New York, NY 10022.

Corporate Travel, Gralla Publications, 1515 Broadway, New York, NY 10036.

Courier: Official Magazine of the National Tour Association, National Tour Association, P.O. Box 3071, 546 East Main Street, Lexington, KY 40596–3071.

Cruise Digest, Box 886, FDR Station, New York, NY 10150–0886.

Cruise Travel, World Publishing Company, 990 Grove Street, Evanston, IL 60201.

EnRoute, Airmedia Division, Southam Inc., 150 John Street, Suite 900, Toronto, ON M5V 3E3.

Entree, Entree Travel, 1470 East Valley Road, Suite W, Santa Barbara, CA 93108.

Family Motor Coaching, Family Motor Coach Association, 8291 Clough Pike, Cincinnati, OH 45224.

Flying, D C 1, Inc., 1633 Broadway, New York, NY 10009.

Fodor's Canada: The Complete Guide to Cities, Parks, and Outdoor Adventures. Toronto: Random House of Canada, 1994.

Go Greyhound, Greyhound Corporation, Greyhound Tower, Phoenix, AZ 85077.

Group Travel, 425 Harris, St-Laurent, PQ H4N 2G8.

Hotel and Motel Management, Edgell Communications, 7500 Old Oak Boulevard, Cleveland, OH 44130.

Hotels, Cahners Publishing Company, 1350 East Touhy Avenue, Des Plaines, IL 60017–5080.

ICTA News, Institute of Certified Travel Agents, P.O. Box 82-56, 148 Linden Street, Wellesley, MA 02181.

Incentive, Bill Communications Inc., 633 Third Avenue, New York, NY 10017.

Introduction to Successful Cruise Selling, CLIA, 500 Fifth Avenue, Suite 1407, New York, NY 10110.

Jax Fax Travel Marketing, Jet Airtransport Exchange, 280 Tokeneke Road, Darien, CT 06820.

Lodging, American Hotel and Motel Association, 1201 New York Avenue NW, Suite 600, Washington, DC 20005-3917.

APPENDIX C: Travel and Tourism Publications

Lodging Hospitality, Penton Publishing, 1100 Superior Avenue, Cleveland, OH 44114.

Marketing News, American Marketing Association, 250 South Wacker Drive, Suite 200, Chicago, IL 60606.

Mass Transit, PTN Publishing Corporation, 210 Crossways Park Drive, Woodbury, NY 11797.

Meeting News, Gralla Publications, 1515 Broadway, New York, NY 10036.

Meeting Planners Guidebook, M P G Productions, 6 Morton Court, Suite C, Mill Valley, CA 94941.

Meetings and Conventions, Reed Travel Group, 500 Plaza Drive, Secaucus, NJ 07096.

Meetings and Incentive Travel, Maclean-Hunter Ltd., Maclean-Hunter Building, 777 Bay Street, Toronto, ON, M5W 1A7.

MLD Canadian Traveller, Suite 210, 1015 Burrard Street, Vancouver, BC V6Z 1Y5.

National Geographic, National Geographic Society, 17th and M Streets NW, Washington, DC 20036.

OAG Frequent Flyer, Official Airline Guides, Inc., Dun and Bradstreet, 888 Seventh Avenue, New York, NY 10016.

OAG Pocket Flight Guides, Official Airline Guides, Inc., 2000 Clearwater Drive, Oak Brook, IL 60521.

Passenger Transport, American Public Transportation Association, 1201 New York Avenue NW, Washington, DC 20005.

Premium Incentive Business, Gralla Publications, 1515 Broadway, New York, NY 10036.

Progressive Railroading, Murphy-Richter Publishing Company, 2 North Riverside Plaza, Room 2115, Chicago, IL 60606.

Public Relations News, 127 East 80th Street, New York, NY 10021.

Recreation Executive Report, Leisure Industry-Recreation News, Box 43563, Washington, DC 20010.

Resort and Hotel Management, Source Communications, Inc., Del Mar, CA 92014.

RV Business, 29901 Agoura Road, Agoura, CA 91301.

Sailing Canada, 95 Berkeley Street, Toronto, ON M5A 2W8.

Sales and Marketing Management, Bill Communications Inc., 633 Third Avenue, New York, NY 10017.

Ski Canada, 19 Albany Drive, Toronto, ON M5R 3C2.

Specialty Advertising Business, Specialty Advertising Association International, Walnut Hill Lane, Irving, TX 75038.

Successful Meetings, Bill Communications Inc., 633 Third Avenue, New York, NY 10017.

The Tourism Intelligence Bulletin, Tourism Canada, 235 Queen Street, 4th Floor, Ottawa, ON K1A 0H6.

Touring & Travel, Groupmark Canada Ltd., 480 University Avenue, Suite 1100, Toronto, ON M5G 1V2.

Tradeshow Week, 12333 West Olympic Boulevard, Suite 236, Los Angeles, CA 90064–9956.

Trailer Life, T L Enterprises, Inc., 29901 Agoura Road, Agoura, CA 91301.

Training, International Association of Conference Centers, Lakewood Publications, Inc., 900 South Highway Drive, Fenton, MO 63026.

Travel Age East, OAG Publications Inc., 888 Seventh Avenue, New York, NY 10106.

Travel Age Mid-America, Official Airline Guides, Inc., 320 North Michigan Avenue, Suite 601, Chicago, IL 60601–5901.

Travel Age West, OAG Publications Inc., 100 Grant Avenue, San Francisco, CA 94108.

The Travel Agent, American Traveler, Inc., 825 Seventh Avenue, New York, NY 10019.

Travel and Leisure, American Express Publishing Company, 1120 Avenue of the Americas, New York, NY 10036.

Travel Destination Canada, Royal Life Centre, 288 Lakeshore Road E., Oakville, ON L6L 6L9.

Travel-Holiday, Reader's Digest Association, Inc., Pleasantville, NY 10570.

Travelling on Business, Royal Life Centre, 288 Lakeshore Road E., Oakville, ON L6L 6L9.

Travel-Log, Publications Division, Statistics Canada, Ottawa, ON K1A 0T6.

Travel Trade Canada, 1015 Burrard Street, Suite 210, Vancouver, BC V6Z 1Y5.

Travel Trade, Travel Trade Publishing Company, 6 East 46th Street, New York, NY 10017.

Travelweek Bulletin, 553 Church Street, Toronto, ON M4Y 3E2.

Travel Weekly, Reed Travel Group, 500 Plaza Drive, Secaucus, NJ 07096.

Voyageur, Publications Vacance Québec, 575 Arago, W., Quebec City, PQ G1N 2M4.

APPENDIX C: Travel and Tourism Publications

INDUSTRIAL SOURCES

Airlines

ABC Air Travel Atlas, Reed Travel Group, Reed International Place, Church Street, Dunstable, Bedfordshire LU 4HB, U.K.

ABC Executive Flight Planner, Reed Travel Group, Reed International Place, Church Street, Dunstable, Bedfordshire LU 4HB, U.K.

The Air Charter Guide, 55B Reservoir Street, Cambridge, MA 02138.

ATPCO Passenger Tariff set, Airline Tariff Publishing Company, Washington-Dulles International Airport, P.O. Box 17415, Washington, DC 20041.

IATA/ATAC Travel Agent's Handbook (1994), International Air Transport Association, 2000 Peel Street, Montreal, PQ H3A 2R4.

IATA Ticketing Handbook—International Air Tariffs, International Air Transport Association, 2000 Peel Street, Montreal, PQ H3A 2R4.

The Industry Agents Handbook, Airline Reporting Corporation, 1709 New York Avenue NW, Washington, DC 20006.

Official Airline Guide—North American Edition and *Official Airline Guide—Worldwide Edition*, Official Airline Guides Inc., 2000 Clearwater Drive, Oak Brook, IL 60521.

Cruises

ABC Passenger Shipping Guide, Reed Travel Group, Reed International Place, Church Street, Dunstable, Bedfordshire LU 4HB, U.K.

CLIA Cruise Manual, CLIA, 500 Fifth Avenue, New York, NY 10010.

Ford's Deck Plan Guide, Ford's Travel Guides, 19448 Londelius Street, Northridge, CA 91324.

Ford's Freighter Travel Guide, Ford's Travel Guides, 19448 Londelius Street, Northridge, CA 91324.

Ford's International Cruise Guide, Ford's Travel Guides, 19448 Londelius Street, Northridge, CA 91324.

Garth's Profile of Ships, Cruising with Garth, P.O. Box 34697, Omaha, NE 68134.

Official Steamship Guide International, Transportation Guides Inc., 111 Cherry Street, New Canaan, CT 06840.

Surface Travel

ABC Rail Guide, ABC Star Service, Reed Travel Group, Reed International Place, Church Street, Dunstable, Bedfordshire LU 4HB, U.K.

American Sightseeing International Worldwide Tour Planning Manual, American Sightseeing International, 211 East 43rd Street, New York, NY 10017.

Amtrak Sales Guide, Amtrak, 60 Massachusetts Avenue NE, Washington, DC 20002.

Consolidated Tour Manual, 11510 Northeast Second Avenue, Miami, FL 33161.

Gray Line Sightseeing Sales and Tour Guide, Gray Line Worldwide, 13760 Noel Road, Dallas, TX 75240.

Official Railway Guide—North American Edition, Thompson Transport Press, 424 West 33rd Street, New York, NY 10001.

Official Tour Directory, Thomas Publishing Company, 5 Penn Plaza, New York, NY 10001.

Russell's Official National Motorcoach Guide, Russell's Guides Inc., 834 Third Avenue SE, Box 278, Cedar Rapids, IA 52403.

Thomas Cook European Timetable and *Thomas Cook Overseas Timetable*, Thomas Cook Ltd., P.O. Box 36, Peterborough PE3 6SB, U.K.

Worldwide Travel Planner, Wineberg Publications, 7842 North Lincoln Avenue, Skokie, IL 60077.

Hotels/Motels, Meetings, and Conventions

ABC Star Service, Reed Travel Group, Reed International Place, Church Street, Dunstable, Bedfordshire LU 4HB, U.K.

Directory of Conventions, Successful Meetings, Directory Department, 633 Third Avenue, New York, NY 10017.

Hotel and Travel Index, Reed Travel Group, 500 Plaza Drive, Secaucus, NJ 07096.

International Youth Hostels Handbook, A H Y, Inc., Box 37613, Washington, DC 20013–7613.

OAG Travel Planners Hotel and Motel Redbook—European, North American, and Pacific Asia editions, Official Airline Guides Inc., 2000 Clearwater Drive, Oak Brook, IL 60521.

APPENDIX C: Travel and Tourism Publications

Official Hotel Guide, Reed Travel Group, 500 Plaza Drive, Secaucus, NJ 07096.

Official Meeting Facilities Guide, Reed Travel Group, 500 Plaza Drive, Secaucus, NJ 07096.

Star Service, Reed Travel Group, 131 Clarendon Street, Boston, MA 02116.

TOURISM CANADA

Tourism Canada publishes several reports, some of them annually. Please request the Tourism Information Directory from Industry Canada, 235 Queen Street, Ottawa, ON K1A 0H5.

APPENDIX D

Occupational Titles in Travel and Tourism

Airline baggage and freight handler
Airline instrument technician
Airline mechanic
Airline meteorologist
Airline pilot
Airline reservations agent
Airline ticket agent
Airplane safety inspector
Airport manager
Airport operations agent
Association executive
Baggage porter
Business travel agent
Bus mechanic
Bus sales representative
Bus ticket agent
Bus tour representative
Cabin steward
Captain
Car maintenance/service worker
Car reservations agent
Chef
Civil engineer
Concession vendor
Concierge
Conductor
Convention planner
Cook
Cruise director
Cruise line reservations agent
Cruise office salesperson
Cruise operational officer
Destination developer
Dining room steward
Engineer
Environmentalist
Exposition manager
Fitness instructor
Fixed-base operator
Fleet service clerk
Flight attendant
Flight engineer
Food and beverage manager
Forest ranger
Freight airport agent
Front desk manager
Golf course supervisor
Graphic artist
Groom
Historic-site supervisor
Hotel bellstaff
Hotel cashier
Hotel comptroller
Hotel desk clerk
Hotel director of catering
Hotel director of personnel
Hotel engineer
Hotel executive housekeeper
Hotel houseworker
Hotel information clerk
Hotel manager
Hotel valet
Hunting and fishing guide
Inbound tour operator
Incentive tour planner
Landscape architect
Layout artist
Lifeguard
Limousine driver
Local transit driver
Marina worker
Market analyst
Meeting planner
Museum curator
Museum director
Museum worker
Outbound tour operator
Outside sales representative
Package tour dealer
Passenger service agent
Pastry chef and baker
Photographer
Provincial tourism department clerk
Provincial tourism department worker
Publications representative
Purser
Railway reservations clerk
Receptive operator
Restaurant host and hostess
Restaurant manager
Restaurant steward
Sales agent
Sales representative
Server
Ship engineer
Ship purser
Social director at a resort
Sociologist
Stadium manager
Stadium worker
Subway driver
Subway operator
Surveyor
Taxi driver
Theme park worker
Ticket taker
Tour creator
Tour distributor
Tour escort
Tour guide
Tour manager
Tour operator
Tour operator reservationist
Tour organizer
Translator
Transportation engineer
Travel agency manager
Travel agency owner
Travel agency receptionist
Travel agent
Travel club director
Travel journalist
Wholesale tour packager
Wildlife manager
Zoo administrator
Zoo caretaker
Zoologist

GLOSSARY

advertising The use of paid media space or time to promote a product.

affinity charter A private charter for members of an organization who are bound together by a common interest.

airport limousine A privately operated bus, van, or extended car that provides passenger service between airports and city centres.

air report An accounting of a travel agency's weekly sales of airline tickets.

à la carte A meal choice from a complete menu, regardless of price.

all-inclusive package A vacation package in which the traveller pays one price that covers almost all trip expenses, including transportation, accommodations, meals, and sightseeing.

allocentric personality According to Stanley Plog, a type of personality that seeks adventure, variety, and excitement.

all-suite A type of hotel that offers units which include a living room and kitchen as well as a bedroom.

American Plan (AP) A hotel rate that includes the room and continental or full breakfast, lunch, and dinner.

Area Settlement Plan A system whereby a specific bank handles all the transactions involved in the sale of airline tickets by travel agents.

area tour A tour that spends a limited amount of time in several countries.

association executive A full-time professional administrator who is employed by an association and is responsible for planning and promoting annual conventions and association meetings.

atrium An architectural feature consisting of a roof-high central lobby courtyard.

attraction A natural or constructed feature that attracts tourists.

automated ticketing machine (ATM) A self-service machine that provides customers with flight information, reservations, tickets, and boarding passes.

back office system A computer system used for behind-the-scenes business operations.

bed-and-breakfast Lodging that provides a room, full breakfast, and a shared bathroom.

berth A sleeping place within a cabin.

bias The preferential display on a CRS of host-carrier flight schedules.

booth The display space rented by a vendor at an exhibition.

break-even point The point at which total revenues equal total operating costs.

breakout A term used to describe small-group meetings that are held as part of a general convention.

BritRail Pass A pass used for train travel in Great Britain.

business class An airplane seating section designed to satisfy the needs of the business traveller.

business travel department (BTD) The department in a corporation that handles travel arrangements for the corporation's employees.

cargo terminal One or more separate buildings at an airport where mail or freight is processed.

carrying capacity The amount of tourism a destination can handle.

charter (1) To hire an airplane, bus, or ship for group travel, usually at lower rates than regularly scheduled transportation. (2) The purchase of the use of transportation equipment at a cut price.

charter airline See *supplemental airline*.

charter tour A tour taken by a club, organization, or other preformed group.

circle trip A type of round-trip journey in which the return journey differs from the outbound journey in terms of routing or class of service.

city package tour A tour that is similar to an independent package tour, but visits only one city.

clinic A small group session of drills and instructions in specific skills.

code sharing An agreement between a major airline and a small regional airline, under which the small airline flies under the larger company's code.

co-host An airline that does not own its own CRS but that shares a database with a host vendor.

cold call A personal sales visit to a prospective client, made without any advance warning.

commercial recreation system Recreational products, services, and facilities created and operated by privately owned small businesses or large corporations.

commission The percentage of a selling price paid to a retailer by a supplier.

common carrier A privately owned air carrier offering public transportation of passengers, cargo, and mail.

compact An average-size car.

competitive marketing decision The decision by the American Civil Aeronautics Board to open up the travel industry to new channels of distribution.

computer reservations system (CRS) A computer system that provides information on schedules, seat availability, and fares, and permits travel agents to make reservations and print itineraries and tickets.

concession A private business that operates at a public recreation facility.

concierge A hotel employee who handles restaurant and tour reservations, travel arrangements, and other details for hotel guests.

conference A large meeting convened to deal with a specific problem or development.

conference-appointment system A system whereby regulatory bodies formulate standards for acceptance of new travel agencies and discipline existing agencies.

configuration An airplane seating arrangement.

congress An international gathering, similar to a conference.

consortium A group of independent firms that band together to pool their financial and company resources.

consulate A branch office of an embassy that is located in a major city other than a capital.

Continental Plan (CP) A hotel rate that includes the room and a continental breakfast.

control tower A tower from which air traffic controllers direct planes in the air and on the ground.

convention A meeting involving a general group session followed by committee meetings in breakout rooms.

convention and visitors' bureau (CVB) An organization that promotes travel to the city it represents and assists in servicing conventions and trade shows held in the city.

convention hotel A hotel that caters to large group gatherings.

convention tour A tour for members of an association or group attending such events as conventions, trade shows, or conferences.

co-op advertising Advertising that promotes and is sponsored by two or more companies.

cooperative A group of independent travel agencies formed temporarily out of a joint interest in promoting a product or event.

corporate rate A reduced room rate that hotels offer employees of large companies.

couchette A sleeping bunk in a second-class train compartment.

cross-adoption A process by which local residents adopt tourists' values and tourists adopt values of the countries that they visit.

customs The government regulation of goods that enter and leave a country.

deluxe A large luxury car, usually equipped with many amenities.

demographics Statistics and facts, such as age, sex, marital status, occupation, and income, that describe a human population.

demonstration effect The tendency of local people to adopt practices and consumption patterns of tourists visiting their region.

departure tax A tax that visitors to a country must pay when they leave that country.

deregulation Removal of government control over the operation of an industry.

destination A location that travellers choose to visit and where they spend time.

destination management company (DMC) A company that provides on-the-scene meetings assistance for corporations and associations.

dine-around plan A plan that permits tourists to dine at a variety of restaurants using vouchers and coupons.

directional advertising Advertising in directories and other sources that customers seek out.

direct spending Money that goes directly from a tourist into the economy of the destination.

discretionary travel Travel undertaken voluntarily or by choice.

documentation Government-issued papers used to identify travellers.

Domestic Independent Tour (DIT) A custom-made tour of a part of Canada planned exclusively for a client by a travel agent.

double occupancy Hotel accommodations for two people who share a room.

drop-off charge A fee charged for dropping a rental car at a different location than the one where it was picked up.

duty A tax paid on items purchased abroad.

duty free A term used to describe overseas purchases that are exempt from taxes.

eco-tourism A type of tourism in which vacationers travel to unusual places to observe ecological systems and endangered species in their natural habitat.

electronic flight information system (EFIS) State-of-the-art technology in the cockpit of newer aircraft; it replaces the dials and gauges found in older planes.

electronic ticket delivery network (ETDN) A ticket printer that is similar to an STP but owned by an outside vendor rather than a travel agency.

embarkation The boarding of passengers onto a ship, plane, train, etc.

embassy The official residence of an ambassador representing his or her country in a foreign capital.

escorted tour An organized tour led by a professional tour manager.

Eurailpass A pass that allows unlimited train travel throughout certain European countries.

European Plan (EP) A hotel rate that includes the room only and no meals.

event An occurrence that attracts tourists.

exhibition A display of goods and services staged as part of a convention or conference.

family plan A hotel rate that allows children to share their parents' room at no extra cost.

FAM trip A familiarization trip for travel professionals to inspect hotels and restaurants, sample attractions, and experience local culture.

fare construction The process of computing international airfares.

fixed-base operator (FBO) A company that rents space at an airport and that provides a particular service.

flag carrier A national airline representing an individual nation.

flag of convenience A flag flown by a ship of one nation that is registered under the flag of another nation.

fly/cruise package A vacation package that includes the air transportation to the port of embarkation and the cruise itself.

fly/drive package A vacation package that includes air transportation and rental car use.

foreign flag A term for any carrier registered in a nation other than Canada.

Foreign Independent Tour (FIT) An international tour planned exclusively for a client by a travel agent.

forum A meeting involving discussion on a specific issue, usually led by panellists and involving audience participation.

franchise A contract between a company owner and an established chain under which the owner pays a fee to operate the company under the chain name.

free enterprise system A system that permits competition among privately owned businesses with a minimum of government interference.

free upgrade A switch to a higher class of service or product, for which no charge is made.

frequent-flier program A program that awards travellers free travel, discounts, and upgrades for flying a certain number of miles on a single airline.

frequent-stay program A program that awards discounts and other incentives to customers who use a particular hotel chain frequently.

gateway airport An airport that services international flights.

gross registered tonnage (GRT) A number representing the amount of enclosed space on a ship.

hangar A place where airplanes are stored and repaired.

hosted tour A tour whose members are assisted by a host, who arranges optional excursions and answers questions.

host vendor An airline or other organization that owns and operates a computer reservations system.

hub-and-spoke route A flight pattern whereby a major airport is the centre point, or hub, for arrivals from and departures to smaller airports that surround it. The smaller airports are considered the rim; the connecting flights the spokes.

hypersonic A term used to describe transportation that can travel at five or more times the speed of sound.

inbound tourism Vacation and leisure travel to Canada from overseas.

incentive tour A tour offered by companies to employees as a reward for achieving a corporate goal.

incoming tour A tour that originates in a foreign country and has Canada as its destination.

independent package tour A tour that visits several cities or places of interest on regular scheduled buses.

indirect spending Money that is spent initially by a tourist and then respent within the destination.

industry A group of businesses or corporations that provide a product or service for profit.

infrastructure The basic facilities of a site, such as local roads, sewage system, electricity, and water supply.

inside cabin A ship's cabin that has no access to natural light and faces a central passageway.

inside sales Sales efforts conducted within the employer's office.

intangible A term used to describe a product that is experienced rather than seen or touched, such as an airplane flight, a family reunion, or an ocean vista.

interface To work together. Used to describe computer reservations systems that can transmit information to and receive information from each other.

interline connection A flight during which the passenger changes both airplanes and airlines.

interlining The use of one standard type of airline ticket that is recognized and honoured by all scheduled airlines.

intermediary A person or company that acts as a link between the producer of a product or service and the consumer of that product or service.

intermodal package A vacation package that includes more than one form of transportation.

intermodal tour A motorcoach tour that ties in with other forms of transportation, such as airline service or cruise line transportation.

International Certificate of Vaccination A certificate that lists the immunizations that a traveller has received.

interpretation The process of educating visitors to national parks and other recreation facilities through the use of marked trails, signs, and so on.

intrusive advertising Advertising that forces itself upon the consumer's attention with a persuasive message.

itinerary A planned route for a trip.

IT number A registration number that is assigned to a tour package.

joint venture A business partnership between two companies, two individuals, or a company and an individual.

junket An all-expenses-paid trip.

kilometre cap A car rental plan that allows clients a certain number of free kilometres each day and charges an extra fee for each additional kilometre driven.

land/cruise package A vacation package that includes a cruise and hotel accommodations at or near the port of embarkation.

leakage The amount of income that flows out of a local economy to purchase outside resources needed to generate that income.

lecture A formal presentation in which an expert addresses the audience from a platform.

leisure The time people use to engage in pleasurable and relaxing activities.

lighter See *tender*.

light-rail transit Trolley car.

limousine A privately owned and operated chauffeur-driven car, often hired for special occasions or for business purposes.

linear route A flight pattern in which an airplane flies to its destination in one direction, turns around, and repeats the flight in the opposite direction.

liner An oceangoing passenger vessel that runs over a fixed route and on a fixed schedule.

loading apron A parking area at an airport terminal where the airplane is refuelled, loaded, and boarded.

local tour A tour that is marketed to a local group or organization.

loss/damage waiver (LDW) An option offered by car rental firms that relieves clients of their liability for an initial amount of damage to a rental car; it also provides coverage for loss of the use of the rental car should an accident occur.

magrodome A sliding roof on a cruise ship that is used to cover a deck area in bad weather.

management contract An agreement under which one company owns a property and pays a management fee to a chain to operate the property.

GLOSSARY

manifest A passenger list.

maritime Any type of transportation that crosses water, such as ocean cruise liners, river ferries, and harbour cruises.

marketing The promotional activities that bring buyers and sellers together.

market price The average price consumers are willing to pay for a product based on supply and demand.

market research The gathering and analysing of information about products and consumers.

market segmentation The concept of dividing a market into different parts.

mart Marketplace.

mass transit The movement of people in large metropolitan areas, usually via buses, subways, and taxis.

mega-agency A large travel agency with branch offices in many cities, primarily interested in multimillion-dollar corporate accounts.

megamall A vast indoor shopping and entertainment complex consisting of hundreds of shops and restaurants.

midcentric personality According to Stanley Plog, a type of personality that enjoys the experience of travelling but that tends to travel to familiar destinations.

model culture A facility in which the houses, artifacts, and way of life of another age or nation are displayed.

Modified American Plan (MAP) A hotel rate that includes the room and continental breakfast or full breakfast and dinner.

monorail An elevated urban transit system that runs on one rail.

motel A type of accommodation, usually built near a highway and catering to motorists.

motorcoach A bus that provides transportation between cities.

motor hotel A hotel catering primarily to motorists, and usually located in a downtown area or near an airport. Also known as a motor inn.

motor inn See *motor hotel*.

nationalize To bring an industry under the control of the federal government.

nationwide tour A tour that is promoted and sold to people throughout the nation.

new-entrant carrier Any one of the airlines that came into business after the deregulation of the airlines.

nondiscretionary travel Travel undertaken out of necessity, such as business or professional travel.

no-show A person who makes a reservation but fails to use it.

oceanarium A type of aquarium that features saltwater animals.

off-site meeting A meeting held at a location other than the sponsoring company's premises.

on-demand public transportation Those transportation services, such as taxis and limousines, that don't have regular schedules; passengers arrange individually for service.

one-way trip A journey that begins in one city and ends in another.

on-line connection A flight during which the passenger changes airplanes but remains on the same airline.

open-jaw trip An air journey interrupted by surface travel, or a flight that has a return destination other than the originating city.

outside cabin A ship's cabin that has a porthole or window and a view of the ocean.

outside sales Sales efforts that involve personal calls by the sales staff on prospective accounts.

overbook To sell more seats or rooms than are available.

override A financial incentive paid by a supplier to a retailer to encourage high-volume sales.

package A combination of various travel components, which are sold as a single product.

package tour A combination of several travel components provided by different suppliers, which are sold to the consumer as a single product at a single price.

panel A meeting in which at least two speakers give their points of view on a particular subject, followed by discussion among the speakers and the audience.

parador A Spanish castle or historic building that has been converted into a hotel.

pari-mutuel betting Betting on the first three places of horse or dog races or jai alai tournaments.

parity product A product that is similar to other products offered by other producers.

passenger name record (PNR) A record of a passenger's travel arrangements that is stored in a CRS.

passport A document, issued by a government, that enables people to enter a foreign country and to return to their own country.

pension A private home that has been converted into a guest house, found mainly in Europe and Latin America.

per diem A term meaning "by the day," used to indicate the amount of money budgeted each day for travel expenses.

personal accident insurance (PAI) Insurance offered by car rental firms that provides coverage in the case of bodily injury to the client.

point to point Transporting passengers from one destination to another.

port tax Tax paid by passengers on embarkation at any port during a cruise.

posada A Portuguese castle or historic building that has been converted into a hotel.

press conference A conference for the media that is organized by a public relations company to promote that company's client.

press release A document prepared by a public relations company for the media to promote that company's client.

pressurization Artificial increase of air pressure in a jet cabin so that the air pressure is almost equivalent to the air pressure at ground level.

primary research Market research in which product suppliers study consumers' responses to surveys, questionnaires, and interviews.

private charter A charter that is not for sale to the general public.

privatize To transfer control or ownership of an industry from public to private hands.

product life cycle A standard marketing concept that identifies four stages in the life cycle of a product.

proof of citizenship A document, such as an expired passport, birth certificate, or voter registration card, that can be used in lieu of a current passport by travellers entering certain countries.

property In the hospitality industry, any lodging facility, such as a hotel or motel.

psychocentric personality According to Stanley Plog, a type of personality whose thoughts tend to be focused on itself and that tends not to venture far from home.

public charter A charter that is open for sale to the general public, either through a travel agency or by a tour or charter operator.

public recreation system Recreational facilities and events operated by federal, provincial, or local governments, or by nonprofit organizations.

public transportation Organized passenger service available to the general public within a small geographic area.

pure incentive An incentive travel program designed strictly for pleasure.

quad A hotel room that is shared by four people.

rack rate The standard day rate for a hotel room.

rail/sail package A vacation package that includes both train fare and cruise ticket.

rebate Cash returned to a purchaser after a purchase has been made.

receptive operator A travel professional who specializes in arranging tours for visitors from other countries.

recreation The activities that people pursue in their leisure time.

repositioning cruise A cruise organized to transfer a ship from one cruising area to another between seasons.

reregulation The reintroduction of government controls over an industry that has been deregulated.

residential hotel A hotel that caters to guests who are permanent residents.

resort condominium An individually owned residential unit that is under common agreement and is located in a vacation spot.

resort hotel A hotel located in a place where people go to spend a vacation.

rifle approach In advertising, the use of small-circulation media to produce a high percentage of leads.

round trip A journey that begins in one city, goes to another city, and ends in the originating city.

run-of-the-house rate A reduced room rate that hotels offer for block bookings.

runway A strip of land on which airplanes land and from which they take off.

sales incentive An incentive travel program that combines a vacation with scheduled business meetings.

satellite ticket printer (STP) A machine that allows travel agents to deliver tickets electronically to a client's premises.

scheduled airline An airline that offers regular flights that are scheduled to depart and arrive at certain times.

secondary research Market research based on information that has been collected and processed.

seminar An informal meeting in which participants hold discussions under the supervision of a leader.

shotgun approach In advertising, the use of large-circulation media to produce a small percentage of leads.

single-city tour An in-depth tour of an individual city that offers travellers the opportunity to experience that city's culture.

single-country tour A tour of a single country that gives travellers an in-depth view of that country.

single-entity charter A private charter that is paid for in full by a single source.

single supplement Hotel accommodations for a single person in a private room.

site destination selection company A company that investigates and suggests potential meeting sites to suit corporate or association needs.

special-interest group tour A tour for clubs, societies, and organizations whose members share a common interest.

specialty channeller An intermediary, such as an incentive travel company, a meeting/convention planner, or a travel club, that organizes specific kinds of tour packages.

spot A standard length of time used for airing commercials on television and radio.

stabilizer A feature on a ship that minimizes the effects of the ship's side-to-side roll.

stand European term for an exhibitor's booth.

standard A full-size car.

standard ticket stock Airline ticket blanks that are recognized and used throughout the country.

steerage The lowest class of accommodation on board a passenger ship.

stopover An interruption to a trip lasting 12 or more hours.

subcompact A very small car.

subway A rail transportation system that provides local rapid-transit passenger service either wholly or partially underground.

superconductor A substance capable of conducting electricity without losing energy.

supersonic A term used to describe transportation that can travel at between one and five times the speed of sound.

superstructure All the buildings and structures, such as hotels, restaurants, shops, and convention centres, that are built at a tourist destination.

supplemental airline An airline that offers charter flights and other nonscheduled flights. Also called charter airline.

surface transportation Any type of transportation system that runs on the ground; includes buses, rental cars, trains, and taxis.

symposium A formal meeting arranged to discuss a specific issue.

table d'hôte A set three-course meal at a fixed price.

tangible A term used to describe a product that can be seen and touched.

tariff A schedule of fares charged by transportation companies.

taxiway A lane where airplanes travel from the apron to the runway or from the runway to the hangar.

teleconferencing A way of holding a meeting at several locations simultaneously using advanced communications technology that enables participants to see and hear each other.

teleshopping Using a personal computer to obtain flight information and make reservations.

teleticketing The issuing of airline tickets by a machine linked to an airline computer reservations system.

tender A small boat that carries cruise passengers between ship and shore. Also known as a lighter.

TGV A French train that travels at hight speed.

time-sharing Shared ownership of a single condominium unit that each owner can use each year for a specified period of time.

tour guide The leader of a guided tour who possesses in-depth knowledge of an area's attractions.

tourism multiplier A formula used to determine the total income generated from money spent by tourists.

tourist cabin An early form of roadside motel that catered to travelling salespeople.

tourist card A card obtained from a foreign country's embassy or through a travel agency or airline that can be used instead of a passport in some countries.

tourist court An early form of roadside motel that consisted of a group of detached cottages built around a central parking area.

tour manager A person who oversees an escorted tour to make sure that everything runs smoothly.

tour operator A company that contracts with hotels, transportation companies, and other suppliers to create a tour package and then sells that package directly to the consumer.

tour organizer A person who may have little travel expertise and who works with a travel agency and tour operator to organize a specialized tour.

tour wholesaler A company that contracts with hotels, transportation companies, and other suppliers to create a tour package and then sells that package to the consumer through a retail travel agency.

trade fair See *trade show*.

trade show A meeting that features freestanding vendor displays and booths. Also known as a trade fair.

train/drive package A package that includes train transportation as well as automobile transportation.

transfer Any change in transportation in the course of a journey.

transient hotel A hotel that caters to guests who stay for a limited time.

travel management services Services offered by a corporate travel agency to help a client control and monitor its business travel costs.

travel professional A person who has received the specialized training needed to work in the travel industry of today.

trip A journey of at least 40 kilometres from home, excluding commuting to or from work.

triple A hotel room that is shared by three people.

trolley A streetcar that runs on electricity.

two-city tour A tour of two cities, either in the same country or in different countries.

unit In the hospitality industry, a guest bedroom or suite.

unlimited kilometres A car rental plan that allows clients to drive a rental car as far as they want for a flat fee within the allotted rental period.

urban bus A bus that operates over short distances within a city.

vertical marketing The promotion of products or services by several different channels of distribution owned by a single company.

voucher A coupon or document that can be exchanged for a travel product.

video kiosk A booth in which travel consumers can watch promotional videos.

video marketing The use of cable television to promote and sell products and services.

visa A stamp or endorsement issued by a foreign government that is placed in a traveller's passport specifying the conditions for entering the country.

wagon-lit A train coach containing a private sleeping compartment for one or two persons.

wait list A numbering system listing passengers hoping to get a seat on a booked flight.

workshop A small group session of intense study or training that emphasizes an exchange of ideas or demonstration of skills.

youth hostel A facility that offers basic overnight lodging at rock-bottom prices for younger travellers.

INDEX

A
À la carte, 248
Abbreviations, commonly used, 379
ACCESS, 316, 328, 372
ACCESS Certified Travel Manager (ACTM), 328
Accor Group, 273
Action park, 220
ADS (Agency DataSystems), 63
Adventure and academic cruises, 140
Adventure tours, 227, 242-244
Adventure travel agencies, 317
Adventure travellers, 201, 242
Advertising, 338-342. *See also* Marketing, Promotion
    car rental industry, in, 119
    defined, 338
    major media, listed, 338
    necessary leakage, as, 199
    public relations, and, contrasted, 343
    railways, by, 111
    rifle approach to, 338
    shot-gun approach to, 338
    use of frequent flier mailing lists, 269
Affinity charters, 253
Africa, 367
Age, 368
Agricultural fairs, 217
Air Canada
    advertising by, 347
    affiliated carriers, 89, 90
    computer reservation system used by, 59, 319
    executive class service, 336
    national carrier, as, 79, 89
    privatization of, 89
Air Canada Vacations, 239
Air Maritime, 89
Air taxis, 7, 80
Air traffic controllers, 96
Air Transport Association (ATA), 91
Air Transportation Association of Canada (ATAC), 321, 323
Air/sea packages, 143
Airbus, 77
Airbus A310-300, 75
Aircraft
    airbus, 77
    categories of, 80
    civilian, 80
    early airplanes, 73
    engine type, 77
    hypersonic transport, 77, 362
    jet age, 75
    jumbo jet, 77
    national carriers, 79, 89
    supersonic transport (SST), 77
Airline dispatchers, 96
Airline flights
    long-haul flights, 78
    short- to medium-range flights, 78
    short-haul flights, 78
    special purpose flights, 78
Airline Reporting Corporation (ARC), 91, 323, 325
Airline reservation agents, 64, 66, 96
Airline restructuring, 90
Airline routes, 83, 84
Airline service
    business- or executive-class ("Y class"), 93, 268, 336
    first-class ("F class"), 93
    kosher/vegetarian meals, 93
    "R class", 93
Airline ticket agents, 96
Airlines, 7. *See also* Airports, Aircraft
    advertising by, 347
    airfare, 93, 94
    amenities offered after flight, 269
    application for licence, 79
    automated reservation systems, 59–61
    business-class service, 93, 268, 269, 336
    cabin crew, 96
    carriers, types of, 78
    classification systems in Canada, 79
    classification systems in U.S., 78, 79
    cockpit (flight deck) crew, 94, 96
    connecting flight, 92
    corporate discounts, 272
    corporate rebates, 272
    development of industry in Canada, 79
    direct/through service, 92
    distribution of tickets by retail outlets, 52
    employment opportunities, 94-97
    flights. *See* Airline flights
    frequent flier programs, 269, 271
    general office (GO), 97
    history of, 72-77
    hypersonic transport, 77, 362
    information on flight schedules/fares, 54, 55
    international airfare, 93, 94
    international travel by, 85-88
    local/commuter, 79
    nonstop service, 92
    "official carrier", as, 302
    penalties for cancellation, 93
    price increases/decreases, 56
    publications, 390
    regional, 79

regulation of. *See* Regulation of airline industry
regulatory reform, 89, 268, 277, 279, 318
restrictions on travel, 93
route structures, 83, 84
sales office, 97
security at, 84
station manager, 96
stopover, 92
technology, future, 362
traffic conferences, 87
traffic rights, 85
transit rights, 85
types of journeys (trips), 92
vertical marketing, 54
Airport limousines, 121
Airport manager, 96
Airports
   business centres, 270, 272
   car rentals, and, 118
   conference rooms at, 272
   development of hotels at/near, 170
   layout, 82, 83
   location of, 82
   ownership of, 82
   parts of, 83
   special facilities for business travellers, 270, 272
   types, 82
   world's ten busiest, 82
All-inclusive packages, 238, 239, 251
All-suite hotels, 170, 275
Alliance of Canadian Travel Associations (ACTA), 249, 273, 312, 316, 326, 348, 372
Allocentric personality, 31
Allocentric traveller, 194
Altitude sickness, 39
American Airlines Advantage Club, 271
American Bus Association (ABA), 117
American Express, 322
   independent tour operator, as, 239
   mega-agency, as, 278
   origins, 318
   tour packages offered by, 245
   use of glamorous brochures, 57
   vertical marketing, 54
American plan (AP), 172, 248
American Sightseeing International, 116
American Sightseeing International World Tariff, 116
American Society of Association Executives (ASAE), 295
American Society of Travel Agents (ASTA), 326, 327, 348, 371
Amex. *See* American Express
Amish, 202
Amtrak, 64, 107, 108, 111, 112, 274, 321, 323, 347
Amusement parks, 220, 221, 226
Animal curators, 228
Anne Murray Centre, 221

Anne of Green Gables, 42, 195, 222
Anthropologists, 205
APOLLO, 59
Aquariums, 216
Architects, 205
Arctic Edge, 219
Area Settlement Plan (ASP), 325
Area tours, 242
Areas of concern, 361
ARROW, 64
Art museums, 215
Association executives, 295
Association of Conference and Events Directors-International (ACED-I), 295
Association of Retail Agents (ARTA), 327
Associations
   exhibitions, and, 299, 300
   motivations, needs and expectations, 293
   types, 291, 293
Associations and organizations, 381–85
ATAC Traffic Conference, 321
Atlantic City, 226
ATPCO Tariff, 56
Atrium, 163
Attractions, 8
   defined, 211
   events, and contrasted, 8
Attractions/events in Canada, 34. *See also* Canada, Destinations in Canada
   Anne Murray Centre, 221
   Anne's Land, 222
   Calgary Stampede, 217
   Canada's Wonderland, 218
   Canadian National Exhibition (CNE), 216
   Crystal Beach, 220
   Crystal Palace, 220
   Pacific National Exhibition, 216
   West Edmonton Mall, 224
   Woodleigh Replicas, 222
Automated systems of information, 58–62
Automated ticketing machines (ATMs), 52, 62, 365
Automobile Association of America (AAA), 170
Avis, Warren E., 118

B
Back office systems, 63
Baldwin, F.W., 72
Bank Settlement Plan, 323, 325
Baryshnikov, Mikhail, 346
Bates, Paul, 199
Beckley, Michael, 370
Bed-and-breakfast (B&B), 173, 174
Bell, Alexander Graham, 72
Bermuda System, 85, 86
Berths, 147
Best Western, 8
Bias, 61

INDEX

Bilevel distribution system, 52, 53
Billboards, 341
Blass, Bill, 322
Blue Train, 111
Boeing 737, 75
Boeing Company, 76
Boeing, William E., 76
Bombardier Inc. (of Montreal), 109
Bon Voyage Travel Insurance, 43
Books, 386, 387
Booths, 299
Break-even point, 165
Breakout, 290
Brewster Transportation and Tours, 243
Brewster, Jim and Bill, 243
BritRail pass, 110, 111
BritRail Seapass, 110
Broadcast media, 340, 341
Brochures, 342
BSP Manual for Agents, 323
Budget hotels, 275
Budget travel, 43
Bus industry. *See* Motorcoach
Business centres, 270, 271, 276
Business class service, 93, 268, 336
"Business loungers", 268
Business travel, 28, 29, 264-286. *See also* Business Travel Departments (BTDs), Corporations, Meetings and Conventions
   average distance of business trips, 278
   Canadian domestic spending patterns, 266
   characteristics, 266
   destination, choice of, 190
   employment opportunities, 279, 280
   future trends, 358
   growth of, 265, 266
   history of, 264, 265
   last-minute changes to itineraries, 266, 279
   methods used to arrange, 278
   profile of frequent business traveller, 267
   women, by, 35
Business travel departments (BTDs), 8, 9, 326
   car rentals, and, 120
   in-house, 52
   keeping track of travellers' points, 269
   managers of, 280
   overview, 278
   travel agencies, and, contrasted, 8, 9
   use by suppliers, 52

C

Cable cars, 122
Cajuns, 202
Calgary Stampede, 217
Campgrounds, 224
Canada
   age of population, 368
   airline regulation, 88–90
   attractions/events. *See* Attractions/events in Canada
   development of airline industry in, 79
   destinations. *See* Destinations in Canada
   international visitors to, 44
   major conferences, 321
   major convention centres, 289
   major tourist attractions, 34
   most travelled air routes, 80
   northernmost part, 201
   proposed developments, 359, 360
   ranking as global destination, 357
   southernmost part, 201
   travel deficit, 197, 357
   travel to. *See* Inbound tourism
   travel within, 33, 34
Canada 3000, 253
Canada CHRIE, 371
Canadian Airlines, 81
   advertising by, 347
   affiliated carriers, 89, 90
   business class service, 336
   computer reservation system used by, 319
   Empress Lounge system, 270
   frequent flier program, 269
   Mileage Plus, 274
   national carrier, as, 79, 89
   official carrier, as, 302
   Orient Business Card Service, 269
Canadian Automobile Association (CAA), 170
Canadian Bus Association, 117
Canadian Federation of Students (CFS), 43
Canadian Holidays, 239, 2349
Canadian Institute of Travel Counsellors (CITC), 316, 328, 372
Canadian National Exhibition (CNE), 216
Canadian Pacific, 53
Canadian Plus, 269
Canadian provincial and territorial tourism offices, 380
Canadian Society of Association Executives (CSAE), 295
Canadian Tourism Authority (CTA), 359, 360
Canadian Transport Commission (CTC), 88
Canadian travel industry associations, 380, 381
Car rental agent, 124
Car rental industry, 7, 117-120
   business travel, and, 271, 272, 274
   "buy back" programs, 118
   charges, special, 120
   classes of rental cars, 119, 120
   club memberships, 119
   companies, types of, 118
   discounts, 272, 274
   employment opportunities, 123
   fly/drive packages, 118
   foreign travel/companies, 120
   history, 118

makes/models, 119, 120
mobile telephones in cars, 274
off/on airport locations, 118
"official car rental agency", as, 302
qualifications needed to rent cars, 119
rates, 119
reservation agents, 64
reservation systems, 64
reservations, 120
train/drive packages, 118
use of airline computer reservation systems, 120
Car transportation, 103
Career opportunities
airline industry, in, 94–97
business travel, 279, 280
car rental industry, 123
casinos, 229
channels of distribution, in, 66
computer-related, 66
cruise industry, 150
destination development, 204, 205
hospitality industry, 177, 178
hunting and fishing lodges, 229
mass transit, 123
meetings and conventions, 303, 304
motorcoaches, 123
museums, 228
parks and forests, 228
private sector tourism agencies, 351
public sector tourism agencies, 350, 351
railways, 123
reservation agents, as, 66
resorts, 229
ski resorts, 229
stadiums, 228, 229
tennis camps, 229
theme parks, 228
tour industry, 255
travel/tourism distributors, 328
zoos, 228
Cargo building, 83
Carlson Travel Group, 273, 278, 319
Carlson Wagonlit Travel, 273
Carlson, Curt, 273
Carnival Cruise Lines, 135, 138, 142, 144, 271, 347
Carnivals, 221
Carrying capacity, 191, 195
Carter, Jimmy, 225
Cartier, George Étienne, 104
Casino gambling, 206, 225-227, 229
Casino hotels, 170
Castro, Fidel, 195
Cavendish Resort Community, 222
Celebrity tours, 225
Certification programs, 371, 372
Certified Corporate Travel Executive (CCTE), 372
Certified Hotel Administrator (CHA), 372

Certified Hotel Sales Executive (CHSE), 372
Certified Tour Professional (CTP), 249, 372
Certified Travel Counsellor (CTC), 372
Channels of distribution, 51–70. *See also* Information sources
business travel, and, 277, 278
car rental industry, 120
cruise industry, 148
deregulation, 277, 278
mass transit, 123
meetings and conventions, 300–303
motorcoach, 117
railways, 111
recreational and leisure systems, 227
recreational vehicles, and, 224
technology, future, 364, 365
tour industry, 254
travel/tourism distributors, 326
types, 51-54
Chanute, Octave, 73
Charitable associations, 293
Charter, 7
Charter airlines, 7, 78
Charter companies, 7
Charter flights, 253
Charter operator, 8, 252, 253
Charter tour, 116, 253
Charters
advantages/disadvantages, 252
defined, 252
deregulation, effect of, 253
pricing, 253
publications, 254
terms/concepts, 253, 254
types, 253
yacht, 141
Chateau Montebello, 277
Châteaux, 175
Cher, 346
Children's museums, 215
Choice Hotels International, 336
Chrétien, Jean, 361
Chunnel, 109, 110
Circle trip, 92
Circuses, 221
City package tours, 116
City-pair discount, 272
Civic centres, 290
Civil Aeronautics Board (CAB), 90
CLIA Cruise Manual, 148
Clinics, 290
Clipper ships, 132
Club Méditerranée (Club Med), 164, 170
cruises, and, 196
overview, 196
tenth largest hotel chain, 164
self-contained vacation destination, as, 170

Club Tout D'Suite, 326
Co-host, 61
Co-op advertising, 342
Code-sharing, 91
Cold calls, 350
Colliss, Owen, 370
Commercial recreation, 218–23
Commercial recreation system, 212
Commercial travel agency, 317
Commercial travel agent, 280
Commission, 51, 313
Commissioned sales agents, 325, 327, 349
Common carrier, 78
Compact, 120
CompuServe, 52
Computer reservation systems (CRSs), 58, 59
    bias, issue of, 61
    bus companies, and, 117
    co-host and shared databases, 61
    hardware, 58
    hotel reservations, and, 176
    interface with back office systems, 63
    meetings market, and, 288
    travel agencies, and, 315
    vendors of, 59–61
Concessions and incentives, 13, 14, 212
Concierge, 175, 281
Concorde, 77, 269, 362
Conference appointment system, 323
Conference centres, 277, 289
Conferences, 290, 321
Configuration, 93
Congresses, 290
Conservators, 228
Consolidated Tour Manual (CTM), 57, 252
Consortiums, 320
Consulates, 36
Continental breakfast, 173
Continental plan (CP), 172
Control tower, 83
Convention, 290. *See also* Meetings and Conventions
Convention and visitors' bureaus (CVBs), 303, 345, 351
Convention centres, 277, 289
Convention hotels, 162, 163, 168, 169, 289
Convention planner, 254
Convention service managers, 297, 304
Convention services and facilities companies, 303
Convention tour, 241
Cook, John Mason, 16
Cook, Thomas, 16, 238, 318
"Cook's tour", 16
Cooperative, 320
Corporate airplanes, 80
Corporate meeting planners, 295
Corporate rate, 173
Corporate travel agencies, 278, 279
Corporate travel manager, 279, 280

Corporations
    cost of business travel, 267, 268
    dealings directly with suppliers, 279
    meetings and conventions, and, 294, 295
    travel policies, 268
Cottage industry, 373
Couchette, 110
Council on Hotel, Restaurant and Institutional Education (CHRIE), 371
Country inns, 163
Coupon brokering, 269
Courier, 252
Crocodile Dundee movies, 195, 344
Croisières Pacquet, 140
Cross-adoption, 202
Cruise and steamship industry
    advertising by, 347
    cancellation penalty, 149
    contemporary cruise ship, birth of, 134
    employment opportunities, 145, 150
    end of passenger ship industry, 134
    excluded activities (from cruise price), 147
    fast growing segment in travel/tourism, 131
    general office, 150
    high overheads, 143
    included activities (in cruise price), 146, 147
    information about, 148
    marketing by, 142–44
    operations on shore, 150
    origins, 131–35
    package tours, 143
    physically challenged passengers, 146
    pricing, 143, 147, 148
    promotion, 149
    publications, 390
    registration in foreign country, 134
    regulation of, 149
    reservation process, 148, 149
    safety standards, 149
    shore excursions, 146
    travel agencies for, 317
Cruise lines, 7
    credits for air travel, 136
    information on schedules/fares, 56
    owned by European companies, 135
    reservation agents, 64
    tremendous recent growth, 135, 136
    vertical marketing, 54
Cruise Lines International Association (CLIA), 135, 142, 149, 321, 371
Cruise ships
    activities on, 146
    coastal, 139, 140
    entertainment on, 146
    "floating hotels", as, 145
    hotel crew, 145, 150
    incentive travel programs, and, 290

    meals on, 146
    meetings and conventions, and, 290
    motion sickness, 39
    physical layout of, 147
    ship's crew, 145, 150
    tipping practices on, 147
Cruisefest, 371
Cruisematch, 149
Cruises
    adventure and academic, 140
    Alaska, to, 138
    Caribbean, to, 138
    Club Med, and, 196
    coastal, 139, 140
    Disney World, and, 143
    Eastern U.S./Canada, to, 139
    exotic riverboat, 141
    freighter, 140
    Hawaiian Islands, to, 139
    Mediterranean, to, 139
    meetings and conventions on, 143, 145
    Mexican Rivera, to, 138
    misconceptions about, 142
    Northern Europe, to, 139
    of today, 135–42
    passengers, ages of, 142
    repositioning, 139
    river, 140
    seasonal, 139, 140
    segments of world, 136
    shorter sea, 138, 139
    theme, 140
    three- and four-day, 142, 146
    trans-canal, 138
    world, 136
Crystal Beach, Ontario, 220
Crystal Palace, 220
Csonka, Larry, 137
Cullen Country Barns, 11
Cullen, Len, 11
Cultural effects of tourism, 200–202
Cultural tours, 242
Cunard Line, 132–34, 136, 141
Cunard, Samuel, 132
Cuomo, Mario, 346
Curator, 228
Currency rates, 366, 367
Customs, 37, 38

D
DATAS II, 59
Dealer meetings, 294
Delhi Belly, 39
Delta Chelsea Inn, 8
Delta Privilege, 175
Delta Queen, 140
Deluxe, 120

Demographics, 32, 368, 369
Demonstration effect of tourism, 200–202
Deregulation. *See also* Regulation of airline industry
    airline industry, of, 53, 56, 253, 268, 277, 279, 318, 319, 361
    channels of distribution, 277, 278
    motorcoach industry, in, 115, 116
Designers, 228
Destination development, 190–210
    changing employment patterns, 200
    community involvement, 204
    congestion, and, 200
    economic impact, 195–99
    employment opportunities, 204, 205
    environmental impact, 202–4
    environmental impact studies, 191, 192
    financial studies, 191
    government, role of, 192, 193
    increased income, and, 200
    market analysis, 191
    negative effects, 199–202
    resentment of locals, 200
    rising properties values, and, 200
    site assessment, 191
    social impact studies, 192
    stages in, 194, 195
    synergism in, 204
Destination geography, 15–17
Destination management companies (DMCs), 303
Destination manager, 20, 42
Destination(s)
    choice of, 188–90
    decline in popularity, reasons for, 195
    defined, 188
    increase in popularity, reasons for, 195
    life cycle of, 194, 195
Destinations in Canada. *See also* Canada, Attractions/events in Canada
    Arctic Edge, 219
    Banff National Park, 201
    Canmore, Alberta, 188, 199
    Cavendish, P.E.I., 222
    Chateau Montebello, 277
    Crystal Beach, Ontario, 220
    Cullen Country Barns, 11
    La Station Touristique du Mont, 11
    Lunenburg, Nova Scotia, 188, 189
    Manitou Springs Mineral Spa, 219
    Moncton, New Brunswick, 220
    Oak Bay Marine Group, 219
    Rodd Hotels and Resorts, 11
Diarrhea, 39
Dickinson, Robert, 144
Dine-around plan, 248
Direct mail, 341
Direct spending, 197
Directional advertising, 341

INDEX

Discounting, 272
Discretionary income, 27
Discretionary travel, 27
Disease and poverty, 367. *See also* Health problems
Disney World. *See also* Theme parks
    chairman, profile of, 337
    cruises, and, 143
    employment opportunities, 228
    other Disney Worlds, 194, 195
    overview, 193, 194
    package tours, and, 227
Disney, Roy, 337
Disneyland, 218
Distribution channels. *See* Channels of distribution
Dog racing, 226
Domestic independent tours (DITs), 238, 240, 317
Domestic vacation travel, 33, 34
Double occupancy, 248
Double with bath (DWB), 248
Douglas, Kirk, 346
Drop-off charge, 120
Duty, 37
Duty-free purchases, 37, 38
Dysynchronosis, 39

E
E.F. MacDonald, 298
Eastern Provincial Airways (EPA), 88, 89
Eco-tourism, 8, 201, 244
Economic impact of tourism, 195–199
Educational associations, 291
Educational courses, 359, 371, 372
Educational Institute of the American Hotel & Motel Association (AHMA), 371
Educational tours, 242
Eisner, Michael, 337
Electronic flight information systems (EFISs), 362
Electronic ticket delivery network (ETDN), 62
Ellesmere Island, 201
Embarkation, 136
Embassy, 36
Emergency traveller, 35
Employment. *See also* Career opportunities, Travel professionals
    destination development, and, 200
    direct, 4, 5
    indirect, 5
Employment areas, 4
Empress ships, 133, 134
Encyclopedic or general museums, 215
Endangered species, 38
England
    subways in, 122
    trains in, 110, 111
English Channel tunnel, 109, 110
Entrepreneurs, 257, 304, 321
Environmental impact studies, 191, 192

Escorted tours, 116, 241
Ethics in U.S. Tour Operations: Standards for Integrity, 249
Ethnic organizations, 293
Ethnic travel, 242
Ethnic travel agencies, 317
Eurail Guide: How to Travel Europe and All the World by Train, 112
Eurailpass, 110, 111, 274
Euro Disney, 194
European plan (EP), 172, 248
European Travel Commission (ETC), 344
Events, 8, 190
    attractions, and, contrasted, 8
    defined, 211
    tours, and, 244
Evergreen Travel, 247
Everything You Need to Know Before You're Hijacked, 366
Exchanging money, 39, 40, 366, 367
Executive conferences, 294
Exhibitions, 290, 299, 300, 342
Exposition, 290

F
Factory outlet centres, 224
Fairs and festivals, 216, 217
Familiarization trips/tours (FAM trips/tours), 18, 252, 303, 343
Family hotel operator, 363
Family plan, 173
Family vacation traveller, 35
Far construction, 93, 94
Fares and schedules, 54-64
Fargo, James, 322
Federal Aviation Administration (FAA), 91
Ferries, 141, 142, 347
Festivals, 217
Fielding's guides, 177
Fixed-base operator, 82, 96
Fixed costs, 251
Flag carriers, 87
Flag of convenience, 135
Flight attendant, 95, 96
Flight instruction aircraft, 80
"Floating casinos", 140
Fly/cruise packages, 143
Fly/drive packages, 118
Flyer, 73
Flying Freedoms, 85, 86
Flying Wheels Travel, 247
Fodor guides, 177
Ford, Henry, 114
Ford's Deck Plan Guide, 148
Ford's Freighter Travel Guide, 148
Ford's International Cruise Guide, 148
Foreign currency, 39, 40, 366, 367
Foreign-flag vessels, 134, 149
Foreign flags, 87

Foreign independent tours (FITs), 238, 240, 317
Foreign languages, 40
Foreign travel. *See* International travel/tourism
Forum, 290
Four Seasons Hotels, 30, 167
France
    subways in, 122
    trains in, 110
Franchises, 167, 320
Fraternal associations, 293
Free enterprise system, 12
Free upgrade, 269, 277
Freedom to Move, 89
Freedoms of the Air, 85, 86
Freighter cruises, 140
Frequent flier programs, 269, 271
Frequent stay programs, 271, 276
Friends. *See* Travellers visiting friends/relatives (VFR)
Frommer's guides, 177
Front desk manager, 179
Frost, Dennis, 55
Fulton, Robert, 132
"Fun ships", 138, 144

G
Galileo, 319
Galileo Canada, 59, 61
Gambling and gaming, 225–27, 229
Gambling junkets, 227
Gardiner, Bill, Jr., 301
Gardiner, Bill, Sr., 301
Garth's Profile of Ships, 148
Gateway airport, 84
Gemini, 59
Geography, 15-18
"Getaway" weekends, 369
Glaser, Milton, 346
Global trends in tourism, 370
Glossary, 393–400
Government
    destination development, and, 192, 193
    promotion, and, 13, 14
    proposed developments, 359, 360
Government accounts, 279
Government regulation, 14, 15
Government Services Administration (GSA), 279
Government tourist offices, 344
Graceland, 225
Grand tour, 237
Grand Trunk Railway, 104
Graphic artists, 255
Gray Line Corporation, 116, 252
Gray Line Sales and Tour Guide, 116
Gretzky, Wayne, 119
Greyhound and Trailways Lines, 116
Gross registered tonnage (GRT), 148

Ground transportation, 7, 8. *See also* Car rental industry, Motorcoach, Railways
    information on schedules/fares, 56
    publications, 390
Groundskeepers, 229
Group coordinator, 255
Group discount, 272
Guided Tour Inc., 247
Guides, 229

H
Halls of entertainment, 225
Hangars, 83
Hannah, Michael, 273
Harness racing, 226
Health problems, 38, 39
Health, as reason for travelling, 190
Henry Davis Trade Show, 299
Hindenburg, 73
Historic fairs, 217
Historical museums, 215
Historical tours, 242
History and art tours, 227
Hoffman, Betty J., 247
Hogan, Paul, 344
Holiday Inn
    franchising, and, 167
    history, 163, 164
    largest chain in world, 8, 163
    offers standard service, 168
    reservation system, 63, 176
    upscaling of, 162, 170
Holidex 2000, 63, 176
Horse-drawn coaches, 113, 121
Hospitality industry, 8. *See also* Hotels
    franchises, 167
    future trends, 165
    history of, 159-161
    incentive deals, 165
    individual ownership, 167
    leases/joint ventures, 167
    management contract agreements, 167
    market segmentation, 168
    other lodging places, 173, 175
    overbuilding, 165
    renovation of grand hotels in downtown area, 163
    technology, future, 364
    time-sharing, 175
    types of accommodation, 161-163
Hospitality suite, 300
Host-guest relationship, 10, 11
Host vendor, 59
Hosted tour, 240, 241
Hot Shoppes, 166
Hotel and Travel Index (HTI), 57, 176
Hotel and Travel Index/ABC International Edition (HTI/ABC), 176

INDEX

Hotel chains, 167
    effect on local economy, 199
    growth of, 163–65
    low cost, no-frills, 168
    world's largest chains, 164
Hotel Industry Switching Company, The (THISCo), 60
Hotels, 8. *See also* Hospitality industry
    administration, 175
    advertising by, 347
    airports, development at/near, 170
    all-suite, 170, 275
    architecture, 163
    "back of the house", 175
    break-even point, 165
    budget, 275
    business accommodation/facilities, 275, 276
    business travellers, catering to, 162, 163, 168, 169
    Canada, largest motel operator, 162
    Canada, largest privately owned, 161
    certification program, 372
    chains of. *See* Hotel chains
    children, cost for, 172
    classification by price, 170
    classification by type, 168
    concierge services, 175, 281
    construction costs, increased, 170
    conventions at, 288, 289
    corporate meetings, and, 294, 295
    employment opportunities, 177, 178
    executive floors, 275
    family-run, 363
    food/beverage services, 176
    frequent stay programs, 271, 276
    "front of the house", 175
    front office, 164, 175
    hotel-airport transportation, 175
    housekeeping, 176
    information on schedules/fares, 56, 57
    information sources, 176, 177
    local residents, attractions for, 175
    location of, 169
    low-cost, no-frills chains, 168
    meals, 172
    national parks, in, 201
    no-smoking rooms, 168
    "official hotel", as, 302
    ownership of, 165–67
    physically challenged, accessibility to, 168
    price, factors affecting, 172, 173
    publications, 390, 391
    rating systems, 172
    recreational facilities, 168
    reservation agents, 64
    reservation systems, 63, 176
    security at, 177, 276
    special features, 173, 175
    standard services, 168
    suburban locations, development in, 169
    terminology, 172
    theme parks, in/around, 220
    theme weekends, 175
    units, 162
    valet parking, 175
    wake-up calls, 275
    women, facilities for, 276
Hub-and-spoke route, 84
Hub cities, 288
Hudson, Henry, 265
Hypersonic transport (HST), 77, 362

I

"I Love New York" promotional campaign, 345, 346
Identifying number (IT number), 250
In-plant agency, 326
Inbound operators, 8
Inbound tourism, 40–44
    improvements, possible, 44
    minimizing language difficulties, 44
    persuade visitors to make sidetrip from U.S., 42
Incentive tour, 241
Incentive travel companies, 302
Incentive travel planners, 298
Incentive travel programs, 297–99
Incoming tours, 241
Independent package tours, 116
Independent tours, 240
Indirect spending, 197
Industrial tours, 225, 226
Industry, 6
Industry conferences, 321
Information sources. *See also* Channels of distribution
    automated systems, 58–62
    charters, 254
    hotels/motels, etc., 176, 177
    printed references, 54–57
    tours, 252
Infrastructure, 191
Inside cabins, 147
Inside sales, 350
Institute of Certified Travel Agents (ICTA), 372
Insurance, 324
    car rentals, and, 120
    students, for, 43
Intangible, 9
"Intelligent travel", 242
Interface, 63
Interior designers, 205
Interline connection, 92
Interlining, 92
Intermediaries, 51
Intermodal package, 9
Intermodal tickets/ticketing, 93, 117
Intermodal tours, 116

International Air Transport Association (IATA), 86–88, 250, 321, 323
International air travel, 85–88
International airfare, 93, 94
International Airline Travel Agency Network (IATAN), 91, 321
International Association of Convention and Visitors' Bureaus (IACVB), 303
International Association of Tour Managers (IATM), 255
International Certificate of Vaccination, 37
International Civil Aviation Organization (ICAO), 87
International Concierge Institute, 281
International Exhibitors Association (IEA), 300
International Student Identity Card (ISIC), 43
International trade shows, 299
International travel/tourism, 15, 34, 36
    bus services abroad, 116
    business travel on railways, 274
    Canada has negative balance, 197, 357
    commercial recreation and leisure, 226
    customs, 37, 38
    directory of overseas doctors, 38, 39
    documents required, 36, 37
    driving abroad, 120
    encouraged by government, 13, 14
    exchanging money, 39, 40, 366, 367
    foreign languages, 40
    health problems, 38, 39
    mass transit in foreign cities, 122
    public recreation and leisure systems, 217, 218
    rental companies abroad, 120
    restrictions on, 38
    top four countries, 197
    train travel abroad, 108–111
    United States, as destination. *See* United States, travel to
International Travel Industry Expo, 299
International Union for the Conservation of Nature and Natural Resources (IUCN), 214
Interpretation, 213, 231
Interstate Commerce Commission (ICC), 108
Intrawest Developments, 188
Intrusive advertising, 341
Itinerary, 15

J
Jannus, Tony, 72
Japan
    railways, 110, 111, 275
    subways, 122
JAX FAX Travel Marketing Magazine, 254
Jenkins, Kevin, J., 81, 370
Jet lag, 39
Joint venture, 167
Jones, James E., 298
Jordan, Michael, 137
Junket, 227

K
KAL 007, shooting down of, 85
Kampgrounds of America (KOA), 224
Karment, Steve, 346
Kiely House, 174
Kilometre cap, 119
King, Stephen, 322

L
L'Étudiant Voyageur, 43
La Station Touristique du Mont Orford, 11
Labour unions, 293
Land/cruise package, 143
Landscape architects, 205
Last Minute Club, 326
Lawson Travel, 273, 319
Lawson, Peter, 273
Leakage, 197–99
Lectures, 290
Leisure, 211
Les Clefs d'Or, 281
Light-rail transit (LRT), 121
Lighters, 146
Lilientahl, Otto, 73
Limousines, 8, 122
Linear route, 84
Liner, 133
Live entertainment, 225, 226
Loading apron, 83
Local parks, 214, 215
Local tour, 254
Loeks, David, 219
London Underground, 122
Loss/damage waiver (LDW), 120
Lurer, Gander, 30

M
Macdonald, Sir John A., 104, 201
MacLaine, Shirley, 346
MacPherson Report, 88
Magazines, 339, 340
Magnan, Fernand, 11
Magnetic levitation (Maglev), 110, 111, 364
Magrodomes, 147
Management contract, 167
Management development seminars, 294
Manifest, 57
Manitou Springs Mineral Spa, 219
Mansiones, 159
Maritime transportation, 7. *See* Cruise and steamship industry
Maritz Travel, 298
Market analysis, 191
Market price, 336
Market research, 13, 32, 336
Market researcher, 205
Market segmentation, 32

Marketing, 12, 13. *See also* Advertising, Promotion
   cruise industry, by, 142–44
      defined, 335, 336
      employment opportunities, 350, 351
      four P's of, 12, 336
      strategies, 336
Marketing mix, 12
Marketplace, 12
Marlin Travel, 319
Marriott Corporation, 166
Marriott, Alice, 166
Marriott, J. Willard, Sr., 166
Mart, 8
Maslow's hierarchy of needs, 29, 30
Maslow, Abraham, 29–31
Mass transit systems, 121–23
Master Key, 116
McCurdy, John, 72
McKinnon, Douglas, 366
Meeting planners, 295–97, 303
Meeting Planners International (MPI), 292, 295, 298
Meeting planning companies, 302
Meetings and conventions
   associations, held by, 291–94
   channels of distribution, 300–303
   corporations, held by, 294, 295
   cruise ships, on, 143, 145
   employment opportunities, 303, 304
   expenditures by average delegate, 289
   growth of, 287, 288
   hotels, in, 162, 163
   ideal meeting sites, 288
   kinds, 290
   locations of, 288–90
   meeting planners, 295–97, 303
   need for, 291
   planning, 254
   publications, 390, 391
Mega-agencies, 278, 319, 320, 328
Megamalls, 224
Metroliner, 274
Michelin's Red Guide series, 177
Midcentric personality, 31
Minelli, Liza, 346
Mississippi Queen, 140
Mixed enterprise system, 12
MNEs. *See* Motivation, needs and expectations (MNEs)
Mobil Travel Guide, 170, 172, 177
Mobile telephones, 274
Model structure, 221, 226
Modified American plan (MAP), 172, 248
Molson, John, 104
Mom-and-pop operations, 167, 227
Monorail, 122
Montebello, The, 277
Montezuma's Revenge, 39
Montgomery, Lucy Maud, 222

Morgan, Joe, 137
Motels, 161, 162, 176
Motion sickness, 39
Motivation, needs and expectations (MNEs), 6
   air travel, and, 92–94
   associations conducting meetings/conventions, of, 293
   business travellers, of, 267
   car rental industry, and, 117
   corporations conducting meetings/conventions, of, 294, 295
   cruise industry, and, 136, 139, 140, 145
   destinations, choice of, and, 188–90
   dividing travellers into three categories, 27
   hospitality industry, and, 168
   meeting planners, of, 297
   motorcoaches, and, 112
   tour industry, and, 242–45
   trains, and, 103
Motor hotels, 162
Motor inns, 162
Motorcoach, 7
   advertising by, 347
   associations, 117
   "Big 10" carriers, 113
   charters and tours, 113, 115
   deregulation in U.S., 115, 116
   district manager, profile of, 55
   employment opportunities, 123
   foreign services, 116
   information on fares/schedules, 56
   intermodal tickets, 117
   modern long-distance buses, 117
   origin, 112, 113
   purchase of tickets in advance, 117
   regulation (Canada), 115
   scheduled services, 113, 116
   sightseeing companies, 116
   transfer transportation, as, 117
Multilevel distribution system, 53, 54
Multinational corporations, 199
Multiplier effect, 197–99
Museums
   around the world, 217, 218
   commercial sector, operated by, 221
   curators of, 228
   employment opportunities, 228
   overview, 215
   types, 215

N

Nagelmackers, Georges, 273
Narrow-body, 93
National Association of Cruise Only Agents (NACOA), 317
National Business Travel Association (NBTA), 278
National Cruise Vacation Month, 149

National park interpreter, 213, 231
National parks
    around the world, 217
    Canada, in, 201, 212, 214
    ecosystem-based approach to, 366
    employment opportunities, 228
    international role, 214
    interpreters in, 213, 231
    modern problems, 214
    mountain, 192
    park facilities, 213
    U.S., in, 213, 365
National Tour Association (NTA), 249
National tourism commission, 361
National tourism organizations (NTOs), 192
National tourist offices (NTOs), 251, 344
National Trade Shows, Inc. (NTS), 301
National Transportation Act of 1987, 56, 89
National Transportation Agency, 89
Nationalize, 106
Nationwide tours, 254
Natural history museums, 215
Nature tourism, 244
Necessary leakage, 199
New Canadian Air Policy of 1984, 56, 61, 89
New-entrant carriers, 91
Newsletters, 341
Newspapers, 338, 339
NIMBY (Not In My Back Yard), 194
No-shows, 93
Nonautomated systems of information, 54–58
Nondiscretionary travel, 28
North American trade shows, 299
Norway, The, 134, 137
Norwegian Cruise Line (NCL), 134, 135, 137

O

OAG Business Travel Planner Hotel and Motel Redbook, 176
OAG Travel Planner, 57
OAG Worldwide Cruise and Shipline Guide, 148
Oak Bay Marine Group, 219
Occupational titles, 392
Ocean liners, 133
Oceanariums, 216
Off-site meetings, 288
Official Airline Guide (OAG), 56, 254
"Official carrier/hotel/car rental agency", 302
Official Hotel Guide (OHG), 172, 176
Official Hotel Resort Guide, 57
Official Railway Guide (ORG), 56, 112
Official Sightseeing Sales and Tour Guide, 252
Official Steamship Guide International (OSGI), 56, 148
Official Tour Directory, 57, 252
OHG Cruise Directory, 148
Oil, 366
Omnibuses, 113, 121

On-demand transportation, 268
One-line connection, 92
One-way trip, 92
Open-jaw trip, 92
Open skies, 90
Orient Express, 111
Out-of-home media, 341
Out-plant agency, 326
Outdoor advertising, 341
Outfitters, 223
Outgoing tours, 241
Outside cabins, 147
Outside sales, 348, 350
Outside sales representatives, 325, 327, 349
Overbook, 93
Overcrowding and pollution, 365, 366
Overrides, 53, 314, 315

P

P&O Line, 136
P. Lawson Travel, 273, 319
Pacific Asia Travel Association (PATA), 348
Pacific National Exhibition, 216
Pacific West Airlines (PWA) Corporation, 81
Package, 9
Package tours, 212, 227. *See also* Tour(s)
    accommodations, 248, 249
    age of travellers, 245
    all-inclusive package, 238, 239, 251
    block booking, 251
    brochure production, 251, 252
    components, typical, 238
    costing, 251
    duration, 238
    educational programs, 249
    employment opportunities, 255
    evolution of tour formats, 238
    flexibility/pacing, 245
    fly/cruise packages, 143
    fly/motorcoach tour, 116, 117
    history, 237
    hotel accommodation and train travel, 111
    imaginary tour, 246–49
    international regulation, 250
    itinerary, 246, 249
    land/cruise packages, 143
    meal plans, 248
    pioneer of, 238
    pricing, 245, 251
    production of, 250–52
    promotion, 252
    publications, 252
    rail/sail packages, 111
    requirements of travellers, 244, 245
    sample European tour itinerary, 246
    sample tour, 240, 241
    self-regulation/ethics, 249

statement of terms and conditions, 250
suppliers, 250, 251
transportation, 248
weekend package, 244
when rates quoted separately, 238, 239
Palmer, Arnold, 119
Panel, 290
Parades, 217
Paradors, 173
Pari-mutuel betting, 226
Paris Metro, 122
Parity products, 336
Park rangers, 228
Park, Brad, 137
Parks. *See* Action parks, Amusement parks, Local parks, National parks, Provincial parks, Theme parks
Parks Canada, 201, 212, 366
PARS, 59
Pascal, Blaise, 121
Passenger freighters, 7
Passenger liners, 7
Passenger name record (PNR), 58
Passenger railway, 7, 8. *See also* Railways
Passport, 36
Peck, Gregory, 346
Pensions, 173
Penthouse suite, 173
Per diem, 268
Performance bond, 250
Periodicals, 387-389
Personal accident insurance (PAI), 120
Personal computers, 364
Pets, 38
Pettit, Heather and Ray, 174
Physically challenged travellers
cruises, on, 146
hotels, and, 168
theme parks, and, 228
tours for, 244, 247
travel agencies for, 317
Pilgrimage, 242
Pitch, 93
Planner, 205
Plants, 38
Pleasure seekers as travellers, 27
Plog, Stanley, 29, 30
PODS, 164
Point Pelee, 201
Point-of-purchase materials, 342
Point-to-point, 134
Point-to-point crossings, 141
Political associations, 293
Political instability, 366
Pollution, 18
Polo, Marco, 160, 264
Porman, John, 163

Port taxes, 147
Port-to-port crossings, 141
Posadas, 173
Premier Cruise Lines, 143
Presley, Elvis, 225
Press conference, 343
Press release, 343
Pressurization, 77
Primary research, 32
Print media, 338–40
Private charters, 253
Private sector promoters, 347
Privatize, 362
Prodigy, 52
Product life cycle, 194
Professional associations, 291
Professional travel. *See* Business travel
Promoters, 343–48
Promotion, 13, 336, 338. *See also* Advertising, Marketing
bus industry, in, 117
cruise industry, 149
government, and, 13, 14
tourism organizations, and, 192, 193
tours, of, 252
types of, 342, 343
Promotional activities, 342, 343
Promotional campaigns, 345, 346
Proof of citizenship, 37
Property, 163
Provincial and territorial tourist offices (PTTOs), 345
Provincial parks, 214, 215
Provincial tourism offices, 203
Psychocentric personality, 31
Psychographics, 32, 33
Public charters, 253
Public meetings, 294
Public recreation system, 212
Public relations, 343
Public sector organizations (PSOs), 251
Publications, 386–91
Publicist, 255
Pure incentives, 298
Purser, 151, 152

Q
Quad, 249
Quarter horse racing, 226
Queen Elizabeth 2 (QE2), 134, 136, 141

R
Rack rate, 172
Radio, 340, 341
Rail/sail packages, 111
Rail Traveler's City Planner, 112
Railfone®, 274
Railways, 103–12
advertising by, 347

business travel, and, 274
Canada/U.S. rail service, 107
Canadian passenger railway service, 106, 107
chartering of trains, 253
Eastern Canadian transcontinental services, 107
employment opportunities, 123
Europe, in, 108–10
European/North American trains compared, 110
fares, 111, 112
federal regulation (Canada), 107
golden age of, 105
great trains of the world, 111
high-speed transportation, as, 103, 110, 111, 364
history of, 104–6
industry in decline (North America), 105, 106
information on fares/schedules, 56, 112
Japan, in, 110, 111, 275
publications on fares/schedules, 112
reservation systems, 64, 111
routes offered today, 107
Russia, in, 110
technology, future, 362, 364
train/drive packages, 110
U.S. passenger railways, 107, 108
Railways of the World, 112
Rampal, Jean-Pierre, 140
Reagan, Ronald, 115
Rebate, 272
Reception services, 20, 42
Receptive operator, 20, 42
Recreation, 211
Recreation and leisure system, 211-236
Recreation systems, 211
Recreational shopping, 224, 226
Recreational vehicles (RVs), 224
Regional theatres, 225
Regional tourism organizations, 345
Regulation of airline industry. *See also* Deregulation
    bilateral agreements, 85, 86
    Canada, regulating domestic service in, 88–90
    freedoms of the air, 85, 86
    international system, 85–88
    traffic conferences, 87
    U.S., regulating domestic service in, 90, 91
    worldwide conferences, 85
Relatives. *See* Travellers visiting friends/relatives (VFR)
Religion, as reason for travelling, 190
Religious conventions, 293
Religious tours, 242
Repositioning cruise, 139
Reregulation, 361
Reservation agents, 64, 66
Reservation systems, 58–64, 227
Reservationist, 255
Reservations centre, 57
Residential hotels, 168
Resort condominium, 175

Resort hotels, 162, 170
Resorts. *See also* Hospitality industry, Hotels
    employment opportunities, 229
    information on schedules/fares, 56, 57
    sites for meetings, as, 289
Restorations, 221, 226
Rifle approach, 338
River cruises, 140, 141
Rodd hotels and resorts, 11
Rodd, David, 11
Round trip, 92
Royal Scotsman, 111
Royal York Hotel, 8
Run-of-the-house rate, 173
Runways, 83
Russell's Official National Motor Coach Guide, 56
Russia
    railways, 110
    subways, 122
Rutan, Dick, 362

S
S.S. Norway, 134, 137
SABRE (Semi-Automated Business Research Environment), 59, 61, 319
Safety of Life at Sea (SOLAS) Convention, 149
Sales, 348–50
Sales contests, 343
Sales incentives, 298
Sales meetings, 294
Sales promotions, 342, 343
Sales support, 342
Satellite Ticket Printer (STP), 62, 278
Saturation, 18
Saunders brothers, 118
Scheduled airlines, 7, 78
Schedules and fares, 54–64
Schlösser, 175
Science and technology museums, 215
Scientific and technical associations, 291
Scientific tour, 242
Sea Sell program, 204, 345
Secondary research, 32
Security
    airports, at, 84
    hotels, at, 177, 276
Seminars, 290
Senior citizens, 317, 368, 369
Seniors, travel agencies for, 317
Sharp, Isadore, 30
Shell brochures, 252
Sheraton Centre Hotel and Towers, 8
Shinkansen bullet trains, 111, 275
"Ship Shop", 317
Ships, chartering of, 253
Shopping, 224, 226
Shore excursions, 146

Shorter sea cruises, 138, 139
Shot-gun approach, 338
Sightseeing companies, 116
Sinatra, Frank, 346
Single-city tour, 242
Single-country tours, 242
Single-entity charters, 253
Single supplement, 249
Singles, travel agencies for, 317
Site assessment, 191
Site destination selection company, 302, 303
Ski resorts, 223, 229
Slogans, 345
Smith, Jim, 370
Soapstone carving, 202
Social impact studies, 192
Society for the Advancement of Travel for the Handicapped (SATH), 247
Society of Family Hoteliers, 363
Society of Incentive Travel Executives (SITE), 299
Society of Travel Agents in Government (STAG), 279
Society of Travel and Tourism Educators (STTE), 371
Socioeconomic impact of tourism, 199, 200
Sociologists, 205
Sons of Norway, 7
"Snowbirds", 34, 366
Special event tours, 244
Special-interest associations, 293
Special-interest group tours, 241
Special-interest tours, 244
Special-services airplanes, 80
Specialty advertising, 342
Specialty channeler, 53, 254
Spectator sports, 221, 223
Spectator sports packages, 244
Sports, 221–26, 244
Sports and recreation tours, 244
Sports planes, 80
Spot, 340
Sproule, Lionel, 219
Stabilizers, 135
Stadiums, 228, 229
Stagecoaches, 112, 113
Standard, 120
Standard ticket stock, 325, 399
Stands, 299
STAR SERVICE, 177
Statler, Ellsworth, 161, 163
Stay-put resort vacations, 242
Steamships, 132
Steerage, 132
Stephen, George, 201
Stern, Isaac, 140
Stewart, Darlene, 292
Stopover, 93
Student Traveller, The, 43
Student Work Abroad Program (SWAP), 43

Students, 43, 317
    educational tours for, 242
    Eurail Youthpasses, 110
Subcompact, 119
Subways, 121, 122
Superconductors, 362
Supersonic, 362
Superstructure, 191
Superstuff, 362
Supplemental airlines (carriers), 7, 78, 253
Symposium, 290
Synergism, 204
System geography, 17
System One, 59
Systemwide discount, 272

T
Table d'hôte, 248
Tall ships, 141
Tangible, 9
Tariffs, 14
Taxicabs, 122
Taxidermists, 228
Taxiways, 83
Taylor, Elizabeth, 346
Technical meetings, 294
Technological advances, 362–65
Tele-Trip Company, 270
Teleconferencing, 290, 364
Teleshopping, 52
Teleticketing, 62
Television, 340
Tenders, 146
Tennis camps, 223, 229
Terminal building, 82, 83
TGV (train grande vitesse), 110
Theme cruises, 140
Theme parks, 218-220. *See also* Disney World
    advertising by, 220
    around the world, 226
    Canada, in, 218
    employment opportunities, 228
    hotels, restaurants surrounding, 220
    impact on marketing methods, 227
    package tours, and, 227
    participatory, 220
THISCo, computer service provided by, 60
Thomas Cook & Son, 16, 318
    purchase of Marlin Travel, 319
    use of glamorous brochures, 57
Thomas Cook Continental Timetable, 112
Thomas Cook Overseas Timetable, 56, 112
Three-day weekends, 369
"Throwaway", 240
Ticketron, 227
Tie-in program, 269, 270, 276
Time sharing, 175

Tour conductor, 248, 251, 255, 256
Tour escort, 248, 251, 255, 256
Tour guide, 248, 255
Tour manager, 248, 251, 255, 256
Tour operators, 8
    advertising by, 347
    bus companies, and, 117
    certification program, 372
    conventions, and, 302
    function, 251
    in-house, 239
    licensed by provinces, 249
    performance bonds, 250
    receptive operators, 20, 42
    reservation agents, 64
    risk-takers, as, 239, 250, 251
    tour wholesaler, and, contrasted, 239
Tour organizer, 248, 254, 255
Tour packages. *See* Package tours
Tour wholesaler, 239
Tour(s). *See also* Package tours
    advantages, 239, 240
    adventure, 227
    celebrity, 225
    charter, 253
    defined by destination, 242
    defined by package format, 240, 241
    defined by purpose, 242–44
    escorted, 241
    history and art, 227
    hosted, 240, 241
    incoming, 241
    industrial, 225, 226
    information on schedules/fares, 57
    local, 254
    motorcoach, by, 113, 115, 116
    nationwide, 254
    not available to general public, 241
    outgoing, 241
    physically challenged, for, 244, 247
    seasonal, 239
    special-interest, 244
Tourism. *See also* Destination development
    balance of payments, and, 198, 199
    cultural effects, 200-202
    export industry, as, 198
    socioeconomic impact of, 199, 200
Tourism bureaus, 203
Tourism Canada, 192, 251, 344, 350, 391
Tourism multiplier, 197
Tourism offices, 380–85
Tourism organizations, 192, 193, 343
Tourist attractions. *See* Attractions
Tourist cabins, 162
Tourist card, 37
Tourist offices (TOs), 193
Trade associations, 291

Trade fairs, 217, 290
Trade Show Bureau, 299
Trade shows, 290, 299, 301
Traffic conferences, 87
Train/drive packages, 118
Training, 292
Training meetings, 294, 295
Trains. *See* Railways
Trans-Canada Airlines (TCA), 88, 287
Trans-Siberian Special, 111
Transfer, 117
Transient hotels, 168
Transit signs, 341
Travel
    budget, 43
    factors impacting on, 18
    growth of, 2–6
    history of, 25, 26
    industry, as. *See* Travel industry
    product, as. *See* Travel products
    restrictions on, 38
    service, as, 10–12
    student, 43
Travel agencies, 8, 9. *See also* Travel agents
    advertising by, 347
    airline commissions as major source of revenue, 53
    airlines, sending payments to, 325
    associations, 326, 327
    automation, and, 319
    business travel departments, and, contrasted, 8, 9
    business travel, and, 278, 279
    car rentals, and, 120
    classification by size, 319
    commissions, 313
    commissions from cruise bookings, 148
    consortium, as part of, 320
    consulting fees, 314
    conventions, and, 302
    corporate, 278, 279
    counselling customers, 314, 315
    deregulation, effect of, 318, 319
    employment in, 312
    franchise group, as part of, 320, 328
    frequent flier clubs, and, 271
    full-service, 315
    globalization of, 319
    government accounts, and, 279
    growth of, 318
    impartiality of, 315
    information needed to book flight, 54
    larger, 315
    number of, in Canada, 312
    opening, procedure for, 321–24
    outside sales representatives, 325, 327, 349
    overrides, 314
    payments, sending, to suppliers/airlines, 325
    products sold by, 324

INDEX

rebates, 314
sale of Eurail/Britrail passes, 111
sale of tour packages to public, 251
service charges, 314
small, 320, 321
staff, 325
suppliers, and, 314, 315
tour operator, functioning as, 239, 246
types, 315–17
use of computers to access CRS vendors, 58
Travel Agent, The, 252
Travel Agent's Handbook, 323
Travel agents, 325. *See also* Travel agencies
career path for, 328
educational course, 316, 328
how they sell, 350
knowledge/skills required, 327
profile, 329
Travel Agents Computer Society (TACOS), 58
Travel and Tourism Research Association (TTRA), 371
Travel assistance, 324
Travel Channel, The, 52, 53
Travel clubs, 9, 326
Travel CUTS, 43, 317
Travel fairs, 342
Travel guides, 248, 255
Travel industry
associations, listed, 380, 381
business travel and, 265, 266
components, 6-9
components, interrelationship between, 9
effect of changing demographics, 368, 369
free or mixed enterprise, as, 12
geography and, 15–18
government control of, 12–15
increased education and professionalism, 359, 369–72
increased recognition, 359–61
largest industry worldwide, 357
other industries, and, contrasted, 51
recreation, and, 212
service vs. self-service, 365
world problems, 365–68
Travel insurance. *See* Insurance
Travel management services, 279
Travel mart, 8, 9, 343
Travel nights, 343
Travel photographers, 351
Travel products
intangible products, 9, 51
perishable products, 51
seasonal products, 51
tangible products, 9
Travel professionals
car rentals, and, 119
defined, 371
inform clients about requirements of international travel, 17

knowledge of destinations/systems, 17, 18
required characteristics, 5, 6
trains, and, 104
Travel retailers, 51. *See* Travel agents
Travel seminars, 343
Travel trade shows, 343
Travel videos, 342
Travel Weekly, 252
Travel writers, 351
Travellers
business/professional. *See* Business travel
three special types, 35
vacation and leisure. *See* Vacation and leisure travellers
Travellers visiting friends/relatives (VFR), 29
destination, choice of, and, 190
future trends, 358
limited interest in cruises, 145
travel agencies for, 317
use of tour packages, 240
Trentway-Wagar, 55, 115
Trigano, Gilbert, 196
Trip, 2, 3
Triple, 249
Trolleys, 121
Twin with bath (TWB), 248
Two-city tours, 242

U

Unilateral distribution system, 52
Unique Reservations, 247
Unit, 162
United Bus Owners of America (UBOA), 117
United Nations Education, Scientific and Cultural Organization (UNESCO), 214
United States
high-speed train transportation, 110
regulation of domestic airline service, 90, 91
United States, travel to, 34
inbound travel, 41, 42
restrictions, 40
U.S. Department of Transportation (DOT), 108
United States Tour Operators Association (USTOA), 249
United States Travel and Tourism Administration (USTTA), 192, 251, 344, 361
Universal Federation of Travel Agents' Associations (UFTAA), 316
Unlimited kilometres, 119
Urban bus, 121

V

Vacancepass, 274
Vacation and leisure agency, 317
Vacation and leisure travellers, 27, 28
future trends, 358, 369
purchase of restricted airfares, 93

travel agencies for, 317
who are they, 32, 33
why they travel, 29–31
Vaccination certificate, 37
Van Horne, Sir William, 161
Variable costs, 251
Vertical marketing, 53
Veterans' and military associations, 293
VIA Rail, 8
    advertising by, 347
    Canadian agent for Amtrak, 321
    connection to U.S., 107
    Crown corporations, as, 125
    discount fares, 107
    first-class service offered by, 107, 274
    history, 106, 107
    reservations system, 64
Video kiosks, 364
Video marketing, 52, 53
Visa, 36
Volunteer Abroad Program, 43
Vouchers, 325

W
Wagonlit Travel, 273, 319
Wagons-lits, 110
Wait list, 57
Wake-up call, 275
Walt Disney World. *See* Disney World
Wardair, 253
Warner, Don, 243
Waterfront marketplaces, 224
Weekend packages, 244
Weekend travel, 369
Wells, Frank, 337
West Edmonton Mall, 224, 226
Westervelt, G. Conrad, 76
White Glove, 303
Wholesale companies, 8
    role in distribution system, 53

tour wholesaler, 239
Wide-body, 93
Wilson, Kemmons, 163, 167
"WKRP in Cincinatti", 195
Women
    business travellers, as, 35, 267
    facilities for, in hotels, 276
    first-time entry into job market, 200
    number of, who are business travellers, 265
Woodleigh Replicas, 222
Woodside Travel Management Corp., 320
Workshops, 290
World cruises, 136
World problems, 365–68
World Tourism Organization (WTO), 192
World's fairs, 217
WORLDSPAN Travel Agency Information Services, 59, 60
Worldwide Cruise and Shipline Guide, 56
Wright, Bob, 219
Wright, Orville and Wilbur, 73
Writer, 255

Y
Yacht charters, 141
Yams, 159
Yeager, Jeana, 362
"Yellow card", 37
Yellow pages, 341
Yellowstone National Park, 365
Yourtown, 19
Youth hostels, 173
Youth standby fares, 43
Youths. *See* Students

Z
Zoo director, 228
Zoo veterinarians, 228
Zoos, 216, 217, 228

To the owner of this book

We hope that you have enjoyed *Passport: An Introduction to the Travel and Tourism,* Canadian edition, and we would like to know as much about your experiences with this text as you would care to offer. Only through your comments and those of others can we learn how to make this a better text for future readers.

School _____ Your instructor's name _____

Course _____ Was the text required? _____ Recommended? _____

1. What did you like the most about *Passport*?
   _____
   _____
   _____

2. How useful was this text for your course?
   _____
   _____
   _____

3. Do you have any recommendations for ways to improve the next edition of this text?
   _____
   _____
   _____

4. In the space below or in a separate letter, please write any other comments you have about the book. (For example, please feel free to comment on reading level, writing style, terminology, design features, and learning aids.)
   _____
   _____
   _____
   _____

Optional

Your name _____ Date _____

May Nelson Canada quote you, either in promotion for *Passport* or in future publishing ventures?

Yes _____   No _____

Thanks!

FOLD HERE

MAIL / POSTE
Canada Post Corporation / Société canadienne des postes

Postage paid | Port payé
if mailed in Canada | si posté au Canada

Business Reply | Réponse d'affaires

0107077099 01

Nelson

TAPE SHUT

0107077099-M1K5G4-BR01

Nelson Canada
College Editorial Department
1120 Birchmount Rd.
Scarborough, ON M1K 9Z9

PLEASE TAPE SHUT. DO NOT STAPLE.